Beckett®

The World's Most Trusted Source In Collecting™

COLLECTOR'S GUIDE TO
SPORTS ILLUSTRATED
& SPORTS PUBLICATIONS

By Philip W. Regli
Author of
The Collectors' Guide to Sports Illustrated, and
Collectors' Guide to Sports Illustrated and Sports Publications

Published by Beckett Publications
Dallas, Texas

Manufactured in the United States of America
First Printing
ISBN 1-887432-49-3

Published by Beckett Publications
15850 Dallas Parkway
Dallas, Texas 75248
(972) 991-6657

Third Edition

Collector's Guide to *Sports Illustrated* and Sports Publications
Table of Contents

Index to Advertisers

About the Author

 Phil Regli has been a national sports memorabilia dealer since 1976 and is recognized as a leading authority on sports publications. He owns and operates P&R Publications, one of the largest Sports Publications trading houses in the country. He has written various articles for trade magazines and has written the Collectors Guide to Sports Illustrated and the 2nd edition Collectors Guide to Sports Illustrated and Sports Publications. Phil also is a Director of Marketing in the Internet Software industry. He has masters degrees in economics and business and has published in the areas of finance and statistics. His address is: P.O. Box 65778, Tucson, AZ 85728-5778, (520) 531-8880, fax (520) 531-8881. You can also e-mail him at Regli@aol.com or visit his website at www.asportmall.com.

Introduction

 Why a book on collecting sports publications and autograph and sports publications? Strangely, as American demand for pro sports continues to grow a decline has occurred in the sports cards market. Kids and fans have gone elsewhere to fulfill there sports collecting needs. For many, they turned to what they have been reading and decided that it was more fun to enjoy 'collecting' thier favorite sports subjects by gathering actual historical material on the person, team, and sport than it was just to collect cardboard. Thus the rebirth of sports publications in the 1990's occurred.

The 90's rebirth is driven by collectors looking for historical items to get autographed. The majority of sports publication collectors are looking for quality historical dated items (Sports Illustrated, Sport) with their favorite player(s) or team on them. This new rebirth has caused the demand for all general sports covers (Time, Life, Look, Colliers, Newsweek) to grow.

This book is devoted to the collector who enjoys publications and getting publications autographed of their favorite stars. However, I also recognize that the demand for their favorite player starts to fall into specific sports teams and magazines. Many true sports fans are just looking for quality information on thier subject and do not have any interest in getting material autographed. To address these needs the book has been and will continue to be expanded to cover as much subject material as possible.

Anything that is not found in this book will be placed on the Collectors Guide to Sports Publications web site: 'www.asportmall.com'.

If you are looking for assistance in a particular sports subject area, you can e-mail me at Regli@aol.com and I will try to accommodate you.

Reasons for This Book

The first reason for this book is the fact that Sports Illustrated and sports publications collecting is one of the fastest-growing niches in the sports memorabilia market. No more than seven years ago only a handful of dealers stocked sports publications. Now ads offering magazines abound in hobby publications and collectors compete fiercely for choice issues. Sports Illustrateds are popular because they are inexpensive, informative, and attractive. While a Mickey Mantle rookie card in nice condition will set you back thousands of dollars, an equally nice copy of Mantle's first SI cover (the magazine collector's equivalent of a rookie card) can be had for about $160. And while Topps makes an effort to provide information about a player on his card, an SI feature written by a top-flight sports journalist obviously offers greater insights. SI covers are also a much more attractive medium for signatures than are sports cards. Get your magazine cover signed and framed, and you have a spectacular and valuable display piece for your home or office.

A second reason for this update is the tremendous growth in autograph collecting on Sports Illustrated over the last four years. Many fellow collectors want a reference that shows them the value of getting their magazine autographed. Until now, only a handful of nationally known dealers have any idea of the scarcity of autographed Sports Illustrateds.

A third and final reason for this update is the demand for all sports publications outside of autographed sports publication collecting. Most sports publication collectors enjoy their favorite player, team and sport and want to find everything out about them. The reference material is rather scattered on what is available and what is not. This book attempts to address the keys in each sport by addressing them team by team.

What to Expect

So what should you expect from this book? The chapter, "Collecting Sports Illustrated," explains why SI is the most popular magazine among sports collectors. This chapter details the magazine's history from its beginnings in August of 1954 until this, its 44th season, and discusses some of the most popular cover stars. It also suggests a number of ways to build an SI collection.

"Autographed Sports Publications," the second chapter, also responds to inquiring collectors. "What is the best way to get SI's (or any publication) autographed?" "Should I send them through the mail?" "If so, how can I maximize the chances that I'll get them back signed and in good shape?"

In addition to answering these questions, the book includes in its third chapter, "Address List," hundreds of addresses you can use to contact individuals who have appeared on a publication cover. In an effort to respect the privacy of cover stars, I have listed institutional rather than individual addresses — teams, colleges, halls of fame, etc. Many of these organizations will gladly forward mail to athletes.

A fourth chapter responds to the questions, "How should I grade my magazines?" and "How should I store and preserve them over time?" Grading, of course, is an inexact science, but here I have done my best to make the art more exacting. And I have offered tips on how to keep your SI's in tip-top shape.

Although I have done my best to respond to a wide variety of questions, the fifth chapter on Sports Illustrated is the heart of the book. Mindful of the fact that the values of magazines vary, like sports cards, according to condition, I have listed not one but three prices for most chapters and two for others. But the price guide, which constitutes the bulk of this book, contains much more information than current values for mint (Mt), excellent-to-mint (Em), and very good (Vg) copies. For example, it lists not only the cover athlete but also his or her team or sport.

Just as critical as condition to a magazine is whether or not it is autographed. The autograph price applies to clean and clear signatures on a Mint (Mt) or Excellent Mint (Em) sports publication. Autograph prices are more subjective than magazine prices. The value for some of the deceased players covers are not known because an autographed magazine may not even exist! However, in most situations, the autographed magazine cover carries the same or more value than an 8x10 autographed photo. For example, deceased baseball player autograph values tend to be more closely to a clean single signed baseball than an 8x10.

Certain issues list key feature articles and ads. Over the years, I have been asked for magazines that contain articles on "Pistol Pete" Maravich, Roberto Clemente, and other athletes that command a strong collectors' following. Corvette enthusiasts, for example, have asked me for magazines with ads of that classic American car, and Sam Snead fans have requested ads featuring "Slammin' Sam." In response to this interest, I have listed articles and ads that in my experience have been widely collected. I have also informed my readers of Sports Illustrated which famous athletes have appeared as youngsters on the popular "Faces in the Crowd" (FIC) page.

In a number of cases, I have also noted when a particular athlete is appearing on the cover for the first time (FC = first cover). I have done this because, like rookie cards, first cover appearances typically bring a premium price. Some collectors, in fact, insist on nothing less than a star's first cover. Because some athletes shared cover honors with others the first time they appeared on it, I have also noted in some cases when an athlete earned his or her first solo cover (FSC).

Also included in the fifth chapter is a section devoted to Sports Illustrated for Kids. This is the child of SI and is geared toward the youth market (6-13). Each magazine has a great cover with great ads and a set of nine sports cards that cover every sport imaginable! Many of these cards are sought after by the player collector (Michael Jordan fans stand up) and usually drive the price of the individual issues. I listed every magazine cover and the cards since both drive the market for these collectibles.

The sixth chapter is devoted to Sport Magazine. This chapter celebrates Sport magazine's 50th anniversary by going into every issue and examining its cover, its photos, its feature articles and its ads. Though the number of autograph Sport magazine collectors is small, Sport magazines has some players that do not appear on Sports Illustrated (Bob Feller, Bob Lemon, etc.) and so many autograph sports magazine collectors seek out Sport magazine as a good substitute.

The seventh chapter is devoted to Time magazine.

The eighth chapter takes a look at general infor-

mation magazines like Life, Look, Newsweek, Colliers magazines with sports covers. This is one of my favorite subjects and is usually the section that everyone asks me about. The covers and pricing are similar to the Sports Illustrated chapter except there are more subjects.

The ninth chapter is an alphabetical checklist of Beckett publications. This book recognizes Beckett as an alternative collectible for many collectors who want to collect more current and popular players. Many players appear on Beckett that do not grace the cover of Sports Illustrated and therefore it has become an alternative for collectors.

The 10th - 12th chapters are devoted to baseball. These chapters covers baseball team publications, World Series, All-Star, Playoff programs, and general baseball magazines.

The 13th - 15th chapters are devoted to basketball. This is the first book ever to cover all of the basketball team publications, All-Star programs, Championship programs, and general basketball magazines.

The 16th - 18th chapters are devoted to football. These chapters cover college as well as pro football team publications. Chapter seventeen is devoted to bowls and general football magazines.

Chapters 19 - 22 do an overview on hockey, golf, boxing and auto racing publications. These chapters will be expanded in years to come.

The 23rd chapter is focused on sports newspapers. This is an area of growth in the hobby because it allows collectors to capture the moment that a key event in sports history occurs.

The final chapter is an Alphabetical Index of Sports covers by player. It lists every player and then the magazines on which he/she appeared. This feature was added because of frequent requests by people who like to collect by player or who like to know if a particular star ever appeared on a sports publication.

The book has three appendices. The first lists various types of Sports Illustrated games, posters, prints, etc. that have been released over the last 40 years. The second deals with the list of stars who appeared on Sports Illustrated. The final appendice concludes the book with sources for magazine supplies, materials, dealers and suppliers. The dealers and providers mentioned have contributed to the sports publication hobby and are worth noting in this second edition of the collectors guide.

Acknowledgments

This book is a "team effort" in more ways than one. Many dealers and collectors have assisted me in bringing it to publication, and I would like to thank them for all their help. Among the folks on my "team" are folks at Sports Illustrated who provided current publication information. Collectors and dealers in sports publications have made contributions in prices and information. These people are: Steve Prothero, Scott Smith, Rich Behrens, Steven Shaff, Stan Keen, Ed Taylor, Joe Esposito, Joe Campius, Lou Madden, Tom Gitto, Bill Chapman, and the thousands of SI collectors we have met over the years. Special acknowledgment to Steve Prothero for his work on the first edition of the collector guide.

I would especially like to acknowledge Thomas Gitto (7 Wilson St., Staten Island, NY 10304) for contributing photos of his autographed Sports Illustrated and Time Magazines.

In addition to these experts, I would like to thank my wife, Carol, for editing the book and my children, Chad and Sarah, for realizing daddy dreams.

I would also like to thank the staff at Beckett Publications for making this third edition possible. This includes: Mike Jaspersen who is responsible for editing the 368 pages, Paul Kerutis and Phaedra Strecher for the art work and compiling, Pepper Hastings for handling the administration and Kevin King for marketing the book to the thousands of book store and libraries everywhere.

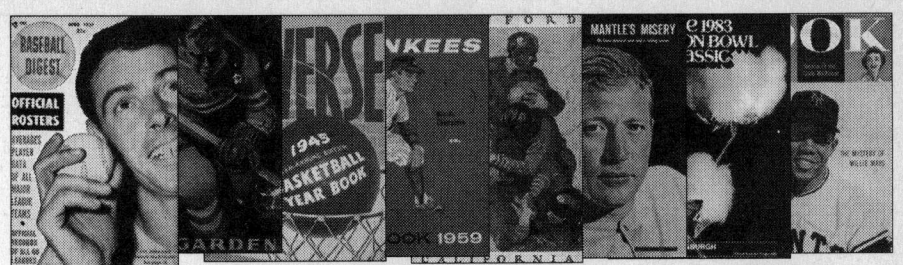

CHAPTER ONE:
COLLECTING SPORTS ILLUSTRATED

Sports Illustrated is an adolescent in the family of American sports magazines. Begun in 1954, it is far younger than, for example, the Sporting News (est. 1886) yet much older than its closest kin, Sports Illustrated for Kids, which began in 1989. Because of its intermediate age, Sports Illustrated is not scarce but chasing down early issues in nice condition is a challenge. This factor, combined with the magazine's runaway popularity among sports fans and the fact that its colorful covers are a near-perfect medium for autograph hunters, contribute to its unparalleled collectibility.

The inspiration behind Sports Illustrated, which is now America's most widely-read sports weekly, was publishing giant Henry R. Luce. Determined to capitalize on the postwar interest among well-to-do American men in the sporting life, Luce (who as the publisher of Time, Life, and Fortune obviously had a penchant for catchy, one-word magazine titles) attempted to buy the name of Sport from McFadden Publications, which in September of 1946 had started the monthly that would become SI's chief rival. Although Luce offered $200,000 for the name, McFadden Publications insisted on a quarter of a million, so Luce shopped around for another title. Jokingly, Luce's associates dubbed his new venture "Jockstrap." But Luce finally settled on "Sports Illustrated."

Unfortunately that moniker too was already taken — by a gentleman named Stuart Scheftel who had inaugurated his monthly Sports Illustrated in an oversized format in the late 1930s. More reasonable than the owners of Sport, Scheftel (who had lent the "Sports Illustrated" name to Dell Publications for a brief run in the 1940s) settled for "something in the low five figures" — plus a lifetime subscription to the new publication — and today's Sports Illustrated was born.

Like Scheftel's Sports Illustrated, which eventually merged with Golf Illustrated, Luce's new magazine began (at a relatively pricey $7.50 a year!) as a highbrow publication aimed at elite sportsmen who had both the money and the leisure to enjoy a week of marlin fishing in the Pacific or an extended safari in East Africa. This fact is reflected in many of the sporting images (now not widely collected) that filled the SI cover in its inaugural year: yacht racers on Long Island Sound, a steeplechase race, a dog with its pheasant prey, etc. Although this well-heeled club had money, it did not have enough members, and Sports Illustrated lost money throughout the 1950s.

In the early 1960s, however, the magazine found its current niche, as a profitable publication devoted primarily, if not exclusively, to major spectator sports such as football, baseball, basketball, hockey, boxing, golf, and tennis. Accompanying this shift in editorial focus (and profitability) was a parallel shift in cover images. Although Sports Illustrated's cover featured some superstars in the mid-1950s — Y.A. Tittle, Ben Hogan, Ted Williams, Rocky Marciano, and Bob Cousy among them — its editors did not discover until later in the decade that covers of dogs and fish and birds would not pay the bills. The decision to jettison the emphasis on the pastimes of elites in favor of an emphasis on popular spectator sports opened the door not only for Sports Illustrated's profitability but also for its current collectibility.

BASEBALL CARD ISSUES

Another factor that contributed to SI's collectibility was its editors' decision to include baseball card inserts in four early issues. The first issue of Sports Illustrated, which hit the newsstands on August 16, 1954, featured on its cover Milwaukee Braves' slugger Eddie Mathews swinging for the fences of Milwaukee's County Stadium. (New York Giants catcher Wes Westrum and umpire Augie Donatelli are also in the shot.) Inside were three fold-out pages of baseball cards made after the manner of regular 1954 Topps cards but printed on paper stock. Among the superstars who appeared on these cards were Willie Mays, Ted Williams, Duke Snider, Richie Ashburn, Jackie Robinson, Ted Kluszewski, and Mathews himself.

SI's second issue, which appeared on August 23, 1954, also included card inserts. Its cover was less interesting (golf bags at the Masters) but its cards are more valuable. Also produced by Topps, this second three-page foldout featured the entire New York Yankee team which included, among them Yogi Berra, Whitey Ford, and Mickey Mantle. Because contractual disagreements prevented Topps from releasing a regular issue card of Mantle, this is the only 1954 Topps Mantle "card" available to collectors.

Conventional wisdom would seem to dictate that the premier issue of a magazine would command the premium price, but conventional wisdom is sometimes wrong. Although SI #1 typically sells for $200 to $300 (a healthy increase over its original price of 25¢), SI #2 retails for around $350 to $500. Why? First and most obviously, the second issue contains not only Yankees cards but a Mantle, and sports collectors are crazy about both New York's most famous team and arguably its most famous modern superstar. Secondly, there were far fewer issues of #2 produced. Luce sent out numerous promotional copies of its inaugural issue, but only subscribers received its next offering. Even today a warehouse find a few years ago has caused the market to be flooded with mint SI #1 issues. Sports Illustrated also has made two recent offerings of its premiere issue through advertisements on its pages and through its collectible marketing arm called the Sports Illustrated Store.

In the spring of 1955, SI produced two more magazines with baseball card inserts. The April 11, 1955 issue showed Giants' legend Willie Mays with Leo Durocher and his wife Laraine Day on the cover. Inside it contained a one-page insert, again produced by Topps but made this time in the image of 1955 cards. Among the stars who appeared on these eight cards were Ernie Banks, Warren Spahn, and Dick Groat. One week later, on April 18, 1955, Sports Illustrated included another page of baseball cards in an issue whose cover featured Cleveland Indians slugger Al Rosen. This less interesting insert contained, along with Rosen, only second-tier stars such as Ferris Fain, Bob Turley, and Roy Sievers.

BUILDING A COLLECTION

There are many ways to build a collection of Sports Illustrated. Usually the easiest way is to subscribe and to save each issue as it is delivered. Many collectors have a run of 10 years or so and are eager to fill in the missing years. The two ways to store entire runs is either with magazine boxes that can be stacked or a library file system in the home that requires magazine (verticle) boxes that are used in libraries.

If, like most collectors, your goal is something less than a complete collection, your first acquisition should be the 35th anniversary issue published as a special supplement by SI on March 26, 1990. Entitled "35 Years of Covers," this magazine pictures every Sports Illustrated cover from 1954 through 1989. Flip through this issue and see what catches your eye. Then fix upon a collecting strategy and stick to it.

One time-honored strategy for SI collecting is to concentrate on a certain sport. This cuts down on both cost and space, but can still be a daunting task. Of all the sports featured on SI covers, football is #1 at 523 covers as of the end of 1995 (not including SI Presents). Baseball and basketball follow with 428 and 324 covers, respectively. Golf (136), boxing, (121), and track (93) come next in popularity, trailed by hockey (83), tennis (73), horseracing (54), and skiing (44).

A third approach is to focus on only your favorite player (or players). Muhammad Ali (a.k.a. Cassius Clay) held the all-time record for cover appearances with 33 until 1996 when Michael Jordan passed it. Third with 28 covers is UCLA Basketball phenom Kareem Abdul-Jabbar [Lew Alcindor], who first appeared on the SI cover on December 5, 1966. Rounding out the current top five are Jack Nicklaus and "Magic" Johnson [see Appendix 1 for cover leaders].

Oddly enough, some SI collectors eschew sports stars entirely, focusing on non-sport celebrities that have appeared on the cover. In this crew are Gary Cooper, Bob Hope, Shirley MacLaine, Steve McQueen, Ernest Hemingway, Burt Reynolds and Arnold Schwarzenegger. Among U.S. Presidents, Ronald Reagan, Gerald Ford, Jack Kennedy and, most recently, Bill Clinton have served as SI cover models.

Clearly the most popular "non-sport" covers, however, are Sports Illustrated's annual swimsuit issues. Swimsuit models appeared on the cover as early as SI's third offering in 1954, but the swimsuit issue did not begin officially until Babette March graced the cover on January 20, 1964. Now a SI institution, this controversial issue prompts cancellations from subscribers every year, but it is also far and away the best seller on the newsstands. A complete run of 33 swimsuit issues from 1964 to 1997 will set a collector back a few hundred dollars.

Given the popularity of the "Sportsman of the Year" (SOY) issue, which Sports Illustrated began on January 3, 1955 with its selection of miler Roger Bannister as 1954's "Sportsman," it should not be surprising that there are collectors who have put together runs of Sportsman (or Sportswoman) of the Year covers. This list includes legends such as Arnold Palmer, Stan Musial, Michael Jordan, Bill Russell, and Billie Jean King (the first Sportswoman of the Year) as well as relative unknowns such as sprinter Bobby Morrow, college quarterback Terry Baker, and miler Jim Ryun.

Collectors specializing in the memorabilia of a particular player may want to track down issues that contain articles featuring their chosen star. There are, moreover, some very interesting and attractive advertisements in the magazine (Corvette ads, etc), especially in the 1950s and 1960s, and some collectors will search for those. (In order to assist those collectors, I have included in the price guide not only the issue date and cover subject but also significant articles and ads.) Nevertheless, collectors primarily interested in the content of the magazine are the exception rather than the rule. Covers, in short, generally drive SI collectibility.

Finally, a growing number of collectors gather only issues that they have a reasonable prospect of getting signed. These folks have merged SI collecting with autograph hunting. (For more on them and their passion, see Chapter 2.)

WHERE TO FIND SI's

There are a number of places to obtain Sports Illustrateds. For people with time on their hands and the desire for a great bargain in their hearts, yard sales, flea markets, and local auctions are good places to start. While the hope of finding baseball cards at bargain basement prices was extinguished years ago, it is still possible to find SI's at these locations for as little as 10 cents apiece. This is especially true at yard sales, where homeowners are frequently ready to throw away anything that doesn't find a buyer over the weekend.

Used book stores, comic book shops, and magazine shops are another good possibility. Most major cities have at least one store devoted exclusively to magazines. Cities that don't have shops specializing in magazines will, no doubt, have stores devoted to used books and comics. These also provide a good opportunity. If when you visit these locations you don't see any SI's, don't give up. Tell the shop owner that you are looking for Sports Illustrated. The next time he's offered a lot, he may give you a call!

If you don't have any luck with these local options, you might want to try national mail-order dealers that specialize in sports-related publications (see Appendix III). You will, of course, pay a little more this way. But your search will be less time consuming, and you are more likely to find the issues you need in collectible condition.

"PERIPHERAL" COLLECTIBLES

Some die-hard SI collectors also chase "peripheral" SI collectibles such as the two "dummy" issues that preceded the magazine's official debut on August 16, 1954. Because Luce hadn't yet settled on a moniker for his new venture, the first "dummy" (December 1953), which featured a crowd of spectators at a football stadium on its cover, was called The New Sport Magazine. The second cover (April 1954) showed a golfer at Pebble Beach and was dubbed, simply, Dummy. These issues, which are frequently accompanied by a letter from Luce asking the reader for helpful comments and criticisms, typically sell for about $400 each in near mint shape.

Also collected by SI buffs are pre-1954 SI's produced either by Scheftel or by Dell. Tops on this list is a May of 1949 Life-sized issue that features Yankee slugger Joe DiMaggio on its cover. Because Dimaggio did not appear on the cover of the "real" SI until 1993, this issue is widely sought-after by SI enthusiasts. It typically commands about $500-700 in nice shape.

Perhaps most difficult to track down are the many "spoofs" of Sports Illustrated published over the years, often by college humor magazines. The most famous and accessible of these is a 1974 parody published by the Harvard Lampoon. Others include Sports Illuminated (1956, Valparaiso), Sports Ill-rated (1956, Maryland), Sports Frustrated (1958, Stanford), and Sports Illiterate (1959, Yale). Mad! magazine has also issued a number of SI parodies.

In addition to these publication "peripherals," some SI collectors also accumulate items sponsored by the magazine and sold through ads on its pages. In this category are Sports Illustrated posters, puzzles, calendars, games, movies, and videos (see Appendix 1). Probably the nicest of these "add-ons" are a set of autographed, limited-edition (1000 or 1500 copies) "Living Legends" lithographs offered to SI readers at $75 and $100 each in the mid-1970s. Some of these signed lithos feature two athletes: Joe Louis and Max Schmeling, Jack Dempsey and Gene Tunney, Wilt Chamberlain and John Havlicek. Others — Stan Musial, Johnny Unitas, Eddie Arcaro, Jack Nicklaus, Rod Laver, Billie Jean King, Red Grange, Arnold Palmer, and Joe DiMaggio, among them — focus on just one superstar. These signed litho's (in

pencil) have commanded prices ranging from $75 - $1,500 depending upon scarcity and demand.

Tomorrow's SI collectibles are also available today through a new venture of Time, Inc.: The Sports Illustrated Store. The SI Store sells a variety of clothing and collectibles, including videos such as "Larry Bird: A Basketball Legend" and "Michael Jordan: Come Fly With Me".

The store also sells oversized, framed lithographs of SI covers signed by superstars such as Larry Bird, Joe Montana, Magic Johnson, Dan Marino, and Reggie Jackson. You can get their current catalog by calling (1-800-274-5200).

CHAPTER TWO:
SPORTS PUBLICATION AUTOGRAPHS

Hunting down signatures of Sports Illustrated cover superstars has in the past few years become an obsession for a growing number of collectors. While many sports fans still prefer autographs on cards, photos, bats, or balls, more and more are turning to magazines such as Life, Time, Sport, Beckett, Look, Colliers, Saturday Evening Post and Sports Illustrated because of their attractive covers, their modest price tags, and the fact that they are dated pieces with interesting historical content. Of all these magazines, Sports Illustrated is far and away the most popular among collectors of sports autographs. In fact, many categorically refuse to meddle with any other magazine. This chapter will fill you in on the autographed publication craze and offer you some tips on how to get autographs for yourself.

GETTING STARTED

There are almost as many ways to build a collection of autographed sports publications as there are collectors. The key is to focus. Some autographed publication collectors chase only Heisman Trophy winners that have appeared on the cover. Others collect only baseball Hall of Famers, or SI's Sportsmen and Sportswomen of the year, or footballers featured on the annual Super Bowl cover. Another simple method is to concentrate on a particular team or city. Start with the Los Angeles Lakers, for example, or, if you're from Philadelphia, fix your sights on the Phillies, Flyers, Sixers, and Eagles.

If you want a slightly broader collection, you might focus on a particular sport. If you're a baseball fan, don't worry about gymnast Mary Lou Retton. And if you're a gymnastics fan, forget about Red Sox slugger Carl Yastrzemski.

The most ambitious approach, of course, is to try to get as many different issues as possible signed. There are over 2,300 different covers (and counting) of Sports Illustrated, but some can never be signed either because they appeared following a star's death (e.g. the Len Bias and Reggie Lewis covers) or because they featured dogs, horses, or other non-signers. Collectors pursuing this diffi-

cult route should emulate Stan Keen of Oregon and Scott Smith of New Jersey, each of whom has amassed a collection of over a thousand signatures.

One modification of this approach adopted by slightly less ambitious collectors is to be satisfied with a single signed issue of any particular player. These folks forget about Muhammad Ali's 33 different covers or even Willie Mays' 8 and are satisfied with one cover signed per athlete (frequently, his or her first!). Even this approach, however, will send you off in hot pursuit of hundreds of different athletes.

If you are new to the signed Sports Illustrated game, you might want to emulate collectors who eschew marquee sports such as baseball, football, and basketball, and concentrate instead on less popular, but equally exciting sports where athletes are often genuinely glad to receive fan mail. These collectors frequently write to stars via their respective halls of fame, which are almost always willing to forward mail to their inductees. (For a list of hall of fame addresses, see Chapter 3.)

No matter which approach you take you will find adventure in each one. Most of the athletes that I meet who sign my cover are delighted to sign the magazine and usually have a story to add to it.

For example, Jim "Toy Cannon" Wynn told me he felt jinxed after he appeared on the cover in 1974. He was not too happy about the jinx but he is happy to sign his magazine cover today.

VALUES OF SIGNED SI'S

Because autographed SI's are not as frequently bought and sold as, for example, signed 8 x 10 photos or "cut" signatures, establishing their value is a bit tricky. One thing is clear, however: unlike baseball cards, which frequently decrease in value when signed, SI's always increase in price when autographed. One "rule of thumb" is that autographed Sports Illustrateds are worth about what the unsigned magazine is worth, plus the value of an autographed 8 x 10. So, for example, if an autographed Carl Yastrzemski 8 x 10 is worth about $25 and his 1967 "Sportsman of the Year" issue also runs $30 in EM shape, the signed SOY magazine should sell for approximately $55. This quick rule works best for relatively common autographs. Signed SI collectors are frequently willing to bid up the value of magazines autographed by "tough" signers or deceased superstars well beyond the combined value of the magazine and the 8 x 10. Signed Ben Hogan and Mickey Mantle SI's, for example, have sold for as much as $350 — well over double what our "rule of thumb" would indicate. In this case (in fact in all cases!), signed SI's are worth no more and no less than what the market will bear.

The price guide section has an autograph additional value to each issue. The autograph price is under the Mt and Em prices on the right hand section of the value list. These are market estimate 'guides' for nice clean autographs on an SI or other magazine. It is critical to note that the prices for tough autographed issues and those of deceased autographed players will be more likely to go for values higher than those prices listed. It should be noted that near mint magazines that are signed sell much faster than EM magazines with a label.

IN-PERSON AUTOGRAPHS

The preferred way to obtain autographs is, of course, in person. Most big-time athletes do not sign through the mail, and almost all current athletes who are on the circuit get too much mail to answer. A few players have resorted to the dreaded autopen while others have been known to use an autograph stamp. So, personally witnessing a sports star signing your magazine is the only sure-fire way to know it's authentic. When you track down Wayne Gretzky after a practice and he agrees to sign your "Sportsman of the Year" SI cover, you know the autograph is legitimate, and you have a memory of your "brush with fame" to boot!

If you live in a major city, go to sporting events early and try to find participants there (before batting practice at the ballpark or before the "shoot-around" at a basketball venue). Better yet, go the day before to where the team works out. Generally, you'll have better luck at the Atlanta Falcons' practice at Suwanee, Georgia than at their game at the Georgia Dome and more success at Pebble Beach practice rounds than at the U.S. Open itself.

These suggestions work for at least some of today's athletes, but what about retired superstars?

One approach is to begin with your local paper and scan it carefully, especially the columns of your local purveyor of celebrity "gossip." There are hundreds and hundreds of SI cover subjects so chances are good that at least one of them will be passing through your city in a given month. If they're appearing at a press conference, playing in an exhibition, filming a commercial, or participating in a celebrity golf tournament, show up. And if you can find out where they are staying, park yourself in the hotel lobby. Some hotels now bar this practice, but many still permit it, especially if you are well-dressed and clean-shaven.

If you're persistent, prepared, and polite, you may get lucky. Bring along your Sharpie pen (the writing implement of choice for SI collectors), and get the attention of the athlete by holding up your magazine. You'll be amazed how frequently you'll hear a star say that he or she is surprised and delighted to see it. If you have duplicates, bring them along too. The athlete might want one or two for himself, and may be willing to sign multiples for you in return. Sound implausible? It's not. Remember that when superstars are in their prime they concentrate on winning championships, not on saving memorabilia. Recently a golf collector encountered Sam Snead after a charity golf tournament with a handful of SI covers. Snead was thrilled to see the November 12, 1962 cover featuring him with a young Arnold Palmer. The collector offered it to him, and he gratefully signed a number of his SI covers in return.

If preparedness is important, remember that the other two "P's" (politeness and persistence) also go a long way. Superstars may be great at shooting a basketball or reading a green, but they are people like you and I. They don't like folks shouting at them or interrupting their meals at restaurants. And believe it or not your chances of getting an autograph actually go up if you avoid pushing, shoving, and screaming. Nonetheless, persistence can pay off. After Jimmy Connors finished playing in a recent team tennis match, he was surrounded by autograph seekers and refused them all. Once he emerged from a press conference, a smaller group of fans besieged him, and again he refused. Undaunted, one SI collector followed him away from the stadium, walking on what he knew was his writing side (his left, of course!). He complimented him on his match, and politely asked Connors for his autograph. Connors, just before jumping into a waiting limousine, signed the magazine in a clear, bold hand.

AUTOGRAPH SHOWS

Sports memorabilia shows with autograph guests are another way to obtain "in person" signatures. Although this route is more expensive than obtaining autographs yourself before a workout or after a spring training game, it is certainly less time consuming. And depending on the athlete, you may also get a handshake and a short conversation for your autograph fee.

Charges for this service vary greatly from athlete to athlete and from show to show. The status of the star in his sport obviously has a lot to do with the cost of his or her autograph. That is why Phillies slugger Mike Schmidt (typically $50) costs more than, say, Pittsburgh shortstop Dick Groat (about $8). But scarcity also plays an important role. Bob Feller may be one of the greatest pitchers who ever lived, but he has been a regular on the baseball card show circuit for years, so his signature is inexpensive (also about $8). Prices really soar when a signer combines greatness with scarcity, as in the case of Celtic legend Bill Russell who until recently categorically refused virtually every autograph request. When he finally agreed to begin signing, collectors didn't blink at fees in triple figures.

If you have paid a lot of money for your autographed sports publication and there is a chance you might want to sell or trade it in the future, you might want to get it notarized. Frequently show promoters contract for the services of a notary public; you can typically obtain their certification on the spot for a nominal fee (about $3-$5). If the autographing fee was modest or you don't want to shell out the money for the notary, save your stamped autograph ticket or a flyer advertising the show. Even better, have your photograph taken with your hero. Some show promoters still allow this, despite the fact that it slows down the line, and you can pull the picture out in the future for "evidence" of your signature's authenticity.

For people who don't live in the vicinity of major card shows, it is possible to obtain autographs from show promoters through the mail. If this is the route you want to go, get references to be sure you are dealing with a legitimate and considerate promoter. In order to preserve the condition of your magazine, take pains to pack your magazine

with a backing board and to mail it in a padded manila envelope. If the show promoter wants you to include return postage (and they usually do), be sure to include an SASE (self-addressed stamped envelope [Priority Mail from the Post Office]) for your SI's safe return trip. However, here is my additional advice on making sure you get your magazine back the same way you sent it.

Type a very clear letter stating the following issues:

a. EXACTLY how you want the magazine signed (Location & personalization & HOF date, etc.),
b. what you want it signed with (Pen, Sharpie, etc.),
c. how you want the magazine handled,
d. how you want it repackaged,
e. How you want it reshipped,
f. State how to identify your magazine (be it with the mailing label name or with your signature penciled lightly on a page inside the magazine.

Be very clear with your instructions. Believe me, it is worth the time. I thought I was getting a super deal from one promoter but found that my magazine was damaged and my complaints were ignored. Also promoters may mix your Mint 1955 Sports Illustrated Ted Williams with someone else's, so tagging your magazine with a pencil mark inside on a specific page (how's page 10) is not a bad idea (your signature is usually good - make sure you can erase it without leaving a mark).

AUTOGRAPHS BY MAIL

Collectors who can't afford to shell out the cash commanded by stars at card shows or who desire signatures of athletes not currently on the autographing circuit will want to contact their heroes directly by mail. The most surprising thing about this strategy is how frequently it works!

The first hurdle to this approach is, of course, obtaining a current address. Here the lists published by autograph collecting newsletters are invaluable. More up-to-date than lists published in a book format, these monthly or bimonthly newsletters routinely publish reports from subscribers regarding addresses that have worked (or failed) and the signing policies of individuals. Clearly the best value of these is "The Autograph Banker," which is published occasionally by George

Haggas of Audubon, New Jersey. An old-fashioned collector, Haggas does his newsletter just for the fun of it. He charges no subscription fees, and asks only that you send him SASE's for as many of his upcoming newsletters as you want. You can reach him at: P.O. Box 42, Audubon, New Jersey 08106. Another source is the internet. You can check out autograph lists and addresses or you can just vist the books website at: www.Asportmall.com.

If you can't get an individual address for an athlete, try his or her college athletic department, pro team, agent, or sponsoring company. (Our address list will help you here.) In fact, sports stars frequently prefer that you write them in this indirect manner, freeing up their home mailboxes for family matters. You will generally have better luck during the off-season or pre season, when athletes have both less mail and more free time to answer it.

Unfortunately, a few of America's most famous superstars will not sign anything through the mail. Don't be too harsh on them, however. Some get practically as much mail as the President and have as little free time. Anything you send to these marquee players will either be returned or, worse, thrown away. As a general rule, therefore, you should never send anything through the mail that you cannot absolutely, positively live without.

Those who will sign through the mail frequently have clear, if unannounced, policies regarding what they will and will not sign, so it may be worth sending a letter (with an SASE) inquiring about policies before you send your publication. Some athletes will return an autographed photo to admirers but will refuse to sign items sent to them. Others will sign only one item, while others will sign up to three. Still others will write back, requesting a fee or referring you to a fan club that offers signed items for sale. In an attempt to frustrate the efforts of dealers who sell autographed items obtained through the mail, some will insist on personalizing (e.g., "To Bill . . ."). Others will refuse to personalize anything on the grounds that it takes up too much time. Sometimes, the secretaries of athletes who are gracious enough to sign through the mail keep track of writers whom their employees have previously accommodated. These athletes will respond to your first request but return a second or third unsigned. The bottom line here is that there are no hard and fast rules about athletes' autographing policies.

IMPROVING YOUR CHANCES

You can do at least four things to improve your chances of getting your SI signed and returned from your favorite athletes. The first rule is to save the athlete both time and money by including a SASE with sufficient return postage. For stars residing outside the United States, use International Reply Coupons (IRC's), which can be exchanged in foreign countries for stamps.

The second rule is to send a thoughtful letter. This letter should be handwritten but legible. It should be concise and to the point. You should tell the athlete why you are writing to him (or her) — you run track, you love three-point shooters, you went to UCLA like he did, you share the same birthday, etc. In short, you should do everything you can to distinguish yourself from all the other requests the athlete receives. DO NOT send a copied letter with the athlete's name filled in, and DO NOT tell the athlete she is the hundred-and-first person you have written to this year (even if she is). Such approaches are, for obvious reasons, doomed to fail.

The third rule is to pack your magazine carefully. My recommendation is the following:

1. Put the SI and backboards in a plastic magazine bag with a backboard on the outside to prevent the magazine from getting bent.
2. Put a RETURN SASE U.S. POST OFFICE PRIORITY MAILER WITH YOUR RETURN ADDRESS and stamp (first class) inside the package, preferably next to the magazine.
3. Put your letter in front of the magazine in the plastic magazine bag, state in the letter how you want the magazine to be shipped back to you. Also attach any donation or check to the letter.
4. Put the bagged SI in a bubble-wrapped manila envelope that you get from an office supply center.
5. Place the bubble-wrapped manila envelope (with the magazine inside it) inside a U.S. Post Office Priority mailer.

These five steps sound like a lot of work, but in my experience it is better to be safe than sorry. The good news is that players usually treat your magazine better than promoters. This is because promoters sometimes hire people to handle the mail who are just not in tune with the hobby at all.

Finally, you might want to include a small check ($2-$10) to speed up the process. Some players will donate the money to charity, while many more will return the check uncashed.

If you are just starting out collecting autographed sports publications through the mail, you might want to begin with individuals who receive only a few pieces of fan mail a month rather than a few hundred a day. Skip big sports names in baseball, and focus on other sports like basketball or football. If you want to make a retired athlete's day, try swimmers or track and field stars.

If you don't have these athletes' individual addresses, try the appropriate hall of fame. If they've been on an SI cover, chances are that they've been inducted into their respective hall. The vast majority of halls of fame are happy to forward mail to their inductees. (For a list of these addresses, see Chapter 3.)

Gathering sports publication autographs through the mail may be a bit risky but it is lots of fun. You will probably, at one time or another, receive a "ghost" signature and you may lose some magazines in the process, but you will go to your mailbox each day with a new sense of adventure!

AUTOGRAPH DEALERS AND OTHER STRATEGIES

If you are serious about collecting autographed sports publications, you may want to call on the services of a reputable autographed publications dealer. Basketball superstar Michael Jordan doesn't do card shows, doesn't sign through the mail, and is a very tough signature in person, so if you absolutely, positively must have an autographed Jordan cover, you will probably have to go through a dealer. The same is true, for obvious reasons, if you want an autographed SI cover of deceased athletes such as Arthur Ashe or if you want a "cut" autograph to frame with an unsigned SI.

When buying through a dealer, the most important advice is to be cautious. There are some cheats out there, so get references. Ask about how and when the dealer obtained the autograph and why he or she thinks it's legitimate. Then, after you are convinced of the story, get a money-back guarantee (It should be automatic and save your receipts!). Finally, don't put too much stock in so-called "certificates of authenticity." If a dealer is unscrupulous enough to be peddling fake autographs, he is probably not going to worry too much about distributing fake "certificates."

Once you have determined that a dealer is reputable, educate yourself about the value of autographs. Sections of this book are devoted to helping educate the collector on the autograph value of a sports publication. However, it is also good to know why certain autographs are more valuable than others. Celtics great Bill Russell is a tough signature and his signed SI (assuming you can find one) rightfully commands a premium price ($250-$300) because he has only done three signings in his entire career! But Eddie Mathews is a show circuit regular whose signature doesn't add more than $10 or $15 to the cost of his magazine covers. Some autographs are hard to obtain because they do not sign through the mail and do not do shows. Try, for example, finding autographed SI's of great Russian athletes...good luck.

Finally, be picky about condition. Don't pay a "mint" price for a "very good" magazine. Make sure the signature is legible and placed in a good spot on the cover. The bottom line here is that you should be certain the cover is something you would be proud to frame and display before you agree to buy it.

There are, of course, other ways to get your magazines signed. If you have a friend who's going to spring training, give him two of your Frank Robinson covers and tell him you expect one back, signed, in return. You might also want to engage in the ancient practice of horse trading. Even if you are only interested in one signed SI per player, get two whenever you have a chance. The second can be used in the future for "trade bait." The lesson here is to keep your ears and options open. Get to know other collectors. Let friends know that you collect autographed SI's. Soon you will discover that a co-worker lives next door to swimming great Donna de Varona or that an acquaintance works for a network and can hit up ex-Steeler Terry Bradshaw. Before you know it, you'll be on your way!

CHAPTER THREE:
ADDRESS LISTS

What follows is a list of addresses you can use to contact sports publication cover subjects. I have not listed individual addresses for two reasons. First, I want to respect the privacy of cover stars who understandably prefer not to be contacted, even by their most admiring fans, at their homes. Second, I have discovered over the years that many athletes prefer to be reached indirectly (via their team, for example) rather than directly (via their residence). As a result, you are in many cases likely to have greater signing success through the institutional addresses I have listed here than through home addresses.

Among the addresses I have included are those for MLB, NBA, NFL, and NHL teams and for colleges whose stars have appeared on the SI cover. I also fill you in on how you can contact key halls of fame and I have provided listings for other associations and key corporations through which you are likely to have signing success. If you need home, business or charity addresses you can request that by subscribing to the SPN, at PO Box 26596, Las Vegas NV 89126-0596 ($24/yr). Many collectors share addresses of people who sign through the mail. The chapter concludes with a list of deceased sports publication cover stars dated through June of 1996.

Major League Baseball Team Addresses

Office of the Commissioner
350 Park Ave., 17th Floor
New York, NY 10022

American League Office
350 Park Ave.
New York, NY 10022

National League Office
350 Park Ave.
New York, NY 10022

Anaheim Angels
2000 Gene Autry Way
Anaheim, CA 92806

Atlanta Braves
P.O. Box 4064
Atlanta, GA 30302

Baltimore Orioles
333 W. Camden St.
Baltimore, MD 21201

Boston Red Sox
4 Yawkey Way
Boston, MA 02215

Chicago Cubs
1060 W. Addison St.
Chicago, IL 60613-4397

Chicago White Sox
333 W. 35th St.
Chicago, IL 6061

Cincinnati Reds
100 Cinergy Field
Cincinnati, OH 45202

Cleveland Indians
2401 Ontario St.
Cleveland, OH 44115

Colorado Rockies
Coors Field
2001 Blake Street
Denver, CO 80205-2000

Detroit Tigers
Tiger Stadium
Detroit, MI 48216

Florida Marlins
2269 NW 199th St.
Miami, FL 33056

Houston Astros
P.O. Box 288
Houston, TX 77001-0288

Kansas City Royals
P.O. Box 419969
Kansas City, MO 64141

Los Angeles Dodgers
1000 Elysian Park Ave.
Los Angeles, CA 90012

Milwaukee Brewers
County Stadium
P.O. Box 3099
Milwaukee, WI 53201-3099

Minnesota Twins
501 Chicago Ave. S.
Minneapolis, MN 55415

Montreal Expos
4549 Pierre-de-Coubertin Ave.
Montreal, PQ H1V 3N7

New York Mets
Roosevelt Ave. & 126th St.
Flushing, NY 11368

New York Yankees
Yankee Stadium
E. 161 St. and River Ave.
Bronx, NY 10451

Oakland Athletics
Oakland Coliseum
7000 Coliseum Way
Oakland, CA 94621-1918

Philadelphia Phillies
P.O. Box 7575
Philadelphia, PA 19101

Pittsburgh Pirates
600 Stadium Circle
Pittsburgh, PA 15212

St. Louis Cardinals
250 Stadium Plaza
St. Louis, MO 63102

San Diego Padres
P.O. Box 2000
San Diego, CA 92112-2000

San Francisco Giants
3Com Park at
Candlestick Point
San Francisco, CA 94124

Seattle Mariners
P.O. Box 4100
411 First Ave. S.
Seattle, WA 98104

Texas Rangers
1000 Ballpark Way
Arlington, TX 76011

Toronto Blue Jays
One Blue Jay Way,
Suite 3200
Toronto, ONT M5V 1J1

National Basketball League Team Addresses

Eastern Conference
Atlanta Hawks
One CNN Center
South Tower, Ste. 405
Atlanta, GA 30303

Boston Celtics
151 Merrimac St.
Boston, MA 02114

Charlotte Hornets
100 Hive Drive
Charlotte, NC 28217

Chicago Bulls
1901 West Madison St.
Chicago, IL 60612

Cleveland Cavaliers
1 Center Court
Cleveland, OH 44115-4001

Detroit Pistons
The Palace of Auburn Hills
Two Championship Drive
Auburn Hills, MI 48326

Indiana Pacers
300 E. Market St.
Indianapolis, IN 46204

Miami Heat
Sun Trust International Cntr.
One S.E. 3rd Ave., Suite 2300
Miami, FL 33131

Milwaukee Bucks
Bradley Center
1001 N. Fourth St.
Milwaukee, WI
53203-1312

New Jersey Nets
Meadowlands Arena
405 Murray Hill Parkway
East Rutherford, NJ 07073

New York Knicks
Madison Square Garden
Two Pennsylvania Plaza
New York, NY 10121-0091

Orlando Magic
One Magic Place
Orlando Ave.
Orlando, FL 32801-1114

Philadelphia 76ers
1 CoreStates Complex
Philadelphia, PA
19148

Toronto Raptors
20 Bay Street
Suite 1702
Toronto, Ontario M5J 2N8

Washington Wizards
1 Harry S. Truman Dr.
Landover, MD 20785

Western Conference
Dallas Mavericks
Reunion Arena
777 Sports St.
Dallas, TX 75207

Denver Nuggets
McNichols Sports Arena
1635 Clay St.
Denver, CO 80204-1799

Golden State Warriors
550 10th St.
Oakland, CA 94612

Houston Rockets
The Summit
Two Greenway Plaza
Houston, TX 77046-3865

Los Angeles Clippers
L.A. Memorial Sports Arena
3939 S. Figueroa St.
Los Angeles, CA 90037

Los Angeles Lakers
Great Western Forum
3900 West Manchester Blvd.
P.O. Box 10
Inglewood, CA 90306

Minnesota Timberwolves
Target Center
600 First Ave. North
Minneapolis, MN 55403

Phoenix Suns
201 E. Jefferson St.
Phoenix, AZ 85004

Portland Trail Blazers
One Center Court
Ste. 200
Portland, OR 97227

Sacramento Kings
One Sports Parkway
Sacramento, CA 95834

San Antonio Spurs
Alamodome
100 Montana
San Antonio, TX 78203-1031

Seattle SuperSonics
190 Queen Anne Ave. N.
Ste. 200
Seattle, WA 98109-9711

Utah Jazz
Delta Center
301 West South Temple
Salt Lake City, UT 84101

Vancouver Grizzlies
800 Griffiths Way
Vancouver, BC V6B 6G1

National Football League Team Addresses

AFC

Baltimore Ravens
11001 Owings Mills Blvd.
Owings Mills, MD 21117

Buffalo Bills
One Bills Drive
Orchard Park, NY 14127

Cincinnati Bengals
One Bengals Drive
Cincinnati, OH 45204

Denver Broncos
13655 Broncos Pkwy.
Englewood, CO 80112
Indianapolis Colts
7001 W. 56th St.
Indianapolis, IN 46254

Jacksonville Jaguars
One Alltel Stadium Place
Jacksonville, FL 32202

Kansas City Chiefs
One Arrowhead Drive
Kansas City, MO 64129

Miami Dolphins
7500 S.W. 30th St.
Davie, FL 33314

New England Patriots
60 Washington St.
Foxboro, MA 02035

New York Jets
1000 Fulton Ave.
Hempstead, NY 11550

Oakland Raiders
1220 Harbor Bay Pkwy.
Alameda, CA 94502

Pittsburgh Steelers
300 Stadium Circle
Pittsburgh, PA 15212

San Diego Chargers
P.O. Box 609609
San Diego, CA 92160

Seattle Seahawks
11220 N.E. 53rd St.
Kirkland, WA 98033

Tennessee Oilers
P.O. Box 198497
Nashville, TN 37219

NFC

Arizona Cardinals
P.O. Box 888
Phoenix, AZ 85001

Atlanta Falcons
One Falcon Place
Suwanee, GA 30024-2198

Carolina Panthers
Ericsson Stadium

800 South Mint St.
Charlotte, NC 28202-1502

Chicago Bears
Halas Hall at Conway Park
1000 Football Drive
Lake Forest, IL 60045-4829

Dallas Cowboys
One Cowboys Pkwy.
Irving, TX 75063

Detroit Lions
1200 Featherstone Road
Pontiac, MI 48342

Green Bay Packers
1265 Lombardi Ave.
P.O. Box 10628

Green Bay, WI 54307-0628

Minnesota Vikings
9520 Viking Drive
Eden Prairie, MN 55344

New Orleans Saints
5800 Airline Highway
Metairie, LA 70003

New York Giants
Giants Stadium
East Rutherford, NJ
07073

Philadelphia Eagles
Veterans Stadium
3501 South Broad St.
Philadelphia, PA 19148-5201

St. Louis Rams
One Rams Way
St. Louis, MO 63045

San Francisco 49ers
4949 Centennial Blvd.
Santa Clara, CA 95054

Tampa Bay Buccaneers
One Buccaneer Place
Tampa, FL 33607

Washington Redskins
P.O. Box 17247
Dulles Airport
Washington, D.C. 20041

National Hockey League Team Addresses

Boston Bruins
One Fleet Center
Suite 250
Boston, MA 02114-1303

Buffalo Sabres
Marine Midland Arena
One Seymour H. Knox III Plaza
Buffalo, NY 14203

Calgary Flames
Canadian Airlines Saddledome
P.O. Box 1540, Station M
Calgary, Alberta T2P 3B9

Carolina Hurricanes
5000 Aerial Center Pkwy. Suite 1000
Morrisville, NC 27560

Chicago Blackhawks
United Center
1901 W. Madison St.
Chicago, IL 60612

Colorado Avalanche
McNichols Arena
1635 Clay St.
Denver, CO 80204-1799

Dallas Stars
StarCenter
211 Cowboys Parkway
Irving, TX 75063

Detroit Red Wings
Joe Louis Arena
600 Civic Center
Detroit, MI 48226

Edmonton Oilers
11230-110 Street

Edmonton, Alberta
T5G 3G8

Florida Panthers
110 N.E. 3rd Ave.
2nd Floor
Ft. Lauderdale, FL 33301

Los Angeles Kings
The Great Western Forum
3900 W. Manchester Blvd.
P.O. Box 17013
Inglewood, CA 90308

The Mighty Ducks
of Anaheim
2695 E. Katella Ave.
P.O. Box 61077
Anaheim, CA 92803

Montreal Canadiens
Molson Centre
1260 Rue de la Gauchetiere W.
Montreal, Quebec
H3B 5E8

New Jersey Devils
Continental Airlines Arena
50 Route 120 North
P.O. Box 504
East Rutherford, NJ 07073

New York Islanders
Nassau Coliseum
Uniondale, NY 11553

New York Rangers
Madison Square Garden
Two Pennsylvania Plaza
New York, NY 10001

Ottawa Senators
1000 Palladium Drive
Kanata, Ontario K2V IA5

Philadelphia Flyers
1 CoreStates Complex
Philadelphia, PA 19148

Phoenix Coyotes
1 Renaissance Square

2 N. Central, Suite 1930
Phoenix, AZ 85004

Pittsburgh Penguins
Civic Arena
66 Mario Lemieux Place
Pittsburgh, PA 15219

St. Louis Blues
Kiel Center
1401 Clark Ave.
St. Louis, MO 63013

San Jose Sharks
San Jose Arena
525 W. Santa Clara St.
San Jose, CA 95113

Tampa Bay Lightning
401 Channelside Dr.
Tampa, FL 33602

Toronto Maple Leafs
Maple Leaf Gardens
60 Carlton St.
Toronto, Ontario M5B 1L1

Vancouver Canucks
General Motors Place
800 Griffiths Way
Vancouver,
British Columbia V5K 3N7

Washington Capitals
MCI Center
601 F Street NW
Washington, DC 20001

Major College Addresses

University of Alabama
Tuscaloosa, AL 35487

University of Arkansas
Fayetteville, AR 72701

Army
West Point, NY 10996

Auburn University
Auburn, AL 36831

Boston College
Chestnut Hill, MA 02167

Brigham Young University
Provo, UT 84602

University of California
Berkeley, CA 94720

UCLA
Los Angeles, CA 90024

Clemson University
Clemson, SC 29633

University of Cincinnati
Cincinnati, OH 45221

University of Colorado
Boulder, CO 80309

Cornell University
Box 729
Ithaca, NY 14853

Davidson College
Davidson, NC 28036

Duke University
Durham, NC 27708

University of Florida
Gainesville, FL 32604

Florida State University
Tallahassee, FL 32316

Georgetown University
Washington, DC 20057

University of Georgia
Athens, GA 30613

Georgia Tech
Atlanta, GA 30332

Harvard University
60 John F. Kennedy St.
Cambridge, MA 02138

University of Houston
Houston, TX 77204

Indiana University
Bloomington, IN 47405

University of Iowa
Iowa City, IA 52242

University of Kansas
Lawrence, KS 66045

Kansas State University
Manhattan, KS 66506

University of Kentucky
Lexington, KY 40506

Louisiana State University
Baton Rouge, LA 70894

University of Louisville
Louisville, KY 40292

Marquette University
Milwaukee, WI 53233

Loyola Marymount
Los Angeles, CA 90045

University of Maryland
College Park, MD 20740

University of Miami
Coral Gables, FL 33124

University of Michigan
Ann Arbor, MI 48109

Michigan State University
East Lansing, MI 48824

University of Minnesota
Minneapolis, MN 55455

University of Mississippi
Oxford, MS 38677

Navy
Annapolis, MD 21402

University of Nebraska
Lincoln, NE 68588

UNLV
Las Vegas, NV 89154

University of North Carolina
Chapel Hill, NC 27514

North Carolina State
Releigh, NC 27695

Northwestern University
Evanston, IL 60208

University of Notre Dame
Notre Dame, IN 46556

Ohio State University
Columbus, OH 43210

University of Oklahoma
Norman, OK 73109

University of Oregon
Eugene, OR 97403

Oregon State University
Corvallis, OR 97331

Penn State University
Univ. Park, PA 16802

University of Pittsburgh
Pittsburgh, PA 15213

Princeton University
Box 71/Jadwin Gym
Princeton, NJ 08544

Purdue University
West Lafayette, IN 47907

St. John's University
Jamaica, NY 11439

University of San Francisco
San Francisco, CA 94117

Santa Clara University
Santa Clara, CA 95053

Seton Hall University
South Orange, NJ 07079

University of South Carolina
Columbia, SC 29208

Southern Methodist University
(SMU)
Dallas, TX 75275

USC
Los Angeles, CA 90089

Stanford University
Stanford, CA 94305

Syracuse University
Syracuse, NY 13244

Temple University
Philadelphia, PA 19122

University of Tennessee
Knoxville, TN 37901

University of Texas
Austin, TX 78713

Texas A&M
College Station, TX 77843

Texas Christian University
Fort Worth, TX 76129

University of Utah
Salt Lake City, UT 84112

Villanova University Villanova,
PA 19085

University of Virginia
Charlottesville, VA 22903

University of Washington
Seattle, WA 98195

Yale University
Box 208216A Yale Station
New Haven, CT 06520

Halls of Fame

College Football Hall of Fame
5440 Kings Island Dr.
Kings Island, OH 45034

Collegiate Tennis Hall of Fame
University of Georgia
Athens, GA 30613

Hall of Fame of the Trotter
240 Main St.
Goshen, NY 10924

Indianapolis Motor Speedway
Hall of Fame Museum
4790 West 16th St.
Indianapolis, IN 46222

International Boxing Hall of
Fame
1 Hall of Fame Dr.
Canastota, NY 13032

International Gymnastics Hall
of Fame
227 Brooks St.
Oceanside, CA 92054

International Motorsports Hall
of Fame (NASCAR)
4000 Speedway Boulevard
Talladega, AL 35160

International Swimming Hall of
Fame
One Hall of Fame Dr.
Fort Lauderdale, FL 33316

International Tennis Hall of
Fame
194 Bellevue Ave.
Newport, RI 02840

International Women's Sports
Hall of Fame
Eisenhower Park
East Meadow, NY 11554

Hockey Hall of Fame
Exhibition Place
Toronto, Ontario
Canada M6K 3C3

Museum of Yachting
Fort Adams State Park
Newport, RI 02840

Naismith Memorial Basketball
Hall of Fame
1150 W. Columbus Ave.
Springfield, MA 01101

National Baseball Hall of Fame
Main Street
Cooperstown, NY 13326

National Bowling Hall of Fame
& Museum
111 Stadium Plaza
St. Louis, MO 63102

National Jockey Hall of Fame
Pimlico Racetrack
Belvedere & Park Heights Ave.
Baltimore, MD 21210

National Museum of Racing and
Hall of Fame (Horseracing)
Union Ave. & Ludlow St.
Saratoga Springs, NY 12866

National Rowing Foundation
Philadelphia Maritime Museum
321 Chestnut St.
Philadelphia, PA 19101

National Soccer Hall of Fame
5-11 Ford Ave.
Oneonta, NY 13820

National Track and Field Hall of
Fame
200 South Capitol
(One Hoosier Dome)
Indianapolis, IN 46225

National Wrestling Hall of Fame
405 W. Hall of Fame Ave
Stillwater, OK 74075

PGA World Golf Hall of Fame
SR 2 • Pinehurst, NC 28374

PGA Hall of Fame
Box 109601
100 Ave. of Champions
Palm Beach Gardens, FL 33418

Pro Football Hall of Fame
2121 George Halas Dr. NW
Canton, OH 44708

Santa Cruz Surfing Museum
Lighthouse Point
Santa Cruz, CA 95060

Speedskating Hall of Fame
371 Washington St.
Newburgh, NY 12550

Stock Car Hall of Fame
SR 34 & US 52
Darlington, SC 29532

U.S. Bicycling Hall of Fame
34 East Main St.
Somerville, NJ 08876

U.S. Hockey Hall of Fame
Frontage & Hat Trick
Eveleth, MN 55734

U.S. National Ski Hall of Fame
Route 41
Ishpeming, MI 49849

U.S. Olympic Committee Hall of
Fame
1750 East Boulder St.
Colorado Springs, CO 80909-
5760

World Figure Skating Hall of
Fame
20 First St.
Colorado Springs, CO 80906

Other Sports Addresses

ABC Sports
47 W. 66th St., 13th Fl.
New York, NY 10023

Association of Tennis
Professionals
200 ATP Tour Blvd.
Ponte Vedra Beach, FL 32082

CBS Sports
51 W. 52nd St., 25th Fl.
New York, NY 10019

ESPN
ESPN Plaza
Bristol, CT 06010

Harlem Globetrotters
15301 Ventura Blvd., Suite
430
Sherman Oaks, CA 91403

IndyCar
390 Enterprise Court
Bloomfield Hills, MI 48302

Ladies' Professional Golf
Association
2570 Volusia Ave., #B
Daytona Beach, FL 32114

NASCAR
Box 2875
Daytona Beach, FL 32120

NBC Sports
30 Rockefeller Plaza
New York, NY 10112

PGA Tour
112 TPC Blvd.
Ponte Vedra Beach, FL 32082

U.S. Figure Skating Association
20 First St.
Colorado Springs, Co 80906

U.S. Olympic Committee
1 Olympic Plaza
Colorado Springs, CO 80909

U.S. International Speedskating
Association
Box 16157
Rocky River, OH 44116

U.S. Skiing
Box 100
1500 Kearns Blvd.
Park City, UT 84060

U.S. Swimming, Inc.
1 Olympic Plaza
Colorado Springs, CO 80909

U.S.A. Gymnastics
Pan American Plaza, #300
201 South Capitol Avenue
Indianapolis, IN 46225

U.S.A. Track & Field
1 Hoosier Dome, #140
Indianapolis, IN 46225

Women's Tennis Association
133 1st St. NE
St. Petersburg, FL 33701

Heaven Hall of Fame
Deceased Cover Stars of Sport, Sports Illustrated, Time and Life.

Allen, George
Alston, Walter (84)
Alzado, Lyle (93)
Armour, Tommy
Ashburn, Richie (97)
Ashe, Arthur (94)
Barber, Jerry (95)
Barney, Rex (97)
Bell, Gus (95)
Bell, Ricky (84)
Bias, Len (86)
Boros, Julius (93)
Boyer, Ken (82)
Brown, Paul (93)
Bryan, Jim
Bryant, Paul (Bear) (83)
Burton, Ernest
Busch, Gussie
Cagle, Christian
Campanella, Roy (93)
Carnera, Primo
Cerdan, Marcel (49)
Chabot, Lorne
Chandler, Happy (91)
Chambers, John
Clark, Jim (68)
Clemente, Roberto (73)
Cochrane, Mickey (62)
Conigliaro, Tony (95)
Connerly, Charles (96)

Cooper, Gary (60)
Cosell, Howard (95)
Cox, Bill (96)
Cramm, Von Gottfried
Crawford, Jack
Cronin, Joe (84)
Davis, Ernie (62)
Dean, Dizzy (74)
Dempsey, Jack (83)
Dixon, Hewritt (92)
Donatelli, Augie
Donohue, Mark (72)
Drysdale, Don (93)
Durocher, Leo (91)
Dyer, Ed (64)
Finley, Charlie (96)
Fox, Nellie (66)
Foxx, Jimmy (67)
Flood, Curt (97)
Galimore, Willie (64)
Gathers, Hank (89)
Gehrig, Lou (41)
Goodman, Johnny
Gomez, Lefty (89)
Goren, Charles
Grange, Red (91)
Grove, Lefty (75)
Gutowski, Bob
Haney, Fred (77)
Harmon, Claude
Harmon, Tom (90)
Harris, Gypsy Joe
Hayes, Woodie (87)
Henie, Sonja (69)
Hill, Phil
Hill, Graham (75)
Hoad, Lew (95)
Hodges, Gil (72)
Hogan, Ben (97)
Holleder, Don
Holman, Nat (95)
Hornsby, Roger (63)
Howard, Elston (95)
Hubbell, Carl (88)
Jacobs, Hellen (97)
Jacobs, Louie
Jensen, Jackie (82)
Johnson, Floyd (46)
Johnson, Gus (87)
Johnson, Jack (46)
Jones, Ben (61)

Jones, Bobby (71)
Jones, Calvin
Jones, Howard
Kennedy, John (63)
Kennedy, Jackie (94)
Kerr, Dave
Kim, Duk Koo
Kimberly, Jim
Kirby, Clay (95)
Kluszewski, Ted (88)
Krebs, Jim (65)
Kuenn, Harvey (88)
Layne, Bobby (86)
Lavagetto, Cookie (90)
Leahy, Frank (73)
Lema, Tony (67)
Lewis, Reggie (95)
Liston, Sonny (70)
Lombardi, Vince (70)
Long, Dale (91)
Louis, Joe (81)
Luce, Clare Boothe
Mack, Connie (56)
Maglie, Sal (94)
Mantle, Mickey (95)
Maravich, Pete (88)
Marciano, Rocky (69)
Maris, Roger (85)
Marston, Ann
Martin, Billy (89)
Matuszak, John (89)
Mayer, Dick
McGraw, John (34)
McMillian, Roy (97)
McQuire, Frank (94)
McQueen, Steve
Monzon, Carlos (94)
Munson, Thurman (79)
Murchison, Clint
Murtaugh, Danny (76)
Nagy, Steve
Nance, Jim (92)
Niarchos, Stavros (96)
Norgay, Tenzing
Nuthall, Betty
O'Connor, Pat
Olin, Mr./Mrs.
O'Malley, Walter (79)
Ott, Mel (58)
Owen, Lawrance (61)
Peck, A. Wells

Perry, Fred (95)
Pietrosante, Nick (88)
Pinson, Vida (96)
Plante, Jacques (86)
Post, Wally (82)
Prefontaine, Steve (75)
Reynolds, Allie (95)
Repulski, Rep
Revson, Pete
Riggs, Bobby (95)
Rockne, Knute (31)
Robinson, Jackie (72)
Robinson, Sugar Ray (89)
Robinson, William (34)
Rodriguez, Ricardo
Roch, Max
Rupp, Adolph (77)
Ruppert, Jacob (39)
Ruth, Babe (48)
Sanders, Mrs. Doug
Sawchuck, Terry (70)
Schaddelee, Hugh
Shor, Toots
Sisler, George (73)
Snite, Betsy
Stagg, Nonagenarian (65)
Stengel, Casey (75)
Street, Gabby (53)
Sullivan, Ed
Sweikert, Bob
Tilden, Bill
Tunney, Gene (78)
Turner, Curtis
Valvano, Jim
Van Brocklin, Norm (83)
Vanderbilt, Alfred
Vanderbilt, Harold (70)
Veeck, Bill (86)
Vines Jr., Ellsworth
Werner, Buddy
Wilkinson, Bud
Willard, Jess
Williams, Edward B.
Wills, Helen (98)
Wise, Mike
Wrigley, W.

CHAPTER FOUR:
GRADING AND PRESERVING MAGAZINES

The biggest change for collectors over the last two years is an increasing concern about the condition of their sports publications. This does not mean they are as fanatical as card collectors who demand PSA grades 8 or above, but it does mean that they will be more sensitive to condition than they are to price.

Grading, however, is only half the battle. Once you have obtained your publications, you will want to preserve them. Unlike baseball cards, which are printed on heavy stock, the thin pages of magazines are extremely sensitive to changes in temperature and humidity. As anyone knows who has seen SI's that resided for years in a dank basement, poor storage circumstances can quickly transform prized magazines into worthless trash. Also using the proper bags and boards and storage material will make a difference in how well they are preserved.

GRADING

Basically there are five major grades with which everyone who buys or sells sports publications should be familiar with. In my price guide I refer to the grades as mint (MT), excellent/mint (EM), excellent (EX), very good (VG) and good (GD). While some may want to add to this list grades of F (fair), and P (poor), I am convinced that such grading only confuses matters for publication collectors. While collectors of World Series programs might be willing to spring for a "good" copy of a 1913 program, knowledgeable collectors of publications simply won't be interested in a "good" example of even the most desirable magazines.

SI's that you might want to get signed and framed in order to display in your home or office typically fall into either the Mint (MT) or Excellent Mint (EM) categories.

Mint magazines are perfect with no mailing labels and no flaws. Of course, only a magazine hot off the press is truly "mint." But what "mint" means here is that the magazine looks like new and, most importantly, has no mailing label. Because the vast majority of Sports Illustrated magazines (97%) are sold through the mail rather than off the newsstand, almost all have mailing labels. "Mint" issues without mailing labels are tremendously difficult to find and, as a result, command premiere prices (50% to 300% higher than EM items).

Excellent Mint (EM) magazines have a mailing label or minor cover flaws such as slight corner creases or some wear along the spine. But the flaws are only minor; covers will not have any significant creases, water stains, finger smudging, loose bindings, etc. As a result, these magazines are desirable for showcasing. Magazines that have the label removed but still show marks are still graded Ex-Mt but may garner a little more if the markings are small and the buyer is willing.

Vg or Ex magazines, on the contrary, have enough cover flaws to make them unsuitable for autographing and framing. They might have, for example, a cover crease, smudging, significant binding wear or rolled bindings. But they will not have major cover flaws — pen or pencil marks, tears or rips (including torn-away labels), water or coffee stains, etc. — that drop them down to the not collectible category. These issues are generally collected for their contents (ads and features, especially) and not for their covers, so they must, like EM and MT issues, have all their pages intact.

PRESERVING MAGAZINES

Like other forms of collectible paper (old money, stamps, prints, etc.), magazines are extremely susceptible to variations in temperature and humidity. So ideally they should be stored in heated and air-conditioned rooms that are neither too humid in the summer nor too dry in the winter. Attics and basements make bad storage spots for publications! If you live in a house without central air conditioning, you might want to think about installing a window AC unit in the room where you keep your magazines. In addition to regulating the temperature, air conditioners also regulate humidity, so they will tend to keep your publications from mildewing.

Perhaps the simplest thing you can do to preserve your publications is to bag, backboard, and box them. Some hobby dealers and comic book shops carry magazine bags with convenient fold-over flaps specifically designed for modern magazines but which may not meet your needs. For example, bags that I use are 9 by 12 inches with a 2-inch flap. I order them from a large distributor in the midwest (Appendix III). As collectors of comics discovered long ago, bagging your magazines will tend to keep your collectibles free from the ill-effects of excess (or too little!) humidity and extreme temperatures. Bags will also prevent covers from picking up finger smudges, coffee stains, binding tears, etc. and protect your autographed magazine from getting smeared!!

Backing boards help to preserve your magazines by preventing them from bending. Slightly smaller than magazine bags, these boards are slipped into the bag behind the magazine before the bag is sealed with scotch tape. Because acid is a great destroyer of paper, a good bet here is acid-free boards.

I've found that boards 8 6/8 by 11 5/8 work well for early *Time*, *Sports Illustrated*, and *Sport* magazines. To get these bags and boards you might try one of the suppliers in the back (Appendix III).

Magazine boxes also make it easy for you to thumb through your collection. Dealers who sell magazine bags and backing boards also typically offer magazine boxes, which like comic book boxes are designed to prevent binding damage by storing your collectibles standing up. Another way to store them, especially if you are only going to collect a few hundred is to buy specially made magazine shelf boxes. These will allow you to store them in your sports library along with your other sports memorabilia. It will give your office or sports den a very official look while preserving the magazines.

The cost of all of these preservation techniques adds up, but it is worth the expense. As our price guide indicates, there is a significant difference in value between a MT and EM and a VG *Sports Illustrated*. So 10¢ for a bag here and $5 for a box there is money well spent.

REMOVING LABELS

After you have taken pains not to ruin your magazines, you might be tempted to improve them. For most collectors, this means removing the mailing labels that appear on the covers of subscriber copies. Happily, this is a simple task for most issues in the 1980s and early 1990s. (Recently, SI jettisoned the mailing label entirely and began "inkjetting" addresses directly onto its covers; this ink, unfortunately, cannot be removed.) Mailing labels can also be removed rather simply from some random issues in the mid- to late-1970s, but it is impossible to be precise about which ones work and which ones don't.

Among the methods that will remove labels are steam, heat, lighter fluid, and turpentine. If you are using steam, a good source is your kitchen's tea kettle. Hold the label up to the steam and let a bit sink in. Be careful, however, that the water in the steam does not seep beyond the label into the cover, since that seepage could cause permanent water damage. If you don't mind the smell and the clean up afterwards, turpentine also works well. Take a Q-tip and lightly dab it on the label until it appears to be soaked. Then lift off. Probably the simplest method is the blow dryer. Turn it on, heat up the label for 30 seconds or so, and then peel away! With any of these methods, you should go slowly, being careful not to tear away any part of the cover as you lift off the label.

It is also possible to remove labels from 1950s and 1960s *Sports Illustrateds*, but because the printers used glues during those decades that discolored its covers, it will typically be obvious afterwards that the label has been removed. (Two or three unsightly white glue lines are the tell-tale signs.) In the future, SI collectors may join movie poster enthusiasts in employing paper conservators to remove labels and then to restore their magazines to something approximating their original condition, but for the time being, it is probably best, at least for pre-1980s issues, to leave your mailing labels alone.

The value of an EM issue after a label has been removed but which has a stain remaining changes little. It just makes it a nicer EM issue. However, I have been lucky making some issues like new (Mt).

Before you take out your expensive issues and try removing your label, just remember that you can easily damage the issue as well!!!

CHAPTER FIVE:
COLLECTING SPORTS ILLUSTRATED

The Sports Illustrated Price Guide section is the most comprehensive price guide on the subject. The guide works chronologically from the earliest known Sports Illustrated to December of 1997. If you need to find the issues of your favorite player, you need too first refer to Chapter 24: Alpha Index.

Each issue of Sports Illustrated is organized by date. Then the person or feature is listed. Under the person name is either the team they played on (example 'Rams') or the sport (Swimming). Then this is followed by the key articles, features and ads. The advertisements are put into brackets. Under the Features/(Ads) section you will find Faces in the Crowd (FIC), Regional Cover mentions, cover variations, and other unique differences that are worth noting on the cover.

It should be noted that between 1954-1967 store variations may have a paper flap promoting a special feature in the issue. The paper flap will add at least a 10% premium to the mint issue and sometimes even more based on the content of the flap.

In some store variations there are actually differences in the headers and borders. These would add at least a 10% premium. During the 1950's for example, I have run across 1/2 off cover price as a promotion. The Canadian versions (1993-1995) will have Canada written on the top. These versions should have at least a 10% premium over the American editions.

Finally there are three prices for different graded Sports Illustrateds and one price for the added autographed value. The mint grade refers to magazines in nr-mt to mint condition. These magazines have no labels, no flaws and look new. A magazine that has no label but has a minor flaw (a bend in the corner, minor rubbing, minor corner bend or crease) will often be priced at a nr-mt to mt magazine and is usually worth it for pre-1980 magazines. However, when the mailing label is off and the magazine has a noticeable flaw, then the magazine will drop down to an EM price. Excellent-Mint price is for magazines that have a mailing label with no noticeable flaws. Most magazines will have a flaw but to be ex-mt it needs to be a clean cover with no cover creases, tears, or damage caused by water, oil, coke, etc. Magazines with a major flaw (crease, finger tears, cover wears, fingerprints) will be graded 'Excellent' and are very common to find at card shows and at the swap meet. These magazines tend to go for 50% of the EM grade. You will see a lot of these with the 50% off sign. The VG grade has serious cover problems (major crease or tear does it) and is only good for ads and articles.

The Autographed add value (+20) is shown in the last column. This means that the value of your SI increases at least by the added value. Sometimes the magazine goes for significantly more than the added value in auctions but it will at least be worth the noted added value for EM and MT prices. The added value does not necessarily apply to VG or EX grade or cover only magazines since collectors tend not to collect that grade. The only exception is autographed magazines of deceased athletes (Rocky Marciano) where the autograph is rarer than the magazine. This is especially true for rare autographed magazine covers. When there is more than one added value (+20/+15) it means the added value of the other person on the cover who is listed second. The (d) behind the (+20) means the person is deceased.

The most expensive Sports Illustrateds tend to be the most popular stars in the sporting world. Therefore, the most expensive SI's tend to be '49 Joe DiMaggio, '55 Ted Williams and the '54 second edition with the baseball card fold out of Mickey Mantle and the rest of the '54 NY Yankee team cards.

The price guide is just a guide, built upon the reports from nationally known dealers and collectors who sell or collect sports publications. When you use this guide to buy and sell, remember that the more expensive items tend to be the most popular and sell the quickest while the cheaper SI's are usually not heavily collected and should be treated like common baseball cards.

PRE 1954 ISSUES

Sports Illustrated (by Stuart Scheftel)

1930s

DATE	COVER	FEATURE	Nr-Mt	Ex	+Auto

The first incarnation of Sports Illustrated, this highbrow magazine eventually merged into Golf Illustrated. The magazine has great car ads and is sought after by advertising and golf enthusiasts. Here mass spectator sports such as football, baseball, and basketball take a back seat to skiing, fishing, golf, and other outdoor sporting activities. Magazine values range depending on ads.

	Typical Issues		200	100	

Sports Illustrated (by Dell Publications)

The second Sports Illustrated, this short-lived Dell Publications offering came in a large, Life-sized format (13 1/2 x 11). The covers are color and the photos inside are black and white. The DiMaggio issue is the prize here.

DATE	COVER	FEATURE	Nr-Mt	Ex	+Auto
☐ 2/49	Ralph Beard		200	150	
	Kentucky BKB	*Ben Hogan*			+30
☐ 3/49	Marcell Cerdan	*Casey Stengel*	125	75	
	Boxing				+1500(d)
☐ 4/49	Lou Boudreau	*Indians*	225	125	
	Indians	*(Joan Crawford/Chesterfield)*			+50
☐ 5/49	Joe DiMaggio		700	500	
	Yankees				+225
☐ 6/49	Rex Barney	*Leo Durocher, Giants,*	150	75	
	Dodgers	*Bob Hope/Chesterfield*			+100(d)

"Dummy" Sports Illustrated Issues (by Time-Life, Inc.)

These promotional issues were issued by Time-Life publisher Henry Luce to potential advertisers and other reviewers in an effort to "test the waters" for the publication that would follow. (The letters that Luce sent out with these issues are, by the way, also collectible.) Dummy #1 appeared as The New Sport Magazine. Its cover depicted a crowd rooting wildly at a football stadium. Dummy #2 was titled, simply, Dummy. Its cover depicted Pebble Beach and inside the magazine featured the Bing Crosby Pro-Am Tournament. The first SI golf issue, this second dummy is desired by golf collectors.

1953

DATE	COVER	FEATURE	Nr-Mt	Ex	+Auto
	Letter/Articles	*Group of Articles*	500	400	
☐ 12/53	Stadium Fans	*Dummy #1, Football*	500	400	
☐ 4/54	Pebble Beach	*Dummy #2, Sam Snead, Ben Hogan*	500	400	

1954

DATE	COVER	FEATURE	Nr-Mt	Ex	+Auto
☐ 8/16	Eddie Mathews*	*1st Issue, Baseball Cards*	250	175	
	Braves	*(24 cards-Mays, Williams, etc)*			+20
		*(*also Wes Westrum (Giants), Augie*			
		Donatelli (umpire))			
☐ 8/23	Masters Golf	*Clubs US Amateur, Yankees Cards,*	500	400	
		(24 cards Mantle, Berra, etc)			
☐ 8/30	Pamela Nelson	*Yankee Stadium, Palmer, Indians,*	40	25	
	Swimsuit	*Eisenhower*			+20
☐ 9/07	Sailing	*Robin Roberts*	40	25	
☐ 9/14	Jim Kimberley	*College Football, Marciano,*	20	15	
	Car Racing	*(Ford Skyline)*			+100(d)
☐ 9/21	Cowboys	*Football, Indians*	15	10	
☐ 9/28	Calvin Jones	*Stadiums, Notre Dame, Rocky*	20	12	
	Iowa	*Marciano, (SI, Cadillac)World Series*			+200(d)
☐ 10/04	Joyce Sellers	*T-Birds, Baseball*	15	10	
	Horserider				+100(d)
☐ 10/11	Bandsman	*Monroe/DiMaggio, Durocher, Giants,*	15	10	
	Oklahoma	*World Series, Mays Catch*			
☐ 10/18	Steeplechase	*Porsche, Hockey Preview*	15	10	
☐ 10/25	English Setter	*(T-Bird)*	15	10	
	Hunting				
☐ 11/01	Football Fans		15	10	
	Oklahoma Stadium				
☐ 11/08	Surfcasting	*Teddy Roosevelt, Pro Football,*	15	10	
		(Studebaker)			
☐ 11/15	Snowbill Duck	*Duck Foldout, (Model Toys)*	25	10	
☐ 11/22	Y.A. Tittle (FC)	*Army/Navy Football, (55 Ford)*	60	30	
	49ers				+20

Cover Variations - Newstand has strip at Top.

	DATE	COVER	FEATURE	Nr-Mt	Ex	+Auto
☐	11/29	Hef Parkins	Beau Jack, Swimsuits, Hoover,	15	10	
		Old Cars	(55 Lincoln)			+100(d)
☐	12/06	African Lion	Redwings, (55 Mercury, Desoto)	15	10	
☐	12/13	Horse Show	Tom Gola, Churchill, Basketball Preview	15	10	
☐	12/20	Ken Sears	Swimsuits	25	15	
		Santa Clara BKB				+20
			Variation at Top: "First Weekly Golf			
			Tip From a Top Pro"			
☐	12/27	Klosters Skiing	Bowl Preview, Tom Gola, (Studebaker)	15	10	

1955

	DATE	COVER	FEATURE	Nr-Mt	Ex	+Auto
☐	1/03	Roger Bannister	Mays, Cars	120	35	
		Track (SOY)				+25
☐	1/10	Horseracing	Bowl Results, Dempsey,	12	6	
		Santa Monica	(Studebaker, Jaguar)			
☐	1/17	Rafael Rodriquez	(55 Ford)	12	6	
		Bullfighting				+100(d)
☐	1/24	Dorris Hedberg	Gordie Howe, Pistons, (55 Studebaker)	12	6	
		Maud Karten/Gymnasts				+20
☐	1/31	Jill Kilmont	James Naismith, College Basketball	12	6	
		Skier				+25
☐	2/07	Carol Heiss	(Studebaker)	20	10	
		Figure Skating				+25
☐	2/14	Great Dane	Dog Foldout, Baseball Hall of Fame	12	6	
☐	2/21	Betty DiBugnano	Lakers/Knicks, Mays, (Studebaker)	20	10	
		Swimsuit Model	Bill Russell			+40
☐	2/28	Race Horses	Mays, Lakers, (Corvette, Dodge)	12	6	
☐	3/07	Jo Alston	Branch Rickey, (T-Bird)	12	6	
		Badminton	Spring Training			+20
☐	3/14	Buddy Werner	Yankees, (Studebaker)	12	6	
		Skier				+100(d)
☐	3/21	Parry O'Brien	Giants, (DeSoto)	12	6	
		Shotputter				+20
☐	3/28	Steve Nagy	Bill Russell, NCAA BKB Tourney	12	6	
		Bowler				+20
☐	4/04	Ben Hogan (FC)	Masters	120	50	
☐	4/11	Willie Mays(FC)	NL Baseball Review	250	125	
		Leo Durocher	(Ted Williams Glove)			
						+50/+100(d)/+100(d)
		Laraine Day	Baseball Card Insert			
			Giants			
☐	4/18	Al Rosen/B.Lope	AL Baseball Review	100	50	
		Indians	Baseball Card Insert			+20/+10
☐	4/25	Tenzing Norgay	(Chrysler, Pepsi, Corvette, Ford)	12	6	
		Mountain Climber	Nixon, A's			+100(d)
☐	5/02	Tom Courtney	Brooklyn Dodgers	12	6	
		Track				+20
☐	5/09	Shields/Fairbanks		12	6	
		Balloonists	Kentucky Derby, Swaps, Stadiums			+20each
☐	5/16	American Birds	Swaps, Marciano, Bird Foldout	12	6	
☐	5/23	Zale Perry	Durocher, (Pepsi)	12	6	
		Skin Diver				+20
☐	5/30	Herb Score	Durocher, Indy 500, (Snead, Corvette)	40	20	
		Indians				+20
☐	6/06	Rainbow Trout	Durocher, Brigg Stadium (55 T-Bird)	12	6	
☐	6/13	Magnus Johnson	LeMans Race, Swaps, (Kiner, Dodge)	12	6	
		Ocean Racing	Indy 500			
☐	6/20	Ed Furgol	Golf Stars Foldout of Hogan, Palmer,	25	15	
		Golf	Snead, etc. U.S. Open Preview			+20
☐	6/27	Duke Snider (FC)	Kluszewski, Mays, Musial	150	60	
		Dodgers				+30
☐	7/04	Bulldog	Dog Show	12	6	
☐	7/11	Yogi Berra (FC)	All Star Game Preview, Alston, Fox	125	50	
		Yankees	(Studebaker)			+25
☐	7/18	Swaps	(Pepsi)	15	8	

	DATE	COVER	FEATURE	Nr-Mt	Ex	+Auto
		Horseracing				
☐	7/25	Marylee Davey	1880s Baseball Player Photos	12	6	
		Emil/Max Julen				+20
		Mountain Climbing				
☐	8/01	Ted Williams (FC)		350	175	
☐	8/08	Ann Marston	Ben Hogan, DiMaggio, (Triumph)	12	6	
		Archery				+20
☐	8/15	Ed Mathews	SI's 1st Anniversary, Ben Hogan	65	25	
		Braves				+20
☐	8/22	Don Newcombe	Red Sox	45	15	
		Dodgers				+15
☐	8/29	Tony Trabert	Babe Ruth	16	8	
		Tennis				+20
☐	9/05	Fred & Art Pinder	Yankees, Pro Football	12	6	
		Fisherman				+100(d)
☐	9/12	Bud Wilkinson	Bobby Jones, (Triumph)	40	20	
		Oklahoma Football				+50(d)
☐	9/19	Rocky Marciano	Bobby Jones, (Lincoln)	75	30	
		Boxer				+1500(d)
☐	9/26	Walt Alston (FC)	Yankees, (Corvette)	45	20	
		Dodgers				+300(d)
☐	10/03	Doak Walker	Notre Dame, Marciano/Moore, (56 Ford)	50	25	
		Lions				+25
☐	10/10	Partridge	World Series, Hunting	12	6	
☐	10/17	Princeton Band	Dodgers, (Chrysler, Bob Hope)	12	6	
☐	10/24	Hopalong Cassady	Hockey Preview, Colts/Bears	55	25	
		Ohio State Football	Woody Hayes			+20
☐	10/31	Pamela Phillips	Notre Dame's Frank Leahy,	12	6	
		Horse Show	(Rolex, Ted Williams)			+20
☐	11/07	Bob Pellegrini	(Ted Williams, GE)	15	8	
		Maryland Football				+20
☐	11/14	Ernest Burton	Yankees, Babe Ruth	12	6	
		Hunter				+100(d)
☐	11/21	Skeeter Werner	Bears/Colts, (T-Bird)	12	6	
		Skier				+10
☐	11/28	Don Holleder	Swimsuit, (Dodge)	20	12	
		Army Football	Army/Navy Football			+20
☐	12/05	Louise Dyer		12	6	
		Fencing				
☐	12/12	Mini Dachshunds	Bill Russell	12	6	
		Dogs				
☐	12/19	Skiing	Sugar Ray Robinson, (Cadillac)	12	6	
☐	12/26	Jim Swink	Bowl Preview, (Chrysler, Dodge)	15	8	
		TCU Football				+20

1956

	DATE	COVER	FEATURE	Nr-Mt	Ex	+Auto
☐	1/02	Johnny Podres	Sports Year in Review	85	35	
		Dodgers (SOY)	Classic American Cars			+20
☐	1/09	Bob Cousy (FC)	Bowls, Bill Russell, (56 T-Bird)	100	35	
		Celtics				+45
☐	1/16	Mike Souchak	Hogan, Cousy, Crosby Pro-Am,	25	15	
		Golf	(Corvette, Porsche)			+25
☐	1/23	Jean Beliveau	Marciano	25	15	
		Canadiens				+20
☐	1/30	Hayes Jenkins	Olympics, Floyd Patterson, (Studebaker,	12	6	
		Tenley Albright	Plymouth)			+20 each
		Figure Skating				
☐	2/06	Ralph Miller	Olympics, (Porsche, Cadillac)	12	6	
		Skier				+20
☐	2/13	Charles Maute	Olympic Results, Dick Irvin,	12	6	
		Seton Hall	Track Classic American Cars			+15
☐	2/20	White Heron	Connie Mack's Death,	12	6	
☐	2/27	Nashua	Baseball Owners	12	5	
		Horseracing				
☐	3/05	Stan Musial/Wally Moon/		75	35	
		Rip Repulski/Bill Virdon	(Jaguar, Studebaker, Porsche)			+20/+10 ea

	DATE	COVER	FEATURE	Nr-Mt	Ex	+Auto
		Cardinals	Spring Training			
☐	3/12	Afghan Dog Dog	Red Sox, Mercedes 300SL, (T-Bird)	12	6	
☐	3/19	Alfred Glassell Marlin Fishing	Dodgers, Red Wings	12	6	+20
☐	3/26	Jim Kimberly Auto Racing	NCAA Basketball (Trabert, Corvette, Jaguar)	15	7	+100(d)
☐	4/02	Al Wiggins Ohio State	Spring Training, (Pepsi, T-Bird, Studebaker,Porsche)	14	7	+20
☐	4/09	56 Baseball Issue	Cleveland Stadium, Flannels,(Robin Roberts)Campy,Berra	50	25	
☐	4/18	Barbara Romack Golf	Patterson, (Porsche, Corvette, Piersall)	12	6	
☐	4/23	Billy Martin(FC)	Babe Didrikson, (Porsche, Jaguar)	40	20	
☐	4/30	Trout Fisherman	Mantle, Bogart, Eisenhower	10	6	
☐	5/07	Needles Kentucky Derby	Marciano, (Kluszewski, Studebaker, Cadillac)	12	5	
☐	5/14	Al Kaline (FC) Harvey Kuenn Tigers	Didrikson, (T-Bird, Porsche, Snead, Mantle) Kentucky Derby,	100	35	+20/+150(d)
☐	5/21	John Landy Runner	(Jaguar, Snead, Motorola) Athea Gibson [FIC]	10	6	+20
☐	5/28	Bob Sweikert	Sugar Ray Robinson (Chrysler, Porsche)	10	6	
☐	6/04	Floyd Patterson	Dale Long, Pirate HR record	50	20	
☐	6/11	Sam Snead(FC) Golf	U.S. Open, Indy 500, (Snead) (Sam Snead)	100	35	+35
☐	6/18	Mickey Mantle Yankees (FC)	Patterson, Gehrig, (Pepsi, Jaguar, Continental)	250	125	+200(d)
☐	6/25	Warren Spahn	US Open, Olympics, Swimsuits,	125	55	

1956

	DATE	COVER	FEATURE	Nr-Mt	Ex	+Auto
☐	7/02	Dave Sime Bobby Morrow Track & Field	Althea Gibson, Phillies, (Billy Pierce)	12	6	
☐	7/09	All Star Preview*	[*Cover shows Snider, Long, Mays, Mantle, Musial, Kuenn, Berra, Friend, Boyer, Brewer,Hogan, (Porsche)]	65	30	
☐	7/16	Reds' Gus Bell Wally Post Ted Kluszewski	Mantle, Wimbledon, (Cadillac, Pepsi, Rafer Johnson)	60	30	+50(d),+10 +50(d)
☐	7/23	Adios Harry	Martin, All Star Game, Marty Marion,	12	6	
☐	7/30	Joe Adcock Braves	Dodgers, (Chrysler)	40	15	+15
☐	8/06	Jeanne Stunyo Diver	Olympics, Greenberg, Cronin HOFer, Orioles, (Campbell Soup)	12	6	+20
☐	8/13	Olympic Sailer	Dodger, Olympics Issue	12	6	
☐	8/20	Ed Mathews Braves	Ted Williams, (Pepsi, Ford) 2nd Aniversary	95	35	+20
☐	8/27	Dorris/Gissy Horse Show	Dodgers	12	6	+20 each
☐	9/03	Lew Hoad Tennis	Forest Hills, Eisenhower, Ken Boyer	12	6	+20
☐	9/10	Whitey Ford (FC) Yankees	Yankee Stadium, Dodgers, Roger Hornsby Mantle, (Cadillac)	100	45	+20
☐	9/17	Willie Hartack Jockey	Black Sox Scandal	12	6	+20
☐	9/24	Football Preview		25	15	
☐	10/01	Mickey Mantle Yankees	World Series, Casey Stengel	125	40	+200(d)
☐	10/08	Paul Brown George Ratterman Browns	Braves, Didrikson Dies Pro Football Preview,(Jaguar)	40	20	+100(d)/+20
☐	10/15	Harold S. Vanderbilt Yachtsman		12	6	+100(d)

DATE	COVER	FEATURE	Nr-Mt	Ex	+Auto
☐ 10/22	John Chambers Duck Hunter	World Series, Yogi Berra	12	6	
☐ 10/29	Paul Hornung (FC) Notre Dame Football	Oklahoma Football	100	35	+25
☐ 11/05	Yale Bulldog	College Football, (T-Bird, Plymouth)	12	6	
☐ 11/12	Tom Maentz Ron Kramer Michigan Football	(Triumph, Mercury)	25	20	+20 each
☐ 11/19	Olympic Preview	(Sam Snead)	10	6	
☐ 11/26	Marching Band	USC/UCLA Football (Plymouth)	10	6	
☐ 12/03	Chuck Connerly Giants Football	Army/Navy Football, Olympics, (Mercury, Pepsi, Ford, Chrysler)	40	20	+100(d)
☐ 12/10	Olympics Runners Patterson, Swimsuits, Bill Russell		20	10	
☐ 12/17	Elizabeth Gurst Fashion Model	Chamberlain	12	6	+30
☐ 12/24	Bowl Preview Christmas Issue	Jackie Robinson, (Ferrari)	12	7	

1957

DATE	COVER	FEATURE	Nr-Mt	Ex	+Auto
☐ 1/07	Bobby Morrow Texas Track (SOY)	NFL Championship, Olympics	20	10	+20
☐ 1/14	Wes/Betty Sime Skiers	Sugar Ray Robinson	12	6	+20 each
☐ 1/21	Johnny Lee Yale Basketball	(Chrysler)	12	6	+20
☐ 1/28	Bill Roberts, Jack Bionda, Cal Gardner, Allan Stanley John Peirson, Larry Regan Boston Bruins	Swimsuits, (Mercury)	40	20	+10 each
☐ 2/04	Huga Schaddlee Yachtsman	Yachting, (Triumph, Hogan)\	12	6	+100(d)
☐ 2/11	Boxer Dog	Wilt Chamberlain,	12	6	
☐ 2/14	Jim Krebs SMU Football	(Chrysler, Mercury)	12	6	+20
☐ 2/25	Johnny Saxton* Carmen Basilio Boxing	Birdie Tebbetts, (Corvette, Mercury)	25	20	+20 each
☐ 3/04	Mickey Mantle Yankees	Spring Training, (Chevrolet)	150	65	+200(d)
☐ 3/11	Ben Hogan Golf	Bob Cousy, Celtics Spring Training, (Corvette)	75	45	+200(d)
☐ 3/18	Gordie Howe (FC) Ted Lindsay Red Wings	Ben Hogan, Basketball Braves, (Schoendienst)	150	50	+25/+15
☐ 3/25	Carroll Shelby Autoracing	Hogan, Roger Maris, B. Robinson (Chevrolet)NCAA Basketball	45	20	+25
☐ 4/01	Dan Hodge Oklahoma	Ben Hogan, Dodgers (Mercury, Robin Roberts)	45	20	+20
☐ 4/08	A.Wells Peck Fisherman	Ben Hogan, Indiana Basketball (Whitey Ford, Cousy, Pepsi)	14	7	+100(d)
☐ 4/15	1957 Baseball	Williams, Ruth, Masters	60	30	
☐ 4/22	Wally Moon Cardinals	(Plymouth,Triumph,Bing Crosby)	35	15	+20
☐ 4/29	Sugar Ray Robinson Gene Fullmer Boxing	Roger Maris, L. Burdette, (Chrysler, Mercury)	40	20	+150(d)/+20
☐ 5/06	Jockey	Kentucky Derby, Pirates, (Corvette)	12	6	
☐ 5/13	Billy Pierce White Sox	(Ted Kluszenski,Jaguar) (Chrysler)	40	15	+20
☐ 5/20	Gussie Busch Horse Show	(Pontiac, Dodge)	12	6	+50(d)
☐ 5/27	Jim Bryan Indy 500	(Chrysler 300, Mercury)	12	6	+50(d)
☐ 6/03	Clem Labine		45	15	

	DATE	COVER	FEATURE	Nr-Mt	Ex	+Auto
		Dodgers				+25
☐	6/10	Cary Middlecoff	U.S. Open, (Mercury, Chrysler)	45	20	
		Golf				+25
☐	6/17	Eddie Arcaro	Hank Aaron, Yogi Berra	35	12	
		Jockey	(Triumph, Dodge)			+25
☐	6/24	Bob Gutowski	US Open, Phillies,	12	6	
		Pole Vaulter	(Chrysler, Dodge)			+20
☐	7/01	Yachting Flags	Al Lopez	12	6	
☐	7/08	Ted Williams	All Star Preview	250	125	
		Stan Musial				+200/+35
		Red Sox/Cardinals				
☐	7/15	Monkey	Wimbledon, Althea Gibson,	12	6	
			(Mercury)			
☐	7/22	Hank Bauer		50	20	
		Yankees				+25
☐	7/29	Floyd Patterson		35	15	
		Boxing	(Plymouth, Porsche, Triumph)			+20
☐	8/05	Bonnie Prudden	Mays, PGA, Ted Williams	12	6	
		Fitness				+20
☐	8/12	Russell Schleeh	Hank Aaron	12	6	
		Hydroplanes	(Chrysler, Pepsi, Bud)			+50
☐	8/19	Johnny Simpson	Hickory Smoke	12	6	
		Jockey	(Triumph, Mercury)			+20
☐	8/26	Consuelo Crespi	Braves	12	6	
		Model				+50
☐	9/02	Althea Gibson	Nicklaus [FIC], Giants	30	15	
		Tennis	(Bud, Kodak)			+100(ill)
☐	9/09	Roy McMillan	White Sox	30	12	
		Reds				+100(d)
☐	9/16	Carmen Basilio	Dodgers	25	12	
		Boxing				+20
☐	9/23	1957 Football Preview		25	12	
☐	9/30	Yankees Pitcher World Series		40	20	
☐	10/07	Ollie Matson	Pro Football Issue	35	15	
☐	10/14	Charles Goren	World Series, (Jaguar)	12	6	
		Bridge				+100(d)
☐	10/21	Ducks	Hunting Preview	12	6	
			(Frank Gifford)			
☐	10/28	Autumn Trees	Hockey	12	6	
☐	11/04	Bobby Cox	Pro Basketball Preview	30	15	
		Minnesota FB	Cousy, (58 Chevy)			+20
☐	11/11	Jay Utz	Car Issue, (Corvette, Jaguar)	12	6	
		Horses				+20
☐	11/18	Oklahoma Band	Football	12	6	
			(Imperial, MG, Lincoln)			
☐	11/25	Willy Scherffler	(Triumph, Mercury)	12	6	
		Skier				+20
☐	12/02	USSR Athlete	Army/Navy, Lions	12	6	
			(Lincoln, Plymouth)			+50
☐	12/09	College BKB Issue	Wilt Chamberlain	30	15	
☐	12/16	Amy Baird	49ers, (Mercury)	12	6	
		Ski Fashion Model				+20
☐	12/23	Stan Musial	Bowl Preview, 49ers	85	35	
		Cardinals (SOY)	Lions, (Lincoln), Sportsman			+30

1958

	DATE	COVER	FEATURE	Nr-Mt	Ex	+Auto
☐	1/06	Wasserman Family	Lions, (Plymouth)	25	15	
		Vacation				+20each
☐	1/13	Bill Mauldin	Bing Crosby, (Corvette)	20	10	
						+25
☐	1/20	Neil Johnston	NBA All Star Game,(Triumph)	35	15	
		Warriors				
☐	1/27	Willie Shoemaker	NY Rangers,	40	20	
		Jockey	(Lincoln, Imperial)			+100(can't sign)
☐	2/03	Seals	Bill Russell,(Mercury, MG)	10	5	

Date	Subject	Description	Val1	Val2	Val3
☐ 2/10	Henri Salem	Wilt Chamberlain, (DeSoto)	10	5	
	Diehl Matcer	Elgin Baylor [FIC],			+20 each
	Squash				
☐ 2/17	Jacques Plante	Bill Sharman, Celtics,	45	20	
	Canadiens	Hockey (Triumph) Chevrolet, Bonneville)			+20
☐ 2/24	Phil Reavis	(Plymouth,Lincoln,	10	5	
	Villanova Track	Thunderbird)			+20
☐ 3/03	Andy Carey	Spring Training, Musial,	35	15	
	Yogi Berra,	(Corvette, Porsche, Ford)			+ Varies
	Enos Slaughter/Gil McDougald/				
	Elston Howard				
☐ 3/10	Surf Australia	NCAA Basketball, Reds,	15	7	
☐ 3/17	Sal Maglie	(Triumph, Bonneville, Mercury)	40	20	
☐ 3/24	Carmen Basilio	LA Stadium, SF Stadium,	20	10	
	Boxing	NCAA Final Four, Walter O'Malley,			+20
		Chevrolet)			
☐ 3/31	Roy Sievers	Billy Martin, (T-Bird, Pepsi)	40	20	
	Senators				+20
☐ 4/07	Masters Golf	Basilio/Robinson,	30	15	
		(Mathews, Ford)			
☐ 4/14	1958 Baseball Issue	Masters, Snider, Mays, Braves,	50	25	
		Cubs,Palmer			
		(Pee Wee Reese, Ted Williams)			
☐ 4/21	Del Crandall	(Lincoln, Sam Snead)	50	25	
	Braves				+20
☐ 4/28	Silky Sullivan	Kentucky Derby, Dodgers/Giants	28	10	
	Horseracing	(Nellie Fox)			
☐ 5/05	Gil McDougald	Dodgers, Giants,	40	20	
	Yankees	(Jaguar, Porsche)			+20
☐ 5/12	American Cup	White Sox,	20	10	
	Yachting	(Ed Mathews, Corvette, Ford)			
☐ 5/19	Richie Ashburn	Musial, (Porsche)	60	25	
	Phillies				+100(d)
☐ 5/26	Pat O'Connor	Indians, Orioles	12	5	
	Indy 500	(Continental)			
☐ 6/02	Eddie Mathews		100	30	
	Braves				+25
☐ 6/09	Dick Mayer	US Open Tennis, Yankees,	20	10	
	Tennis	(7-Up, Chevrolet)			+20
☐ 6/16	Lew Hoad	Forest Hills, Mays,	15	5	
	Pancho Gonzales	(Jaguar, Bud)			+20/+100(d)
	Tennis				
☐ 6/23	Jackie Jensen		40	15	
	Red Sox				+150(d)
☐ 6/30	Tennis Doubles	Dodgers, (Renault)	10	5	
☐ 7/07	Al-Star Preview*	(T-Bird) [* Cover shows Mays,	70	35	
		Jensen, Auto varies, Mantle, Triandos)			
☐ 7/14	Dog & Girl	(Corvette, Kodak)	10	5	
☐ 7/21	Chris Von Saltza		10	5	
	Swimmer				+20
☐ 7/28	Frank Thomas	(Pepsi, Renault)	30	15	
	Pirates				+20
☐ 8/04	Vacationers		10	5	
☐ 8/11	Clare Luce	Rafer Johnson, Giants	10	5	
	Scuba Diving	(T-Bird, Chevrolet)			+100(d)
☐ 8/18	Roy Harris	Cobb, Mantle	10	5	
	Boxing				+20
☐ 8/25	Pine Valley	Yankees,	30	12	
	Golfer	(Pepsi, Lincoln, Triumph)			
☐ 9/01	Floyd Patterson/Roy Harris		30	15	
	Boxing				+20/+100(d)
☐ 9/08	Fisherman	(7-Up, Jaguar)	10	5	
☐ 9/15	Sceptre Yacht	(Grange, Ted Williams, Bob Cousy)	10	6	
	America's Cup				
☐ 9/22	1958 Football	College Football Issue	20	10	
	Issue				

DATE	COVER	FEATURE	Nr-Mt	Ex	+Auto
☐ 9/29	World Series Stadium Drawing	Mantle, Hank Aaron\ (7-Up, Ashburn)	24	12	
☐ 10/06	Goose Hunting	Stengel, YA Title (Jaguar, Buick)	10	5	
☐ 10/13	Ohio State Band	World Series Preview	10	5	
☐ 10/20	James McCarthy Cliff Hanging	World Series Game 7, (Feller, Ford, GM, Dodge)	10	5	+20
☐ 10/27	Chick Zimmerman Syracuse Football	Pro Basketball Preview,(7-Up)	18	9	+20
☐ 11/03	Hugh Wiley Equestrian	Mercedes 300sl, (Chevy)	10	5	+20
☐ 11/10	Herb Elliott Track	Jim Brown, (Buick)	10	5	+20
☐ 11/17	Mr./Mrs. Olin Hunters	(DeSoto)	10	5	+50 each(d)
☐ 11/24	Pete Dawkins Walters, Anderson Army Football	Swimsuits, (7-Up, Arnett Rams, 59 Mercury)	50	20	+25 each
☐ 12/01	Montana Skiers	Montana Skiing	10	5	
☐ 12/08	1958 BKB Preview	College Basketball Issue, Oscar Robertson, (Mark 4)	30	15	
☐ 12/15	Barbara Wagner Figure Skating	(Mercury) Bob Paul	10	5	+20 each
☐ 12/22	Holiday Issue	Bowl Preview, (7-Up)	14	7	

1959

DATE	COVER	FEATURE	Nr-Mt	Ex	+Auto
☐ 1/05	Rafer Johnson Track (SOY)	Colts Championship, UCLA Track, Notre Dame Stengel	60	25	+40
☐ 1/12	Andy Bathgate Rangers	Davis Cup, Swimsuits, (Corvette, 7-Up)	35	15	+20
☐ 1/19	Hal Roach Phesant Hunter	Bob Pettit (Bing Crosby, T-Bird, Renault)	10	5	+100(d)
☐ 1/26	Horseracers	I. Johansson, Robertson (Studebaker, Dodge, Mercury)	10	5	
☐ 2/02	Ron Delany Track	Black Hawks (DeSoto, Lincoln, Triumph)	10	5	+15
☐ 2/09	Skiers	Vince Lombardi, (Imperial)	10	5	+15
☐ 2/16	John Longden Jockey	(T-Bird, 7-Up, Corvette, Buick, Bob Hope, Desoto)	10	8	+15
☐ 2/23	Bill Cox Sailing	(Coke, MG, Rambler)	10	5	+100(d)
☐ 3/02	Casey Stengel Fred Haney/Umpire Yankees/Braves	Spring Training, Yogi Berra, (Volvo, Triumph, Continental)	25	17	+250/+125(d)
☐ 3/09	Ed Sullivan Golf	Hot Rod Henley (Corvette, Mercedes, Austin)	25	7	+300(d)
☐ 3/16	Phil Hill Autoracing	Pirates, Basketball Issue, (T-Bird, Coke, 7-Up, Jaguar)	10	5	+20
☐ 3/23	Aly Khan Polo	Giants, Ashburn, (Willie Mays, Lincoln, Dodge)	10	5	+100(d)
☐ 3/30	Tommy Armour Golf	NCAA Final Four (Stengel, Chevy, Gill McDonald)	10	6	+200(d)
☐ 4/06	Bobby Jones Golf	Masters, Elgin Baylor, Lakers, (Palmer, Mercedes)	125	35	+2500(d)
☐ 4/13	Willie Mays (FC) Giants	59 Baseball Issue, Masters, (Stengel, Dodge, 7-Up, Ted Williams, T-Bird)	100	35	+45
☐ 4/20	Bill Talbert Tennis	Ingemar Johansson Poster (Bob Hope, Coke, Jaguar, Chevrolet)	10	5	+10
☐ 4/27	Silver Spoon Horseracing	Kentucky Derby (Bob Cousy, Continental)	10	5	
☐ 5/04	Bob Turley Yankees	(Triumph, MG)	65	20	+20

☐	5/11	Gambling	*Swimsuits, Indians, Patterson* *(T-Bird, 7-Up, Hogan/Snead)*	10	5	
☐	5/18	Bob/Bus Mosbacher Yachting	*Tigers, Ben Hogan, Oscar Robertson,* *(Mays, Hank Aaron, Chrysler)*	10	5	+20 each
☐	5/25	Indy 500 Cars	*Yankees, Hank Aaron* *(Coke, Ted Williams, Corvette)*	10	5	
☐	6/01	Gary Cooper/Family Scuba Diving	*Yankees, Killebrew,* *(Ashburn, Corvette, Gifford)*	10	5	+200(d)
☐	6/08	Tom Bolt Art Wall Don Finsterwald Peter Thomson Golf	*US Open, Indy 500, Braves,* *(Coke)*	25	12	+20 each
☐	6/15	Dodger Stadium	*Mickey Mantle, Willie Mays, Dodgers,* *(Mercedes, T-Bird, Venturi)*	25	10	
☐	6/22	Ingemar Johansson Boxing	*US Open, Arcaro, Casper,* *(Snead, Chrysler, Continental)*	20	10	+35
☐	6/29	Golden Eagle	*Mantle, Wilhelm, Colavito Poster*	10	5	
☐	7/06	Ingemar Johansson Boxing	*All Star Game, Tigers,* *Floyd Patterson (Mantle, Imperial, 7-Up)*	30	15	+35/+20
☐	7/13	Becky Collins Swimmer	*Patterson/Johansson,* *(Corvette, Coke, Lincoln)*	10	5	+20
☐	7/20	Vasily Kuznetsov Dodgers USSR Track	*(Mercedes, Rambler)*	10	5	+50
☐	7/27	Toots Shor/ John Wayne	*Track, Indians* *(Drysdale, Chrysler)*	10	5	+50(d)/+200(d)
☐	8/03	Horsetrotter	*Giants, (7-Up, VW)*	10	5	
☐	8/10	Nellie Fox/ Luis Aparicio White Sox	*McCovey,* *(Wheaties, Coke, VW, Chevy, MG)*	95	35	+20/+150(d)
☐	8/17	Anne Quast Golf	*Ernest Hemingway, Willie McCovey*	10	5	+20
☐	8/24	Stavros Niarchos Yachting	*Archie Moore, Dodgers,* *Yaz [FIC], (VW)*	10	5	+100(d)
☐	8/31	Parry O'Brien Shot Putter	*Braves, Dodgers* *Drysdale, Coke, (7-Up)*	10	5	+20
☐	9/07	Alex Olmedo Tennis	*Giants, White Sox, Davis Cup* *(Crandall, Coke)*	10	5	+20
☐	9/14	Charlie Coe Golf	*Yankees* *(Warren Spahn, Pat Boone, Roy Rogers)*	10	5	+20
☐	9/21	1959 Football Issue	*Dodgers, Reds, Giants,* *(Spahn, Triumph)*	30	15	
☐	9/28	White Sox Team Aparicio,Fox, ETC	*Nicklaus, World Series,* *(Colavito, Spahn)*	75	30	+ varies
☐	10/05	Johnny Unitas (FC) Colts	*Pro Football Preview* *Dodgers, (Mickey Mantle, Bob Hope)*	150	40	+25
☐	10/12	Duck Hunting	*World Series, Sam Snead* *(Falcon, VW, Dodge)*	10	5	
☐	10/19	Auto Racing	*Dodgers, World Series* *(Plymouth, Porsche)*	10	5	
☐	10/26	George Izo Notre Dame	*Pro Basketball Issue,* *Gifford Poster, Football Issue* *(Gifford, Mercedes, 7-Up)*	40	20	+20
☐	11/02	Golfers	*(Coke, Desoto, Corvair)*	10	5	
☐	11/09	Bob/Mrs. Lackey Texas Football	*(Tennis, Triumph, Mercury)*	10	5	+20(each)
☐	11/16	Daytona 500 NASCAR	*Russell/Wilt Chamberlain* *(Imperial, VW, Snead)*	10	5	
☐	11/23	Ski Season	*(Mercedes, Andy Bathgate, Chevy)*	10	5	
☐	11/30	Hunting Dog	*Colts, (Lincoln, Desoto,*	10	5	
☐	12/07	College BKB Issue	*John Brodie, C. Connerly*	20	10	
☐	12/14	Tom Watson/Family skiing	*Colts/Giants,* *Skiing (Volvo, Porsche, Imperial)*	10	5	+100(d)

DATE	COVER	FEATURE	Nr-Mt	Ex	+Auto
☐ 12/21	Holiday Issue	Bowl Preview, Football's Babe Ruth, Wilt Chamberlain, Silver Anniversary, (Mercedes, Volvo)	14	7	

1960

DATE	COVER	FEATURE	Nr-Mt	Ex	+Auto
☐ 1/04	Ingemar Johansson Boxer (SOY)	Sportsman, Colts/Giants Bobby Hull, Snead	75	25	+30
☐ 1/11	Jerry Lucas Ohio State Basketball		50	20	+20
☐ 1/18	Art Wall Golfer	Golf Preview (Plymouth, Desoto)	35	10	+20
☐ 1/25	Russian Boys	AFL (Bing Crosby, T-Bird)	10	5	
☐ 2/01	Betsy Snite US Skier	Royals, Oscar Robertson (Lincoln, Mercury)	10	5	+10
☐ 2/08	Bedlington Dog	Richard Nixon, willie Mays (Corvette, Pan Am, Olds 60)	10	5	
☐ 2/15	Gennady Voronia Speedskater	Olympics (Dodge, Ford, Chevy, Imperial)	10	5	+50
☐ 2/22	Elliot Burch/ Sword Dancer Horse Trainer	Chamberlain vs Russell (Corvair, VW, Coke)	10	5	+100(d)
☐ 2/29	Squaw Valley Skiing	Yankees, Olympics (Chevy, Plymouth, Continental)	10	5	
☐ 3/07	Phillies Cartoon Baseball	Winter Olympics (Corvette, Oldsmobile, Imperial)	15	10	
☐ 3/14	Family Bowling	NCAA Tourney, (Coke, Sprite, 7-up, VW, Corvair)	10	5	
☐ 3/21	Maurice Richard Montreal Canadiens	Cardinals, NCAA Tourney (Dart, A.Palmer, Lincoln)	45	20	+15
☐ 3/28	Fisherman	James Leisenring NCAA Tourney, Dodgers (Desoto, Chevy, T-bird, Ford, Rambler)	10	5	+45
☐ 4/04	Masters Golf	The Masters, W. Chamberlain, (Coke, A.Palmer, Corvette, S.Snead, Oldsmobile)	15	10	
☐ 4/11	1960 Baseball Preview	E.Banks, N.Fox, Olympics,Giants (Harmon Killebrew, White Sox, Pontiac)	40	20	
☐ 4/18	Carin Cone Swimmer	Arnold Palmer-Masters, (Indians, Mercedes, Corvair, Chrysler)	10	5	+10
☐ 4/25	Dallas Long Shotputter	Giants, Stanley Cup Finals (Gene Sarazen, Porsche, Chrysler, Lincoln)	20	10	+10
☐ 5/02	Jockey	Kentucky Derby, Ted Williams (Thunderbird)	10	5	
☐ 5/09	Boating	Luis Aparicio Dodge Dart, Corvette, Ambassador V-8)	10	5	
☐ 5/16	Australian Sport	Kentucky Derby (Corvair, Coke, 7-Up, Pontiac)	10	5	
☐ 5/23	Charles Goren Bridge	Indians, Orlando Cepeda (Sam Snead, Chevy, Contential)	10	5	+100(d)
☐ 5/30	Herb Elliott* Running	Indy 500-Watson, Senators (Valient) (* Cover includes Dyrol Burleson)	20	10	+20
☐ 6/06	Red Schoendienst Braves	(Chevy, Coke, VW Van)	75	35	+20
☐ 6/13	Arnold Palmer* Golfers (FC)	US Open Golf (Corvair, Volvo, Chrysler) (* Cover also includes Ken Venturi, Don Finsterwald)	100	40	+40/+15
☐ 6/20	Ingemar Johansson Boxing	Indians (Corvette, Thunderbird)	30	15	+25
☐ 6/27	Glen Davis Track	Floyd Patterson, US Open (Campbell, Chevy, Rambler)	10	5	+10

	DATE	COVER	FEATURE	Nr-Mt	Ex	+Auto
☐	7/04	Comiskey Park	Maris/Mantle, Archie Moore	30	15	
☐	7/11	Jim Beatty	A's, Arnold Palmer	10	5	
		Track	(Corvair, Lincoln, Ambasador)			+10
☐	7/18	Candlestick Park	Arnold Palmer - British Open	35	20	
		Baseball	(7-Up, Chevy)			
☐	7/25	Yachting -Art	All Star Game, John Kennedy	12	7	
☐	8/01	Mike Troy	PGA	10	5	
		Swimmer				+10
☐	8/08	Dick Groat*		60	25	
		Pirates	(Campbell Soup, Coke)			+15
			(* Cover includes Phillies #20)			
☐	8/15	Olympics Flag	Olympics, Dodgers	10	5	
		Olympics				
☐	8/22	Barbara McIntire	Cardinals	25	10	
		Golfer				+10
☐	8/29	Mountain Climber	Roth	10	5	
			(VW)			
☐	9/05	Olympic Team	*Olympics Rafer Johnson	10	5	
		Olympics	Mantle/Maris			
☐	9/12	Jack Nicklaus	Olympics, Stan Musial	175	55	
		Golf (FC)				+100
☐	9/19	Lois Goetz	College Football Preview	12	5	
		Cheerleader-Syracuse				+20
☐	9/26	Jim Brown	Pro Football Preview	125	50	
☐	10/03	Bob Schloredt	Pirates, World Series	30	15	
		Washington	(VW Valiant)			+15
☐	10/10	Vernon Law	Jack Nicklaus, Thompson Home Run	50	25	
		Pirates	Bob Clemente (Corvair, Oldsmobile,			+15
			Falcon, Plymouth)			
☐	10/17	Model	Swimsuits, World Series,	15	7	
		Fashion Model	Pro Basketball Preview			
			(Corvette, VW)			
☐	10/24	Football Players	World Series, Hawks	10	5	
		Football				
☐	10/31	Jack Brabham	Casey Stengel	15	5	
		Car Racing	(Coke, Chevy, Pontiac)			+20
☐	11/07	James Thurber	Bobby Jones Series #1	10	5	
		Cartoon	(Bob Hope, VW, Buick, Ford)			+15
☐	11/14	Bobby Hull	Oscar Robertson, Bobby Jones	50	25	
		Blackhawks	Series #2 (T-bird)			+20
☐	11/21	Skiers		10	5	
			(Cadillac, Mercedes, Chrysler)			
☐	11/28	Joe Bellino	Norm Van Brocklin	15	8	
☐	12/05	Sam Snead	Eagles, Sam Snead	60	30	
		Golf	(Corvette, Bud)			+35
☐	12/12	Basketball Issue	10	5	3	
☐	12/19	Norm Van Brocklin	Hockey	45	20	
		Eagles	(Coke, T-Bird)			+150(d)
☐	12/26	John Kennedy/	Rose Bowl, Bowl Preview	75	40	
		Jackie Kennedy	Bear Bryant, (Huff)			+1500(d)/+700(d)

1961

	DATE	COVER	FEATURE	Nr-Mt	Ex	+Auto
☐	1/09	Arnold Palmer	Sportsman, Bowl Review,	125	45	
		Golf (SOY)	Eagles, (61 Buick)			+50
☐	1/16	Bob Cousy	Bill Russell, Tom Heinshon	100	40	
		Celtics				+35
☐	1/23	Golfers	Crosby Pro Am, Bobby Fisher	10	5	
			(61 Chevy, Dart)			
☐	1/30	Safe Driving	Crosby, Thunderbirds	10	5	
		Cars	(Corvette)			
☐	2/06	Track Runners		10	5	
			(Lincoln, Pontiac, VW)			
☐	2/13	Laurence Owen	Yogi Berra	15	5	
		Figure Skater	(Corvette, MG)			+15

☐	2/20	Billy Casper		35	12	
		Golf	(Buick)			+15
☐	2/27	Bobsledders	Duke	10	5	
			(T-Bird, Lincoln, Cadillac, Chrysler)			
☐	3/06	Raul Sanchez	Spring Training, Dodgers	35	12	
		Miquel Cueller	Yankees (Maris, Colovito, Palmer Ads)			+10/+10
		Reds				
☐	3/13	Floyd Patterson	Yankees, NCAA Tournament	35	15	
		Boxer	(Arnold Palmer)			+20
☐	3/20	Lynn Pyland	Floyd Patterson, Celtics	10	5	
		Sky Diver	(Corvette, George Mikan)			+10
☐	3/27	Jerry Lucas	NCAA Tournament,	35	15	
		John Havlicek	(Dodge, T-bird, Rambler, Lincoln)			+20 each
		Ohio State				
☐	4/03	The Masters	NCAA, Marlyn Monroe	40	15	
		Golfer	Joe DiMaggio, Carl Yaz			
			(Chevy, A.Palmer)			
☐	4/10	Cardinal Player	1961 Baseball Issue,	25	20	
		Cardinals	B. Robinson, R.Maris,			
			M. Mantle, N.Fox			
☐	4/17	Fishing - Art	Masters, Mickey Mantle,	10	5	
			Orioles,(Dodge, Corvette)			
☐	4/24	Hot Rodders	Angels, Senators	10	5	
			(VW, Dodge, Continental)			
☐	5/01	Kentucky Derby	Yankees	10	5	
			(Pontiac, T-Bird)			
☐	5/08	Gary Player	Warren Spahn	45	20	
		Golfer (FC)	(Corvair)			+15
☐	5/15	Cookie Lavagetto	Kentucky Derby, Sam Snead	30	15	
		Twins	(VW)			+100(d)
☐	5/22	Snorkling	Giants, Tigers, Swimsuits	10	5	
			(Porsche, Corvette, VW, Pontiac)			
☐	5/29	Indy 500 Racer	Orioles	10	5	
			(Skylark, VW, T-Bird)			
☐	6/05	Sailing Racing	Charlie Finley-A's	10	5	
			(VW, Cadillac, Chrysler)			
☐	6/12	Golfers	U.S. Open Golf, Reds	10	5	
		(T-Bird, VW)				
☐	6/19	Earl Young	Indians	10	5	
		Track	(Skylark, Lincoln, VW)			+10
☐	6/26	Ernie Broglio*	US Open Golf Results	25	10	
		Cardinals	(VW)			+15
			(* Cover includes Willie Mays)			
☐	7/03	Swimmer	Pirates, Jack Nicklaus	12	5	
☐	7/10	Tennis	Tigers, Norm Cash	10	5	
			(Sprite, Ford V-8)			
☐	7/17	Valeri Brumel	Reds, Sonny Liston	10	5	
		Track	Joe Dimaggio			+50
☐	7/24	Fish	W.Ford, Pirates, A. Palmer	10	5	
		Fishing	(Skylark)			
☐	7/31	Baseball Umpire	Reds, Muhammad Ali	10	5	
		Mickey Mantle, Roger Maris				
☐	8/07	Lisa Lane	Herb Score	10	5	
		Chess	(Ford V8, MG, VW)			+20
☐	8/14	Murray Rose	Dodgers, Willie Mays	10	5	
		USC Swimmer	Reds (Skylark)			+10
☐	8/21	Judy Torluennke	Ty Cobb's Death	10	5	
		Golfer				+10
☐	8/28	John Sellers		10	5	
		Jockey	(Kodak)			+10
☐	9/04	Forest Hills	Dodgers, Tigers, Senators	10	5	
		Tennis	(Bart Starr, Ford)			
☐	9/11	Deane Beman	Yankees	25	12	
		Golf				+25
☐	9/18	College Football	College Football, Dodgers	20	8	
			(MG, Buick Skylark, John Unitas)			

	DATE	COVER	FEATURE	Nr-Mt	Ex	+Auto
☐	9/25	Bart Starr Packers (FC)	Swimsuit Issue	65	30	+25
☐	10/02	Roger Maris Yankees (FC)	Maris #60 Home Run (D. Drydsdale, Buick, R.Maris, M.Mantle, Corvair)	150	35	+1000(d)
☐	10/09	Joey Jay Reds	Maris breaks record (S.Snead, Chevy, Corvette, Chrysler, Buick)	45	25	+15
☐	10/16	Terry Baker Oregon State	World Series, Cassius Clay (Mercedes, VW, Chevy)	40	25	+12
☐	10/23	Jon Arnett* Roy Hord Rams	Ryder Cup, AFL, Reds (Dodge, T-Bird, Buick)	25	10	+20
☐	10/30	Wilt Chamberlain Warriors	NBA Preview, Bears (Chevy, VW, Chrysler) (* Cover includes Dick McGuire)	75	35	+75
☐	11/06	Jockey - Kelso Horseracing	Hockey Preview (Cadillac, Buick)	10	5	
☐	11/13	Tom McNeeley Boxer	(VW, Rambler, Lincoln)	10	5	+10
☐	11/20	Y.A. Tittle Giants	Paul Hornung, Jerry West (Ford, Buick, VW, Chrysler)	65	25	+20
☐	11/27	Jimmy Saxton Texas		40	15	+10
☐	12/04	Skiing	(Buick, Dodge, Olds F-85)	10	5	
☐	12/11	Basketball Preview (T-Bird)	Patterson, B. Bryant	30	15	
☐	12/18	Dan Currie Packers	Packers, Giants (Buick)	20	10	+10
☐	12/25	Francine Breaud	Giants/Browns, Bowling	10	5	

1962

	DATE	COVER	FEATURE	Nr-Mt	Ex	+Auto
		Skier	(Lincoln, Porsche, Buick, Ford V-8)			+35
☐	1/08	Jerry Lucas Ohio State (SOY)	Sportsman, Packers Champs (Bart Starr, Buick-Skylark)	50	25	+20
☐	1/15	Don Heal Bruins	A. Palmer, J. Nicklaus (Rambler, T-Bird, Imperial, Pontiac)	20	7	+20
☐	1/22	Mr./Mrs.D.Sanders Golfer	Knicks (Corvette, Dodge, Lincoln, Cutlass)	10	5	+15/+100(d)
☐	1/29	Chet Jastremski Swimmer	Swimsuit Issue (Studenbaker, Ford, Buick)	10	5	+10
☐	2/05	Joan Hanah Skiing	Wilt Chamberlain (Cadillac, T-bird)	10	5	+10
☐	2/12	Sonny Liston (FC) Boxing	Figure Skating (62 Chevy)	30	15	+750(d)
☐	2/19	Mickey Wright Golfer	(VW Ghia, Corvette)	10	5	+10
☐	2/26	John Uelses Pole Vault	(Valiant)	10	5	+10
☐	3/05	Casey Stengel Mets	(Don Drysdale, Ted Williams, VW)	45	20	+400(d)
☐	3/12	Horses Racing Kentucky Derby	Jack Nicklaus (Grand Prix)	15	8	
☐	3/19	Gary Cunningham & John Green* UCLA/USC	(UCLA, * also John Rudometkin(USC)	30	15	+10
☐	3/26	Ricardo Rodriguez Race Car Driver	NCAA Tournament (Imperial, T-bird, Pontiac)	15	7	+100(d)
☐	4/02	Arnold Palmer Golf	Masters,Spring Training, NCAA Finals, Mantle/Maris Movie (Babe Ruth, (Mantle/Maris/Ford)	75	40	+40
☐	4/09	Frank Lary Tigers	Baseball Issue, W.Mays S.Koufax, E.Banks (Babe Ruth, Mantle/Maris/Ford)	60	30	+15

☐	4/16	Donna DeVarona Swimmer	Arnold Palmer (Buick, Corvette, Chrysler)	10	5 +10
☐	4/23	Jerry Schmidt Lacrosse	Dodger Stadium (Casey Stengel, Whitey Ford)	10	5 +10
☐	4/30	Luis Aparico White Sox	Celtics Champs,Stanley Cup Finals, Willie Mays, Stan Mikita (VW Van, Casey Stengel, Corevette, Valient)	60	25 +20
☐	5/07	Horses Racing Kentucky Derby	Sonny Liston, Hoston Colts (Buick, VW)	12	8
☐	5/14	Gene Littler Golfer	(Sam Snead, Avanti, VW Van)	75	35 +20
☐	5/21	Water Skiing	E. Hemingway, Reds, Twins (Roger Maris, Don Drysdale)	10	5
☐	5/28	Floyd Patterson Boxing	Yankees-Mantle (Chevy II)	35	15 +20
☐	6/04	Willie Mays Giants	Floyd Patterson, J.Nicklaus (VW, Mercedes, Corvette, Cadillac)	120	35 +45
☐	6/11	US Open Golf Course	US Open Preview, (Ben Hogan, Bob Hope)	40	20
☐	6/18	Crew Team* Cornell	[*includes John Beeman/ William Stowe/ Michael McGuirk/ Richard Thackaberry /John Abele/ Victor Erickson/ Donald Light/ David Nisbet/ Gary Brayshaw.] Nicklaus, (T-Bird, Triumph, VW)	10	5
☐	6/25	Jack Nicklaus Golfer	U.S. Open	65	35 +60
☐	7/02	Mickey Mantle Yankees	Yankees, J. Nicklaus (Imperial)	175	55 +250(d)
☐	7/09	Gretel- Yacht American Cup	Angels, Yankees (Lincoln)	10	5
☐	7/16	Igor Ter-Ovanesyan Long Jump	(Triumph, Chevy, VW, Sunbean)	10	5 +25
☐	7/23	Barbara McAlister Diving	Arnold Palmer, Braves (VW)	10	5 +10
☐	7/30	Ken Boyer Cardinals	Gary Player	20	12 +125(d)
☐	8/06	Paul Runyan Golfer	Cubs (VW)	20	10 +20
☐	8/13	Dick Fortenberry Sky Diving	Wilt Chamberlain, Mets (Bart Starr)	10	5 +10
☐	8/20	Don Drysdale (FC) Dodgers	(Porsche, Corvair)	60	25 +150(d)
☐	8/27	Helga Schultze Tennis	Nicklaus (Triumph)	10	5 +10
☐	9/03	California Beaches Art Drawing	(P. Hornung, B. Cousy, K. Venturi, Triumph, VW)	10	5
☐	9/10	Jim Taylor (FC) Forrest Gregg* Packers	Pro Football Issue, Yankees (*Also includes Packers/49ers Players)	60	25 +20each
☐	9/17	Sonny Liston Boxer	Giants,Palmer/Nicklaus (Maris/Mantle/Ford ad, Crazy Leg Hirsh)	30	15 +300(d)
☐	9/24	Flag Girls Texas	College Football Issue J. Nicklaus, S.Liston (Ted Williams, Whitey Ford)	25	12
☐	10/01	Baseballs 1962 World Series	World Series, Yankees, Frank Gifford (Corvette, T-Bird, Chevy, Ted Williams, Sunbeam)	30	15
☐	10/08	Tommy McDonald Eagles	Willie Mays	35	15 +15
☐	10/15	Sonny Gibbs TCU	World Series, Whitey Ford (Jack Nicklaus)	35	12 +10
☐	10/22	Hunter Art	World Series (Corvette)	10	5

	DATE	COVER	FEATURE	Nr-Mt	Ex	+Auto
☐	10/29	Fran Tarkenton	Pro Basketball Issue, J. West	75	35	
		Vikings (FC)	(VW Van, Sunbean, Rambler, Ford)			+35
☐	11/05	Mary Anderson	Dallas Texans	10	5	
		Skin Diving	(Lincoln, Pontiac, Dodge)			
☐	11/12	Sam Snead/Arnold Palmer		85	35	
		Golfer				+35/+55
☐	11/19	Nick Pietrosante	Lions, Giants, A.Palmer, S.Snead	15	8	
		Lions	(Dart, VW, Lincoln, Chrysler, Rambler)			+10
☐	11/26	Paul Dietzel	Clay	10	5	
		Army	(Corvette, VW, Triumph, Skylark)			+10
☐	12/03	Skier	Detroit/Packers, Celtics	10	5	
		Montana	Jack Nicklaus (Cadillac, Lincoln)			
☐	12/10	Cotton Nash	Basketball issue,	40	15	
		Kentucky	Tom/Dick Van Arsdales			+20
☐	12/17	Frank Gifford	Bill Bradley	65	35	
		Giants	(Ford, 7-Up, T-Bird, Pontiac)			+35
☐	12/24	Bold Americans	Swimsuits, John Kennedy	10	5	
		Sky Diving	(Lincoln)			

1963

	DATE	COVER	FEATURE	Nr-Mt	Ex	+Auto
☐	1/07	Terry Baker	Packer Champs	50	25	
		Oregon (SOY)				+15
☐	1/14	Phil Rodgers		20	10	
		Golfer	(A.Palmer/G.Player)			+20
☐	1/21	Vacationer	Arnold Palmer	10	6	
			(Chrysler, Cadillac, Rambler, Bob Cousy)			
☐	1/28	Howie Young		20	10	
		Red Wings	(7-Up)			+20
☐	2/04	Valeri Brumel	Jack Nicklaus	10	6	
		High Jump	(Chrsyler, Chevy, Volvo)			+25
☐	2/11	Cathy Nagel	Jack Nicklaus	10	6	
		Skier	(VW, Pontiac, Dodge, Mercedes)			+10
☐	2/18	Jerry Barber	Leo Durocher	25	10	
		Golfer	(VW)			+100(d)
☐	2/25	Rex Ellsworth	Celtics vs Lakers	10	6	
		Horseracing	(Triumph, Volvo)			+100(d)
☐	3/04	Sandy Koufax (FC)	Spring Training	100	40	
		Dodgers	(Ted Williams, Stan Musial,			+50
			Ralph Kiner)			
☐	3/11	Chuck Ferries	Cassius Clay,	10	6	
		Skier	(VW, Corvair, Rambler)			+10
☐	3/18	Larry Singleton	Jack Nicklaus, NCAA Basketball	20	10	
		Cincinati-Basketball	(Ted Williams, Ford, MG,			+10
			Cadillac, Sam Snead)			
☐	3/25	Sonny Liston	Cassius Clay	30	15	
		Boxer	(VW, GM, Triumph, Casey Stengel)			+750(d)
☐	4/01	Ken Venturi	NCAA-Finals, Masters	50	25	
		Golfer	Ben Hogan			+25
			(Jack Nicklaus/Arnold Palmer)			
☐	4/08	Harmon Killebrew	Baseball Preview, N. Fox	125	40	
		Twins	Walt Alston, Arthur Ashe(FACES)			+25
			(Ted Williams, Barbara Streisand)			
☐	4/15	Bill Talbert		10	6	
		Tennis	(Corvette, Jaquar, Studenbaker)			+20
☐	4/22	Fishing	Bob Cousy,	10	6	
		Fishing	J. Nicklaus, Masters			
			(Mercedes, GM, Ford, Yankees)			
☐	4/29	Art Mahaffey	Stanley Cup Finals	50	22	
		Phillies	(Sam Snead, Arnold Palmer,			+20
			T-Bird, Chrysler)			
☐	5/06	Candy Spot	Kentucky Derby, Celtics,	10	6	
		Horse	Mets (Stan Musial, S.Snead, VW,			
			Corvair, T-Bird)			

☐	5/13	Boat	W.Alston, Yankees, J.Nicklaus	10	6	
			Masters, (Corvette, Rambler, 7-Up, Cadillac)			
☐	5/20	Paul Hornung	Ernie Davis, Roger Maris	50	25	
		Packers	(Golf Ball History, Jaquar, J.Nicklaus)			+20
☐	5/27	Dan Gurney	Indy 500, Roger Maris, Angels	10	6	
		Car Racing	(Chevy, Ford)			+15
☐	6/03	Bob Hope	Arnold Palmer	150	45	
		Indians Owner	(Chevy, Nicklaus)			+50
☐	6/10	Cassius Clay		200	95	25
		Boxer (FC)	(Corvette, Bud)		+90 (Ali)	+120 (Clay)
☐	6/17	Jack Nicklaus	US Open/Golf	75	35	
		Golfer				+50
☐	6/24	Roy Face	A.Palmer, J. Nicklaus	30	15	
		Pirates	(Corvette, J. Nicklaus, Rambler)			+15
☐	7/01	Julius Boros	US Open Golf, Twins,	30	15	
		Golfer	W.McCovey, C. Clay (S.Musial, Chevy)			+100(d)
☐	7/08	Jon Tarantino	Mickey Mantle	10	6	
		Fisherman	(Cadillac)			+10
☐	7/15	Arnold Palmer	Wimbledon, White Sox	60	30	
		Golfer	(Corvette, Volvo, GM, VW)			+40
☐	7/22	Dick Groat	A. Palmer	50	20	
		Cardinals	(Ted Williams)			+15
☐	7/29	Sonny Liston	J. Nicklaus, S. Koufax	30	15	
		Boxing	A. Palmer, (Ford, VW, MG)			+750(d)
☐	8/05	Nancy Vonderheide	(Bing Crosby)	10	6	
		Archery				+10
☐	8/12	Alfred Vanderbilt		10	6	
		Horseracing	Red Sox, Arnold Palmer (7-Up, VW)			+10
☐	8/19	Ron Vanderkelen	Phillies	10	6	
		Vikings				+10
☐	8/26	Dennis Ralston	Alvin Dark, Mickey Mantle	10	6	
		Tennis				+10
☐	9/02	Ron Fairly	(Schwinn)	35	15	
		Dodgers	(Sam Huff, Bob Cousy, Bob Feller)			+20
☐	9/09	Dallas Cowboys*	Pro Football Preview [*Cover includes	50	25	
			George Andrie/ Chuck Howley/ Bob Lilly/			+10/auto
			Lee Roy Jordan]			
☐	9/16	Yachting	S. Koufax, J. Nicklaus	10	6	
			A. Palmer, Ron Mix (Koufax, VW)			+10
☐	9/23	George Mira	Dodger, Cardinals	20	10	
		Dolphins	(Bart Starr)			+10
☐	9/30	Whitey Ford*	Bear Bryant, World Series	125	35	
		Yankees	(T-Bird, M. Mantle, Corvette, B.Feller)			+25
			(* Also Al Downing on fold)			
☐	10/07	Deer Hunter	Jim Brown, Stan Musial	10	6	
			(Ford Fairlaine, Dodge, Sam Huff)			+10
☐	10/14	Ronnie Bull	Sandy Koufax, World Series	45	15	
		Bears	(Dodge Dart, VW Ghia, Chevy, Comet)			+15
☐	10/21	Duke Carlisle		10	6	
		Texas	(Mercury, GM Rambler, Cadillac)			+10
☐	10/28	Jerry Lucas*	Pro Basketball Preview	35	10	
		Royals	(Pontiac, Chrysler, Honda, Dodge)			+15
			(* includes Art Heyman Knicks)			
☐	11/04	Jack Cvercko	Raiders, 49ers, YA Title	10	6	
		Northwestern	(Comet, Corvair)			+10
☐	11/11	Referee	Texas Football (64 Rambler, Chevy	10	6	
			Dodge 880, Spitfire, 7-Up, Galaxia, Riveria)			
☐	11/18	Cindy Hollingworth	C. Clay, S. Liston, Bill Russell,	10	6	
		Skier	YA Title (Cadillac, Ford, T-Bird)			+10
☐	11/25	Willie Galimore	J. Nicklaus	25	10	
		Bears	(Studenbacker, Squirt, YA Title)			+150(d)
			(VW Ghia, Falcon)			
☐	12/02	Roger Staubach	Army/Navy	150	35	
		Navy (FC)	(Chevy II, Schwinn, Stan Musial, VW)			+35
☐	12/09	Frank Ramsey	Basketball Preview	65	30	

	DATE	COVER	FEATURE	Nr-Mt	Ex	+Auto
		Celtics	*(Corvette, Ford, Skylark,*			+20
			LeMans, Cadillac)			
☐	12/18	Tobin Rote	*Bob Cousy, AFL/NFL*	25	10	
		Paul Lowe	*(VW, 7-Up, Squirt, Ford)*			+15 each
		Chargers				
☐	12/23	C.K. Yang	*YA Title, Bowl Preview,*	10	6	
		Decathalon	*(T-Bird, Squirt)*			+40

1964

	DATE	COVER	FEATURE	Nr-Mt	Ex	+Auto
☐	1/06	Pete Rozelle	*Championship*	60	25	
		Commissioner	*NFL Commissioner (SOY)*			+150(d)
☐	1/13	Jack Dempsey*	*AFL Champs*	65	35	
		Boxing	*(* Cover includes Willard)*			+700(d)
☐	1/20	Babette March	*First Swimsuit Issue*	150	50	
☐	1/27	Buddy Werner	*A. Palmer, Winter Olympics*	10	6	
		Skiing	*(Chevy, Dodge, Chrysler,*			+100(d)
			Wilt Chamberlain)			
☐	2/03	Bobby Hull	*Olympics*	50	25	
		Blackhawks	*(Corvair, Ford)*			+20
☐	2/10	Egon Zimmermann	*Olympics, Sonny Liston*	10	6	
		Skier	*(Sam Snead,7-Up, Chevy, Porsche)*			+10
☐	2/17	Charles Goren	*Olympics, Cassius Clay*	10	6	
		Bridge Card	*(Corvette, Chrysler, Mercury)*			+100(d)
☐	2/24	Cassius Clay		120	45	
		Boxing	*(Covair, GM, Imperial, Triumph,*			+100
			Imperial)			
☐	3/02	Casey Stengel	*Wilt Chamberlain*	45	20	
		Yogi Berra	*(Waren Spahn, VW Van)*			+250(d)/+30
		Mets/Yankees				
☐	3/09	Cassius Clay	*Cassius Clay, Jerry West*	120	40	
		Sonny Liston	*(Bobby Hull, Stan Musial, 7-Up,*			
		Boxing	*Cadillac)*			+100/+750(d)
☐	3/16	Gordon Howe	*NCAA Basketball Tourney*	50	25	
		Red wings				+20
☐	3/23	Tony Lema		30	15	
		Golf	*(Grand Prix, Triumph, Chevy, Dart)*			+100(d)
☐	3/30	Walt Hazard/*	*UCLA NCAA Champs (Corvair, VW Ghia)*	30	15	
		Jeff Mullins	*(Cover includes Duke)*			+10
		UCLA				
☐	4/07	Jack Nicklaus	*Masters, Senators*	100	35	
		Golf	*(7-Up)*			+60
☐	4/13	Sandy Koufax	*Baseball Issue (Schwinn, Corvette*	120	35	
		Dodgers	*Riveria, LeMans, Whitey Ford)*			+50
☐	4/20	Janis Rinchlott	*A.Palmer-Masters,*	35	12	
		Texas Sprinters	*Richie Allen*			+10 each
			(64 Mustang, Stan Musial, YA Title, Corvair)			
☐	4/27	Claude Harmon	*Willie Mays*	25	10	
		Golf	*Lew Alcindor [fic]*			+25
☐	5/04	Kentucky Derby	*Celtics NBA Champs*	10	7	
		Horseracing	*(Triumph, 7-Up)*			
☐	5/11	Al Kaline (FSC)	*Kentucky Derby, Jack Nicklaus*	120	30	
		Tigers	*(Corvette, Chevy)*			+20
☐	5/18	Joey Giardello	*Twins, Juan Marichal (64 Mustang,*	10	6	
		Boxing	*J.Nicklaus, Buick, YA Title)*			+10
☐	5/25	Frank Howard	*Nothern Dancer*	30	15	
		Dodgers	*(Mercury, Jaquar, Barracuda, Chevy, VW)*			+10
☐	6/01	AJ Foyt	*Indy 500, Cassius Clay, Jim Fregosi*	20	10	
		Car Racing	*(T-Bird, 7-Up, Jack Nicklaus)*			+15
☐	6/08	Bill Hartack	*Robin Roberts, AJ Foyt*	10	6	
		Horseracing	*(VW, Warren Spahn, Chrysler, Bob Cousy)*			+10
☐	6/15	Arnold Palmer	*US Open, Roberto Clemente*	75	25	
		Golf	*(Stan Musial)*			+50
☐	6/22	Tom O'Hara	*Cassius Clay, Mickey Mantle,*	10	6	
		Loyola	*Brooks Robinson (VW, Chrysler)*			+10

	DATE	COVER	FEATURE	Nr-Mt	Ex	+Auto
☐	6/29	Ken Venturi	*U.S. Open Golf, White Sox*	55	20	
		Golf	*(7-Up, Volvo)*			+25
☐	7/06	Alvin Dark	*Giants, Angels, Floyd Patterson*	35	15	
		Giants				+20
☐	7/13	Bill Talbert	*Orioles, Brooks Robinson*	10	6	
		Tennis	*F.Patterson*			+10
			(Jack Nicklaus, Buick)			
☐	7/20	Shirley Maclaine	*Angels*	45	20	
		Actress				+20
☐	7/27	Tommy McDonald	*Yogi Berra*	35	12	
		Cowboys	*(Cadillac, 7-Up)*			+10
☐	8/03	Betsy Rawls	*Tony Congiliaro*	20	10	
		Golf				+25
☐	8/10	Johnny Callison	*Chi Chi Rodriguez*	50	20	
		Phillies	*Astrodome*			+15
☐	8/17	Don Trull	*10 Years of SI, Swimsuit*	20	10	
		Oilers	*Frank Robinson (Mustang)*			+20
☐	8/24	Sovereign*	*Americn Cup, Yogi Berra,*	10	6	
		Yachting	*Reds (Paul Hornung)*			+10
			*(*Cover includes Yachting Team)*			
☐	8/31	Brooks Robinson	*[* also Gerry McNerty (White Sox)/*	65	25	
		Orioles	*Earl Robinson (Orioles)]*			+25
			(VW Van)			
☐	9/07	YA Title	*Pro Football Preview*	45	15	
		Browns				+15
☐	9/14	Jim Ryun	*Rollie Fingers(FIC)*	25	6	
		Track	*(VW)*			+15
☐	9/21	Jimmy Sidle	*College Football Preview*	20	10	
		Auburn				+10
☐	9/28	Tommy Mason	*Yankees,*	15	8	
		Vikings	*(Corvair, Grand Prix, Rambler, Riveria)*			+10
☐	10/05	Tokyo Olympics*	*Dyrol Burleson, Marie Walther, Donna*	10	6	
			DeVarona, Don Schollander, Henry Carr,			+10each
			Fred Hansen. (Mustang, Mercury,			
			Packers, Pontiac, Comet, Buick, Cadillac)			
☐	10/12	Dick Butkus (FC)		130	45	
		Illinois	*(Corvair, VW, Yogi Berra)*			+25
☐	10/19	Yoshinori Sakai	*Floyd Patterson,*	10	6	
		Olympics	*Cardinals World Series (7-Up)*			+35
☐	10/26	Tommy Heinsohn	*Pro Basketball Issue,*	65	30	
		Celtics	*Olympic Games, World Series*			+25
☐	11/02	John Huarte	*Olympics*	60	25	
		Notre Dame	*(Green Bay Packers - Schick, Corvette)*			+20
☐	11/09	John David Crow	*Bill Russell-Celtics, Bear Bryant*	30	10	
		Cardinals	*(Micky Mantle, Ford Galaxie, YA Tittle)*			+15
☐	11/16	Cassius Clay*		120	30	
		Boxer	*(Comet, Bud, Impala, Gene Sarazen,*			+100/+750(d)
			(Also Sonny Liston), VW, Grand Prix)*			
☐	11/23	Helmut Falch	*Muhammad Ali (Saab, VW,*	10	6	
		Skier	*Mustang, Rambler, Dart, Corvair)*			+15
☐	11/30	Alex Karras	*Jack Nicklaus, Arnold Palmer*	20	10	
		Lions	*(T-Bird, Jerry West, Pontiac)*			+15
☐	12/07	Bill Bradley	*College Basketball Issue (Squirt,*	60	30	
		Princeton	*Corvette, Gordie Howe, Mickey Mantle)*			+50
☐	12/14	Charley Johnson	*Arnold Palmer, Jack Nicklaus*	25	12	
		Cardinals	*(7-Up, Comet, Gordie Howe, Cadillac)*			+10
☐	12/21	Ken Venturi	*Bowl Preview, Sportsman*	60	35	

1965

	DATE	COVER	FEATURE	Nr-Mt	Ex	+Auto
☐	1/04	Frank Ryan	*Browns win Championship*	50	20	
		Browns	*Jack Kemp*			+20
☐	1/11	Ernie Koy	*Namath, Bradley, Shula*	50	20	
		Texas	*(Jerry West, VW, Eva Gabor)*			+20

	Date	Subject	Cover/Contents			
☐	1/18	Sue Patterson Swimsuit Model	Swimsuit Issue #2 (Corvette, Pontiac)	150	50	+100
☐	1/25	Bobby Hull Black Hawks	Wilt Chamberlain All Star Basketball Game	55	20	+25
☐	2/01	George Chuvalo Boxing	Crosby Golf (Rivera, Oldsmobile, Ford, Chevy)	25	5	+20
☐	2/08	Jerry West Lakers	Floyd Patterson, Joe Namath (Grand Prix, Fairlane)	75	25	+25
☐	2/15	Golf Courses	Muhammad Ali (Coke, Mustang, VW Van, Sam Snead)	10	5	
☐	2/22	Golf Courses	(VW Ghia, Rambler, Buick Skylark, Sam Snead, Grand Prix)	10	5	
☐	3/01	Jim Bunning/ Bo Belinsky Phillies	(Volvo, Chevy, Eva Gabor, Mustang)	50	20	+20/+10
☐	3/08	Billy Kidd Skiing	NY Rangers, Bill Bradley (Arnold Palmer, Pepsi, 65 Olds, Jim Brown)	10	5	+10
☐	3/15	Tony Lema Golf	NCAA, Joe Garagiola (O.Robertson, G.Howe, Mustang, Corvair, Lincoln)	35	12	+100(d)
☐	3/22	Willie Pastrano Boxing	Bill Bradley, Al Lopez (Rambler 65, Johnny Carson RCA, VW)	10	5	+10
☐	3/29	Gail Goodrich UCLA	NCAA Champs, Bronco Dodge (Ford, Chevy, Ralph Terry)	40	15	+25
☐	4/05	A.Palmer/ J.Nicklaus Golf	Masters (Corvette, Tony Lema, S.Snead, A. Palmer, B. Hogan)	120	35	+40/+60
☐	4/12	Wilt Chamberlain Warriors	Cardinals, Astrodome (Ben Hogan, Rivera, Le Mans GTO, Barracuda)	65	20	+90
☐	4/19	1965 Baseball Issue	Baseball, Jack Nicklaus, Wilt Chamberlain,(J. Bunning, R.Roberts, Farlane)	50	20	
☐	4/26	Sonny Liston Boxing	Jack Nicklaus, Masters, Celtics (Bob Hope, Impalla, Mustang)	25	10	+750(d)
☐	5/03	Kentucky Derby Horseracing	Celtics NBA Champs,Yankees (Cadillac, Coke, Bonneville, Corvette)	15	6	
☐	5/10	Janell Smith Track	Kentucky Derby, Willie Shoemaker, VW Ghia, Mustang)(Stanley Cup Final)	10	5	
☐	5/17	Bill Veeck Baseball Owner	Twins (Marlin, Chevelle, Sprite, T-bird)	20	10	+125(d)
☐	5/24	Cassius Clay Boxing	AJ Foyt -Indy, Yankees (VW, Ford Galazie, Corvair, Schwinn)	65	25	+100
☐	5/31	Lloyd Ruby Car Racing	Indy 500 (Bob Hope, Coke, Plymouth, Mustang)	10	5	
☐	6/07	Cassius Clay/ Sonny Liston Boxing	White Sox (Tony Lema, Bob Hope)	50	20	+100/+750(d)
☐	6/14	US Open Golf	US Open, Bear Bryant (Rambler, Warren Spahn, Coke, Pontiac)	30	15	
☐	6/21	Mickey Mantle Yankees	Yankees (Galaxie, Sprite)	150	55	+250(d)
☐	6/28	Harry Parker/	Boston, US Open,Gary Player	10	5	
☐	7/05	Bill Talbert Tennis	Jim Ryun, Sam Snead (VW, Sprite)	10	5	+15
☐	7/12	Maury Wills Dodgers	Atlanta Stadium	45	15	+15
☐	7/19	Joe Namath (FC) Jets	(Sprite)	120	45	+40
☐	7/26	Arnold Palmer Golf	(Coke)	65	25	+40
☐	8/02	Powerboating Fishing	Sandy Koufax (Sprite)	10	5	
☐	8/09	Juan Marichal Giants	Arthur Ashe (Coke)	125	30	+25
☐	8/16	YA Title Giants Football	Pro Football Quarterback	60	20	+25

	DATE	COVER	FEATURE	Nr-Mt	Ex	+Auto
☐	8/23	Tony Oliva	YA Title, Arnold Palmer	55	20	
		Twins	(Budweiser, Ford)			+10
☐	8/30	Michel Jazy	Juan Marichal bat hit SF/LA,	10	5	
		Track	YA Title (Sprite)			+10
☐	9/06	Sugar Ray Robinson	Don Drysdale	20	9	
		Stan Harrington	(Coke, Zsa Zsa Gabor)			+175(d)
		Boxing				
☐	9/13	Fran Tarkenton	Tommy Mason, Pro Football Issue	50	20	
		Vikings	(Ed Mathews, Bart Starr,Lance Alworth)			+35
☐	9/20	Frank Solich	College Football Issue	50	20	
		Nebraska	Arthur Ashe			+15
☐	9/27	Frank Ryan	Green Bay, Giants,	35	12	
		Browns	Willie Mays (Coke)			+25
☐	10/04	Zoilo Versalles	World Series	40	15	
		Twins	(Ford Mustang, Bob Hope,			+125(d)
			Porsche, Mercury Comet)			
☐	10/11	Ken Willard	Alabama	35	10	
		49er's	(Bill Russell, Corvette,			+20
			Plymouth, Impalla)			
☐	10/18	Tommy Nobis	World Series	60	25	
		Texas	(T-Bird)			+20
☐	10/25	Bill Russell (FC)	Pro Basketball Issue	45	15	
		Celtics	Sandy Koufax, World Series			+195
			(Bronko Naqurski, SS Chevy, Dart)			
☐	11/01	Sonny Randle/Charley Johnson		25	15	2
		Cardinals	Satchel Paige			+10/+10
☐	11/08	Harry Jones	Gale Sayers	35	15	
		Arkansas Football	(Barracuda, T-Bird, Mercury, Chevy SS)			+10
☐	11/15	Ted Johnson	Cassius Clay, Wilt Chamberlain,	7	5	
		Skiing	B.Russell (Corvette, TV, Bonneville,			
			Maurice Richard)			
☐	11/22	Cassius Clay/		65	20	
		Floyd Patterson	(Mustang, Squirt, Corvette, Sprite)			+100/+20
		Boxing				
☐	11/29	Dennis Gaubatz	Cassius Clay	10	5	
		Colts	(Buick, T-Bird, Dart)			+10
☐	12/06	UCLA	College Basketball Issue	20	15	
		Basketball	G.Sayers, C.Clay, L.Alcindor, Rick Mount(FIC)			
			(Coke, GTO, Sprite)			
☐	12/13	Lance Alworth	(Squirt)	120	40	
		Chargers	(Willie Mays Coke Ad, Budweiser,			+20
☐	12/20	Sandy Koufax	Sportsman, Paul Hornung,	120	35	
		Dodgers (SOY)	(Squirt)			+50

1966

	DATE	COVER	FEATURE	Nr-Mt	Ex	+Auto
☐	1/03	Bowls Preview	AFL Championship	30	15	
			(GT Fairlane)			
☐	1/10	Jim Taylor	Bowl Games (Coke, Galaxie,	75	35	
☐	1/17	Sunny Bippus	Swimsuit Issue, Arnold Palmer	120	40	
		Model				+65
☐	1/24	George Peeples	Golf Courses	20	10	
		Iowa Basketball	(Bob Cousy, Dodge Charger, VW Van)			+15
☐	1/31	Stan Mikita (FC)	George Halas, Jo Jo White	45	20	
		Black Hawks	Calvin Murphy(FIC)			+20
			(Corvette, Jerry West, Ford Galaxie)			
☐	2/07	Billy Casper	Royals, Bill Bradley, Peggy Fleming	35	15	
		Golf	(Bob Hope, Mustang, Malibu, A.Palmer)			+20
☐	2/14	Rick Mount		40	15	2
		Basketball	(Mustang)			+20
☐	2/21	Jean-Claude Killy	Joe Frazier	12	9	
		Skier	(Pan Am, T-Bird, Corvette, Toranado)			+10

☐	2/28	Leo Durocher/Eddie Stanky Cubs / White Sox		35	15	+125(d)/25
☐	3/07	Adolph Rupp Kentucky	R. Clemente, M. Ali, P.Riley R. Petty,(Mustang, Porsche)	55	25	+300(d)
☐	3/14	Richmond Flowers Tennessee -Track	Dodgers, B.Bradley (VW Bug, Pam Am, Mustang)	10	5	+10
☐	3/21	Gary Player Golf	Bobby Hull (Polara, Porsche, Corvette, T-bird)	40	20	+15
☐	3/28	Hem Flournou/ Pat Riley Texas Western/Kentucky	NCAA Championship, Ted Turner (Mustang, Chevy SS, Lincoln)	40	20	+10/+25
☐	4/04	Jack Nicklaus/ Arnold Palmer Golf	Masters, Drysdale/Koufax (VW, Tony Lema, Gary Player)	75	30	+50/+40
☐	4/11	George Chuado/ Muhammad Ali	Celtics, M. Ali (Corvette, Starfire, Whitey Ford, T-bird)	50	20	+100/+25
☐	4/18	Dick Groat Phillies	Baseball Issue, Masters, C. Clay (T-Bird, VW, Bob Hope, Bing Crosby)	50	20	+15
☐	4/25	Bill Gadsby/ Chicago/Detroit	Jack Nicklaus, Cassius Clay, Lakers	25	10	
☐	5/02	Peggy Fleming	Cassius Clay	45	15	
☐	5/09	John Havlicek Celtics (FC)	Muhammad Ali (Volvo, Buick, Palmer)	65	20	+20
☐	5/16	Don Brunfield/Kauai King Horseracing	Kentucky Derby, Yankee (Budweiser, Ford, Coke, Charger)	10	5	+10 each
☐	5/23	Sam McDowell Indians	Giants, Willie Mays, Gary Player (Falcon, Schwinn)	25	10	+10
☐	5/30	John Boyd Indy 500	Brooks/Frank Robinson Cassius Clay, Mario Andretti (Sam Snead, Comet, Coke)	10	5	+10
☐	6/06	Joe Morgan/ Sonny Jackson Astros	Indy 500, Jack Nicklaus (J. Brown, B. Cousy, F. Gifford, B. Hull)	45	15	+25/+15
☐	6/13	Ken Venturi Golfer	Indy 500, US Open (VW, Coke)	50	20	+25
☐	6/20	Jim Ryun Kansas	Dodgers, Sandy Koufax, Yankees (Le Mans)	25	10	+20
☐	6/27	Billy Casper Golf	Mets, Rick Mount US Open Golf (Coke)	40	20	+20
☐	7/04	Ocean Sailors	Warren Spahn (VW Van)	10	5	
☐	7/11	Andy Etchebarren Tony Oliva, Denny McLain	(Coke)	25	10	2 +15
☐	7/18	Phil Edwards Surfer	Jack Nicklaus (Sprite)	45	12	+20
☐	7/25	Otto Graham/ Edward Williams Redskins	Jim Brown, Jack Nicklaus (Coke)	35	15	+20/+50(d)
☐	8/01	Jim Ryun Track	Orioles, Hank Aaron, Brooks Robinson	30	10	+15
☐	8/08	Frank Emanual Dolphins	Casey Stengel/Ted Williams to HOF, Steve McQueen	30	10	+10
☐	8/15	Paul Bryant (FC) Alabama Football	Cassius Clay, Bear Bryant #1 (VW,Coke)	120	35	+300(d)
☐	8/22	Paul Hornung/* Jim Taylor Packers	Bryant Series #2 (Coke) [* Flap has Jim Grabowski/Donny Anderson]	85	35	+20/+15
☐	8/29	Arthur Ashe Tennis	U.S. Open Tennis, John Brodie Bear Bryant #3, Don Drysdale	35	15	+120(d)
☐	9/05	Harry Walker Pirates	Bear Bryant #4 (Jack Kemp, Joe Namath)	25	10	+15
☐	9/12	Gale Sayers/ Randy Bukuich Bears Football	Pro Football Issue Jack Kemp, John Unitas, Bart Starr, Paul Hornung (VW)	60	35	+20/+10
☐	9/19	Gary Beban UCLA	College Football Issue Packers, Dodgers, Cassius Clay	20	10	+10

	DATE	COVER	FEATURE	Nr-Mt	Ex	+Auto
			(Paul Hornung, Sean Connerly, Sam Huff)			
☐	9/26	Gaylord Perry(FC) Giants	Giants, Dallas, D.Reeves (Lance Alworth, Bob Cousy)	50	25	+15
☐	10/03	Roman Gabriel Tommy McDonald Rams Team	(Rams) Orioles, (Pontiac GTO, Camaro, Dart, Delta 88)	20	10	+10
☐	10/10	Brooks Robinson/ World Series Frank Robinson/ Hank Bauer - Flap	(Willie Mays)	75	35	+20/+20
☐	10/17	Joe Namath Jets	World Series, Bobby Orr (Camero, Mustang)	65	25	+50
☐	10/24	Elgin Baylor Lakers	Pro Basketball Issue, Pele, W.S. (Sprite, Dart, Cadillac)	50	20	+15
☐	10/31	Bart Starr Packers	(Chevy SS, 67 Olds, T-Bird)	50	20	2 +25
☐	11/07	Terry Hanratty Notre Dame		40	15	2 +15
☐	11/14	Skier	(Corvette, T-Bird)	10	5	
☐	11/21	Ross Fichtner Browns	C. Clay (SI, Sean Connery, Mustang GT, Squirt)	15	7	+10
☐	11/28	Football Players Billy Casper, Notre Dame vs Mich State	Koufax Retires	40	20	
☐	12/05	Lew Alcindor (FC) UCLA	College Basketball Issue Cowboys	70	25	+45 "Jabbar"
☐	12/12	Jim Nance* Patriots/Buffalo	(T-Bird, Squirt, Bob Hope) (* Cover includes Buffalo players)	15	6	2 +10
☐	12/19	Jim Ryun Track (SOY)	F.Robinson Bobby Hull, Lew Alcindor (Sean Connery, Squirt)	55	25	+20

1967

	DATE	COVER	FEATURE	Nr-Mt	Ex	+Auto
☐	1/02	Kitty McManus Nebraska Cheerleader	Bowls, Jack Kemp (Mustang, Buick)	25	10	+10
☐	1/09	Bart Starr Packers	Playoffs, Bowls (Coke)	65	20	+15
☐	1/16	Marilyn Tindall Model	Swimsuit Issue, Vince Lombardi	70	30	+50
☐	1/23	Max McGee Packers	Superbowl #1, Len Dawson (Chevy SS, Mercury)	150	45	+20
☐	1/30	Rod Gilbert Rangers	(Frank Sinatra, Bud, Corvair, Mustang)	20	10	5 +10
☐	2/06	Cassius Clay Boxing	(Bob Hope)	50	20	3 +100
☐	2/13	Rick Barry (FC) Warriors	Cassius Clay (Olds, Mustang, Corvette,Sammy Davis Jr.)	20	10	+15
☐	2/20	Bob Seagren USC Pole Vaulter	(Ken Venturi, T-Bird, VW Ghia, Coronet)	10	6	+10
☐	2/27	George Walters/Chris Thomforde Princeton	(67 Chevy)	10	6	+10
☐	3/06	Mr/Mrs. Arnold Palmer Golf	(Corvair, Firebird)	45	15	+40/+15
☐	3/13	Jim Nash A's	A.Palmer, Peggy Fleming (T-Bird, Corvette, Cougar)	20	10	+10
☐	3/20	Stan Mikita/ Kenny Wharram/ Doug Mohns Blackhawks	NCAA, Bobby Hull (Ford Galaxia)	30	15	+15
☐	3/27	Jean-Claude Killy Skiing	Lew Alcindor, A.Palmer (Camero, Elgin Baylor, Brooks Robinson, Fairlane)	10	6	+15
☐	4/03	Lew Alcindor UCLA	Muhammad Ali, NCAA Champs (Firebird, VW Van)	45	15	+40

	Date	Cover / Team	Notes				
☐	4/10	Jack Nicklaus / Golf	*Masters, M. Ali, Orioles* / *(G Player, Galaxia, Corvair, A. Palmer)*	65	20		+50
☐	4/17	Maury Wills / Pirates	*Baseball Issue, Chamberlain* / *Masters, Maris* / *(Chevy SS, Golf Dress)*	30	12		+15
☐	4/24	Rick Barry / Warriors	*Roger Maris* / *(GT)*	20	10		+15
☐	5/01	Jim Hall / Car Racing	*(Firebird, Shelby GT, Mantle, Galixie)*	10	6		+10
☐	5/08	Ken Berry/ Mickey Mantle / White Sox/Yankees	*M.Ali, W. Chamberlain* / *(White Sox, Palmer, Sam Snead, VW Van)*	40	20		+10
☐	5/15	Sandy Koufax/Maury Wills / Walt Alston / Don Drysdale	*(Cadillac), Stanley Cup Finals*	30	15		+50/+150(d) +120(d)/+10
☐	5/22	Tommie Smith / San Jose -Track	*(Plymouth, B. Hull, P.Hornung, B.Cousy)*	10	6	2	+20
☐	5/29	Indy 500 - Art	*(Bud, Coke, Red Ruffing, Mustang)*	10	6		
☐	6/05	Al Kaline / Tigers	*(Volvo, GM, Hull)*	65	25	2	+25
☐	6/12	Billy Casper/ Arnold Palmer	*U.S. Open*	40	15		+10/+40
☐	6/19	Joe Harris / Boxing	*Bill Russell*	10	6		+10
☐	6/26	Jack Nicklaus / Golf	*U.S. Open, Tom Seaver* / *Ronald Reagan (Camaro)* / *Ralph Garr(FIC)*	45	15		+50
☐	7/03	Roberto Clemente / Pirates (FC)		200	40		+600(d)
☐	7/10	Muhammad Ali / & Challengers* / Boxing	*[*George Chivalo, Ernie Terrell,* / *Karl Mildenberger, Joe Frazier.]* / *Baseball Stadiums*	40			+100/+15
☐	7/17	Fran Tarkenton / Giants	*Orioles, Swimsuits*	55	20		+35
☐	7/24	Surfer Girls	*Fran Tarkenton, Orlando Cepeda*	10	6		
☐	7/31	Spitball	*Fran Tarkenton*	20	10		
☐	8/07	Gay Brewer / Golf	*Willie Mays, F. Tarkenton* / *Masters*	30	10		+100(d)
☐	8/14	Jim Taylor/ Gary Cuozzo / Saints	*Muhammad Ali, Rick Barry, Swaps*	40	15		+15/+10
☐	8/21	Carl Yastrzemski / Red Sox	*Muhammad Ali, Ted Williams*	120	35		+25
☐	8/28	Intrepid / Yachting	*Muhammad Ali* / *(Paul Hornung)*	10	6		
☐	9/04	Tim McCarver / Cardinals		40	15		+15
☐	9/11	Terry Hanratty* / Notre Dame	*Colleges Football Issue* / *(* Also includes Bill* / *Bradley,Ted Henricks, Kirby Moore)*	40	15		+20
☐	9/18	Tommy Mason / Rams	*Pro Football Issue, G.Sayers, Killebrew* / *Leroy Kelly, Ed Mathews*	15	8		+10
☐	9/25	Nino Benvenuti / Boxing	*(Corvette)*	10	6		+10
☐	10/01	John McKay / USC Coach	*John Unitas* / *(Chrysler, GTO, T-Bird, Buick)*	10	6		+20
☐	10/08	Mike Phipps	*W.Shoemaker, Red Sox, Cards*	10	6		
☐	10/15	Lou Brock (FC) / Cardinals	*World Series, Joe Namath* / *(Mustang, Star Trek)*	45	15		+25
☐	10/22	Pro Basketball / Knicks names	*Pro Basketball Issue, OJ Simpson* / *World Series (Shelby Cobra GT)*	15	8		+10/+40/+10
☐	10/29	Dennis Homan/ Jimmy Weatherford / Alabama/Tenn. Football		30	15		+15 each

DATE	COVER	FEATURE	Nr-Mt	Ex	+Auto
☐ 11/06	Dan Reeves Cowboys	Pro Hockey Issue (Toronado, Star Trek)	20	10	+10
☐ 11/13	Ski Fashions France	(VW, Chrysler, Cadillac)	10	5	
☐ 11/20	OJ Simpson,Gary Beban USC/UCLA		35	15	+40/+15
☐ 11/27	Jim Hart Cardinals	OJ Simpson (VW Van, Mercury, Buick)	15	7	+10
☐ 12/02	Basketball Art	College Basketball Issue (Coke, VW Gia, Firebird, Rivera)	20	10	
☐ 12/09	Bobby Orr (FC) Bruins	Raiders, R. Mount, C. Murphy	75	25	+50
☐ 12/18	Roman Gabriel/Willie Davis Rams/Packers	Bill Bradley, Vince Lombardi	20	10	+15
☐ 12/25	Carl Yastrzemski Red Sox (SOY)	Holiday (Cadillac, Torino)	120	30	+25

1968

DATE	COVER	FEATURE	Nr-Mt	Ex	+Auto
☐ 1/08	Chuck Mercein/ Hewitt Dixon Packers/Raiders	George Blanda, Bowl Games (Cadillac, Coke)	30	15	+10/+15
☐ 1/15	Turia Mau Swimsuit Model	Swimsuit Issue	60	20	+45
☐ 1/22	Vince Lombardi/ Jerry Kramer Packers	Superbowl II (Chevy, Bud)	120	40	+300(d)/+15
☐ 1/29	Lew Alcindor/ Elvin Hayes UCLA/Houston	Olympics	30	15	+45/+35
☐ 2/05	Billy Kidd/ Jimmy Heuga Skier	Winter Olympics (GTO, Fury III)	10	6	+10
☐ 2/12	Bobby Hull Bruins	Olympics (Camaro, Corvette)	35	15	+15
☐ 2/19	Peggy Fleming Ice Skating	Muhammad Ali, Olympics (Cadillac, Toronado, Bonneville)	35	15	+15
☐ 2/26	Curtis Turner NASCAR	(Corvette) John Havlicek, Olds, Camaro)	10	5	+20
☐ 3/04	Pete Maravich* LSU	Joe Frazier (Corvette)(* Also includes Pete's Dad)	120	35	+300(d)/+100(d)
☐ 3/11	Johnny Bench* Reds	(*Cover includes Alan Foster, Mike Torrez, Don Pepper, Cisco Carlos)	65	30	+25/10 each others
☐ 3/18	Bill Bradley Knicks	NCAA, Joe Frazier (Camaro, Mustang)	60	25	+50
☐ 3/25	Julius Boros Golfer	NCAA, Carl Yaz (GTO, Toronado)	10	5	+100(d)
☐ 4/01	Lew Alcindor/ Elvin Hayes UCLA/Houston	NCAA final (T-Bird, Camaro)	20	10	+50/+30
☐ 4/08	Goalie LA Kings	Stanley Cup, Masters,Pete Maravich (AMX, Cougar, Arnold Palmer, Bonneville)	10	5	
☐ 4/15	Lou Brock Cardinals	1968 Baseball Issue, Pete Rose (Corvette, Palmer, Carl Yaz, YA Title)	40	15	+25
☐ 4/22	B.Goalby/R.DeVicenzo Golf	Masters (Satellite, Firebird)	25	6	+15/+15
☐ 4/29	Elgin Baylor/ Jerry West Lakers	Harmon Killebrew, Reggie Jackson Bill Russell (Chevy SS 396)	55	25	+25 each
☐ 5/07	Ron Swoboda Mets	Nolan Ryan, Tom Seaver (Chrysler, Harmon Killebrew, Schwinn)	35	12	+10
☐ 5/13	Graham Hill Car Racing	Indy 500, Kentucky Derby, Celtics Champs (Corvette, Cadillac, Brooks Robinson)	10	6	+10

☐	5/20	Dancer Image Horse	Kentucky Derby (Charger, Plymouth, T-Bird)	10	6	
☐	5/27	Pete Rose Reds (FC)	VW, Chevy SS) (Palmer, Torino, Harmon Killebrew)	100	30	+25
☐	6/03	Dave Patrick Villanova- Track		10	5	+10
☐	6/10	Arnold Palmer/ Jack Nicklaus Golf (Corvette, Campaneris, Unser)	U.S. Open Preview, Willie Mays Ted Williams	65	15	+40/+50
☐	6/17	Don Drysdale Dodgers	Ted Williams	50	20	+120(d)
☐	6/24	Lee Trevino (FC) Golf	U.S. Open, Ted Williams (Cadillac, Chevy SS)	45	15	+25
☐	7/01	Black Athlete	Ted Williams (Gatorade)	10	5	
☐	7/08	Ted Williams Red Sox	'The Science of Hitting'	35	15	+200
☐	7/15	Ray Nitschke Packers	Olympics (Harmon Killebrew, VW Ghia, Bud, Johnny Bench)	120	25	+20
☐	7/22	Mark Spitz Swimmer		10	5	+15
☐	7/29	Denny McLain (FC) Tigers	(VW Van)	45	20	+10
☐	8/05	Nevele Pride Harness racing	Orioles (Roman Gabrial)	10	5	
☐	8/12	Paul Brown Bengals	Jack Nicklaus	20	10	+120(d)
☐	8/19	Curt Flood Cardinals	(Coke)	25	10	+100(d)
☐	8/26	Rod Laver Tennis	U.S. Open, Joe Namath	15	6	+10
☐	9/02	Ken Harrelson Red Sox	Bobby Orr	24	12	+10
☐	9/09	Leroy Keyes Purdue Football	College Football Issue John Riggens (Charley Taylor, Dan Reeves, Frank Ryan)	15	7	+10
☐	9/16	Don Meredith Cowboys	Pro Football Issue, Carl Yaz. Arthur Ashe,(FB Hall of Fame, H. Killebrew)	60	20	+25
☐	9/23	Denny McLain/ Al Kaline Tigers	McLain's 30th Victory, Bobby Jones (Charger, Chrysler)	65	25	+10/+20
☐	9/30	Jim Ryun*/ Kip Keino Olympics Preview	World Series. (Cadillac, Chevy) (*Also Harry Edwards/Avery Brundage)	20	10	+15

☐	10/07	Roger Maris/Lou Brock/Tim McCarver Bill Shannon/Orlando Cepeda, Curt Flood Julius Javiar, Bill Maxwill, Red Schoendiest Cardinals		100	30	5	

+600(d)/+20/+10/+10
+10/+100(d)/+10/+10
+20

☐	10/14	OJ Simpson USC	Hockey Preview, World Series (Ray Nitschke, LeMans, SS)	30	10	+40
☐	10/21	Sotela Basilio/ Norma Enriqueta Olympic Torchbearers	Pro Basketball Preview, Olympics (Unitas, Crosby, Cougar) World Series	10	6	
☐	10/28	F.Gregg/Bob Brown Packers	Olympics (VW Ghia, Toronado, Nova, Dart)	40	12	+15/+10
☐	11/04	Earl Monroe Bullets	Olympics (Coronet, Bud)	20	10	+25
☐	11/11	Bruce Jankowski Ohio State	Peggy Fleming (Pontiac, Charger, Buick GS)	30	10	+15
☐	11/18	Jean-Claude Killy Skiing	OJ Simpson (VW Van, Unitas, Camaro, Palmer)	10	5	+15
☐	11/25	Earl Morrall Colts	(Charger, Squirt, Nicklaus)	65	25	1 +25
☐	12/02	Mike Casey* Kentucky	College Basketball Issue (J.Havilek, J. Unitas, J. West) (*Cover includes Charlie Scott-NC, Mike Malloy-Davidson)	35	12	+10

	DATE	COVER	FEATURE	Nr-Mt	Ex	+Auto
☐	12/09	Joe Namath Jets	OJ Simpson, Notre Dame, Gordie. Howe, Royals (Delta, Squirt)	45	15	+40
☐	12/16	Rick Volks/ Donny Anderson Colts/ Packers	Bart Starr, Connie Hawkins (Coronet, Imperial) (*Cover includes Dennis Gabatz)	35	12	+15 each
☐	12/21	Bill Russell (SOY) Celtics	Colts, J. Kelly, Bowls (Squirt, J. Unitas)	75	20	+200

1969

	DATE	COVER	FEATURE	Nr-Mt	Ex	+Auto
☐	1/06	Tom Matte* Colts	John Wooden, Joe Namath (*also shows Charley Talyor)	30	12	+10
☐	1/13	Jamee Becker Swimsuit Model	1969 Swimsuit Issue (GTO)	100	25	+50
☐	1/20	Joe Namath Jets	Superbowl III (Wilt Chamberlain, Don Maynard)	150	55	+50
☐	1/27	Wilt Chamberlain Lakers	 (Imperial, Bob Hope, John Havlicek)	40	15	2 +80
☐	2/03	Bobby Orr Bruins	Frank Robinson	40	20	+40
☐	2/10	Bud Ogden Santa Clara	(Bob Hope, John Havlicek, Wilt Chamberlain, GTO)	10	5	+15
☐	2/17	Bob Lunn Golf	Jack Nicklaus (Chrysler, Bud, T-Bird)	25	8	+20
☐	2/24	Willis Reed/ Billy Cunningham Knicks/ 76ers	Ted Williams, Earl Monroe (Bonnyville, W.Chamberlain)	20	6	+15
☐	3/03	Vince Lombardi Redskins	Tom McMillen(FIC) (Nicklaus, Toronado, Nova)	35	10	+300(d)
☐	3/10	Puma's & Adidas Shoe Scandal	 (Elgin Baylor, Wilt Chamberlain, Jack Nicklaus, T-Bird)	10	5	
☐	3/17	Ted Williams Senators	Lew Alcindor (Bud, Playboy Club, Camaro, Opel GT, Grand Prix)	35	15	+185
☐	3/24	Richie Guerin/ Jeff Mullins Hawks/ Warriors	Charlie Scott, Dan Gable (Chamberlain, Dodge, Imperial)	10	9	+15/+15
☐	3/31	Lew Alcindor UCLA	NCAA Champ, Johnny Bench George McGinnis (fic) (T-Bird, Al Kaline, Charger, G.Howe)	35	15	+40
☐	4/07	Red Berenson Blues	Tony Conigliaro, Masters (Arnold Palmer, Wilt Chamberlain, Volvo)	25	12	+15
☐	4/14	Bill Freeham Tigers	Baseball Issue, John Havlicek, T.Seaver (P.Rose, J.Nicklaus, A.Kaline, Bud)	40	15	+15
☐	4/21	George Archer Golf	Willie Mays, Masters	20	10	+10
☐	4/28	Bill Russell Celtics	Bobby Orr, Bobby Murcer (Camaro)	30	15	+200
☐	5/05	Muhammad Ali Boxing	 (Maverick, Lee Trevino, Mercedes)	45	15	+100
☐	5/12	John Havlicek Celtics	Kentucky Derby (Chevelle SS, Roy Campanella, Pepsi)	45	15	+20
☐	5/19	Walt Alston* Dodgers	(*Cover shows: Ted Sizemore, Bill Sudakis, Bill Grabarkewitz.) Jack Nicklaus, (VW, Casper)	35	15	+250(d)/+15 each
☐	5/26	Grizzly Bear	 (Mercedes, Pete Rose)	10	5	
☐	6/02	Water Scooter	Frank Robinson, Lee Trevino, Billy Casper) Steve Prefontaine (fic)	10	5	
☐	6/09	Lee Trevino Golf	Indy 500-Mario Andretti OJ, US Open	40	15	+25
☐	6/16	Joe Namath Jets	Arnold Palmer (Opel GT)	40	15	+40
☐	6/23	Drugs	US Open Golf (Fresca, Olympic Beer, Arnold Palmer, MG)	10	5	

	DATE	COVER	FEATURE	Nr-Mt	Ex	+Auto
☐	6/30	Ron Santo / Cubs	(Mercedes)	45	15	+15
☐	7/07	Reggie Jackson (FC) / A's		70	30	+35
☐	7/14	O.J. Simpson / Bills	Billy Casper (VW)	30	15	+40
☐	7/21	Billy Martin / Twins	(VW)	45	15	+100(d)
☐	7/28	Sonny Jurgensen/Vince Lombardi / Redskins	(Pete Rose)	20	10	+15/+350(d)
☐	8/04	Bill Russell / Celtics	All Star Game, Willie McCovey (Olympic Beer, Pepsi, Gatorade)	30	15	+200
☐	8/11	Joe Namath / Jets		30	15	+40
☐	8/18	Henry Aaron (FC) / Braves		65	20	+35
☐	8/25	O.J. Simpson / Bills	Luis Aparico (Gatorade, OJ Simpson)	30	15	+40
☐	9/01	Arnold Palmer / Golfer		45	15	+40
☐	9/08	Pete Rose/Ernie Banks / Reds / Cubs		60	25	+25/+25
☐	9/15	Woody Hayes/ Rex Kern / Ohio State Football	College Football Issue Willie McCovey, Nancy Lopez (FIC) (Bear Bryant, Ernie Banks)	30	15	+200(d)/+15
☐	9/22	Jim Turner / Jets	Pro Football Issue (Vince Lombardi, Cutlass, Gale Sayers, GTO, Budweiser)	30	15	+15
☐	9/29	Jimmy Jones / USC	Willie Mays, Ernie Banks (Mustang, Pete Rose, SS)	20	10	+15
☐	10/05	Frank Robinson/ Boog Powell (Flap) / Orioles	(G.Howe, Cyclone, Monte Carlo, Pee Wee Reese)	30	15	+20/+15
☐	10/12	Bruce Kemp / Georgia	Pro Hockey Issue (Impalla, John Havlicek, Charger, Toronado)	20	9	+15
☐	10/20	Brooks Robinson* / Orioles	Connie Hawkins, Lew Alcindor (Arnold Palmer, Buick) (* Cover includes: Paul Hendricks)	45	20	+15/+10
☐	10/27	Lew Alcindor / Bucks	Pro Basketball Issue World Series	35	15	+40
☐	11/03	Alan Page/Roy Winston / Carl Eller / Vikings Football	Lew Alcindor, Joe Kapp (Imperial, J.Kramer)	30	12	+15 each
☐	11/10	Steve Owens / Oklahoma Football	Archie Manning, Joe Namath L. Alcindor (John Wayne, Mach 1 Mustang)	10	5	+15
☐	11/17	Beredette Barzini / Ski Model	Jerry Lucas, Jack Nicklaus (Porsche, Mustang)	10	5	+25
☐	11/24	Len Dawson* / Chiefs	Joe Namath (Olympic, G. Sayers, P. Rose, Squirt) (* Cover includes Chiefs 45,21,55,84)	40	15	+25
☐	12/01	Pete Maravich / LSU Basketball	College Basketball Issue (Gale Sayers, Joe Montana)	125	35	+200(d)
☐	12/08	Walt Frazier/ Bob Weiss / Knicks/ Bulls	Jack Nicklaus (Bud, Willis Reed, Duster)	35	15	+15
☐	12/15	James Street / Texas Football		35	15	+15
☐	12/22	Tom Seaver* / Mets (SOY)	Notre Dame, Stadium (Torino, R. Gabrial, Rose Bowl) (*flap cover includes Joe Namath, Muhammad Ali)	150	35	+25

1970

	DATE	COVER	FEATURE	Nr-Mt	Ex	+Auto
☐	1/05	Dave Osborn/ Deacon Jones / Vikings/ Rams	(Lee Trevino, Joe Kapp, Darryl Lamonica, Craig Morton)	35	12	+15 each

	Date	Cover	Feature			
☐	1/13	Cheryl Tiegs (FC) Model	Swimsuit Issue Playoffs, D.Lamonica	100	30	+30
☐	1/19	Len Dawson Chiefs	Superbowl IV (Bud)	100	35	+25
☐	1/26	Bob Cousy Royals	Ted Williams [Bill Walton (FIC)] (Don Maynard)	30	15	+30
☐	2/02	Environment	(AMX)	10	5	
☐	2/08	Terry Bradshaw La Tech	(Bob Hope, VW, Lee Trevino)	75	25	+45
☐	2/16	Tom McMillen HS Basketball	Joe Frazier (Jerry West)	15	7	+12
☐	2/23	Denny McLain Tigers	(Toronado)	25	10	+15
☐	3/02	Eddie Giacomin Rangers	Spring Training (Mustang, Camaro)	10	7	+10
☐	3/09	Lew Alcindor Bucks		35	15	+40
☐	3/16	Dan Issel* Kentucky	(* Includes Bob Lanier-St. Bonaventure, Jim Collins New Mexico, J. Vallely-UCLA)	25	10	+15
☐	3/23	Richie Allen Cardinals	Steve Carlton, Bob Gibson (Sam Snead, Stan Mikita)	45	15	+15
☐	3/30	Sidney Wicks/ Art Gilmore UCLA/Jacksonville	Basketball Final Four Pete Maravich	24	12	+15
☐	4/06	Keith Magnuson Black Hawks	Pete Maravich, Masters, (Williams/Hodges,Koosman, Ben Hogan, Sam Snead)	25	8	+15
☐	4/13	Jerry Koosman Mets	Baseball Issue, W.McCovey, Rod Carew (J. Wayne, Bud, Lou Brock, Arnold Palmer, Jack Nicklaus)	25	8	+15
☐	4/20	Billy Casper Golf	Master (Pepsi)	35	12	+15
☐	4/27	Lew Alcindor/ Willis Reed Bucks/Knicks	Wilt Chamberlain (Peggy Fleming)	35	10	+40/+15
☐	5/04	Bobby Orr Bruins		55	20	+40
☐	5/11	David Smith Peace Pentathlon	Mario Andretti (Camaro, Gil Hodges, Earl Weaver)	10	5	+15
☐	5/18	Dave Debusschere Knicks	NBA Champs, Ben Hogan (Datzun 280z, Brooks Robinson)	35	12	+25
☐	5/25	Hank Aaron Braves	(Firebird, Arnold Palmer)	65	20	+25
☐	6/01	Jack Nicklaus/ Arnold Palmer Golf	Bob Griese, Tom Seaver	55	17	+50/+40
☐	6/08	Al Unser Indy 500	Bill Russell (Cary Middlecoff)	20	6	+15
☐	6/15	Steve Prefontaine Oregon-Track	Jack Nicklaus (Bud)	120	20	+500(d)
☐	6/20	Tony Conigliaro Red Sox		60	15	+300(d)
☐	6/29	Tony Jacklin Golf	US Open, Denny Mclain, Pele Tony Conigliaro (Lee Trevino)	24	12	+100(d)
☐	7/06	George Frenn Hammer throw	Frank/Brooks Robinson Willie Mays, Luis Aparico, (Pepsi), Orlando Cepeda	10	4	+15
☐	7/13	Johnny Bench Reds	Tony Perez (Jerry Koosman)	50	20	+25
☐	7/20	Joe Kapp Vikings	Jack Nicklaus	25	12	+15
☐	7/27	Willie Mays Giants	Joe Kapp	50	20	+40
☐	8/03	Frank Shorter* Track	(* Also Mikitenko)	10	4	+15

DATE	COVER	FEATURE	Nr-Mt	Ex	+Auto
☐ 8/10	Mike Garrett Chiefs		10	6	+15
☐ 8/17	Joe Namath Jets	George Foreman, Tony Oliva	25	10	+40
☐ 8/24	Rick Barry Squires - ABA	PGA	10	6	+15
☐ 8/31	Les Sly Cowboys	Roger Staubach (Gale Sayers)	15	6	+15
☐ 9/07	Bud Harrelson* Mets	(* cover include Pete Rose)	25	10	+15
☐ 9/14	Archie Manning Mississippi	College Football Issue, Muhammad Ali (Joe Namath)	65	25	+20
☐ 9/21	Dick Butkus Bears	Pro Football Issue	120	40	+20
☐ 9/29	Danny Murtaugh* Pirates	Roberto Clemente (Mustang) (* Also Leo Durocher- Cubs & Gil Hodges - Mets)	15	10	+120(d)/+120(d)/250(d)
☐ 10/05	Football players Colorado/Penn State	Willie Stargell, Frank/Brooks Robinson	10	7	
☐ 10/12	Alex Karras Lions		15	7	+15
☐ 10/19	Brooks Robinson* Orioles	World Series (Mickey Mantle, Camaro, Joe Namath) (* Cover includes P. Hendricks, Boog Powell, C.Carbo, L. May, T.Perez)	45	15	+15/+10each
☐ 10/26	Oscar Robertson Bucks	NBA Pro Basketball, Joe Theisman, Pete Maravich (Challenger)	45	15	+25
☐ 11/02	Monday Night Footbal	Muhammad Ali (Jaquar)	10	4	
☐ 11/09	Joe Theismann* Notre Dame	(*Cover includes Jack Tatum - Ohio State, Steve Worster - Texas)	35	12	+15
☐ 11/16	Calvin Murphy Rockets	(Joe Namath)	30	12	+15
☐ 11/23	George Blanda / Daryl Lamonica Raiders		35	12	+20
☐ 11/31	Sidney Wicks	College Basketball Issue	24	12	
☐ 12/07	Roman Gabriel Rams	Jack Kemp	20	10	+15
☐ 12/14	Steve Worster Texas	Muhammad Ali, Notre Dame	10	5	+15
☐ 12/30	Bobby Orr Bruins (SOY)	Raiders, Muhammad Ali	75	25	+50

1971

DATE	COVER	FEATURE	Nr-Mt	Ex	+Auto
☐ 1/04	John Roche South Carolina	49ers, Bowl Games	30	15	+15
☐ 1/11	Joe Theismann Notre Dame		30	15	+15
☐ 1/18	Craig Morton Cowboys		40	15	+15
☐ 1/25	Jim O'Brien Earl Morrell Cowboys	Superbowl V	45	20	+15/+20
☐ 2/01	Tannia Rubiano Model	Swimsuit Issue, Muhammad Ali	50	20	+40
☐ 2/08	Willis Reed Lew Alcindor Knicks	Tony Conigliaro	15	7	+15/+40
☐ 2/15	Jim Plunkett Stanford	Muhammad Ali	15	7	+15
☐ 2/22	Del Meriwether Track	Joe Frazier	10	5	+30

☐ 3/05	Joe Frazier/Muhammad Ali Boxing		50	22	+25/+90
☐ 3/08	Jack Nicklaus Golf	PGA, Pete Maravich Spring Training	35	12	+60
☐ 3/15	Joe Frazier/Muhammad Ali Boxing		50	22	+25/+90
☐ 3/22	Wes Parker Dodgers		20	10	+15
☐ 3/29	Phil & Tony Esposito Bruins/Blackhawks		40	20	+15/+15
☐ 4/05	Steve Patterson UCLA	NCAA Championship	10	5	+15
☐ 4/12	Boog Powell Orioles	Baseball Issue (SI, Lou Brock, Pete Rose, Corvette)	20	10	+15
☐ 4/19	Willis Reed Abdul-Jabbar Knicks/Bucks	Lew Alcindor, Bobby Orr (Johnny Carson, Porsche)	10	6	+20/+45
☐ 4/26	Derek Sanderson Bruins		10	5	+15
☐ 5/03	Dave Duncan Jim Fregosi A's/Angels	Jack Nicklaus, A's, Derby Chris Evert(FACES) (Mustang)	15	7	+15/15
☐ 5/10	Oscar Robertson* Bucks	NBA Title (Porsche, Jerry Lucas, Ted Williams) *Cover also shows Wes Unseld/Gus Johnson	35	12	+30
☐ 5/17	James McAlister UCLA	Giants (Mustang, Phil Esposito)	10	4	+10
☐ 5/24	Liquori/Jim Ryun Villanova Track	Kentucky Derby, Red Sox (VW Ghia)	15	5	+15/+15
☐ 5/31	Vida Blue A's	Pete Maravich	30	12	+15
☐ 6/07	Al Unser/Pete Revson Indy 500	All Star Game, Jack Nicklaus (Porsche, All Star Ballot-Gilette,Foyt)	20	10	+10
☐ 6/14	Canonero II Horseracing	Bobby Jones	7	4	
☐ 6/21	Jerry Grote Mets		15	7	+15
☐ 6/28	Lee Trevino Golf	US Open (Corvette)	30	12	+25
☐ 7/05	Alex Johnson Angels	(Brooks Robinson)	15	6	+15
☐ 7/12	Evonne Goolagong Tennis	Wimbledon, Vida Blue	10	4	+15
☐ 7/19	George Blanda Raiders	Tony Conigliaro, Boug Powell (Brooks Robinson)	25	10	+15
☐ 7/29	Muhammad Ali Boxing	George Blanda (Porsche)	30	12	+80
☐ 8/02	Willie Stargell Pirates (FC)	Muhammad Ali, Lee Trevino, George Blanda, Roberto Clemente	40	15	+15
☐ 8/09	Mike Peterson Kansas		10	6	+15
☐ 8/16	Calvin Hill Cowboys	(Porsche)	15	6	+15
☐ 8/23	Steve McQueen Actor		20	5	+350(d)
☐ 8/30	Ferguson Jenkins (FC) Cubs	(Ferrari)	30	15	+15
☐ 9/06	Jackie Stewart Auto Racing	OJ Simpson	15	4	+25
☐ 9/13	Tommy Casanova LSU	College Football Issue Bear Bryant	15	6	+15
☐ 9/20	John Brodie 49ers	Pro Football Issue	25	10	+20
☐ 9/27	Maury Wills Dodgers	Giants/Dodgers	25	10	+15

	DATE	COVER	FEATURE	Nr-Mt	Ex	+Auto
☐	10/04	Sonny Sixkiller		20	12	
		Washington	(Gale Sayers, Porsche)			+15
☐	10/11	Joe Greene		30	15	
		Steelers	(Willie Mays)			+20
☐	10/18	Frank Robinson	Willie Stargell	40	15	
		Orioles	(Alex Karras, Bob Griese, Bart Starr)			+20
☐	10/25	Gus Johnson*	Pro Basketball Issue	15	6	
		Dave Debuschere				+15/+25
		Bullets/Knicks				
☐	11/01	Ed Marinaro		15	6	
		Cornell				+15
☐	11/08	Norm Bulaich		12	6	
		Colts				+15
☐	11/15	Ski Jumper	Olympics	12	4	
		Olympics Sapporo	(Bob Griese)			
☐	11/22	Football Players		20	10	
		Oklahoma/Nebraska	(Johnny Unitas)			
☐	11/29	Tom Burleson	College Basketball	15	6	
		North Carolina State				+15
☐	12/06	Johnny Musso		15	5	
		Alabama				+15
☐	12/13	Gail Goodrich		15	7	
		Lakers				+15
☐	12/20	Lee Trevino	Sportsman	45	20	
		Golf (SOY)	(Gale Sayers)			+30

1972

	DATE	COVER	FEATURE	Nr-Mt	Ex	+Auto
☐	1/03	Garo Yepremian	Playoffs, Bruins	15	7	
		Dolphins				+20
☐	1/10	Janssen/Terrio	Bowl Games, Bill Walton,	25	10	
		Nebraska Football	UCLA Basketball			+15 each
☐	1/17	Sheila Roscoe	Swimsuit Issue, Cheryl Tiegs, Lakers	50	20	
		Swimsuit				+25
☐	1/24	Duane Thomas	Super Bowl VI: Cowboys Beat Dolphins	35	16	
		Dallas Cowboys	Jack Nicklaus, (Mustang)			+20
☐	1/31	Annie Henning	Nolan Ryan, George McGinnis,	8	4	
		Speedskating	Olympics			+15
☐	2/07	Cowens/Frazier	Jerry West, John Havlicek,	14	7	
		Celtics/Knicks	Fran Tarkenton			+15 each
☐	2/14	Ken Dryden (FC)	Olympics, (Bob Hope)	12	6	
		Canadiens				+15
☐	2/21	Al McGuire	Olympics, (Mustang)	8	4	
		Marquette Basketball				+15
☐	2/28	AJ Foyt	Daytona 500	10	5	
		Autoracing				+15
☐	3/06	Bill Walton (FC)	NCAA Basketball	25	12	
		UCLA Basketball				+15
☐	3/13	Johnny Bench	Pete Rose	35	15	
		Reds				+25
☐	3/20	College Basketball		10	5	
		NCAA Final 4,	(Pinto, Mustang, Porsche)			
☐	3/27	Vida Blue	UCLA Basketball	20	10	
		A's				+15
☐	4/03	Bill Walton		20	10	
		UCLA Basketball				+20
☐	4/10	Joe Torre	Baseball Issue, Brooks Robinson,	20	10	
		Cardinals	Tom Seaver, Carl Yaz, (Jesse Owens)			+15
☐	4/17	Jack Nicklaus	Masters	25	8	
		Golf				+60
☐	4/24	Lew Alcindor*	[*Cover also shows Jim McMillan/Dave	20	10	
		Bucks	Meyers/Flynn Robinson (Bucks/Lakers).]			+60
		Steve Carlton, Juan Marichal,	(Hank Aaron)			
☐	5/01	Willie Davis		12	6	
		Dodgers				+15

☐ 5/08	Phil Esposito/Bobby Orr Bruins		25	12	+20/+35
☐ 5/15	Wilt Chamberlain Lakers	Kentucky Derby, (Porsche)	30	15	+65
☐ 5/22	Willie Mays Mets	Stanley Cup, Orr, Indy 500	35	15	+40
☐ 5/29	Louie Jacobs	Pacers ABA Champs	10	4	+15
☐ 6/05	Mark Donohue Car Racing	Indy 500, Astros, Jim Palmer, (SI/Goudeys)	12	6	+15
☐ 6/12	Dick Allen White Sox	US Open Golf, (Hogan)	18	8	+15
☐ 6/19	Bobby Hull Black Hawks		25	10	+20
☐ 6/26	Jack Nicklaus Golf	US Open Golf, (Boog Powell) Johnny Unitas	25	15	+60
☐ 7/03	Steve Blass Pirates	Roberto Clemente	15	6	
☐ 7/10	Johnny Unitas Colts	Muhammad Ali	30	15	+20
☐ 7/17	Jim Ryun Track		10	10	+15
☐ 7/24	Tommy Prothro Rams	Lee Trevino, (Hank Aaron)	12	6	+10
☐ 7/31	Robyn Smith Jockey	A's, (Porsche)	10	4	+10
☐ 8/07	Larry Csonka Jim Kiick Dolphins		20	9	+20/+10
☐ 8/14	Bobby Fischer Chess	Joe Morgan, (SI)	10	4	+60
☐ 8/21	Sparky Lyle Yankees		15	6	+10
☐ 8/28	Olympics Preview	Cathy Rigby	10	4	
☐ 9/04	Mark Spitz Swimmer	Jack Nicklaus, Olympics, (Porsche)	10	6	+20
☐ 9/11	Bob Devaney Nebraska	College Football Issue, (Joe Namath, SI)	16	8	+100(d)
☐ 9/18	Walt Garrison Cowboys	Pro Football Issue, Mark Harmon, Tom Landry, Olympics, (Bob Griese, SI)	20	10	+20
☐ 9/25	Carlton Fisk Red Sox		30	15	+20
☐ 10/02	Greg Pruitt Oklahoma Football	Orioles, Muhammad Ali	8	4	+10
☐ 10/09	Joe Namath Jets	World Series	20	10	+60
☐ 10/16	Wilt Chamberlain Lakers	World Series, (Brooks Robinson),Pro Basketball Issue,	25	10	+60
☐ 10/23	Jim Hunter A's	World Series, (Bart Starr)	25	10	+20
☐ 10/30	Dave/Don Buckey NC State Football	World Series, (Johnny Carson, Porsche)	10	4	+10 each
☐ 11/06	Larry Brown Redskins		10	5	+20
☐ 11/13	John Havlicek* Celtics	[*Cover also shows Mike Riodar.] Sugar Ray Robinson	25	12	+25
☐ 11/20	Terry Davis Alabama Football		12	6	+20
☐ 11/27	Walter Luckett Ohio State Basketball	College Basketball, Dolphins	12	6	+10
☐ 12/04	Steve Spurrier 49ers	(Jack Nicklaus)	15	7	+15
☐ 12/11	Campy Russell Michigan Basketball	Franco Harris, Dr. J, Oscar Robertson, (Roger Staubach) Pete Maravich,	10	5	+15

DATE	COVER	FEATURE	Nr-Mt	Ex	+Auto
☐ 12/18	Lee Roy Jordan	Colts, (Roger Staubach)	20	10	
	Cowboys				+15
☐ 12/25	John Wooden (SOY)		40	15	
	Billie Jean King (SOY)				+20 each
	UCLA Basketball/Tennis				

1973

DATE	COVER	FEATURE	Nr-Mt	Ex	+Auto
☐ 1/08	Mercury Morris	Playoffs, Dolphins, Bowls, (Opel GT,	15	6	
	Dolphins	Roger Staubach)			+20
☐ 1/15	Doug Collins	Sam Snead, Redskins,George Foreman,	12	6	
	Illinois State	Stan Mikita,(John Wooden)			+15
☐ 1/22	Bob Griese	Super Bowl VII: Dolphins Beat Redskins	45	15	
	Dolphins				+35
☐ 1/29	Dayle Haddon	Swimsuit Issue	45	20	
	Swimsuit Model				+40
☐ 2/05	Bill Walton*	[*Cover also shows Keith Wilkes, Larry	15	7	
	UCLA Basketball	Hollyfield, John Schumate (UCLA/Oregon)]			+20
		George Foreman, (Bob Hope, Jack Nicklaus)			
☐ 2/12	Steve Smith	Notre Dame, (Bobby Orr)	10	4	
	Pole Vault				+10
☐ 2/19	Kareem Abdul-Jabbar	Bobby Knight, Jack Nicklaus	12	6	
	Wilt Chamberlain				+45/+95
	Bucks/Lakers				
☐ 2/26	Gil Perreault	Muhammad Ali, (Mustang, SI)	12	6	
	Sabres				+15
☐ 3/05	Broadway Actors	Lee Trevino	8	4	
☐ 3/12	Bill Melton	Chris Evert, (Willie Mays, VW, Schwinn)	10	6	
	White Sox				+15
☐ 3/19	Olga Korbut	Pirates, NCAA Tournament	40	17	
	Gymnastics				+25
☐ 3/26	Bill Walton*	[*Cover also shows Marvin Barnes-	15	6	
		(Providence), Steve Downs (Indiana),			+20
		Larry Kenon (Memphis State).]			
		Secretariat, (Mustang)			
☐ 4/02	Henry Richard	UCLA NCAA Champs, Masters,	20	10	
	Canadiens	Cowens, (Gale Sayers)			+15
☐ 4/09	Steve Carlton	Baseball Issue, Joe Morgan,(Bobby Hull,	20	10	
	Phillies	J. Garagiola, M.Ali, J. Nicklaus)			+20
☐ 4/16	Earl Monroe*	[*shows Phil Chenier/Walt Frazier.]	12	6	
	Knicks	Masters, (Nicklaus, Palmer, SI Posters)			+20
☐ 4/23	Muhammad Ali		20	9	
	Boxing				+95
☐ 4/30	Chris Speier	49ers, Kentucky Derby	20	9	
	Giants				+15
☐ 5/07	Frazier/West	Bill Russell	20	10	
	Knicks/Lakers	(VW Bug, Corvette, SI Posters)			+20/+20
☐ 5/14	Spitz/Weiner	Kentucky Derby, Nolan Ryan, (Mustang,	15	6	
	Swimmers	Johnny Bench)			+10 each
☐ 5/21	Bobby Riggs	Knicks NBA Champs, Pacers ABA Champs,	10	5	
	Tennis	Stanley Cup, (Toyota, Johnny Miller)			+50(d)
☐ 5/28	Women in Sports	Secretariat, Hank Aaron, (Fergie Jenkins)	6	3	
☐ 6/04	Wilbur Wood	(J.Nicklaus, SI, Porsche, Tom Seaver)	14	7	
	White Sox				
☐ 6/11	Secretariat		35	12	
	Penny Tweedy				
	Horseracing				
☐ 6/18	George Foreman	Secretariat, A's	14	7	
	Boxing				+30
☐ 6/25	Johnny Miller	US Open Golf, Reds, (Arnold Palmer,	20	10	
	Golf	Len Dawson, Mustang, Porsche)			+20
☐ 7/02	Bobby Murcer	Bob Hayes	18	9	
	Ron Blomberg				+15each
	Yankees				

DATE	COVER	FEATURE	Nr-Mt	Ex	+Auto
☐ 7/09	George Allen Redskins	Secretariat, Willie Mays	12	6	+20
☐ 7/16	Billie Jean King Tennis	Wimbledon, Gaylord Perry	20	10	+20
☐ 7/23	Tom Weiskopf Golf	Don Maynard, (Fergie Jenkins) British Open	12	6	+20
☐ 7/30	Carlton Fisk Red Sox	(Pinto)	20	10	+25
☐ 8/06	John Matuszak Houston Football	(SI)	12	6	+15
☐ 8/13	Children Motorcross	Secretariat, B. Williams, L. Durocher	12	4	
☐ 8/20	Claude Osteen Bill Russell Dodgers	Nicklaus, Steelers, Negro Baseball	12	6	+20each
☐ 8/27	Duane Thomas Redskins	(Fergie Jenkins)	12	6	+15
☐ 9/03	Bob Rigby Soccer	Orioles, Bubba Smith	10	5	+15
☐ 9/10	Texas Football	College Football Issue	12	6	
☐ 9/17	Larry Csonka Bob Griese Dolphins	Pro Football Issue	25	10	+30each
☐ 9/24	Danny Murtaugh Pirates		12	6	+100(d)
☐ 10/01	Anthony Davis USC Football	Mets	12	6	+15
☐ 10/08	Fran Tarkenton Vikings	Jerry Lucas	30	15	+30
☐ 10/15	Tiny Archibald Rick Adleman Kings/Trailblazers	Pro Basketball Issue, Tracy Austin [FIC] (Walt Frazier, Joe Namath, Bill Bradley)	12	6	+15each
☐ 10/22	Campaneris/Milner A's/Mets	Hockey Issue, World Series	14	7	+15each
☐ 10/29	OJ Simpson Bills	Reggie Jackson, World Series Bill Russell	18	7	+40
☐ 11/05	Anthony Davis USC	(Johnny Carson, Porsche, Camaro) Secretariat	18	6	+20
☐ 11/12	Pete Maravich* Hawks	*Cover shows Garfield Heard (Suns) & Lou Hudson (Hawks). (SI Posters)	35	10	+250(d)
☐ 11/19	Phil Esposito Bruins	(Camaro, Porsche, Bob Griese)	18	7	+20
☐ 11/26	David Thompson NC State Basketball	College Basketball Issue	20	9	+20
☐ 12/03	Paul Bear Bryant Gary Rutledge Alabama Football	Harlem Globetrotters, OJ Simpson, (Schwinn)	20	10	+200(d)/+15
☐ 12/10	Bill Walton/ Len Elmore UCLA/Maryland Basketball		12	6	+30/+20
☐ 12/17	Marv Hubbard Raiders	Warriors, (Jack Nicklaus, Johnny Bench, Dick Butkus)	15	6	+15
☐ 12/24	Jackie Stewart Auto Racing (SOY)	OJ Simpson, Walt Frazier, George Foreman	25	10	+40

1974

DATE	COVER	FEATURE	Nr-Mt	Ex	+Auto
☐ 1/07	Fran Tarkenton* Vikings	Playoffs, Bowls [*Grady Alderman (Vikings)]	30	15	+25
☐ 1/14	Julius Erving Nets (FC)	Bob Griese, Fran Tarkenton (SI Poster)	50	20	+25
☐ 1/21	Larry Csonka Dolphins	Superbowl VIII Issue, M. Ali (Joe Namath, Sonny/Cher)	40	15	+25
☐ 1/28	Ann Simonton Model	Swimsuit Issue Cheryl Tiegs	50	25	+50

☐ 2/04	Muhammad Ali	Bill Cartwright (FIC)	40	15	
	Joe Frazier	(Corvette, Bob Hope)			+90/+25
	Boxing				
☐ 2/11	Ben Crenshaw		24	12	
	Golf	(Pete Maravich-SI Ad)			+15
☐ 2/18	John Havlicek		30	12	
	Celtics	(Porsche, Bart Starr)			+15
☐ 2/25	Bill Walton/Gerald Lillett		15	8	
	UCLA/Oregon	(Walt Frazier, Reggie Jackson)			+15
☐ 3/04	Jimmy Connors (FC)		20	10	
	Tennis	(Sam Snead)			+15
☐ 3/11	Gordie Howe	Elvin Hayes, Walt Alston	30	12	
	WHA Houston Aeros	(Sean Connery, Jack Nicklaus)			+20
☐ 3/18	Babe Ruth	Babe Ruth	15	7	
	Yankees	(Camaro, Porsche)			
☐ 3/25	Bill Walton	Babe Ruth	25	10	
	UCLA	(Johnny Carson)			+15
		(* Cover includes Tom Burleson/NC state)			
☐ 4/01	Bill Walton*	Babe Ruth	25	10	
	UCLA	(* Cover includes Thompson, Burleson NC State)			
☐ 4/08	Pete Rose	Baseball Issue, Bobby Bonds,	35	15	
	Reds	Jim Palmer, Reggie Jackson, Hank Aaron			+25
		(Hank Aaron)			
☐ 4/15	Henry Aaron #715	Home Run #715, Masters	95	35	
	Braves	(Porsche, Jack Nicklaus)			+30
☐ 4/22	Gary Player	Masters, Hank Aaron	30	12	
	Golf	(Jack Nicklaus)			+15
☐ 4/29	Bruce Hardy	Kentucky Derby	7	3	
	Utah Football	Dick Allen, Bart Conners(FIC)			+15
☐ 5/06	Bobby Clarke (FC)	(Brooks Robinson)	10	4	
	Fliers	(* Cover includes Pete Stenkowski/NY)			+15
☐ 5/13	Cannonade/	Kentucky Derby, Dave Cowens	7	3	
	Angel Cordero	Jack Nicklaus			+15
	Horse	(Arthur Ashe, Hank Aaron-SI ad)			
☐ 5/20	John Havlicek	A's, Celtics NBA Champs	20	9	
	Lew Alcindor	(Porsche) Nets ABA Champs			+15/+40
	Celtics/Bucks				
☐ 5/27	Jim Wynn	Stanley Cup, Steve Garvey	15	6	
	Dodgers				+15
☐ 6/03	John Rutherford	Indy 500	12	6	
	Car racer				+15
☐ 6/10	Johnny Miller	US Open	25	10	
	Golf	(Bill Russell, Porsche, Camaro,			
		Hank Aaron, Mercedes 450 SL)			+15
☐ 6/17	Reggie Jackson		40	15	
	A's	(Car foldout - Goodyear)			+35
☐ 6/24	Hale Irwin	US Open, Reds, Bjon Borg	25	10	
	Golf	(Hank Aaron, SI Poster ad)			+15
☐ 7/01	Rod Carew (FC)	Moses Malone, Arnold Palmer,	35	12	
	Twins	Braves			+20
☐ 7/08	Gerald Ford		50	20	
	Vice President	(Don Schula, Porsche, Camaro)			+40
☐ 7/15	Jimmy Connors	Wimbledon	20	10	
	Chris Evert	(Willie Mays)			+25
	Tennis				
☐ 7/22	Lou Brock	Superdome, Gary Player	24	12	
	Cardinals	(Willie Mays, AJ Foyt)			+25
☐ 7/29	Terry Bradshaw	Indians	40	15	
	Steelers				+40
☐ 8/05	Football Strike	Dodger, Golf Hall of Fame	5	3	
		(Porsche, Bill Russell, SI Poster)			
☐ 8/12	Mike Marshall		15	6	
	Dodgers				+25
☐ 8/19	Lee Trevino	PGA, Reds, OJ	35	15	
	Golf	(Sean Connery, Willie Mays, SI Poster)			+25

DATE	COVER	FEATURE	Nr-Mt	Ex	+Auto
☐ 8/26	John Newcombe Golf	Red Sox	20	9	+15
☐ 9/02	Evel Knievel Stuntman	Browns, A's	35	12	+25
☐ 9/09	Archie Griffin Ohio State	College Football Issue	35	12	+15
☐ 9/16	OJ Simpson Bills	Pro Football Issue (AJ Foyt, Lee Roy Jordan, VW)	30	15	+40
☐ 9/23	Joe Gilliam Steelers	Yankees, 49ers	15	5	+15
☐ 9/30	Tom Clements Notre Dame		20	10	+15
☐ 10/07	Jim Hunter A's	World Series , Wilt Chamberlain (Don Schula, Terry Bradshaw)	35	15	+15
☐ 10/14	Bill Walton K.Abdul-Jabbar Trailblazers/ Lakers	Jim Plunkett, Playoffs Arnold Schwarzenegger	20	10	+15/+40
☐ 10/21	Rollie Fingers* A's / Dodgers	Arnold Schwarzenegger Frank Robinson (Phil Esposito) (* Also includes Steve Garvey, Steve Yeager, Bill Butler)	35	12	+15each
☐ 10/28	Muhammad Ali Boxing	Pro Basketball Issue Secretariat, A's, Sunny Jurgenson (Wilt Chamberlain Poster ad for Spalding)	35	15	+90
☐ 11/04	Joe Washington Oklahoma	Moses Malone (Don Schula)	15	6	+15
☐ 11/11	Muhammad Ali George Foreman Boxing	Muhammad Ali (Corvette, Sports Poster ad, Johnny Carson)	35	15	+90/+40
☐ 11/18	Woody Green Chiefs	Wes Unseld (Porsche)	12	6	+15
☐ 11/25	Ken Dryden Canadiens	(Tyco Trains, Hank Aaron)	12	6	+15
☐ 12/02	Louisville* Basketball Mascots	College Basketball Preview Raiders, C. Murphy (Jack Nicklaus) (*includes Marquette, UCLA, NC State, Indiana, Alabama, Maryland, S.Carolina)	15	7	
☐ 12/09	Anthony Davis USC Football	Kareem Abdul Jabbar	20	9	+15
☐ 12/16	Rick Barry* Warriors	(* Also Keith Erickson(Suns)) (Porsche)	30	12	+15
☐ 12/23	Muhammad Ali Boxing (SOY)	Dick Butkus	50	25	+100

1975

DATE	COVER	FEATURE	Nr-Mt	Ex	+Auto
☐ 1/06	Franco Harris Bubba Smith	Playoffs, Bobby Orr (Superbowl, Don Schula) Steelers/ Raiders	20	10	+15
☐ 1/13	Bill Tilden Tennis	Fran Tarkenton, Bowls Terry Bradshaw	10	4	
☐ 1/20	Terry Bradshaw Steelers	Superbowl IX	30	15	+25
☐ 1/27	Cheryl Tiegs Model	Swimsuit Issue, C. Brinkley, B. Walton (Bear Bryant)	50	25	+25
☐ 2/03	John Laskowski Indiana-Basketball	(Bob Hope, Telly Salvas)	10	5	+15
☐ 2/10	Rogie Vachon Kings	Walt Frazier (SI Poster ad - Dr. J)	10	5	+15
☐ 2/17	Dave Meyers UCLA	Pete Maravich (OJ Simpson, Arthur Ashe)	10	5	+15
☐ 2/24	Sheep dog		10	3	
☐ 3/03	Cincinnati Reds* Reds	Spring Training, Celtics, Tom Seaver	20	10	+15 each

[*also shows Clay Kirby/ Gary Nolan/ Clay Carroll/ Jack Billingham/ Don Gullett]

☐ 3/10	Lee Elder	Dr. J, Arthur Ashe	25	10	
	Golf	Foolish Pleasure (OJ Simpson)			+15
☐ 3/17	Phil Ford/ Mo Rivers		25	15	
	UNC/ NC State Basketball				+15
☐ 3/24	Chuck Wepner	Frank Robinson	20	6	
	Boxing	(Johnny Carson, Terry Salvas)			+100(d)
☐ 3/31	Mike Flynn/Benson	Final Four, Sam Snead	10	4	
	Kentucky	(Jack Nicklaus)			+15
☐ 4/07	Steve Garvey (FC)	Baseball Issue, Carlton Fisk	45	15	
	Dodgers	NCAA Champions			+15
		(Mercury, Corvette, OJ Simpson)			
☐ 4/14	Vasili Alexeyev		10	5	
		Weightlifting (Bear Bryant)			+35
☐ 4/21	Jack Nicklaus	Masters, Giants	35	10	
	Golf	(Terry Salvas)			+60
☐ 4/28	Garfield Heard*		10	5	
	Braves	(* also includes Bob McAdoo, Smith)			+15
☐ 5/05	Jimmy Conners		12	5	
	Tennis	(Jack Nicklaus)			+20
☐ 5/12	Foolish Pleasure*	Kentucky Derby (* Also Jaciata Vasquez)	10	5	
	Horse	(NBA Players -John Havlicek, SI Poster Ad)			
☐ 5/19	A.J. Foyt	Indy 500, A's	10	6	
	Auto Racing				+15
☐ 5/26	Filbert Bayi	Cubs	10	5	
	Track				+15
☐ 6/02	Billy Martin	Indy 500, Warriors-Champs	15	7	
	Rangers	Stanley Cup			+100(d)
☐ 6/09	Rocky Bleier	Reds, Pete Rose	20	10	
	Steelers	Steve Prefontaine (Budweiser)			+15
☐ 6/16	Nolan Ryan		85	32	
	Angels	(Bill Russell)			+25
☐ 6/23	Pele		25	8	
	Soccer	(OJ Simpson)			+40
☐ 6/30	Lou Graham	US Open	20	10	
	Golf				+15
☐ 7/07	Fred Lynn (FC)	Carlton Fisk, Thurmon Munson	30	15	
	Red Sox	Orioles			+15
☐ 7/14	Arthur Ashe	Wimbledon, Richard Petty	30	15	
	Tennis	(Willie Mays, Bear Bryant)			+100(d)
☐ 7/21	Jim Palmer	Arthur Ashe	40	10	
	Tom Seaver				+20/+25
	Orioles/Mets				
☐ 7/28	Paul Warfield/Larry Csonka/Jim Kiick		40	15	
	Memphis Grizzlies				+15each
☐ 8/04	Tim Shaw		10	3	
	Swimming				+15
☐ 8/11	Baseball Boom	Fans	5	3	
☐ 8/18	Jack Nicklaus	Bruce Jenner, PGA	25	12	
	Golf	(SI Poster ad, Johnny Miller)			+60
☐ 8/25	Bart Starr		25	12	
	Packers				+20
☐ 9/01	Brian Oldfield	Alex Grammas, Jim Brown	10	3	
	Track				+15
☐ 9/08	Terry Davis	College Football Issue,	15	6	
	Barry Switzer	Nolan Ryan, A's, Archie Griffin			
	Joe Washington				
	Oklahoma				+15 each
☐ 9/15	Muhammad Ali/Don King/Joe Frazier		20	10	-
	Boxing	Dave Kingman, Tony Dorsett			+80/+20/+25
☐ 9/22	Joe Greene	Pro Football Issue,Joe Namath	30	15	
	Steelers	(Baseball Card Ad- Duke Snider)			+15

	DATE	COVER	FEATURE	Nr-Mt	Ex	+Auto
☐	9/29	Rick Slager/Dan Devine Notre Dame	Joe Namath, Muhammad Ali, Pete Rose, Reds Stadium	20	10	+15/+15
☐	10/06	Reggie Jackson A's Babe Dickerson	Red Sox, A's, Pirates, World Series (Jack Nicklaus, Terry Bradshaw)	35	15	+25
☐	10/13	Muhammad Ali Joe Frazier Boxing	Manilia fight, OJ, Babe Dickerson	35	12	+80/+25
☐	10/20	Luis Tiant Johnny Bench Red Sox/Reds	Pro Hockey Preview, Bobby Orr Babe Dickerson, World Series	35	15	+15/+25
☐	10/27	George McGinnis 76ers	Pro Basketball Issue, World Series	12	6	+15
☐	11/03	Will McEnaney Reds	World Series	15	7	
☐	11/10	Fran Tarkenton* Vikings	Pete Maravich (Tom Selleck, Willie Mays) [*Cover also shows Ed Marinaro (Vikings)]	35	12	+35
☐	11/17	Hockey Players	Violence, Terry Bradshaw	12	5	+15
☐	11/24	Chuck Muncie Cal Bears	Tony Dorsett (Yul Bryner ad)	12	7	+15
☐	12/01	Kent Benson Indiana	College Basketball	12	6	+15
☐	12/08	Bubba Bean Texas A & M	Indiana, Robert Parrish	10	5	+15
☐	12/15	George Foreman/Muhammad Ali Boxing		25	12	+25/+80
☐	12/22	Pete Rose Reds (SOY)		60	25	+25

1976

	DATE	COVER	FEATURE	Nr-Mt	Ex	+Auto
☐	1/05	Preston Pearson Cowboys	[*Cover also shows Wally Hilgenberg (Vikings)]	30	15	+15
☐	1/12	Franco Harris* Steelers	Cowboys, Cav's, Bowls (Dick Butkus) [*Cover also shows Gerry Mullens/Otis Sistrunk]	20	15	+20
☐	1/19	Sylvander Twins Models	Swimsuit Issue, Dorthy Hamill Christy Brinkley, Cheryl Tiegs (* Model names are Yvette & Yuonne)	45	20	+25each
☐	1/26	Lynn Swann Steelers	Superbowl X (Giants/Yankees)	35	15	+15
☐	2/02	Sheila Young Speedskating	Olympic Issue, Bulls (Johnny Miller)	8	4	+15
☐	2/09	Ernie Grunfield* Tennessee	Olympics (Teamster, Datsun 280z) (* Cover includes Bernard King)	30	12	+10/+15
☐	2/16	Franz Klammer Skier	UCLA, Warriors (Tom Seaver, Bud History)	12	5	+25
☐	2/23	Bobby Clarke Flyers	UNLV, Dorthy Hamell, Sonics	10	5	+15
☐	3/01	Muhammad Ali Boxing	(SI Poster ad- Pete Maravich) (* Cover includes Jean Piere Coopman)	25	12	+80/+20
☐	3/08	Bob McAdoo Buffalo		10	5	+15
☐	3/15	Bill Veeck Owner	Dr J, ABA Championship	10	5	+100(d)
☐	3/22	Tracy Austin Tennis		10	6	+15
☐	3/29	Kent Benson Indiana	Nuggets, Spring Training		10	+15
☐	4/05	Scott May Indiana	NCAA Final (Johnny Carson, Merc. 450sl)	15	5	+15
☐	4/12	Joe Morgan Reds	Baseball Issue,Jerry Rice, Fred Lynn, J.Jensen, (Tom Seaver, Bob Griese) (SI poster ad, Jim Hunter, Nolan Ryan)	45	20	+20

☐	4/19	Raymond Floyd Golf	Masters,Giants (Johnny Miller)	25	12 +20
☐	4/26	Evonne Goolagong Tennis	Yankees Stadium, Tom Landry, Dr J.	10	4 +25
☐	5/03	Mike Schmidt Phillies		35	17 +35
☐	5/10	Angel Cordero Bold Jockey	Kentucky Derby, Muhammad Ali, Arnold Palmer, Jim Palmer (Gale Sayers, Bob Griese)	10	4 +15
☐	5/17	Julius Erving* Nets	[* Cover includes Chuck Williams] (SI ad)	60	25 +35
☐	5/24	Larry Robinson Montreal	Stanley Cup, Suns,Rick Barry (Carlton Fisk)	10	5 +15
☐	5/31	Carlton Fisk Lou Pinella Red Sox/Yankees	Larry Holmes (Arnold Palmer)	30	12 +25
☐	6/07	Alvan Adams Dave Cowens Suns/Celtics	Indy 500, Giants,John Montefusco	20	10 +15/+15
☐	6/14	Dwight Stones High Jump Track	Bobby Jones, Boston Celtics Phillies,Dave Cash	12	4 +15
☐	6/21	George Brett Royals	Bobby Orr Joe Namath	45	15 +35
☐	6/28	Bowie Kuhn Baseball		15	4 +100(d)
☐	7/05	Frank Shorter Track	Mark Spitz	10	4 +15
☐	7/12	Randy Jones Padres	Jack Lambert	10	5 +15
☐	7/19	Frank Shorter Track	Olympic Issue, Braves (Datsun 280z, Heineken) (* Cover includes Shirley Babashoff, Scott May)	10	4 +15
☐	7/26	Torch Carriers Olympics	OJ Simpson, Jim Palmer	10	4
☐	8/02	Nadia Comaneci Gymnastics	Olympic, Oklahoma (SI Poster ad)	40	20 +20
☐	8/09	Bruce Jenner Track	Olympics	20	10 +15
☐	8/16	Calvin Hill Redskins	(Heineken)	10	5 +15
☐	8/23	Steve Spurrier Tampa Bay	Stan Musial, Bernard King (Bill Cosby, Johnny Miller)	20	5 +15
☐	8/30	Reggie Jackson Orioles	Tennis US Open, Chris Evert	35	15 +30
☐	9/06	Rick Leach Michigan	College Football Issue Reds,Tony Dorsett,Earl Campbell	10	4 +15
☐	9/13	Bert Jones Colts	Pro Football Issue, Thurmon Munson	15	6 +15
☐	9/20	Jimmy Connors Tennis	A's, Tony Dorsett (Bill Cosby, Ben Hogan, SI Poster)	15	4 +15
☐	9/27	Ken Norton Boxing	OJ Simpson, Muhammad Ali	12	4 +15
☐	10/04	Mark Manges Maryland	Raiders (Ben Hogan)	12	4 +15
☐	10/11	George Foster Reds	Reds, M. Ali,World Series (Lou Brock/Steve Garvey, MG)	35	15 +15
☐	10/18	Chuck Foreman Vikings	Playoffs, Reds, Bobby Orr (Gail Goodrich) Hockey Issues	12	5 +15
☐	10/25	Dave Cowens/Dr J Boston	Pro Basketball Issue World Series	35	10 +15/+25
☐	11/01	Johnny Bench Reds	World Series, Dr J, 49ers Steve Cauthen(FIC) (SI Poster ad, Jack Nicklaus)	35	15 +25

DATE	COVER	FEATURE	Nr-Mt	Ex	+Auto
☐ 11/08	Tony Dorsett	*Pete Maravich*	20	10	
	Pittsburgh	*John McEnroe(FIC)*			+20
☐ 11/15	David Thompson	*Michigan, Dr J, Artis Gilmore*	20	8	
	Nuggets				+20
☐ 11/22	Walter Payton	*Dave Cowens*	45	20	
	Bears	*(Porsche, Dave Cowens)*			+30
☐ 11/29	Rickey Green	*College Basketball Issue*	10	5	
	Michigan	*USC,Cav's (Dave Cowens, Schwinn)*			+15
☐ 12/06	Rocky Bleier	*Bruins*	20	7	
	Sam Davis	*(Dave Cowens)*			+20
	Steelers				
☐ 12/13	Bill Walton	*Raiders, Reggie Jackson*	10	5	
	Trail Blaziers	*Oklahoma*			+15
☐ 12/20	Chris Evert	*Muhammad Ali, Tony Dorsett*	35	15	
	Tennis (SOY)	*(Squirt)*			+15
	Year In Sports	*Muhammad Ali, Reggie Jackson*	10	6	

1977

DATE	COVER	FEATURE	Nr-Mt	Ex	+Auto
☐ 1/03	Clarence Davis/Mel Blout/Glen Edwards		15	6	
	Raiders/ Steelers	*(TR7)*			+15
☐ 1/10	Tony Dorsett	*Playoff, Bowls*	35	15	
	Pittsburgh				+25
☐ 1/17	Ken Stabler	*Superbowl XI, Moses Malone*	35	15	
	Raiders				+15
☐ 1/24	Lena Kansbod	*Swimsuit Issue, Bobby Orr*	35	12	
	Model	*Dave Cowen, Cheryl Tiegs*			+35
☐ 1/31	Bill Cartwright		10	6	
	USF				+10
☐ 2/07	Guy Lafleur	*Bernard King (Camaro,*	15	7	
	Montreal	*Walt Frazier, Gale Sayers, Tom Selleck)*			+15
☐ 2/14	Kareem Abdul-Jabbar		12	5	
	Lakers				+40
☐ 2/21	NBC TV Deal	*UNLV*	10	4	
	Olympics	*(Tom Selleck, Mustang, SI Poster)*			
☐ 2/28	Carl Yarborough	*Daytona 500*	35	12	
	Car Racer-Nascar	*(Joe Morgan, SI Ad, Pinto)*			+25
☐ 3/07	Steve Cauthen		12	5	
	Jockey				+15
☐ 3/14	Tom Lasorda	*(Mariners-Tickets)*	45	15	
	Dodgers	*(SI poster- Pete Maravich, Camaro)*			+25
☐ 3/21	George McGinnis/ Dr J,	*Atlanta Stadium*	12	5	
	Paul Silas	*(Tom Selleck,Dr J-Converse,Bob Griese)*			+15/+15
	76'ers/Nuggets				
☐ 3/28	Bump Wills		12	5	
	Rangers	*(McDonalds Basketball - Magic Johnson)*			+15
☐ 4/04	Butch Lee	*Seattle Slew, NCAA 4*	10	4	
	Walt Davis	*(Dr J-Converse)*			+15
	Marquette/NC				
☐ 4/11	Joe Rudi	*Baseball Issue, Rollie Fingers*	10	6	
	Angels	*(Lou Brock-Converse, Jack Nicklaus)*			+15
☐ 4/18	Tom Watson	*Masters(Kareem Abdul-Jabbar,*	25	10	
	Golf	*BMW, Ford, Tom Seaver)*			+15
☐ 4/25	Sidney Wicks*	*Joe Namath*	15	6	
	Celtics	*(SI Poster-Dr J., Pete Rose, Roger*			+15
		Staubach,[also C.Scott/Billy Paultz]*			
☐ 5/02	Reggie Jackson	*Thurmon Munson, Willie McCovey*	35	12	
	Yankees	*(Arthur Ashe, Horseracing,*			+25
		Roger Staubach Tom Selleck, Ford)			
☐ 5/09	Brad Park*	*(Johnny Bench RC Can ad)*	20	6	
	Bruins	*(SI poster ad- Dr J, Ben Hogan)*			+15
		(Also Garry Cheevers)*			
☐ 5/16	Seattle Slew	*Kentucky Derby*	15	5	

	J Cruguet	(Arthur Ashe)		+15
	Horse			
☐ 5/23	Bill Walton*	[*also shows Lanny, K. Abdul-Jabbar,	12	8
		Steelers (Blazers). Magic Johnson[FIC]		
	Trailblazers/Lakers	Stanley Cup, (McDonalds-/Magic Johnson)		
☐ 5/30	Dave Parker	Roger Staubach, Budweiser Ad)	20	8
	Pirates	Pirates, Busch Stadium,		+15
☐ 6/06	Mark Fidrych	AJ Foyt, Dr J	35	12
	Tigers	(SI poster - Dr J, The Deep poster)		+15
☐ 6/13	Bill Walton*	[* Cover includes Joe Bryant/76ers]	55	20
	Trailblazers	(SI poster-C.Evert, Dave Cowens-YMCA)		+15
☐ 6/20	Seattle Slew*	Triple Crown, Roger Maris	20	5
	Horse	(* Also Jean Cruguet)		+15
☐ 6/27	Tom Seaver		25	12
	Reds			+25
☐ 7/04	Ted Turner	American Cup, Indians	25	10
	Yachting			+15
☐ 7/11	Bjorn Borg (FC)	Wimbledon, Dave Winfield	15	5
	Tennis			+15
☐ 7/18	Rod Carew/Ted Williams		35	12
	Twins	(Joe Namath, Danny White)		+20/+180
☐ 7/25	Conrad Dobler	Cubs	10	4
	Cardinals			+15
☐ 8/01	Colorado Rapids		6	3
☐ 8/08	Carlos Monzom*	Orioles	10	5
	Boxing	(* Cover includes Rodrigo Valdes)		+50(d)
☐ 8/15	Sadaharu Oh	Joe Namath	40	16
	Tokoyo Giants			+45
☐ 8/22	Lanny Wadkins	PGA, Reds, Lou Brock	20	10
	Golf	Pete Rose, Ty Cobb		+15
☐ 8/29	Greg Luzinski	Archie Manning, Mike Schmidt	10	5
	Phillies	(Tom Selleck,US Open)Jackie Joyner(FIC)		+15
☐ 9/05	Ross Browner	College Football Issue	10	5
	Notre Dame	Pele (Mickey Mantle -AMC)		+15
☐ 9/12	Alberto Juantoren	Meadows Stadium	10	4
	Track	(* Cover include Boit)		+25/+15
☐ 9/19	Kenny Stabler	Pro Football Issue	35	15
	Raiders	Tony Dorsett		+15
☐ 9/26	Robert Duran	Cowboys, Yankees (Tom Selleck)	20	10
	Edwin Viruet	(Lite Beer Fold Out 15 Jocks)		+25/+10
	Boxing			
☐ 10/03	Billy Sims	Raiders	10	5
	Oklahoma	(Jack Nicklaus, Arnold Palmer)		+15
☐ 10/10	Muhammad Ali	Pele, Yankee Stadium	20	12
	Ernie Shavers	(World Series, Jack Nicklaus)		+80/+15
	Boxing			
☐ 10/17	Rubin Carter	Pro Hockey Preview	10	4
	Denver	Dodgers, Raiders		+15
☐ 10/24	Thurmon Munson	World Series	50	15
	Bill Russell	(Rowan/Martin-Laugh in)		+300(d)/+10
	Yankees/Dodgers			
☐ 10/31	Maurice Lucas	Pro Basketball Issue Reggie Jackson,	15	7
	Blaziers	Joe Montana, Bill Bradley		+15
☐ 11/07	Burt Reynolds*	Oakland, Indians	20	7
	Movie Star	(Danny White, Camaro)		+25/+20/+10
		(* Also Kris Kristofferson, Jill Clayburn)		
☐ 11/14	Belmont Swindle		10	4
	Crime	(Chuck Munice, BMW, Joe Namath)		
☐ 11/21	Dave Casper*		25	10
	Raiders	(Tom Selleck)		+10each
		(* Also Pruitt, Cunningham, Lambert, Jones)		
☐ 11/28	Larry Bird (FC)	First Issue	100	40
	Indiana State	College Basketball Issue		+60
☐ 12/05	Earl Campbell	Pete Maravich	35	15
	Texas			+15

DATE	COVER	FEATURE	Nr-Mt	Ex	+Auto
☐ 12/12	Bryan Trottier	*Lyle Alzado*	15	5	
	Islanders	*(Chuck Munice)*			+15
☐ 12/19	Steve Cauthen	*Sportsman*	40	15	
	Horseracing	*(Danny White, Champion plug)*			+15
	Year In Sports	*Joe Montana, Munson, Dr J*	20	10	
		(Mickey Mantle -AMF, Roger Staubach, SI Poster)			

1978

DATE	COVER	FEATURE	Nr-Mt	Ex	+Auto
☐ 1/02	Mark Van Eeghan	*NFL Playoffs*	35	15	
	Raiders				+15
☐ 1/09	Terry Eurick	*Bowls, Playoffs*	25	10	
	Notre Dame	*(Superbowl)*			+15
☐ 1/16	Maria Joao	*Swimsuit Issue*	40	20	
	Model				+35
☐ 1/23	Randy White	*Dallas Superbowl*	40	20	
	Harvey Martin	*(Magic Johnson)*			+15/+15
	Cowboys				
☐ 1/30	Robert Duran*		25	12	
	Boxing	*(Corvette, Ken Stabler)*			+20/+15
		(* Cover includes Esteban DeJesus)			
☐ 2/06	Dick Buerkle/Filbert Bayi		15	5	
	Miler	*Carl Lewis(FIC),(Reggie Jackson)*			+15
☐ 2/13	Sidney Moncrief		20	7	
	Arkansas Basketball				+15
☐ 2/20	Walter Davis		15	7	
	Suns				+15
☐ 2/27	Leon Spinks		12	5	
	Boxing				+15
☐ 3/06	Houston McTear	*Spring Training(Ferrari,*	12	5	
	Track	*Dr. J, Jack Nicklaus, Walt Frazier)*			+15
☐ 3/13	Gene Banks	*White Sox, Leon Spinks*	12	5	
	Duke Basketball	*(Dr. J)*			+15
☐ 3/20	Clint Hurdle	*UCLA*	12	5	
	Royals				+15
☐ 3/27	Jack Nicklaus	*TPC, NCAA final four*	35	15	
	Golf				+60
☐ 4/03	Goose Givens	*NCAA Finals,*	10	5	
	Duke-Gene Banks	*(Red Holtman)*			+15
	Kentucky Basketball				
☐ 4/10	George Foster	*Baseball Issue*	16	8	
	Rod Carew	*John Havlicek*			+15/+20
	Reds/Twins	*(Reggie Jackson, Lou Brock)*			
☐ 4/17	Gary Player	*Bill Walton, Masters*	25	10	
	Golf	*(Meadowlark Lemon, John Bench)*			+15
☐ 4/24	Mark Fidrych	*Bucks*	20	10	
	Tigers	*(Dr. J)*			+15
☐ 5/01	Gary Player	*Red Sox, Bill Walton*	20	10	
	Golf				+15
☐ 5/08	Elvin Hayes/Mike Green		20	10	
	Bullets				+15/+10
☐ 5/15	Steve Cauthen	*Kentucky Derby,76ers*	15	7	
	Affirmed	*Pete Rose, (Terry Bradshaw)*			+15
	Jockey				
☐ 5/22	Marvin Webster/Jack Silema		10	5	
	Sonics				+15/+10
☐ 5/29	Leroy Robinson/Ken Dryden		10	5	
	Canadiens	*(Jim Palmer, Corvette)*			+10/+10
☐ 6/05	Al Unser	*Indy 500, Sonics, Stanley Cup*	20	10	
	Auto Racing	*Ted Simmons*			+15
☐ 6/12	Kenny Norton	*Sonics*	20	10	
	Boxing				+15
☐ 6/19	Affirmed/Alydar	*Belmont,Rod Carew*	10	4	
	Horse				+15
☐ 6/26	Andy North	*US Open Golf*	20	8	
	Golf				+15

	DATE	COVER	FEATURE	Nr-Mt	Ex	+Auto
☐	7/03	Daniel Passarella Argentina Soccer	World Cup	10	4	+40
☐	7/10	Nancy Lopez Golf		20	7	+15
☐	7/17	Money & Sports	Wimbeldon, Celtics	10	3	
☐	7/24	Jack Nicklaus Golf	British Open, Orioles Larry Bowa	20	10	+60
☐	7/31	Billy Martin Yankees	Reggie Jackson	20	8	+100(d)
☐	8/07	Pete Rose Reds	Giants/Dodgers (Tom Selleck)	40	15	+20
☐	8/14	Brutality/Football	Giants/Dodgers	10	4	
☐	8/21	Bill Walton Trail Blazers	Tigers	25	10	+15
☐	8/28	Maxie Anderson, Ben Abruzzo Ballooning	Larry Newman - US Open,	10	5	+10each
☐	9/04	Roger Staubach Cowboys	Pro football Issue (Jim Palmer)	50	20	+25
☐	9/11	Lou Holtz* Arkansas	College Football Issue, M. Ali (Lite Miller Jock Foldout) (* Cover includes Calcagni, D. Cowins)	20	5	+15 each
☐	9/18	Jimmy Conners Tennis	US Open, Red Sox White Sox-Harry Carey	15	5	+25
☐	9/25	Muhammad Ali* Boxing	(* Cover includes Michael Spinks)	30	10	+80/+15
☐	10/02	Charles White USC	Dodger -Reggie Smith (Corvette, Camaro-fold out)	20	8	+15
☐	10/09	Terry Bradshaw Steelers	Yankee/Red Sox (World Series)	30	15	+25
☐	10/16	Marvin Webster Knicks	Pro Basketball Issue Elvin Hayes (Camero, World Series, Willis Reed)	10	5	+15
☐	10/23	Lee Lacy Brian Doyle Dodgers/ Yankees	World Series, Hockey Issue (Ben Crenshaw, Terry Bradshaw)	15	6	+15
☐	10/30	Bill Rogers Runner	NY Marathon,World Series (Sylvester Stalone Movie, Dr.J)	10	4	+15
☐	11/06	Race Fixer	Pete Rose, Larry Holmes, Dr. J, (Tom Selleck)	5	4	
☐	11/13	Chuck Fusina Penn State	Sonics, Cowboys (Tom Selleck, Roger Staubach, SI Poster)	15	8	+15
☐	11/20	Rick Berns* Nebraska	Nebraska, Rams, Charlie White (Tom Selleck, Willis Reed) (* Cover includes Oklahoma #85)	15	5	+15
☐	11/27	Magic Johnson (FC) Michigan State	College Basketball Issue Celtics, Magic foldout, Tom Selleck)	100	25	+75
☐	12/04	Earl Campbell* Houston	[*Cover includes Ross Browner (Bengels)]	35	12	+15
☐	12/11	Jeff Love Mountain Climber		10	3	+15
☐	12/18	John McEnroe Tennis	Davis Cup, Indiana Terry Bradshaw, Jimmy Carter	8	5	+15
☐	12/25	Jack Nicklaus Golf (SOY) Year In Sports 1978	Sportsman Terry Bradshaw, Muhammad Ali (Willis Reed)	50 20	25 10	+60

1979

	DATE	COVER	FEATURE	Nr-Mt	Ex	+Auto
☐	1/08	Alabama/Penn St	Bowls Games, Pro Playoffs	25	12	
☐	1/15	Terry Bradshaw Steelers	Tony Dorsett (SI Poster ad)	35	12	+25
☐	1/22	Herb Willie Ohio State		10	4	+15

	Date	Cover	Description			
☐	1/29	Rocky Bleier Steelers Sam Bowie (FIC)	Superbowl, Ron Guidrey Roger Staubach	35	15	+20
☐	2/05	Christie Brinkley Model	Swimsuit Issue, Larry Bird (SI Poster Ad)	60	25	+50
☐	2/12	Danny Lopez Boxing		12	4	+15
☐	2/19	Moses Malone (FC)* Rockets	[*Cover also shows Mike Dunleavey/Rick Barry/Rudy Tomjanovich (Rockets) and Leon Douglas/ML Carr (Pistons)]	25	10	+30
☐	2/26	Eamonn Coghlan Runner	Eric Heiden	10	3	+15
☐	3/05	#42 -art Reds	Baseball Spring Training	20	10	
☐	3/12	Dudley Bradley North Carolina	Rod Carew, Arnold Palmer	35	15	+15
☐	3/19	Harry Chappas White Sox	(Roger Staubach)	10	5	+15
☐	3/26	Larry Bird Indiana State		50	20	+60
☐	4/02	Magic Johnson Michigan State	NCAA Basketball/	40	20	+70
☐	4/09	Jim Rice Red Sox	Pro Baseball Issue, Trailblazers,Q.Dailey(FACES) [(* Cover includes Dave Parker/Pirates)]	25	10	+15each
☐	4/16	Denis Potvin Islanders		10	4	+15
☐	4/23	Fuzzy Zoeller Golf	Masters, Ken Stabler, K.Jabbar (Roger Staubach, Tom Watson)	25	10	+15
☐	4/30	George Bamberger Brewers	Magic Johnson (SI Poster ad)	15	5	+15
☐	5/07	Elvin Hayes* Bullets	Bryon Nelson (* Cover includes Ray Dandridge)	10	5	+15
☐	5/14	Spectacular Bid* Horse	Kentucky Derby (SI Poster) (* Also Ronnie Franklin)	8	5	+15
☐	5/21	Giorgio Chinaglia Cosmos	Sonics, A's Tony Cousineau, Lou Brock	10	5	+40
☐	5/28	Pete Rose Phillies	George Gervin,	25	10	+25
☐	6/04	Tom Watson Golf		30	12	+15
☐	6/11	Gus Williams* Sonics	[*Cover also shows Wes Unseld/Bob Dandridge (Bullets)]. Sonics NBA Champs.	12	5	+15
☐	6/18	Earl Weaver Orioles	Edwin Moses	35	15	+20
☐	6/25	Hale Irwin Golf	US Open	30	15	+15
☐	7/02	Robert Duran/Palomino Boxing	Mike Marshall, Billy Martin	25	10	+25/+15
☐	7/09	Eamonn Coghlan Track	Dave Winfield,Jack Nicklaus (SI Poster Ad)	6	4	+20
☐	7/16	Bjorn Borg Tennis	Alan Page Don Mattingly(FACES)	20	10	+20
☐	7/23	Nolan Ryan Angels	Pan Am Games	60	25	+25
☐	7/30	Sebastian Coe Track	Boston Red Sox. Larry Csonka	15	3	+15
☐	8/06	Kenny Stabler Raiders		35	15	+15
☐	8/13	25th Anniversary	Year of Photos, Orioles,Russell/Cousy (Wilt Chamberlain/Rick Barry) PGA	12	6	

DATE	COVER	FEATURE	Nr-Mt	Ex	+Auto
☐ 8/20	John Jefferson	Dave Kingman, Willie Stargell	20	10	
	Chargers	(US Open)			+15
☐ 8/27	Baseball's	[*Cover shows Rose,Yastrzemski,Stargell,	15	7	
	Oldies*	P. Nieckro,G.Perry, M.Mota.L. Brock]			+varies each
☐ 9/03	Earl Campbell	Pro Football Issue, Reds	30	15	
	Oilers	(Steelers, Joe Greene, T. Bradshaw)			+15
	Hershel Walker (FIC)				
☐ 9/10	Charle White	Col Football Issue	15	7	
	Billy Simms	(Muhammad Ali)			+15
	USC/Oklahoma				
☐ 9/17	Tracy Austin	US Open Tennis	10	5	
	Tennis				+15
☐ 9/24	Vagas Ferguson		10	5	
	Notre Dame				+15
☐ 10/01	Dewey Selmon	Pete Rose	10	5	
	Buc's	(SI Poster Ad)			+15
☐ 10/08	Larry Holmes	Pro Hockey Issue, Reggie Jackson	20	8	
	Ernie Shavers	(World Series insert)			+15 each
	Boxing				
☐ 10/15	Bill Walton	Pro Basketball Issue	10	7	
	Clippers	Larry Bird, Magic Johnson			+15
☐ 10/22	Doug Decinces	World Series	15	7	
	Phil Garner				+15
	Orioles/Pirates				
☐ 10/29	Bill Rogers	World Series	10	4	
	Runner				+15
☐ 11/05	Franco Harris		20	8	
	Steelers				+15
☐ 11/12	Jarvis Redwine	College Football Issue	12	6	
	Nebraska	Greg Lemond (FACES), Mark Spitz			+15
		(Cover includes Jimmy Jordan- Florida St., Steadman Shealy, Alabama, Art Schlichter -Ohio S., Delrick Browner- Houston)			
☐ 11/19	Magic Johnson/George McGinnis		25	15	5
	Lakers/Denver	Nolan Ryan, Curtis Dickey			+70/+10
☐ 11/26	Art Schlichter	Sugar Ray Robinson	10	3	
	Ohio State	OJ Simpson (Earl Campbell)			+15
☐ 12/03	Indiana Jersey	College Basketball Issue,Larry Bird	7	5	
	Indiana	(Bruce Jenner-Boy Scout)			+15 (Knight)
☐ 12/10	Sugar Ray Leonard	Lynn Swann	20	8	
	Boxing (FC)	(Paul Newman)			+15
☐ 12/17	Ralph Sampson		15	5	
	Virgina				+15
☐ 12/24	Willie Stargell/Terry Bradshaw Sportsman		40	15	
	Pirates/Steelers(SOY)	Bowl Preview			+15/+25
	Year In Sports		15	7	

1980

DATE	COVER	FEATURE	Nr-Mt	Ex	+Auto
☐ 1/07	Ricky Bell	Bowl	10	5	
	Bucs				+15
☐ 1/14	L.C. Greenwood/Don Pasorini		10	5	
	Steelers/Oilers				+15
☐ 1/21	Gordie Howe		20	8	
	Whalers				+15
☐ 1/28	John Stallworth	Superbowl XIV	30	15	
	Steelers				+15
		(* Cover includes Rams player)			
☐ 2/04	Christie Brinkley Swimsuit		50	25	
	Model				+40
☐ 2/11	Eric Heiden		15	6	
	Ice Skater				+20
☐ 2/18	Mary Decker	Olympic	10	4	
	Speed Skating				+15

	Date	Cover	Notes			
☐	2/25	Eric Heiden	Winter Olympics	10	5	
		Speed Skating				+15
☐	3/03	USA Hockey Team		50	25	
		Olympic Hockey				+10 each
☐	3/10	Jim Craig		15	5	
		Flame				+15
☐	3/17	Albert King*	NCAA Tournament	10	4	
		Maryland	[*Cover includes Steve Johnson (Tennessee)]			+15
☐	3/24	Kirk Gibson		15	7	
		Tigers				+15
☐	3/31	Darrell Griffith	NCAA Finals	10	4	
		Lousiville Basketball	Kareem Abdul Jabbar			+15
☐	4/07	Keith Hernandez	Baseball Issue	10	6	
		Cardinals				+15
☐	4/14	Muhammand Ali		28	10	
		Boxing				+15
☐	4/21	Steve Ballesteros Masters		10	5	
		Golf				+15
☐	4/28	Larry Bird/Dr J*	[*Cover includes Darryl Hawkins]	35	15	
		Celtics/76ers				+50
☐	5/05	Kareem Abdul-Jabbar*		10	7	
		Lakers	(* Also Sonics Dennis Johnson, other)			+35
☐	5/12	Geniune Risk	Kentucky Derby	5	3	
		Horse				
☐	5/19	Athlete Hoax	Dr. J	6	3	
☐	5/26	Magic Johnson	Lakers NBA Champs	30	15	
		Lakers				+60
☐	6/02	John Rutherford	Indy 500, Stanley Cup - Islanders	10	4	
		Car Racing				+15
☐	6/09	Darrell Porter		15	5	
		Royals				+15
☐	6/16	Roberto Duran		20	10	
		Boxing				+25
☐	6/23	Jack Nicklaus	US Open, Reggie Jackson	20	10	
		Golf				+50
☐	6/30	Roberto Duran/		20	10	
		Sugar Ray Leonard				+25 each
		Boxing				
☐	7/07	Steve Scott		10	4	
		Track				+15
☐	7/14	Bjorn Borg	Wimbledon	10	4	
		Tennis				+15
☐	7/21	Steve Carlton		30	15	
		Phillies				+15
☐	7/28	Olympics - Moscow		5	3	
☐	8/04	Reggie Jackson		22	10	
		Yankees				+25
☐	8/11	Sebastian Coe		10	3	
		Track				+15
☐	8/18	J.R. Richard	Roger Staubach	30	12	
		Astros				+20
☐	8/25	Yankees/Orioles*	[*Cover shows Bucky Dent/	25	10	
			Fred Stanley(Yankees) &			+25
			Al Bumbry (Orioles)]			

	DATE	COVER	FEATURE	Nr-Mt	Ex	+Auto
☐	9/01	Hugh Green Pittsburgh Football	College Football Issue George Brett	7	3	+15
☐	9/08	Dave Logan Browns	Pro Football Issue	8	6	
☐	9/15	John McEnroe Tennis	US Open	7	5	+15
☐	9/22	Billy Sims Lions		7	5	+15
☐	9/29	Muhammad Ali Boxing		15	7	+80
☐	10/06	Gary Carter (FC) Expos		20	10	+15
☐	10/13	Muhammad Ali Boxing	Pro Hockey Issue	20	10	+80
☐	10/20	Paul Westphal Sonics	Pro Basketball Issue Bill Walton	15	6	+15
☐	10/27	Mike Schmidt (FC) Darrell Porter Phillies/Royals	World Series	15	7	+25/+10
☐	11/03	Alberto Salazar Track		10	5	+15
☐	11/10	L.C. Greenwood Steelers		7	5	+15
☐	11/17	Herschel Walker (FC) Georgia		20	10	+15
☐	11/24	Sugar Ray Leonard Boxing		20	10	+15
☐	12/01	Ralph Sampson Virignia	College Basketball Issue	7	3	+15each
			(* Cover includes Bernard King-Maryland, Mark Aquirre-DePaul)			
☐	12/08	Vince Ferragamo Rams	James Worthy	10	5	+15
☐	12/15	Loyld Free* Warriors	[*Cover shows Kareem Abdul-Jabbar/Lakers]	7	3	+15
☐	12/22	USA Hockey Team* Hockey (SOY)	[*Team: Bill Bake/Neil Broton/ Dave Christian/Steve Christoff/ Jim Craig/Mike Eruzione/JohnHarrington/Steve Janaszak/ Mark Johnson/Rob McClanahan/Ken Morrow/John O'Callahan/ Mark Pavelich/Mike Ramsey/BuzzSchneider/Dave Silk/Erik Strobel Bob Suter/Phil Verchota/Mark Wells/ Herb Brooks.]	40	20	+10each
		Year in Sports		15	5	

1981

	DATE	COVER	FEATURE	Nr-Mt	Ex	+Auto
☐	1/05	Dave Winfield (FC) Yankees		20	10	+20
☐	1/12	Chuck Muncie* Chargers	[*Cover also shows Rod Kush/Steve Freeman (Bills)]	20	10	+15
☐	1/19	Mark Van Eeghan Raiders		20	10	+15
☐	1/26	Bobby Knight Indiana		15	5	+15
☐	2/02	Rod Martin Raiders	Superbowl XV	22	10	+15
☐	2/09	Christie Brinkley Swimsuit Issue Model		50	25	5 +25

☐	2/16	Point Shaving Scheme Dr. J		5	3
☐	2/23	Bobby Carpenter Hockey		10	3 +15
☐	3/02	J.R. Richard Astros		20	10 +20
☐	3/09	Magic Johnson Lakers		20	10 +50
☐	3/16	Rollie Fingers Brewers		20	10 +15
☐	3/23	Rolando Blackman* Kansas State	[*Cover also shows Mark Radford/Ray Blume(Oregon State).]	10	5 +15
☐	3/30	Ralph Sampson* Virginia	[*Cover also shows Danny Ainge (BYU)]	10	3 +15
☐	4/06	Isaiah Thomas Indiana (FC)	Indiana NCAA Champs Dr J	20	10 +15
☐	4/13	George Brett/ Mike Schmidt Royals/Phillies	Baseball issue	25	12 +25each
☐	4/20	Tom Watson Golf	Masters Wayne Grettzky, Danny Ainge	20	10 +15
☐	4/27	Oakland A's Pitchers*	[**Cover Shows Brian Kingman Mike Norris, Matt Keogh, Rick Langford, Steve McCantey]	10	7 +10each
☐	5/04	Gerry Cooney Boxing		15	7 +15
☐	5/11	Larry Bird/Kevin McHale* Celtics	(* Cover includes Maurice Cheeks-76ers)	30	15 +50/+15
☐	5/18	Fernando Valenzuela Dodgers	ad George Brett	10	5 +15
☐	5/25	A.J. Foyt Car Racing	Indy 500, Celtic Champs Larry Bird	10	5 +15
☐	6/01	Joe/Marvis Frazier Boxing		10	5 +20/+10
☐	6/08	Greg Luzinski Phillies		10	4 +15
☐	6/15	Bjorn Borg Tennis		10	4 +15
☐	6/22	Baseball Strike		5	3
☐	6/29	David Graham Golf	US Open	10	7 +15
☐	7/06	Sugar Ray Leonard* Boxing	(* Cover includes Ayub Kalule)	20	10 +20
☐	7/13	John McEnroe Tennis	Wimbledon	10	4 +15
☐	7/20	Vince Ferragano Rams		10	6 +10
☐	7/27	Tom Seaver Reds		25	12 +25
☐	8/03	John Hannah Patriots		10	6 +15
☐	8/10	George Brett Mike Schmidt Royals/Phillies	Baseball issue	20	10 +25 each
☐	8/17	Gary Carter/Dick Williams Expos		15	7 +15 each

	DATE	COVER	FEATURE	Nr-Mt	Ex	+Auto
☐	8/24	Wendell Tyler*	[*Cover also shows Kent Hill	10	6	
		Rams	(Rams) and Randy White/			+15
			Bill Gregory/Bob Breunig(Cowboys)]			
☐	8/31	Herschel Walker	College Football Issue	20	7	
		Georgia				+15
☐	9/07	Jim Plunkett	Pro Football Issue	20	7	
		Raiders				+15
☐	9/14	Thomas Hearns		10	8	
		Boxing				+15
☐	9/21	John McEnroe	US Open	10	5	
		Tennis				+15
☐	9/28	Sugar Ray Leonard/		10	6	
		Thomas Hearns				+15 each
		Boxing				
☐	10/05	Marcus Allen (FC)		18	7	
		USC				+15
☐	10/12	Wayne Gretzky	Pro Hockey Issue	50	25	
		Oilers (FC)				+35
☐	10/19	Texas Players		10	5	
		Texas				
☐	10/26	Graig Nettles	World Series	10	5	
		Yankees				+15
☐	11/02	Dave Lopes	World Series	10	6	
		Dodgers				+15
☐	11/09	Larry Bird	Pro Basketball Issue	30	15	
		Celtics	World Series			+50
☐	11/16	Larry Holmes*		10	5	
		Boxing	(* Cover includes Renaldo Snipes)			+15 each
☐	11/23	Bear Bryant		25	10	
		Alabama				+200(d)
☐	11/30	Dean Smith/James Worthy/Sam Perkins		25	15	
		Jimmy Black/Matt Doherty				+15 each
		North Carolina	College Basketball Issue			
☐	12/07	Tony Dorsett		25	15	
		Cowboys				+15
☐	12/14	Cris Collinsworth		10	5	
		Bengals				+15
☐	12/21	Earl Cooper		15	7	
		49ers				+15
☐	12/28	Sugar Ray Leonard		30	15	
		Boxing (SOY)				+25
		Year in Sports		10	6	

1982

	DATE	COVER	FEATURE	Nr-Mt	Ex	+Auto
☐	1/11	Perry Tuttle	Bowl Games	25	10	
		Clemson				+15
☐	1/18	Dave Clark	"The Catch"	75	35	
		49ers				+20
☐	1/25	Joe Montana (FC)		60	25	
		49ers				+50
☐	2/01	Earl Cooper	Superbowl XVI	20	10	
		49ers				+15
☐	2/08	Carol Alt	Swimsuit Issue	40	20	
		Model				+30
☐	2/15	Wayne Gretzky		40	15	
		Oilers				+30

☐ 2/22	Sidney Moncrief		12	6	
	Bucks	Ralph Sampson			+15
☐ 3/01	Herschel Walker		10	6	
	Georgia	George McGinnis			+15
☐ 3/08	The Banzai Pipeline		5	3	
	Surfer				
☐ 3/15	Reggie Jackson		25	10	
	Angels				+35
☐ 3/22	Patrick Ewing (FC)		15	5	
	Georgetown				+25
☐ 3/29	Sam Perkins*		30	15	
	North Carolina	(* Cover includes James Worthy)			+15/+20
☐ 4/05	James Worthy*	(* Cover includes NC Brust, #45;	30	15	
	North Carolina	Georgetown Ewing, 50)			+20
☐ 4/12	Steve Garvey	Baseball Issue	20	10	
	Dodgers				+15
☐ 4/19	Craig Stadler		15	7	
	Golfer	Larry Bird			+15
☐ 4/26	Renaldo Nehemiah		10	5	
	49ers	Dan Issel			+15
☐ 5/03	Moses Malone/Jack Skima		20	5	
	Rockets/Sonics				+20/+10
☐ 5/10	Georgia Frontier/Bert Jones		10	3	
	Rams	Rickey Henderson			+15 each
☐ 5/17	Gaylord Perry		25	10	
	Mariners				+15
☐ 5/24	Magic Johnson*		30	12	
	Lakers	(* Cover includes Michael Cooper)			+50
☐ 5/31	Julius Erving		25	10	
	76ers	(* Cover includes Parrish, Ford,Cheeks)			+25/+15
☐ 6/07	Gerry Cooney		10	4	
	Boxing	NBA LA vs Philly			+15
☐ 6/14	Don Reese		5	3	
	Special Report "Cocaine"				
☐ 6/21	Larry Holmes/Gerry Cooney*		10	3	
	Boxing	Eddie Murray			+15 each
☐ 6/28	Tom Watson	US Open Golf	10	5	
	Golf				+15
☐ 7/05	Kent Hrbek		15	8	
	Twins				+15
☐ 7/12	Jimmy Conners	Wimbeledon	10	3	
	Tennis	Don Sutton			+15
☐ 7/19	Pete Rose/Carl Yastrezemski		25	10	
	Reds	Hal McRae			+20 each
☐ 7/26	Mary Decker Tabb		15	5	
	Track				+15
☐ 8/02	Ray Mancini/Ernesto Espana		10	3	
	Boxing	Reggie Jackson			+15
☐ 8/09	Dale Murphy		15	8	
	Braves	Bill Walton, Tom Glassic			+15
☐ 8/16	Walter Payton (FC)		25	15	
	Bears				+35
☐ 8/23	Franco Harris		25	10	
	Steelers	Mychal Thompson			+15

	DATE	COVER	FEATURE	Nr-Mt	Ex	+Auto
☐	8/30	Tom Cousineau		10	4	
		Browns				+15
☐	9/01	Football	Pro/College Football, Dan Marino	10	5	
☐	9/06	Rickey Henderson (FC)		20	10	
		A's				+25
☐	9/13	Wayne Peace		10	3	
		Florida				+15
☐	9/20	Jimmy Conners	US Open	10	3	
		Tennis	Dan Marino			+15
☐	9/27	NFL Strike		5	3	
☐	10/04	Todd Blackledge		10	3	
		Penn State	Herschel Walker			+15
☐	10/11	Robin Yount (FC)	Pro Hockey Issue	25	12	
		Brewers				+20
☐	10/18	Marvin Hagler		10	5	
		Boxer				+15
☐	10/25	Robin Yount/Lonnie Smith		20	10	
		Brewers/Cards	World Series			+15
☐	11/01	Moses Malone	Pro Basketball Issue	10	5	
		76ers	World Series			+25
☐	11/08	John Elway (FC)		40	20	
		Stanford				+45
☐	11/15	Sugar Ray Leonard		25	10	
		Boxing				+15
☐	11/22	Ray Mancini/Duke Koo Kim		10	4	
		Boxing	(Does not sign)/(d)			
☐	11/29	Ralph Sampson/	College Basketball Issue	10	6	
		Patrick Ewing				+15
		Virginia/Georgetown				
☐	12/06	Lyto Kaab		10	3	
		Eagles				
☐	12/13	Marcus Allen*		20	8	
		Raiders	(*also Keith Butler (Seahawks)			+15
☐	12/20	Ralph Sampson		10	5	
		Virginia				+15
☐	12/27	Wayne Gretzky	Sportsman	50	25	
		Oilers	Bear Bryant Retires			+40
		Year In Sports		10	6	

1983

	DATE	COVER	FEATURE	Nr-Mt	Ex	+Auto
☐	1/10	Greg Garrity	Bowls	10	5	
		Penn State				+15
☐	1/17	Chuck Muncie*	Michael Jordan article	15	10	
		Chargers	(*also Jack Lambert/Donnie Shild)			+15
☐	1/24	Andra Franklin		12	5	
		Dolphins				+15
☐	1/31	Darrell Grant		12	5	
		Redskins				+15
☐	2/07	John Riggins	Superbowl XVII Issue	15	6	
		Redskins				+15
☐	2/14	Cheryl Tiegs	Swimsuit Issue	40	25	
		Model				+25
☐	2/21	Terry Cummings		15	6	
		Clippers				+15
☐	2/28	Julius Erving	(*also Andrew Toney (76ers))	25	12	
		76ers	(*also Moses Malone/Marc Iavaroni)			+30

	Date	Cover	Note			
☐	3/07	Hershel Walker		15	8	
		Generals				+15
☐	3/14	Pete Rose/Joe Morgan/Tony Perez		35	12	
		Reds	Herschel Walker			+20/+15/+15
☐	3/21	Billy Goodwin		10	3	
		St. John's				+10
☐	3/28	Michael Spinks		10	3	
		Boxing	(* Cover includes Dwight Braxton)			+15
☐	4/04	Gary Carter	Baseball Issue	15	6	
		Mets				+15
☐	4/11	Thurmon Bailey*	NCAA Champs,John Elway	10	3	
		NC State	(* Cover includes Sidney Lowe, Derrick Whittenburg)			+15
☐	4/18	Tom Seaver	Masters	20	7	
		NY Mets				+20
☐	4/25	Steve Garvey		15	6	
		Padres				+15
☐	5/02	Larry Bird	(* Cover includes Robert Parrish, Danny Ainge;	30	15	
		Celtics	Hawks-Tree Rollins, Johnny Davis)			+50
☐	5/09	Kareem Abdul-Jabbar		12	6	
		Lakers				+35
☐	5/16	Sunny Halo	Kentucky Derby	5	3	
		Horse				
☐	5/23	Billy Smith	Stanley Cup	10	3	
		Islanders	Moses Malone			+15
☐	5/30	Larry Holmes		10	6	
		Boxing				+15
☐	6/06	Moses Malone/Jamael Wilkes		10	6	
		76ers/Lakers				+20
☐	6/13	Rod Carew	76ers NBA Champs	16	8	
		Angels				+20
☐	6/20	Marcus Dupree	Jackie Robinson pt 1	12	5	
		Oklahoma				+15
☐	6/27	Robert Duran	(* Cover incldues Davey Moore)	20	8	
		Boxing	Jackie Robinson pt 2			+20
☐	7/04	Dale Murphy		20	8	
		Braves				+15
☐	7/11	John McEnroe	Wimbledon, Herschel Walker	10	3	
		Tennis				+15
☐	7/18	Andre Dawson/Dave Steib		15	8	
		Expos/Blue Jays				+15 each
☐	7/25	Tom Watson	British Open Golf, Mel Blount	10	5	
		Golf				+15
☐	8/01	Richard Todd		10	4	
		Jets				+15
☐	8/08	Howard Cosell	Dave Parker	10	3	
						+100(d)
☐	8/15	John Elway		35	15	
		Bronco's				+35
☐	8/22	Carl Lewis (FC)		25	10	
		Track				+15
☐	8/29	Tony Dorsett	College/Pro Football Issue	25	10	
		Cowboys				+15
☐	9/05	Mike Rozier		10	6	
		Nebraska Football				+15
☐	9/12	Edwin Moses		20	5	
		Track				+15

DATE	COVER	FEATURE	Nr-Mt	Ex	+Auto
☐ 9/19	Martina Navratilova (FC) Tennis		10	3	+30
☐ 9/26	Doug Flutie (FC) Boston College		10	8	+15
☐ 10/03	Steve Carlton Phillies		20	10	+20
☐ 10/10	Joe Washington Redskins	Pro Hockey Issue	10	3	+15
☐ 10/17	Eric Dickerson Rams		10	6	+15
☐ 10/24	Rick Dempsey Orioles	World Series	10	3	+15
☐ 10/31	Ralph Sampson Rockets	Pro Basketball Issue	10	3	+15
☐ 11/07	Marvin Hagler/Roberto Duran Boxing		10	3	+15
☐ 11/14	Dan Marino (FC) Dolphins		50	20	+45
☐ 11/21	Marvin Hagler/Roberto Duran Boxing		25	10	+25 each
☐ 11/28	Michael Jordan (FC)/Sam Perkins North Carolina		275	150	+250/+15
☐ 12/05	Sam Bowie Kentucky		6	3	+15
☐ 12/12	Jim Brown Raiders		20	10	+25
☐ 12/19	John Riggins* Redskins	(also George Strake (Redskins))	10	5	+15
☐ 12/26	Mary Decker Track (SOY)		30	15	+15
	Year In Sports		10	5	

1984

DATE	COVER	FEATURE	Nr-Mt	Ex	+Auto
☐ 1/09	Keith Griffith Dolphins	Bowl Games	10	6	+15
☐ 1/16	Joe Theismann Redskins	(* Cover includes Tucker-49ers)	10	6	+15
☐ 1/23	Wayne Gretzky Oilers		25	15	+35
☐ 1/30	Jack Squirek Raiders	Superbowl XVIII Dan Isse, Tommy Lasorda	25	15	+15
☐ 2/06	Scott Hamilton/Tamara McKinney Rosalynn Summers/Phil Mahre Olympic Americans		10	3	+15 each
☐ 2/13	Paulina Porizkova Swimsuit, Pete Rose, Bernard King Model		30	15	+35
☐ 2/20	Debbie Armstrong Olympics, Darry Dawkins Skier		10	3	+15
☐ 2/27	Bill Johnson Skier	Olympics	10	3	+15
☐ 3/05	Magic Johnson* Lakers	(*also Mo Cheeks, Dr J, Clint Richardson)	20	10	+50
☐ 3/12	George Brett Royals	Steve Young, Charles Barkley	30	12	+35
☐ 3/19	Patrick Ewing Georgetown		20	10	+35

	Date	Subject	Note	Val1	Val2	Plus
☐	3/26	Sam Perkins		20	10	
		North Carolina				+15
☐	4/02	Yogi Berra	Baseball Issue	20	10	
		Yankees	Michael Jordan, Cal Ripken Jr			+20
☐	4/09	Michael Graham	NCAA Finals	10	3	
		Georgetown`	(*also Winslow & Anderson)			+15
☐	4/16	Graig Nettles/Rich Gossage		10	5	
		Padres				+15
☐	4/23	Darryl Strawberry (FC)		10	6	
		Mets				+15
☐	4/30	Bull Cyclones Coach		6	3	
☐	5/07	Bernard King*	Reggie Jackson	10	5	
		Knicks	(*Kelly Tripuka/Len Robinson)			+15
☐	5/14	Mike Bossy		25	10	
		Islanders				+15
☐	5/21	Soviet Boycott		6	3	
☐	5/28	Alan Trammell (FC)		20	10	
		Tigers	Stankley Cup			+15
☐	6/04	Magic Johnson*	(* cover includes Kurt Rambis	15	7	
		Lakers	/Dennis Johnson)			+50/+10
☐	6/11	Leon Durham		10	3	
		Cubs				+15
☐	6/18	Martina Navartilova		10	3	
		Tennis	French Open			+30
☐	6/25	Carl Lewis		10	4	
		Track	Celtics NBA Champs			+15
☐	7/02	Dwight Stones		10	4	
		High Jump				+15
☐	7/09	Jeff Float		10	3	
		Swimming				+10
☐	7/16	John McEnroe	Wimbledon	10	3	
		Tennis	Preview of Summer Olympic Issue	10	5	+10
☐	7/23	Michael Jordan		150	50	
		US Olympic Team				+250
☐	7/30	Jack Lambert		35	15	
		Steelers				+20
☐	8/06	Rafer Johnson	Jim Rice	10	4	
		Olympics	Olympics			+35
☐	8/13	Mary Lou Retton		10	4	
		Gymnastics	Olympics			+10
☐	8/20	Carl Lewis		20	9	
		Track	Olympics			+12
☐	8/27	Pete Rose	Dr J	15	8	
		Reds				+20
☐	9/03	Joe Theismann		10	5	
		Redskins				+10
☐	9/10	Clayton/Green		7	4	
		Dolphins/Redskins	Dave Winfield			+10 each
☐	9/05	Dan Marino/Bernie Kosar		40	15	
		Dolphins	Col/Pro Football Issue			+45/+15
☐	9/17	John McEnroe	US Open Tennis	10	4	
		Tennis				+15
☐	9/24	Dwight Gooden/Rick Sutcliffe		20	8	
		Mets/Cubs				+15 each
☐	10/01	Jeff Smith		15	5	
		Nebraska	Reggie Jackson, Carlton Fisk			+15

DATE	COVER	FEATURE	Nr-Mt	Ex	+Auto
☐ 10/08	Sammy Winder		10	3	
	Broncos				+15
☐ 10/15	Walter Payton	Payton Breaks Record	35	15	
	Bears	Pro Hockey Issue			+35
☐ 10/22	Alan Trammell	World Series	25	12	
	Tigers				+15
☐ 10/29	Larry Bird/Bill Russell		35	15	
	Celtics	Pro Basketball Issue, Dan Marino, Dr J			+50/+200
☐ 11/05	Gerry Faust		12	5	
	Notre Dame	Akeem Olajuwon			+15
☐ 11/12	NFL Issue/Trouble		5	3	
☐ 11/19	Mark Duper		10	3	
	Dolphins				+15
☐ 11/26	Patrick Ewing/John Thompson/Ronald Reagan		20	6	
	Georgetown	College Basketball Issue			+25/+15/+200
☐ 12/03	Doug Flutie		10	5	
	Boston College				+15
☐ 12/10	Michael Jordan*		150	50	
	Bulls	(*also Mike Dunleavy/Sidney Moncrief)			+200
☐ 12/17	Eric Dickerson		10	5	
	Rams				+15
☐ 12/24	Mary Lou Retton/Edwin Moses		30	15	
	Gymnastics (SOY)				+15/+20
	The Year In Sports		15	5	

1985

DATE	COVER	FEATURE	Nr-Mt	Ex	+Auto
☐ 1/07	Walter Abercrombie		10	6	
	Steelers	Bowls, Patrick Ewing			+15
☐ 1/14	Dan Marino		40	15	
	Dolphins	Karl Malone			+35
☐ 1/21	Dan Marino/Joe Montana		40	15	
	Dolphins/49ers				+35/+40
☐ 1/28	Roger Craig	Superbowl XIX	20	10	
	49ers				+15
☐ 2/04	Walter Berry*		10	5	
	St Johns	(*Mike Gminski (St John))			+15
☐ 2/11	Paulina Porizkova Swimsuit Issue		30	15	
	Model				+30
☐ 2/18	Wayne Gretzky		20	10	
	Oilers				+35
☐ 2/25	Doug Flutie		10	5	
	Generals				+15
☐ 3/04	Mike Schmidt		20	10	
	Phillies	Larry Bird			+35
☐ 3/11	Jack/Gary Nicklaus		12	8	
	Golf	Charles Barkley			+50/+15
☐ 3/18	Fred Lynn		10	6	
	Red Sox				+15
☐ 3/25	Peter Ueberroth/Willie Mays/Mickey Mantle		10	6	
	Commissioner				+15/+50/+175(d)
☐ 4/01	Patrick Ewing/Chris Mullin/Dwayne McLain		10	6	
	Georgetown/St John's/Villanova				+35/+15/+10
☐ 4/08	Ed Pinckney	NCAA Finals	10	5	
	Villanova				+15
☐ 4/15	Dwight Gooden	Baseball Issue	10	6	
	Mets	Pete Rose, Ron Cey			+15

	Date	Subject	Notes			
☐	4/22	Marvin Hagler / Thomas Hearns / Boxing		10	6	+25 each
☐	4/29	Hulk Hogan / Wrestling		20	10	+15
☐	5/06	Billy Martin / Yankees	*Patrick Ewing*	15	6	+100(d)
☐	5/13	Magic Johnson / Lakers	*Charles Barkley*	15	7	+50
☐	5/20	Patrick Ewing / Knicks	*Reggie Jackson*	15	5	+25
☐	5/27	Herschel Walker / Generals	*Dr J* / *Indy 500, Stanley Cup*	16	8	+15
☐	6/03	Danny Sullivan / Auto Racing		10	3	+15
☐	6/10	Kareem Abdul-Jabbar* / Lakers	*(* Larry Bird)*	10	5	+35
☐	6/17	Kareem Abdul-Jabbar/Michael Cooper Danny Ainge / Lakers/Celtics	*(Cover Inset Chris Evert)* / *Lakers NBA Champs* / *(* Cover includes Danny Ainge/Celtics)*	10	4	+35
☐	6/24	Andy North / Golf	*US Open Golf* / *(* Corner inset Earl Weaver/Orioles)*	10	6	+15
☐	7/01	Larry Holmes / Boxing		10	3	+15
☐	7/08	Fernando Valenzuela / Dodgers	*Ricky Henderson*	20	7	+15
☐	7/15	Boris Becker / Tennis		10	4	+15
☐	7/22	Howie Long / Raiders		10	6	+15
☐	7/29	Mary Decker Slaney/Zola Budd / Track		10	4	+15
☐	8/05	Pedro Guerrero / Dodgers	*Bobby Orr*	10	6	+15
☐	8/12	Tony Dorsett / Cowboys	*Tom Seaver, Rod Carew*	20	6	+15
☐	8/19	Pete Rose / Reds		20	10	+20
☐	8/26	Bernie Kosar / Browns		16	9	+15
☐	9/02	Dwight Gooden / Mets		12	6	+15
☐	9/04	Eric Dickerson / Rams	*College & Pro Football* / *(* Cover includes McCullin-Navy)*	10	6	+15
☐	9/09	Bill Elliott / Car Racing		30	15	+25
☐	9/16	Joe Louis / Boxing	*Pete Rose*	10	3	+15
☐	9/23	Ozzie Smith (FC) / Cardinals		35	12	+15
☐	9/30	Michael Spinks / Boxing	*(* Cover includes Larry Holmes)*	10	5	+15
☐	10/07	Tony Robinson / Tennessee	*Joe Namath*	10	5	+15

Date	Cover	Feature	Nr-Mt	Ex	+Auto
☐ 10/14	Eddie Robinson	(*Robinson Breaks Bryant Record)	10	7	
	Grambling				+15
☐ 10/21	Jim McMahon		10	5	
	Bears	George Brett			+15
☐ 10/28	Ozzie Smith	World Series	25	10	
	Cardinals	Pro Basketball Issue			+15
☐ 11/04	Royals Players	World Series	8	6	
	Royals				+10 each
☐ 11/11	Roy McDonald/DJ Dozier		10	3	
	Florida/Penn State				+15
☐ 11/18	Dale Brown		10	3	
	LSU				+15
☐ 11/20	Cheryl Miller/Mark Price/Bruce Dalrymple			10	6
	USC/Georgia Tech				+15
☐ 11/25	Danny White*	(*Cover also shows Dave	10	7	
	Cowboys	Dureson/Otis Wilson)			+15
☐ 12/02	Bo Jackson/Chuck Long/Joe Dudek		25	10	
	Auburn/Iowa/Plymouth State				+25/+10 each
☐ 12/09	Kirk Gibson		15	7	
	Tigers				+15
☐ 12/16	Marcus Allen		15	7	
	Raiders				+15
☐ 12/23	Kareem Abdul-Jabbar		35	17	
	Lakers (SOY)	Sportsman			+35
	The Year In Sports		12	6	

1986

DATE	COVER	FEATURE	Nr-Mt	Ex	+Auto
☐ 1/06	Mike Tyson (FC)		20	10	
	Boxing				+45
☐ 1/13	Craig James		10	5	
	Patriots	[Corner Oklahoma Player]			+15
☐ 1/20	Jim McMahon*		10	5	
	Bears	[Cover shows Jerry Gray-Rams]			+15
☐ 1/27	Mike Singletary		10	5	
	Bears				+15
☐ 2/03	Hampton/Eason	Superbowl XX	20	10	
	Bears				+15 each
☐ 2/10	Elle MacPherson	Swimsuit issue	30	15	
	Model (FC)				+35
☐ 2/17	Danny Manning		20	10	
	Kansas				+15
☐ 2/24	Networks	Celtics	10	3	
☐ 3/03	Larry Bird		20	10	
	Celtics	Mario Lemieux			+50
☐ 3/10	Gambling		4	3	
☐ 3/17	Mark Alarie		10	4	
	Duke				+15
☐ 3/24	Marvin Hagler	Charles Barkley	10	6	
	Boxing	(* Cover includes John Mugabi)			+15
☐ 3/31	LSU #44*	Reggie Jackson	10	5	
	LSU	(* also Louisville/Duke/Kansas)			
☐ 4/07	Pervis Ellison		20	6	
	Louisville	NCAA Finals			+15
☐ 4/14	Wade Boggs (FC)	Baseball 86	10	6	
	Red Sox	Don Mattingly			+15

	Date	Cover		Price 1	Price 2	Bonus
☐	4/21	Jack Nicklaus		25	10	
		Golf				+50
☐	4/28	Dominique Wilkins		10	6	
		Hawks	*Jack Nicklaus*			+20
☐	5/05	Ernest Hemingway Stanley Cup		10	3	
☐	5/12	Roger Clemens		30	12	
		Red Sox				+35
☐	5/19	James Worthy*		20	8	
		Lakers	*(*Cover shows Rodney McCray)*			+25
☐	5/26	Akeem Olajuwan (FC)/Kareem Abdul-Jabbar			30	15
		Rockets/Lakers	*[* Corner is Naratovia/Evert]*			+35/+35
☐	6/02	Montreal Canadiens		10	5	
		Canadiens				
☐	6/09	Larry Bird		20	10	
		Celtics				+50
☐	6/16	Kevin McHale		10	5	
		Celtics				+15
☐	6/23	Christine/Raymond Floyd		10	8	
		Golf				+10/+15
☐	6/30	Len Bias		10	7	
		Cocaine		-		
☐	7/07	Diego Maradona		15	5	
		Argentina Soccer				+50
☐	7/14	Bo Jackson		25	12	
		Chicks				+25
☐	7/21	Jim Kelly (FC)	*Generals*	25	12	
		Generals				+25
☐	7/28	Rickey Henderson		10	7	
		Yankees				+15
☐	8/04	"Oil Can" Boyd		12	6	
		Red Sox	*Mike Tyson*			+20
☐	8/11	William Perry/Too Tall Jones		10	6	
		Bears/Cowboys	*(Reggie Jackson)*			+15 each
☐	8/18	Herschel Walker		10	6	
		Cowboys	*John Mcenroe/Wilt Chamberlain*			+15
☐	8/25	Ron Darling		10	5	
		Mets				+15
☐	9/01	Kristie Phillips		10	3	
		US Gymnaists	*Marcus Allen*			+15
☐	9/08	Sugar Ray Leonard		10	5	
		Boxer				+15
☐	9/15	Ivan Lendl		10	3	
		Tennis				+15
☐	9/22	Football Players		10	5	
		Michigan/Notre Dame	*Ralph Sampson*			
☐	9/03	Jim McMahon/Brian Bosworth		10	5	
		Bears/Oklahoma	*Col/Pro Football 86*			+15 each
☐	9/29	Mark Gastneau/Lawrence Taylor		10	6	
		Jets	*Nolan Ryan*			+15 each
☐	10/06	Darryl Strawberry		10	5	
		Mets				+15
☐	10/13	John Elway		10	5	
		Broncos	*Pro Hockey Issue*			+25
☐	10/20	Bobby Grich/Doug DeCinces		10	6	
		Angels	*Steve Largent*			+15 each

	DATE	COVER	FEATURE	Nr-Mt	Ex	+Auto
☐	10/27	Gary Carter/Jim Rice		10	6	
		Mets/Red Sox				+15 each
☐	11/03	Ray Knight	World Series	10	5	
		Mets	Pro Basketball Issue			+15
☐	11/10	Injuries		4	3	
☐	11/17	Michael Jordan	(* Cover includes M. Thompson/Alvin	50	25	
		Bulls	Robertson- San Antonio)			+75
☐	11/19	Dave Robinson	Basketball Issue	20	10	
		Navy	Reggie Miller			+20
☐	11/24	Vinny Testaverde		10	5	
		Miami				+15
☐	12/01	Mike Tyson/Trevor Berbick		10	5	
		Boxing				+15
☐	12/08	Walter Payton		20	7	
		Bears				+30
☐	12/15	Mark Bavaro		10	6	
		Giants				+10
☐	12/22	Joe Patereno	Sportsman	30	15	
		Penn State (SOY)				+15
		Year In Sports		12	6	

1987

	DATE	COVER	FEATURE	Nr-Mt	Ex	+Auto
☐	1/05	Brian Bosworth		10	6	
		Oklahoma	[Corner Kentucky-Rex Chapman]			+15
☐	1/12	Ozzie Newsome*		10	5	
		Browns	[Corner Penn State]			+15
☐	1/19	Rich Karlis*		10	5	
		Broncos	[*also Gary Kubiak]			+15
☐	1/26	Lawrence Taylor		10	6	
		Giants	John Elway			+20
☐	2/02	Phil Simms/Simon Fletcher		10	5	
		Giants/Denver	Superbowl XXI			+15 each
☐	2/09	Elle Macpherson	Swimsuit Issue	30	15	
		Model	Michael Jordan			+25
☐	2/16	Ronald Reagan/Dennis Conner		20	10	
		President/Yachting				+200/+15
☐	2/23	Magic Johnson/Dennis Johnson		20	10	
		Lakers/Celtics				+50/+15
			[Corner Bill Elliott- Daytona]			
☐	3/02	JR Reid		10	6	
		North Carolina				+15
☐	3/09	Ripken's (Cal, Jr, Billy)		30	15	
		Orioles	[Corner Variations #1 Notre Dame; #2 SMU]			+15/+45/+15
☐	3/16	Gary McLain		10	3	
		Cocaine	Moses Malone			+10
☐	3/23	Bobby Knight		10	5	
		Indiana				+10
			[Corner variations #1 Wyoming, #2 Rebels, #3 DePaul]			
☐	3/30	Marvin Hagler/Sugar Ray Leonard		10	3	
		Boxing	[Corner variation #1 Indiana #12]			+15
☐	4/06	Cory Snyder/Joe Carter Baseball Issue		10	5	
		Indians	(* Cover includes Joe Carter)			+10/+15
			[Corner - Indiana #12]			

☐	4/13	Sugar Ray Leonard/Marvin Hagler		10	5	
		Boxing				+20 each
☐	4/20	Baseball Players (Cover has 43 players)			10	4
		Salaries	(*Puckett,Mattingley,Schmidt,Brett,Smith,Jackson,etc)			
☐	4/27	Rob Deer	Larry Bird	10	5	
		Brewers	[Corner - Hockey Thriller]			+15
☐	5/04	Julius Erving		30	15	
		76ers	Bo Jackson			+35
☐	5/11	Reggie Jackson		25	10	
		A's	[Corner -Alysheba- Horse Race]			+30
☐	5/18	Isaiah Thomas		20	7	
		Pistons	[Corner - Indy 500]			+15
☐	5/25	Eric Davis		10	5	
		Reds	[Corner - Larry Bird]			+15
☐	6/01	Wayne Gretzky		25	10	
		Oilers	[Corner - Wayne Gretzky]			+35
☐	6/08	Larry Bird	Stanley Cup - Gerry Cooney	20	10	
		Celtics	[Corner - Wayne Gretzky]			+50
☐	6/15	Byron Scott*	(*also McHale/Roberts-Celtics)	10	5	
		Lakers	(*also Kurt Rambus-Lakers)			+10 each
☐	6/22	Kareem Abdul-Jabbar		10	5	
		Lakers				+35
☐	6/29	Scott Simpson	US Open	10	5	
		Golf	Larry Bird/Magic Johnson			+15
			(Cover includes Tom Watson)			
☐	7/06	One Day in Baseball		10	5	
☐	7/13	Don Mattingly/Darrell Strawberry		10	6	
		Yankees	[Corner - Martina Navratilova]			+15 each
☐	7/20	Andre Dawson		10	6	
		Cubs				+15
☐	7/27	Pit Bull Terrier		5	4	
		Dog	[Corner includes Don Mattingly]			
☐	8/03	Vinny Testaverde		10	6	
		Tampa Bay				+15
☐	8/10	Mike Tyson		10	6	
		Boxing	[Corner - Pete Rose]			+20
☐	8/17	Alan Trammell		10	6	
		Tigers	[Corner - 49er player]			+15
☐	8/24	Jim McMahon		10	5	
		Bears				+15
☐	8/31	Tim Brown	College Football Issue	10	6	
		Notre Dame	[Corner-Oklahoma Football Insert]			+15
☐	9/07	Surfs Up	George Bell - Dale Earnhardt	4	3	
☐	9/09	Mark Bavaro	Pro Football Issue	10	6	
		Giants				+15
☐	9/14	Jackie Joyner Kersee		25	12	
		Track	[Corner var. #1LSU,#2Wash,#3 Kirby Puckett]			+15
☐	9/21	John Elway		25	12	
		Broncos	Hockey Olympics			+35
☐	9/28	Ozzie Smith	Jerry Rice - Marvin Hagler	25	10	
		Cardinals	(* Cover includes Ray Collins - Reds)			+25
☐	10/05	Lloyd Moseby		10	5	
		Blue Jays	[*Corner variations #1 Strike, #2 SEC]			+15
☐	10/12	Steve Walsh	Pro Hockey Issue	10	5	

DATE	COVER	FEATURE	Nr-Mt	Ex	+Auto
	Florida State	[* Corner is Alan Trammell]			+15
☐ 10/19	Greg Gagne		10	5	
	Twins	(* Cover includes Darrell Evans- Tigers)			+15
☐ 10/26	Dan Gladden	World Series	10	6	
	Twins	Mike Tyson			+15
☐ 11/02	Twins Team	World Series	20	9	
					+10 each
☐ 11/09	Eric Dickerson*	Pro Basletball Issue	10	6	
	Colts	(*Michael Jordan Inset)			+15
☐ 11/16	Rotnei Anderson		10	4	
	Oklahoma				+15
☐ 11/18	Fennis Dembo	College Basketball Issue	10	4	
☐ 11/23	Dexter Manley		10	4	
	Redskins				+15
☐ 11/30	Oklahoma/Nebraska		10	4	
		[Corner variations #1 North Carolina, #2 USC]			
☐ 12/07	Arnold Schwarzenegger		20	7	
	Movie Star				+40
		[Corner variations #1 Saints, #2 Lee Trevino]			
☐ 12/14	Bo Jackson		20	7	
	Royals/Raiders				+20
☐ 12/21	Dale Murphy*	Sportsman	20	10	
	Braves				+10 each
		(* Also Rory Sparrow, Patty Sheeham, Reggie Williams, Chip Rives,			
		Bobby Bourne, Judy Brown King, Kip Keino)			
	Michael Jordan	Year In Pictures	10	8	
	Bulls				

1988

DATE	COVER	FEATURE	Nr-Mt	Ex	+Auto
☐ 1/11	Miami	Bowls	10	5	
☐ 1/18	Anthony Carter		10	5	
	Vikings				+15
☐ 1/25	John Elway		10	6	
	Broncos				+25
☐ 1/27	Winter Olympics		5	3	
☐ 2/01	Mike Tyson		10	5	
	Boxing				+35
☐ 2/08	Doug Williams	Superbowl	20	10	
	Redskins				+15
☐ 2/15	Elle Macpherson	Swimsuit Issue	30	15	
	Model				+25
☐ 2/22	Wilt Chamberlain/Bill Russell		30	10	
	Warriors/Celtics				+75/+200
☐ 2/29	Brian Boitano	Ice Skating	10	5	
	Ice Skating				+15
☐ 3/07	Kirk Gibson		10	5	
	Dodgers	[Corner Kathy Witt/Ice Skating]			+15
☐ 3/14	Pam Postema	Woman Ump	10	3	
					+15
☐ 3/21	Larry Bird		20	10	
	Celtics				+50
☐ 3/28	Mark Macon/Mark Tillmon	[Corner var.#1 Arizona,	10	5	
	Temple/Georgetown	#2 Oklahoma, #3 Michigan,#4 RI]			+15
☐ 4/04	Will Clark/Mark McGwire		20	10	
	Giants/A's	Baseball 88			+15 each
☐ 4/11	Danny Manning	NCAA Champs	10	4	
	Kansas				+15
☐ 4/18	Lakers Team (Players/Coaches)		15	7	
	Basketball				+10each +35 Kareem +50 Magic +200 all
☐ 4/25	Muhammad Ali		10	5	

	Date	Description	Notes			
		Boxing				+95
☐	5/02	Billy Ripken		10	5	
		Orioles	[Corner - Wayne Gretzky]			+15
☐	5/09	Pete Rose		15	7	
		Reds				+20
☐	5/16	Michael Jordan/Scotty Pippen*		40	15	
		Bulls	[Lady - Horseracing]			+70/+25
			(*also Brad Daugherty/Cavs)			
☐	5/23	Magic Johnson/Karl Malone		15	7	
		Lakers/Jazz				+50 each
☐	5/30	Wayne Gretzky		25	10	
		Oilers				+35
☐	6/06	Bill Russell*	(* Cover includes C. Ripken Sr.,	8	4	
			Chuck Tanner, Larry Bowa			+200/15 each
			John Wetzel, Larry Keenan)			
☐	6/13	Mike Tyson/Robin Givens		10	5	-
		Boxing				+50/+20
☐	6/20	Michael Spinks		10	5	
		Boxing	[Corner AC Green - Lakers]			+15
☐	6/27	Magic Johnson/Bill Lambeer		15	6	
		Lakers/Pistons	[Corner - Curtis Strange/Golf]			+50/+15
☐	7/04	Mike Tyson/Michael Spinks		10	4	
		Boxing				+25/+15
☐	7/11	Darryl Strawberry		10	5	
		Mets				+15
☐	7/18	Actor Mike Regan		10	5	
		"Casey at the Bat"				
☐	7/25	Florence Griffith Joyner		25	10	
		Track				+20
☐	8/01	Tony Dorsett		20	5	
		Bronco's	[Corner Wade Boggs- Red Sox]			+15
☐	8/06	Beer		5	3	
☐	8/14	China Kids		5	3	
☐	8/22	Wayne Gretzky/Magic Johnson		35	15	
		Kings/Lakers				+35/+50
☐	8/29	Bernie Kosar	NFL Preview	15	7	
		Browns				+15
☐	9/05	Florida	College Football Issue	10	4	
☐	9/12	Jim McMahon		12	5	
		Bears	[Corner - Jose Canseco]			+15
☐	9/12	Matt Biondi		10	4	
		Olympics	Summer Olympic Preview			+15
☐	9/19	Steffi Graf		10	3	
		Tennis				+15
☐	9/26	Dwight Evans		15	7	
		Red Sox	Olympics			+15
☐	10/03	Ben Johnson		10	3	
		Track	Olympics			+20
☐	10/10	Florence Griffith Joyner/Jackie Joyner Kersee			25	10
		Track				+15 each
☐	10/17	Jose Canseco (FC)		15	6	
		Athletics				+15
☐	10/24	Tony Rice*	(Also Russell Maryland/Miami)	15	6	
		Notre Dame	[Corner - Kirk Gibson/Dodger]			+15
☐	10/31	Orel Hershiser/Rick Dempsey		15	6	
		Dodgers				+15
☐	11/07	Karl Malone*	Pro Basketball Issue	20	6	
		Utah	(*Rod Higgens (Warriors))			+15
☐	11/14	Tom Landry/Chuck Knoll		10	6	
		Cowboys/Steelers				+15
		Billy Owens	College Basketball Issue	10	5	
		Syracuse				+15
☐	11/21	Saints/Rams		10	5	
			(*shows Greg Bell (Rams))			
☐	11/28	Rodney Peete		10	4	
		USC				+15

DATE	COVER	FEATURE	Nr-Mt	Ex	+Auto
☐ 12/05	Tony Rice		10	4	
	Notre Dame				+15
☐ 12/12	Charles Barkley (FC)		15	8	
	76ers				+25
☐ 12/19	Orel Hershiser Sportsman		38	10	
	Dodgers				+15
	Flo Joyner Kersee Pictures - 1988		20	10	
	Track				+20

1989

DATE	COVER	FEATURE	Nr-Mt	Ex	+Auto
☐ 1/09	Tony Rice	Bowls	10	5	
	Notre Dame				+15
☐ 1/16	Ickey Woods		10	4	
	Bengels				+10
☐ 1/23	Kareem Abdul-Jabbar		10	5	
	Lakers				+35
☐ 1/30	Jerry Rice	Superbowl XXIII	50	20	
	49ers				+45
☐ 2/07	Kathy Ireland	Swimsuit Issue	25	15	
	Model (FC)				+20
☐ 2/06	Mario Lemieux		25	10	
	Penquins (FC)				+25
☐ 2/13	Patrick Ewing		10	4	
	Knicks				+25
☐ 2/20	Chris Jackson		10	4	
	LSU				+25 (Islamic)
☐ 2/27	Charles Thompson/Barry Switzer		10	4	
	Sooners				+10 each
☐ 3/06	Wade Boggs		10	5	
	Red Sox	[Corner - Mike Tyson]			+15
☐ 3/13	Michael Jordan		40	15	
	Bulls				+75
☐ 3/20	Jimmy Johnson		10	5	
	Cowboys				+10
☐ 3/27	Steffi Graf		10	4	
	Tennis	[Corner - NC State]			+15
☐ 4/01	Benito Santiago	Baseball Issue	10	5	
	Padres				+15
☐ 4/03	Pete Rose		10	5	
	Reds	[Corner -Danny Ferry- Duke]			+20
☐ 4/10	Rumeal Robinson		10	5	
	Glen Rice	NCAA Champs			+15 each
	Michigan				
☐ 4/17	Nick Faldo - Golf Masters		20	9	
	Golf	[Corner-Magic Johnson/Lakers]			+15
☐ 4/24	Tony Mandarich		10	4	
	Football Player				+10
☐ 5/01	Nolan Ryan		35	12	
	Texas				+25
☐ 5/08	Jon Peters -	High School Pitcher	10	4	
	Baseball	[Corner - Chris Mullin/Warriors]			+10
☐ 5/15	Michael Jordan		35	15	
	Bulls				+75
☐ 5/22	Julie Krone		10	3	
	Woman Jockey				+15
☐ 5/29	Kentucky Basketball		10	3	
☐ 6/05	James Worthy	Stanley Cup Final	10	6	
	Lakers				+20
☐ 6/12	Bo Jackson		10	5	
	Royals				+20
☐ 6/19	Sugar Ray Leonard/Thomas Hearns		10	5	
	Boxing	[Corner- Michael Chang Tennis]			+20
☐ 6/26	Curtis Strange	US Open	15	5	
	Golf	NBA Finals			+15

	DATE	COVER	FEATURE	Nr-Mt	Ex	+Auto
☐	7/03	Pete Rose Reds		20	6	+20
☐	7/10	Rick Reuschel Giants		10	5	+15
☐	7/17	George Foreman Boxing		15	7	+20
☐	7/24	Greg Jefferies Mets		12	6	+15
☐	7/31	Greg Lemond Cycling	Tour De France	10	7	+15
☐	8/07	Boomer Esiason Bengels		12	6	+15
☐	8/14	Michael Jordan Golf		25	15	+75
☐	8/21	Troy Aikman (FC) Cowboys		35	12	+35
☐	8/27	Chris Evert Tennis	[Corner - Pete Rose]	10	5	+15
☐	9/04	Lou Holtz Notre Dame	Col Football Issue (*Ernie Davis/Lafeyette/Pete Rose)	7	4	+15
☐	9/11	Randall Cunningham Eagles	Pro Football Issue	10	5	+15
☐	9/18	Boris Becker Tennis	U S Open Tennis	10	4	+15
☐	9/25	Raghib Ismail Notre Dame		10	4	+15
☐	10/02	Joe Montana 49ers		25	10	+40
☐	10/09	Sergiei Starikov Viacheslav Fetisov	Pro Hockey Issue	10	5	+15
☐	10/16	Rickey Henderson* A's	(*also Kelly Gruber (Jays))	10	6	+15
☐	10/23	Herschel Walker Vikings		12	6	+15
☐	10/30	Kelly Downs Giants	[Corner Dave Stewart, Wayne Gretzky] Earthquake	12	5	
☐	11/06	Joe Dumars Michael Jordan Pistons/Bulls		35	15	+15/+$75
☐	11/13	Deion Sanders Atlanta		20	10	+20
☐	11/15	Muhammad Ali Boxing	35th Anniversary	20	10	+95
☐	11/20	Rumeal Robinson Michigan	College Basketball Issue	12	6	+15
☐	11/27	Harris/Rice/Smith/Thompson/Ware UWV/N.Dame/FL/Ind/Houston		10	4	+10 each
☐	12/04	Steve McGuire Miami		10	4	+15
☐	12/11	Larry Bird Celtics	(Cover shows Randolph Keys(Cavs) [Corner Nadi Comaneci, Mark Langston]	20	10	+50
☐	12/18	Joe Montana- 49ers Magic Johnson - Lakers Wayne Gretzky - Kings		35	15	+30/+50/+35
☐	12/31	Greg Lemond - Sportsman* Cycling The Year In Photo's		30 10	12 7	+20

1990

	DATE	COVER	FEATURE	Nr-Mt	Ex	+Auto
☐	1/08	Craig Erickson Miami	Bowls	8	5	+20
☐	1/15	Jerry Rice 49ers		35	12	+50

	Date	Description	Notes			
☐	1/22	John Elway Bronco's		30	12	+45
☐	1/29	Dave Robinson Spurs		10	6	+30
☐	2/05	Joe Montana/ McIntyre - 49ers	*49ers Superbowl XXIV*	10	4	+40/+15
☐	2/12	Judit Mascow Model	*Swimsuit issue*	20	12	+45
☐	2/19	Mike Tyson Boxing		5	3	+40
☐	2/26	Buster Douglas Boxing	*(Michael Jordan)*	5	3	+20
☐	3/05	Gary Payton Oregon State	*College Basketball Issue*	5	3	+15
☐	3/12	Tony LaRussa Athletics		5	3	+15
☐	3/19	Jennifer Capriati Tennis		20	8	+20
☐	3/26	Bo Kimble Loyola Marymount		5	3	+15
☐	4/02	Stacey Augmon/Chris Knight UNLV/LOYOLA	*NCAA Basketball*			+10/+10
☐	4/09	Rod Scurry/Brian Davis UNLV/Duke	*NCAA Finals*	5	3	+15/+10
☐	4/16	Ted Williams Red Sox	*Baseball Issue, Masters*	25	10	+175
☐	4/23	Thomas Sandstrom LA Kings	*[Corner Bo Jackson, Steffi Graf]*	5	3	+15
☐	4/30	Jeff George Colts		10	5	+15
☐	5/07	Ken Griffey Jr. (FC) Mariners		35	15	+40
☐	5/14	Sneakers		5	3	
☐	5/21	Michael Jordan Bulls		35	15	+75
☐	5/28	Will Clark (FSC) Giants		10	5	+15
☐	6/04	Lenny Dykstra Phillies		10	5	+15
☐	6/11	Isaiah Thomas Pistons		8	4	+15
☐	6/18	Jack Nicklaus/Monica Seles/George Steinbrenner Golf/Tennis/Baseball		10	5	+40/+15/+10
☐	6/25	Hale Irwin Golf	*US Open*	12	6	+20
☐	7/02	Marvin Hagler Boxer		4	3	+25
☐	7/09	Darryl Strawberry Mets		10	4	+15
☐	7/16	Martina Navratilova Tennis	*NBA Finals*	5	3	+25
☐	7/23	Narciso Elrira Dodgers	*Minor Baseball Teams* *Pistons NBA Champs*	5	3	+15
☐	7/30	Greg Lemond Cycling		9	5	+15
☐	8/06	Joe Montana 49ers		25	10	+30
☐	8/13	Autograph Madness		5	1	
☐	8/20	Jose Canseco A's		10	5	+15
☐	8/27	Troy Aikman* Cowboys	*[*Also Mike Wise - Raiders]*	15	7	+35

	DATE	COVER	FEATURE	Nr-Mt	Ex	+Auto
☐	9/03	Todd Marinovich USC	College Football Issue	5	2	+10
☐	9/10	Barry Sanders (FC) Lions		10	5	+25
☐	9/17	Peter Sampras Tennis		10	4	+25
☐	9/24	Rick Mirer Notre Dame		10	5	+15
☐	10/01	Bobby Bonilla Pirates		10	5	+15
☐	10/08	OJ Simpson Bills	Pro Hockey Issue	10	5	+40
☐	10/15	Burt Grossman Chargers	Pro Football Issue	20	5	+15
☐	10/22	Dennis Eckersley A's	World Series	10	4	+10
☐	10/29	Chris Sabo Reds	World Series	10 .	4	+15
☐	11/05	Bill Laimbeer Pistons	Pro Basketball Issue	5	4	+15
☐	11/12	William Bell Georgia Tech		5	3	+15
☐	11/19	Stacey Augmon/Larry Johnson UNLV	College Basketball Issue	10	5	+15/+20
☐	11/26	Notre Dame/Penn State		7	4	
☐	12/03	Magic Johnson Lakers		10	5	+50
☐	12/10	Ty Detmer BYU		8	4	+15
☐	12/17	Michael Jordan* Bulls	[*also Kevin Duckworth-Blazers]	30	15	+50
☐	12/24	Joe Montana 49ers	Sportsman	40	15	+50
☐	12/31	Chiefs Player	Pictures of 1990	10	5	

1991

	DATE	COVER	FEATURE	Nr-Mt	Ex	+Auto
☐	1/14	Dan Marino Dolphins	Bowls	40	15	+35
☐	1/21	Shaquille O'Neal (FC) LSU		40	12	+35
☐	1/28	Otis Anderson Giants		7	4	+15
☐	2/04	Everson Walls Giants	Superbowl XXV	7	5	+15
☐	2/11	Robert Parrish Celtics		15	5	+15
☐	2/18	Michael Jordan/Charles Barkley/Patrick Ewing Karl Malone/Magic Johnson		40	15	
		+70 Jordan/ Olympic Team Johnson/Ewing +25 for others				
☐	2/25	Rocket Ismail Notre Dame		7	4	+15
☐	3/04	Darryl Strawberry Dodgers		10	3	+15
☐	3/11	Ashley Montana Model	Swimsuit Issue	20	10	+15
☐	3/18	Brett Hull Blues		10	5	+15
☐	3/25	Mike Tyson/ Razor Ruddock Boxing		10	5	+20
☐	4/01	Mark Randall Kansas	NCAA	10	4	+15

☐	4/08	Grant Hill Duke	Duke NCAA Champs	20	10	+15
☐	4/15	Nolan Ryan Rangers	Baseball Issue	35	15	+25
☐	4/22	Ian Woosnam Golf	Masters	10	6	+10
☐	4/29	Evander Holyfield George Foreman Boxing		10	4	+15 each
☐	5/06	Bjorn Borg Tennis		10	4	+15
☐	5/13	Roger Clemens* Red Sox	[*Corner Nolan Ryan]	10	5	+35
☐	5/20	Michael Johnson Track		10	5	+15
☐	5/27	Mickey Mantle Roger Maris Yankees		20	10	+225(d)
☐	6/03	Michael Jordan Bulls	Stanley Cup	30	15	+75
☐	6/10	Magic Johnson/Michael Jordan Lakers/Bulls	NBA Finals	25	15	+70 each
☐	6/17	Michael Jordan Bulls	NBA Finals	30	15	+75
☐	6/24	Mike Tyson Boxing	[* Corner inset -Michael Jordan]	10	5	+20
☐	7/01	Orel Hershiser Dodgers		10	5	+15
☐	7/08	Lyle Alzado Football		5	2	+100(d)
☐	7/15	Steffi Graf Tennis		15	9	+25
☐	7/22	Fans World		2	1	
☐	7/29	Cal Ripken Jr (FSC) Orioles		35	12	+40
☐	8/05	Michael Jordan (Black Athlete)		30	10	+75
☐	8/12	Eric Dickerson Colts		5	2	+15
☐	8/19	John Daly Golf	[Corner inset George Bush]	20	7	+15
☐	8/26	David Klingler Houston	College Football Issue	5	3	+15
☐	9/02	Bruce Smith Bills	Pro Football Issue	7	4	+15
☐	9/09	Mike Powell Long Jump		7	4	+15
☐	9/16	Jimmy Connors Tennis	US open Tennis	7	4	+15
☐	9/23	Desmond Howard Michigan		7	2	+15
☐	9/30	Ramon Martinez Dodgers		7	4	+15
☐	10/07	Bobby Hebert Saints	Pro Hockey Issue	7	3	+15
☐	10/14	Gary Clark Redskins		7	3	+15
☐	10/21	Kirby Puckett (FC) Twins		20	8	+25
☐	10/28	Dan Gladden Gregg Olson Twins	World Series	10	5	+10 each

	DATE	COVER	FEATURE	Nr-Mt	Ex	+Auto
☐	11/04	Twins	World Series	10	3	
						+10 each
☐	11/11	Michael Jordan Phil Jackson/ Scotty Pippen Bulls	Pro Basketball Issue	35	15	+75/+20/+25
☐	11/18	Magic Johnson Lakers		12	6	+40
☐	11/25	Christian Laettner Duke	College Basketball Issue	5	2	+15
☐	12/02	Jim McMahon Eagles	100 yrs of Basketball	5	2	+15
☐	12/09	Desmond Howard Michigan		5	2	+15
☐	12/16	Buffalo Bills		4	3	+15
☐	12/23	Michael Jordan Bulls (SOY)	Sportsman of the Year	40	20	+125
☐	12/30	Pictures of 1991	(Discus Thrower)	10	4	
☐	FI/91	Red Grange	Classic SI	10	5	

1992

	DATE	COVER	FEATURE	Nr-Mt	Ex	+Auto
☐	1/13	Muhammad Ali Boxing	Bowl Games	6	3	+95
☐	1/20	Thurman Thomas Bills		8	3	+15
☐	1/27	AJ Kitt Skier	Olympics	4	2	+15
☐	2/03	Mark Rypien Redskins	Redskins Win Super Bowl XXVI	8	3	+15
☐	2/10	Patrick Ewing Chris Mullin Knicks/Warriors		5	2	+40/+20
☐	2/17	Mike Tyson Boxing	Olympics	4	2	+40
☐	2/24	Bonnie Blair Speedskating	Olympics	8	4	+15
☐	3/02	Kristi Yamaguchi Figure Skating	Olympics	35	15	+20
☐	3/09	Kathy Ireland Model	Swimsuit Issue	20	10	+20
☐	3/16	Ryne Sandberg Cubs		10	5	+25
☐	3/23	Larry Bird Celtics		8	4	+40
☐	3/30	Malcolm Mackey Georgia Tech	NCAA Basketball	4	2	+15
☐	4/06	Kirby Puckett Twins	Baseball Issue	20	6	+25
☐	4/13	Bobby Hurley Duke	Duke NCAA Basketball Champs	6	4	+15
☐	4/20	Fred Couples Masters	Masters	6	3	+15
☐	4/27	Deion Sanders Braves		12	4	+20
☐	5/04	Barry Bonds (FC) Pirates		12	6	+40
☐	5/11	Michael Jordan Clyde Drexler Bulls/Trailblazers		30	15	+70/+25
☐	5/18	Baseball Errors		4	2	
☐	5/25	Michael Jordan* Patrick Ewing Bulls/Knicks	[*also Gerald Wilkins (Knicks)] (also Scottie Pippen (Bulls))	35	15	+75/+40

	Date	Subject	Notes			
☐	6/01	Mark McGwire (FSC) A's		4	3	+15
☐	6/08	Mario Lemieux Penguins	Stanley Cup	25	10	+20
☐	6/15	Michael Jordan Bulls		30	12	+70
☐	6/22	Michael Jordan Bulls	NBA Finals	30	12	+70
☐	6/29	Tom Kite Golf		15	5	+15
☐	7/06	Steve Palermo Baseball Umpire		4	2	+10
☐	7/13	Andre Agassi Tennis		10	4	+20
☐	7/20	Jackie Joyner Kersee Track	Summer Olympic Preview	20	9	+25
☐	7/27	Joe Montana 49ers	Olympics	20	5	+35
☐	8/03	Nelson Diebel Swimmer	Olympics	4	2	+10
☐	8/10	Gail Devers Track	Olympics	8	5	+10
☐	8/17	Carl Lewis Dennis Mitchell Track	Olympics	8	4	+10 each
☐	8/24	Deion Sanders Braves/Falcons		12	5	+20
☐	8/31	Miami Football	College Football Issue	4	2	
☐	9/07	Jerry Rice 49ers	Pro Football Issue	20	5	+50
☐	9/14	Jim Harbaugh Bears		5	2	+10
☐	9/21	Stefan Edberg Tennis		5	2	+10
☐	9/28	Tony Mandarich Packers		4	2	+10
☐	10/05	George Brett Royals		20	5	+30
☐	10/12	Randall Cunningham Eagles	Pro Hockey Issue	8	4	+10
☐	10/19	Dave Winfield Walt Weiss Blue Jays/A's		10	5	+20/+10
☐	10/26	John Smoltz* Braves	[*also Roberto Alomar (Jays)/ Mike Reilly (Ump)] World Series, SI FIRST Sideways Cover	25	10	+20/+10 +20
☐	11/02	Blue Jays Team	Blue Jays Win Series	8	4	
☐	11/09	Charles Barkley Suns	Pro Basketball Issue	10	5	+25
☐	11/16	Everett/Norton Cowboys		10	5	+20 each
☐	11/23	Riddick Bowe Evander Holyfield Boxing	College Basketball Issue	4	2	+15/+20
☐	11/30	Shaquille O'Neal Magic		10	5	+50
☐	12/07	Campten/Blackmon Packers		5	2	+10
☐	12/14	Larry Bird Magic Johnson Celtics/Lakers		25	10	+40 each
☐	12/21	Arthur Ashe (SOY) Tennis		16	8	+200(d)
☐	12/28	Year In Pictures		12	6	
		Fall/92 Willie Mays Giants	(Classic SI)	25	10	+40

1993

DATE	COVER	FEATURE	Nr-Mt	Ex	+Auto
☐ 1/11	Jim Valvano	*Bowl Games*	8	4	
	Coach				+100(d)
☐ 1/11	Derric Lassic	*(Regional Issue-Alabama state)*	30	15	
	Alabama				+15
☐ 1/18	Steve Young (FC)		25	12	
	49ers				+40
☐ 1/25	Emmitt Smith (FC)		25	12	
	Cowboys				+50
☐ 2/01	Dr Z on Football (Eastern US)"Bad News Buffalo"			8	4
	(Western US)'Good News Dallas'		8	4	
☐ 2/08	Troy Aikman	*Cowboys Win Super Bowl XXVII*	10	5	
	Cowboys				+40
☐ 2/15	Arthur Ashe		6	3	
	Tennis		(Deaceased)		
☐ 2/22	Vendala	*Swimsuit Issue*	16	8	
	Swimsuit				+40 each
☐ 3/01	George Steinbrenner		6	3	
	Yankees				+15
☐ 3/08	Brian Reese		6	3	
	North Carolina				+10
☐ 3/15	Reggie White		8	4	
	Football				+15
☐ 3/22	Dwight Gooden		6	3	
	Mets				+15
☐ 3/29	Jason Kidd/ Bobby Hurley	*NCAA Basketball*	6	3	
	California/Duke BKB				+15 each
☐ 4/05	Larry Walker	*(FIRST CANADIAN ISSUE)*	60	30	
	Expos				+20
☐ 4/05	David Cone	*Baseball Issue*	6	3	
	Royals				+15
☐ 4/12	Eric Montross*	**Cover also shows George Lynch (UNC)/*	6	3	
	UNC Basketball	*Chris Webber/Juwan Howard (Michigan)*			+10
☐ 4/19	Mario Lemieux	*Masters*	20	5	
	Penquins				+25
☐ 4/26	Joe Montana		6	3	
	49ers				+40
☐ 5/03	Joe DiMaggio (FC)		16	8	
	Yankees				+180
☐ 5/10	Monica Seles		15	5	
	.Tennis				+25
☐ 5/10	Doug Gilmour	*(Canadian Issue)*	45	25	
	Mapleleaf				
☐ 5/17	Hakeem Olajuwon		6	4	
	Rockets				+40
☐ 5/24	Barry Bonds		6	4	
	Giants				+40
☐ 5/31	Patrick Ewing		6	3	
	Bill Cartwright				+40/+10
	Knicks/Bulls				
☐ 6/07	Michael Jordan		30	10	
	Bulls				+70
☐ 6/14	Mathieu Schneider	*Stanley Cup*	6	3	
	Tomas Sandstrom				+10 each
	Canadiens/Kings				
☐ 6/21	Michael Jordan		30	10	
	Charles Barkley				+70/+30
	Bulls/Suns				
☐ 6/21	Patrick Roy	*(Canadian Issue)*	50	25	
	Canadians				
☐ 6/28	Michael Jordan	*Bulls NBA Champs*	30	10	
	Scottie Pippen				+40/+30
	Bulls				
☐ 7/05	Mike Piazza (FC)		15	5	
	Dodgers				+25

	DATE	COVER	FEATURE	Nr-Mt	Ex	+Auto
☐	7/12	Laurie Crews/Patti Olin Indians' Wives		4	2	+15 each
☐	7/19	Bob Gibson Denny McLain Cardinals/Tigers		10	5	+15 each
☐	7/26	Greg Norman (FC) Golf	British Open	6	3	+15
☐	8/02	John Elway Dan Reeves Broncos		15	7	+40/+10
☐	8/09	Reggie Lewis Celtics		6	3	+100(d)
☐	8/16	Nike's Phil Knight		4	2	+10
☐	8/23	Mary Pierce Tennis		15	5	+10
☐	8/30	Scott Bentley Florida State Football	College Football Issue	4	2	+10
☐	9/06	Junior Seau Chargers	Pro Football Issue	8	5	+15
☐	9/13	Joe Montana Chiefs		15	5	+40
☐	9/20	Pernell Whitaker Julio Cesar Chavez Boxing		6	3	+20 each
☐	9/27	Ron Gant Braves		5	3	+15
☐	10/04	Boomer/Gunnar Esiason Jets		6	3	+15
☐	10/11	Chuck Cecil Cardinals Football	Hockey Preview	6	3	+10
☐	10/11	Kirk Muller/Doug Flutie Canadian	(Canadian issue)	50	25	+15 each
☐	10/18	Michael Jordan Bulls	Jordan Retires ("Why?")	30	10	+40
☐	10/25	Michael Irvin Cowboys	World Series	15	6	+40
☐	11/01	Joe Carter Blue Jays	Blue Jays Win World Series	12	5	+30
☐	11/08	Alonzo Mourning (FC) Bill Russell Hornets/Celtics	Pro Basketball Issue	8	4	+30/+200
☐	11/15	Evander Holyfield Boxing		8	4	+15
☐	11/22	Jim Flanigan Notre Dame Football		6	3	+10
☐	11/29	BC/Notre Dame FB	College Basketball Issue	6	3	
☐	12/06	Football Player		4	2	
☐	12/13	Damon Bailey Indiana Basketball		4	2	+15
☐	12/20	Don Shula (SOY) Dolphins		20	7	+30
☐	12/27	Uniforms	Year In Pictures	10	5	

1994

	DATE	COVER	FEATURE	Nr-Mt	Ex	+Auto
☐	1/10	Florida State	#1 Bowl Games	6	4	
☐	1/17	Nancy Kerrigan Ice Skating		10	5	+15
☐	1/24	Joe Montana Kansas City Chiefs		10	6	+40
☐	1/31	Emmitt Smith Cowboys		12	6	+45
☐	2/07	Emmitt Smith Cowboys	Superbowl	10	6	+45

	Date	Subject	Category			
☐	2/14	Kathy Ireland/Rachel Hunter/El Macpherson			25	12
		Swimsuit Issue				+40 each
☐	2/21	Tommy Moe	Olympics		6	4
		Skier				+10
☐	2/28	Dan Jansen/	Olympics		10	6
		Bonnie Blair				
		Skaters				+10 each
☐	3/07	David Robinson			10	5
		Spurs				+20
☐	3/14	Michael Jordan			30	12
		White Sox				+70
☐	3/21	Bill Clinton			10	4
		President				+100
☐	3/28	Boston College	Basketball Players		6	4
		Basketball				+10 each
☐	4/04	Ken Griffey Jr/	Baseball Issue		10	7
		Mike Piazza				+70/+30
		Mariners/Dodgers				
☐	4/04	Ken Griffey Jr	(Canadian Issue)		60	30
		Mariners				+50
☐	4/11	Corliss Williamson			6	4
		Arkansas	NCAA Finals			+10
☐	4/18	Mickey Mantle			14	7
		Yankees				+250(d)
☐	4/25	Dan Wilkinson			6	4
		Ohio State				+10
☐	5/02	Gary Payton			6	4
		Sonics				+20
☐	5/09	Tennis in Crisis			5	3
☐	5/09	Felix Potvin	(Canadian Issue)		60	25
		Toronto				
☐	5/16	Florida	State Football		6	4
☐	5/23	Atlanta vs Mets			6	4
☐	5/30	John Starks			6	4
		Knicks				+10
☐	6/06	Ken Griffey Jr			15	7
		Seattle				+35
☐	6/09	Joe Carter	(Canadian Issue)		75	35
		BlueJays				
☐	6/13	Mark Messier			10	5
		Rangers				+25
☐	6/21	Mike Richter/Pat Ewing			6	4
		Rangers/Knicks				+20
☐	6/20	Mike Richter	Regional Cover		30	15
		Rangers				+25
☐	6/27	OJ Simpson	Murder		6	4
						+100
☐	7/04	Ernie Stewart	US Soccer/NBA Finals		6	4
		US Soccer				+10
☐	7/04	Hakeem Olajuwon	(regional cover) NBA Finals		35	20
		Rockets				+35
☐	7/11	Pete Sampras	Wimbledon		8	5
		Tennis				+15
☐	7/18	Mike Mussina/Ben McDonald			6	4
		Orioles				+15 each
☐	7/25	Via Brazil	World Cup		6	3
		Soccer				+25
☐	8/01	Emmitt Smith			10	6
		Cowboys				+40
☐	8/08	Frank Thomas			10	6
		White Sox				+25
☐	8/16	Ed Mathews	40th Anniversary		10	6
		Braves				+20
☐	8/29	Wildcats	College Football Issue		10	5
		Arizona				+10 each

	DATE	COVER	FEATURE	Nr-Mt	Ex	+Auto
☐	9/05	Will Wolford		6	4	
		Colts				+10
☐	9/12	Dan Marino		20	10	
		Dolphins				+40
☐	9/19	Muhammad Ali, Jim Brown, Olga Korbut			20	10
		Hank Aaron, Billy Jean King, Larry Bird				
		Magic Johnson	(flap has 33 others)			+varies
		40 most Influencial People In Sports				
☐	9/26	Steve McNair		6	4	
		Alcorn State				+10
☐	10/03	Michael Westbrook		10	5	
		Colorado				+10
☐	10/10	Pernell Whitaker		6	4	
		Boxing				+15
☐	10/17	Natrone Means		10	6	
		Chargers				+10
☐	10/24	Freddie Scott		6	4	
		Penn State				+10
☐	10/31	Hisanobu Watanabe		6	4	
		Seibu - Japan				+35
☐	11/07	Charles Barkley	Basketball Issue	10	5	
		Horance Grant				
		Suns/Magic				+30/+10
☐	11/14	George Foreman/Michael Moore		6	4	
		Boxing				+30/+10
☐	11/21	Ricky Watters		7	5	
		49ers				+15
☐	11/28	Felipe Lopez		6	4	
		St Johns				+10
☐	12/07	Steelers/Raiders		6	4	
☐	12/12	Emmitt Smith/Others		6	4	
		Dallas				
☐	12/19	Bonnie Blair/Johann Koss - Sportsman		10	5	
		Ice Skating (SOY)				+15 each
☐	12/26	Jerry Rice		12	5	
		49ers				+40

1995

	DATE	COVER	FEATURE	Nr-Mt	Ex	+Auto
☐	1/09	Tom Osborne		12	6	
		Nebraska				+10
☐	1/16	Steve Young/Troy Aikman		10	6	
		40ers/Cowboys				+40 each
☐	1/23	Steve Young		12	6	
		49ers				+40
☐	1/30	Derric Coleman		6	3	
		Nets				+10
☐	2/06	Steve Young		12	6	
		49ers	NFL Champs			+40
☐	2/13	Penny Hardaway		12	6	
		Magic				+40
☐	2/20	Daniela Glisten	Swimsuit Issue	15	10	
		Swimsuit Issue				+40
☐	2/27	Darryl Strawberry/Dwight Gooden		6	3	
		Mets				+10/+10
☐	3/06	Jerry Stackhouse		6	3	
		NC				+10
☐	3/13	Andre Aggasi		7	4	
		Tennis				+20
☐	3/20	Michael Jordan		25	10	
		Bulls				+70
☐	3/27	Michael Jordan		25	10	
		Bulls				+70
☐	4/03	Arkansas Basketball		6	3	

☐	4/10	Ed O'Bannon UCLA	UCLA Champs	8	4
					+15
☐	4/10	Jennifer Rizzotti Univ. Of Conn.	(Connecticut Regional)	45	15
					+15
☐	4/17	Ben Crenshaw Golf	Masters	8	4
					+15
☐	4/24	Joe Montana Chiefs		10	5
					+40
☐	5/01	Cal Ripken Jr Orioles		10	6
					+40
☐	5/08	Vlade Divac Lakers		6	3
					+15
☐	5/15	Erickson, Moeller, Cox Coaches		6	3
					+10 each
☐	5/22	Michael Jordan/Shaq Bulls/Magic		20	10
					+70/+40
☐	5/29	Dennis Rodman Spurs		20	10
					+35
☐	6/05	Matt Williams Giants		8	4
					+20
☐	6/05	Sergei Fedorov Redwings	(Canadian Only)	45	25
					+20
☐	6/12	University of Miami		6	3
☐	6/19	Clyde Drexler Rockets		6	3
					+20
☐	6/26	Kevin Garnett High School		20	5
					+25
☐	7/03	Mike Tyson Boxing		6	3
					+40
☐	7/10	Hideo Nomo Dodgers		10	5
					+30
☐	7/17	Monica Seles Tennis		8	4
					+10
☐	7/24	Car Racing		6	3
☐	7/31	John Daily Golf		12	5
					+20
☐	8/07	Cal Ripken Jr Orioles		15	8
					+40
☐	8/14	Greg Maddux Braves		25	10
					+40
☐	8/14	Gene Stallings Alabama	(Southeast Region)	25	15
					+15
☐	8/21	Mickey Mantle	Yankees (Special Story)	15	7
☐	8/28	Keyshawn Johnson USC		6	3
					+10
☐	9/04	Dan Marino Dolphins		18	7
					+40
☐	9/11	Cal Ripken Jr Orioles		10	7
					+40
☐	9/18	Emmitt Smith Cowboys		10	7
					+40
☐	9/25	Danny Wuerfel Gators		6	4
					+10
☐	10/02	Mo Vaughn Red Sox		8	5
					+20
☐	10/09	Deion Sanders Cowboys		6	4
					+25
☐	10/09	Eric Lindros Flyers	(Canadian Only)	50	25
					+25
	FI/95		Bobby Layne (Lions) Sports History	6	4
☐	10/16	Ken Griffey Jr Mariners		10	5
					+35
☐	10/23	Michael Jordan/Dennis Rodman Bulls		20	10
					+70/+30

DATE	COVER	FEATURE	Nr-Mt	Ex	+Auto
☐ 10/30	Bo Jackson Raiders		8	5	+30
☐ 11/06	Greg Maddux & Team Braves	World Series Champs	12	5	+40
☐ 11/13	Northwestern		6	4	
☐ 11/20	Elvis 49ers		6	4	+15
☐ 11/27	Jacque Vaughn Kansas		6	4	+10
☐ 11/27	Mike Keenan Blues	(Canadian Issue)	50	25	+15
☐ 12/4	Mark Modell Browns - owner		6	3	
☐ 12/11	Pat Riley/Don Shula Heat/Dolphins		6	4	+20 each
☐ 12/19	Cal Ripken Jr Orioles	Sportsman	20	10	+40
☐ 12/25	Shaq Magic	(National)	35	10	+40
☐ 12/25	Steve Spurrier Florida	(South East Issue)	35	10	+10
☐ 12/25	Steve Tasker Bills	(Eastern Cover)	45	25	+10
☐ 12/25	Barry Sanders Lions	(Central Michigan Area)	45	25	+15
☐ 12/25	Tommy Frazier Nebraska	(Central Nebraska Area)	45	25	+15

1996

DATE	COVER	FEATURE	Nr-Mt	Ex	+Auto
☐ 1/08	Billy Payne Olympics	Playoff & Bowl	5	3	+10
☐ 1/15	Brett Favre (FC) Packers	Playoff, Wade Boggs	25	10	+35
☐ 1/22	Emmitt Smith Cowboys	Playoff, Mario Lemieux	10	5	+35
☐ 2/05	Emmitt Smith Cowboys	Superbowl	15	6	+40
☐ 2/12	Magic Johnson Lakers	Magic Johnson Returns	8	4	+40
☐ 2/19	Marcus Stroud Georgia Football		5	2	+10
☐ 2/21	Tyra Banks Model	Swimsuit annual	20	10	+25
☐ 2/26	Rick Pitino Kentucky		5	2	+20
☐ 3/04	Dennis Rodman Bulls		10	5	+20
☐ 3/11	Wayne Gretzky/Neil O'Donnell Blues/Steelers		7	2	+40/+10
☐ 3/18	Jay Buhner/Son Mariners		5	2	+10
☐ 3/25	#20 Texas Tech Texas Tech	Final 16 NCAA	5	2	+10
☐ 4/01	Manny Ramirez Indians	Baseball Issue	5	3	+10
☐ 4/08	Antoine Walker Kentucky	NCAA Finals	5	3	+10
☐ 4/15	Christy Martin Boxing	Female Boxer	5	2	+10
☐ 4/22	Greg Norman Golfer	Masters	7	3	+25
☐ 4/29	Dave Robinson Spurs	Bulls	5	3	+25

	Date	Subject	Note			
☐	5/06	Albert Belle Indians		5	3	+20
☐	5/13	Dan Marino/Jimmy Johnson Dolphins		7	3	+40/+10
☐	5/20	Marge Schott Reds	Shaq	5	3	+10
☐	5/27	Phil Jackson/Michael Jordan Bulls		20	10	+10/+70
☐	6/03	Michael Jordan Bulls	Playoffs	15	5	+70
☐	6/10	Gary Payton Sonics		5	3	+10
☐	6/17	Michael Jordan Bulls	NBA Playoffs/NHL Finals	8	4	+70
☐	6/17	Patrick Roy Avalanche	[Regional Cover] NHL Championship	25	15	+15
☐	6/24	Richie Parker Basketball Scandal		6	2	+10
☐	7/01	Emmitt Smith Cowboys		10	7	
☐	7/08	Alex Rodriquez (FC) Mariners		20	10	
☐	7/15	Drew Rosenhaus Agent		5	3	
☐	7/22	Sheryl Swoopes* Basketball US	Olympic Issue Katrina McClain, Ruthie Bolton, Lisa Leslie, Teressa Edwards, Coach Tark VanDerveer	10	5	+10 each
☐	7/29	Tom Dolan Swimmer	Olympics	5	3	+10
		Michael Johnson Track	OLYMPIC ISSUE	10	5	+$20
☐	8/05	Carl Lewis Track		10	5	+$15
☐	8/19	Al Simmons Athletics		5 (D)	3	
☐	8/26	Peyton Manning /Archie Manning	College Football Issue	20	10	
☐	9/02	Brett Farve* Packers/Chiefs	Pro Football Issue (*also Reggie White/Robert Brooks /Marcus Allen, Neil Smith, Steve Bono)	15	5	varies
☐	9/02	Marcus Allen* Chiefs/Packers	Regional Cover in KC (same as above but in reverse)	45	25	varies
☐	9/09	Dolpins #94/#99		5	3	
☐	9/16	Ahman Green Nebraska		5	3	+10
☐	9/23	Ron Powlus Notre Dame		5	3	+$10
☐	9/30	Muhammad Ali/Joe Frazier Boxing		5	3	+$95/+$30
☐	10/07					
☐	10/14	Roberto Alomar Orioles		7	4	+$20
☐	10/21	Derek Jeter Yankees		7	4	+$20
☐	11/4	Joe Girardi/John Wetteland Yankees		10	5	+$10 each
☐	11/11	Shaq/George Mikan/Kareem Lakers	NBA Preview	20	5	+$40/+$20/+$30
☐	11/18	Holyfield/Mike Tyson Boxing		5	3	+$20/+$40
☐	11/25	Ted Williams Red Sox		5	3	+$195
☐	12/02	Danny Fortson Cincinnati	College Basketball Issue	5	3	+$10
☐	12/09	Warrick Dunn Florida State		5	3	+$10

Date	Cover	Feature	Nr-Mt	Ex	+Auto
☐ 12/16	Brett Farve		10	5	
	Packers				+$25
☐ 12/20	Tiger Woods		20	10	
	Golf	Sportsman of the Year			+$100

1997

DATE	COVER	FEATURE	Nr-Mt	Ex	+Auto
☐ 1/08	John Elway		15	10	
	Broncos				+$45
☐ 1/13	Mark Brunell/Kerry Collins		10	5	
	Jaquars/Panthers				+$15 each
☐ 1/20					
☐ 1/27	Brett Farve/Mike Holmgren		10	5	
	Packers				+$25/+$10
☐ 2/03	Desmond Howard		10	5	
	Packers	Superbowl			+$10
☐ 2/10	Terrell Brandon		5	3	
	Cav's				
☐ 2/17	NFL Blueprint		4	2	
☐ 2/24	Derek Jeter/Alex Rodriquez		10	5	
	Yankees/Mariners				+15/+15
☐ w/97	Tyra Banks	Swimsuit Annual	7	4	
	Swimsuit				
		International Editions of Swimsuit Issue	25	15	
	Norway Edition		25	15	
	Argentina Edition		25	15	
	14 other different editions		25	15	
☐ 3/03	Sugar Ray Robinson		4	2	
	Boxer		(D)		
☐ 3/10	Michael Jordan*		10	5	
	Bulls Cartoon	(*also Barkely, Shaq, Grant Hill, Shawn Kemp, Pat Ewing)			+70/varies
☐ 3/17	Jamila Wideman/John Wideman		4	2	
	Stanford/writer				+$10
☐ 3/24					
☐ 3/31	Randy Johnson	Baseball Issue	5	3	
	Mariners				+$20
☐ 4/07	Miles Simon	NCAA Champs	5	3	
	Arizona				
☐ 4/14	Drugs		3	1	
☐ 4/21	Tiger Woods		5	3	
	Golf				
☐ 4/28	Jock Schools - Bulldog		3	1	
☐ 5/05	Jackie Robinson		4	2	
	Dodgers		(d)		
☐ 5/12	Karl Malone	(Ken Griffey Jr)	5	3	
	Jazz				
☐ 5/19	Steve Smith/Michael Jordan		10	5	
	Hawks/Bulls				+$10/+$70
☐ 5/26	Deion Sanders		5	3	
	Reds				
☐ 6/02	Detroit #18/Colorado#29		4	2	
☐ 6/09	Michael Jordan/Dennis Rodman		10	5	
	Bulls				+$70/+$20
☐ 6/16	Karl Malone/Dennis Rodman		5	3	
	Jazz/Bulls	(Barry Sanders)			
☐ 6/23	Michael Jordan		10	5	
	Bulls				+$70
☐ 6/30	Mike Tyson		5	3	
	Boxing				+$40
☐ 7/07	Mike Tyson/Evander Holyfield		5	3	
	Boxing				+$40/+$20
☐ 7/14	Pete Sampras		10	5	
	Tennis				+$35
☐ 7/21	Frank Gifford		10	5	
	Giants				+$25

☐ 7/28	Tony Gwynn		10	5
	Padres			+$20
☐ 8/04	Steve Young		10	5
	49ers			+$35
☐ 8/11	Pudge Rodriquez		5	3
	Texas			+$5
☐ 8/18				
☐ 8/25	Joe Jurevicius	(College Football Issue)	5	3
	Penn State			+$5
☐ 9/01	Kordell Stewart*	(Pro Football Issue)	5	3
	Packers	*also Steve McNair (Oilers), Mark Brunel (Lions),	Varies	
		Jeff Black (Bengals), Vinny Testaverde (Ravens)		
☐ 9/08	Steve Young		5	3
	49ers			+$35
☐ 9/15	Venus Williams		5	3
	Tennis			+$10
☐ 9/22	Peyton Manning		10	5
	Tennessee			+$15
☐ 9/29	Warrick Dunn		5	3
	Tampa Bay Bucs			+$10
☐ 10/06	Tiger Woods		10	5
	Golf			+$40
☐ 10/13				
☐ 10/20	Kevin Faulk		5	3
	LSU			+$10
☐ 10/27	Larry Bird		5	3
	Pacers			+$40
☐ 11/04	Edger Ranteria	(World Series)	5	3
	Marlins			+$10
☐ 11/10	Grant Hill	(Pro Basketball Issue)	5	3
	Pistons			+$20
☐ 11/17	Steve Wojciechowski*	(Col Basketball Issue)	5	3
	Duke	*Cameron Crazies		+$10
☐ 11/24	Jerome Bettis		5	3
	Steelers			+$15
☐ 12/01	Boston		5	2
	Ohio State Football			+$10
☐ 12/08	Basketball Players		5	3
☐ 12/15	Latrell Sprewell		3	1
	Warriors			+$10
☐ 12/22	Dean Smith		10	5
	NC	Sportsman of the Year		+$25
☐ 12/29	Evander Holyfield		5	3
	Boxing	Year in Review		+$25

SI PRESENTS/SPECIAL ISSUES

In addition to its regular issues, Sports Illustrated has published a number of special or commemorative issues over the years. The best-known special issues are the annuals that feature photos of the preceding sport year. There seems to be a misconception in the hobby that these issues are rare or especially valuable. As this price guide indicates, most "Year in Sports" and "Pictures" were released with the regular issues and go for slightly more than a regular issue. The most collectible of the special issues is the 1978 "25th Anniversary" magazine, which was distributed to advertisers and has a low circulation. Like the later "35th Anniversary" issue (also desirable, largely as a reference, among SI collectors), this issue is comprised largely of color images of covers and was sold on the newsstand.

Sports Illustrated did not begin to produce commemorative covers until 1989 when it started with a test issue "Sports Illustrated Presents the Superbowl" (Life magazine size) with the 1968 Superbowl cover of Vince Lombardi. A second test issue occurred in 1990 with a Life size magazine format with Joe Montana which covered 25 years of Super Bowls. However, it was in 1993 when they began using the 1993 Sports Illustrated Presents as an official commemorative issue. On January 11 of that year, after Alabama had won college football's National Championship SI ran a cover of NC State basketball coach Jim Valvano. This decision incensed Alabama fans, who communicated their ire in a barrage of letters and phone calls to Time, Inc. SI responded to the outcry with their first commemorative issue, which featured Crimson Tide star Derek Lassic on its cover. The commercial success of that effort prompted a series of commemorative issues, which SI continues to produce to this day. Rumor has it that Sports Illustrated had a commemorative issue ready to go to celebrate the New York Knicks' victory in the 1994 NBA Finals, but had to hold it back when Olajuwon and the Rockets snatched the title away from Ewing and the Knicks. SI Presents also handles special advertiser commemorative issues that are done with a specific advertiser (Kelloggs, etc). These issues are only obtained through the particular product promotion and not through Sports Illustrated. These are footnoted in the list below.

SPECIAL & PROMOTIONAL ISSUES

DATE	COVER	FEATURE	Nr-Mt	Ex	+Auto
☐ 1978	25TH ANN.	*Depicts SI Covers 54-78 ($75-100)			
☐	Distributed to Advertisers only.				
☐	Multiple covers of SI shown				
☐					

☐ 1977-1984 Hardbound version of the 'Year in Sports'and 'Sportsman of the Year' were also used as sales promotion tools. These books are worth two times the regular cover (approximately $30 each).

SPORTS ILLUSTRATED AUSTRALIA

In 1992, SI tried to make a go of it in Australia. Six issues were released all with Cricket and Rugby players. The issues were never released in the United States. I value the issues around 25 each. The magazine covered both local and international sports.

"YEAR IN SPORTS" SERIES

DATE	COVER	FEATURE	Nr-Mt	Ex	+Auto
☐ 1976	Year In Sports		15	10	
	NASTASE/ALEXEYEV/PAYTON.	*Cover shows M.Ali/D.Hamill/R.Jackson/			
☐ 1977	The Year in Sports		15	6	
☐ 1978	The Year in Sports		15	6	
		Cover shows Navratilova/Yarborough/Staubach/ Elvin Hayes/Passarella/Spinks/Affirmed/Lopez/ Lafleur.			
☐ 1979	The Year in Sports		15	6	
		**Cover shows Rose/McEnroe/Heiden/Maravich.			
☐ 1980	The Year in Sports		15	6	
☐ 1981	The Year in Sports		15	6	
		**Cover shows Bird/Erving/McEnroe/Borg/ Leonard/Valenzuela/Montana/Gretzky/Austin			
☐ 1982	The Year in Sports		15	7	
		*Cover shows Evert/Holmes/Dorsett/Yount Parish/Gretzky/Nicklaus/Connors/Walker/ Ricky Henderson/Billy Smith.			
☐ 1983	The Year in Sports		15	6	
		*Cover shows: Marino/NC State BKB/McEnroe/ Riggins/Moses/Holmes/Cosell/Tiegs/Carlton /Billy Smith/Watson/ Bowie/Andra Franklin/ Navratilova/Walker/Lewis/Carew/Rozier/Hagler/ Sunny's Halo/Cummings/Dickerson/Murphy/Abdul-Jabbar.			

The concept "The Year in Sports" shifted to "Pictures of." These issues were given at the end of the year instead of a month or two later in "The Year of Sports". In 1994 "The Year In Pictures" Life magazine format was introduced and is given out as a promotional subscription offer and therefore more scarce.

"PICTURES OF"

DATE	COVER	FEATURE	Nr-Mt	Ex	+Auto
☐ 1987	Michael Jordan	*Pictures '87*	20	10	
	Bulls				+75
☐ 1988	Florence Joyner	*Pictures '88*	20	10	
	Track				+20
☐ 1990	Stephone Paige	*Pictures '90*	15	7	
	Chiefs				+15
☐ 1991	Christian Schenk Pictures '91		10	5	
					+15
☐ 1992	Carl Lewis	*Pictures '92*	20	10	
	Track				+20
☐ 1993	Uniforms	*Pictures '93*	10	5	
☐ 1993	Troy Aikman	*Year In Pictures*	20	10	
	Cowboys	*(Life Magazine Size)*			+40
☐ 1994	Akeem Olajuwon	*Pictures '94*	25	5	
	Rockets				
☐ 1995	Jerry Rice	*Pictures of the Year*	20	6	
	49ers				+40
☐ 1995	Michael Jordan	*Year In Pictures*	25	15	
	Bulls	*(Life Magazine Size)*			+40
☐ 1996	Bret Favre	*The year In Pictures*			
	Packers	*NFL & College Football*			
☐ 1997	Michael Jordan	*Year in Pictures*	25	15	
	Bulls				

SPORTS ILLUSTRATED PRESENTS SERIES

Sports Illustrated Presents is a separate division within the Sports Illustrated family. The group develops the Football, Baseball, and Basketball Annuals as well as special commemorative issues for both sport championships and marketing promotionals. SI Present issues are not available through subscriptions and are sometimes only available in very local markets. The scarcity and demand for the issue influences the value of the magazine.

DATE	COVER	FEATURE	Nr-Mt	Ex	+Auto
☐ 1989	Vince Lombardi	*"Dr Z's Great Moments in*	35	25	
	Jerry Kramer	*Super Bowl History"*			+15
☐ 1990	Shaq O'Neal	*'NBA Hot Shot*	25	15	
	LSU	*Young Upcoming Players*			
☐ 1990	Joe Montana	*Super Bowl History*	35	25	
	49ers	*(Test Issue)*			+40
☐ 1990		*35 Years of Covers*	25	15	
	1954-1989				
	(Newstands Only)				
☐ 1991	Eric Heiden	*Golden Winter Olympic*	35	15	
		Moments'			
		(Kelloggs Premium)			
☐ F 91		*SI's 25 Unforgettable*	15	7	
		Moments			
☐ F 93		*Baseball Greatest Teams*	25	15	
		(Kelloggs Premium)			
☐ 1993	Gene Stallings	*Alabama Championship*	25	10	
	Alabama	*Commemorative Issue*			+20
☐ 1993	Derick Lassic	*Alabama Championship*	25	10	
	Alabama	*Regional Issue*			
☐ 1993	Ace Atkins	*Auburn Championship*	25	10	
	Auburn	*Commemorative Issue*			+15
☐ 1993	Michael Jordan Bulls NBA Champions				
	Phil Jackson	*Commemorative Issue*	20	10	
	Bulls	*'Three Peat'*			+25/+10
☐ 1993	Dean Smith	*North Carolina NCAA Champs*			
	UNC	*Commemorative Issue*	25	10	
					+15
☐ 1993	Michael Irvin	*Cowboys NFL Champs*	15	10	
	Cowboys	*Commemorative Issue*			+20
☐ 1994	Shaq*	*NBA Hot Shots*	25	15	
	Magic	*Gatorade Promotional*			
		*(*also Barkley, Pippen, Hardaway, Mourning)*			

	DATE	COVER	FEATURE	Nr-Mt	Ex	+Auto
☐	1994	Emmitt Smith Cowboys	Cowboys NFL Champs Commemorative Issue	15	7	+20
☐	1994	N.Richardson Arkansas	Arkansas NCAA Champs Commemorative Issue	25	10	+15
☐	1994	Mike Richter Rangers	Rangers NHL Champs Commemorative Issue	35	15	+20
☐	1995	Kathy Ireland Model	'Best of the Swimsuit Models'	40	20	+25

SI PRESENTS COMMEMORATIVE ISSUES

	DATE	COVER	FEATURE	Nr-Mt	Ex	+Auto
☐	1995	Penn State Commemorative Issue	NCAA Championship Issue	25	10	
☐	1994	Lawrence Phillips Nebraska	NCAA Championship Issue College Football Champs	25	10	+10
☐	1995	S.Young/J.Rice 49ers	49ers Commemorative Issue NFL Champs	25	10	+30
☐	1995	Cal Ripken Jr. Orioles	Breaks Lou Gehrig Record Commemorative Issue	25	15	+40
☐	1995		200 Moments to Remember Life Magazine Size Jim Beam Promotional	20	10	
☐	1995		NFL Classics (Ford) Ford Promotional	20	10	
☐	1995	Dave Justice Braves	World Series Issue Commemorative Issue	15	7	+15
☐	1995	Tyrus Edney UCLA	UCLA Championship Issue	25	10	+10
☐	1995	Olajuwon/Drexler Houston	NBA Champions	25	10	+25
☐	1995	Mickey Mantle Yankees	Mantle Remembered (hard-cover book) First book in series	25	10	
☐	1996	Tom Frazier Nebraska	Nebraska Commemorative Issue College Football Champs	25	10	+10
☐	1996	Emmitt Smith Cowboys	Cowboys Commemorative Issue NFL Champs	15	7	+40
☐	1996	Kentucky	Kentucky Commemorative Issue NCAA Basketball Champs	15	7	
☐	1996	Michael Jordan Bulls	Bulls NBA Champions	15	7	+70
☐	1996	Michael Johnson Track	Olympic Track Issue	10	5	+15
☐	1996	Torch Hologram	Olympic Issue Official Souvenir Program	10	5	
☐	1996	Yankees Yankees	World Series	20	10	
☐	1997	NASCAR	NASCAR racing special issue	15	5	
☐	1997	Eric Lindros Pittsburgh	Commemorative	25	15	+25
☐	1997	Miles Simon Arizona	NCAA Champions	25	15	+10
☐	1997	Brett Farve Packers	NFL Superbowl Champs	20	10	+25
☐	1997	Miami Florida	NCAA Football Champs	20	10	
☐	1997	El MacPherson	'Around the World with Swimsuit	15	5	

	Model	*Models'*	
		+20	
☐ 1997	Mickey Mantle	*SI Classic*	
25	15		
	Yankees		
☐ 1997	Tiger Woods	*SI Golf Plus*	
Special Preview Issue		*35*	
15			
	Golf	*This was*	
only released to Golf subscribers			
☐ 1997	Ted Williams	*Boston*	
sports Commemorative		*15*	
5			
	Red Sox		
☐ 1998	Jeff Gordon	*Nascar -*	
Winston Cup	15	*5*	
	NASCAR	*Racing Issue*	
		+15	
☐ 1998	Michael Jordan	*Chicago City*	
Commemorative Issue		*10*	
5			
	Bulls		
☐ 1998	Dean Smith	*Retirement*	
Commermorative		*20*	
10			
	NCAA		
		+20	

1995 SI PRESENTS
COLLEGE FOOTBALL ANNUAL ISSUE

COVER	Nr-Mt	Ex	+Auto
☐ Lawrence Phillips	20	10	
☐ Bobby Engram	30	15	
☐ Nebraska (National)			+10
☐ Penn State			+10
☐ Peyton Manning	30	15	
☐ Shawn Walters	30	15	
☐ Tennessee			+10
☐ USC			+10
☐ S.Davis/Bryan Bufgdorf	30	15	
☐ J. Brown/L. McElroy	30	15	
☐ Auburn/Alabama			+10
☐ Texas/Texas A&M			+10
☐ Wuerffel/Kanell/Collins	30	15	
☐ D.Huard/C. McLemore	30	15	
☐ Florida/Fl.St/Miami			+10
☐ Washington/Oregon			+10
☐ Ron Poulus	30	15	
☐ Pete Kendall	30	15	
☐ Notre Dame			+10
☐ Boston College			+10
☐ Tshimanga Biakabutuka	30	15	
☐ Brice Hunter	30	15	

☐ Michigan	....		+10
☐ Georgia	....		+10

1996 SI PRESENTS
COLLEGE FOOTBALL ANNUAL ISSUE

COVER		Nr-Mt	Ex	+Auto
☐ Almon Green		10	5	
☐ Ron Polulus		10	5	
☐ Nebraska (National)				+10
☐ Notre Dame				+10
☐ Jarrett Irons		10	5	
☐ Heines Ward		10	5	
☐ Michigan				+10
☐ Georgia				+10
☐ Todd Pollack		10	5	
☐ Donovan McNabb		10	5	
☐ Boston College				+10
☐ Syracuse				+10
☐ Mike Vrable		10	5	
☐ Clay Etmer		10	5	
☐ Ohio State				+10
☐ Colorado				+10
☐ Kevin Falk		10	5	
☐ Danny Weurffel		10	5	
☐ LSU				+10
☐ Florida				+10
☐ Payton Manning		15	5	
☐ James Brown		10	5	
☐ Tennessee				+20
☐ Texas				+10
☐ Dennis Riddle		10	5	
☐ Tony Graziana		10	5	
☐ Alabama				+10
☐ Oregon				+10
☐ Brad Ohon		10	5	
☐ W. Dunn/Ferguson			10	5
☐ USC				+10
☐ Florida State				+10 each

1995 SI PRESENTS PRO FOOTBALL ANNUAL ISSUE

COVER	Nr-Mt	Ex	+Auto
☐ Troy Aikman/Steve Young	7	3	
☐ Tim Brown	15	10	
☐ Cowboys/49ers (Nat)			+40ea
☐ Raiders			+20
☐ Drew Bledsoe	15	10	
☐ Bruce Smith	20	10	
☐ Patriots			+15
☐ Bills			+20
☐ Brett Farve	20	10	
☐ Kenny Collins	20	10	
☐ Packers			+15
☐ Carolina			+10
☐ Jerome Bettis	20	10	
☐ James Stewart	20	10	
☐ Rams			+15
☐ Jacksonville			+10
☐ Ricky Watters	15	10	
☐ Kevin Green	15	10	
☐ Eagles			+15
☐ Steelers			+10

1996 SI PRESENTS PRO FOOTBALL ANNUAL ISSUE

COVER	Nr-Mt	Ex	+Auto
☐ Troy Aikman	5	2	
☐ Cordell Stewart	10	5	
☐ Cowboys (National)			+40
☐ Steelers			+10
☐ Steve Young	10	5	
☐ Brian Cox	10	5	
☐ 49ers			+40
☐ Bears			+10
☐ Thurmon Thomas	10	5	
☐ John Elway	10	5	
☐ Bills			+10
☐ Broncos			+25
☐ Derrick Thomas	10	5	
☐ Jim Harbaugh	10	5	
☐ Chiefs			+20
☐ Colts			+10
☐ Dan Marino	15	5	
☐ Rodney Peete	10	5	
☐ Dolphins			+35
☐ Eagles			+10
☐ Neil O'Donnell	10	5	
☐ Barry Sanders	10	5	
☐ Jets			+10
☐ Lions			+10
☐ Brett Farve	15	5	
☐ Kerry Collins	10	5	
☐ Packers			+20
☐ Panthers			+10
☐ Drew Bledsoe	10	5	
☐ Vinny Testaverde	10	5	
☐ Patriots			+10
☐ Ravens			+10

1995 SI PRESENTS
COLLEGE BASKETBALL ANNUAL ISSUE

COVER	Nr-Mt	Ex	+Auto
☐ Tony Delk National Issue	15	10	
☐ University of Kentucky			+10
☐ Keyana Garris Illinois Aera	15	10	
☐ University of Il.			+10
☐ Ray Allen Connecticut Region	15	10	
☐ University of Ct.			+10
☐ Marice Taylor Michigan Area	15	10	
☐ Michigan			+10
☐ Marcus Camby Massachusetts	15	10	
☐ Univ. Of Mass			+25
☐ Don Te Calabria North Carolina	15	10	
☐ North Carolina			+10
☐ Marvin Organe Alabama Area	15	10	
☐ Univ. of Alabama			+10
☐ Allen Iverson Washington DC Area	15	10	
☐ Georgetown			+10
☐ Bryan Evans Indiana Region	15	10	
☐ Indiana University			+10
☐ Jacque VaughnKansas Region	15	10	
☐ Univ. Of Kansas			+10

1995 SI PRESENTS
PRO BASKETBALL ANNUAL ISSUE

COVER	Nr-Mt	Ex	+Auto
☐ Eric Montross (Boston Area)	25	10	
☐ Celtics			+10
☐ Michael Jordan (National Issue)	25	10	
☐ Bulls			+40
☐ Kendall Gill (Charlotte Area)	25	15	
☐ Heat			+15
☐ Grant Hill (Detroit Region)	25	15	
☐ Pistons			+25
☐ Hakeem Olajuwon (Texas Area)	25	15	
☐ Rockets			+30
☐ Reggie Miller (Indianapolis Area)	25	15	
☐ Pacers			+25
☐ Nick Van Exel (LA Region)	25	10	
☐ Lakers			+15
☐ Patrick Ewing (New York Area)	25	10	
☐ Knicks			+30
☐ Shaq O'Neal (Florida Area)	25	15	
☐ Magic			+40
☐ Chris Webber (Philadelphia Area)	25	15	
☐ Sixers			+20
☐ Damon Stoudamire (Toronto Area)	30	15	
☐ Raptors			+10
☐ Bryant Reeves (Vancouver Area)	25	15	
☐ Grizzlies			+10
☐ Juwan Howard (Washington D.C. Area)	2515		
☐ Bullets			+10

To get the National issue of the SI Annual you can contact Sports Illustrated at 1-800-528-5000.

1996 SI PRESENTS PRO BASEBALL ANNUAL ISSUE

COVER	Nr-Mt	Ex	+Auto
☐ Greg Maddux	10	5	
☐ Jack McDowell	10	5	
☐ Braves (National Issue)			+25
☐ Indians			+10
☐ Cal Ripken Jr.	10	5	
☐ Mo Vaugh	10	5	
☐ Orioles			+40
☐ Red Sox			+15
☐ Ryne Sandberg	10	5	
☐ Barry Larkin	10	5	
☐ Cubs			+20
☐ Reds			+10
☐ Dante Bichette	10	5	
☐ Gary Shepfield	10	5	
☐ Rockies			+10
☐ Marlins			+10
☐ Mike Piazza	10	5	
☐ Dennis Eckersley	10	5	
☐ Dodgers			+25
☐ Blue Jays			+15
☐ Dave Cone	10	5	
☐ Greg Jefferies	10	5	
☐ Yankees			+15
☐ Phillies			+15
☐ Ken Griffey Jr.	10	5	
☐ Mariners			+30

SPORTS ILLUSTRATED 1996 OLYMPIC DAILY

In 1996, Sports Illustrated became the official 1996 Atlanta games Olympic magazine. Over 16 daily issues were released which captured the daily games. This was a first for a daily magazine (not a newspaper).You can order the complete set through Sports Illustrated (1-800-274-5200). Approximately 250,000 were printed.

DATE	COVER	Nr-Mt
☐ July 19, 1996	The Olympic Torch	5
☐ July 20, 1996	The Olympic Stadium	5
☐ July 21, 1996	Toni Kukoc (Croatia) vs Lithuania #12	7
☐ July 22, 1996	Tom Dolan - US Swimmer wins Gold	5
☐ July 23, 1996	Naim Suleymanoglu - Weightlifting	5
☐ July 24, 1996	Dominique Dawes - US Gymanist Gold!	5
☐ July 25, 1996	Australia - Equestrian Champs	5
☐ July 26, 1996	Brooke Bennett - Swimming Champion!	5
☐ July 27, 1996	Randy Barnes - Shot Putter Champion!	5
☐ July 28, 1996	Donovan Bailey - 100 Champion	5
☐ July 29, 1996	Shannon MacMillian - US Soccer	5
☐ July 30, 1996	Carl Lewis - Long Jump Champion	5
☐ July 31, 1996	Fidel Castro & Primo Nebiolo - Cuba	5
☐ Aug. 1, 1996	Lisa Leslie - US Basketball	5
☐ Aug. 2, 1996	Michael Johnson - Track	5
☐ Aug. 3, 1996	Omar Linares - Cuba Baseball	5
☐ Aug. 4, 1996	John Stockton - USA Basketball	20
☐ Aug. 5, 1996	Woman Basketball Players - Win Gold	5

SPORTS ILLUSTRATED FOR KIDS

Sports Illustrated for Kids started in 1989 and is produced every month. The issues are unique in the Sports Illustrated family because of the cards, ads, features and posters that are in each issue. The SI for Kids is the last of the magazines that continue with a card insert tradition. Many of these cards are of the current great stars (Jordan, Ripken, Ryan, for example), however, they do have older stars (Ruth) as well. Just as important, the SI for Kids card set is now the most diverse and well represented card set ever developed. More sports and more athletes are represented in this series than any other card set ever issued. Many of these cards are sought after by player and sport collectors. Many times the price of the magazine is driven by a highly collectible card included inside.

However, the ads, features and posters should not be neglected. Some of the most unique ads only seem to appear in the SI for Kids magazine (then again, I don't read every kid magazine). The features ask players questions reporters normally don't seem interested to ask about, like the game and favorite food (innocent stuff).

The magazine is geared toward kids and will have a lack of adult collecting appeal, except for those who collect players on the cover, ads, articles, and cards. Yet, it is exactly that reason why these magazines may be great sleepers in the years to come. Many of these issues are already becoming popular in the hobby because collectors of favorite players never seem to be able to find enough of their favorite player's cover (or cards).

Many SI for Kids issues are cut up for the cards and therefore the number of mint issues left in the market will be continually shrinking. Currently SI for Kids has a circulation of 1.1 million issues a month. The autograph value is more subjective since very few of the issues have been traded after they have been signed.

SI for Kids has produced their own series of extras. A few books and magazines have appeared and are offered through SI for Kids. In 1995 SI released a special magazine called "Michael" on Michael Jordan, and a paperback called Emmitt Smith/Barry Sanders. Two magazines were released in 1996 called "Amazing Sports Photo's I" with Michael Jordan and "Amazing Sports Photo's II" with Barry Sanders. A third mailed packet focused on the Olympics called "The Kids' Guide to the 1996 Summer Olympics" with Carl Lewis, Scotty Pippen and others appearing on the cover, and two paperback books "Frank Thomas and Ken Griffey Jr" and "The Everything you want to know about Sports Encyclopedia" with Michael Jordan on the cover. There is also a list of SI For Kids for Parents. This add on magazine comes with subscriptions about two to three times a year.

The Price guide is similar to Sports Illustrated with the exception that every card and its number is listed (listed in italics). The SI for Kids did start the numbering cards twice (1989 & 1992). They also had Olympic cards issued in 1996. Ads, articles, and posters are not listed. Since this is a recent magazine, a collectible condition magazine is in mint or ex-mt condition.

SPORTS ILLUSTRATED FOR KIDS

1989

Date	Cover - Team /Cards	NrMt	Ex	+Auto
☐ 1/89	Michael Jordan - Bulls	40	30	+50

#1-9 Howie Long,Steffi Graf, Mario Lemieux,Isaiah Thomas, Orel Hershiser, Larry Bird, Florence Griffith Joyner, Tom Curren, Doug Williams

☐ 2/89	Wayne Gretzky - Oilers	40	30	+30

#10-18 Mark Jackson, Jose Canseco, Katrarina Witt, Dante Muse, Alberta Tomba, Joe Nieuwendyk, Michael Jordan, Herschel Walker, Jackie Joyner- Kersee

☐ 3/89	Spud Webb -Hawks	30	20	+10

#19-27 Wayne Gretzky, Darryl Strawberry, Janet Evans, Martina Navratlova, Dominique Wilkens,Maria Walliser, Steve Yzerman, Carl Lewis, Magic Johnson

☐ 4/89	Tony Gwynn - Padres	35	20	+15

#28-36 Sean Burke, Charles Barkley, Keba Phiipps, Tony Gwynn, Camille Duvall,Mike Greenwell,Mary Decker Slaney,Frank Viola, Alex English

☐ 5/89	Kenny Walker - Knicks	30	20	+10

37-45 Mike King, Louise Ritter, Don Mattingly, Kareem Abdul-Jabbar, Mario Andretti, Zina Garrison, Nancy Lopez, Akeem Olajuwon, Ozzie Smith

☐ 6/89	Janet Evans - Swimmer	25	20	+10

#46-54 Chris Sabo, Andre Agassi, Rickey Henderson, Evelyn Ashford, Curtis Strange,Connie Young, Lyn St. James, Roger Kingdom, Andrew Dawson

☐ 7/89	Jessee Roach - Skateboarder	20	10	-

#55-63 Kirsten Hanssen, Alan Trammell, Kristin Otto, Roger Clemens, Jerry Rice, Ricky Davis, Andres Galarraga, Gabriela Abatini, Butch Reynolds

☐ 8/89	Little League	35	20	-

#64-72 Kim Gallagher, Al Toon, John Franco, Cal Ripken Jr, Ivan Lendl, Mike McGill, Patty Sheehan, Karch Kiraly, Will Clark

☐ 9/89	Boomer Essiason - Bengels	20	10	+10

#73-81 Frida Zamba, Inerid Kristiansen, Bo Jackson, Boomer Esiason, Patrick Ewing, Mike Singletary, Brandy Johnson, Tab Ramos, Nolan Ryan

☐ 10/89 Hershal Walker - Vikings 25   15   +15
82-90 Al Macinnis, Sandra Farmer-Patrick, Dan Marino, Mike Stewart, Eric Dickerson, Said Aouita, Chris Evert, Karl Malone, Mike Schmidt

☐ 11/89 Karl Malone - Utah Jazz 25   15   +20
#91-99 Chris Mullin, Kristi Yamaguchi,Joe Dumars, Pat LaFontaine, Greg Lemond,Reggie Roby, Ruth Lawanson, Bobby Hebert, Rbidgette Gordon

☐ 12/89 Magic Johnson - Lakers 30   20   +40
#100-108 Tamara McKinney, Nancy Liberman-Cline, Mark Messier,Mike Rozier John Stockton, John Elway, HugoPerez, Michael Cooper, Lynnette Love

1990

Date	Cover - Team /Cards	NrMt	Ex	+Auto
☐ 1/90	Buzz to the Future	15	10	-

#109- 117 Christy Henrich, Randall Cunningham, Midori Ito, Jon Lugbill, James Worthy, Kevin Mitchell, Jack Sikma, Brian Leetch, Lori McNeil

☐ 2/90   Snowboarding 15   10   -
#118-126 Preki, Sandra Hodge, Denis Savard, Brad Daugherty, Paula Ivan, Ryne Sandberg, Kale Hawerchuk, Wendy Bruce, Dale Ellis

☐ 3/90   Jackie Joyner Kersee - Track 20   10   +15
127-135 Robin Yount, Kent Desormeaux, Bill Laimbeer, Aranhxa, Sanchez Vicario, David Robinson, Diane Dixon, Dave Stewart, Ray Bourque, Jeannie Loneo

☐ 4/90   Dave Stewart - A's 15   10   +10
#136-144 Cathy Hearn, Moses Malone, Vicki Huber, Charla Hartness, Eric Davis, JR Reid, Mike Scott, Grant Fuhr, Paul Caligiuri

☐ 5/90   Ed and Tony George - kid car racers. 10   5   +10
#145-153 Merlene Ottey, Mark McGwire, Reggie Miller, Rex Chapman, Boris Becker, Wendy Williams, Sheryl Johnson, Tony Hawk, Dwight Gooden,

☐ 6/90   Paul Caligiuri - Soccer 10   5   +10
#154-162 Monica Seles, Steve Ballesteros, Rosa Mota, Tony Meola, Ken Griffey Jr.,Mike Barrowman, George Brett, Michelle Gilman, Scottie Pippen

☐ 7/90   Eric Davis - Reds 15   10   +10
#163-171 Ruben Sierra, Jennifer Azzi, Diego Maradona, Joe Montana, Kirby Puckett, Inga Thompson, Carlton Fisk, Jolanda Jones, Robby Naish

☐ 8/90   Martina Navratilova - Tennis 10   5   +15
#172-180 John Tomac, Joetta Clark, Fred McGriff, Lynn Jennings, Wade Boggs, Michael Chang, Bobby Humphrey, Kris Karlson, Tim Raines

☐ 9/90   Dan Marino - Miami Dolphins........... 30   20   + 40
#181-189 Shannon Higgin, Jack Nicklaus, Bobby Bonnilla, Jimmy Connors, Ronnie Lott, Sinjin Smith, Kelly Gruber, Ana Quirot, Danny Sullivan also Jackie Joyner Kersee McDonalds Cards

☐ 10/90 Dave Robinson - San Antonio Spurs 20   10   + 20
#190-198 Dennis Rodman, Tatu, Pam Shriver, Paula Newby Fraser, Bernie Kosar, Brett Hull, Bo Jackson, Dennis Eckersley, Lori Johns, Michael Jordan McDonalds cards

☐ 11/90 D'Shaun Crockett - football player kid 10   5   +5
#199-207 Kim Zmeskal, Terry Cummings, Lynettte Woodard, Kevin Johnson, Patti Sue Plumer, Barry Sanders,Randy Barnes, Willie Anderson, Cecil Fielder

☐ 12/90 Kevin Johnson - Phoenix Suns......... 20   10   + 10
#208-216 Billie Jean King, Jesse Owens, Wilt Chamberlain, Pele, Jackie Robinson, Babe Didrikson, Babe Ruth, Wilma Rudolph, Gordie Howe: Michael Jordan McDonalds

1991

Date	Cover - Team /Cards	NrMt	Ex	+Auto
☐ 1/91	Bobsledder kids B. Shimer, K. Beach	10	5	-
☐ 2/91	Charlie Barkley - Sixers	15	10	+ 20

#226-234 Bernie Nicholls, Lori Norwood, Ricky Pierce, Suzy Favor, Bernard King, Barry Bonds, KarlMecklenburg, Jill Trenary, Warren Moon

☐ 3/91   Monica Seles - Tennis 10   5   + 15
#235-243 Rochelle Stevens, Christian Hosoi, Kevin McHale, Jose Rijo, Charles Smith, Chris Chelios, Jennifer Capriati, John Smith, Donna Weinbrecht

☐ 4/91   Cecil Fielder - Tigers 15   10   + 15
#244-252 Vlade Divac, Maureen Mendoza, Rolando Blackman, Beth Daniel, Sandy Alomar, Erin Baker, Joe Mullen, Ron Gant, Mike Liut

☐ 5/91   Robert Parrish - Celtics 15   10   + 10
#253-261 Kevin Duckworth, Steve Larmer, Michael Johnson, Mary Joe Fernandez, Al Unser Jr, April Heinrichs, Bob Welch, Angela Cochran, Dave Justice

☐ 6/91   Kids of Famous Fathers 10   5   -
#262-270 Desmond Armstrong, Alvin Robertson, Michelle Finn, Bunki Davis, Doug Drabek, Todd Holland, Leroy Burrell, Deena Mapple, Rafael Palmeiro

☐ 7/91   BMX Champs Gary and
          Rich Houseman 10   5   -
#271-279 Sergei Bubka, Kim Jones, Paul Molitor, Ned Overend, Bobby Thigpen, Daedra Charles, Edgar Martinez, Summer Sanders, OJ Anderson

☐ 8/91   Darryl Strawberry - Dodgers............. 15   10   +5
#280-288 Dave Winfield, Sonja Henning, Terry Schroeder, Betsy King, Thurmon Thomas, Mark Grace, Dwight Evans, Anne Marden, Mark Allen

☐ 9/91   Nolan Ryan - Rangers...................... 30   20   + 25
#289-297 Dave Henderson, Rick Mears, Derrick Thomas, Carev Kemnex, Victor Nogueira, Lee Smith, Emmitt Smith, Shannon Miller, Jennifer Leachman

☐ 10/91 Barry Sanders - Lions...................... 20   10   + 20
#298-306 Paul Coffey, Michelle Stahl, Art Monk, Ramon Martinez, Tim Hardaway, Sanna Neilson, Mark Carrier, Lance Ringnald, Gwen Torrence

☐ 11/91 Chris Mullin/Manute Bol -
          Warriors 20   10   +5ea
#307-315 Hersey Hawkins, Gail Roberts, Chuck Person, Karolyn Kirby, Keith Jackson, Venus Lacy, Morten Andersen, Javier Gaspar, Mark Gonzales

☐ 12/91 Reggie White - Eagles...................... 20   10   + 15
#316-324 Wyomia Tyus, Bobby Orr, Joe Louis, Ty Cobb, Jim Thorpe, Althea Gibson, Sonja Henie, Bill Russell, Red Grange

1992

Date	Cover - Team /Cards	NrMt	Ex	+Auto
☐ 1/92	Bo Jackson - WhiteSox/Raiders........	20	10	+ 15

#1-9 Jim Kelly, Monica Seles, Mike Powell, Bonnie Blair, Christian Okoye, Michael Jordan, Tom Barrasso, Dee Brown, Kerri Strug

☐ 2/92   Mogul Skiing star Donna Weinbrecht 10   5   +5
#10-18 Matti Nykanen, Eric Heiden, Mike Eruzione, Toni Sailer,

Paul Hildgartner, Scott Hamilton, Dorthy Hamill, Wolfgang Hoppe, Hannie Wenzel

☐ 3/92   Isaiah Thomas - Pistons 20   10   + 20
#19-27 Pam Burridge, Brian Bellows, Dominique Wilkins, Terry Pendleton, Mark Rypien, Meg Mallon, Roswitha Raudaschl, Fernando Clavijo, Derrick Coleman

☐ 4/92   Sandy Alomar Jr./Roberto Almor...... 20   10+10ea
#28-36 Greg Barton, Kirby Puckett, Francie Larrieu Smith, Mitch Richmond, Martina Navratilova,Ed Belfour, Angela Rock, David Robinson, Roger Clemens

☐ 5/92   Michael Jordan - Bulls 30   20   + 40
#37-45 Jim Courier, Pat Bradley,Robert Parish, Mark Messier, D. Mutombo, Tom Glavine, Frank Thomas, J. Eickhoff, Liz McColgan

☐ 6/92   Cal Ripken Jr - Orioles 25   20   +30
#46-54 D. Waltrip, J. Driscoll, Shawn Kemp, N. Morceli, Jim Abbott, W. Botha, Roberto Alomar, C. Guidry, John Daly

☐ 7/92   Janet Evans & Matt Biondi - Divers .. 10   5+10 ea
#55-63 Al Oerter, T. Stevenson, D. Fraser, N.Comaneci, G.Louganis, A. Bilkila, M. Spitz, F. Koen, V. Alexeyev

☐ 8/92   Kirby Puckett - Twins 25   15   + 20
☐ #64-72 Richard Petty, Anita Nall, Matt Williams, Deion Sanders, Bobby Bonilla, Dawn Staley, Chuck Finley, Mia Hamm, Fred Couples

☐ 9/92   Michelle Akers - Stahl - Soccer Player 10   5   + 5
☐ #73-81 Danny Tartabull, Troy Aikman, T. Larsen, B Murray, J Krone, Marcus Allen, Jack Morris, S.Edberg, K. Smyers

☐ 10/92 Warren Moon - Oilers 20   10   + 10
☐ #82-90 K. Steffes, C. Burnsside, L. Russell, C. Jennings, Will Clark, Larry Johnson, Tom Kite, Anthony Carter, Karen Neville

☐ 11/92 Patrick Ewing - Knicks 20   10   + 20
#91-108 Patrick Roy, Michael Adams, Gao Min, Lori Endicott, Q.Watts, Haywood Jeffires, Bruce Smith, K.Yamaguchi, Detlef Schrempf

☐ 12/92 Jerry Rice - 49ers 30   15   + 25
#109-#117 Sugar Ray Robinson, R. Laver, W White, Olga Korbut, Julius Erving, R. Bannister, L. Gehrig, M. Wright, J. Brown

1993

Date	Cover - Team /Cards	NrMt	Ex	+Auto

☐ 1/93 Buzz Beamer - Maniac Sports........... 20   10   -
#118-126 M.Washington, E. Mataya, D. Petrovic, N. Mansell, Dan Marino, H. Boulmerka, J. Jagr, K Sprague, A. Munoz

☐ 2/93 Clyde Drexler - Trailblazers............... 20   10   + 15
#127-135 S. Billmeier, Steve Young, N. Kerrigan, A. Rison, Karl Malone, J. Gonzalez, M.Maleeva, M. Lemieux, Horace Grant

☐ 3/93   Kevin Johnson, Tony Gwynn,
         Troy Aikman 20   10Varies
#136-#144 D. Mochrie, Pete Sampras, C. Mullin, Cal Ripken Jr., Shaquille O'Neal, D. Steirotter, Eric Lindros, K. Lende, Rod Woodson

☐ 4/93   Ken Griffey Jr. - Seattle..................... 20   10 + 20
#145-153 Junior Seau, Maria Mutola, Jack McDowell, K. Oden, Charles Barkley, J. Furtado, Marquis, Grissom, M. Balboa, N.Diebel

☐ 5/93   Scottie Pippen - Bulls 20   10   + 15
#154-162 Spud Webb, J. Thompson, Andy Van Slyke, L. Fernandez, K Young, Andre Agassi,Wayne Gretzky, Dennis Eckersley, Tish Johnson

☐ 6/93   Karl Malone - Jazz 20   10   + 15

#163-171 Dana Chladek, Cliff Robinson, A. Mogilny, S.Scott, Steffi Graf, Barry Bonds, Greg Maddux, Matt Hoffman, Amy Alcott

☐ 7/93   Frank Thomas -White Sox 20   10   + 15
#172-180 M. Indurain, Val Whitting, B. Becker, Nolan Ryan, L. Maskayan, Patrick Ewing, Dan O'Brien, Dave Winfield, J. Cooper

☐ 8/93   Barry Bonds - Giants 20   10   +20
#181-189 R. Erbesfield, Ken Griffey Jr., O. Markova, A. Medvedev, D. Dawes, K. Slater, S. Sharpe, Nick Faldo, Wade Boggs

☐ 9/93   Girls in Sports................................... 10   5   -
#190-198 N. Lowery, S. Webber, R. Scarpa, T. Dees, Kirk Gibson, S. Swoopes, M. Gould, Randal Cunningham, Albert Belle

☐ 10/93 John Elway - Broncos 20   10 + 15
#199-207 C. Kennedy, Manon Rheaume, John Burkett, K. Grissom, Barry Foster, C. Laettner, John Harkes, Holli Hyche, John Kruk

☐ 11/93 Steve Young - 49ers 20   10   + 15
#208-216 J. Parisien, T. Selanne, Randy Johnson, Lou Whitaker, Brett Favre, Barbara Marois, Tony Meola, Lisa Ondieki, Clye Simmons

☐ 12/93 Mario Lemieux - Pittsburgh.............. 20   10 + 15
#217-225 Johnny Unitas, M.Ali, Helen Wills, Oscar Robertson, Yogi Berra, Bobby Hull, K. Whitworth, Jim Ryun, K. Ender

1994

Date	Cover - Team /Cards	NrMt	Ex	+Auto

☐ 2/94   Oksana Baiul - Ice Skater 10   5   + 5
#226 -234 Katarina Witt, Gustav Weder, Donna Wenbrecht, Cathy Turner, T. Nieminen, Tovill & Dean, A. Tomba, Bonnie Blair, V. Ulvang

☐ 3/94   Bryce Joradan - Snow Boarding 10   5   -
#235-243 W. Wnia, L. Dykstra, T. Dooley, P. Simms, Breinalda,Hakeem Olajuwon, R. Twigg, Dennis Rodman, U. Robitaille

☐ 4/94   Juan Gonzalez - Rangers 10   5   -
#244 -252 Mike Gartner, J. Rodriguez, Caros Baerga, Alonzo Mourning, Tim Brown, M. Jones, H. McPeak, James Briggs, John Starks

☐ 5/94   Charles Barkley - Suns...................... 10   5   +20
#253 - 261 Joe Amato, Joe Carter, L. Butler, T. Martin, K. Quance, Emmitt Smith, L. Hill, Chris Webber, Sergei Fedorov

☐ 6/94   Cobi Jones & Alexi Lalas - Soccer 10   5   + 7
☐ #262-270 Danny Manning, Ricky Watters, Derek Ho, S. Gunnell, Chuck Carr, Cam Neely, Michael Jordan, L. Leslie, J. Croteau

☐ 7/94   Pets Pals... 10   5   -
#271-279 L. French, J. Bettis, Greg Norman, L. Armstrong, Gwen Torrence, Andres Galarraga, Anfernee Hardaway, Jeff Bagwell, Janet Evans

☐ 8/94   Deion Sanders - Reds 10   5   +15
#280-288 Brandi Hunt, John Olerud, K. Lilly, B. Kempainen, Mike Richter, Reggie White, Tony Gwynn, M. Clark, Mark Price

☐ 9/94   Jim Abbott - Yankees........................ 10   5   +10
#289-297 Drew Bledsoe, M. Giove, L. Davies, B. Miller, S. Bruguera, G. Jefferies, Mo Vaughn, John Taylor, L. Sprewell

☐ 10/94 Emmitt Smith,Troy Aikman -
         Dallas Cowboys 10   5+30ea
#298-306 U. Pippig, Dikembe Mutombo, M. Alou, Pavel Bure, Joe Montana, C. Martinez, T. Zorn, J. Key, R. Turnbull

☐ 11/94 Junior Seau - Chargers..................... 10   5 + 10
#307-315 D. Gilmour, BJ Armstrong, J. Golay, Amy Feng, M.Mussina, Eric Metcalf, S. Joyner, A.Marsh, Mike Piazza

☐ 12/94 Shawn Kemp - Sonics 10   5   + 10
#316 -324 M. Connolly, Phil Esposito, Ann Meyers, Walter Payton, Stan Musial, Bobby Jones, S. Gould, Rafer Johnson, Bill Bradley

1995

Date	Cover - Team /Cards	NrMt	Ex	+Auto

☐ 1/95 Jennie Thompson & Dominique Moceanu - Gymnasts 10   5   + 5
#325-333 Matt Williams, G. Tamega, Kim Batten, H. Alfredsson, Mugsy Bougues, T. Dolan, J.Roenick, J. Foudy, Mel Gray

☐ 2/95 Greed!! 5   3   -
#334-342 Reggie Miller, B. Lancer, G. Bodine, C. Hearn, J. Vanbiesbrouck, D. Meggett, N. Price, Shaquille O'Neal, Liz Mcintyre

☐ 3/95 Shaq - Magic 5   3   +20
#343-351 Karl Malone, Steffi Graf, Frank Thomas, Janet Evans, Mike Messier, Scottie Pippen, Dan Marino, Joyner Kersee, Michael Jordan

☐ 4/95 Grant Hill - Pistons 5   3   +20
#352-360 Mary Price, David Robinson, R. Wegerle, Barry Sanders, Felix Potvin, T.Loroupe, H. Lindh, Kenny Lofton, Pat Smith

☐ 5/95 Ken Griffey Jr. - Mariners 5   3   +20
#361-369 R. Lobo, R. Mondesi, Grant Hill, S. Stevens, T. Hughes, N. Means, S. Persons, J. Mashburn, M. Smith

☐ 6/95 Mike Piazza - Dodgers 5   3   +10
#370-378 Ben Coates, Lisa Andersen, Larry Johnson, T. Roberts, Michael Jordan, L. Davenport, John Stockton, P. Kariya, Colin Jackson

☐ 7/95 Buzz Beamer 5   3   -
#379-387 David Cone, S. Bonaly, Dana Barros, M. Faulk, Gary Payton, Jim Carey, C.Teuscher, Brady Anderson, Cindy Blodgett
☐ Olympic Cards #1-4: Tommy Kno, Tracy Caulkins, Jesse Owens, Ulrike Meyfarth

☐ 8/95 Cal Ripken Jr - Orioles........................ 5 3+ 25
#388-396 Tisha Nenturini, Cosmas Ndeti, Eric Karros, Paul O'Neill, Bruce Baumgartner, Nicole Bobek, Bev Odenn, Jason Kidd, Chris Carter
Olympic Cards #5-8 Lis Hartel, Mark Spitz, Abebe Bikila, Mary Lou Retton

☐ 9/95 Emmitt Smith - Cowboys 5   3   +30
#397-405 Eric Lindros, Eddie Murray, M. Moses, Barry Larkin, T. Muster, S. Slone, Picabo Street, Horace Grant, K. Greene, Olympic cards #9-12 Wilma Rudolph, Matt Biondi, Vera Caslavska, Rafer Johnson

☐ 10/95 Dan Marino - Dolphins....................... 7   4   +20
#406-414 M.Stewart, Edgar Martinez,Nikki McCray, Clyde Drexler,J. Benedict, Rodney Hampton, J Facett, M.Brodeur, Mark McGwire

☐ 11/95 Shaq - Magic 5   3   +20
#415-423 Vin Baker, Albert Belle, Jerry Rice, P. Coffey, Shaq O'Neal, Grant Hill, V. Williams, Chris Webbe
Olympic Card 13-16 Babe Didrikson Zaharias, Karoly Takacs, Olga Korbut, Billy Mills

☐ 12/95 Penny Hardaway - Magic 5   3   +20
#424-432 B. Bennett, P. Forsberg, N. Exel, J. Seau, Glen Robinson, D. Moceani, K. Bye, Steve Young, Mark Grace
Olympic Cards #17-20 Fanny Blankers-Koen, Dawn Fraser, Paavo Nurmi, Jeff Blatnick

1996

Date	Cover - Team /Cards	NrMt	Ex	+Auto

☐ 1/96 Hakeem Ojajowon - Rockets 5   3   +20
#433-441 Peter. Bondra, Meredith Rainey, Chuck Knolauch, Trica Saunders, John Elway, John Roethlisberger, Terance Mathis, Glen Rice, Dot Richardson
Olympic Cards #21-24 Shun Fujimoto, Patricia McCormick, Jim Thorpe, Mary Meagher

☐ 2/96 Gheorghe Muresan - Washington Bullets........................... 5   3   +10
#442-450 Katrina McClain, Cammy Potter, Dominik Hasek, Chipper Jones, Alexi Lalas, Deion Sanders, Brett Favre, Alonzo Mourning, Nancy Reno
Olympic Cards #25-28 Nadia Comaneci, Edwin Moses, Naim Suleymanoglu, Wyomia Tyus

☐ 3/96 Michael Jordan - Bulls 15   5   +40
#451-459 Mario Lemieux, Teresa Edwards, Tom Glavine, Mia Hamm, Cal Ripken, Jr., Barry Sanders, Troy Aikman, David Robinson, Gabriela Sabatini

☐ 4/96 Ken Griffey Jr. - Seattle Mariners....... 5   3   +40
#460-468 Jeff Conine, Mahmoud Abdul-Rauf, Amy Van Dyken, Brendan Shanahan, Kristin Folk, Jonathan Edwards, Rik Smits, Kordell Stewart, Annika Sorenstam
Olympic Cards #29-32 Cassius Clay, Gabriela Andersen, Alice Coachman, Pablo Morales

☐ 5/96 Shaquille O'Neal - Magic.................. 5   3   +40
#469-477 Michelle Kawn, Hideo Nomo, Juwan Howard, Steve Yzerman, Magic Johnson, Monica Seles, Jenny Spangler, Jim Harbaugh, Bernie Williams
Olympic Cards #33-36 Al Oerter, Gao Min, Carl Lewis, Lyudmila Tourischeva

☐ 6/96 Kenny Lofton - Cleveland Indinas 5   3   +20
#478-486Dale Jarrett, Jeannie Longo, Craig Biggio, Darrell Green, Dennis Rodman, Karrie Webb, Loretta Claiborne, Jose Mesa, Clifford Robinson
Olympic Cards 37-40 Shane Gould, Teofilo Stevenson, Dan Gable, Joan Benoit

☐ 7/96 Gail Devers and Grant Hill - Olmpics.. 5   3+15ea
#487-495Oscar robertson, Daley Thompson, Irena Szewinska, Steffi Graf, Sammy Lee, Oscar De La Hoya

☐ 8/96 Deon Sanders/Mo Vaughn/ Rebecca Lobo 5   3+15ea
#496-504Stephanie Petterson, Roberto Alomar, Ronne Irvine, Herman Moore, Jennifer Calleri, Joe Sakic, Jennifer Rizzotti, John Smoltz, Danny Wuerffel, (SI legends) #45-48 Sadaharu Oh, Larry Bird, Florence Joyner, Joe Montana.....

☐ 9/96 Kordell Stewart - Pittsburgh Steelers.. 5   3   +15
#505-513Kelly Amonte, Tasha Hodgson, Henry Rodriquez, Bryce Paup, Mia Axon, Pete Sampras, Rey Ordonez, Preki, Ricky Watters (legends 49-52) Bobby Clarke, Marina Navratilova, Pete Maravich, Willie Mays

☐ 10/96 Cris Carter - Vikings.......................... 5   3   +10
#514-522 Ellis Burks, Cara Dunne, Shawn Kemp, Oksana Baiul, Ivan Rodriquez, Willie Roaf, Gheorge Muresan, Jeff George, Cindy Parlow

☐ 11/96 Juwan Howard - Bullets..................... 5   3   +10
#523-531 Jaromiar Jaga, Kerri Strug, Arvydas Sabonis, Donovan Bailey, Cammi Granato, Neil O'Donnell, Darren Bennett,Troop Johnson, Amy Van Dyken (special #53-56) Jack Kemp, Bob Dole, Al Gore, Bill Clinton

☐ 12/96 Larry Johnson - Knicks 45   40   +20
#532-540 Lisa Leslie, Jerry Stackhouse, Curtis Martin, Michael Finley, Tiger Woods, Martina Hingis, Ed Jovanouski, Chen Lu, Doug Flutie (First Tiger Woods card ever made)

1997

Date	Cover - Team /Cards	NrMt	Ex	+Auto
☐ 1/97	Reggie White - Packers	5	3	+15

#541-549 Alex Rodriquez, Cammy Myler, Kevin Garnett, Daren Puppa, Shaquille O'Neal, Steffi Graf, Kara Wolters, Brian Mitchell, Wayne Gretzky

☐ 2/97 Jackie Robinson, Michael Jordan, Emmitt Smith, Ken Griffey, Jr... 5   3Varies
#550-558 Damon Stoudamire, Erin Whitten, Becky Sundstrom, Mo Vaughn, Terrell Davis, Leigh Donovan, Shawn Bradley, Sergei Fedorov, Stan Humphries (#57-60) Allen Iverson, Marcus Camby, Kobe Bryant, Kerry Kittles

☐ 3/97 Dominique Moceanu - Gymnast 5   3   +10
#559-567 Patrick Roy, Charles Barkley, Andy Pettitte, Barry Bonds, Joyce Luncher, Justin Huish, Jeremy McGrath, Nikki Stone, Jackie Joyner Kersee

☐ 4/97 Bernie Williams - NY Yankees............. 5   3   +10
#568-576 Emmitt Smith, Mia Hamm, Randy Johnson, Michael Jordan, Ken Griffey Jr, Muggsy Bougues, Kerri Strug, Sheryl Swoopes, Andre Agassi

☐ 5/97 Gary Payton & Shawn Kemp - Sonics. 5   3+20 ea
#577-585 Lisa Fernandez, Marco Etcheverry, Tony Hawk, Kevin Johnson, Jackie Gallangher, Andrew Jones, Kristi Overton-Johnson, Penny Hardaway, Chris Chelios (61-64) Hank Aaron, Lee Smith, Rickey Henderson, Nolan Ryan

☐ 6/97 Rebecca Lobo/Lisa Leslie - WNBA...... 5   3+ 10 ea
#586-594 Amanda Beard, Grant Hill, Brian Jordan, Derek Jeter, Eric Wynalda, Sudsy Monchik, Jerome Bettis, Alison Sydor, Marisa Baena (65-68) Edwin Moses, Mike Schmidt, Chris Evert, Tony Dorsett

☐ 7/97 Alex Rodriquez - Mariners 5   3   +20
#595-603 Tara Lipinski, Juan Gonalez, Tom Gugliotta, Andres Galarraga, Hakeem Olajuwon, Monicque Kalkman, Mats Sundin, Jeff Gordon, Chamique Holdsclaw (Major League Soccer) 69-72 Mark Dodd, Carlos Valderrama, John Doyle,Steve Ralston

☐ 8/97 Tiger Woods - Golf 5   3   +40
#604-612Drew Bledsoe, Mark Jackson, Lindsay Davenport, Misty Hyman, Mark McGwire, Derek Downing, Mark Chmura, Pat Hentgen, Michele Timms...............................

☐ 9/97 Brett Farve - Packers 5   3   +20
#613-621Tino Martinez, Tim Hardaway, Simeon Rice, Holly McPeak, Deoin Sanders, Claude Lemieux, Julie Foudy, Mark Brunell, Stacy Dragila

☐ 10/97 Deion Sanders - Cowboys / Reds
#622-630 Dominique Moceanu, eric Lindros, Patrick Ewing, Cal Ripken Jr, Lisa Leslie, Troy Aikman, Donovan Bailey, Picabo Street, Pete Sampras: Also Milk Cards: Alex Rodriquez, Nomar Garciaparra, Andy Pettitte, Darin Erstad, Jason Kendall, Vladimir Guerrero, Scott Rolen, Tony Clark........

☐ 11/97 Karl Malone - Jazz 5   3   + 20
#631-639Scottie Pippen, Jerry Rice, Fabiola da Silva, Sandy Alomar, Jr., Cynthia Cooper, Vinny Testaverde, John Stockton, Brett Hull, Mehgan Heaney-Grier........................

☐ 12/97 Michael Jordan - Bulls 5   3   +70
#640-648 Rod Woodson, brady anderson, Bolton Holifield, Gary Payton, Dan Marino, Wilson Kipketer, Iva Majoli, Eric Bergoust, Jessica Burke

☐ 12/97 Michael Jordan, Tiger Woods, Ken Griffey Jr, Brett Farve others

☐ Special SI For Kids issue 5   3 Varies

1954

1955

1956

1957

  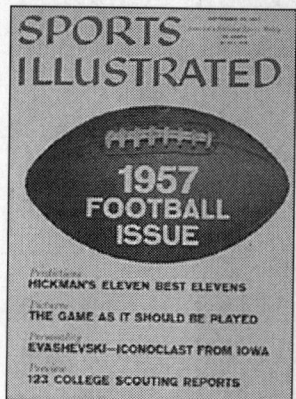

1958

1959

  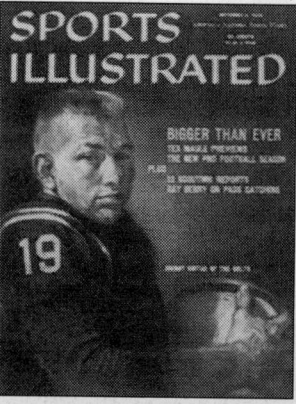

1960

1961

1962

1963

1964

1965

1966

1967

1968

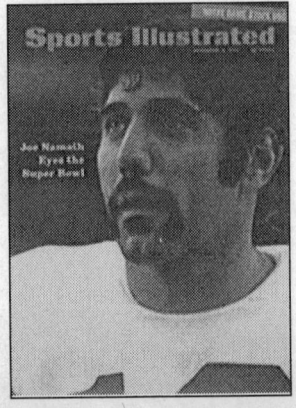

1969

1970

1971

1972

1973

1974

1975

1976

1977

1978

1979

1980

1981

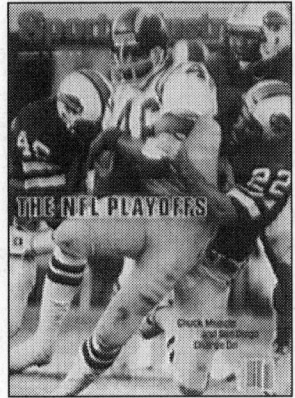

1982

1983

1984

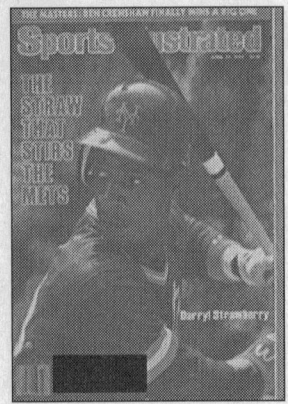

1985

1986

1987

1988

1989

1990

1991

1993

1995

1996

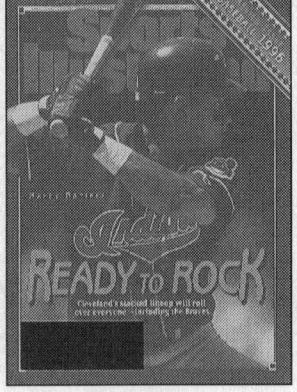

1997

SI SPECIAL ISSUES

1958

1988

1989

1974

1994

1995

1989

1995

1996

SI AUTOGRAPHED

1955

1955

1955

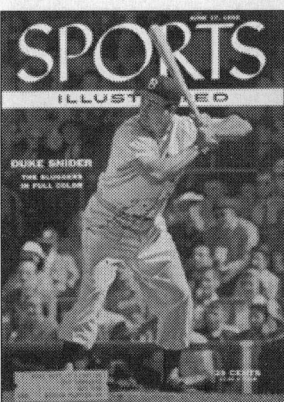

SI AUTOGRAPHED

1955

1955

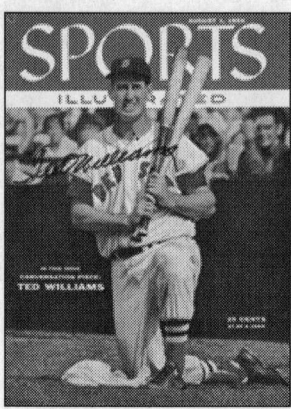

1955

1956

1956

1956

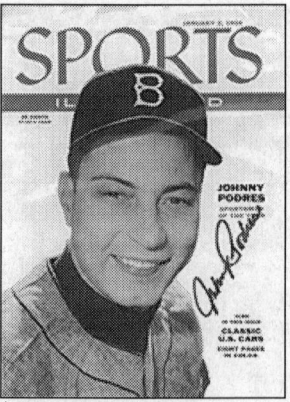

1956

1957

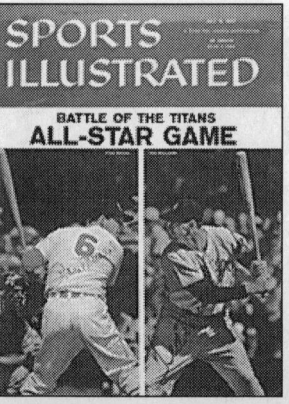

1962

1962

1964

1964

1965

1969

1970

1982

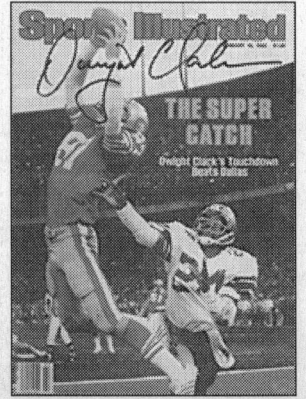

1991

1995

Figurines, Autographs and Other Sports Collectible News...

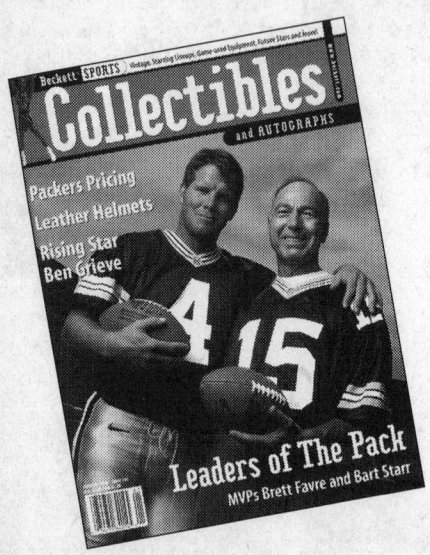

From vintage sports cards and collectibles to draft picks cards and autographed memorabilia, you won't find better coverage of today's sports collectibles hobby. With your subscription to *Beckett Sports Collectibles and Autographs*, you get regular and bonus Price Guides for the most popular collectibles.

Plus get sports auctions coverage, a figurine market watch, Kenner Starting Lineup info, autograph news and answers to your hobby questions, too!

Subscribe to *Beckett Sports Collectibles and Autographs* today!

CHAPTER SIX:
Collecting Sport Magazine

Sport magazine is the oldest running continuous sports magazine and is best remembered for being the greatest magazine during the Golden Era of sports publications. The Golden Era occurred from 1946 to 1959, a time when the primary information came via radio and publications. Sport distinguished itself in the print arena by focusing on major sports, using glossy covers and following up with color photos inside. The combination of great sports stories and great photographs made Sport the leader until the late 1950s when Sports Illustrated changed its marketing style to focus only on major sports.

Sport magazine articles, ads and photos are some of the best during this era. The color pages are the most remembered (and most removed from magazines). These pages are still shots taken for the magazine stories. The photograph fills the entire page and is known for being cut up and made into pinups for display on walls. Many of the pages were used by collectors as autograph pieces.

Many of the articles in Sport were written by the leading sportswriters of that era. The features range from the greatest athletes to unknown rookies. It is important to note that the Golden Era and Silver Era (1960s) had many classic feature articles as well. The Corvette giveaway and the College Girl section were classics of an innocent era long gone.

The ads in Sport feature many sports celebrities in color pushing every product under the sun. If you are a collector of a particular player, pay attention to the ads mentioned. Ads range from underwear to cars and are marked below by parenthesis (). Color ads are underlined.

Finally, the covers are just awesome. Some of the best, if not the best, covers were found during the Golden Era on Sport. These pictures are remembered by every elder sports fan that ever read the magazine. The 1960s brought us television and the faster pace of gathering information. This lead to changes in the marketing of sports information and Sports Illustrated took the powerful lead in providing information quickly. This forced Sport to change its style to appeal to a broader audience. Consequently, the marketing of Sport in recent years has shifted to key proven superstars, key events, preseason issues and swimsuits. Marketing efforts have shown multiple covers (retail vs. mail) and (East vs. West) regional versions.

The Sport magazine price guide section is similar to Sports Illustrated with the Date, Cover, Articles and Prices. However, the price guide underlines key color pictures and ads because so many collectors ask about the color photographs.

The prices for Sport have an extreme wide range based on condition. The magazine is so easily damaged that it is rather rare to find the popular issues in top condition. The NM means Near Mint to mint condition magazines. The EM means Excellent to Mint and this usually means there is some flaw in the magazine. Most quality Sport magazines have a flaw in the spin and/or the cover and usually fall under EM.

However, most Sport magazines that exist are usually in Excellent condition or Very Good condition. Excellent condition means that it has at least one serious flaw (such as spin or splitting over an inch or a creased corner). Very Good condition magazines have two serious flaws. Issues with serious flaws are not used at all for autographing and mostly for research and content. The value for Ex grade issues is 50% of the EM price. VG is 25% of the EM price.

The autograph value of Sport is less than Sport Illustrated or Time, but it is collected at times for players who do not appear on any other magazine. Autographed magazines of deceased players still can command a premium when found in quality condition.

1946

DATE	COVER	FEATURE	Nr-Mt	Ex	+Auto
☐ 9/46	Joe DiMaggio & Son	Joe DiMaggio, Joe Lewis, Bob Feller, Mel Ott/John McGraw, Ben Hogan,	700	450	+200
☐ 10/46	Glenn Davis Doc Blanchard	Stan Musial, Joe Cronin, Bob Waterfield, Bobby Doer Doc Blanchard, Hal Newhouser, Eddie Arcaro Army	200	100 + 10 each	
☐ 11/46	Johnny Lujack Frank Leahy* Notre Dame	Charley Trippi, Bobby Riggs, Babe Didrikson (*also Wedemeyer-St Mary's, Bechtol-Texas, Davis-Army, Trippi-Georgia)	150	75	+20 each
☐ 12/46	Tom Harmon Rams	Harry Gilmer, Green Bay Packers, Tom Harmon, Ace Parker, Jack Krame	150	75	+50 (d)

1947

DATE	COVER	FEATURE	Nr-Mt	Ex	+Auto
☐ 1/47	Andy Phillips Illinois	Jackie Robinson, Babe Ruth, Bill Veeck Frank Brimsek	60	40	+20
☐ 2/47	Doug/Max Bentley Blackhawks	Ted Williams, Jack Dempsey, Bentley Brothers, Bucky Harris	50	30	+25 each
☐ 3/47	Alex Groza Kentucky	Joe DiMaggio, Maurice Richard/Toe Blake 1927 Yankees	50	30	+50 (d)
☐ 4/47	Leo Durocher* Dodgers	Happy Chandler, Leo Durocher, Howie Pollet, Walter Johnson History, National League (*also Bob Feller, Stan Musial, Howie Pollet, Ted Williams)	63	36	+75 (d)
☐ 5/47	Horse Racing History, Johnny Pesky	Reese/Reiser, Bonnie Baker, American League	40	20	
☐ 6/47	Bob Feller Indians	Hank Greenberg, Bob Feller, Ben Hogan, Enos Slaughter, Charley Keller, Dixie Walker	70	40	+20
☐ 7/47	Joe Cronin /Ed Dyer Cardinals/Red Sox	Joe Cronin, Eddie Dyer, Lou Boudreau Graziano/Zale, Larry McPhall	40	24	+100(d)
☐ 8/47	Ted Williams Red Sox	Pittsburgh Pirates, Clint Hartung, Tommy Henrich Bill Nicholson, Ted Williams	150	75	+200
☐ 9/47	Joe DiMaggio Dom DiMaggio Red Sox/Yankees	Joe DiMaggio, Knute Rockne, Jackie Robinson, John Mize, Billy Southworth	150	75	+200/20
☐ 10/47	Harry Gilmer Alabama	Leo Durocher, Lujack, Leahy & Notre Dame, World Series Thrills Johnny Jorgensen, Charley Justice, Harry Brecheen, Sugar Ray Robinson, George McQuinn, Babe Didrikson (Rita Hayworth)	42	24	+20
☐ 11/47	Johnny Lujack Notre Dame	Jersey Joe Walcott, Branch Rickey, Notre Dame/Army	40	24	+25
☐ 12/47	Charley Trippi Cards	Joe Louis, Chicago Sports Teams, George Weiss, Red Grange	35	20	+25

1948

DATE	COVER	FEATURE	Nr-Mt	Ex	+Auto
☐ 1/48	Ralph Beard* Kentucky	Joe DiMaggio, Bill Klem, Rocky Graziano, Joe McCarthy Bobby Layne (Gary Cooper - Chesterfield) (*also Arnold Ferrin - Utah)	35	20	+20
☐ 2/48	Frank Brimsek Bruins	Maurice Richard, Walter Hagen, Primo Carnera	35	20	+15
☐ 3/48	George Kaftan Holy Cross	Joe Louis, Connie Mack, Ralph Kiner, Syl Apps, Red Barber	35	20	+20
☐ 4/48	Ted Williams Red Sox	Leo Durocher, Ted Williams, Ewell Blackwell, Howie Morenz, Stanley Ketchel	88	50	+100
☐ 5/48	Babe Ruth* Yankees	Bob Elliott, Dizzy Dean, Joe Page/Hugh Casey (*also Johnny Mize, Ralph Kiner, Ted Williams)	112	60	
☐ 6/48	Joe Louis Boxing	Bob Feller, Mel Ott, Joe Louis, George Kell, Babe Didrikson, Luke Appling, Vern Stephens	56	36	+400(d)
☐ 7/48	Ewell Blackwell Reds	Baseball HOF, Lou Boudreau, Charley Grimm, Art Houtteman, Carl Hubbell/'34 All Star game, Harry Walker	42	24	+20
☐ 8/48	Stan Musial Cardinals	Stan Musial, Hal Newhouser, Eddie Stanky, Eddie Joost, (Gregory Peck -Beer, William Bendix 'Babe Ruth Story')	88	50	+20
☐ 9/48	Ted Williams/ Joe DiMaggio	Babe Ruth, Bill Veeck, Walker Cooper, Hank Greenberg, Sammy Baugh, Richie Ashburn, (Indian Motorcycle)	350	125	+200/200

	Red Sox/Yankees				
☐ 10/48	Lou Gehrig	Dom DiMaggio, Lou Gehrig, Joe Gordon, Jackie Robinson	100	50	
	Yankees	Marty Marton, Frank Leahy, World Series (Jane Wyman - Chesterfield)			
☐ 11/48	Doak Walker	Turk Broda, Alvin Dark, Ty Cobb, Doak Walker	49	25	+25
	SMU				
☐ 12/48	Johnny Lujack	Branch Rickey, George Halas, Satchel Paige, Casey Stengel	42	25	+25
	Bears	(Bob Hope - Beer)			
	Blackhawks				

1949

DATE	COVER	FEATURE	Nr-Mt	Ex	+Auto
☐ 1/49	Ed Macauley*	Lou Boudreau, John McGraw, Ed Macauley,	35	20	+20
	St Louis	Johnny Sain, Jim Conacher, George Mikan (Harley Davidson)			
		(*also Jim Conacher-Redwings, Lou Boudreau, , Rod Franz)			
☐ 2/49	Lou Boudreau*	Clark Griffith, The Celtics, Max Bentley, Gene Bearden	42	20	+20
	Indians	(*also Jim McIntyre, Sandy Saddler, Buddy O'Connor)			
☐ 3/49	Ralph Beard*	Joe Louis, Stan Musial, Ralph Beard, Larry Dolby, Ted Lindsay	35	20	+20
	Kentucky	(*also Larry Doby-Indians, Ted Atkinson-Jockey, Ted Lindsay-Redwings)			
☐ 4/49	Bob Feller*	Happy Chandler, Ewell Blackwell, Bob Feller, Babe Herman,	70	35	+20
	Indians	Pete Reiser, Jim Thorpe			
		(*Also Bob Mathias-track, John Palmer-Golf, Victor Seixas-Tennis)			
☐ 5/49	Enos Slaughter*	Ted Williams, Willie Pep, Pee Wee Reese,	49	25	+20
	Cardinals	Veeck/Boudreau, Dempsey/Tunney, Eddie Arcaro, Sam Snead,			
		Enos Slaughter (NY Yankees -Jock Strap, Joe DiMaggio- Vitallas)			
		(Also Beverly Baker-Tennis, Jimmy Demaret-Golf, Eddie Arcaro-Jockey)			
☐ 6/49	Hal Newhouser*	Joe McCarthy, Honus Wagner, Hal Newhouser, Joe Louis,	42	24	+20
	Tigers	Tinker/Evers/Chance, Birdie Tebbetts (Bob Hope - Chesterfield)			
		(Also Birdie Tebbits-Redsox, Joe Louis-Boxing, Don Gehrmann-Track)			
☐ 7/49	Lou Boudreau	Joe Gordon,Bill Dickey, Phil Marchildon, Ralph Kiner,	42	24	+20
	Joe Gordon	Rogers Hornsby & Joe Gordon			
	Indians				
☐ 8/49	Jackie Robinson	Vern Stephens & Bobby Jones, Babe Ruth, Rocky Graziano,	88	50	+400 (d)
	Dodgers	Jackie Robinson, Yogi Berra			
☐ 9/49	Joe DiMaggio	Ben Hogan, Joe DiMaggio & Mickey Walker, Dale Mitchell ,	140	70	+200
	Yankees	George Stallings, Mel Parnell, Red Schoendienst			
☐ 10/49	Christy	Shoeless Joe Jackson, Christy Mathewson & Tommy Henrich,	56	30	-
	Mathewson	Billy Goodman			
	NY Giants				
☐ 11/49	Charlie Justice	Bob Dillinger, Frank Leahy & Francis Ouimet, Charlie Justice,	35	20	+20
	North Carolina	Dempsey/Rickard, Bill Durnan, Eddie LeBaron			
☐ 12/49	Johnny Lujack/	Maurice McDermott, Jim Thorpe & Sid Luckman,	42	24	+20 each
	Sid Luckman	Roland LaStarza			
	Bears				

1950

DATE	COVER	FEATURE	Nr-Mt	Ex	+Auto
☐ 1/50	Don Lofgran	Phil Rizzuto, Walter Johnson & Bing Crosby, Lofgren/Herrerias	30	12	+15 each
	/Rene Herrerias	Roy Conacher (Bing Crosby - Chesterfield)			
	USF				
☐ 2/50	Tommy Henrich	Tommy Henrich, Jake LaMotta & Eddie Shore, Preacher Roe	40	24	+15
	Yankees				
☐ 3/50	George Mikan	Kenny Reardon, Joe Page & John L. Sullivan, Joe Louis,	40	20	+20
	Lakers	George Mikan, Bill Veeck			
☐ 4/50	Casey Stengel	Leo Durocher, Casey Stengel & Grover Alexander, Eddie Waitkus	40	20	+100 (d)
	Yankees	Sam Snead, Bill Veeck, Sid Abel, Andy Pafko (Kirk Douglas - Chesterfield)			
☐ 5/50	Ralph Kiner	Gene Tunney & Dom DiMaggio, Ralph Kiner, Virgil Trucks,	40	20	+10
	Pirates	Bobby Thomson, Glenn Davis, Bill Veeck			
☐ 6/50	Bob Lemon	Ted Williams, Bob Lemon & Kenesaw M. Landis, Ezzard Charles	40	20	+10
	Indians	Whiz Kids, Connie Mack, Charley Faust, Carl Furillo			
☐ 7/50	Stan Musial	Happy Chandler, Jerry Priddy, Stan Musial, Luke Easter,	75	40	+20
	Cardinals	Warren Spahn, Earl Sande & Sugar Ray Robinson			
☐ 8/50	Art Houtteman	Art Houtteman, Max Baer & Joe McCarthy, Roy Campanella,	33	20	+10
	Tigers	Willie Jones			

			Nr-Mt	Ex	+Auto
☐ 9/50	Don Newcombe Dodgers	Don Newcombe, Baseball Club History series Chicago Cubs, Ben Hogan, Vic Wertz, Walt Dropo, Allie Reynolds	40	24	+10
☐ 10/50	World Series Painting	Brooklyn Dodgers, Bob Williams, Hoot Evers, Bronko Nagurski Chico Carrasquel, Dick Sisler	33	20	
☐ 11/50	Harry Aganis Boston Col.	Detroit Tigers, Earl Blaik, Joe DiMaggio, Harry Agganis, Ruth/Wagner/Cobb	33	20	+250 (d)
☐ 12/50	Football Painting	Boston Red Sox, Red Grange, Ted Kluszewski	30	15	-

1951

DATE	COVER	FEATURE	Nr-Mt	Ex	+Auto
☐ 1/51	Basketball Painting	St. Louis Cardinals, Ezzard Charles, '50 Phillies, Jerry Coleman,	25	15	-
☐ 2/51	Nat Holman Basketball	Philadelphia Athletics, Bill Tilden, Ted Williams, Jake Lamotta, Sugar Ray Robinson, Branch Rickey	25	15	+ 100 (d)
☐ 3/51	George Mikan Lakers*	Boston Braves, Hank Greenberg, Eddie Stanky (*the cover is art with other athletes)	25	15	+ 20
☐ 4/51	Baseball Art	Lee Durocher, St. Louis Browns, Andy Seminick ("Follow The Sun"-Ben Hogan)	33	20	-
☐ 5/51	Joe DiMaggio Stan Musial*	Reds, 1927 Yankees, Jim Konstanty, Ty Cobb, Rabbitt Maranville (Ben Hogan) Baseball Jubliee issue (*the cover is art with many deceased HOF, Ruth etc)	100	40	+200/+20
☐ 6/51	Sugar Ray Robinson Boxing	Chicago White Sox, Pee Wee Reese, Sugar Ray Robinson Early Wynn, Sam Jethroe, Mickey Mantle	40	24	+150 (d)
☐ 7/51	Ewell Blackwell Reds	Ewell Blackwell, New York Giants, Chico Carrasquel, Duke Snider, Lou Boudreau, Basketball Fix (Harly Davidson)	25	15	+15
☐ 8/51	Yogi Berra Yankees	Philadelphia Phillies, Ezzard Charles, Larry Jansen, Bob Feller, Ferris Fain, Kid Gavilan, Bob Mathias, (Ted Williams Car Wax)	50	30	+20
☐ 9/51	Ted Williams Red Sox	New York Yankees, Otto Graham, Richie Ashburn, Enos Slaughter Gil Hodges, Eddie Robinson, Ted Williams, Sal Maglie	75	45	+100
☐ 10/51	Jackie Robinson Dodgers	Pittsburgh Pirates, Jackie Robinson, Wally Westlake, Vic Raschi , Bobby Doerr, Joe Walcott, Doak Walker, Bob Feller, Luis Firpo, Rocky Marciano (Marlyn Monroe)	75	45	+250 (d)
☐ 11/51	Bill McColl Stanford	Bob Waterfield, Cleveland Indians, Willie Mays, Charley Gehringer, Nelson Fox	25	15	+10
☐ 12/51	Johnny Lujack Bears	Johnny Lujack, Washington Senators, Gordie Howe, Mike Garcia, Mickey Mantle, Maureen Connolly	30	12	+20

1952

DATE	COVER	FEATURE	Nr-Mt	Ex	+Auto
☐ 1/52	No Issue Published				
☐ 2/52	Sugar Ray Robinson Boxing	Minnie Minoso, Maurice Richard, Jim Corbett, Larry Doby Leo Durocher, Joe DiMaggio, Ted Williams	30	15	+250 (d)
☐ 3/52	Gil McDougald Yankees	Rocky Marciano, Gil McDougald, Dick Groat, Willie Shoemaker, Art Houtteman, Roy Campanella, Roger Hornsby, Rocky Graziano, Jimmie Foxx, Babe Ruth ((Liz Taylor Pin up ad)	30	15	+15
☐ 4/52	Chico Carrasquel Reds	Terry Sawchuk, Bobby Thomson, Gus Zernial, Chicago White Sox Ellis Kinder, Marty Marion, (Joe DiMaggio -Spalding)	25	15	+20
☐ 5/52	Alvin Dark Giants	Eddie Stanky, Earl Torgeson, Al Rosen, Ralph Branca, Murry Dickson, Alvin Dark ("The Story of Dizy Dean" Pride of St Louis)	25	15	+10
☐ 6/52	Ralph Kiner Pirates	Ralph Kiner, Johnny Pesky, Robin Roberts, Hal Newhouser, Jim Rivera, Billy Cox, Dizzy Dean, Eddie Lopat, Ben Hogan	35	20	+10
☐ 7/52	Stan Musial Cardinals	Tris Speaker, Bobby Shantz, Ted Williams, Sugar Ray Robinson Stan Musial, Whitey Ford, Jeck Dempsey, Chuck Connors	65	40	+20
☐ 8/52	Allie Reynolds Yogi Berra Yankees	Allie Reynolds, Red Schoendienst, Del Ennis, Leo Durocher, Bob Feller, Jim Piersall, Marty Marion	30	12	+50 (d) +15
☐ 9/52	Mike Garcia Indians	Sal Maglie, Gran Hamner, Andy Pafko, Tommy Byrne, Ewell Blackwell, Augie Donatelli, Football Club history- L.A. Rams, Dixie Walker, Ballpark series- Fenway Park (Otto Graham -Battaries)	25	15	+15
☐ 10/52	Jackie Robinson/ Pee Wee Reese Dodgers	Curt Simmons, Jim Hegan, George Kell, Gerry Staley, Monte Irvin, Charlie Dren, Joe Walcott, Hank Sauer, Billy Martin, Chicago Bears	150	60	+450 (d) +40
☐ 11/52	J. Robinson* Dodgers	Archie Moore, Doak Walker, Joe DiMaggio, Satchel Paige, Whitney Lockman, Cleveland Browns, Henry Armstrong (*also Allie Reynolds, Harry Agganis, Doak Walker)	50	20	Varies

	DATE	COVER	FEATURE	Nr-Mt	Ex	+Auto
☐	12/52	Johnny Olszewski Cal Bears	Harry Agganis, Jackie Jensen, Johnny Olszewski, Green Bay Packers, Bill Veeck, Russ Myer	25	15	+20

1953

	DATE	COVER	FEATURE	Nr-Mt	Ex	+Auto
☐	1/53	Rocky Marciano Boxing	Rocky Marciano, Joe Black, Johnny Mize, Clint Courtney, S.F. 49ers, Boom Boom Geoffrion	40	25	+400(d)
☐	2/53	Bobby Shantz A'S	Jimmie Dykes, Gene Woodling, Milt Schmidt, Jackie Robinson, Florence Chadwick	30	15	+20
☐	3/53	Bob Cousy Celtics	Frank Frisch, Red Kelley, Frank Shea, Bob Cousy, Duke Snider, Ralph Kiner, Ten Greatest Fights, Stanley Ketchel, Bob Pettit	30	15	+25
☐	4/53	Mickey Mantle Yankees	Mickey Mantle, Larry Doby, Branch Rickey, Ford Frick, Roger Hornsby	150	90	+250 (d)
☐	5/53	Bob Lemon Indians	Roy McMillan, Bob Lemon, Carl Hubbell, Ewell Blackwell, Jim Piersall, (Phil Rizzuto - Spalding)	25	15	+15
☐	6/53	Hank Sauer Cubs	Hank Sauer, Luke Easter, Bucky Harris, Bill Veeck, Bobby Thomson, Pepper Martin, Billy Loes, (Joe DiMaggio-Reach, Mantle-Camels)	25	15	+10
☐	7/53	Ferris Fain White Sox	Gil Hodges, Sid Gordon, Ferris Fain, Charley Gehringer, Ted Williams, Solly Hemus, Vic Wertz	25	15	+10
☐	8/53	Warren Spahn Braves	Warren Spahn, Ted Klu, Walt Dropo, Jim Braddock, Ezzard Charles, Ed Yost, Don Zimmer (George Mikan -Sports Star Shoes)	33	20	+20
☐	9/53	Robin Roberts Phillies	Kid Gavilan, Bobby Avila, Ed Mathews, Johnny Mize, Robin Roberts, Babe Didrikson, Detroit Lions, (Bobby Layne - Batteries)	33	20	+15
☐	10/53	Roy Campanella Dodgers	Charlie Grimm, Whitey Ford, Billy Pierce, Rocky Marciano, Roy Campanella, Gus Bell, Mickey Vernon, Pittsburgh Steelers, Peanuts Lowery	50	30	+200 (d)
☐	11/53	Phil Rizzuto/ Johnny Lattner Yankees/Notre Dame	Willie Pep, Enos Slaughter, Knute Rockne, Phil Rizzuto Carl Furillo, Washington Redskins, Three-Finger Brown	33	20	+30 each
☐	12/53	Michigan State Football Issue	Ben Hogan, Norm Van Brocklin, Elmer Lach, Michigan State Football, Benny Leonard, Ralph Kiner, Philadelphia Eagles, Virgil Trucks	20	12	Varies

1954

	DATE	COVER	FEATURE	Nr-Mt	Ex	+Auto
☐	1/54	Eddie Le Baron Redskins	Eddie Le Baron, Mickey Mantle, Ted Willliams, N.Y. Giants	20	12	+10
☐	2/54	Ed Mathews Braves	1953 N.Y. Yankees, Danny O'Connell, Bob Porterfield, Charlie Dressen, Robin Roberts, Jean Beliveau	40	24	+15
☐	3/54	Casey Stengel Yankees	Harlem Globetrotters, Jim Piersall, Willlie Shoemaker, George Mikan, Walter Alston, Harvey Kuenn (Goose Tatum - Globetrotters)	33	20	+100 (d)
☐	4/54	Don Newcombe Dodgers	Jesse Owens, Lew Burdette, Al Rosen, Ted Williams, Don Newcombe, Eddie Stanky, Floyd Patterson, Joe McGinnity (Yogi Berra - Spalding)	30	12	+15
☐	5/54	Ted Kluszewski Reds	Mel Parnell, Harvey Haddix, Billy Martin, Joe Black, Bill Terry, Bobby Bragan, Germany Schafer (Milky Way Candy Bar Phil Rizzuto-Spalding)	30	12	+50 (d)
☐	6/54	Rocky Marciano Boxing	Andy Pafko, Carl Erskine, Chico Carrasquel, Terry Brennan, Rocky Marciano, Branch Rickey, Bill Dickey (Ted Kluzenski - MacGregor)	33	20	+400 (d)
☐	7/54	Stan Musial Cardinals	Eddie Matthews, Rocky Marciano, Casey Stengel, Ray Boone Stan Musial	60	36	+20
☐	8/54	Minnie Minoso White Sox	Ted Williams, Leo Durocher, Jim Busby, Vic Raschi, Minnie Minoso (John Wayne - Camels)	30	12	+15
☐	9/54	Duke Snider Dodgers	Birdie Tebbetts, Bob Turley, Bear Bryant, Sal Maglie, Bobo Olson, George Strickland, Vic Power, Rudy York	75	30	+20
☐	10/54	Al Rosen Indians	Babe Ruth, Willie Mays, Al Rosen, Mickey McDermott	30	12	+15
☐	11/54	Larry Morris* Georgia Tech	Bronko Nagurski, Stan Musial, Art Houtteman, Josh Gibson (*also Stan Musial, Crazy Legs Hirsch, Roy Campanella)	20	12	+15
☐	12/54	Pete Vann Army	Paul Brown, Charlie Justice, Phil Rizzuto, Pete Vann, Baltimore Colts	20	12	+15
☐	1/55	Pete Philos* Eagles	Henry Armstrong, Pete Philos, Wally Moon, Lester Patrick Chicago Cardinals (George Mikan - Keds, Corvette) (*also Don Schlundt-Basketball , Cisco Andrade,Art Houtteman)	16	10	+15

1955

DATE	COVER	FEATURE	Nr-Mt	Ex	+Auto
☐ 2/55	Alvin Dark Giants	*Alvin Dark, Eddie Stankey, Jackie Jensen, (Coke, Rock Hudson - Camel) (*Also Nino Valdes Boxing, Bob McKeen Cal bears, Terry Sawchuk -Redwings)*	20	12	+10
☐ 3/55	Rocky Marciano Boxing	*Bob Cousy, Leo Durocher, Frank Thomas, Vic Wertz, Wilt Chamberlain*	25	15	+400 (d)
☐ 4/55	Bob Turley Yankees	*Montreal Canadiens, Dusty Rhodes, Floyd Patterson, Ralph Kiner, Gene Conley, Bob Turley, (Wilson Gloves) (*also Joe Norris-Bowling, Ralph Kiner-Indian, Maurice Richard-Hockey)*	20	12	+15
☐ 5/55	Bobby Thomson Braves	*Bobby Thomson, Walter Alston, Jack Harshman, Ray Jablonski, Carmen Basilio*	20	12	+15
☐ 6/55	Johnny Antonelli Giants	*Johnny Antonelli, Ed Mathews, Yogi Berra, Joe Louis Schoendiest/Musial, Hal Smith, (Ted Kluszenski - MacGrego)r*	20	12	+15
☐ 7/55	Ned Garver Orioles	*Pepper Martin, Minnie Minoso, Ned Garver, Pee Wee Reese, Fred Hutchinson (Musial - Rawlings)*	16	10	+10
☐ 8/55	Paul Richards	*Paul Richards, Rogers Hornsby, Herb Score, Joe Adcock Don Mueller, Don Newcombe, Al Kaline, Sammy White*	20	12	+10
☐ 9/55	Duke Snider Dodgers	*Duke Snider, Jim Hegan, Nellie Fox, Roger Hornsby Curt Simmons, Hank Bauer*	60	35	+20
☐ 10/55	Yogi Berra Yankees	*Archie Moore, Jackie Robinson, Jim Rivera, Jim Finigan, Pete Reiser, Yogi Berra (Corvette)*	40	24	+15
☐ 11/55	Eddie Erdelatz* Navy	*Eddie Erdaletz, Carmen Basilio, Johnny Podres, Lefty O'Doul,(*also Johnny Podres, Carmen, Basilio, Whitey Rouviere)*	16	10	+10
☐ 12/55	Hugh McElhenny 49ers	*Glenn Davis/Doc Blanchard, Robin Roberts, The Heavyweight Champs, Hugh McElhenny, Mickey Cochrane*	20	12	+10

1956

DATE	COVER	FEATURE	Nr-Mt	Ex	+Auto
☐ 1/56	Doak Walker Lions	*Rocky Graziano, Doak Walker, Tommy Byrne, Willie Mosconi*	16	10	+15
☐ 2/56	Sihugo Green* Basketball	*Howie Morenz, Dick Donovan, Mickey Mantle, '55 Dodgers (Coke, Rock Hudson)(*also Mickey Mantle, Marcino, Boffoon)*	16	10	+10
☐ 3/56	Walter Alston Dodgers	*Early Wynn, Floyd Patterson, Frank Lane, Maurice Stokes*	20	12	+150 (d)
☐ 4/56	Larry Doby White Sox	*Larry Doby, Wally Post, Jean Beliveau, Larry MacPhail (Chevy 56', Robin Roberts - MacGregor, Harlem Globetrotters)*	20	12	+15
☐ 5/56	Bob Lemon Indians	*Marty Marion, Bob Lemon, Del Ennis, Sugar Ray Robinson Larry MacPhail, Horace Stoneham, Bob Friend (Rock Hudson - Camels)*	20	12	+15
☐ 6/56	Willie Mays Giants	*Willie Mays, Johnny Logan, Bill Hoeft, Mickey Vernon Willie Pep (Ted Williams - Wilson)*	50	30	+30
☐ 7/56	Ted Williams Red Sox	*Ted Kluszewski, Ted Williams, Ernie Banks, Ray Boone*	75	36	+200
☐ 8/56	Vinegar Minell Cardinals	*Robin Roberts, Bob Feller, Vinegar Bend Mizell, Vic Power Ford Frick, Archie Moore (Al Kaline - Wilson)*	16	10	+15
☐ 9/56	10th Anniversary Issue	*Joe DiMaggio, Curt Simmons, Gus Bell, Al Smith, Top Performer of the Decade*	33	20	-
☐ 10/56	Mickey Mantle Yankees	*'56 Brooklyn Dodgers, Mantle/Martin, Floyd Patterson, Hank Aaron (500 photo's, Van Broklin - Spalding, Corvette)*	125	60	+250(d)
☐ 11/56	Paul Hornung Notre Dame	*Bud Wilkinsom, Jackie Robinson, Paul Hornung, Whitey Ford (George Mikan - Keds, Ted Williams, Wilson, 56 Chevy, Yogi Berra NSC, Howard Cassady -Wilson)*	16	10	+20
☐ 12/56	Bobby Morrow Track	*Rocky Marciano, Casey Stengel*	16	10	+10

1957

DATE	COVER	FEATURE	Nr-Mt	Ex	+Auto
☐ 1/57	Wilt Chamberlain Kansas	*Alan Ameche, Don Larsen, Bobo Olson, Ted Williams, Doug Harvey, Frank Lane, Harvey Kuenn*	25	15	+75
☐ 2/57	Jacques Plante* Canadiens	*'56 Cincinnati Reds, Sal Maglie, Al Rosen, Hockey's Goalie's (Herb Score - Wilson, 57 Pontiac) (*also Sal Maglie, Art Aragon, Jack George)*	20	12	+15
☐ 3/57	Mickey Mantle Yankees	*Gene Conley, Don Newcombe, Detroit Red Wings, Al Lopez, Dale Long*	125	50	+250 (d)
☐ 4/57	Ed Mathews Braves	*Don Larson, Bob Pettit, Gene Fullmer, Tony Galento, (Corvette)*	25	15	+15

DATE	COVER	FEATURE	Nr-Mt	Ex	+Auto
☐ 5/57	Robin Roberts	Lou Boudreau, Floyd Patterson, Hank Greenberg Roy Campanella/ Warren Spahn/ Ted Kluzewski/ Phillies/Reds/Dodgers/Braves	25	15	Varies
☐ 6/57	Early Wynn Indians	Pee Wee Reese, Leo Durocher, Gil McDongald, Early Wynn (Corvette, Ted Williams -Wislon, Musial - Rawling)	25	15	+10
☐ 7/57	Al Kaline Tigers	Walter O'Malley, Ralph Kiner, Vic Raschi, Sam Jones (Ford 57, Spalding)	40	25	+15
☐ 8/57	Joe Adcock Braves	Mickey Mantle, Joe Adcock, Score/Colavito, Willie Mays, Roberto Clemente, Joe Garagiola (Corvette)	25	15	+10
☐ 9/57	Duke Snider Dodgers	Fred Haney, Duke Snider, Sugar Ray Robinson, Ed Bailey, Sherm Lollar, Joe DiMaggio (Ford 57)	50	30	+20
☐ 10/57	Billy Pierce White Sox	Carmen Basilio, Mantle/Ford/Martin, Frank Robinson, Gil Hodges, Billy Pierce (John Wayne - Movie)	20	12	+10
☐ 11/57	Don Stephenson* Georgia Tech	Berra/Newcombe, Floyd Patterson, Jackie Robinson, Ted Lindsay (Bob Pettitt-Rawlings; Frank Gifford - Wilson) (*also includes Yogi Berra and Don Newcombe)	16	10	+10
☐ 12/57	Chicago Bears	Chicago Bears, Mickey Mantle/Willie Mays, Henri Richard) (Herb Score-Wilson, Pontiac)	16	10	Varies

1958

DATE	COVER	FEATURE	Nr-Mt	Ex	+Auto
☐ 1/58	Snider/Reese/ Robinson/Mays/* Durocher/ Dodgers/Giants	Lew Burdette, Ted Williams, Norm Van Brocklin Don Hoak, Chuck Stobbs , Sugar Ray Robinson Giants/Dodgers Feud (Geroge Mikan - Keds, Chevy 57) (*also Johnny Antonelli)	25	15	Varies
☐ 2/58	Carmen Basilio Boxing	Stan Musial, Carmen Basilio, Terry Sawchuk, Robin Roberts, Ted Klu	20	12	+15
☐ 3/58	Lew Burdette Braves	Lew Burdette, Cousy/Sharman/Russell & Co., Wilt Chamberlain, Hockey's All-Time All-Star Team (Lew Burdette - Rawlings, Corvette)	20	12	+10
☐ 4/58	Nellie Fox White Sox	Nellie Fox, Don Drysdale, Rocky Marciano, Harvey Kuenn) Dick Groat - Shoes, Ted Williams - Wilson, Stan Musial - Rawlings)	40	24	+175 (d)
☐ 5/58	Yogi Berra Yankees	Larry Doby, Wes Covington, Duke Snider, Joe Louis, Don Blasingame, Bear Bryant	30	12	+20
☐ 6/58	Willie Mays Giants	Warren Spahn, Ted Williams, Billy Loes, S.F. Giants (Nellie Fox - Wilson)	33	20	+30
☐ 7/58	Herb Score* Indians	Herb Score, Chicago White Sox, Alvin Dark, Ken Venturi (Al Dark - Wilson) (*also Hot Rod Rodriquez, Duke Snider, Ken Venturi)	20	12	+10
☐ 8/58	Billy Martin Tigers	Ted Klu, Enos Slaughter, Gene Littler, Frank Leahy, Minnie Minoso, Eddie Arcaro	20	12	+75
☐ 9/58	Ed Mathews Braves	Sports Hall of Fame series begins: Ed Mathews, Lou Gehrig, Roy Campanella, Jackie Jensen, Arnold Palmer	35	15	+15
☐ 10/58	Bob Turley* Yankees	Sam Snead, Jim Thorpe, Bob Turley, Hank Aaron, Orlando Cepeda, Bill Mazeroski (Corvette) (* also Mel Allen, Hank Aaron, Sam Snead)	16	10	+10
☐ 11/58	Bob Anderson Army	Lou Groza, Ty Cobb, Bob Anderson, World Series Heroes (Bob Pettit - Rawlings)	20	10	+10
☐ 12/58	John Unitas* Colts	Whitey Ford, S.F. Giants, Red Grange, Ernie Banks, John Unitas (Mantle - Rawlings) (* Willie Mays, Bob Pettit, Tom Bolt)	20	12	+20

1959

DATE	COVER	FEATURE	Nr-Mt	Ex	+Auto
☐ 1/59	Maurice Richard	Bill Sharman, Richie Ashburn, Jack Dempsey, Maurice Richard Jack Twyman, Tony Kubeck	25	15	+15
☐ 2/59	Rafer Johnson Track	Lew Burdette, Eddie Shore, '59 Yankees, Maurice Stokes, Bob Cerv	20	12	+25
☐ 3/59	Al Kaline* Tigers	Adolph Rupp, L.A. Dodgers, Al Kaline, Sugar Ray Robinson, George Mikan, Andy Bathgate, Oscar Robertson (* also Oscar Robertson, Ron Delany, Floyd Patterson)	35	20	+15
☐ 4/59	Rocky Colavito Indians	Rocky Colavito, Bob Skinner, Elgin Baylor, Elston Howard, Ed Litzenberger, Solly Hemus, Wilt Chamberlain, Elston Howard (Harvey Kuenn-Wilson, Bill Mazeroski, Mays, Aaron, F. Robinson, -MacGregor, Johnny Unitas - (Corvette)	40	24	+25
☐ 5/59	Hank Bauer/* Gil Hodges Yankees/Dodgers	Willie Mays, Archie Moore, Gil Hodges, Roger Hornsby, Billy O'Dell (Corvette, Hodges, Mays, Bauer-Bats, Nellie Fox - Wilson, Mickey Mantle -Rawlings), (*Also Terry Brennan-ND)	20	12	+10/ +100 (d)

	COVER	FEATURE	Nr-Mt	Ex	+Auto
☐ 6/59	MickeyMantle/* Ted Williams Yankees/Red Sox	Floyd Patterson, Mickey Mantle, Duke Snider, Walter Hagen Nellie Fox, Billy Martin, (Corvette, Harley Davidson) (*Also Floyd Patterson), Ted Williams	75	35	+200 (d) +150
☐ 7/59	Don Newcombe/ Jimmy Piersall Reds/Indians	Don Newcombe, Jim Piersall, Fred Haney, Sal Maglie Bill Skowron, Ken Boyer (Harvey Kuenn-Wilson, Harley Davidson)	16	10	+10 +10
☐ 8/59	Mantle/Mays/ Matthews Colavito	Rocky Colavito, Joe DiMaggio, Bill Rigney & Giants, Bill Veeck Vic Power, Del Crandall (Nellie Fox-Wilson)	40	24	varies
☐ 9/59	Ted Williams/ Stan Musial Red Sox/Cards	Hank Aaron, Williams/Musial, John McGraw, Dick Stuart, Hoyt Wilhelm, Cal McLish	60	36	+150 +20
☐ 10/59	Warren Spahn/ World Series Braves	Casey Stengel, Warren Spahn, Dizzy Dean, Bob Feller, Ten Greatest World Series Games, Chicago Black Sox Harmon Killebrew	33	20	+20
☐ 11/59	Coach Dietzel Billy Cannon* LSU	Basilio/Sugar Ray Robinson, Luis Aparicio, Don Meredith, Sam Baugh, Orlando Cepeda (Corvette, Nellie Fox-AMF, Corvair) (Nellie Fox-Wilson)(*also Roger Maris, Harmon Killebrew, Milt Pappas, Vada Pinson)	16	10	+15
☐ 12/59	Johnny Unitas Colts	Johnny Unitas, Ingemar Johansson, Johnny Antonelli, Red Schoendienst, Sam Huff, Early Wynn Babe Didrikson	20	12	+25

1960

DATE	COVER	FEATURE	Nr-Mt	Ex	+Auto
☐ 1/60	Bob Cousy Celtics	Bob Cousy, Floyd Patterson, Honus Wagner, Tito Francona, Johnny Temple	15	10	+35
☐ 2/60	Ingemar Johansson* Boxing	L.A. Dodgers, Ingemar Johansson, Ted Kluzewski, Don Budge Enos Slaughter, Joe Gordon, Gordie Howe, Sonny Liston, Gene Conley (Stan Musial - Rawlings) (*Also Larry Sherry - Dodgers)	12	8	
☐ 3/60	J. Robinson Willie Mays Chamberlain Althea Gibson	Jackie Robinson, Bob Pettit, Joe Louis, Dickie Moore, Ernie Banks, Chamberlain/Russell (Corvette, John Taylor, Ken Boyer)	24	16	varies
☐ 4/60	Duke Snider Dodgers	Duke Snider, Willie Mays, Mickey Cochrane, Roy Face, Gene Fullmer (Banks, Nellie Fox-Wilson, Corvette, Bill Sharman-Spalding, George Mikan-Keds, Stan Musial-Spalding)	24	16	+20
☐ 5/60	Willie McCovey/ Har. Killebrew Giants/Senators	Al Kaline, Johnny Temple, Willie McCovey, Bobby Jones, Roger Maris, Harmon Killebrew, Stan Musial, Sugar Ray Robinson, White Sox (Corvette)	30	20	+15 each
☐ 6/60	Don Drysdale Dodgers	Sam Jones, Don Drysdale, Gene Woodling, Casey Stengel Hank Greenberg, Jim Lemon, (Corvette, Nellie Fox - BB Guns)	18	12	+100 (d)
☐ 7/60	Luis Aparicio/ Frank Howard WhiteSox/Dodgers	Ingemar Johansson, Frank Howard, Vada Pinson, Johnny Weismuller, Bob Shaw (Corvette, Nellie Fox -BB Guns) (*also Ingemar Johansson)	15	10	+15/+10
☐ 8/60	Mickey Mantle Yankees	Gil Hodges, Mickey Mantle, Wilt Chamberlain, Tris Speaker Jim Landis	50	30	+200 (d)
☐ 9/60	Colavito/ Mays/Fox	Bill Skowron, Rocky Colavito, Bob Mathias, Vern Law, Bill White	30	20	Varies
☐ 10/60	Babe Ruth/ Larry Sherry	Harvey Kuenn, Larry Sherry, Roberto Clemente, Floyd Patterson Babe Ruth, Stan Musial, Jack Nicklaus	24	16	+15
☐ 11/60	Roger Maris* Yankees	Roger Maris, Floyd Patterson, Ernie Davis,Paul Hornung, Jim Gentle, Davis/Blanchard, Joe Adcock (Also Ernie Davis - Syracuse)	45	30	+450 (d)
☐ 12/60	Johnny Unitas Colts	Baltimore Colts, Willie Mays, Bobby Hull, Bronko Nagurski Sonny Liston, Jim Brown (Corvette)	12	8	+25

1961

DATE	COVER	FEATURE	Nr-Mt	Ex	+Auto
☐ 1/61	Bobby Lane Steelers	Bobby Lane, Herb Score, Norm Larker, Bill Russell, Joe Garagiola, Benny Leonard	12	8	+10
☐ 2/61	Danny Murtaugh* Pirates	Ted Williams, Danny Murtaugh, N.Y. Yankees, Jackie Jensen, Vinegar Bend Mizell, John L. Sullivan, Gordie Howe, Jerry Lucas (*also Ted Williams, Jerry Lucas, Bobby Richardson)	15	10	+50 (d)
☐ 3/61	Jack Twyman/ Oscar Robertson Royals	Wilt Chamberlain, Jimmy Piersall, Twyman/Robertson Henri Richard, Spahn/Wynn, Stengel/Martin, Wilma Rudolph Gene Tunney, Brooks Robinson	15	10	+10 +20

	COVER	FEATURE	Nr-Mt	Ex	+Auto
☐ 4/61	Frank Howard Dodgers	Frank Howard, Bill Mazeroski, Elgin Baylor, Floyd Patterson, Ron Hansen, Carl Yastrzemski, Frank Mahovlich (Stan Musial/Ken Boyer Rawlings)	12	8	+10
☐ 5/61	Dick Groat/ Mickey Mantle Pirates/Yankees	Dick Groat, Gene Fullmer, Ernie Broglio, Mickey Mantle Jim Brosnan, Minnie Minoso, Mel Ott (Ken Boyer Rawlings, Corvair, Yogi Berra - Spalding)	50	25	+20 +200 (d)
☐ 6/61	Willie Mays* Giants	Willie Mays, Frank Robinson, Leo Durocher, Yogi Berra Johnny Longden, Jim Bunning (*also Yogi Berra/Roy Face) (Roger Maris-Spalding, Mickey Mantle -Rawlings)	24	16	+35
☐ 7/61	Rocky Colavito* Tigers	Arnold Palmer, Rocky Colavito, Jim Perry, Bob Allison, Orlando Cepeda, Bill Dickey, L.A. Dodgers (Yogi Berra - Spalding)(*Also Orlando Cepeda/Arnold Palmer)	30	20	+20
☐ 8/61	Warren Spahn* Braves	Ken Boyer, Warren Spahn, Woodie Held, Frank Lary, Strangler Lewis, Maury Wills, Frank Malzone (*also Ken Boyer, John Thomas)	18	12	+15
☐ 9/61	Joe DiMaggio/ Mickey Mantle Yankees	Bob Friend, Top Performers of 1946-1961 - Sport's Special 15th Anniversary Issue (Musial -Rawlings)	60	30+150 each	+200(d)
☐ 10/61	Wally Moon Dodgers	Ed Mathews, John Romano, Wally Moon, Hoyt Wilhelm Al Dark, Norm Cash (Norm Van Broklin-Spalding)	12	8	+10
☐ 11/61	Paul Hornung Packers	Paul Hornung, Sandy Koufax, Gene Freese, Walter Johnson	12	8	+20
☐ 12/61	Sam Huff Giants	Sam Huff, Frank Robinson, Glen Hall, Elston Howard (Harley Davidson)	12	8	+15

1962

DATE	COVER	FEATURE	Nr-Mt	Ex	+Auto
☐ 1/62	Jim Brown Browns	Jim Brown, Mickey Mantle. Roger Maris, Don Mossi, Frank Thomas, Boom Boom Geoffrion (Corvette)	20	10	+25
☐ 2/62	Roger Maris Yankees	Jerry Lucas, Bob Cousy, Roger Maris, Gordon Coleman, Steve Barber, Ty Cobb (Bob Cousy-Seamless, Roger Maris-Spalding)	45	30	+450 (d)
☐ 3/62	Wilt Chamberlain Warriors	Floyd Patterson, Wilt Chamberlain, Frank Lary, Jim Gentle (Don Drysdale-Vitalis(2pg)	15	10	+75
☐ 4/62	Vada Pinson/ Norm Cash Reds/Tigers	Orlando Cepeda, Pinson/Cash, Vern Law, John Blanchard (Stan Musial-Rawlings)	12	8	+40 (d) +20
☐ 5/62	Baseball Sluggers	Harmon Killebrew, Roberto Clemente, Branch Rickey, Robin Roberts, Mantle/Maris, (Mickey Mantle-Rawlings, Bobby Richardson-Vitalis, Harly Davidson)	18	12	varies
☐ 6/62	Hank Aaron Braves	Luis Aparicio, Sport's Greatest Team series- '55 Dodgers, Whitey Ford, Floyd Patterson, Hank Aaron, Roy Sievers (Galexie, Ken Boyer-Spalding) (*also Whitey Ford, Floyd Patterson, Luis Aparicio)	21	14	+25
☐ 7/62	Mickey Mantle Yankees	Mickey Mantle, Sonny Liston, Early Wynn, Ron Santo Milt Pappas, Al Kaline, Pie Traynor	45	30	+200 (d)
☐ 8/62	Rocky Colavito/ Harvey Kuenn Giants/Tigers	Colavito/Kuenn, Dick Stuart, Roger Maris, '34 Cards (Don Drydale - Vitalis)	24	16	+20 + 100 (d)
☐ 9/62	Stan Musial/ Ken Boyer Cardinals	Don Drysdale, Felipe/Matty Alou, Bobby Richardson, Charlie Finley, Arnold Palmer, Bo Belinsky, Paavo Nurmi (Mantle & Maris - Big Yank, Bob Cousy, Frank Gifford, Ken Venturi, Mike Ditka, RogerMaris-Camel, 63 Crovair, Bob Pettit-Rawlings)	24	16	+20/50(d)
☐ 10/62	Willie Mays Giants	Maury Wills, Willie Mays, Liston/Patterson, Rich Rollins Chuck Essegian, '27 Yankees	18	12	+30
☐ 11/62	Tommy Davis Jim Taylor Dodgers/Packers	Tommy Davis & Jim Taylor, Ralph Houk, Jim Davenport, '24 Notre Dame, Dick Donovan, Curt Flood	12	8	+10 each
☐ 12/62	Johnny Unitas/ Jim Brown Colts/Browns	Y.A. Tittle, Stan Mikita, Clete Boyer, Casey Stengel, Willie Davis, Cassius Clay	15	10	+25 each

1963

DATE	COVER	FEATURE	Nr-Mt	Ex	+Auto
☐ 1/63	Paul Hornung Packers	Packers Sonny Liston , Mickey Mantle, Paul Hornung Leon Wagner , Dave Keon , Jim Gilliam	12	8	+20
☐ 2/63	Maury Wills* Dodgers	Dodger, Bill Russell , Willie Mays , Maury Wills , Jim Piersall Marcel Cerdan , Tom Tresh (*Bill Russell, Jim Perisall)	15	10	+10
☐ 3/63	Bob Cousy	Celtics, Elgin Baylor , Bob Cousy , Jack Sanford , Jim Brown ,	12	8	+25

		Celtics	Jerry Lucas , George Sisler (Chevy II)			
☐ 4/63	Stan Musial/ Wilt Chamberlain	Cardinals/Warriors	Ernie Banks , Wilt Chamberlain , Stan Musial , Ed Mathews , Hank Aguirre (Stan Musial Rawlings, Boby Cousy Seamless Maris, Mantle, Ford - Big Yaks, B. Robinson- Rawlings, Bob Cousy -Jentzen)	15	10	varies
☐ 5/63	Mickey Mantle/ Yogi Berra	Yankees	Vic Power , Berra/Mantle , Arnold Palmer , Bart Starr , Bill Mazeroski , Boston Bruins	45	30	+200 (d) +20
☐ 6/63	Maury Wills	Dodgers	Frank Robinson , Maury Wills , Henry Armstrong Dick Stuart , Luis Aparicio , Juan Marichal	15	10	+10
☐ 7/63	Rocky Colavito/ Al Kaline	Tigers	Jack Nicklaus , Colavito/Kaline , Willie McCovey , '42 cards , Ralph Terry (Arnold Palmer - Ford)	30	20	+15 each
☐ 8/63	Willie Mays	Giants	Joey Jay , Willie Mays , John Unitas Boog Powell , HOF , Johnny Podres , Ted Williams	18	12	+30
☐ 9/63	Sandy Koufax	Dodgers	Sandy Koufax & Babe Ruth, Special Babe Ruth section , Paul Hornung , Yaz	30	20	+30
☐ 10/63	Mickey Mantle	Yankees	Brooks Robinson , Cassius Clay , Mickey Mantle , Dick Groat , Casey Stengel , Ernie Davis , '05 Giants , Ron Fairly (Paul Hornung, Bob Cousy - Jantzen)	36	24	+200 (d)
☐ 11/63	Whitey Ford	Yankees	Fred Hutchinson , Ford/Musial , Felipe Alou , Nellie Fox , Lefty Grove	15	10	+20
☐ 12/63	Del Shofner	Giants	Bobby Mitchell , Sonny Liston , Jerry Kramer , Jerry Lucas , Jim Maloney , Dick Ellsworth , Joe Pepitone	12	8	+10

1964

DATE	COVER		FEATURE	Nr-Mt	Ex	+Auto
☐ 1/64	Jim Taylor	Packers	Allie Sherman , Stan Musial , Pierre Pilote , Elston Howard , Gary Peters	15	10	+10
☐ 2/64	Sandy Koufax	Dodgers	Gordie Howe , Yogi Berra,Wilt Chamberlain , Al Kaline , Curt Simmons , Floyd Patterson , '40 Chicago Bears , Zoilo Versalles , Bill Bradley , John Callison	30	15	+30
☐ 3/64	Cassius Clay	Boxing	Frank Howard , Bob Cousy , Jim Bouton , Frank Frisch	30	16	+75
☐ 4/64	Oscar Robertson	Royals	Elgin Baylor, Bobby Hull , Rocky Colavito , Joe Torre (Al Kaline-Wilson) (YA Title, Rocky Colavito)	15	10	+15
☐ 5/64	Warren Spahn	Braves	Steve Barber , Alex Karras , Jean Beliveau , Vada Pinson , Warren Spahn	15	10	+15
☐ 6/64	Dick Stuart*	Red Sox	Dick Stuart , Cassius Clay , Willie Mays , Pete Rose , Tommy Davis , The Whiz Kids, Jerry Lumpe (*Also M. Ali) (Ford Mustang, Al Lopez-MacGregor)	15	10	+10
☐ 7/64	Tommy Davis/ Tom Tresh/Yaz	Dodgers/Yankees/Red Sox	Bill White , Vic Davalillo , Orlando Cepeda , Tony Lema ,	15	10	varies
☐ 8/64	Joe DiMaggio/ Willie Mays	Yankees/Giants	Joe Nuxhall , Bill Skowron , Luke Appling, Hank Aaron , Jim Brown , Billy Williams	50	30	Varies
☐ 9/64	Mickey Mantle	Yankees	Jaun Marichal , Mickey Mantle , Jim Taylor , Ted Williams , Richie Allen , Casey Stengel , Bob Allison , John Roseboro (Bart Starr-MacGregor)	45	25	+200 (d)
☐ 10/64	Willie Mays	Giants	Bobby Richardson , Willie Mays , Tony Oliva , Willie Stargell , Jesse Owens , Norm Siebern	20	12	+25
☐ 11/64	Harmon Killibrew*	Twins	Jim Bunning , Harmon Killebrew, Paul Hornung , Sandy Koufax , '14 Boston Braves , Dusty Rhodes , Jackie Brandt , Dick Butkus (Oscar Roberson-Macgregor) (*also Paul Hornung)	25	12	+15
☐ 12/64	Jim Brown	Browns	Mike Ditka, Mickey Mantle, Brooks Robinson , '64 Phillies Roger Staubach , Deron Johnson , Juan Pizzaro (Oscar Roberson-Macgregor, Mickey Mantle-Rawlings)	15	10	+20

1965

DATE	COVER		FEATURE	Nr-Mt	Ex	+Auto
☐ 1/65	Johnny Unitas	Colts	Cookie Gilchrist , Johnny Unitas,Dean Chance , Richie Allen , Eric Nesterenko , Pedro Ramos	15	10	+20
☐ 2/65	Fred Hutchinson	Reds	Bob Pettit , Bob Pulford , Warren Spahn , Bill Sharman Ray Sadecki , Bill Freehan (* also Oscar Robertson-Royals/Lenny Moore)	10	6	+10
☐ 3/65	Jerry West*	Lakers	Red Auerbach , Jerry West , Bobby Hull , Curt Flood , Phil Linz , Bob Bailey , Mickey Lolich (*also Brooks Robertson)	20	10	+15

	DATE	COVER	FEATURE	Nr-Mt	Ex	+Auto
☐	4/65	Dean Chance Angels	Jerry Lucas , Dean Chance, Ron Hunt , Tony Conigliaro , Cassius Clay , Jack Nicklaus , Bill Bradley , Rico Carty (Corvette, 7-up, Stan Musial-Macgregor, Ron Santo - Rawlings)	12	6	+10
☐	5/65	Sandy Koufax Dodgers	Roberto Clemente , Elston Howard , Floyd Patterson , Lou Brock , Bill Terry (Stan Musial - Macgregor, Ron Santo - Rawlings)	30	15	+25
☐	6/65	Willie Mays Giants	Willie Mays, Tim McCarver , Ed Mathews , ' 48 Indians , Wally Bunke, Arnold Palmer	25	12	+25
☐	7/65	Johnny Callison* Phillies	Johnny Callison , Rocky Colvavito , Bob Gibson , Larry Jackson , Don Zimmer, (Ford Auora Model) (*also Rocky Colavito)	15	10	+10
☐	8/65	Mickey Mantle Yankees	Mickey Mantle , Joe Namath , Max Alvis, Hank Bauer , Ron Santo, Sam Ellis (7-up)	40	25	+150 (d)
☐	9/65	Gehrig/DiMaggio, Frank Robinson Yankees/Orioles	Pete Ward , Frank Robinson ,Willie Horton , Mudcat Grant , Charlie O. Finley , Jim Ryun , Ron Swoboda , Jesus Alou (7-up)	30	16	varies
☐	10/65	Sandy Koufax/ Maury Wills Dodgers	Vada Pinson , Hank Aaron ,Wilt Chamberlain , Al Kaline , Jim Taylor , Al Lopez , Sam McDowell (Babe Ruth-Aurora Model, 7-up)	25	12	+30/+10
☐	11/65	Johnny Unitas/ Tommy Mason Colts/Vikings	Ray Nitschke , Jack Kemp , Harmon Killebrew , Lujack , Leahy & Notre Dame , Ron Fairly , Roseboro/Marichal , Norm Ullman (Ford Mustang)	15	10	+20/+10
☐	12/65	Fran Tarkenton/ Sonny Jurgensen Vikings/Redskins	Sonny Jurgensen , Willie Mays Sid Luckman , Hank Thompson , Pete Rose , John Havlicek (7-up)	12	8	+15 each

1966

	DATE	COVER	FEATURE	Nr-Mt	Ex	+Auto
☐	1/66	Charley Johnson Cardinals	Charley Johnson , Don Drysdale , Yaz , Brooks Robinson (Coke)	12	8	+10
☐	2/66	Sandy Koufax Dodgers	Bobby Hull , Sandy Koufax, , Gale Sayers , Special Ted Williams section (Dodger-Chargers, Cyclone GT)	30	12	+25
☐	3/66	Bill Russell Celtics	Zoilo Versalles , Bill Russell, Tony Zale , Gordie Howe , Lou Johnson , Judge Landis , Rick Barry (Wilt Chamberlain-Spalding, Coke, Pontiac GTO)	20	10	+200
☐	4/66	Willie Mays/ Paul Hornung Giants/Packers	Jerry West , Bobby Rousseau , Roger Maris , Vern Law , Willie Mays , Paul Hornung , Sam Mele (Bob Hope-Chrysler)	20	10	+25/+10
☐	5/66	Maury Wills Dodgers	Maury Wills , Arthur Ashe , Richie Allen , Denny McLain 55-'56 Montreal Canadiens , Bert Campaneris (Harmon Killebrew-shoes, Dr. Pepper, Paul Hornung Jantzen, Coke)	15	10	+10
☐	6/66	Joe Namath Jets	Joe Torre , Joe Namath , Frank Howard Juan Marichal , Special Lou Gehrig section (55 Chevy, Coke, [Juan Marichal fights back]	25	16	+30
☐	7/66	Mickey Mantle Yankees	Deron Johnson , Mickey Mantle, Orlando Cepeda , Arnold Palmer , Bobby Hull , Don Buford , Bob Feller (Coke)	30	20	+150(d)
☐	8/66	Frank Robinson Orioles	Tony Oliva , Frank Robinson , Ed Mathews , Dick Butkus Jim Pagliaroni, (Coke)	15	10	+20
☐	9/66	Willie Mays Giants	Sam McDowell , Top Performers of1946-1966 (Sports Special 20th Anniversary Issue)	25	15	+25
☐	10/66	Sandy Koufax Dodgers	Alex Karras , Sandy Koufax , Brooks / Frank Robinson Thompson/Branca , George Scott , Dick McAuliffe (Coke)	25	12	+25
☐	11/66	John Brodie 49ers	John Brodie , Jim Brown , Boog Powell (Corvette) Steve Spurrier , Leo Durocher , Roger Crozier , Gaylord Perry	12	8	+15
☐	12/66	Gale Sayers Bears	Gale Sayers , Jim Kaat , Jim Thorpe , Ralph Kiner Bears (Mickey Mantle-Rawlings)	20	10	+15

1967

	DATE	COVER	FEATURE	Nr-Mt	Ex	+Auto
☐	1/67	Don Meredith Cowboys	Don Meredith & Lance Alworth, Joe Morgan Mickey Mantle , Phil Regan , Ted Green ,	20	10	+15
☐	2/67	Frank Robinson Orioles	Rick Barry , Frank Robinson , Babe Ruth , Earl Wilson , Tommy Helms (Camero)	15	10	+15
☐	3/67	Wilt Chamberlain Warriors	Wilt Chamberlain , Bart Starr, Sandy Koufax , Bobby Hull Warriors , Knute Rockne , Dave DeBusschere , Jim Nash (Supremes - Coke, GTO,Charger)	15	10	+75
☐	4/67	Lew Alcindor UCLA	Lew Alcindor , Willie Davis , Bill Russell , Tommie Agee WalterJohnson , Rod Gilbert , Sam McDowell (Ford Mustang, Corvette, Moody Blues-Coke)	15	10	+35

	COVER	FEATURE	Nr-Mt	Ex	+Auto
☐ 5/67	Mickey Mantle Yankees	Ron Santo , Mickey Mantle , Jack Nicklaus , Dave Boswell Jim Lefebvre Barney Ross , Ken Wharram (Firebird, Rawling Gold Glove)	40	25	+200 (d)
☐ 6/67	Willie Mays Giants	Felipe Alou , Willie Mays , Bear Bryan, Roy Campanella (The Fortunes - Coke)	20	10	+30
☐ 7/67	Richie Allen/ Jim Ryan Phillies/Runner	Richie Allen & Jim Ryan , Sandy Koufax , Sonny Siebert Bill Tilden , Lee May , Bobby Orr	15	10	+10
☐ 8/67	Roberto Clemente Pirates	Frank Robinson , Dean Chance , Ernie Banks Joe McGinnity , Jim Northrup (Vaudeville Band - Coke)	40	25	+450 (d)
☐ 9/67	Pete Rose Reds	Pete Rose , Juan Marichal , Rico Petrocelli , Lou Brock Joe Horlen	30	20	+20
☐ 10/67	Orlando Cepeda/ Johnny Unitas Cards/Colts	Eddie Stanky , Orlando Cepeda , Johnny Unitas, Lew Alcindor Tony Perez , Harmon Killebrew (Ray Charles - Coke, Dodge Charger)	15	10	+10/20
☐ 11/67	Joe Namath Jets	Joe Namath , Tim McCarver , Yaz, Elgin Baylor , Jimmy Wynn , Colavito/K. Boyer'47-'49 Toronto Maple Leafs , Rod Carew	15	10	+30
☐ 12/67	Bart Starr Packers	Bart Starr , '67 Red Sox , Ed Giacomin , Musial/Schoendienst Oscar Robertson , Mike McCormick , Rusty Staub, (Bob Hope-Chrysler, Firebird)	15	8	+15

1968

DATE	COVER	FEATURE	Nr-Mt	Ex	+Auto
☐ 1/68	Mike Garrett Chiefs	Mike Garrett , Rick Barry , Julian Javier , Mickey Mantle, (Coke)	15	8	+10
☐ 2/68	Carl Yastrzemski Red Sox	Stan Mikita & Wilt Chamberlain , Yaz , Ferguson Jenkins Joe Frazier , Elvin Hayes (Sandy Posey - Coke, Ford Torino)	20	12	+15
☐ 3/68	Lew Alcindor UCLA	Nate Thurmond , Lew Alcindor , Roberto Clemente , Tom Seaver Maurice Stokes , Johnny Unitas	15	10	+40
☐ 4/68	Bobby Hull Black Hawks	Vince Lombardi , Bobby Hull , Jim Bouton , Bill Bradley , Reggie Smith , Paul/Lloyd Waner , Juan Marichal (Bobby Hull-Black Hawks)	20	12	+10
☐ 5/68	Willie Mays Giants	Bob Gibson , Al Kaline , Baseball '68 Special section, (Roberto Clemente - Louisville Slugger, GTO, Corvette, Coke Camaro)	15	10	+35
☐ 6/68	Carl Yastrzemski Red Sox	Carl Yastrzemski, Jim Bunning , Jim Beliveau , '31 A's Cesar Tovar (Coke)	20	10	+20
☐ 7/68	Hank Aaron Braves	St. Louis Cardinals , Tony Conigliaro , Tommy Davis , Hank Aaron (Coke)	20	10	+20
☐ 8/68	Pete Rose Johnny Unitas,	Bill Freehan , Pete Rose , Joe DiMaggio , Dal Maxvill , Curt Blefary (Coke)	24	10	+20
☐ 9/68	Don Drysdale Dodgers	Frank Howard , Don Drysdale , Luis Tiant , Alex Johnson (Harmon Killebrew-Head Shoulders, Jim Ryan Olympics)	15	10	+100 (d)
☐ 10/68	Fran Tarkenton Giants	Curt Flood & Randy Matson, Denny McLain , Matty Alou (Bob Hope Chrysler, Harmon Killebrew Head Shoulders)	15	6	+15
☐ 11/68	Don Meredith Cowboys	Leroy Kelly , Don Meredith , Lew Alcindor, Willie Horton Lou Brock , Hoyt Wilhelm (Johnny Unitas -Head & Shoulders)	15	6	+15
☐ 12/68	O.J. Simpson USC	Bob Hayes , O.J. Simpson , Denny McLain , Bert Campaneris , Arnold Palmer , Phil Esposito	30	20	+30

1969

DATE	COVER	FEATURE	Nr-Mt	Ex	+Auto
☐ 1/69	Deacon Jones Rams	Deacon Jones , Mike Shannon , Boom Boom Geoffrion Joe Namath , Tommy John , Satchel Paige , Johnny Bench (Bob Hope - Chrysler)	12	6	+10
☐ 2/69	John Havlicek/ O.J. Simpson Celtics/USC	John Havlicek , O.J. Simpson , Glenn Beckert , Celtics/Bills Maravich , Stan Musial , Lee Trevino (Camaro/Corvette, Wilt Chamberlain Head & Shoulders, Coke)	15	6	+10
☐ 3/69	Chamberlain/ West/Baylor Lakers	Chamberlain , West , Baylor , Bobby Hull , Mickey Stanley Rick Barry , Felix Millan , Frank Robinson , Jerry Koosman, Camaro)	20	12	Varies
☐ 4/69	Mickey Mantle Yankees	Bobby Orr , Joe Namath , Mickey Mantle John Unitas , Charlie Gehringer , Bill Mazeroski	60	40	+150 (d)

	DATE	COVER	FEATURE	Nr-Mt	Ex	+Auto
☐	5/69	Babe Ruth/ Willie Mays/Ty Cobb/ Sandy Koufax/Joe DiMaggio	Babe Ruth , Special Issue: 100 Years of Baseball	24	16	Varies
☐	6/69	Ted Williams Senators	Willie McCovey , Ted Williams , Sonny Liston , Dave McNally Pele , Bo Belinsky , Ernie Banks , Willie Shoemaker	25	15	+125
☐	7/69	Tony Conigliaro Red Sox	Lou Brock , Tony Conigliaro , Reggie Jackson Sugar Ray Robinson , Elgin Baylor	20	12	+250(d)
☐	8/69	O.J. Simpson Bills	Willie Mays , O.J. Simpson , Wilt Chamberlain , Bobby Murcer Don Kessinger , Phil Niekro , Jim Palmer	24	16	+20
☐	9/69	Durocher/Banks Cubs	Durocher & '69 Cubs , Joe Namath , Graziano/Zale Santo/B. Williams Chico Cardenas , Paul Blair , Blue Moon Odom	36	24	Varies
☐	10/69	Sonny Jurgensen Redskins	Rod Carew & Notre Dame , Randy Hundley , Cleon Jones , Doak Walker	10	6	+10
☐	11/69	Gale Sayers Bears	Roman Gabriel , Gale Sayers , Maurice Richard , Jim Maloney , Killebrew/Powell , Bill Russell Vada Pinson , Sal Bando	12	8	+20
☐	12/69	O.J./McLain Orr/Unseld Bills/Tigers/Bruins/Bullets	Johnny Bench & Morton/Staubach , '69 Mets , Richie Hebner 10 Greatest Sporting Events of the 60's	15	8	Varies

1970

	DATE	COVER	FEATURE	Nr-Mt	Ex	+Auto
☐	1/70	Calvin Hill Cowboys	Viking Front Four , Calvin Hill , '69 World Series , Joe Namath Bobby Bonds , Mike Cuellar	12	6	+10
☐	2/70	Lew Alcindor/ Gil Hodges Bucks/Mets	Lew Alcindor , Gil Hodges , Rico Carty	12	6	+35/ +100 (d)
☐	3/70	Jerry West Lakers	Pete Maravich , Curt Flood , Ted Williams , Tommie Agee (Mustang Mach 1)	12	6	+20
☐	4/70	Willis Reed Knicks	Willis Reed , Joe Pepitone , Ernie Banks/ Ron Santo	10	6	+10
☐	5/70	Tom Seaver Mets	Tom Seaver , Bill Freehan , Walt Alston Tony/Phil Esposito (Paper Flap - Camaro)	15	10	+25
☐	6/70	Harmon Killebrew Twins	Rico Petrocelli , Harmon Killebrew , Denny McLain Bobby Tolan , Carlos May (Paper Flap - Camaro, Paul Hornung/Roger Maris - Champion Spark plug)	15	10	+15
☐	7/70	Johnny Unitas/ Bart Starr Colts/Packers	Richie Allen , Wilt Chamberlain , Starr/Unitas , Jim Bouton , Andy Messersmith	12	10	Varies
☐	8/70	Hank Aaron Braves	Hank Aaron , Mickey Mantle (Lee Tevino)	15	10	+20
☐	9/70	Johnny Bench Reds	Billy Williams , O.J.Simpson , Pete Maravich Nolan Ryan Derek Sanderson , Reggie Jackson (Johnny Unitas -v-8)	22	15	+20
☐	10/70	Plunkett/Kern/ Theismann Manning	Tony Perez , Alex Johnson , Jim Bouton, Vince Lombardi Stanford, Ohio St, ND, Ol Miss	15	10	Varies
☐	11/70	Dick Butkus Bears	Dick Butkus , Clemente/Oliva , Bud Harrelson Jim Merritt	25	10	+20
☐	12/70	Roman Gabriel Rams	Bob Lilly , Roman Gabriel , Joe Namath, Luis Aparicio (Dodge Charger, Triump GT)	12	6	+10

1971

	DATE	COVER	FEATURE	Nr-Mt	Ex	+Auto
☐	1/71	Larry Brown/ Mike Lucci Redskins	Detroit Lions , Jerry Lucas , Frank Robinson/ World Series , Keith Magnuson , Bill Bradley	10	6	+10
☐	2/71	Dave Bing Pistons	Dave Bing , Bobby Orr	15	6	+10
☐	2/71	Bobby Orr Bruins (regional)	Dave Bing , Bobby Orr , Merv Rettenmund	40	20	+30
☐	3/71	Pete Maravich Hawks	Walt Frazier , Pete Maravich , Muhammad Ali , Pete Rose , Manny Sanguillen	35	15	+225 (d)
☐	4/71	John Havlicek Celtics	Phil Esposito , Pete Rose , John Havlicek , History of the NHL Stanley Cup (Paul Newman-Coke, Phil Esposito-Gillette, Ed Giacomin, Brooks Robinson)	15	10	+20

DATE	COVER	FEATURE	Nr-Mt	Ex	+Auto
☐ 5/71	Ted Williams/ D. McLain/ C. Flood Senators	Dave DeBusschere , Joe Frazier , Lew Alcindor , Sam McDowell	20	10	Varies
☐ 6/71	Boog Powell Orioles	Calvin Murphy, Billy Martin , Maury Wills	15	10	+10
☐ 7/71	Carl Yastrzemski Red Sox	Bob Gibson , Yaz , Seaver/Hodges/ Swoboda , Cesar Cedeno (Yaz, Bob Gibson, Coke)	15	10	+20
☐ 8/71	Mike Curtis Colts	Willie Stargell , Vida Blue , Jim Bouton , Bobby Hull	10	6	+10
☐ 9/71	Willie Mays Giants	Joe Torre , Top Performers of 1946-1971 (Coke , Joe DiMaggio) (Sports Special 25th Anniversary Issue)	25	15	+35
☐ 10/71	Vida Blue A's	Top Performers of 1946- 1971, Vince Lombardi, Willie Davis Bill Russell	10	6	+10
☐ 11/71	Ken Willard 49ers	Ken Willard , Top Performers of 1946-1971 Roberto Clemente / Bill Mazeroski , Catfish Hunter	10	6	+10
☐ 12/71	Bob Griese Dolphins	Bob Griese , Pete Maravich , Ernie Banks , Jackie Robinson	12	6	+20

1972

DATE	COVER	FEATURE	Nr-Mt	Ex	+Auto
☐ 1/72	Larry Brown Redskin	Satchel Paige, Artis Gilmore	10	6	+10
☐ 2/72	Spencer Haywood Supersonics	Tony Esposito, Lance Alworth, Sandy Koufax Kareem Abdul- Jabbar	10	6	+10
☐ 2/72	Tony Esposito (regional)		15	10	+15
☐ 3/72	Wilt Chamberlain Gene Washinton	Larry Csonka, Johnny Bench, Rod Gilbert, Wilt Chamberlain, (Ford Mustang-mach1)	15	9	+75
☐ 4/72	Bobby Orr Bruins	Joe Theisman, Connie Hawkins, Lee Trevino, (Cowens, Staubach)	25	15	+35
☐ 5/72	Bobby Hull Blackhawks	Richie Allen, F. Robinson, Bobby Hull (Blackhawk), (Richard Petty-Sunglasses-Mustang) Walt Frazier, Tom Seaver	15	8	+15
☐ 6/72	Brooks Robinson Orioles	Hank Aaron, Steve Prefontaine, (Ford Mustang)	15	10	+10
☐ 7/72	Joe Namath Jets	Freguson Jenkins	15	10	+35
☐ 8/72	Tom Seaver Mets	Bobby Orr	20	10	+20
☐ 9/72	Frank Robinson Orioles		15	10	+15
☐ 10/72	Jim Plunkett Stanford	Willie Mays, Johnny Bench	10	6	+10
☐ 11/72	Johnny Bench Reds		25	12	+20
☐ 11/72	Otis Taylor Chiefs (regional)	Red Auerbach	15	10	+10
☐ 12/72	Fran Tarkenton Viking	Lakers, Dick Allen (Bob Griese) , Duke Snider	15	8	+20

1973

DATE	COVER	FEATURE	Nr-Mt	Ex	+Auto
☐ 1/73	Merlin Olson Rams		10	6	+10
☐ 2/73	Rick Barry Warriors (regional)	Mark Spitz, Knicks	15	10	+10
☐ 2/73	Willis Reed Knicks (regional)	Mark Spitz, Bobby Fisher, OJ Simpson, Knicks Carlton Fisk	15	10	+10
☐ 3/73	Ken Dryden Canadians	Nate Archiblad, Dr J, Yankees (Mustang)	12	6	+10
☐ 4/73	Oscar Robertson Bucks (regional)	Steve Carlton, Lakers, 76ers, Roberto Clemente, Super Bowl VII	12	6	+20
☐ 4/73	Steve Carlton Phillies (regional)		20	12	+15

DATE	COVER	FEATURE	Nr-Mt	Ex	+Auto
☐ 5/73	Dave Cowens Celtics		10	6	+15
☐ 6/73	A.J. Foyt Car Racing	Nolan Ryan, Dr J (Mustang)	12	9	+15
☐ 7/73	George Foreman Boxing		12	9	+40
☐ 8/73	Bobby Murcer Yankees	Joe Morgan	12	7	+10
☐ 9/73	Gaylord Perry Indians	Cards	12	6	+10
☐ 10/73	Pete Rose * Reds	Pete Rose, Ferguson Jenkins, Cowboys (*also Ron Blomberg-Yanks, John Mayberrry -Royals Ferguson Jenkins - Cubs, Ken Holtzman-A's)	15	10	+20
☐ 11/73	Franco Harris Steelers	Anthony Davis, Dave Bing	12	6	+10
☐ 12/73	Joe Namath Jets	(Flap-Norm Snead-Giants, John Huarte -Chiefs) Pete Maravich, Philadelphia Flyers	15	8	+40

1974

DATE	COVER	FEATURE	Nr-Mt	Ex	+Auto
☐ 1/74	Larry Little/ Manny Fernandez Dolphins	SF Giants, Jackie Stewart, Reggie Jackson, Dolphins, Gordie Howe, M. Fernandez	10	6	+10
☐ 2/74	Karem Abdul Jabbar Bucks	Secretariat, Dr J, Arthur Ashe	10	6	+35
☐ 3/74	Bill Russell Wilt Chamberlain Celtics/Lakers	(B Robinson-Rawlings), Giants, Bill Russell, Buffalo Braves, Dave Thompson	10	6	+200/+75
☐ 4/74	Dave Debusschere Knicks	Jerry Tarkanian, Dodgers, Fran Tarkenton, Gaylord Perry	10	6	+10
☐ 5/74	Hank Aaron Braves (#715)	Phil Esposito, Babe Ruth, John Havlicek Home Run Record	25	15	+20
☐ 6/74	Pete Rose Reds	Johnny Miller, Rod Carew (B. Robinson-Rawlings)	15	10	+20
☐ 7/74	Chris Evert Jimmy Connors Tennis	Charlie Finley, Yogi Berra, Thurmon Munson, Dr J, Johnny Bench	12	6	+20 each
☐ 8/74	Larry Csonka/Calvin Hill Dolphins/Cowboys		12	8	+20
☐ 9/74	Muhammad Ali Boxing		14	8	+75
☐ 10/74	Reggie Jackson A's	Jackie Jensen, Mario Andretti	16	8	+25
☐ 11/74	Joe Namath* Jets	(*also Palmer, Chamberlain),(VW-Earl Monroe)	12	8	+40
☐ 12/74	O.J. Simpson, Bills	(Ed Giacomin-VW, Rick Barry, Wilt Chamberlin Pistol Pete Spalding Poster promotion -life size) Pro Keds shoes - Kareem & Others) Rangers, Mike Schmidt, Knicks, Notre Dame	12	9	+30

1975

DATE	COVER	FEATURE	Nr-Mt	Ex	+Auto
☐ 1/75	Fran Tarkenton Viking	Maury Wills, Wilt Chamberlain, Moses Malone (Lee Roy Jordan-Cowboys-VW) Rollie Fingers	12	8	+25
☐ 2/75	Muhammad Ali Boxing	NC State, Bobby Hull, Don Sutton, Dr J, Suns	12	8	+75
☐ 3/75	Julius Erving 76ers	Jim Palmer, ABA	25	15	+40
☐ 4/75	Rick Barry Warriors	Bill Sharmon (Kareem & Others- Pro Keds)	12	6	+10
☐ 5/75	Frank Robinson Indinas	Bobby Orr, Tom Heinsohn, Tony Congliaro	12	6	+15
☐ 6/75	Johnny Miller Golf	Steve Garvey, (Joe Torre-VW Bug)	10	6	+10
☐ 7/75	Bobby Bonds Yankees		12	9	+10
☐ 8/75	Billy Martin Rangers	Mickey Mantle, Bill Walton	12	9	+50 (d)

DATE	COVER	FEATURE	Nr-Mt	Ex	+Auto
☐ 9/75	Jimmy Connors Tennis		10	5	+20
☐ 10/75	James Harris Rams	*World Series, Reggie Jackson*	10	6	+10
☐ 11/75	Joe Namath Jets	*Fran Tarkenton, Rick Barry*	12	9	+35
☐ 12/75	Joe Greene Steelers	*Green Bay Packers*	10	6	+15

1976

DATE	COVER	FEATURE	Nr-Mt	Ex	+Auto
☐ 1/76	Super Bowl Preview	*Superbowl*	10	6	-
☐ 2/76	Fran Tarkenton Viking		10	6	+15
☐ 3/76	George McGinnis 76ers	*Bob Gibson*	10	6	+10
☐ 4/76	Steve Garvey Dodgers	*National League 100th Anniversary Issue*	15	8	+ 5
☐ 5/76	Tom Seaver Mets	*Celtics*	15	8	+10
☐ 6/76	Ronald Reagan/Gerald Ford Jimmy Carter/George Wallace Presidental Hopefuls		10	6	
☐ 7/76	Bruce Jenner Track	*Olympic Issue*	10	6	+10
☐ 8/76	Pete Rose/ Joe Morgan Reds		15	10	+20 each
☐ 9/76	Franco Harris Steelers	*Arthur Ashe*	10	6	+10
☐ 10/76	Bert Jones Colts		10	6	+10
☐ 11/76	George Simpson		10	6	+ 5
☐ 12/76	Pill-Popping Pete Maravich, Jack Lambert		10	4	

1977

DATE	COVER	FEATURE	Nr-Mt	Ex	+Auto
☐ 1/77	Roger Staubach Cowboys		15	8	+25
☐ 2/77	Julius Erving 76ers	*Performer of the Year*	25	10	+30
☐ 3/77	Joe Namath Bobby Orr OJ Simpson		15	6	+30
☐ 4/77	Bill Walton Trailblazers	*Bill Walton, Tom Lasorda, Dr J (Magic Johnson-McDonalds) OJ- Dingo, Raiders, Roger Staubach- Hagger, Johnny Bench -Batter up, Lou Brock -Converse, Coke)*	15	6	+20
☐ 5/77	Jan Stephenson Golfer	*Reds, Knicks (see through shirt on cover)*	20	12	+20
☐ 6/77	Greed in Sports	*George Brett, Vida Blue, Reggie Jackson (Coke)*	15	6	
☐ 7/77	Mark Fidrych Tigers	*Suns, Bill Cosby (Coke)*	10	6	+10
☐ 8/77	Boxing	*Davey Lopez, Muhammad Ali, Sugar Ray Leonard, Carlton Fisk*	10	6	
☐ 9/77	Leonard Willis* Vikings	*Dan Pastorini-Oilers, Raiders, Broncos (*Also Floyd Rice - Raiders)*	10	6	+ 5
☐ 10/77	Rod Carew Twins	*Rod Carew, World Series, Bruce Sutter*	10	6	+15
☐ 11/77	Earl Monroe* Bulletts	*Curt Flod, Joe Namath, Tony Dorsett (*also Woodie Allen)*	10	6	+10
☐ 12/77	Ken Stabler Raiders		10	6	+15

1978

DATE	COVER	FEATURE	Nr-Mt	Ex	+Auto
☐ 1/78	Tony Dorsett Cowboys	*Superbowl*	10	6	+15
☐ 2/78	Kareem Abdul-Jabbar Lakers	*Performer of the Year*	10	6	+35
☐ 3/78	Maurice Lucas Trailblazers	*Marice Lucas, Tarkanian, Mario Andretti, OJ-Dingo*	8	6	+10
☐ 4/78	Rich Gossage Jim Hunter Yankees	*Lou Brock-Cards*	8	6	+10 each
☐ 5/78	Graig Nettles Yankees	*Celtics, Paul Westphal, (R Jackson-Rabbit)*	8	6	+10
☐ 6/78	Julius Erving 76ers	*NBA Finals*	20	12	+30
☐ 7/78	Jim Rice Red Sox	*Ted Simmons, Bobby Bonds*	10	6	+10
☐ 8/78	Tom Seaver Reds	*Bob McAdoo, Nolan Ryan*	15	9	+20
☐ 9/78	Cliff Branch Raiders	*Football Preview Issue*	10	6	+10
☐ 10/78	Carl Yastrzemski Red Sox	*Gary Carter, Yaz, (Dr J), (Tony Dorsett-Underwear)*	12	8	+20
☐ 11/78	O.J. Simpson 49ers	*Earl Campbell, Jack Clark*	12	8	+25
☐ 12/78	Jack Lambert Steelers	*Don Shula, Paul Newman, Kyle Macy , Larry Bird*	12	6	+10

1979

DATE	COVER	FEATURE	Nr-Mt	Ex	+Auto
☐ 1/79	Harvey Martin Raiders	*Howard Cosell, Cowboys* *(*Also Jim Hart/Cardinals)*	12	6	+10
☐ 2/79	Julius Erving 76ers		25	12	+30
☐ 3/79	John Drew Hawks	*NBA Basketball Issue*	10	6	+ 5
☐ 4/79	Pete Rose Reds	*Baseball Preview Issue*	12	9	+20
☐ 5/79	Ron Guidry Yankees	*Elvin Hayes, Jim Palmer, Joe Louis*	8	6	+ 5
☐ 6/79	Dave Parker Pirates	*Red Auerbach*	8	6	+ 5
☐ 7/79	Graig Nettles Yankees (regional)		12	6	+ 5
☐ 7/79	J.R. Richard Astros (regional)		12	6	+15
☐ 8/79	Rod Carew Angels		10	6	+15
☐ 9/79	Tony Dorsett Cowboys		10	6	+15
☐ 10/79	Reggie Jackson Yankees	*World Series Issue*	15	8	+30
☐ 11/79	Raiders/Patriots Raiders	*NBA Basketball Preview*	8	6	
☐ 12/79	Pat Haden Chargers	*College Baskeball Preview*	8	6	+ 5

1980

DATE	COVER	FEATURE	Nr-Mt	Ex	+Auto
☐ 1/80	Jack Ham Steelers	*Playoff*	10	4	+ 5
☐ 2/80	Magic Johnson Lakers		25	16	+40
☐ 3/80	Larry Bird Celtics		20	12	+40
☐ 4/80	Willie Stargell Priates (regional)	*Pro Baseball Preview Issue* *Nolan Ryan*	15	6	+10

DATE	COVER	FEATURE	Nr-Mt	Ex	+Auto
☐ 4/80	Nolan Ryan Astros (regional)	Pro Baseballl Preview Willie Stargell	30	15	+25
☐ 5/80	Lou Piniella Yankees (regional)		8	6	+ 5
☐ 5/80	Steve Garvey Dodger (regional)		8	6	+ 5
☐ 5/80	George Brett Royals (regional)		20	10	+40
☐ 6/80	Bill Russell Dodgers	Indy 500	6	4	+ 5
☐ 7/80	Gorman Thomas Brewers	Muhammad Ali, Roger Staubach	6	4	+ 5
☐ 8/80	Terry Bradshaw Steelers	Pro Football Issue	10	4	+10
☐ 9/80	Tommy John White Sox(regional)	Bear Bryant, College Football Issue	6	4	+10
☐ 9/80	Art Schlicter Ohio State (regional)		6	4	+ 5
☐ 10/80	Earl Campbell Oilers	Terry Bradshaw, Pro Basketball Preview	10	4	+15
☐ 11/80	Lee Roy Selmon Tampa Bay Buccaneers	Pro Basketball Previw	6	4	+ 5
☐ 11/80	Dan Pastorini Chiefs (regional)		10	5	+10
☐ 12/80	Louie Gicmmon Eagles	FB's Special Teams, Col Basketball Issue	6	4	+10
☐ 12/80	Herschel Walker Georgia	(Regional Cover) Col Baskeball Preview	10	5	+15

1981

DATE	COVER	FEATURE	Nr-Mt	Ex	+Auto
☐ 1/81	Billy Sims Lions	Al Davis, Wayne Gretzky	6	4	+ 5
☐ 2/81	Danny White Cowboys		6	4	+10
☐ 2/81	Ron Jaworski Eagles	Danny White	6	4	+ 5
☐ 3/81	Kelly Tripucka Notre Dame (regional)	Dave Winfield, Final Four	6	4	+ 5
☐ 3/81	Rod Foster UCLA (regional)	Boxing, Final Four, Dave Winfield	10	5	+ 5
☐ 4/81	Tug McGraw Phillies(regional	Baseball Issue	8	4	+ 5
☐ 4/81	George Brett Royals(regional)		10	5	+40
☐ 5/81	Billy Martin A's	Mike Schmidt, Reggie Jackson	8	6	+50 (d)
☐ 6/81	Don Sutton Astros (regional)		10	4	+10
☐ 6/81	Dave Parker Pirates(regional)		10	4	+ 5
☐ 7/81	Goose Gossage or Bruce Sutter Yankees(regional) or Cubs (regional)		10	4	+ 5
☐ 8/81	Jim Plunkett Raiders	Frank Robinson	6	4	+ 5
☐ 9/81	Earl Campbell Oilers	Football Preview	7	4	+10
☐ 10/81	Doug Plank-Bears Jackie Slater - Rams		6	4	+ 5
☐ 11/81	Lester Hayes Raiders		6	4	+ 5
☐ 12/81	Steve Bartkowski Falcons	College Basketball Issue	6	4	+ 5

1982

DATE	COVER	FEATURE	Nr-Mt	Ex	+Auto
☐ 1/82	Tony Dorsett Cowboys	*NFL Playoff Preview*	16	4	+10
☐ 2/82	Magic Johnson Lakers		20	10	+40
☐ 3/82	Gerry Cooney Boxing		6	4	+20
☐ 4/82	Fernando Valenzuela* Dodgers	*(*also Larry Bird in corner) Baseball Preview Issue*	6	4	+10
☐ 5/82	Reggie Jackson Angels	*[Wayne Gretzky in corner] NBA Issue*	12	6	+35
☐ 6/82	Tom Seaver Reds	*Nolan Ryan*	8	6	+20
☐ 7/82	Billy Martin A's	*Cowboys*	8	5	+50 (d)
☐ 8/82	Joe Montana 49ers	*NFL Preview*	20	10	+50
☐ 9/82	Herchel Walker Georgia	*College Football Issue*	12	6	+20
☐ 10/82	Los Angeles Rams*	*[* Reggie Jackson in corner] World Series*	8	5	
☐ 11/82	Lawrence Taylor Giants	*Magic Johnson*	10	5	+20
☐ 12/82	Patrick Ewing Georgetown	*Baskeball Preview*	10	5	+35

1983

DATE	COVER	FEATURE	Nr-Mt	Ex	+Auto
☐ 1/83	John Elway* Stanford	*Fearless Predictions* *(*Also Kareem abdul-Jabbar, Walker, Garvey, Leonard, Evert)*	15	6	+25
☐ 2/83	Tony Dorsett* Cowboys	*(*Kurt Rambis in Corner)*	10	6	+20
☐ 3/83	Moses Malone Gary Carter*	*Top 100 Salaries* *(*Martina Navratilova, Angel Cordero)*	6	4	Varies
☐ 4/83	Steve Garvey Padres	*Baseball Issue*	6	4	+ 5
☐ 5/83	Steve Carlton* Phillies	*(* Also Wayne Gretzky)*	6	4	+10
☐ 6/83	Gary Carter* Mike Schmidt Expos/Phillies	*(*Also Robin Yount, Andre Dawson)*	8	6	+10 +40
☐ 7/83	Reggie Jackson Angels		8	6	+35
☐ 8/83	Marcus Allen Raiders	*NFL Preview*	6	4	+15
☐ 9/83	Marcus Dupree Oklahoma	*College Football Preview*	6	4	+10
☐ 10/83	Mark Gastineau Jets	*NHL preview, John Elway*	6	4	+10
☐ 11/83	Franco Harris Pirates	*NBA Preview*	6	4	+10
☐ 12/83	Lyle Alzado Raiders	*Colege Basketball Preview*	6	4	+50 (d)

1984

DATE	COVER	FEATURE	Nr-Mt	Ex	+Auto
☐ 1/84	Dan Marino Dolphins	*Playoffs*	20	10	+40
☐ 2/84	Mary Decker * Runner	*(*also Dickerson, Hagler, Landry, Ewing, Cosell, Rose, Noah)* *Fearless Predictions Issue*	6	4	-
☐ 3/84	Marina Navratilova* Tennis	*(*also Dale Murphy, Joe Theisman, Magic Johnson,* *Mavin Hagler, Herschel Walker) Salaries Issue*	6	4	-
☐ 4/84	Cal Ripken Jr. Orioles	*Baseball Preview Issue*	20	10	+ 40
☐ 5/84	Wayne Gretzky Oilers		20	15	+ 40

DATE	COVER	FEATURE	Nr-Mt	Ex	+Auto
☐ 6/84	Dale Murphy Braves	NBA Playoff	6	4	+ 10
☐ 7/84	Tom Lasorda,* Sparky Anderson	(*Also Herzog, Joe Torre)	6	4	Varies
☐ 8/84	Eric Dickerson Colts	NFL Preview	6	4	+ 10
☐ 9/84	Darryl Clack ASU	College Football Preview	6	4	+ 5
☐ 10/84	Walter Payton Bears		6	4	+ 30
☐ 11/84	Betting Football NBA Preview		6	4	-
☐ 12/84	Chris Mullin Patrick Ewing St Johns/Georgetown	College Basketball Preview	6	4	Varies

1985

DATE	COVER	FEATURE	Nr-Mt	Ex	+Auto
☐ 1/85	Dan Marino Dolphins		15	10	+ 40
☐ 2/85	Mary Lou Retton* Gymnast	Fearless Predictions (*also Ralph Samson, Alzado, Gooden, Joe Montana)	6	4	-
☐ 3/85	Joe Montana Magic Johnson Gary Carter	Salaries Preview USFL	6	4	+ 10
☐ 4/85	Dwight Gooden Mets	Baseball Issue	8	6	+ 10
☐ 5/85	Gary Matthews Keith Hernandez Cubs/Mets		6	4	+10
☐ 6/85	George Brett Royals	Baseball Issue	12	6	+ 30
☐ 7/85	Model (Regional cover)	Baseball season	6	4	
☐ 7/85	Kirk Gibson Tigers (regional)	Baseball Issue	6	4	+ 10
☐ 8/85	Joe Montana 49ers	NFL Preview Issue	15	10	+ 35
☐ 9/85	John Maarleveld/Rick Badanjek Maryland (Regional)		6	4	+ 5
☐ 9/85	Robbie Bosco BYU	College Football Issue	6	4	+ 5
☐ 10/85	Dan Marino Dolphins	Football Issue	10	6	+ 40
☐ 11/85	Lawrence Taylor & Marcus Allen Giants/Raiders	NHL Preview	8	5	+ 20 ea
☐ 12/85	Patrick Ewing Knicks	College & Pro Baseketball Preview	6	4	+ 15

1986

DATE	COVER	FEATURE	Nr-Mt	Ex	+Auto
☐ 1/86	Jim McMahon Bears		6	4	+ 10
☐ 2/86	William Perry "The Fridge" Bears		6	4	+ 10
☐ 3/86	Stacy Oversier Gymnast	"The Most Beautiful Women In Sports (See Through Swimsuit)	6	4	Varies
☐ 4/86	Bret Saberhagen Royals		6	4	+ 10
☐ 4/86	Dwight Gooden Mets	Baseball Preview Issue	6	4	+ 10
☐ 5/86	George Brett Royals	Larry Bird	8	4	+ 30
☐ 6/86	Wayne Gretzky*	"Top 100 Salaries"	6	4	-

DATE	COVER	FEATURE	Nr-Mt	Ex	+Auto
	Oilers	(*Cover Includes others)			
☐ 7/86	Hall of Fame Prospects		6	4	-
☐ 8/86	Howie Long		6	4	+ 15
	Raiders				
☐ 9/86	Jim Harbaugh		6	4	+ 10
☐ 10/86	Dan Marino		20	10	+ 35
	Dolphins				
☐ 10/86	Magic Johnson		15	10	+ 40
	Lakers (regional)				
☐ 11/86	Pervis Ellison		10	5	+ 5
	Louisville	College/Pro Basketball Preview			
☐ 11/86	Terry Cummings		6	4	+ 10
☐ 12/86	40th Anniversary Issue		10	5	-

1987

DATE	COVER	FEATURE	Nr-Mt	Ex	+Auto
☐ 1/87	John Elway		20	10	+ 30
	Broncos				
☐ 2/87	Montana/Dent/		10	5	Varies
	M. Allen	Superbowl Issue			
	49ers/Raiders/Bears				
☐ 3/87	M. Jordon/M. Schmidt/		25	15	Varies
	R. Clemens/Eric Davis				
☐ 4/87	Darryl Strawberry Cal Ripken Jr, baseball Preview		6	4	+10
	Mets				
☐ 5/87	Dominique Wilkins		6	4	+10
	Hawks	NBA/ NHL Playoff			
☐ 6/87	Michael Jordan*	(*also Tyson, Conner, Woodard, Schmidt	6	4	-
	Bulls	Hogan, Flutie, Madden, Joyner, Graf) "Top 100 Salaries"			
☐ 7/87	Dave Parker vs.		6	4	+10
	Mike Scott				
	Pirates/Astros				
☐ 8/87	Roger Craig &		6	4	+10
	The 49ers	NFL Preview			
	49ers				
☐ 9/87	Lawrence Taylor		6	4	+10
	Giants	College Football Preview			
☐ 10/87	Jim Kelly		6	4	+25
	Bills	NHL Preview			
☐ 11/87	Larry Bird		25	15	+35
	NBA Preview				
☐ 12/87	"10 Most Intriguing		6	4	-
	Sports Stories"				

1988

DATE	COVER	FEATURE	Nr-Mt	Ex	+Auto
☐ 1/88	Boomer Esiason		6	4	+10
☐ 2/88	NFL's All -Time		6	4	-
	Greatest Coaches				
☐ 3/88	Jack McDowell/ Greg Jefferies/		6	4	Varies
	Don Lovell				
	Mets/Indians/White Sox				
☐ 4/88	Don Zimmer	Baseball Preview Issue (Regional Cover)	6	4	+10
☐ 4/88	K. Hernandez/	Baseball Preview Issue	6	4	+10 ea
	W. Clark				
	Mets/Giants (regional Cover)				
☐ 5/88	Isaiah Thomas		6	4	+15
	Pistons				
☐ 6/88	"Top 100 Salaries"		6	4	-
☐ 7/88	Mike Tyson		8	5	+40
	Boxing				
☐ 8/88	Howie Long & Marcus Allen		6	4	Varies
	& Todd Christianson				
	Raiders				
☐ 9/88	Troy Aikman	College Football Preview	12	8	+40
	Cowboys				

DATE	COVER	FEATURE	Nr-Mt	Ex	+Auto
☐ 10/88	Cornelius Bennett Bills	Football Issue	6	4	+ 5
☐ 11/88	Michael Jordan Bulls	NBA Preview	25	10	+40
☐ 12/88	Stacey King Oklahoma	College Basketball Issue, Wayne Gretzky	6	4	+ 5

1989

DATE	COVER	FEATURE	Nr-Mt	Ex	+Auto
☐ 1/89	Dennis Gentry Bears		6	4	+ 5
☐ 2/89	Cindy Crawford Swimsuit Issue	Swimsuit	25	15	+40
☐ 3/89	Orel Hershiser Dodgers	Baseball Spring Training Issue	6	4	+10
☐ 4/89	Don Mattingley Yankees*	Baseball Preview Issue (*also Eckersley, Gibson, Hernandez)	10	6	+15
☐ 5/89	Magic Johnson Lakers	NBA/NHL Playoff Preview	10	5	+40
☐ 6/89	Wayne Gretzky Oilers	Top 100 paid atheletes (* also Tyson, Marino, Graff, Ewing, Clemens)	20	10	+40
☐ 7/89	Jose Canseco A's		6	4	+ 10
☐ 8/89	Joe Montana 49ers*	NFL Preview (also Randall Cunningham, Troy Aikman)	10	5	+30
☐ 9/89	Emmitt Smith* Gators	(* also Scott Mitchell, Tony Rice) College Football preview	25	10	+25
☐ 10/89	Dan Marino Dolphins	43rd Anniversary Issue (*also Dwight Gooden)	15	5	+30
☐ 11/89	Michael Jordan Larry Bird Magic Johnson		20	10	+40 +35 +35
☐ 12/89	Hank Gathers Loyola*	College Basketball Preview (*also Trevor Wilson, David Butler)	8	5	+100 (d)

1990

DATE	COVER	FEATURE	Nr-Mt	Ex	+Auto
☐ 1/90	Jim Everett Rams	NFL Playoff Issue	8	5	+10
☐ 2/90	Swimsuit Model	Swimsuit Issue	20	10	+20
☐ 3/90	Bo Jackson Royals	Baseball Spring Training issue	10	6	+25
☐ 4/90	Jose Canseco A's	Baseball Issue (*Orel Hershiser, Wally Joyner)	7	4	+10
☐ 5/90	Rickey Henderson A's	Baseball Preview	7	4	+10
☐ 6/90	Michael Jordan* Bulls	100 Top paid players (*Montana, Gretzky, Stockton, etc)	20	9	+40
☐ 7/90	Will Clark Giants		7	4	+10
☐ 8/90	Joe Montana 49ers	Football Issue (* also Willie Anderson, Bobby Humphry)	12	8	+30
☐ 9/90	John Elway* Broncos	NFL Preview (*also Roger Craig, Jim Everett, Bo Jackson	15	8	+20
☐ 10/90	Joe Montana 49ers	'100 best sports stories' (*also Wayne Gretzky, Michael Jordan, others)	12	8	+20
☐ 11/90	Joe Montana 49ers	NHL Preview, Swimsuit Calendar	12	5	+20
☐ 12/90	Randall Cunningham Lawrence Taylor*	NBA/College Basketball Issue (*KJ, Thomas, others)	6	4	+10

1991

DATE	COVER	FEATURE	Nr-Mt	Ex	+Auto
☐ 1/91	Michael Jordan Bulls	NFL Playoff Preview	20	10	+40

	DATE	COVER	FEATURE	Nr-Mt	Ex	+Auto
☐	2/91	Rowanne Swimsuit	Swimsuit Issue	20	10	+15
☐	3/91	Ken Griffey Jr. Mariners		20	10	+40
☐	4/91	Jose Canseco A's*	Baseball issue (* also Ryan Sandberg, Dwight Gooden)	6	4	+10
☐	5/91	Matt Williams Giants*	Baseball Poster of Nolan Ryan, Ken Griffey Jr (* also Eddie Murray, Benito Santiago)	6	4	+10
☐	6/91	Darryl Strawberry Dodgers	Sports Salary Survey	6	4	+10
☐	7/91	Joe Montana 49ers*	NFL Hottest Cheerleader poster, NFL Preview (* also Lenny Dykstra, Elliott, King)	10	6	+20
☐	8/91	Ronnie Lott Raiders	Football Poster	6	4	+10
☐	9/91	Joe Montana 49ers*	NFL & College Preview (* also Marcus Allen, Jim Everett, Bobby Humphrey)	10	6	+20
☐	10/91	Bo Jackson Raiders	45 Great years of Sport	6	4	+10
☐	11/91	Michael Jordan Bulls*	NBA Preview (Swimsuit Calendar) (*also C. Drexler, David Robinson, Magic Johnson, Charles Barkley)	20	10	+40
☐	12/91	Michael Jordan Bulls		20	10	+30

1992

	DATE	COVER	FEATURE	Nr-Mt	Ex	+Auto
☐	1/92	Jim Kelly Bills	NBA Pictorial	10	5	+25
☐	2/92	Charles Barkley 76ers		6	4	+10
☐	3/92	Swimsuit Model	Swimsuit Issue	20	10	+ 15
☐	4/92	Eric Davis, Darry Strawberry, Dodgers	Brett Butler Baseball Preview issue	6	4	+ 10 ea
☐	5/92	Michael Jordan Bulls	NBA Playoff Issue, Cheerleaders (*also Tim Hardaway, Patrick Ewing	20	10	+40
☐	5/92	Cal Ripken Jr. Orioles	NBA Playoff Issue, Cheerleaders	10	5	+40
☐	6/92	Michael Jordan Scottie Pippen Bulls	(*also Magic Johnson)	20	10	+40
☐	7/92	Troy Aikman Cowboys	NFL Preseason	10	5	+30
☐	8/92	Mark Rypien Redskins*	NFL Hottest Cheerleaders (*also Jerry rice, Tommy Maddox)	6	4	+10
☐	9/92	Eric Dickerson Raiders	Football Preview Issue	6	4	+10
☐	10/92	Larry Johnson Hornets	NBA Issue	6	4	+10
☐	11/92	Tim Hardaway Warriors*	NBA PREVIEW (*also Pete Rose)	6	4	+10
☐	12/92	Chargers/Steelers	Swimsuit Calendar	6	4	+ 5

1993

	DATE	COVER	FEATURE	Nr-Mt	Ex	+Auto
☐	1/93	Charles Barkley* 76ers	(*also Jerry Rice, Magic Johnson,others) Top 40	6	4	Varies
☐	2/93	Jill Model	Swimsuit Issue (Newstand version)	20	10	+ 15
☐	2/93	Charles Barkley Model	Swimsuit Issue Hank Aaron	20	10	+ 15
☐	3/93	Dave Winfield* Toronto Blue Jays	Inside Baseball Issue	6	4	+ 10
☐	4/93	Barry Bonds Giants	Baseball 12993 preview edition (* also Bonila, Canseco, Clemens)	6	4	+ 15
☐	5/93	Michael Jordan Bulls	NBA PLAYOFF ISSUE (*also Pat Ewing)	20	10	+ 40

	COVER	FEATURE	Nr-Mt	Ex	+Auto
☐ 6/93	Michael Jordan Bulls	NBA Final Edition (*also C. Barkley, D. Robinson, P. Ewing)	20	10	+ 40
☐ 7/93	Troy Aikman Cowboys	Football Issue	10	5	+ 20
☐ 8/93	Steve Young 49ers	(*also Joe Montana, Reggie White, Troy Aikman) Football Preview Issue	10	5	+ 20
☐ 9/93	Joe Montana Chiefs	Football Issue	10	5	+ 20
☐ 10/93	Steve Young 49ers*	Whos the Best QB? (*also Troy Aikman, Joe Montana, Randall Cunningham, Dan Marino)	6	3	+ 15
☐ 11/93	Michael Jordan Bulls	NBA Preview (*also Barkley, Shaq, Ewing)	20	10	+ 30
☐ 12/93	Michael Jordan Bulls	10 years of Michael Jordan (swimsuit Calendar)	20	10	+ 40

1994

DATE	COVER	FEATURE	Nr-Mt	Ex	+Auto
☐ 1/94	Steve Young 49ers	The Best 40 (* also Bonds, Barkley, Jordan, Thomas, Smith)	10	5	+ 20
☐ 2/94	Joe Montana Chiefs*	SuperBowl (*also Troy Aikman, Jerry Rice)	10	5	+ 20
☐ 3/94	Alison Armitage Actress	Swimsuit Issue	15	10	+ 15
☐ 4/94	Barry Bonds Giants*	Baseball 1994 isue (* also Joe Carter, David Justice, Juan Gonzalez)	10	6	+ 20
☐ 5/94	Mike Piazza Dodgers	NBA Showtime Pictorial	12	6	+ 15
☐ 6/94	Scottie Pippen Bulls	NBA Playoffs (*background with Jordan)	8	5	+ 25
☐ 7/94	Aikman/Smith Cowboys	NBA Draft Preview, Swimsuit	8	6	+ 25
☐ 8/94	Dan Marino Dolphins*	Football Preview (*Thurman Thomas, Jerry Rice, Troy Aikman)	12	8	+ 30
☐ 9/94	75th Pro Football Cowboys*	75 Yeras of Pro Football (Mail Version) (* also Walter Payton, Joe Montana, Joe Namath, Jim Brown)	6	4	+ 20
☐ 9/94	Troy Aikman Cowboys*	75 Yeras of Pro Football (Store Verison) (* also Walter Payton, Joe Montana, Joe Namath, Jim Brown)	12	8	+ 20
☐ 10/94	Marcus Allen Chiefs	NBA Preseason	6	4	+ 10
☐ 11/94	Michael Jordan Bulls*	Basketball Preview (*Charles Barkley, Patrick Ewing, Hakem Olajuwon)	15	10	+ 30
☐ 12/94	Shaq Magic	College Basketball Preview Swimsuit Calendar	10	6	+30

1995

DATE	COVER	FEATURE	Nr-Mt	Ex	+Auto
☐ 1/95	Frank Thomas White Sox*	Athlete of the Year (*Emmit Smith, Ken Griffey Jr, Troy Aikman, Olajuwon)	10	6	+20
☐ 2/95	Jerry Rice 49ers*	SuperBowl Issue, Swimsuit sneak Peek (*also Troy Aikman & others)	6	4	+20
☐ 3/95	Shanna Model	Swimsuit Issue	15	10	+10
☐ 4/95	Michael Jordan White Sox*	(*also Thomas, Bonds, Ripken)	15	10	+30
☐ 5/95	Charles Barkley Suns	Baseball predictions (*Rodman)	6	4	+15
☐ 6/95	Michael Jordan Bulls	NBA Playoff Preview	15	10	+25
☐ 7/95	Steve Young 49ers*	Swimsuit Special (*Troy Aikman)	6	4	+15
☐ 8/95	Steve Young 49ers*	Football Preview (*Jeff Hosteler, Emmitt Smith, John Elway)	6	4	+15
☐ 9/95	Steve Young 49ers*	Pro Football 95 (*Marino, Aikman, Cunnigham, Elway)	6	4	+15
☐ 10/95	Dan Marino/Jerry Rice /Irvin/Warren Moon		6	4	+15

	DATE	COVER	FEATURE	Nr-Mt	Ex	+Auto
		49ers*	*Subsription Version*			
☐	10/95	Steve Young		6	4	+15
		49ers*	*(*also Jerry Rice) Store Version*			
☐	11/95	Michael Jordan	*Pro preview Issue*	15	8	+15
		Bulls*	*(*also Shaq,Olajuwon, Johson, Exel)*			
☐	12/95	Dennis Rodman	*Baslektball Preview*	6	4	+15
		Spurs*	*(* UCLA)*			

1996

	DATE	COVER	FEATURE	Nr-Mt	Ex	+Auto
☐	1/96	Michael Jordan		15	8	+15
		Bulls				
☐	2/96	Dan Marino/Troy Aikman		6	4	+15
		Dolphins/Cowboys	*Superbowl Dream Team*			
☐	3/96	Swimsuit	*Swimsuit Issue*	12	8	+15
☐	4/96	Penny Anfernee Hardaway		6	4	+15
		Magic	*Baseball Issue*			
☐	5/96	Magic Johnson/Dennis Rodman/Michael Jordan		6	4	+15
		Lakers/Bulls	*NBA Playoff*			
☐	6/96	Michael Jordan/Scottie Pippen/Dennis Rodman		6	4	+15
		Bulls				
☐	7/96	Jerry Rice/Joe Montana		6	4	+ 35
		49ers				
☐	8/96	Emmitt Smith/Junior Seau/Dan Marino/Brett Farve		6	4	Varies

---

1946

1947

1948

1949

1949

1949

1950

1951

1951

1979

1980

1987

CHAPTER SEVEN:
Collecting Time Magazine

Time magazine has been covering historical events for seven decades through portraits of individuals who impact our history. Alongside presidents, villains, artists, scientists and a load of politicians is a significant representation on the front cover of movie stars and athletes. Since the audience for this book is more interested in athletes than Marilyn Monroe, I will cover the likes of Marilyn's ex, Joe DiMaggio, and the like first.

Time began making sports covers in 1923 with a dummy issue featuring on the front cover a boxer named Floyd Johnson. In all, there are 170-plus sports-related front covers. Baseball and football players dominate, followed by stars from tennis and boxing. However, the most popular magazine covers for collectors are baseball players and then golfers.

The most popular issue of Time is the 1936 Joe DiMaggio because of the immense demand to get the issue autographed. An ExMt issue of Joe DiMaggio went for more than $500 in a recent auction. Just as valuable but rarely seen are the two issues with Bobby Jones on the covers. Both of these are on every golf magazine collector's want list. The rarest issue of all the sports covers is the dummy issue of Johnson, which rarely trades hands.

I have diligently compiled a listing of all the key covers by subject for you below. However, if you are serious about collecting Time magazines you need to obtain the book "The Faces of History - TIME magazine covers 1923-1991." This book, released by Time-Warner, shows every Time magazine from that period.

GRADING OF TIME MAGAZINE

Grading of Time magazines is similar to Sports Illustrated. However, labels were placed on the back of the magazine before 1945. After 1945 you will find magazines with the label on the front. Most collectors want the magazine to be Ex-Mt or better with or without the label. Issues used for autograph purposes are preferred without a label. Most of the magazines will be used for framing purposes, so it is critical that the cover be clean

without any major flaws. However, the early issues (pre-1940) may be acceptable in Excellent grade. The most common flaw with Time magazines is flaking along the spine. The paper stock is excellent, so the issues that have survived the paper drives over the years tend to be in nice condition.

COLLECTING TIME MAGAZINE

Collecting every sports issue of Time is a challenge because there is no easy source. You can contact sports publication dealers across the country and discover that they have just a handful in stock at any given time.

For example, I have seen just three George Sisler issues in the last four years. Some of the most advanced sports collectors usually have a George Sisler on their want lists.

Many, people only collect their favorite player. A few people collect every baseball cover and even fewer collect every sport cover. However, the challenge is fun and rewarding and you will meet a lot of interesting people along the way.

TIME MAGAZINE VARIATIONS

Another important aspect of Time magazine collecting is the variations that are available. Time magazine began to make variations as early as World War II with the 1945 Pony editions. I do not know all of the variations that exist, but I have compiled the variations of which I am aware:

1. Pacific Edition - currently produced for the Far East.

2. Pacific Edition (Pony) - small format used during and after World War II. Mel Ott was on a cover.

3. Time International - currently produced for Europe.

4. Atlantic Edition (Pony) - small format used during and after WW II. Mel Ott was on a cover in 1945.

5. Latin American Edition - These started as early as 1948 with Joe DiMaggio on the cover. The paper is a thinner, different stock.

6. Canadian Edition - These have "Canada" written on them. In the earlier years a Canadian maple leaf was on the center page. I also have a version with a different red-color variation

than the American version. Later have a small maple leaf. From the late 1950s through today, the Canadian versions just state "Canada" on them.

7. Atlantic/East Coast Edition - In the 1960s it stated "Atlantic Edition" on the cover.

8. Classroom Edition - This was designed for school education, and it has a statement across the middle saying "Classroom Edition."

AUTOGRAPHED TIME MAGAZINES

Time is one of the most popular magazines in the world to have autographed. A collection of autographed Time magazine covers sold for over $170,000 in a 1996 auction. Many great men and woman of this century have appeared on the cover and were willing signers through the mail. The autograph price list is based on complete magazines; however, autographed covers of deceased players will still command a quality price.

My success at getting Time magazines signed through the mail has been just as good or better than getting my Sports Illustrateds signed. Many collectors treasure their Time autographed issues. I recommend that you review the Sports Illustrated chapter on autographs for further details on how to obtain signatures.

As for values of recent issues, most autographed Time magazines will retain the cumulative value of the magazine. The older issues have extreme limits on availability and thus an increasing in demand for key covers. Values for autographed covers of deceased individuals are estimates because so few will be in existence and may go for higher prices. When paying high premiums on autographed magazines make sure that they have a certificate of authenticity. It is always a concern to spend hundreds to thousands of dollars on a key magazine to find out later on that the signature is a fraud.

BASEBALL COVERS		Nr-Mt	Em	Ex	+Auto
☐ 3/30/25	George Sisler - Browns	1200	750	450	+1000 (d)
☐ 4/11/27	Connie Mack - A's	400	250	100	+1000 (d)
☐ 7/09/28	Roger Hornsby - Braves	750	500	250	+1000 (d)
☐ 7/29/29	Jimmie Foxx - A's	750	500	250	+1000 (d)
☐ 10/14/29	W. Wrigley Jr - Cubs	200	125	50	+1000 (d)
☐ 8/25/30	W. Robinson - Dodgers	200	125	50	+500 (d)
☐ 3/28/32	Gabby Street - Cardinals	200	100	45	+300 (d)
☐ 9/19/32	Col Jacob Ruppert - Owner	200	75	40	+250 (d)
☐ 7/09/34	Lefty Gomez - Yankees	250	150	55	+750 (d)
☐ 4/15/35	Dizzy Dean - Cardinals	250	150	40	+600 (d)
☐ 10/07/35	Mickey Cochrane-Tigers	200	100	40	+500 (d)

☐ 7/13/36	Joe DiMaggio - Yankees	550	450	150	+250 (d)
☐ 10/05/36	Lou Gehrig - Yankees/				
	Carl Hubbell - Giants	350	250	100	+1500/+250(d)
☐ 4/19/37	Bob Feller - Indians	350	200	50	+50
☐ 8/01/38	Happy Chandler - Commissioner	100	65	35	+250 (d)
☐ 7/02/45	Mel Ott - Giants	100	50	20	+500 (d)
☐ 7/02/45	Mel Ott - Giants				
	(pony East/West Edition)	100	65	35	+500 (d)
☐ 4/14/47	Leo Durocher - Dodgers	100	40	25	+300 (d)
☐ 4/14/47	Leo Durocher (Classroom ed)	200	100	25	+300 (d)
☐ 9/22/47	Jackie Robinson - Dodgers	300	175	60	+1000 (d)
☐ 10/04/48	Joe DiMaggio - Yankees	375	250	75	+200
☐ 9/05/49	Stan Musial - Cardinals	250	150	50	+35
☐ 4/10/50	Ted Williams - Red Sox	350	200	100	+210
☐ 10/01/51	Bert Lahr - (Comedy)	40	30	15	+150 (d)
☐ 4/28/52	Eddie Stanky - Cardinals	60	45	15	+ 35
☐ 7/01/53	Mickey Mantle - Yankees	275	175	75	+350 (d)
☐ 7/26/54	Willie Mays - Giants	300	200	75	+50
☐ 6/13/55	Gwen Verdon (Actress)				
	Damn Yankees	35	25	10	+50
☐ 7/11/55	A. Busch - Owner Cardinals	35	25	5	+150 (d)
☐ 8/08/55	Roy Campanella - Dodgers	150	65	25	+400 (d)
☐ 10/03/55	Casey Stengel - Yankees	50	40	15	+300 (d)
☐ 5/28/56	Robin Roberts - Phillies	100	40	10	+20
☐ 7/08/57	Berdie Tebbetts - Reds	50	25	5	+55
☐ 4/28/58	Walley O'Malley - Dodgers	50	25	10	+200 (d)
☐ 8/24/59	Rocky Colavito - Indians	100	40	10	+35
☐ 9/11/64	Hank Bauer - Orioles	100	35	10	+15
☐ 6/10/66	Juan Marichal - Giants	150	40	15	+20
☐ 9/13/68	Denny Mclain - Tigers	100	30	15	+20
☐ 9/05/69	NY Mets	80	30	5	Varies
☐ 8/23/71	Vida Blue - A's	50	25	5	+15
☐ 7/10/72	Johnny Bench - Reds	50	25	5	+25
☐ 6/03/74	Reggie Jackson - A's	60	30	5	+40
☐ 8/18/75	Charlie Finley - A's	35	15	5	+150 (d)
☐ 4/26/76	Babe Ruth - Yankees	20	10		+15 (artist)
☐ 7/18/77	Rod Carew - Twins	35	15		+25
☐ 5/11/81	Billy Martin - A's	20	10		+150 (d)
☐ 8/19/85	Pete Rose - Reds	25	10		+25
☐ 4/07/86	Dwight Gooden - Mets	15	5		+15
☐ 7/10/89	Pete Rose - Reds	15	5		+25
☐ 1/06/92	Ted Turner - Owner	10	5		+20
☐ 8/22/94	Strike	5			+15 (artist)
☐ 9/11/95	Cal Ripken Jr - Orioles				
	(corner only)	15	5		+40

BASKETBALL COVERS		Nr-Mt	Em	Ex	+Auto
☐ 10/20/58	Nonagenarian Stagg	40	25	5	+500 (d)
☐ 3/17/61	Oscar Robinson	80	35	5	+40
☐ 3/18/85	Larry Bird/Wayne Gretzky	60	30	5	+ 75/+50
☐ 2/12/96	Magic Johnson - Lakers	20	5		+120

BOXING COVERS		Nr-Mt	Em	Ex	+Auto
☐ 2/27/23	Floyd Johnson (dummy)	600	400	250	+2000(d)
☐ 9/17/23	Jack Dempsey	350	250	125	+ 500(d)
☐ 8/30/26	James Tunney	250	150	50	+ 500(d)
☐ 6/24/29	Max Schmeling	200	150	35	+ 75
☐ 10/01/31	Primo Carnera	100	55	15	+ 350(d)
☐ 9/29/41	Joe Louis	100	50	25	+ 450 (d)
☐ 6/25/51	Sugar Ray Robinson	100	45	20	+ 450 (d)
☐ 3/22/63	Cassius Clay	150	75	35	+ 120
☐ 3/08/71	Ali vs Frazier	65	35	15	+ 100/35
☐ 2/27/78	Muhammad Ali	40	20	10	+ 100
☐ 6/14/82	Gerry Cooney	15	5		+ 25
☐ 6/27/88	Mike Tyson	5	2		+ 45

FOOTBALL COVERS		Nr-Mt	Em	Ex	+Auto
☐ 10/05/25	Red Grange	550	350	150	+ 300 (d)
☐ 11/07/27	Knute Rockne (Notre Dame)	350	150	75	+1200 (d)
☐ 9/23/29	Christian Cagle (Army)	75	50	25	+ 250 (d)
☐ 11/17/30	Football Crowd	35	25	10	

		Nr-Mt	Em	Ex	+Auto
☐ 11/21/31	Captain Wood (Harvard) ...	50	40	20	+ 250 (d)
☐ 11/14/32	Howard Jones (USC)	200	100	20	+ 400 (d)
☐ 11/11/33	Football Crowd	40	20	10	
☐ 11/11/35	Football Crowd	40	20	10	
☐ 10/25/37	Duke Wade (Football)	60	30	15	+ 125
☐ 11/06/39	Tom Harmon (Michigan) ...	60	40	25	+ 150 (d)
☐ 11/12/45	Blanchard/Davis (Army) ..	75	35	15	+ 25 each
☐ 10/14/46	Frank Leahy (Notre Dame)	50	30	15	+ 50
☐ 11/03/47	Chappuis (Michigan)	55	35	20	+ 40
☐ 11/19/51	Dick Kazmaier (Princeton)	55	35	15	+ 25
☐ 11/09/53	Lattner - Notre Dame ...	55	35	20	+ 20
☐ 5/24/54	Clint Murchison (owner)	25	15	5	+ 200 (d)
☐ 11/29/54	Bobby Layne(Lions)	45	25	15	+ 200 (d)
☐ 10/08/56	Daugherty (Michigan St) ..	55	30	15	+ 55
☐ 11/30/59	Sam Huff (Giants)	55	20	5	+ 35
☐ 6/16/61	Clint Murchison (Owner) ..	35	15	2	+ 100 (d)
☐ 12/21/62	Vince Lombardi (Packers) ..	55	20	5	+ 550 (d)
☐ 10/18/63	Roger Staubach -Navy ...	55	20	10	+ 35
☐ 11/20/64	Parshian (Notre Dame) ...	55	25	10	+ 35
☐ 11/26/65	Jimmy Brown (Browns) ...	60	30	15	+ 35
☐ 10/28/66	Seymour/Hanratty (Notre Dame)	55	20	15	+ 25 each
☐ 1/17/72	Staubach & Griese	55	25	15	+ 45 each
☐ 10/16/72	Joe Namath (Jets)	55	35	15	+ 50
☐ 12/11/72	Don Shula (Dolphins)	55	25	10	+ 25
☐ 12/08/75	White, Greene, Holmes,				
	Greenwood (Steelers)	55	25	10	+ 25 each
☐ 1/10/77	Superbowl (Raiders vs Vikings)	20	10		Varies
☐ 1/10/78	Superbowl (Denver vs Cowboys)	15			Varies
☐ 9/29/80	Bear Bryant - Alabama ...	45	25		+ 250 (d)
☐ 1/12/82	Joe Montana - 49ers	45	25		+ 50
☐ 1/27/86	Payton & Fridge	15	5		+ 55/+15
☐ 6/27/ 94	OJ Simpson	15	5		+ 50

GOLF COVERS

		Nr-Mt	Em	Ex	+Auto
☐ 8/30/25	Bobby Jones	800	650	350	+2500 (d)
☐ 9/21/30	Bobby Jones	800	650	350	+2500 (d)
☐ 6/06/38	Johnny Goodman	65	35	15	+ 250 (d)
☐ 1/10/49	Ben Hogan	250	175	35	+300 (d)
☐ 6/21/54	Sam Snead	150	75	15	+ 50
☐ 5/02/60	Arnold Palmer	150	55	15	+100
☐ 6/29/63	Jack Nicklaus	150	55	15	+100
☐ 7/19/71	Leo Trevino	65	35	10	+ 35
☐ 1996	Tiger Woods	20	5		+ 75

HOCKEY COVERS

		Nr-Mt	Em	Ex	+Auto
☐ 2/11/35	Lorne Chabot - Blackhawks .	100	45	15	+250 (d)
☐ 3/14/38	Dave Kerr - Rangers	100	45	15	+250 (d)
☐ 3/01/68	Bobby Hull - BlackHawks ...	70	35	15	+ 25
☐ 10/09/72	Phil Esposito (Canadian only)	150	45	15	+ 25
☐ 10/14/74	Mele - Gordie Howe				
	(Canadian only)	100	45	10	+ 25
☐ 2/24/75	Bernie Parent	35	15	10	+ 15
☐ 6/26/78	Woman in Sports Field Hockey	10	5		+ 15
☐ 3/18/85	Wayne Gretzky/Larry Bird	35	25	15	+ 40

OTHER SPORTS COVERS

		Nr-Mt	Em	Ex	+Auto
☐ 9/05/27	Deverux Milburan (Polo) ..	50	25		+ 150 (d)
☐ 1/13/30	Domingo Ugalde (Jai Alai)	40	25		+ 150 (d)
☐ 3/03/30	Pointer Mary Blue (Hunting)	45	25		+ 150 (d)
☐ 5/26/30	Edward Statley (Horse Owner)	45	25		+ 150 (d)
☐ 9/15/30	Mike Vanderbilt (Yachting)	40	20		+ 50
☐ 3/14/31	David Ingalls (Polo)	45	25		+ 50
☐ 7/11/32	Ben Eastman - Stanford (Track)	50	20		+ 50
☐ 3/27/33	John Whitney (Polo)	40	20		+ 50
☐ 5/07/34	Edward Bradley (Horse Owner)	40	20		+ 150(d)
☐ 8/20/34	Calvalcade (Horse)	45	25		
☐ 5/10/37	Matt Winn (Horse Owner) ..	45	25		+ 150(d)
	Horses [Blue Grass,Bourbon,Bands,Build Up]				
☐ 5/17/48	Eddie Arcaro - Jockey	40	25		+ 25
☐ 8/02/48	Mel Patton (Olympic Hurdler)	30	20		+ 20

		Nr-Mt	Em	Ex	+Auto
☐ 5/39/49	Ben Jones (Horse Owner)	30	20		+ 150(d)
☐ 7/21/52	Bob Mathias (Track)	35	20		+ 25
☐ 5/31/54	Native Dancer (Horse) .	55	35		
☐ 12/03/56	Parry O'Brian (Track)	40	25		+ 25
☐ 2/10/58	Willie Hartak (Jockey) ..	40	25		+ 35
☐ 8/29/60	Rafer Johnson (Decathlon)	45	25		+ 35
☐ 7/09/65	Jim Clark (Car Racing) ..	40	20		+ 25
☐ 9/11/72	Mark Spitz (Swimmer) ...	40	20		+ 25
☐ 6/11/73	Secretariat (Horse)	55	25		
☐ 9/01/76	Nadia Comaneci (Gymnastics)	40	20		+ 25
☐ 6/13/77	Steve Cauthen (Jockey)	25	15		+ 15
☐ 5/29/78	Steve Cauthen (Jockey)	25	1 5		+ 15
☐ 7/28/84	Carl Lewis (Track)	25	1 5		+ 25
☐ 8/13/84	Carl Lewis (Track)	25	. 15		+ 25
☐ 2/09/87	Dennis Conners- American Cup	25	10		+ 15
☐ 9/19/88	Jackie Joyner Kersee (Track)	25	10		+ 25
☐ *1996	Michael Johnson (Track) .	10	2		+ 20
☐ *8/1/96	Michael Johnson (Track) .	10	2		+ 20

WINTER SPORTS COVERS

		Nr-Mt	Em	Ex	+Auto
☐ 2/17/36	Leni Riefenstahl (Skiing) .	45	25	10	+ 350(d)
☐ 7/17/39	Sonja Henie (Ice Skating)	75	45	20	+ 400(d)
☐ 2/03/48	Barbara Ann Scott (Ice Skating)	35	15	10	+ 25
☐ 1/21/52	Andrea Lawrence (Skiing)	35	20	10	+ 25
☐ 2/02/76	Dorthy Hamill (Ice Skating)	25	10		+ 20
☐ 2/12/80	Eric Heiden (Speed Skating)	20	10		+ 20
☐ 10/17/83	Peter Ueberoth (Olympics)	20	10		+ 20
☐ 1/30/84	Phil Mahre & Tamara Mckinney	20	10		+ 20 Each
☐ 2/15/88	Debbie Thomas (Ice Skating)	20	10		+ 20
☐ 1/24/94	Tony Harding/Nancy Kerrigan	10	5		+ 20 Each

TENNIS COVERS

		Nr-Mt	Em	Ex	+Auto
☐ 7/16/26	Helen Wills	150	100	25	+ 150 (d)
☐ 6/31/29	Helen Wills	150	100	25	+ 150 (d)
☐ 7/06/31	Betty Nuthall	45	25	15	+ 150 (d)
☐ 8/01/32	Ellsworth Vines Jr. ...	45	25	15	+ 150 (d)
☐ 9/04/33	Jack Crawford	45	20		+ 150 (d)
☐ 9/03/34	Fred Perry	45	15		+ 150 (d)
☐ 9/02/35	Donald Budge	45	15		+ 25
☐ 9/14/36	Helen Jacobs	45	15		+ 100 (d)
☐ 9/13/37	Gottfried Von Cramm ..	40	15		+ 150 (d)
☐ 9/02/46	Pauline Betz	35	15		+ 25
☐ 9/01/47	Jake Kramer	35	15		+ 15
☐ 8/27/51	Dick Savitt	35	10		+ 15
☐ 8/26/57	Althea Gibson	35	15		+ 45
☐ 6/10/73	Bobby Riggs	25	5		+150 (d)
☐ 4/28/75	Jimmy Conners	25	5		+ 25
☐ 6/30/80	Bjorn Borg	15	5		+ 20

TIME: NON-SPORTS COVERS

Since the second edition, people have been requesting informtion on non-sport related Time Magazine covers. These covers are just as tough, or tougher, to find. The value for them has gone up just as much or more than the related sports. The popular non-sport Time magazines are those covers of popular movie stars, gangsters and entertainers. However, there is a demand for war heros and villians as well as a few noted politicians.

Time magazine covers mostly featured politicians over the years. Presidents obtain the most attention followed by other leading politicians of each generation. During the war years, many generals graced the cover of Time. Sports covers were more common that movie stars. However, the movie stars selected were the biggest names of the time period. Today many of those covers are coveted by movie star collectors. The biggest demand I have had is for Al Capone Time magazine. This was his only major national magazine appearance and it is sought after by all the autograph collectors who want to frame it with his autograph cut.

Many early Time magazines were paintings. The artwork was fantastic during those years and many of the original paintings can be viewed at key institutions. Other pieces disappeared and have only reappeared in some sports auctions. The pieces can be worth $5,000 and up.

The values of these older issues are based both on year (scarcity) and by who is on the cover (popularity). Many of these issues, if signed, would be worth a mini fortune. However, this is an overview of key issues from 1924-1978. Most issues since 1978 are still available through Time magazine and have little more than what they are willing to charge.

Since this is the first official price guide on Time, it should be noted that the prices can easily go up in value. Especially, the autograph price add on value. Very few if any of these autographed issues exist. The total number of buyers will far exceed the amount that is going to be made available to the market.

NON-SPORTS COVERS		Nr-Mt	EM	+Auto
☐ 1923	Dummy Issues	300	200	
☐ 1924	First Issue	1000	400	
☐ 1924	Common Issue	150	100	
☐ 1925-30	Common Issues	75	50	
☐ 1928	Charles Lindbergh	100	75	+400(d)
☐ 1928	Calvin Coolidge	100	75	+400(d)
☐ 1929	JP Morgan	100	75	+400(d)
☐ 1929	Queen of England	100	75	+400
☐ 1930	Al Capone	200	125	+1000(d)
☐ 1931-39	Common Issues	50	35	
☐ 1931	Charlie Chaplan	200	100	+500(d)
☐ 1931-45	Adolf Hitler	150	75	+1000(d)
☐ 1932	Marx Brothers	200	100	+500(d)
☐ 1931-45	Nazi Leaders/War Generals	75	45	+200(d)
☐ 1934	Irvin Berlin	100	50	+200(d)
☐ 1931-45	FDR	75	45	+500(d)
☐ 1935	J. Edgar Hoover	100	65	+250(d)
☐ 1935	Helen Hayes	100	65	+350(d)
☐ 1936	Clark Gable	150	75	+350(d)
☐ 1937	Walt Disney	150	75	+1000(d)
☐ 1937	Joesph Stalin	75	50	+1000(d)
☐ 1938	Betty Davis	100	75	+400(d)
☐ 1939	Charles Lindbergh	100	75	+300 (d)
☐ 1940	Mickey Rooney	100	50	+ 50

☐ 1940-49	Common Issues	40	20	
☐ 1940	Mussolini	75	50	+500 (d)
☐ 1941	Gary Cooper	75	50	+200 (d)
☐ 1941	Rita Hayworth	75	50	+300 (d)
☐ 1943-55	Harry Truman	75	50	+350 (d)
☐ 1943	Ingrid Bergman	75	50	+250 (d)
☐ 1944	Jimmy Durante	75	50	+250 (d)
☐ 1946	Lawrence Olivier	75	50	+250 (d)
☐ 1948	Howard Hughes	65	40	+250 (d)
☐ 1949-54	John Macarthur	65	50	+250 (d)
☐ 1949	Milton Berle	65	40	+ 50
☐ 1949	Elizabeth Taylor	75	50	+150
☐ 1950-59	Common Issues	30	15	
☐ 1951	Ave Gardner	50	25	+100
☐ 1951	Groucho Marx	75	50	+250 (d)
☐ 1952	John Wayne	75	50	+350 (d)
☐ 1952	Kate Hepburn	75	50	+200
☐ 1954	Humphrey Bogart	75	50	+250 (d)
☐ 1954	Marlon Brando	75	50	+150
☐ 1954	Walt Disney	100	75	+1000 (d)
☐ 1955	Grace Kelly	75	50	+250(d)
☐ 1955	Frank Sinatra	75	50	+200
☐ 1955	Ed Sullivan	65	35	+250 (d)
☐ 1956	Maryln Monroe	200	100	+1500 (d)
☐ 1959	Shirley Maclaine	50	35	+ 35
☐ 1960-70	Common Issues	25	15	
☐ 1961	Jackie Gleason	50	35	+250 (d)
☐ 1962	Sophia Loren	50	35	+ 50
☐ 1963	Richard Burton	50	35	+150 (d)
☐ 1966	Lauren Bacall	50	35	+ 50
☐ 1966	Julia Child	50	35	+ 20
☐ 1966	Walter Cronkite	50	35	+ 25
☐ 1966	Julie Andrews	50	35	+ 20
☐ 1967	Johnny Carson	50	35	+ 25
☐ 1967	The Beatles	75	50	+Varies
☐ 1968	Aretha Franklin	50	35	+ 25
☐ 1969	Raquel Welch	50	35	+ 25
☐ 1969	Dustin Hoffman/Mia Farrow		35	+ 25 each
☐ 1970	Jane Fonda	50	35	+ 25
☐ 1971	Ali MacGraw	40	25	+ 10
☐ 1971	James Taylor	40	25	+ 25
☐ 1972	Woody Allen	30	15	+ 20
☐ 1973	Marlon Brando	25	10	+ 35
☐ 1973	Peter Falk	20	10	+ 20
☐ 1973	Carole King	15	10	+ 20
☐ 1974	Joni Mitchell	15	10	+ 20
☐ 1974	Mary Tyler Moore/V. Harper	15	10	+ 20
☐ 1974	Merle Haggard	15	10	+ 20
☐ 1974	Robert Redford/Mia Farrow	15	10	+ 20
☐ 1975	Elton John	15	10	+100
☐ 1975	Cher	15	10	+ 20
☐ 1976	Charlie Angels	15	10	+ 20each
☐ 1976	Robert Redford/Dustin Hoffman	15	10	+ 25 each
☐ 1977	Diane Keaton	15	10	+ 20
☐ 1977	Lilly Tomlin	15	10	+ 20
☐ 1978	Burt Reynolds/Clint Eastwood	15	10	+ 20
☐ 1978	John Travolta	15	10	+ 20

1927

1929

1929

1930

1934

1936

1936

1937

1930

1939

1949

1953

1954

1959

1961

1962

1963

1963

CHAPTER EIGHT:
Collecting General Magazines

LIFE MAGAZINE

Life Magazine is an icon like Time but it is more known for pictures and covers. Life is heavily collected by non-sport magazine collectors for the purpose of getting autographed and framed. While this is popular to do, only a few Life magazines are used heavily for this purpose. Joe DiMaggio, Mickey Mantle, Ted Williams and Ben Hogan are the four most popular Life magazines used for autographing. The other issues are also used but clean copies are required for the avid autographed magazine collector.

Life is more common than any other magazine from the 1930's - 1960's period. This is because people love to save these big picture magazines. However, this also keeps the price of these magazines down compared to Time or other publications of the same era.

The magazine was a weekly but went down to bi-annual in the 1970's. It was reintroduced as a monthly in 1978 and has continued on that track since.

BASEBALL COVERS

	Nr-Mt	Em	Ex	+Auto
☐ 4/25/38 John Thomas Winsett - Dodgers	25	15		+40
☐ 5/01/39 Joe DiMaggio- Yankees	150	100	50	+195
☐ 4/01/40 John Rucker- Giants	25	15		+40
☐ 9/01/41 Ted Williams - Red Sox	150	75	25	+150
☐ 4/01/46 Charles "Red" Barrett - Cardinals	25	15		+40
☐ 4/05/48 Dodgers Rookies	20	10		
☐ 5/02/49 Arnold Galiffa- Army	20	10		+40
☐ 8/01/49 Joe DiMaggio - Yankees	150	55	20	+150
☐ 5/08/50 Jackie Robinson- Dodgers	60	40	15	+450 (d)
☐ 6/08/53 Roy Campanella- Dodgers	60	40	10	+250 (d)
☐ 9/14/53 Casey Stengel- Yankees	45	25	5	+300 (d)
☐ 6/25/56 Mickey Mantle- Yankees	75	55	20	+250 (d)
☐ 10/14/57 Milwaukee Braves Victory Parade	30	20	5	Varies
☐ 4/28/58 Willie Mays - Giants	45	25	5	+40
☐ 7/21/58 Roy Campanella - Dodgers	60	40	20	+300 (d)
☐ 8/18/61 M. Mantle & R. Maris- Yankees	75	45	20	+250(d)
				+600 (d)
☐ 4/13/62 Richard Burton & Liz Taylor	200	125	85	
(Baseball cards of Mickey Mantle/Maris)				
☐ 9/28/62 Don Drysdale - Dodgers	40	20	5	+150 (d)
☐ 8/02/63 Sandy Koufax - Dodgers	40	25	10	+50
☐ 7/30/65 Mickey Mantle - Yankees	60	40	10	+250 (d)
☐ 7/30/65 M. Mantle - Yankees (newsstand)	75	55	15	+250 (d)
☐ 9/08/67 Carl Yastrzemski - Red Sox	45	25	5	+25
☐ 9/26/69 Jerry Koosman - Mets	35	15	5	+10

BASKETBALL COVERS

	Nr-Mt	Em	Ex	+Auto
☐ 1/15/40 Ralph Vaughn/Tom McGarvin - USC	25	15	5	+20 each
☐ 1/22/45 Bill Kotsores/Ivor Summer - St Johns	25	15	5	+20 each
☐ 3/24/72 Kareem Jabbar/Wilt Chamberlain	25	15	5	+40/+75

BOXING COVERS

	Nr-Mt	Em	Ex	+Auto
☐ 5/16/49 Child Boxer	15	10	5	
☐ 4/07/58 Sugar Ray Robinson	25	15	5	+200 (d)
☐ 7/20/59 Ingemar Johansson / Birgit Lundgren	20	10	5	+35/+20
☐ 3/06/64 Cassius Clay	45	35	5	+100
☐ 10/23/70 Muhammad Ali	30	20	5	+100
☐ 3/05/71 Muhammad Ali/Walt Frazier	30	20	5	+100/+25
☐ 3/19/71 Joe Frazier / Muhammad Ali	30	20	5	+100/+25
☐ 1/19/81 Muhammad Ali	20	10	5	+100

FOOTBALL COVERS

	Nr-Mt	Em	Ex	+Auto
☐ 10/11/37 Chuck Williams -USC	25	15	5	+40
☐ 10/24/38 Sid Luckman - Columbia	25	15	5	+40
☐ 10/09/39 Child Football Player	15	5		
☐ 11/11/40 Tom Harmon - Michigan	35	25	5	+150 (d)
☐ 11/17/41 Texas Football Players	25	10	5	
☐ 10/22/45 Paul Sarringhaus - Ohio State	20	10	5	+20
☐ 9/16/46 Glen Davis/Doc Blanchard - Army	40	25	5	+40
☐ 9/29/47 Johnny Lujack - Notre Dame	35	15	5	+25
☐ 10/25/48 Football Crowd	15	5		
☐ 9/27/48 Doak Walker - SMU	35	20	5	+25
☐ 10/03/49 Charles Justice - UNC	20	10	5	+20
☐ 11/13/50 Kyle Rote-SMU	20	10	5	+20
☐ 12/05/60 Pro Football Kickoff	15	5		
☐ 11/17/61 Minnesota Vikings Team	30	15	5	Varies
☐ 12/10/65 Tommy Nobis - Texas	30	15	5	+20
☐ 4/08/66 Pete Dawkins - Army	25	15	5	+20
☐ 10/14/66 Brown vs Packers	25	15	5	
☐ 12/13/68 Baltimore Colts	25	15	5	
☐ 6/20/69 Joe Namath - Jets	25	15	5	+ 65
☐ 12/03/71 Baltimore Colts	25	15	5	
☐ 1/14/72 Roger Staubach & Tom Landry	25	15	5	+25 each
☐ 10/06/72 Football's Tough Guys	15	10	5	
☐ 11/03/72 Joe Namath - Jets	25	15	5	+65

TENNIS COVERS

	Nr-Mt	Em	Ex	+Auto
☐ 2/01/37 Tennis at Vassar College	15	10	5	
☐ 8/28/39 Alice Marble	15	10	5	+25
☐ 7/06/59 Gardner McKay	15	10	5	+10
☐ 9/20/68 Arthur Ashe	25	15	5	+100 (d)
☐ Jan /83 Jimmy Conners	20	10	5	+25

OLYMPIC SPORTS COVERS

	Nr-Mt	Em	Ex	+Auto
☐ 08/02/48 Mel Patton - Track	25	15	5	+25
☐ 07/11/49 Bob Mathias- Track	25	15	5	+25
☐ 07/23/51 Mary Freeman- Swimming	15	10	5	+10
☐ 02/11/52 Henri Oreiller- Skiing	15	10	5	+10
☐ 12/10/56 Bobby Morrow -Track	25	10	5	+10
☐ 02/08/60 U.S. Skiers	15	10		
☐ 02/29/60 Tamas Sudar- Ski Jumping	15	10		
☐ 08/22/60 Chris Von Saltza &Lynn Burke	15	10		+10 each
☐ 09/12/60 Doris Fuchs &Sharon Richardson	15	10		+10 each
☐ 02/14/64 Ski Jumper	15	10		
☐ 07/31/64 Diver	15	10		
☐ 10/09/64 Donna de Varona- Swimming	15	10		+10
☐ 10/30/64 Don Schollander- Swimming	15	10		+10
☐ 02/23/68 Peggy Fleming- Figure Skating	15	10		+15
☐ 02/18/72 Yukio Kasaya- Ski Jumping	15	10		+10
☐ 05/05/72 Cathy Rigby- Gymanastic	15	10		+10
☐ 08/18/72 Mark Spitz- Swimmer	15	10		+15
☐ 09/15/72 Munich Murders	15	10		
☐ 09/22/72 Frank Shorter- Marathon	15	10		+15
☐ Sum/ 84 Mary Decker -Track	15	10		+10
☐ Jan/ 85 Mary Lou Retton-Gymnastics	25	10		+10
☐ Feb/ 88 Bonnie Blair- Speedskating	15	10		+10

MISC. SPORTS COVERS

	Nr-Mt	Em	Ex	+Auto
☐ 12/07/36 Skier	15	10		
☐ 03/08/37 Skier	15	10		
☐ 07/26/37 Polo Horse	15	10		
☐ 01/03/38 Vivi-Anne Hulten-Figure Skating	15	10		+20
☐ 01/24/38 Skiers	15	10		
☐ 03/21/38 Squash Players	15	10		
☐ 06/19/39 Payton Jordan - USC	25	15	5	+20
☐ 08/05/40 Sailer	15	10		
☐ 12/02/40 Balloonist	15	10		
☐ 01/20/41 Army Ski Patrol	15	10		
☐ 07/14/41 Sand Sailors	15	10		
☐ 04/17/44 Esther Williams- Skiing	15	10		+20
☐ 02/19/45 Ski Fashions	15	10		
☐ 03/26/45 Carol Lynn -Figure Skating	15	10		+20

Cover/Feature	Em	Ex		+Auto
☐ 03/04/46 Gretchen Merrill- Figure Skating	15	10		+20
☐ 05/20/46 Ice Show -Skaters	15	10		
☐ 02/17/47 Water Skier	15	10		
☐ 05/05/47 Equestrian Fashions	15	10		
☐ 09/01/47 John Cobb- Autoracing	15	10		+20
☐ 04/26/48 Rugby Week	15	10		
☐ 06/21/48 Sailers	15	10		
☐ 06/28/48 Stuart Auchincloss-Rowing	15	10		
☐ 06/27/49 Sailer	15	10		
☐ 01/16/50 Child Ice Skater	15	10		
☐ 04/16/51 Esther Williams- Swimming	15	10		
☐ 07/13/53 Everst Mountain Climbers	15	10		
☐ 07/20/53 John Kennedy- Sailing	15	10		
☐ 08/05/55 Ben Hogan -Golf	85	65	30	+200(i)
☐ 12/28/59 Diver & Figure Skater	15	10		
☐ 04/07/61 Ocean Fishing	15	10		
☐ 01/19/62 Ice Sailers	15	10		
☐ 07/06/62 Ballooning	15	10		
☐ 04/09/65 Robert Kennedy- Mountain Climbing	25	15		+450(d)
☐ 05/14/65 Skateboarder	15	10		
☐ 07/09/65 Yachting	15	10		
☐ 07/31/70 Bebe Rebozo- Golf	15	10		+20
☐ 11/12/71 Bobby Fischer-Chess	15	10		+50
☐ 06/02/72 Raquel Welch- Roller Skating	15	10		+40

NON-SPORT LIFE MAGAZINE

This is the most common magazine found at flea markets, garage sales and in used book stores. The issues were saved because of the great photographs that were captured in the day. Today, many of these magazines can be ordered through many of the magazine dealers across the country. These are issues you can be picky about and wait for a nice condition issue.

The concept of getting them autographed is rather recent. A nicely framed autographed magazine of your favorite hero is perhaps the nicest item one can display.

Cover/Feature	Em	Ex	+Auto
☐ 11/23/36 First Cover (Peak Dam)	150	100	
☐ 1936 Common	20	10	
☐ 1937 Common	20	10	
☐ 11/8/37 Greto Garbo - Actress	40	20	1000+(d)
☐ 1938 Common	20	10	
☐ 5/23/38 Errol Flynn - Actor	20	10	300+(d)
☐ 7/11/38 Shirly Temple - Actress	50	25	35+
☐ 8/22/38 Ginger Rogers & Fred Astaire	40	20	100+ ea(d)
☐ 1939 Common	20	10	
☐ 1/23/39 Betta Davis - Actress	25	10	300+(d)
☐ 12/11/39 Betty Grable - Actress	40	20	300+(d)
☐ 1940 Common	20	10	
☐ 7/15/40 Rita Hayworth - Actress	25	15	200+(d)
☐ 10/7/40 Gary Cooper - Actor	30	15	250+(d)
☐ 12/9/40 Ginger Rogers - Actress	35	20	100+(d)
☐ 1941 Common	20	10	
☐ 1/6/41 Katharine Hepburn - Actress	50	25	200
☐ 8/11/41 Rita Hayworth - Actress	40	20	250+(d)
☐ 8/25/41 Fred Astaire - Actor	40	20	100+(d)
☐ 10/13/41 Turner & Clark Gable	40	20	350+(d)
☐ 1942 Common	20	10	
☐ 3/2/42 Ginger Rogers - Actress	40	25	100+(d)
☐ 3/30/42 Shirley Temple - Actress	40	25	35
☐ 1943 Common	20	10	
☐ 1/18/43 Rita Hayworth - Actress	40	25	250+(d)
☐ 7/12/43 Roy Rogers - Actor	40	25	100+(d)
☐ 1944 Common	20	10	
☐ 1/10/44 Bob Hope - Actor	50	25	50+
☐ 2/7/44 George Bernard Shaw	20	10	200+(d)
☐ 12/11/44 Judy Garland - Actress	50	25	250+(d)
☐ 3/26/45 Carol Lynne - Skater	20	10	100+
☐ 11/12/45 Ingrid Bergman - Actress	50	25	200+(d)
☐ 12/3/45 Spencer Tracy - Actor	40	25	200+(d)
☐ 1946 Common	15	10	
☐ 2/4/46 Bob Hope/Bing Crosby	40	25	50/300(d)

Cover/Feature	Em	Ex	+Auto
☐ 7/29/46 Vivien Leigh - Actress	40	25	+300(d)
☐ 10/7/46 Bing Crosby/Caulfield	35	20	+300(d)
☐ 12/2/46 Ingrid Bergman - Actress	40	25	+200(d)
☐ 1947 Common	10	15	
☐ 7/14/47 Elizabeth Taylor - Actress	40	25	+100(d)
☐ 11/10/47 Rita Hayworth - Actress	40	20	+200(d)
☐ 12/1/47 Gregory Peck - Actor	30	15	50
☐ 1948 Common	15	10	
☐ 8/9/48 Marlene Dietrich- Actress	15	10	+300(d)
☐ 11/15/48 Ingrid Bergman - Actress	35	15	+200(d)
☐ 12/6/48 Montgomery Clift - Actor	20	10	+200(d)
☐ 1949 Common	12	10	
☐ 1950 Common	15	10	
☐ 2/6/50 Eve Gardner - Actress	30	20	+200(d)
☐ 2/20/50 Gregory Peck - Actor	30	15	+100(d)
☐ 12/11/50 Rex Harrison - Actor	30	15	+150(d)
☐ 1951 Common	15	10	
☐ 2/26/51 Debbie Reynolds - Actress	35	15	+ 25
☐ 6/25/51 Janet Leigh - Actress	15	10	+200(d)
☐ 8/13/51 Dean Martin/Jerry Lewis	35	15	+100(d)/25
☐ 10/15/51 ZsaZsa Gabor - Actress	35	20	+ 35
☐ 11/5/51 Ginger Rogers - Actress	30	20	+100(d)
☐ 12/17/51 Leigh/Olivier - Actors	30	15	+200(d)/150(d)
☐ 4/7/52 Marilyn Monroe - Actress	85	50	1000(d)+
☐ 9/1/52 Ernest Hemingway - Author	30	15	200(d)+
☐ 1953 Common	15	10	
☐ 4/20/53 Marlon Brando - Actor	30	15	100+
☐ 5/23/53 Marlyn Monroe/Jane Russell	85	50	1000(d)/25
☐ 12/7/53 Audrey Hepburn - Actress	35	20	150+(d)
☐ 4/26/54 Grace Kelly - Actress	35	20	250+(d)
☐ 9/13/54 Judy Garland - actress	35	20	250+(d)
☐ 1954 Common	15	10	
☐ 1/10/55 Greta Garbo - Actress	20	15	250+(d)
☐ 1/31/55 Spencer Tracy - Actor	20	15	150+(d)
☐ 4/11/55 Grace Kelly - Actress	25	15	200+(d)
☐ 6/6/55 Henry Fonda - Actor	20	15	100+(d)
☐ 7/18/55 Kathren Hepburn - Actress	20	15	150+(d)
☐ 8/22/55 Sophia Loren - Actress	30	15	75
☐ 9/26/55 Harry Truman - President	20	15	200+(d)
☐ 10/3/55 Rock Hudson - Actor	20	15	150+(d)
☐ 1956 Common	15	10	
☐ 1/23/56 Harry Truman - President	20	15	200+(d)
☐ 2/6/56 Shirley Jones - Actress	20	15	25
☐ 2/13/56 Harry Truman/McArthur	20	15	
☐ 3/5/56 Kim Novak - Actress	20	15	25
☐ 3/12/56 Dwight Eisenhower - President	20	15	200+(d)
☐ 3/26/56 Julie Andrews - Actress	25	15	25
☐ 4/9/56 Grace Kelly - Actress	20	15	200+(d)
☐ 4/23/56 Jayne Mansfield - Actress	25	15	25
☐ 8/20/56 Audrey Hepburn - Actress	20	15	150+(d)
☐ 10/15/56 Elizabeth Taylor - Actress	35	20	100+
☐ 11/26/56 Ingrid Bergman - Actress	20	15	150+(d)
☐ 1957 Common	12	10	
☐ 5/6/57 Sophia Loren - Actress	20	15	100+
☐ 7/1/57 Billy Graham - Preacher	20	15	20+
☐ 11/4/57 Elizabeth Taylor - Actress	20	15	100+
☐ 1958 Common	12	10	
☐ 11/24/58 Kim Novak - Actress	20	15	25+
☐ 1959 Common	12	10	
☐ 2/2/59 Pat Boone - Actor	20	15	20+
☐ 2/23/59 Gwen Verdon - Actress	20	15	20+
☐ 4/20/59 Marilyn Monroe - Actress	50	35	1000+(d)
☐ 6/29/59 Zsa Zsa Gabor - Actress	20	15	25+
☐ 8/3/59 Kingston Trio - Singers	20	15	20+ ea
☐ 8/24/59 Jackie & John Kennedy	20	15	1000+(d)
☐ 9/14/59 Seven Astronauts	25	20	Varies
☐ 11/2/59 Jackie Gleason - Actor	20	15	150+(d)
☐ 11/9/59 Marilyn Monroe- Actress	50	35	1000+(d)
☐ 1960 Common	12	10	
☐ 2/22/60 Jane & Henry Fonda	25	15	25/100+(d)
☐ 3/21/60 Billy Graham - Preacher	20	15	20+
☐ 3/8/60 John Kennedy - President	20	15	1000+(d)
☐ 4/4/60 Marlon Brando - Actor	20	15	100+
☐ 8/15/60 Marilyn Monroe - Actress	50	35	1000+(d)
☐ 10/10/60 Doris Day - Actress	20	15	20+

11/14/60	Sophia Loren - Actress	20	15	100+
11/21/60	John & Jackie Kennedy	25	20	1000+(d)
12/19/60	John & Jackie Kennedy	25	20	1000+(d)
1961	Common	12	10	
1/13/61	Clark Gable - Actor	15	10	200+(d)
1/27/61	John & Jackie Kennedy	25	20	
2/17/61	Shirley MacLaine - Actress	20	15	20+
3/3/61	Astronaunts	20	15	Varies
4/28/61	Liz Taylor - Actress	20	15	100
5/12/61	Alan Shepard - Astronaut	20	15	25+
6/9/61	John Kennedy - President	20	15	
6/23/61	Grace Kelly - Actress	20	15	200+(d)
7/28/61	Brigitte Bardot - Actress	20	15	20+
8/4/61	John Kennedy - President	20	15	
8/11/61	Sophie Loren - Actress	20	15	100+
9/1/61	Jacqueline Kennedy - First Lady	20	15	1000+(d)
1962	Common	12	10	
1/5/62	Lucille Ball - Actress	20	12	100(d)
2/2/62	John Glenn - Astronaunt	20	15	20+
2/16/62	Rock Hudson - Actor	20	10	100(d)
3/2/62	John Glenn - Astronaunt	20	15	20+
4/13/62	Burton/Taylor (Mantle/Maris Card)	150	100	Varies
5/11/62	Bob Hope - Actor	35	20	50+
6/22/62	Marilyn Monroe - Actress	40	25	1000(d)
8/17/62	Marilyn Monroe - Actress	40	25	
12/14/62	Marlon Brando - Actor	20	15	100+
1963	Common	12	10	
1/11/63	Ann-Margret - Actress	20	15	20+
4/19/63	Richard & Liz	20	15	100+/100
4/26/63	Jackie Kennedy - First Lady	20	15	
5/24/63	Astronaut Cooper	20	15	25+
11/29/63	John Kennedy - President	20	15	
12/6/63	Jackie Kennedy - First Lady	20	15	
12/15/63	John Kennedy - President	20	15	
1964	Common	12	10	
2/14/64	Insbruck - Ski Jumper	12	10	
5/22/64	Barbara Streisand - Actress	35	20	+150
8/7/64	Marilyn Monroe - Actress	45	35	
8/28/64	Beatles - Singers	50	40	varies
9/18/64	Sophia Loren - Actress	20	15	+50
12/18/64	Liz Taylor - Actress	30	20	+75
3/12/65	Julie Andrews- Actress	25	15	+20
3/26/65	Martin Luther King Jr	20	15	+1000(d)
4/23/65	Frank Sinatra - Actor	25	15	+100
5/7/65	John Wayne - Actor	25	15	+500(d)
9/3/65	Astronaut Conrad	20	10	+100
1/7/66	Sean Connery - Actor	30	20	+50
3/11/66	Batman and more	30	20	+20
3/18/66	Barbara Streisand - Actress	20	15	+100
4/1/66	Sophie Loren - Actress	20	15	+50
4/15/66	Louis Armstrong - Music	20	15	+200(d)
5/6/66	Jackie Kennedy	25	15	+1000(d)
6/17/66	Angela Lansbury - Actress	25	15	+25
9/16/66	Sophia Loren - Actress	25	15	+50
9/30/66	Rex Harrison - Actor	20	15	+100(d)
2/24/67	Liz Taylor - Actress	25	15	+100
5/5/67	Mia Farrow - Actress	20	15	+20
5/19/67	Astronaut Wally Shirria	20	15	+25
11/17/67	Jackie Kennedy	20	15	+1000(d)
1968	Common	12	10	
1/5/68	Katharine Hepburn - Actress	20	15	+200
1/12/68	Faye Dunaway - Actress	12	10	+25
3/15/68	Boris Karloff - Actor	25	15	+250(d)
3/29/68	Jane Fonda - Actress	30	20	+35
4/12/68	Martin Lurther King Jr	25	15	
5/10/68	Paul Newman - Actor	25	15	+35
6/28/68	Jefferson Airplane - Singers	30	20	+35
9/13/68	The Beatles - Singers	45	30	Varies
10/18/68	Paul/Joanne Newman	25	20	Varies
2/14/69	Barbra Streisand - Actress	25	15	+100
4/18/69	Mae West - Actress	25	15	+200(d)
5/2/69	Judy Collins - Singer	20	15	+20
5/23/69	Rowan & Martin - Comedy	20	12	Varies
7/4/69	Neil Armstrong- Astronaut	30	15	+50
7/25/69	Astronaut	20	12	Varies
8/15/69	Astronaut on Moon	25	15	+50
9/5/69	Peter Max - Artist	25	15	+35
11/7/69	Paul McCartney - Beatle	35	20	+200
11/21/69	Johnny Cash - Singer	25	15	+35
12/19/69	Charles Manson	20	15	+75
1970	Commons	10	8	
1/23/70	Johnny Carson-Actor	25	15	+40
2/6/70	Robert Redford - Actor	30	15	+50
4/3/70	Lauren Bacall - Actress	25	15	+20
7/24/70	Candice Bergen - Actress	25	15	+20
9/11/70	Angela Davis - Protester	20	10	+20
9/18/70	Tom Jones/Engelbert	15	10	+20 each
1971	Common	10	8	
1/9/71	Bob Hope - Actor	35	20	+40
2/12/71	Jackie Onassis	20	15	+1000(d)
3/26/71	Walter Cronkite - Broadcaster	20	15	+45
4/16/71	Paul McCartney - Singer	30	20	+200
5/14/71	Carol Burnett - Actress	20	15	+25
6/25/71	Frank Sinatra - Singer	25	15	+100
7/23/71	Clint Eastwood - Actor	25	15	+45
8/6/71	Ann Margret - Actress	25	15	+35
9/24/71	Jackson Five - Singers	30	20	Varies
10/29/71	David Cassidy - Singer	20	15	+20
12/10/71	Cybill Shepherd - Actress	35	20	+35
1972	Commons	8	5	
2/25/72	Liz Taylor - Actress	20	15	+100
3/10/72	Marlon Brando - Actor	20	15	+100
3/31/72	Jackie Onassis	25	15	+1000(d)
5/5/72	Cathy Rigby - Gynamist	20	15	+30
6/2/72	Raquel Welch - Actress	20	15	+30
7/14/72	Mick Jagger - Singer	20	15	+200
8/4/72	Flip Wilson - Comedian	15	10	+30
9/8/72	Marilyn Monroe - Actress	25	15	
12/8/72	Diana Ross - Singer	20	12	+20
11/78	Mickey Mouse - Cartoon	15	10	
6/79	Marlon Brando - Actor	15	10	+100
10/79	Dolly Parton - Singer	15	10	+35
3/80	Mickey Rooney - Actor	15	10	+25
11/80	Walter Cronkite - Broadcaster	15	10	+35
4/81	Meryl Streep - Actress	15	10	+35
5/81	Ronald Reagan - President	15	10	+200
10/81	Marilyn Monroe - Actress	15	10	
12/81	Brooke Shields - Actress	15	10	+25
2/82	Christie Brinkley - Model	15	10	+50
3/82	Elizabeth Taylor - Actress	15	10	+100
7/82	Raquel Welch - Actress	15	10	+30
8/82	Marilyn Monroe - Actress	15	10	
2/83	Brooke Shields - Actress	15	10	+25
8/83	Willie Nelson - Singer	15	10	+25
10/83	Nancy Reagan -First Lady	15	10	+20
12/83	Barbra Streisand - Actress/Singer	15	10	+100
2/84	The Beatles - Singers	15	10	Varies
3/84	Daryl Hannah - Actress	15	10	+25
6/84	Harrison Ford - Actor	15	10	+40
9/84	Michael Jackson - Singer	15	10	+200
2/85	Brooke Shields - Actress	15	10	+40
6/85	Bill Cosby - Actor	15	10	+40
2/86	Brooks Shield - Model	15	10	+40
11/86	Tom Cruise/Paul Newman	15	10	Varies
12/86	Madonna - Singer	15	10	+100
2/87	Christie Brinkley - Model	15	10	+50
5/87	Dustin Hoffman/Beatty	15	10	+50
12/87	Meryl Streep - Actress	15	10	+35
2/88	Ice Skater	10	5	

GENERAL INFORMATION MAGAZINE

The most popular magazines after Time and Life is a battle between the large colorful magazine formats (Look, Colliers, Post, Police Gazette) and the standard size newsmagazine (Newsweek). This chapter is devoted to those magazines that are not exclusively dedicated to sports but have many sports covers that need to noted.

The most popular magazines to get autographed after Time, Life and Sports Illustrated tend to be the Looks, Colliers and Post. Newsweek does have a dozen quality covers that are good for autographing. Newsweek magazines are harder to find and tougher to find signed.

The demand for these publications has grown, especially by the player and team collectors. The period that is most sought after is the 50's and thus the names of Joe DiMaggio, Mickey Mantle, Ted Williams and others are the ones that appeared on these magazines.

The values are based on grade and condition. Some of these are more common than others. The list below is not a complete reflection of all the magazines known to exist.

BOYS LIFE MAGAZINE

Boys life magazine is a large magazine format that was geared toward young boys since the early part of this century. It was during the 50's that Boy's Life began to feature major superstars on the cover. Listed below is an incomplete list of Boys Life Magazines.

Date	Player Feature - Team	Nr-Mt	Ex	+Auto
☐ 10/60	Ernie Davis - Syracuse	80	35	+1000(d)
☐ 3/68	Roberto Clemente - Pirates	80	35	+1000(d)
☐ 6/69	Mickey Mantle & Son - Yankees	75	35	+250(d)
☐ 9/71	Brooks Robinson - Orioles	45	15	+35
☐ 3/72	Henry Aaron - Braves	45	15	+35

COLOR MAGAZINE

This is a competitor of Ebony magazine that did not survive. Copies are scarce and rare.

Date	Player Feature - Team	Nr-Mt	Ex	+Auto
☐ 7/52	Willie Mays/H Thompson/ Monte Irvin/Ray Noble/ Leo Durocher - Giants	75	35	Varies

COLLIERS MAGAZINE

Colliers is the least attractive of the large magazines but is still collected by player collectors. These are tough magazines and are usually not found at shows but only through large publication dealers. The early years of Colliers (1920's-1940's) tend to have artistic draw scenes. However, athletic scenes are common throughout their history. Autograph values still are critical on key issues. A complete list of all the baseball issues is not done.

Date	Player Feature - Team	Nr-Mt	Ex	+Auto
☐ 1/15/49	Knicks vs Capitals	50	25	
☐ 3/19/49	Ed Macauley - St Louis Univ.	50	25	+ 25
☐ 3/8/52	Leo Durocher/Family- Giants	75	35	+200(d)
☐ 10/52	Scarbath - MD (Col Foot Pre)	35	20	+ 25
☐ 3/4/55	Willie Mays (Corner)	50	25	
☐ 5/13/55	Rocky Marcino	50	25	+500(d)
☐ 7/20/56	Mantle/Stengel (Corner)	50	25	

EBONY (1946-ON)

Ebony magazine is one of the first black oriented magazines ever made. This magazine had a circulation over 500,000 by the mid 50's. The magazine is known for having some of the greatest black athletes, actresses and models of their day. The magazine has some of the best advertisements of its day. The issues are tough and rarely appear in trade magazines. I had the oppurtunity to go through a collection of the earliest issues in Ebony history.

Date	Player Feature - Sport/Team	Nr-Mt	Ex	+Auto
☐ 5/46	Joe Louis - Boxing	150	50	+500(d)
☐ 10/46	Kenny Washington - UCLA	150	50	+ 50
☐ 9/47	Jackie Robinson – Dodgers	200	75	+500(d)
☐ 9/47	Jackie Robinson - Dodgers	200	75	+500(d)
☐ 6/48	Jackie Robinson - Dodgers	200	75	+500(d)
☐ 5/49	Lary Doby/Bob Feller - Indians	150	75	+ 20 each

☐ 6/49	Joe Louis - Boxing	100	50	+500(d)
☐ 9/49	Sugar Ray Robinson - Boxing	100	50	+300(d)
☐ 6/50	Roy Campenalla - Dodgers	200	75	+200(d)
☐ 10/50	Sam Jethroe - Braves	100	50	+ 25
☐ 7/51	Sugar Ray Robinson - Boxing	50	25	+300(d)
☐ 10/51	Ezzard Charles - Boxing	50	25	+ 25
☐ 5/52	John Davis - Weightlifter	45	20	+ 25
☐ 11/52	Joe Louis - Boxing	75	35	+500(d)
☐ 6/53	Sugar Ray Robinson - Boxing	75	35	+200(d)
☐ 8/53	Joe Louis - Boxing	75	35	+400(d)
☐ 10/53	Kid Gavilan - Boxing	75	35	+ 25
☐ 8/55	Willie Mays/Leo Durocher/ Larine Day - Giants	150	65	+ 65
☐ 6/56	Roy Campanella - Dodgers	150	50	+250(d)
☐ 10/56	Nat King Cole & Daughter	50	35	+300(d)
☐ 12/56	Sammy Davis Jr.	50	35	+300(d)
☐ 3/57	Floyd Petterson & Wife & Child	50	35	+ 25
☐ 10/57	Athlea Gibson - Tennis	50	35	+100
☐ 9/58	Willie Mays - Giants	150	65	+ 65
☐ 5/59	Sidney Pointer - Actor	50	35	+ 35
☐ 8/59	Roy Campanella - Dodgers	150	50	+250(d)
☐ 8/60	Rat Pack - Sammy Davis Jr, Dean Martin, Frank Sinatra	150	50	Varies
☐ 1/75	Muhammad Ali & family - Boxing	35	25	+ 95

LOOK MAGAZINE

These covers actually are prettier than Life and offer very interesting diversity. If you love movie stars Look magazine is the place to go looking. However, some of the most attractive sports covers appeared on Look. The magazine originated in the 30's and ceased publication when the printing cost of the large format put them out of business. Many sports covers were produced and only a limited amount are listed here

Date	Feature	Nr-Mt	Ex	+Auto
☐ 6/21/38	Helen Will's - Tennis	50	25	200(d0
☐ 10/10/39	Joe DiMaggio - Yankees	350	100	250
☐ 4/30/46	Hank Greenberg - Tigers	200	75	500(d)
☐ 10/15/46	Ted Williams - Red Sox	300	100	250
☐ 9/14/48	Doak Walker - SMU	75	35	200
☐ 12/7/48	Barbara Ann Scott - Ice Skater	50	25	25
☐ 9/12/50	Bob Williams - Notre Dame	50	35	25
☐ 11/12/56	John Lujack - Notre Dame	100	50	50
☐ 4/26/49	Joe DiMaggio & Son - Yankees	250	100	250
☐ 4/24/51	Phil Rizzuto & Wife - Yankees	150	50	75
☐ 5/22/51	Joe DiMaggio & others - Yankees	150	50	250
☐ 7/31/51	Stan Musial (corner) - Cardinals	65	35	35
☐ 9/25/51	Campanella (corner) - Yankees	65	35	35
☐ 10/09/51	Ted Williams (corner) - Red Sox	65	25	150
☐ 3/11/52	Bob Feller (corner - Indians	50	25	20
☐ 4/22/52	Casey Stengel(corner) - Yankees	50	25	300(d)
☐ 6/17/52	Roger Hornsby (corner) - Browns	50	25	300(d)
☐ 7/15/52	Al Rosen (corner) - Indians	50	25	35
☐ 8/12/52	Mickey Mantle (corner) - Yankees	75	35	250(d)
☐ 5/3/55	Willie Mays - Giants	75	35	50

NEWSWEEK MAGAZINE

This magazine is growing in popularity. The earily editions are scarce. I have never seen some of the early editions. Newsweek has many baseball cover issues along with other sports. I compiled the baseball issues below along with an overview of other sport covers and celebrities. Newsweek is also released in foreign countries like Japan.

Date	Baseball Cover	Nr-Mt	Em	+Auto
☐ 4/29/33	Carl Hubbell	150	60	+100(d)
☐ 9/09/33	Connie Mack & Others	125	50	
☐ 9/30/33	Clark Griffith & Others	100	50	
☐ 12/25/33	Judge Landis	85	45	
☐ 2/17/34	Babe Ruth & Others	200	75	
☐ 3/17/34	Mel Ott & Others	125	45	
☐ 10/06/34	Mickey Cochrane - Tigers	150	65	
☐ 4/20/35	Judge Landis	75	45	
☐ 10/03/36	Carl Hubbell - Giants	125	75	+100(d)
☐ 10/11/37	Carl Hubbell & Others	100	50	
☐ 4/18/38	Rudy York & Others	75	35	

	Date	Cover	Nr-Mt	Em	+Auto
☐	10/10/38	Joe McCarthy & Gaby Hartnett	75	35	
☐	6/19/39	Abner Doubleday (HOF)	100	45	
☐	9/16/46	Ted Williams - Red Sox	350	200	+225
☐	4/14/47	Cal Hubbard - Umpire	50	35	+ 50(d)
☐	4/14/47	Cal Hubbard - Umpire (Pacific)	60	45	+ 50(d)
☐	6/2/47	Bob Feller - Indians	200	100	+ 50
☐	8/18/47	Jack Kramer - Tennis	50	25	+ 35
☐	10/06/47	NY & Dodgers World Series .	60	45	
☐	4/26/48	Joe MacCarthy-Boston			
		Billy Southworth - Braves ..	65	45	
☐	8/08/49	Branch Rickey - Dodgers	65	45	
☐	4/17/50	Mel Parnell - Braves	60	35	+ 20
☐	3/24/52	Dodger Spring Training	50	30	
☐	10/4/54	Bob Feller/Bob Lemon	60	40	+20 each
☐	10/03/55	World Series	50	25	
☐	6/25/56	Mickey Mantle-Yankees	400	200	+250
☐	7/01/57	Stan Musial - Cardinals	100	65	+ 35
☐	8/03/59	Casey Stengel- Yankees	+ 65	35	
☐	8/14/61	Mickey Mantle (drawing)	200	100	+250
☐	4/26/65	Astros Player	+ 35	15	
☐	10/11/65	Sandy Koufax - Dodgers	75	40	+ 60
☐	10/02/67	Carl Yastrzemski - Red Sox ..	75	35	+ 60
☐	8/13/73	Hank Aaron/Babe Ruth	30	15	+ 45
☐	5/16/75	Nolan Ryan - Angels	45	15	+ 45
☐	6/28/76	Vida Blue - A's	15	10	+ 15
☐	8/6/90	George Steinbrenner-Yankees	20	10	+ 20
☐	8/22/94	Ken Griffey Jr - Mariners	25	10	+ 60
☐	10/25/95	Nomo - Dodgers (Japan only)	50	25	+ 40

NEWSWEEK: PARTIAL OTHER LIST

	Date	Cover	Nr-Mt	Em	+Auto
☐	3/13/34	Bill Tilden - Tennis	50	35	+200(d)
☐	7/14/34	Fred Perry - Tennis	50	35	+100(d)
☐	9/12/36	Fred Perry - Tennis	50	35	+100(d)
☐	7/17/39	Bobby Riggs - Tennis	50	25	+150(d)
☐	7/26/43	General Patton	50	25	+500(d)
☐	9/30/43	Adolf Hitler	40	20	
☐	7/31/44	Adolf Hitler	40	20	
☐	1/28/46	Bing Crosby	40	20	+250(d)
☐	6/17/46	Jimmy Durante	40	20	+200(d)
☐	8/12/46	General MacArthur	40	20	+250(d)
☐	8/20/46	Vivien Leigh	40	20	+250(d)
☐	11/11/46	Football Fan	20	10	
☐	12/30/46	Jimmy Stewart	35	20	+100(d)
☐	1/27/47	Ingram Bergman	40	20	+150(d)
☐	2/17/47	Ice Skater	25	15	
☐	3/10/47	Albert Einstein	40	20	+500(d)
☐	3/31/47	Jack Benny	40	20	+200(d)
☐	6/30/47	Dinah Shore	35	15	+100
☐	9/1/47	Gandi	35	20	
☐	9/8/47	Trotter	25	10	
☐	9/29/47	Lou Little- Columbia	40	20	+100(d)
☐	2/2/48	Winter Olympic	20	10	
☐	3/1/48	Henry Fonda	35	15	+200(d)
☐	8/3/48	Rita Hayworth	40	20	+200(d)
☐	10/25/48	Sonja Henie - Ice Skater ...	60	30	+150(d)
☐	6/10/49	Harrison Dittard - Track	35	15	
☐	12/4/50	Nat Holman - CCNY	50	25	+100(d)
☐	2/13/50	Disney - Cinderella	40	20	
☐	12/5/50	Nate Holman - CCNY	40	20	+100(d)
☐	12/7/53	Frank Leahy - Notre Dame ...	40	20	+100(d)
☐	9/26/55	Brennan - Notre Dame	40	20	+ 50
☐	2/15/60	Penny Pitou - Olympic Skier .	20	10	+ 25
☐	7/17/61	Phil Hill - Auto Racing	30	15	+ 25
☐	2/21/66	Australia - Olympic	20	15	
☐	5/29/67	Mario Andretti - Auto Racing .	40	20	+ 35
☐	12/15/69	Willies Reed/Walt Frazier ...	35	15	+ 25
☐	10/5/70	Terry Bradshaw - Steelers ...	50	25	+ 50
☐	7/19/71	Leo Trevino - Golf	50	25	+ 50
☐	11/1/71	George Allen - Redskins ...	35	15	+ 20
☐	2/14/72	Janet Lynn - Ice Skater ...	25	10	+ 20
☐	9/11/72	1972 Olympics	20	10	
☐	10/2/72	Howard Cosell	30	15	+100(d)
☐	12/4/72	Larry Brown - Redskins	20	10	+ 25
☐	6/11/73	Secretariat - HorseRacing ...	75	35	

☐	7/1/74	Bjorn Borg - Tennis	35	15	+ 25
☐	2/3/75	Johnny Miller - Golf	35	15	+ 25
☐	6/22/79	Terry Bradshaw - Pittsburgh .			
		'Hollywood' Henderson	35	15	Varies
☐	6/16/80	Ted Turner - Owner	20	10	+ 15
☐	8/20/84	Olympics: Hogshead, Miller,			
☐		Louganis, Moses, Vidmar ...	35	15	Varies
☐	5/14/90	Jennifer Capriati - Tennis ...	20	10	+ 20
☐	11/18/91	Magic Johnson - Lakers ...	20	10	+110
☐	6/4/92	Tonya Harding - Ice Skater ..	20	10	+ 20
☐	7/6/92	Michael Jordan/Larry Bird/ ..			
		Magic Johnson	25	10	Varies
☐	2/10/92	Kristi Yamaguchi - Skater ..	25	10	+ 25
☐	2/21/94	Tony Harding - Ice Skater ...	20	10	+ 20
☐	6/20/94	Cobi Jones - Soccer	15	5	+ 20
☐	2/12/96	Magic Johnson - Lakers	15	5	+120

OUR WORLD

This magazine is a competitor to Ebony. The magazine folded. However, it did produce a few quality sports covers. The list is not known.

	Date	Feature	Nr-Mt	Ex	+Auto
☐	6/54	Jackie & Rachel Robinson ...	75	20	+20/+2

PATHFINDER

Pathfinder started before the turn of the century and folded in the 50's. The magazine competed against Newsweek, Time, etc. The magazine has never been cataloged. Listed below is a sample of magazines that I have found.

	Date	Feature on cover	Nr-Mt	Ex
☐	2/27/46	BlackHawks / Canadians	50	25
☐	4/10/46	Chicago Cubs	50	25
☐	1/15/47	Rangers Goalie	60	35
☐	11/5/47	Michigan/?? Football game .	40	20
☐	4/07/48	Leland Brissie - Phil A's	50	25
☐	2/23/49	Kentucky/ St John's -Basketball	50	25
☐	4/20/49	Lou Boudreau - Indians	70	35
☐	10/17/51	Ohio State Player #54	40	20
☐	4/23/52	Bill Veeck - St Louis Browns .	50	35

POLICE GAZETTE MAGAZINE

These magazines span almost 100 years and have some of the greatest sports heroes featured. There are many covers of great boxers, baseball players and other athletes. Great sports and drama (besides police excitement) is captured in every issue. These newspapers (turned magazines) are worth pursuing and are on the very tough list for particular issues. Many issues cut the magazine covers into four pictures of famous (and infamous) personalities. This list is far from complete.

	Year	Feature on cover	Nr-Mt	Ex	+Auto
☐	1940's	Joe DiMaggio	350	250	+225
☐	1950's	Mickey Mantle	100	50	+250(d)
☐	1950's	Ted Williams	200	150	+220
☐	1950's	Joe DiMaggio (shares cover)	125	50	

RADIO & TELEVISION BEST

This magazine was short lived and the list of all magazines is unknown.

	Date	Feature - Team	Nr-Mt	Ex	+Auto
☐	8/48	Leo Dourcher - Dodgers	70	35	+200(d)

POST (SATURDAY EVENING POST) MAGAZINE

These covers are famous for the Norman Rockwell pictures and other great Americana artists. Very few of these survive the ad cutters and the quality magazines demand a premium. A few of these magazine covers grace the baseball Hall of Fame. Articles are throughout the issues. Many feature great baseball players. The early years were art drawings by leading artist of the day (Norman Rockwell) and others. In the 1960's the Post shifted from art work drawings to feature current movie stars and athletes. Listed below is a sampling of values.

Dates	Feature	Nr-Mt	EX	+Auto
☐ 1910's	Common Magazine	35	20	-
☐ 1920's	Common Magazine	35	-	20
☐ 1930's	Common Magazine	30	15	
☐ 1940's	Common Magazine	25	10	
☐ 1950's	Common Magazine	20	10	
☐ 1954	Stan Musial (Norman Rockwell)	75	35	+35
	Ted Williams (Norman Rockwell)	125	45	+230
☐ 1957	Yogi Berra - Yankees	75	35	+ 35
☐ 4/28/62	Dick Stuart - Pirates	25	10	+ 20
☐ 9/8/62	Ray Poage - Texas	25	10	+ 20
☐ 2/2/63	Beverly Hillbillies	25	10	Varies
☐ 5/11/63	Leo Durocher - Cubs	35	10	+200(d)
☐ 1/4/64	Miami Dolphin Player	25	10	
☐ 2/15/64	Sophia Loren (Actress)	35	10	+ 50
☐ 3/21/64	Beatles	55	35	Varies
☐ 8/1/64	Donna de Varone			
	Don Schollander - Swimmer .	35	10	+ 20 each
☐ 12/12/64	Johnny Unitas - Colts	45	25	+ 50
☐ 7/17/65	Sean Connery - Actor	25	10	+ 50

1960 LIFE

1960 BOY'S LIFE

1953 COLLIER'S

1939 LOOK

1946 LOOK

1955 LOOK

1961 NEWSWEEK

1970 NEWSWEEK

1955 POLICE GAZETTE

1950 QUICK

1952 QUICK

1956 HOW TO PLAY...

1948 RADIO & TELEVISION BEST

1954 OUR WORLD

1949 DELL SPORTS ILLUSTRATED

1975 EBONY

1947 AMERICANA

1948 SPORTS PARADE

1952 SPORTS REVIEW

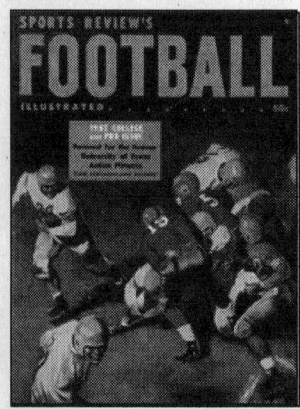

1952 SPORTS REVIEW

1953 OPEN ROAD

1953 PROFESSIONAL FOOTBALL

1962 POST

1977 YOUNG ATHLETE

CHAPTER NINE:
Beckett Alphabetical Checklist

BECKETT BASEBALL CARD MONTHLY

ISSUE #	MONTH	YEAR	FRONT COVER	BACK COVER
☐ BB0001	Nov	1984	Roberto Clemente/Dale Murphy	Ryne Sandberg
☐ BB0002	Dec	1984	Mickey Mantle/Cal Ripken Jr.	Jim Palmer
☐ BB0003	Jan	1985	Willie Mays/Dave Winfield	Roberto Clemente
☐ BB0004	Feb	1985	Hank Aaron/Gary Carter	Tony Gwynn
☐ BB0005	Mar	1985	Stan Musial/Eddie Murray	Alan Trammell
☐ BB0006	Apr	1985	Johnny Bench/Wade Boggs	Dale Murphy
☐ BB0007	May	1985	Steve Garvey	Mike Schmidt
☐ BB0008	Jun	1985	Rick Sutcliffe	Carl Yastrzemski
☐ BB0009	Jul	1985	Cal Ripken Jr.	Julio Franco
☐ BB0010	Aug	1985	Reggie Jackson	Leon Durham
☐ BB0011	Sep	1985	Pete Rose	Stan Musial
☐ BB0012	Oct	1985	Dwight Gooden	Ernie Banks
☐ BB0013	Nov/Dec	1985	Vince Coleman/Willie McGee	Ron Guidry
☐ BB0014	Jan/Feb	1986	Don Mattingly	Brett Saberhagen
☐ BB0015	Mar	1986	Dwight Gooden	Gary Carter
☐ BB0016	Apr	1986	George Brett	Rickey Henderson
☐ BB0017	May	1986	Wade Boggs	Jose Canseco/Billy Jo Robidoux
☐ BB0018	Jun	1986	Dale Murphy	Dave Winfield
☐ BB0019	Jul	1986	Mickey Mantle	Darryl Strawberry
☐ BB0020	Aug	1986	Roger Clemens	Pete Incaviglia/Jose Canseco
☐ BB0021	Sep	1986	Pete Rose	Kirby Puckett
☐ BB0022	Oct	1986	Wally Joyner	Mike Schmidt
☐ BB0023	Nov/Dec	1986	Don Mattingly	Dwight Gooden
☐ BB0024	Jan/Feb	1987	Wade Boggs	Eric Davis
☐ BB0025	Mar	1987	Roger Clemens	Rickey Henderson
☐ BB0026	Apr	1987	Mike Schmidt	Cory Snyder
☐ BB0027	May	1987	Kirby Puckett	Vince Coleman
☐ BB0028	Jun	1987	Eric Davis	Darryl Strawberry
☐ BB0029	Jul	1987	Willie Mays	Pete Incaviglia
☐ BB0030	Aug	1987	Bo Jackson	Mark McGwire/Jose Canseco
☐ BB0031	Sep	1987	Andre Dawson	Don Mattingly
☐ BB0032	Oct	1987	Mark McGwire	Tony Gwynn
☐ BB0033	Nov	1987	George Bell	Kevin Seitzer/George Brett
☐ BB0034	Dec	1987	Kirby Puckett	Mark McGwire/Eric Davis
☐ BB0035	Jan/Feb	1988	Don Mattingly	Will Clark
☐ BB0036	Mar	1988	Seitzer/Boggs	Roger Clemens
☐ BB0037	Apr	1988	Benito Santiago	Dale Murphy
☐ BB0038	May	1988	Eric Davis	Mike Greenwell
☐ BB0039	Jun	1988	Matt Nokes	Dwight Gooden
☐ BB0040	Jul	1988	Jose Canseco	Joe DiMaggio
☐ BB0041	Aug	1988	Dave Winfield	Mark Grace
☐ BB0042	Sep	1988	Darryl Strawberry	Chris Sabo/Bobby Bonilla
☐ BB0043	Oct	1988	Don Mattingly	Andres Galarraga/Tim Raines
☐ BB0044	Nov	1988	Jose Canseco	Gregg Jefferies
☐ BB0045	Dec	1988	Orel Hershiser	Mark McGwire
☐ BB0046	Jan	1989	Will Clark	David Cone
☐ BB0047	Feb	1989	Mike Greenwell	Kirk Gibson
☐ BB0048	Mar	1989	Mark Grace	Johnny Bench
☐ BB0049	Apr	1989	Gregg Jefferies	Gary Sheffield
☐ BB0050	May	1989	Roberto Clemente	Jose Canseco
☐ BB0051	Jun	1989	Bo Jackson	Ellis Burks
☐ BB0052	Jul	1989	Will Clark	Ernie Banks
☐ BB0053	Aug	1989	Kevin Mitchell	Ken Griffey Jr.

ISSUE #	MONTH	YEAR	FRONT COVER	BACK COVER
☐ BB0054	Sep	1989	Jim Abbott	Carl Yastrzemski
☐ BB0055	Oct	1989	Nolan Ryan	Fred McGriff
☐ BB0056	Nov	1989	Kevin Mitchell/Will Clark	Jerome Walton
☐ BB0057	Dec	1989	Rickey Henderson	Matt Williams
☐ BB0058	Jan	1990	Ruben Sierra	Brett Saberhagen
☐ BB0059	Feb	1990	Bo Jackson	Greg Olson
☐ BB0060	Mar	1990	Robin Yount	Todd Ziele
☐ BB0061	Apr	1990	Mark Grace	Howard Johnson
☐ BB0062	May	1990	Don Mattingly	Eric Anthony
☐ BB0063	Jun	1990	Bo Jackson	Tim Raines
☐ BB0064	Jul	1990	Ken Griffey Jr.	Frank Viola
☐ BB0065	Aug	1990	Ryne Sandberg	Roger Clemens/Nolan Ryan
☐ BB0066	Sep	1990	Rickey Henderson	Carlton Fisk
☐ BB0067	Oct	1990	Jose Canseco	Gregg Jefferies
☐ BB0068	Nov	1990	Barry Bonds	Sandy Alomar Jr.
☐ BB0069	Dec	1990	Nolan Ryan	David Justice
☐ BB0070	Jan	1991	Cecil Fielder	Barry Larkin
☐ BB0071	Feb	1991	George Brett	Kevin Maas
☐ BB0072	Mar	1991	Ken Griffey Jr.	Darryl Strawberry
☐ BB0073	Apr	1991	Rickey Henderson	Ramon Martinez
☐ BB0074	May	1991	Cal Ripken	Bobby Bonilla
☐ BB0075	Jun	1991	Joe Dimaggio/M Mantle	Babe Ruth/Lou Gehrig
☐ BB0076	Jul	1991	Roger Clemens	Brooks Robinson
☐ BB0077	Aug	1991	Fred McGriff/Tony Gwynn	Andre Dawson
☐ BB0078	Sep	1991	Dave Justice	Scott Erickson
☐ BB0079	Oct	1991	Frank Thomas	Dave Winfield
☐ BB0080	Nov	1991	Bo Jackson	Howard Johnson
☐ BB0081	Dec	1991	Cecil Fielder	Robin Ventura
☐ BB0082	Jan	1992	Nolan Ryan	Steve Avery/Tom Glavine
☐ BB0083	Feb	1992	Ozzie Smith	Jeff Bagwell
☐ BB0084	Mar	1992	Cal Ripken	Phil Plantier
☐ BB0085	Apr	1992	Frank Thomas	Ron Gant
☐ BB0086	May	1992	Steve Avery	Roberto Alomar
☐ BB0087	Jun	1992	Kirby Puckett	Ruben Sierra
☐ BB0088	Jul	1992	Deion Sanders	Tony Perez/Pete Rose/Johnny Bench
☐ BB0089	Aug	1992	Mark McGwire	Jack McDowell
☐ BB0090	Sep	1992	Robin Yount	John Kruk
☐ BB0091	Oct	1992	Gary Sheffield	Juan Guzman
☐ BB0092	Nov	1992	Tom Glavine	Mike Mussina
☐ BB0093	Dec	1992	Juan Gonzalez	Eric Karros
☐ BB0094	Jan	1993	Frank Thomas	Chuck Knoblach
☐ BB0095	Feb	1993	Ken Griffey Jr.	Pat Listach
☐ BB0096	Mar	1993	Mike Mussina	Joe Carter
☐ BB0097	Apr	1993	Roberto Alomar	Carlos Baerga
☐ BB0098	May	1993	Greg Maddux	George Brett
☐ BB0099	Jun	1993	Jim Abbott	Bo Jackson
☐ BB0100	Jul	1993	Jackie Robinson	Nolan Ryan
☐ BB0101	Aug	1993	R Alomar, J Olerud, J Carter	J.T. Snow
☐ BB0102	Sep	1993	Darren Daulton	Albert Belle
☐ BB0103	Oct	1993	Barry Bonds	Andres Galarraga
☐ BB0104	Nov	1993	Fred McGriff	Don Mattingly
☐ BB0105	Dec	1993	Mike Piazza	Jack McDowell
☐ BB0106	Jan	1994	Frank Thomas	Nolan Ryan
☐ BB0107	Feb	1994	Paul Molitor	Tim Salmon
☐ BB0108	Mar	1994	Juan Gonzalez	Kenny Lofton
☐ BB0109	Apr	1994	Michael Jordan	Mitch Williams/Joe Carter
☐ BB0110	May	1994	Cliff Floyd	Randy Johnson
☐ BB0111	Jun	1994	Ken Griffey Jr.	Jeffrey Hammonds
☐ BB0112	Jul	1994	Manny Ramirez	Ben McDonald

ISSUE #	MONTH	YEAR	FRONT COVER	BACK COVER
☐ BB0113	Aug	1994	Ryne Sandberg	Paul O'Neill
☐ BB0114	Sep	1994	Jeff Bagwell	Kirby Puckett
☐ BB0115	Oct	1994	Matt Williams	Klesko/Tarasco/Lopez
☐ BB0116	Nov	1994	Thomas/Griffey	Mickey Mantle
☐ BB0117	Dec	1994	Raul Mondesi	Will VanLandingham
☐ BB0118	Jan	1995	Cal Ripken Jr.	Eddie Murray
☐ BB0119	Feb	1995	Babe Ruth	Derek Jeter
☐ BB0120	Mar	1995	Gregg Maddux	David Cone
☐ BB0121	Apr	1995	Jose Canseco	Fred McGriff
☐ BB0122	May	1995	Tony Gwynn	Ruben Rivera
☐ BB0123	Jun	1995	Kenny Lofton	Michael Jordan
☐ BB0124	Jul	1995	Ken Griffey Jr.	Ozzie Smith
☐ BB0125	Aug	1995	Frank Thomas	Mike Schmidt
☐ BB0126	Sep	1995	Cal Ripken Jr.	Chipper Jones
☐ BB0127	Oct	1995	Mickey Mantle	Mickey Mantle
☐ BB0128	Nov	1995	Hideo Nomo	Hideo Nomo
☐ BB0129	Dec	1995	Greg Maddux	Garret Anderson
☐ BB0130	Jan	1996	Braves/Indians Series	Sammy Sosa
☐ BB0131	Feb	1996	Mo Vaughn	Johnny Damon
☐ BB0132	Mar	1996	Ted Williams/Stan Musial	Pulsipher/Wilson/Isringhausen/Payton
☐ BB0133	Apr	1996	Barry Larkin	Marty Cordova
☐ BB0134	May	1996	Frank Thomas	Andruw Jones
☐ BB0135	Jun	1996	Chipper Jones	Don Mattingly
☐ BB0136	Jul	1996	Mike Piazza	Tim Salmon
☐ BB0137	Aug	1996	Cal Ripken/Roberto Alomar	Steve Carlton
☐ BB0138	Sep	1996	Alex Rodriguez	Henry Rodriguez
☐ BB0139	Oct	1996	Ken Griffey Jr.	Kirby Puckett
☐ BB0140	Nov	1996	Ozzie Smith	Cecil Feilder
☐ BB0141	Dec	1996	Alex Rodriguez	Year of Home Run
☐ BB0142	Jan	1997	World Series Photo	Todd Hundley
☐ BB0143	Feb	1997	Andruw Jones	Wade Boggs
☐ BB0144	Mar	1997	Juan Gonzalez	Ken Caminiti
☐ BB0145	Apr	1997	Roger Clemens	Andres Galarraga
☐ BB0146	May	1997	Chipper Jones	Fleet 15 Base Stealers
☐ BB0147	Jun	1997	Derek Jeter	Alex Fernandez
☐ BB0148	Jul	1997	Kenny Lofton	Larry Walker
☐ BB0149	Aug	1997	Ken Griffey Jr.	Peter Gammons
☐ BB0150	Sep	1997	Tony Gwynn	Tony Clark
☐ BB0151	Oct	1997	Tino Martinez	Mark McGwire
☐ BB0152	Nov	1997	Nomar Garciaparra	Randy Johnson
☐ BB0153	Dec	1997	Roger Clemens	Scott Rolen

BECKETT BASKETBALL CARD MONTHLY

ISSUE #	MONTH	YEAR	FRONT COVER	BACK COVER
☐ BK0001	Apr	1990	Michael Jordan	Patrick Ewing
☐ BK0002	Jun	1990	David Robinson	Karl Malone
☐ BK0003	Aug	1990	Magic Johnson	Kevin Johnson
☐ BK0004	Sep/Oct	1990	Charles Barkley	Dumars/Green
☐ BK0005	Dec	1990	David Robinson	Hakeem Olajuwon
☐ BK0006	Jan	1991	Patrick Ewing	John Stockton
☐ BK0007	Feb	1991	Larry Bird	Shawn Kemp
☐ BK0008	Mar	1991	Clyde Drexler	Reggie Miller
☐ BK0009	Apr	1991	Dominique Wilkins	Anfernee Hardaway
☐ BK0010	May	1991	Michael Jordan	Coleman
☐ BK0011	Jun	1991	Kevin Johnson	B.King
☐ BK0012	Jul	1991	Kareem Abdul-Jabbar	Scottie Pippen
☐ BK0013	Aug	1991	Magic Johnson	Shaw
☐ BK0014	Sep	1991	Michael Jordan	Larry Johnson
☐ BK0015	Oct	1991	Karl Malone	Isiah Thomas

ISSUE #	MONTH	YEAR	FRONT COVER	BACK COVER
☐ BK0016	Nov	1991	David Robinson	Clyde Drexler
☐ BK0017	Dec	1991	Coleman	Chris Mullin
☐ BK0018	Jan	1992	Mutumbo	S.Smith
☐ BK0019	Feb	1992	Anfernee Hardaway	Simmons
☐ BK0020	Mar	1992	Larry Johnson	D.Brown
☐ BK0021	Apr	1992	Scottie Pippen	Rodman/Price
☐ BK0022	May	1992	Augmon	Rodman
☐ BK0023	Jun	1992	Owens	O'Neal/Laettner
☐ BK0024	Jul	1992	Johnson/Malone/Barkley/Jordan/Ewing	
☐ BK0025	Aug	1992	Michael Jordan	Bird/Parish/McHale
☐ BK0026	Sep	1992	Magic Johnson	Kendall Gill
☐ BK0027	Oct	1992	Shaquille O'Neal	Charles Barkley
☐ BK0028	Nov	1992	Larry Bird	Shawn Kemp
☐ BK0029	Dec	1992	Larry Johnson	Karl Malone
☐ BK0030	Jan	1993	Christian Laettner	LaPhonso Ellis
☐ BK0031	Feb	1993	Michael Jordan	W.Williams
☐ BK0032	Mar	1993	Shaquille O'Neal	Alonzo Mourning
☐ BK0033	Apr	1993	Charles Barkley	Gugliotta
☐ BK0034	May	1993	Harold Miner	Hakeem Olajuwon
☐ BK0035	Jun	1993	Patrick Ewing	Richard Dumas
☐ BK0036	Jul	1993	Alonzo Mourning	Robert Horry
☐ BK0037	Aug	1993	Shaquille O'Neal	Shaquille O'Neal
☐ BK0038	Sep	1993	Michael Jordan	Jim Jackson
☐ BK0039	Oct	1993	Shawn Kemp	Drazen Petrovic/Reggie Lewis
☐ BK0040	Nov	1993	Chris Webber	Oliver Miller
☐ BK0041	Dec	1993	Michael Jordan	Hakeem Olajuwon
☐ BK0042	Jan	1994	Julius Erving/Charles Barkley	Dominique Wilkins
☐ BK0043	Feb	1994	Jamal Mashburn	Isiah Thomas
☐ BK0044	Mar	1994	David Robinson	John Starks
☐ BK0045	Apr	1994	Shaq O'Neal/A. Mourning	Danny Manning
☐ BK0046	May	1994	Anfernee Hardaway	Isaiah Rider
☐ BK0047	Jun	1994	Scottie Pippen	Dan Majerle
☐ BK0048	Jul	1994	Chris Webber	Glen Rice
☐ BK0049	Aug	1994	Dream Team II	Grant Hill
☐ BK0050	Sep	1994	Shaquille O'Neal	Houston Rockets
☐ BK0051	Oct	1994	Hakeem Olajuwon	Juwan Howard
☐ BK0052	Nov	1994	Reggie Miller	Karl Malone
☐ BK0053	Dec	1994	Latrell Sprewell	Dominique Wilkins
☐ BK0054	Jan	1995	Grant Hill	Michael Jordan
☐ BK0055	Feb	1995	Anfernee Hardaway	Jalen Rose
☐ BK0056	Mar	1995	J.Mashburn/J.Kidd/J.Jackson	John Stockton
☐ BK0057	Apr	1995	Shaquille O'Neal	Wesley Person
☐ BK0058	May	1995	Michael Jordan	Brian Grant
☐ BK0059	Jun	1995	Shawn Kemp	Nick Van Exel
☐ BK0060	Jul	1995	Hakeem Olajuwon	Red Auerbach/Larry Bird
☐ BK0061	Aug	1995	Clyde Drexler	Joe Smith
☐ BK0062	Sep	1995	Jason Kidd	Rick Smits
☐ BK0063	Oct	1995	Karl Malone	Mitch Richmond
☐ BK0064	Nov	1995	Kevin Garnett	Robert Horry
☐ BK0065	Dec	1995	D.Robinson/H.Olajuwon	Juwan Howard
☐ BK0066	Jan	1996	Jerry Stackhouse	Antonio McDyess
☐ BK0067	Feb	1996	Michael Jordan	Ed O'Bannon
☐ BK0068	Mar	1996	Anfernee Hardaway	Damon Stoudamire
☐ BK0069	Apr	1996	Magic Johnson	Larry Johnson
☐ BK0070	May	1996	Scottie Pippen	Michael Finley
☐ BK0071	Jun	1996	Shawn Kemp	Kevin Garnett
☐ BK0072	Jul	1996	Dream Team III	Glenn Robinson
☐ BK0073	Aug	1996	Dennis Rodman	Joe Dumars
☐ BK0074	Sep	1996	Michael Jordan	Allen Iverson

ISSUE #	MONTH	YEAR	FRONT COVER	BACK COVER
☐ BK0075	Oct	1996	Shaq O'Neal	Dream Team
☐ BK0076	Nov	1996	Damon Stoudamire	Alonzo Mourning
☐ BK0077	Dec	1996	Kevin Garnett	Juwan Howard
☐ BK0078	Jan	1997	Barkley,Olajuwon,Drexler	Gheorghe Muresan
☐ BK0079	Feb	1997	Chris Webber,Juwan Howard	Shareef Abdur-Rahim
☐ BK0080	Mar	1997	Allen Iverson	Joe Smith
☐ BK0081	Apr	1997	Anfernee Hardaway	Tom Gugliotta
☐ BK0082	May	1997	Grant Hill	Stephon Marbury
☐ BK0083	Jun	1997	Glen Rice	Tim Hardaway
☐ BK0084	Jul	1997	Allen Iverson	Eddie Jones
☐ BK0085	Aug	1997	Michael Jordan	M.Jordan/S.Pippen
☐ BK0086	Sep	1997	D.Robinson/ Tim Duncan	Marcus Camby
☐ BK0087	Oct	1997	Karl Malone	Antoine Walker
☐ BK0088	Nov	1997	Spike Lee	Rasheed Wallace
☐ BK0089	Dec	1997	K.Bryant/Shaq O'Neal	Voshon Lenard

BECKETT FOOTBALL CARD MONTHLY

ISSUE #	MONTH	YEAR	FRONT COVER	BACK COVER
☐ FB0001	Dec	1989	Bo Jackson	Dan Marino
☐ FB0002	Jan	1990	Joe Montana	Eric Dickerson
☐ FB0003	Mar	1990	John Elway	Randall Cunningham
☐ FB0004	May	1990	Barry Sanders	Christian Okoye
☐ FB0005	Jul	1990	Andre Ware	Lawrence Taylor
☐ FB0006	Sep	1990	Jerry Rice	Jim Everett
☐ FB0007	Oct	1990	Majkowski	Walter Payton
☐ FB0008	Nov	1990	Bo Jackson	Warren Moon
☐ FB0009	Dec	1990	Joe Montana	Humphrey
☐ FB0010	Jan	1991	Bo Jackson	Lombardi/Starr
☐ FB0011	Feb	1991	Randall Cunningham	Neal Anderson
☐ FB0012	Mar	1991	Thurman Thomas	E.Smith
☐ FB0013	Apr	1991	Ismail	Ronnie Lott
☐ FB0014	May	1991	Bruce Smith	Johnny Johnson
☐ FB0015	Jun	1991	Boomer Esiason	Marion Butts
☐ FB0016	Jul	1991	Jerry Rice	Jeff George
☐ FB0017	Aug	1991	Barry Sanders	D.Thomas
☐ FB0018	Sep	1991	Warren Moon	Andre Rison
☐ FB0019	Oct	1991	Troy Aikman	Carrier
☐ FB0020	Nov	1991	Lott/Craig	Sharpe
☐ FB0021	Dec	1991	Emmitt Smith	Blair Thomas
☐ FB0022	Jan	1992	Jim Kelly	Joe Namath
☐ FB0023	Feb	1992	Rypien	H.Williams
☐ FB0024	Mar	1992	Dan Marino	Russell
☐ FB0025	Apr	1992	T.Thomas	John Elway
☐ FB0026	May	1992	Desmond Howard	Pat Swilling
☐ FB0027	Jun	1992	Ervins	Irvin
☐ FB0028	Jul	1992	Barry Sanders	Deion Sanders
☐ FB0029	Aug	1992	D.Thomas	McGwire
☐ FB0030	Sep	1992	Emmitt Smith	Randall Cunningham
☐ FB0031	Oct	1992	Art Monk	Nagle
☐ FB0032	Nov	1992	Deion Sanders	Warren Moon
☐ FB0033	Dec	1992	Dan Marino	H.Walker
☐ FB0034	Jan	1993	Ricky Watters	Lawrence Taylor
☐ FB0035	Feb	1993	Barry Foster	Steve Young
☐ FB0036	Mar	1993	Michael Irvin	Brett Favre
☐ FB0037	Apr	1993	Troy Aikman	Cortez Kennedy
☐ FB0038	May	1993	Sterling Sharpe	David Klingler
☐ FB0039	Jun	1993	Drew Bledsoe	Reggie White
☐ FB0040	Jul	1993	Joe Montana	Walter Payton
☐ FB0041	Aug	1993	Emmitt Smith	Jerry Rice

ISSUE #	MONTH	YEAR	FRONT COVER	BACK COVER
☐ FB0042	Sep	1993	Brett Favre	Junior Seau
☐ FB0043	Oct	1993	Steve Young	Desmond Howard
☐ FB0044	Nov	1993	Garrison Hearst	Ken Norton
☐ FB0045	Dec	1993	Barry Sanders	Keith Jackson
☐ FB0046	Jan	1994	Troy Aikman	John Elway
☐ FB0047	Feb	1994	Jerry Rice	Marcus Allen
☐ FB0048	Mar	1994	Rick Mirer	Ron Woodson
☐ FB0049	Apr	1994	Emmitt Smith	Jason Jett
☐ FB0050	May	1994	Montana/Aikman /Namath/Bradshaw	
☐ FB0051	Jun	1994	Heath Shuler	Rodney Hampton
☐ FB0052	Jul	1994	Jerome Bettis	Tony Dorsett
☐ FB0053	Aug	1994	Marshall Faulk	Tim Brown
☐ FB0054	Sep	1994	Drew Bledsoe	Warren Moon
☐ FB0055	Oct	1994	Jerry Rice	Anthony Miller
☐ FB0056	Nov	1994	Dan Marino	Heath Shuler
☐ FB0057	Dec	1994	Joe Montana	Natrone Means
☐ FB0058	Jan	1995	Michael Irvin	Deion Sanders
☐ FB0059	Feb	1994	Troy Aikman	Jeff Blake
☐ FB0060	Mar	1995	Marshall Faulk	Chris Warren
☐ FB0061	Apr	1995	Steve Young	Errict Rhett
☐ FB0062	May	1995	Deion Sanders	Chris Carter
☐ FB0063	Jun	1995	Joe Montana	Steve McNair
☐ FB0064	Jul	1995	Drew Bledsoe	William Floyd
☐ FB0065	Aug	1995	Ki-Jana Carter	Ricky Watters
☐ FB0066	Sep	1995	Emmitt Smith	Kerry Collins
☐ FB0067	Oct	1995	Barry Sanders	J.J. Stokes
☐ FB0068	Nov	1995	Deion Sanders	Rashaan Salaam
☐ FB0069	Dec	1995	Dan Marino	Joey Galloway
☐ FB0070	Jan	1996	Brett Favre	Errict Rhett
☐ FB0071	Feb	1996	Emmitt Smith	Jerry Rice
☐ FB0072	Mar	1996	Deion Sanders	Curtis Martin
☐ FB0073	Apr	1996	Kordell Stewart	Jim Harbaugh
☐ FB0074	May	1996	Kerry Collins	Bryce Paup
☐ FB0075	Jun	1996	Chris Warren	Yancy Thigpen
☐ FB0076	Jul	1996	Keyshawn Johnson	Herman Moore
☐ FB0077	Aug	1996	Curtis Martin	Mark Brunell
☐ FB0078	Sep	1996	Steve Young / Jerry Rice	Carl Pickens
☐ FB0079	Oct	1996	Troy Aikman	Joey Galloway
☐ FB0080	Nov	1996	John Elway	Eddie George
☐ FB0081	Dec	1996	Barry Sanders/Emmitt Smith	Karim Abdul-Jabbar
☐ FB0082	Jan	1997	Brett Favre	Jerome Bettis
☐ FB0083	Feb	1997	Eddie George	Vinny Testaverde
☐ FB0084	Mar	1997	Terrell Davis	Terry Glenn
☐ FB0085	Apr	1997	Mark Brunell	Ricky Watters
☐ FB0086	May	1997	Brett Favre	Jim Kelly
☐ FB0087	Jun	1997	Drew Bledsoe	Isaac Bruce
☐ FB0088	Jul	1997	Emmitt Smith	Jeff George
☐ FB0089	Aug	1997	John Elway	Mike Ditka
☐ FB0090	Sep	1997	Barry Sanders	Reggie White
☐ FB0091	Oct	1997	Kerry Collins/Aikman	Advertisement
☐ FB0092	Nov	1997	Roy Firestone/Eddie George	Advertisement
☐ FB0093	Dec	1997	Warrick Dunn	Advertisement

FUTURE STARS

ISSUE #	MONTH	YEAR	FRONT COVER	BACK COVER
☐ FS0001	May	1991	Van Poppel / Ryan	K.Anderson
☐ FS0002	Jun	1991	Frank Thomas	Shaquille O'Neal
☐ FS0003	Jul	1991	Sierra / Gonzalez	Larry Johnson
☐ FS0004	Aug	1991	Morris	Deion Sanders

ISSUE #	MONTH	YEAR	FRONT COVER	BACK COVER
☐ FS0005	Sep	1991	D.Bell	T.Martinez
☐ FS0006	Oct	1991	Ismail	Bagwell
☐ FS0007	Nov	1991	McRae	Owens
☐ FS0008	Dec	1991	O'Neal	Croel
☐ FS0009	Jan	1992	Howard	Plantier
☐ FS0010	Feb	1992	Klesko	Mutumbo
☐ FS0011	Mar	1992	MacLean / T.Murray	Buckley
☐ FS0012	Apr	1992	Frank Thomas	Avery
☐ FS0013	May	1992	Ken Griffey Jr.	Rodriquez
☐ FS0014	Jun	1992	Taylor	VanPoppel
☐ FS0015	Jul	1992	R.Sanders	McCarty
☐ FS0016	Aug	1992	Mussina	Lofton
☐ FS0017	Sep	1992	Knoblauch	Salmon
☐ FS0018	Oct	1992	Nagle	Karros
☐ FS0019	Nov	1992	Juan Gonzalez	D.McGwire
☐ FS0020	Dec	1992	Faulk / B.Sanders	Eldred
☐ FS0021	Jan	1993	Shaquille O'Neal	Watters
☐ FS0022	Feb	1993	Nied	Toretta
☐ FS0023	Mar	1993	Karros	Rondell White
☐ FS0024	Apr	1993	Mashburn	Mirer
☐ FS0025	May	1993	Shaquille O'Neal	N.Wilson
☐ FS0026	Jun	1993	Salmon / Snow	Tucker
☐ FS0027	Jul	1993	Chipper Jones	M.Jones
☐ FS0028	Aug	1993	Floyd	Rheaume
☐ FS0029	Sep	1993	Hammonds	Gates
☐ FS0030	Oct	1993	Sele	E.Perez
☐ FS0031	Nov	1993	Ramirez	Bettis
☐ FS0032	Dec	1993	Brooks / Bettis / Mirer	Jason Bere
☐ FS0033	Jan	1994	Anfernee Hardaway	Jett
☐ FS0034	Feb	1994	Delgado	R.Smith
☐ FS0035	Mar	1994	Ward	Hunter
☐ FS0036	Apr	1994	Rider	Newfield
☐ FS0037	May	1994	Javier Lopez	T.Kukoc
☐ FS0038	Jun	1994	Glen Robinson	Raul Mondesi
☐ FS0039	Jul	1994	C.Johnson	Mouton
☐ FS0040	Aug	1994	Grant Hill	Tyrone Wheatley
☐ FS0041	Sep	1994	Raul Mondesi	P.Wilson
☐ FS0042	Oct	1994	Manon Rheaume	Kieschnick
☐ FS0043	Nov	1994	Robinson	Faulk
☐ FS0044	Dec	1994	Jason Kidd	C.Johnson
☐ FS0045	Jan	1995	Faulk	Howard / Rose / Webber
☐ FS0046	Feb	1995	Grant Hill	Bam Morris
☐ FS0047	Mar	1995	Corliss Williamson	R.Rivera
☐ FS0048	Apr	1995	Carter	Johnson
☐ FS0049	May	1995	T.Bailey	Wesley Person
☐ FS0050	Jun	1995	Grant Hill	McNair
☐ FS0051	Jul	1995	J.Stackhouse	Grieve
☐ FS0052	Aug	1995	Chipper Jones	Joe Smith
☐ FS0053	Sep	1995	Ki-Jana Carter	Carlos Perez
☐ FS0054	Oct	1995	Garret Anderson	Rasheed Wallace
☐ FS0055	Nov	1995	Michael Westbrook	Jason Isringhausen
☐ FS0056	Dec	1995	Kevin Garnett	Rashaan Salaam
☐ FS0057	Jan	1996	Jerry Stackhouse	Kerry Collins
☐ FS0058	Feb	1996	Damon Stoudamire	Curtis Martin
☐ FS0059	Mar	1996	Michael Jordan	Kordell Stewart
☐ FS0060	Apr	1996	Paul Wilson	Eddie George
☐ FS0061	May	1996	Keyshawn Johnson	Karim Garcia
☐ FS0062	Jun	1996	Andruw Jones	Kerry Kittles
☐ FS0063	Jul	1996	Allen Iverson	Alan Benes

ISSUE #	MONTH	YEAR	FRONT COVER	BACK COVER
☐ FS0064	Aug	1996	Derek Jeter	Ray Allen
☐ FS0065	Sept	1996	Tim Biakabatuka	Kris Benson
☐ FS0066	Oct	1996	Glenn, George	Vladimir Guerrero
☐ FS0067	Nov	1996	Rahim,Marbury	Alex Ochoa
☐ FS0068	Dec	1996	Karim Abdul-Jabbar	Neifi Perez
☐ FS0069	Jan	1997	Eddie George	Paul Konerko
☐ FS0070	Feb	1997	Allen Iverson	Tony Banks
☐ FS0071	Mar	1997	Kenner BK Figures	Tim Duncan
☐ FS0072	Apr	1997	Andruw Jones	Warrick Dunn
☐ FS0073	May	1997	Nomar Garciaparra	Ray Allen
☐ FS0074	Jun	1997	Michael Jordan	Advertisement
☐ FS0075	Jul	1997	Cal Ripken	Jose Cruz Jr.
☐ FS0076	Aug	1997	Ken Griffey Jr.	Orlando Pace
☐ FS0077	Sep	1997	Brett Favre	Advertisement
☐ FS0078	Oct	1997	Derek Jeter	Advertisement
☐ FS0079	Nov	1997	Dan Marino	Advertisement
☐ FS0080	Dec	1997	Cal Ripken Autographed Balls	Advertisement

BECKETT HOCKEY CARD MONTHLY

ISSUE #	MONTH	YEAR	FRONT COVER	BACK COVER
☐ HK0001	Sep	1990	Wayne Gretzky	Patrick Roy
☐ HK0002	Nov	1990	Brett Hull	Mark Messier
☐ HK0003	Jan	1991	Paul Yzerman	Bobby Hull
☐ HK0004	Feb	1991	Mario Lemieux	Joe Sakic
☐ HK0005	Mar	1991	Ray Bourque	Mike Bossy
☐ HK0006	Apr	1991	Patrick Roy	Adam Oates
☐ HK0007	May	1991	Sergi Fedorov	Al MacInnis
☐ HK0008	Jun	1991	Eric Lindros	Cullen
☐ HK0009	Jul	1991	Ed Belfour	Mark Recchi
☐ HK0010	Aug	1991	Mario Lemieux	Potvin / Messier
☐ HK0011	Sep	1991	Jagr	Theorn Fleury
☐ HK0012	Oct	1991	Yari Kurri	Igor Statsny
☐ HK0013	Nov	1991	Brett Hull	Luc Robitaille
☐ HK0014	Dec	1991	Grant Fuhr	Savard
☐ HK0015	Jan	1992	Mark Messier	Pat Falloon
☐ HK0016	Feb	1992	Trevor Linden	Owen Nolan
☐ HK0017	Mar	1992	Pavel Bure	Stevens
☐ HK0018	Apr	1992	Roenick	Linden
☐ HK0019	May	1992	Wayne Gretzky	Amonte
☐ HK0020	Jun	1992	G.Dionne	Lachance
☐ HK0021	Jul	1992	LaFontaine	Brind'Amour
☐ HK0022	Aug	1992	Pittsburgh Celebration	Cherry
☐ HK0023	Sep	1992	Lindros	T.Esposito
☐ HK0024	Oct	1992	Bure	Oates
☐ HK0025	Nov	1992	Wayne Gretzky	Lafleur
☐ HK0026	Dec	1992	Manon Rheaume	Niedermayer
☐ HK0027	Jan	1993	Leetch	Mogilny
☐ HK0028	Feb	1993	Juneau	Jagr
☐ HK0029	Mar	1993	Selanne	Recchi
☐ HK0030	Apr	1993	Lemieux	Sakic
☐ HK0031	May	1993	Potvin	Iafrate
☐ HK0032	Jun	1993	Neely	Daigle
☐ HK0033	Jul	1993	Gilmour	Belfour
☐ HK0034	Aug	1993	Roy	Yzerman
☐ HK0035	Sep	1993	Daigle/Pronger/Gratton	Fuhr
☐ HK0036	Oct	1993	Lindros	Zhamnov
☐ HK0037	Nov	1993	Luc Robitaille	Courtnall
☐ HK0038	Dec	1993	Turgeon	Zhitnik
☐ HK0039	Jan	1994	Mike Modano	Gordie Howe

ISSUE #	MONTH	YEAR	FRONT COVER	BACK COVER
☐ HK0040	Feb	1994	Clark	Renberg
☐ HK0041	Mar	1994	Fedorov	Tkachuk
☐ HK0042	Apr	1994	Wayne Gretzky	Mike Richter
☐ HK0043	May	1994	Patrick Roy	R.Bourque
☐ HK0044	Jun	1994	Eric Lindros	Brett Lindros
☐ HK0045	Jul	1994	Leetch	Pavel Bure
☐ HK0046	Aug	1994	Messier	Rangers Parade
☐ HK0047	Sep	1994	Bonk	McLean
☐ HK0048	Oct	1994	Brodeur	Jagr
☐ HK0049	Nov	1994	Goalie Masks	Vanbiesbrouck
☐ HK0050	Dec	1994	.50 in 50 Club	Mogilny
☐ HK0051	Jan	1995	Pavel Bure	LaFontaine
☐ HK0052	Feb	1995	Wayne Gretzky	Vernon
☐ HK0053	Mar	1995	Shanahan	Roenick
☐ HK0054	Apr	1995	Oates / Neely	Rod Brind "Amor"
☐ HK0055	May	1995	Kariya	Arnott
☐ HK0056	Jun	1995	Eric Lindros	Jim Carey
☐ HK0057	Jul	1995	Jagr	Sundin
☐ HK0058	Aug	1995	Martin Brodeur	Dominik Hasek
☐ HK0059	Sep	1995	Jeremy Roenick	Bryan Berard
☐ HK0060	Oct	1995	Peter Forsberg	Todd Harvey
☐ HK0061	Nov	1995	Mogilny / Bure	Brendan Shanahan
☐ HK0062	Dec	1995	Patrick Roy	Alexi Zhamnov
☐ HK0063	Jan	1996	Brett Hull	Saku Koivu
☐ HK0064	Feb	1996	Mario Lemieux	Vitali Yachmenev
☐ HK0065	Mar	1996	Teemu Selanne	Marcus Ragnarsson
☐ HK0066	Apr	1996	Wayne Gretzky	Eric Daze
☐ HK0067	May	1996	Lindros / LeClair / Renberg	Petr Sykora
☐ HK0068	Jun	1996	Steve Yzerman	Roman Hamerlik
☐ HK0069	Jul	1996	Paul Kariya	John Vanbiesbrook
☐ HK0070	Aug	1996	Joe Sakic	Chris Osgood
☐ HK0071	Sep	1996	Gordie Howe	Chris Philips
☐ HK0072	Oct	1996	Gretzky,Messier	Claude Lemieux
☐ HK0073	Nov	1996	Patrick Roy	'96 World Cup Champs
☐ HK0074	Dec	1996	Mario Lemieux	Theoren Fleury
☐ HK0075	Jan	1997	Keith Tkachuk	Peter Bondra
☐ HK0076	Feb	1997	John Vanbiesbrouck	Doug Weight
☐ HK0077	Mar	1997	Jaromir Jagr	Brian Leetch
☐ HK0078	Apr	1997	Eric Lindros	Andy Moog
☐ HK0079	May	1997	Dominik Hasek	Jarome Iginla
☐ HK0080	Jun	1997	Wayne Gretzky	Brian Berard
☐ HK0081	Jul	1997	Mario Lemieux	Mario Lemieux
☐ HK0082	Aug	1997	Brendan Shanahan	Advertisement
☐ HK0083	Sep	1997	Paul Kariya	Advertisement
☐ HK0084	Oct	1997	Rob Ray	Advertisement
☐ HK0085	Nov	1997	Steve Yzerman	Advertisement
☐ HK0086	Dec	1997	Saku Koivu	Advertisement

BECKETT PROFILES

ISSUE #	MONTH	YEAR	FRONT COVER	BACK COVER
☐ BP0002		1996	Olympians '96	Various
☐ BP0003E		1996	Pro Football '96; Dan Marino	Various
☐ BP0003MW		1996	Brett Favre	Various
☐ BP0003SW		1996	Troy Aikman	Various
☐ BP0003W		1996	Steve Young	Various
☐ BP0004C		1996	Pro Basketball; Michael Jordan	Various
☐ BP0004NE		1996	Allen Iverson	Various
☐ BP0004SE		1996	Anfernee Hardaway	Various
☐ BP0004W		1996	Shaquille O'Neil	Various

ISSUE #	MONTH	YEAR	FRONT COVER	BACK COVER
☐ PF0005		1996	Dennis Rodman	Dennis Rodman
☐ PF0006		1997	Tiger Woods	Tiger Woods
☐ PF0007		1997	Mike Piazza	Advertisement
☐ PF0008		1997	Ken Griffey Jr.	Various

BECKETT RACING HEROES

ISSUE #	MONTH	YEAR	FRONT COVER	BACK COVER
☐ RH0001	Dec	1995	Preview '96 Jeff Gordon	Various
☐ RH0002	Jan	1996	Jeff Gordon	Jeff Gordon
☐ RH0003	Jan	1996	Dale Earnhardt	Dale Earnhardt
☐ RH0004	Jan	1996	Bill Elliott	Bill Elliott

BECKETT RACING MONTHLY

ISSUE #	MONTH	YEAR	FRONT COVER	BACK COVER
☐ RM0001	Sep	1994	Dale Earnhardt	Ernie Irvan
☐ RM0002	Oct	1994	Ernie Irvan	Mario Andretti
☐ RM0003	Nov	1994	Rusty Wallace	Harry Gant
☐ RM0004	Dec	1994	Mark Martin	Ricky Rudd
☐ RM0005	Jan	1995	Bill Elliott	David Green
☐ RM0006	Feb	1995	Jeff Gordon	Geoff Bodine
☐ RM0007	Mar	1995	D.Earnhardt/ R.Petty	Dale Jarrett
☐ RM0008	Apr	1995	Sterling Marlin	Darrell Waltrip
☐ RM0009	May	1995	Al Unser Jr.	Terry Labonte
☐ RM0010	Jun	1995	Jeff Gordon Car	Bobby Labonte
☐ RM0011	Jul	1995	Dale Earnhardt Car	Ken Schrader
☐ RM0012	Aug	1995	Kyle Petty	Robert Pressley
☐ RM0013	Sep	1995	Sterling Marlin	Ron Hornaday truck
☐ RM0014	Oct	1995	Dale Earnhardt	Ted Musgrave
☐ RM0015	Nov	1995	Bobby Labonte	Terry Labonte
☐ RM0016	Dec	1995	Jeff Gordon	Ernie Irvan
☐ RM0017	Jan	1996	Richard Petty	Bobby Hamilton
☐ RM0018	Feb	1996	Ernie Irvan	Ward Burton car
☐ RM0019	Mar	1996	Rusty Wallace	Steve Grissom's car
☐ RM0020	Apr	1996	Dale Jarrett	Patti Moise
☐ RM0021	May	1996	Cars :T.Musgrave / M.Martin	Bill Brodrick
☐ RM0022	Jun	1996	Dale Earnhardt	Ned and Dale Jarrett
☐ RM0023	Jul	1996	Terry Labonte	Advertisement
☐ RM0024	Aug	1996	Dale Earnhardt Olympic Car	Michael Waltrip
☐ RM0025	Sep	1996	Cover Collage	Advertisement
☐ RM0026	Oct	1996	Gordon / Earnhardt	Advertisement
☐ RM0027	Nov	1996	Jeff Gordon	Advertisement
☐ RM0028	Dec	1996	Pit Pros	Advertisement
☐ RM0029	Jan	1997	John Force	Advertisement
☐ RM0030	Feb	1997	Dale Jarrett	Advertisement
☐ RM0031	Mar	1997	Earnhardt,Gord. Cars	Advertisement
☐ RM0032	Apr	1997	Labonte / Gordon / Craven	Advertisement
☐ RM0033	May	1997	Darrell Waltrip	Advertisement
☐ RM0034	Jun	1997	Jeff Burton / Mark Martin	Advertisement
☐ RM0035	Jul	1997	Jeff Gordon	Advertisement
☐ RM0036	Aug	1997	Terry Labonte's Car	Advertisement
☐ RM0037	Sep	1997	Dale Earnhardt	Advertisement
☐ RM0038	Oct	1997	Bobby Labonte's Car	Advertisement
☐ RM0039	Nov	1997	Jeff Gordon	Advertisement
☐ RM0040	Dec	1997	Richard Petty	Advertisement

BECKETT SPORTS HEROES

ISSUE #	MONTH	YEAR	FRONT COVER	BACK COVER
☐ SH0001	Apr	1995	Michael Jordan	No Photo
☐ SH0002	Jul	1995	Mickey Mantle	No Photo
☐ SH0003	Oct	1995	Shaquille O'Neal	No Photo

ISSUE #	MONTH	YEAR	FRONT COVER	BACK COVER
☐ SH0004	Dec	1995	Joe Montana	No Photo
☐ SH0005	Feb	1996	Joe DiMaggio	Joe DiMaggio
☐ SH0006	Jun	1996	Magic Johnson	Magic Johnson
☐ SH0007	Aug	1996	Emmitt Smith	Advertisement

BECKETT TRIBUTES

ISSUE #	MONTH	YEAR	FRONT COVER	BACK COVER
☐ TR0001	Aug	1993	Nolan Ryan	Nolan Ryan
☐ TR0002	Oct	1993	Joe Montana	Joe Montana
☐ TR0003	Dec	1993	Michael Jordan	Michael Jordan
☐ TR0004	Feb	1994	Shaquille O'Neal	Shaquille O'Neal
☐ TR0005	Apr	1994	Frank Thomas	Frank Thomas
☐ TR0006	Jun	1994	Larry Bird, Magic Johnson	Bird/Magic
☐ TR0007	Aug	1994	Emmitt Smith	Emmitt Smith
☐ TR0008	Oct	1994	Wayne Gretzky	Wayne Gretzky
☐ TR0009	Nov	1994	Charles Barkley	Charles Barkley
☐ TR0010	Mar	1995	Dale Earnhardt	Earnhardt's Car
☐ TR0011	Jun	1995	Cal Ripken Jr.	Cal Ripken, Jr.
☐ TR0012	Aug	1995	Dan Marino	Dan Marino
☐ TR0013	Sep	1995	Notre Dame Football	Ron Powlus
☐ TR0014	Jan	1996	Dallas Cowboys	Deion Sanders
☐ TR0014S	Feb	1996	Dallas Cowboys*	Deion Sanders
☐ TR0015	Mar	1996	Ken Griffey Jr.	Ken Griffey, Jr.
☐ TR0016	May	1996	Chicago Bulls	Dennis Rodman
☐ TR0016S	Jun	1996	Chicago Bulls*	Dennis Rodman
☐ TR0017	Jul	1996	Dream Team III	Dream Team III
☐ TR0018	Aug	1996	Troy Aikman	Aikman Advertisement
☐ TR0019	Nov	1996	Brett Favre	Brett Favre
☐ TR0020	Jan	1997	Terry Labonte Winston Cup	Labonte's Car
☐ TR0021	Jan	1997	Super Bowl XXXI Champ.	Sean Jones
☐ TR0022	Jun	1997	Chicago Bulls (NBA Champ.)	Various

BECKETT VINTAGE SPORTS

ISSUE #	MONTH	YEAR	FRONT COVER	BACK COVER
☐ VS0001	Fall	1996	Mickey Mantle	Advertisement
☐ VS0002	Winter	1996	Jim Brown	Advertisement
☐ VS0003	Feb	1997	Joe Namath	Advertisement
☐ VS0004	Mar	1997	Lou Gehrig	Advertisement
☐ VS0005	Apr	1997	Jackie Robinson	Advertisement
☐ VS0006	May	1997	Babe Ruth	Advertisement
☐ VS0007	Jun	1997	Wilt Chamblerlain	Advertisement
☐ VS0008	Jul	1997	All Star Salute	Advertisement
☐ VS0009	Aug	1997	Muhammad Ali	Advertisement
☐ VS0010	Sep	1997	Roberto Clemente	Advertisement
☐ VS0011	Oct	1997	Ruth/Mays/Larsen/Berra	Advertisement
☐ VS0012	Nov	1997	Mickey Mantle	Advertisement
☐ VS0013	Dec	1997	Vincent Lombardi	Advertisement

BECKETT PREVIEWS

ISSUE #	MONTH	YEAR	FRONT COVER	BACK COVER
☐ PR0001		1997	Racing 97; Dale Earnhardt	Earnhardt Pictures
☐ PR0002NE		1997	Baseball 97; Derek Jeter	Advertisement
☐ PR0002SE		1997	Baseball 97; Chipper Jones	Advertisement
☐ PR0002W		1997	Baseball 97; Mike Piazza	Advertisement
☐ PR0002SW		1997	Baseball 97; Ivan Rodriguez	Advertisement
☐ PR0002NW		1997	Baseball 97; Alex Rodriguez	Advertisement
☐ PR0002MW		1997	Baseball 97; Frank Thomas	Advertisement
☐ PR0003NE		1997	Football 97; Drew Bledsoe	Advertisement
☐ PR0003SE		1997	Football 97; Kerry Collins	Advertisement
☐ PR0003W		1997	Football 97; Steve Young	Advertisement
☐ PR0003SW		1997	Football 97; Troy Aikman	Advertisement
☐ PR0003MW		1997	Football 97; Brett Favre	Advertisement

BASEBALL - ISSUE 74

BASEBALL - ISSUE 77

BASEBALL - ISSUE 80

FOOTBALL - ISSUE 3

FOOTBALL - ISSUE 7

FOOTBALL - ISSUE 14

BASKETBALL - ISSUE 13

BASKETBALL - ISSUE 41

BASKETBALL - ISSUE 66

HOCKEY - ISSUE 25

HOCKEY - ISSUE 73

HOCKEY - ISSUE 81

RACING - ISSUE 3

RACING - ISSUE 6

RACING - ISSUE 17

FUTURE STARS - ISSUE 26

FUTURE STARS - ISSUE 34

FUTURE STARS - ISSUE 59

CHAPTER TEN:
Collecting Baseball Team Publications

Baseball traditionally has been the base of sports publication collecting. Baseball sports publications date back into the 1860's. The earliest sports publications were newspapers and game programs. Magazines began to show up in the 1900's. Books date back to the turn of the century as well. In fact, book collecting is perhaps one of the strongest areas in sports publications.

Today, most baseball publication collectors tend to focus on there favorite teams and players. To address their needs this book is divided by teams with a minor focus on the key players on each team. The next chapter is devoted to general baseball sports publications.

It should be noted that many baseball covers appear on the general sports publications that are featured throughout this book like Sports Illustrated, Sport, Beckett, etc. I have developed and index for those magazines. However, all the magazines in the Baseball publications chapter are not in the alpha index.

Finally, the great games in baseball The World Series and the All-Star Game are listed in a special section of this chapter.

ANGELS (LOS ANGELES, ANAHEIM, CALIFORNIA)
The California Angels were a Pacific Coast League team before they became a major league team in the 1960's. The team started in the American League in Los Angeles in 1961 and moved to Anaheim in 1966. Gene Autry was the original owner. Today it is owned by Disney. Most of the sports publication collectors pursue Nolan Ryan, Rod Carew or early unusual Angel publications.

MEDIA GUIDES	Nr-Mt	Ex
☐ 1961 First Guide	70	35
☐ 1962 - 1963	35	20
☐ 1964-1965	35	20
☐ 1966 - 1968	20	10
☐ 1969-1971	20	10
☐ 1972 - 1975 (Nolan Ryan)	20	10
☐ 1976-1980	12	6
☐ 1981 - 1990	10	3
☐ 1991-1997	5	2

PROGRAMS	Nr-Mt	Ex
☐ First Game 1961	200	100
☐ 1961 Program	45	25
☐ 1962-1964 programs	20	10
☐ 1965-1968	15	7
☐ 1969-1972	12	5
☐ 1972 (Nolan Ryan First)	100	50
☐ 1972-1975 (Nolan Ryan)	40	20
☐ 1973-1980	10	4
☐ 1981-1997	6	3
☐ Reggie Jackson cover	12	6
☐ Rod Carew Covers	10	6
☐ Nolan Ryan Cover	30	15

YEARBOOKS	Nr-Mt	Ex
☐ 1962 First Yearbook	95	40
☐ 1963	60	25
☐ 1964-1965	40	20
☐ 1966 (First in Anaheim)	60	20
☐ 1967	25	10
☐ 1983-1985	10	3
☐ 1987-1997	7	2

SCHEDULES	Nr-Mt	Ex
☐ 1961	30	15
☐ 1962-1965	12	8
☐ 1966-1970	5	3
☐ 1971-1979	3	2
☐ 1980-1989	1	.50
☐ 1990-1997	.50	.25

TICKETS	Nr-Mt	Ex
☐ 1961 First Game	100	50
☐ 1961-1962 tickets	10	8
☐ 1963-1969	5	3
☐ 1970-1980	2	1
☐ Nolan Ryan Games	10	5
☐ Nolan Ryan No Hitters	100	50
☐ 1981-1990	2	1
☐ Reggie Jackson record	50	20

PUBLICATIONS	Nr-Mt	Ex
☐ Angel Angles 61-date	20	10
☐ Nolan Ryan Covers	30	15
☐ Books	10	4
☐ General Publications	20	10
☐ Nolan Ryan Pubs Covers	45	20

The team newsletter/newspaper is called "Angel Angles" which started in 1961. Early editions would be in the $20 range. Edition with Nolan Ryan would be in the $40 range.

ASTROS (HOUSTON, ALSO COLTS)
The Houston Astros started out in 1962 as the Houston Colts. They changed their name to the Astros in 1965 when they moved into the Astrodome. There are a few highlights in Astros publications: Early Colts material, Nolan Ryan, and Joe Morgan.

MEDIA GUIDES	Nr-Mt	Ex
☐ 1962 First Guide	65	25
☐ 1963 - 1964 Colts	40	20
☐ 1965-1966	25	15
☐ 1967 - 1969	20	10
☐ 1970-1972	15	8
☐ 1973 - 1975	12	8
☐ 1976-1980	10	5
☐ 1981 - 1990	6	3
☐ 1991-1997	5	2

PROGRAMS	Nr-Mt	Ex
☐ First Game 1962	200	100
☐ 1962 Program	40	20
☐ 1963-1964 programs	20	10
☐ 1965-1968	12	7
☐ 1969-1972	10	5
☐ 1973-1980	10	4
☐ 1981-1997	6	3
☐ Joe Morgan cover	20	10
☐ Nolan Ryan Cover	30	15
☐ Nolan Ryan Games	20	10

YEARBOOKS	Nr-Mt	Ex
☐ 1962 First Yearbook	200	100
☐ 1963 Colts	175	100
☐ 1964 Colts	150	75
☐ 1965 Astros	100	50
☐ 1977,1978,1979	12	7
☐ 1982	15	10
☐ Astrodome YB 65'	25	15

SCHEDULES	Nr-Mt	Ex
☐ 1962	40	15
☐ 1963-1965	25	10
☐ 1966-1970	7	5
☐ 1971-1979	3	2
☐ 1980-1989	2	1
☐ 1990-1997	1	.50

TICKETS	Nr-Mt	Ex
☐ 1962 First Game	100	65
☐ 1962 tickets	14	8
☐ 1963-1969	5	3
☐ 1970-1980	2	1
☐ Nolan Ryan Games	10	5
☐ Nolan Ryan No Hitters	100	50
☐ 1981-1990	2	1

PUBLICATIONS	Nr-Mt	Ex
☐ Astrographs (60's)	20	10
☐ Newsletters 70 - 90's	6	3
☐ Nolan Ryan Covers NL	30	15
☐ Books	10	4
☐ Colts Publication covers	45	20
☐ Nolan Ryan Pubs Covers	45	20
☐ Astros Pubs (60's)	25	10
☐ Astros Pubs (70's-80's)	15	5
☐ Astros Pubs covers (90's)	6	3
☐ The Colt 45's NL (62-64)	30	15

ATHLETICS
(PHILADELPHIA, KANSAS CITY, OAKLAND)

The Athletics have a great tradition. They were the best team at the start of the century with a great leader in Connie Mack. He lead the team for 54 years and won 9 pennants. These early years produced a strong following for quality historical Philadelphia A's sports publications.

The most sought after A's material are the early World Series programs from the start of the century. However, there are a few books on the early A's that are sought after: 'Our Champions' 1902 by Standard Engravings (Est. 2,500), 'The Champion Athletics' 1905 by Charles Drydren (Est. 2,500), 'Portraits of Chicago & Philadelphia A's' 1910 (Est. 2,500), and Connie Mack Philadelphia Athletics' 1929 (Est. 450).

The Kansas City A's had a short history filled with nondescript teams. The publications produced are not common and not highly sought after. The highlight of the Kansas City A's is Roger Maris in1957.

The Oakland A's have a solid collector following but since the team started in 1968, very few publications are expensive. However, collectors still pursue unusual Reggie Jackson sports publications.

MEDIA GUIDES	Nr-Mt	Ex
☐ 1930-1935 Roster list	100	50
☐ 1936-1941	75	35
☐ 1942-1949	60	20
☐ 1950 Connie Mack	60	20
☐ 1951-1954	50	15
☐ 1955 (First Kansas City)	70	20
☐ 1956-1961	40	15
☐ 1962-1967	25	10
☐ 1968 (First Oakland)	50	20
☐ 1969-1974	12	5
☐ 1975-1979	10	2
☐ 1980-1991	6	1
☐ 1992-1997	4	1

PROGRAMS & SCORECARDS	Nr-Mt	Ex
☐ 1901	600	200
☐ 1902 Champs	400	100
☐ 1903-1904	300	100
☐ 1905 League Champs	225	50
☐ 1906-1909	200	50
☐ 1910,1911 Champs	175	50
☐ 1912	150	50
☐ 1913 Champs	175	50
☐ 1914 League Champs	175	50

	Nr-Mt	Ex
☐ 1915-1920	125	35
☐ 1921-1925	100	35
☐ 1926-1929	75	25
☐ 1930-31 Champs	75	20
☐ 1932-40	35	10
☐ 1941-50	20	10
☐ 1951-54	15	10
☐ 1955	25	5
☐ 1956-1960	20	4
☐ 1961-1967	15	3
☐ 1968 (Oakland A's)	20	4
☐ 1969-1972	10	2
☐ 1973-1980	5	1
☐ 1981-1997	3	1

SCHEDULES	Nr-Mt	Ex
☐ 1901-1909	150	50
☐ 1910-1919	100	30
☐ 1920-1929	75	25
☐ 1930-1939	45	15
☐ 1940-1949	30	10
☐ 1950-1954	25	5
☐ 1955	40	20
☐ 1956-1959	30	15
☐ 1960-1965	20	5
☐ 1961-1967	15	3
☐ 1968 (Oakland A's)	20	4
☐ 1969-1972	10	2
☐ 1973-1980	5	1
☐ 1981-1997	2	1

YEARBOOKS	Nr-Mt	Ex
☐ 1949 Connie Mack	200	100
☐ 1950 Connie Mack	150	50
☐ 1951 ,1952	125	50
☐ 1953,1954	95	35
☐ 1955 (KC- black cover)	185	100
☐ 1955 Yellow Cover	185	100
☐ 1956 (First , 2nd edition)	150	75
☐ 1957	125	40
☐ 1958	125	40
☐ 1959	125	40
☐ 1960	125	20
☐ 1961	125	35
☐ 1962	125	15
☐ 1962 (2nd edition)	125	15
☐ 1963	25	12
☐ 1964	25	12
☐ 1965	25	12
☐ 1966	50	12
☐ 1967	35	20
☐ 1968 (Oakland First)	45	20
☐ 1969	20	15
☐ 1970 Reggie Jackson	20	15
☐ 1971	20	10
☐ 1972	20	10
☐ 1973	20	10
☐ 1974	20	10
☐ 1975	12	5
☐ 1976	12	5
☐ 1977	12	5
☐ 1979	12	5
☐ 1978,80,81,84-on		None Issued

GENERAL PUBLICATIONS	Nr-Mt	Ex
☐ Reggie Jackson (60's)	25	10
☐ Connie Mack (40's)	40	15

The A's have multiple newsletters and newspapers released. 'Along the Elephant Trail' was produced and released from 1946-1954. I am not sure if KC A's had a newsletter or the official newsletter from the Oakland A's.

BLUE JAYS (TORONTO)

The Blue Jays is a young team with a short history in sports publications. The amount of sports publications is limited mostly to Canada.

MEDIA GUIDES	Nr-Mt	Ex
☐ 1977	22	10
☐ 1978-1979	12	4
☐ 1980-1993	6	1
☐ 1994-1997	4	1

PROGRAMS & SCORECARDS	Nr-Mt	Ex
☐ 1977	20	4
☐ 1969-1972	10	2
☐ 1973-1980	5	1
☐ 1981-1997	3	1

SCHEDULES	Nr-Mt	Ex
☐ 1977	20	5
☐ 1979-1980	7	3
☐ 1981-1997	2	1

YEARBOOKS	Nr-Mt	Ex
☐ 1977	35	10
☐ 1978 None Issued		
☐ 1979-1986	12	05
☐ 1987-1993	08	02

BRAVES (ATLANTA, MILWAUKEE, BOSTON)

The Braves moved from Milwaukee to Atlanta in 1966. The Milwaukee Brave era (1953-1965) is the most collected Brave era. The Boston Braves (1876-1952) is the least collected. Unusual Milwaukee Braves material is heavily collected, especially in high grade. Atlanta Brave publication collectors focus on Dale Murphy and Greg Maddux..

MEDIA GUIDES	Nr-Mt	Ex
☐ Roster Sheet 1927	150	85
☐ Roster Sheets 28-35	120	65
☐ Roster Sheet 36-49	75	50
☐ Roster Sheets 50-52	50	35
☐ 1953 (First Milwaukee)	65	40
☐ 1954 - 1958	50	35
☐ 1959 - 1965	40	25
☐ 1966 (First Atlanta)	30	10
☐ 1967 - 1969	20	8
☐ 1970 - 1972	15	8
☐ 1973 - 1980	12	8
☐ 1981 - 1997	6	3

PROGRAMS	Nr-Mt	Ex
☐ 1876 Programs	700+	500+
☐ 1877-1880	600+	400+
☐ 1881-1890	500+	300+
☐ 1891-1900	400+	200+
☐ 1901-1904	400+	200+
☐ 1905-1910	200+	100+
☐ 1911-1920	150	75+
☐ 1914 World Champs	200	100
☐ 1921-1930	100	50
☐ 1931-1940	60	30
☐ 1941-1949	40	20
☐ 1941 Boston Bees only	60	30
☐ 1950-1952	30	15
☐ 1953 (First Program)	250	100
☐ 1953	80	50
☐ 1954-1959	25	10
☐ 1960-1965	16	8
☐ First Game 1966	65	35
☐ 1966 Program	20	10
☐ 1967-1970	15	7
☐ 1971-1973	12	5
☐ 1974-1980	10	4
☐ 1981-1997	6	3
☐ Dale Murphy Cover	20	10
☐ Greg Maddux Cover	12	5

YEARBOOKS	Nr-Mt	Ex
☐ 1874 Record Book of the Boston Club (George Wright)	10,000+	7,000
☐ 1936 Who's Who in Boston Major League Baseball	300	150
☐ 1946 First Braves YB	350	200
☐ 1947	200	100
☐ 1950-52	150	70
☐ 1953 (First M. Braves)	150	50
☐ 1954	100	35
☐ 1955	60	20
☐ 1956	125	25
☐ 1957	125	25
☐ 1958	60	20
☐ 1959	60	20
☐ 1960	60	20
☐ 1961	45	15
☐ 1961 (2nd ed)	60	20
☐ 1962	60	20
☐ 1963	40	12
☐ 1964	45	12
☐ 1965	40	12
☐ 1966 First Atlanta	35	15
☐ 1967	15	5
☐ 1968	8	2
☐ 1969	15	5
☐ 1970	20	5
☐ 1971-1972	10	2
☐ 1973-1976	15	3
☐ 1977-1978	10	2
☐ 1979-1982	15	3
☐ 1983-1985	8	2
☐ 1986-1987	12	2
☐ 1988-1989	8	2
☐ 1990-1993	12	2

SCHEDULES	Nr-Mt	Ex
☐ 1900-1909	100	60
☐ 1910-1920	70	35
☐ 1921-1930	60	25
☐ 1931-1940	40	20
☐ 1941-1952	30	15
☐ 1953-1957	40	20
☐ 1958-1960	30	15
☐ 1961-1965	20	10
☐ 1966	12	6
☐ 1967-1971	8	4
☐ 1972-1979	4	2
☐ 1980-1989	2	1
☐ 1990-1997	1	.50

TICKETS	Nr-Mt	Ex
☐ 1876	400	200
☐ 1877-1880	300	150
☐ 1881-1890	200	100
☐ 1891-1899	150	75
☐ 1900-1910	100	50
☐ 1911-1920	75	40
☐ 1921-1930	50	20
☐ 1931-1940	45	15
☐ 1941-1952	30	15
☐ 1953 First Game	300	150
☐ 1953-1955	30	15
☐ 1956-1965	20	10
☐ 1966 First Game	80	40
☐ 1966 tickets	8	4
☐ 1967-1970	6	3
☐ 1971-1972	4	2
☐ 1973-1980	2	1
☐ 1981-1995	2	1

PUBLICATIONS	Nr-Mt	Ex
☐ Eddie Mathews Covers	35	15
☐ Warren Spahn Covers	35	10
☐ Hank Aaron Covers (50's)	70	35

	Nr-Mt	Ex
☐ Hank Aaron covers (60's)	35	10
☐ Braves Pow Wow 68-69	20	10
☐ Hank Aaron Covers (70's)	25	12
☐ Braves Fun Kit 70 - 90's	10	4
☐ Greg Maddux Covers NL	30	15
☐ Books	10	4
☐ Dale Murphy Pubs Covers	20	10
☐ Braves Pubs (70's-80's)	15	5
☐ Braves Pubs covers (90's)	10	3
☐ Braves Bulletin (53-67)	25+	15

BREWERS (MILWAUKEE)

The Milwaukee Brewers are a young team. In the world of sports publications the Brewers history is brief. The hottest Brewers items are those with Seattle Pilot logos (1971) and Robin Yount items.

MEDIA GUIDES

	Nr-Mt	Ex
☐ 1971	20	4
☐ 1972-1974	12	2
☐ 1975-1976	10	2
☐ 1977 Robin Yount	15	2
☐ 1978-1979	10	2
☐ 1980,1982	6	1
☐ 1981,1983 Robin Yount	8	2
☐ 1984-1992	6	1
☐ 1993-1997	4	1

PROGRAMS & SCORECARDS

	Nr-Mt	Ex
☐ 1971	20	4
☐ 1972-1975	10	2
☐ 1976-1980	5	1
☐ 1981-1997	3	1

SCHEDULES

	Nr-Mt	Ex
☐ 1971	35	15
☐ 1972-1975	20	5
☐ 1976-1978	15	5
☐ 1979-1980	7	3
☐ 1981-1997	2	1

YEARBOOKS

	Nr-Mt	Ex
☐ 1970	60	15
☐ 1971-1978 None Issued		
☐ 1979-1980	10	2
☐ 1981 Robin Yount	12	2
☐ 1982	12	3
☐ 1983 Robin Yount	12	2
☐ 1984-1987	10	2
☐ 1988 Paul Molitor	10	2
☐ 1989 Hank Aaron	12	3
☐ 1990	12	3
☐ 1991 Robin Yount	12	3
☐ 1992 Molitor/Yount	12	3
☐ 1993 None Issued	None Issued	

GENERAL PUBLICATIONS

	Nr-Mt	Ex
☐ Hank Aaron (70's)	30	15
☐ Robin Yount (70's)	20	10
☐ Paul Molitor (80's)	15	10
☐ Newsletters	10	3

CARDINALS (ST. LOUIS)

The St. Louis Cardinals are the best in the Midwest. The St. Louis fans are very devoted to their team. There are a lot of sports publications featuring the Cardinals. However the most collected Cardinal player is Stan Musial. He appeared on publications throughout the late 40's through the early 60's. In fact the only players to exceed his popularity from during this time period are Joe Dimaggio, Ted Williams and Mickey Mantle. The great Roger Hornsby and the Dean brothers are collected by pre-war Cardinal fans.

The Cardinals generated a few more world champion teams lead by Bob Gibson and Lou Brock. Then a few decades later they produced more World Champions led by Ozzie Smith.

MEDIA GUIDES

	Nr-Mt	Ex
☐ 1926 Word Champs	200	100
☐ 1927-1929	135	50
☐ 1930-1935 Roster Sheet	115	35
☐ 1936-1940 Roster Sheet	75	25
☐ 1941-1949 Roster Sheet	60	15
☐ 1950-1955	50	10
☐ 1956-1958	40	8
☐ 1959 Stan Musial	50	10
☐ 1960 , 1961	40	8
☐ 1962 Stan Musial	45	10
☐ 1963-1964	40	8
☐ 1965-1968	25	4
☐ 1969-1975	15	2
☐ 1976-1979	10	1
☐ 1980-1990	8	1
☐ 1991-1997	4	1

PROGRAMS & SCORECARDS

	Nr-Mt	Ex
☐ 1900	500	200
☐ 1901	400	200
☐ 1902	400	100
☐ 1903-1904	300	100
☐ 1905-1909	200	50
☐ 1910-1914	175	50
☐ 1915-1920	125	35
☐ 1921-1925	75	35
☐ 1926-1930	50	25
☐ 1931-1940	35	10
☐ 1941-1950	25	10
☐ 1951-1955	20	10
☐ 1956-1960	20	4
☐ 1961-1969	15	3
☐ 1970-1980	10	1
☐ 1981-1997	5	1

SCHEDULES

	Nr-Mt	Ex
☐ 1901-1909	150	50
☐ 1910-1919	100	30
☐ 1920-1929	75	25
☐ 1930-1939	45	15
☐ 1940-1949	30	10
☐ 1950-1959	25	5
☐ 1960-1969	20	5
☐ 1970-1979	9	1
☐ 1980-1997	4	1

YEARBOOKS

	Nr-Mt	Ex
☐ 1951	250	50
☐ 1952	150	50
☐ 1953 Stan Musial	125	35
☐ 1954 Red Schoendienst	100	25
☐ 1955 -1956	75	20
☐ 1957-1958	50	20
☐ 1959 Stan Musial	55	20
☐ 1960 -1961	40	15
☐ 1962	40	15
☐ 1963 Stan Musial	40	15
☐ 1964	35	12
☐ 1965 Bob Gibson	35	10
☐ 1966	65	10
☐ 1967 World Champions	75	20
☐ 1968	35	7
☐ 1969 Gibson/Brock	30	10
☐ 1970 - 1971	15	5
☐ 1972-1973	20	5
☐ 1976-77	15	2
☐ 1978-1979	15	2
☐ 1978,1981-1987 None Issued		
☐ 1988-1993	10	2

GENERAL PUBLICATIONS

	Nr-Mt	Ex
☐ Stan Musial (50's)	50	25
☐ Red Schoendienst (50's)	35	15
☐ Ozzie Smith (70's)	20	10
☐ Bob Gibson (60's)	20	10

The St Louis Cardinals produce a newsletter called 'Cardinal Newsletter' from 1954-to date.

CUBS (CHICAGO)

The Chicago Cubs have some of the most devoted sports fans in the world. Which also means there has been a lot of sports publications made over their 97 year history. The Cubs have had three great dynasties that generate many unique sports publications. The earliest is 1905-1910 which generated the best Cubs teams ever. The special publication devoted to this era is 'Sketch Book & Complete Record of Our Sox and Cubs' (1919) (Estimate 1,000). The second great era is the 1930's. This era generated a few key publications 'The Cubs of 1934' by Murray Book (est. 500), 'The Cubs of 1935' by Harold Speed Johnson (500), 'Who's Who in Chicago Major League Baseball', 1936, 1937,1938 (500 each) and 'Chicago Cubs Autograph Book Chicago National League Ball Club' 1937 (est. 500). The last great era is the 1969 Cubs which never won a championship but has the greatest following. The 1969 Chicago Cubs had the greatest Cub player - Ernie Banks. He has a strong following. To a smaller degree Ryne Sandberg, Ron Santo, and Billy Williams are collected.

MEDIA GUIDES

	Nr-Mt	Ex
☐ 1926 -1927 Roster Bk	175	25
☐ 1928 -1929 Roster Bk	150	35
☐ 1930 Roster Bk	100	25
☐ 1931 Roger Hornsby	125	35
☐ 1932 Roger Hornsby	125	35
☐ 1933-1935 Roster Bk.	100	25
☐ 1936-1938 Roster bk	75	25
☐ 1939-1948 Roster Bk	65	20
☐ 1949-1951 Roster Bk	50	15
☐ 1952-1955	50	10
☐ 1956-1964	30	10
☐ 1965-1968	20	5
☐ 1969-1971	15	3
☐ 1972-1979	10	2
☐ 1980-1989	6	1
☐ 1990-1997	4	1

PROGRAMS & SCORECARDS

	Nr-Mt	Ex
☐ 1900	500	200
☐ 1901	400	200
☐ 1902	400	100
☐ 1903-1904	300	100
☐ 1905-1909	200	50
☐ 1910-1914	175	50
☐ 1915-1920	125	35
☐ 1921-1925	75	35
☐ 1926-1930	50	25
☐ 1931-1940	35	10
☐ 1941-1950	25	10
☐ 1951-1955	20	10
☐ 1956-1960	20	4
☐ 1961-1969	15	3
☐ 1970-1980	10	1
☐ 1981-1997	5	1

SCHEDULES

	Nr-Mt	Ex
☐ 1900-1909	150	50
☐ 1910-1919	100	30
☐ 1920-1929	75	25
☐ 1930-1939	45	15
☐ 1940-1949	30	10
☐ 1950-1959	25	5
☐ 1960-1969	20	5
☐ 1970-1979	9	1
☐ 1980-1997	4	1

YEARBOOKS

	Nr-Mt	Ex
☐ 1934	250	100
☐ 1939	200	100
☐ 1941	225	100
☐ 1942	200	75
☐ 1948	100	50
☐ 1949	35	15
☐ 1950	35	15
☐ 1951	60	20
☐ 1952,1953,1954,1955	50	15
☐ 1956	75	20
☐ 1957	125	25

	Nr-Mt	Ex
☐ 1958-1984	None Issued	
☐ 1985	8	2
☐ 1986 Ryne Sandberg	8	2
☐ 1987 Ryne Sandberg	8	2
☐ 1988 Andre Dawson	8	2
☐ 1989	10	2
☐ 1990	10	2
☐ 1991 Ryne Sandberg	8	1
☐ 1992-1997	10	1

GENERAL PUBLICATIONS

	Nr-Mt	Ex
☐ Ernie Banks (50's)	50	20
☐ Billy Williams (60's)	30	15
☐ Ryne Sandberg (80's)	15	10
☐ Ron Santo (60's)	30	15

Cubs newsletter is called 'Cubs News' from 1936 to present. These newsletters range in value from $20-$40 each during the 30's, $15-$30 during the 40's -50's and $10-$20 in the 60's-70's. Value increases when it features Ernie Banks.

COLORADO ROCKIES

This team is so new that it only has a few years of sports publications history. However this team has taken the National League West by storm by becoming a hitters paradise.

MEDIA GUIDES

	Nr-Mt	Ex
☐ 1993	5	1
☐ 1994-1997	4	1

PROGRAMS & SCORECARDS

	Nr-Mt	Ex
☐ 1993 First Game Program	30	5
☐ 1993-1997	3	1

SCHEDULES

	Nr-Mt	Ex
☐ 1993-1997	2	1

YEARBOOKS

	Nr-Mt	Ex
☐ 1993-1997	4	1

DODGERS (BROOKLYN, LOS ANGELES)

Next to the New York Yankees the Dodgers is the team publications collectors love. The Dodgers have two great eras of collecting. The first era was 1946-1957. This is the era of the 'Bums' that is so loved.

The second era is the LA Dodgers 1958-present.

Most collectors love the Brooklyn Dodgers. They only had one championship (1955) but they captured the hearts of a city. The most popular (collected) player is Duke Snider. He was the home run champion of the 1950's. He had only a handful of publications. This is because he was overshadowed by the great Mickey Mantle. There are many other key Dodger players that are collected (Sandy Koufax, Jackie Robinson, Roy Campanella, Johnny Podres). In fact, Brooklyn Dodger fans collect them all. Sports publications were not generous toward the Brooklyn Dodgers but very generous toward the LA Dodgers.

When the Dodgers moved to LA the number of covers increased 10 fold. Most of the magazines feature the great Sandy Koufax. However, covers of Maury Wills, Don Drysdale had a good representation. When the 60's era ended the cover subject shifted to Steve Garvey. He was (and is) still one of the most popular Dodgers. The 1990's Dodger fans focus their attention on Mike Piazza.

MEDIA GUIDES

	Nr-Mt	Ex
☐ 1927 Roster sheet	195	100
☐ 1928 - 1935 Roster sheet	150	75
☐ 1936 - 1946 Roster sheet	75	45
☐ 1947 - 1949 Roster sheet	50	25
☐ 1950 First media guide	75	35
☐ 1951 - 1954	65	30
☐ 1955 Champions	100	40
☐ 1956 - 1957	55	35
☐ 1958 First LA MG	75	40
☐ 1959 - 1962	45	20
☐ 1963 Champions	55	25
☐ 1964 - 1970	30	15

	Nr-Mt	Ex
☐ 1971 - 1975	20	10
☐ 1976 - 1980	15	8
☐ 1981 - 1990	10	5
☐ 1991 - 1997	5	3

PROGRAMS

	Nr-Mt	Ex
☐ 1889-1890	1000	500
☐ 1890-1900	400	200
☐ 1901-1904	400+	200+
☐ 1905-1913	250	100
☐ 1914-1920	100	50
☐ 1921-1925	65	45
☐ 1926-1930	50	25
☐ 1931-1940	40	20
☐ 1941-1957	40	20
☐ 1955 Champions	60	30
☐ 1958 LA Dodger First Yr	60	30
☐ 1959-1960	25	10
☐ 1961-1966	15	7
☐ 1967-1971	12	5
☐ 1972-1983	6	2
☐ 1984-1997	5	1
☐ Duke Snider cover	25	10
☐ Jackie Robinson cover	30	10
☐ Sandy Koufax cover	25	10
☐ Don Drysdale cover	15	5
☐ Steve Garvey cover	10	5
☐ Roy Campanella cover	40	15

YEARBOOKS

	Nr-Mt	Ex
☐ 1947 First Yearbook	150	75
☐ 1948 No Yearbook		
☐ 1949 (Jackie Robinson)	325	150
☐ 1949 without Jackie	300	150
☐ 1950	175	100
☐ 1951	125	50
☐ 1952	125	50
☐ 1953	125	50
☐ 1954	125	50
☐ 1955 Champions	300	150
☐ 1956	125	50
☐ 1957	125	50
☐ 1958 First LA Dodger	175	60
☐ 1959	100	35
☐ 1960	55	35
☐ 1961	50	20
☐ 1962	35	15
☐ 1963	45	15
☐ 1964-1967	35	15
☐ 1968-1971	15	5
☐ 1972-1975	12	4
☐ 1976-1981	12	5
☐ 1982-1989	10	2
☐ 1990-1997	10	2

SCHEDULES

	Nr-Mt	Ex
☐ 1901	200	100
☐ 1902-1909	120	60
☐ 1910-1920	100	50
☐ 1921-1930	60	30
☐ 1931-1940	50	25
☐ 1941-1950	30	15
☐ 1951-1960	20	10
☐ 1961-1970	15	8
☐ 1971-1979	8	5
☐ 1980-1989	3	1
☐ 1990-1997	1	.50

TICKETS

	Nr-Mt	Ex
☐ 1901 First game	400	200
☐ 1901	200	100
☐ 1902-1909	100	50
☐ 1910-1919	80	40
☐ 1920-1929	50	35
☐ 1930-1939	40	25

	Nr-Mt	Ex
☐ 1940-1949	30	15
☐ 1950-1959	21	7
☐ 1960-1970	10	4
☐ 1971-1980	4	2
☐ 1981-1990	3	1
☐ 1991-1997	2	1
☐ 1958 First Game	200	50
☐ Sandy Koufax Shut out	100	50
☐ Jackie Robinson First game	300	100
☐ Don Drysdale record	200	100

GENERAL PUBLICATIONS

	Nr-Mt	Ex
☐ Duke Snider (50's)	100	25
☐ Duke Snider (60's)	40	15
☐ Roy Campanella (50's)	70	20
☐ Jackie Robinson (50's)	100	35
☐ Sandy Koufax (50's)	70	20
☐ Sandy Koufax (60's)	35	15
☐ Brooklyn Covers	50	15
☐ LA Covers (60's)	30	10
☐ Dodger Doings (38-42)	30	15
☐ Line Drives NL (47-57)	30	15
☐ Line Drive NL (58)	30	15
☐ Line Drive NL (59-65)	25	10
☐ Line Drive (66-79)	12	5
☐ Line Drive (80-on	7	3

EXPOS (MONTREAL)

The Montreal Expos are a young team with a short history in sports publications. Since they never won a World Series and they are located in Canada, the Expos have limited exposure in national sports publications.

MEDIA GUIDES

	Nr-Mt	Ex
☐ 1969	50	10
☐ 1970 -1973	20	8
☐ 1974-1979	12	2
☐ 1980-1987	7	1
☐ 1988-1993	5	1
☐ 1994-1997	4	1

PROGRAMS & SCORECARDS

	Nr-Mt	Ex
☐ 1969 (First Program)	25	4
☐ 1970-1975	15	2
☐ 1976-1980	5	1
☐ 1981-1997	3	1

SCHEDULES

	Nr-Mt	Ex
☐ 1969	35	15
☐ 1970-1972	25	10
☐ 1973-1975	20	5
☐ 1976-1978	15	5
☐ 1979-1980	7	3
☐ 1981-1997	2	1

YEARBOOKS

	Nr-Mt	Ex
☐ 1969 (vol #1)	35	20
☐ 1969 (vol #2,#3,#4)	50	20
☐ 1970 (vol #1,#2,#3)	35	15
☐ 1971 (#1,#2,#3)	25	10
☐ 1972 (vol #1,#2,#3)	25	10
☐ 1973-1981	None Issued	
☐ 1982-1986	10	2
☐ 1987-1991	None Issued	
☐ 1992 Gary Carter	7	1
☐ 1993	None Issued	

GIANTS (NEW YORK, SAN FRANCISCO)

The New York Giants have produced more Hall of Famers than any other baseball team. They are also one of the oldest teams with a heritage in sports publications. The great NY Giants teams were the 1911-1924, 1933-1937, and 1951-1954 teams. One of the most collected players from the early Giants period is Christy Mathewson. He has only a few publications (Baseball Magazine/Sporting News). The most popular Giant player is Willie Mays (1951-1972). He has a strong following among publication collectors. The NY Giants are not heavily collected but the SF Giants have a strong following in the bay area. The key publications for the SF Giants is from 58-60.

Some of the early key Giant publications is 'Sketches of the New York Baseball Club' by June Rankin 1887 (est. 2,500 range), 'Sketches of the New York & Brooklyn Baseball Clubs' by June Rankin 1888 (est. 2,500) and 'Complimentary Testimonial to the Champions' by Digby Bell, DeWitt 1889 (est. 2,500). Also a tough modern era book is 'The Giants of New York' by Gary Schumacher, 1947 (est. 200).

MEDIA GUIDES

	Nr-Mt	Ex
☐ 1927 Roster	150	50
☐ 1928-1935 roster	100	25
☐ 1936-1940 roster	75	20
☐ 1941-1949	60	15
☐ 1950-1955	50	10
☐ 1956-1957	40	10
☐ 1958 (First SF Giants)	50	10
☐ 1959-1961	40	10
☐ 1962-1964	30	8
☐ 1965-1967	20	4
☐ 1968-1969	15	3
☐ 1970 McCovey/Mays	20	5
☐ 1971-1974	15	3
☐ 1975-1979	10	2
☐ 1980-1989	6	1
☐ 1990-1997	4	1

PROGRAMS & SCORECARDS

	Nr-Mt	Ex
☐ 1883-1889	1000	500
☐ 1890-1900	500	200
☐ 1901-1902	400	200
☐ 1903-1904	300	100
☐ 1905-1909	200	50
☐ 1910-1914	175	50
☐ 1915-1920	125	35
☐ 1921-1925	75	35
☐ 1926-1930	50	25
☐ 1931-1940	35	10
☐ 1941-1950	25	10
☐ 1951-1955	20	10
☐ 1956-1960	20	4
☐ 1961-1969	15	3
☐ 1970-1980	10	1
☐ 1981-1997	5	1

SCHEDULES

	Nr-Mt	Ex
☐ 1900-1909	150	50
☐ 1910-1919	100	30
☐ 1920-1929	75	25
☐ 1930-1939	45	15
☐ 1940-1949	30	10
☐ 1950-1959	25	5
☐ 1960-1969	20	5
☐ 1970-1979	9	1
☐ 1980-1997	4	1

YEARBOOKS

	Nr-Mt	Ex
☐ 1947	150	75
☐ 1948-1950	None Issued	
☐ 1951	125	35
☐ 1952	85	25
☐ 1953	85	25
☐ 1954	75	20
☐ 1955	125	25
☐ 1956	85	35
☐ 1957	100	25
☐ 1958 (First SF Cover)	200	50
☐ 1959	85	20
☐ 1959 (2nd Edition)	100	25
☐ 1960	50	15
☐ 1961	50	15
☐ 1962	50	15
☐ 1963	40	15
☐ 1964-1966	30	10
☐ 1967,68 Willie Mays	40	10
☐ 1969,70,71 McCovey	25	10
☐ 1972 Willie Mays	25	5

☐ 1973 Marichal	10	2
☐ 1974	10	2
☐ 1975	12	2
☐ 1976	12	2
☐ 1979 Photo Album	20	5
☐ 1977-1979 None Issued		
☐ 1980-1985	10	2
☐ 1981 Photo Album	20	5
☐ 1986-1991 None Issued		
☐ 1992 Will Clark	10	2
☐ 1993	None Issued	

GENERAL PUBLICATIONS

	Nr-Mt	Ex
☐ Willie Mays (50's)	50	20
☐ Willie Mays (60's)	40	15
☐ Willie McCovey (60's)	35	10
☐ Juan Marichal (60's)	25	10
☐ Barry Bonds (90's)	10	3
☐ Bobby Bonds (70's)	15	5
☐ Christy Mathewson	200	100
☐ Mel Ott (30's)	75	35

One of the modern era Giant newsletters is called 'Giant Jottings'. They started in 1936 and run into the 1970's. The value range based on era and player.

INDIANS (CLEVELAND)

The Cleveland Indians started in 1901 and have been in Cleveland ever since. They were called the 'Blues' in 1901. They were also called the 'Naps' after Napoleon Lajoie until 1915. They were then named the 'Indians'. The team won the championship in 1920, 1948 and 1954. Most collectors focus on the 1948 and 1954 era of Bob Feller, Satchel Paige and Earl Wynn. Since the Indians have been in the World Series in 1995 and 1997 many new Indian publication collectors have appeared.

MEDIA GUIDES

	Nr-Mt	Ex
☐ 1936 Roster	75	15
☐ 1937 - 1940 Rosters	75	10
☐ 1941 - 1947 Rosters	60	10
☐ 1948 World Series	150	50
☐ 1949 - 1953	60	10
☐ 1954 Al Rosen	60	10
☐ 1955-1958	40	10
☐ 1959 Rocky Colovito	60	10
☐ 1960 - 1961	40	10
☐ 1962 - 1964	30	10
☐ 1965 - 1968	20	5
☐ 1969 - 1973	15	3
☐ 1974 - 1979	12	2
☐ 1980 - 1987	7	1
☐ 1988 - 1997	5	1

PROGRAMS & SCORECARDS

	Nr-Mt	Ex
☐ 1901	600	300
☐ 1902	400	200
☐ 1903-1904	300	100
☐ 1905-1909	200	50
☐ 1910-1914	175	50
☐ 1915-1920	125	35
☐ 1921-1925	75	35
☐ 1926-1930	50	25
☐ 1931-1940	35	10
☐ 1941-1950	25	10
☐ 1951-1955	20	10
☐ 1956-1960	20	4
☐ 1961-1969	15	3
☐ 1970-1980	10	1
☐ 1981-1997	5	1

SCHEDULES

	Nr-Mt	Ex
☐ 1901-1909	150	50
☐ 1910-1919	100	30
☐ 1920-1929	75	25
☐ 1930-1939	45	15
☐ 1940-1949	30	10

☐ 1950-1959	25	5
☐ 1960-1969	20	5
☐ 1970-1979	9	1
☐ 1980-1997	4	1

YEARBOOKS	Nr-Mt	Ex
☐ 1948 (First Issue)	125	50
☐ 1949	60	20
☐ 1950	60	20
☐ 1951	55	20
☐ 1952	55	20
☐ 1953	95	30
☐ 1954 Bob Lemon	95	30
☐ 1955	75	20
☐ 1956	75	20
☐ 1957	125	35
☐ 1958 Herb Score	225	75
☐ 1959	50	20
☐ 1960	90	30
☐ 1961	75	20
☐ 1962	75	20
☐ 1963	75	20
☐ 1964	70	20
☐ 1965	65	15
☐ 1966	65	20
☐ 1967	65	20
☐ 1968	30	10
☐ 1969	20	10
☐ 1970	25	10
☐ 1971	15	5
☐ 1972	10	1
☐ 1973	20	5
☐ 1974-1983	None Issued	
☐ 1984	8	2
☐ 1985-1988	None Issued	
☐ 1989-1992	6	1
☐ 1993	None Issued	

GENERAL PUBLICATIONS	Nr-Mt	Ex
☐ Bob Feller (40's-50's)	40	15
☐ Bob Lemon (50's)	35	15
☐ Herb Score (50's)	20	10
☐ Kenny Lofton (90's)	10	5
☐ Satchel Paige (50's)	50	25

The Cleveland Indians Newsletter/Magazine 'Indian News' started in 1947.

MARINERS (SEATTLE)

The Seattle Mariners are such a young team that there are only a handful of publications that are on the subject. Ken Griffey Jr. is the best Mariner player and his face has graced many national magazines.

MEDIA GUIDES	Nr-Mt	Ex
☐ 1977	20	4
☐ 1978-1979	10	2
☐ 1980-1987	7	1
☐ 1988-1997	5	1

PROGRAMS & SCORECARDS	Nr-Mt	Ex
☐ 1977 (First Program)	15	4
☐ 1978-1980	5	1
☐ 1981-1997	3	1

SCHEDULES	Nr-Mt	Ex
☐ 1977-1978	15	5
☐ 1979-1980	7	3
☐ 1981-1997	2	1

YEARBOOK	Nr-Mt	Ex
☐ 1977-1984	None Issued	
☐ 1985	12	2
☐ 1986-1993	None Issued	

MARLINS (FLORIDA)

This team is so new that it only has a few years of sports publications history. However this team has taken baseball by storm by winning the 1997 World Series.

MEDIA GUIDES	Nr-Mt	Ex
☐ 1993 First mg	5	1
☐ 1994-1997	4	1

PROGRAMS & SCORECARDS	Nr-Mt	Ex
☐ 1993 First Game Program	30	5
☐ 1993-1997	3	1

SCHEDULES	Nr-Mt	Ex
☐ 1993-1997	2	1

YEARBOOKS	Nr-Mt	Ex
☐ 1993-1997	4	1

METS (NEW YORK)

The New York Mets are best remembered for the 1969 Miracle Mets. New York fans fell in love with this team and with their leader, Tom Seaver. Tom Seaver is the one of the most collected hall of fame pitchers in the United States. However, the most collected baseball pitcher, Nolan Ryan, began his career with the NY Mets and he is the most collected Met player.

MEDIA GUIDES	Nr-Mt	Ex
☐ 1962 (First MG) (8 pgs)	750	350
☐ 1963 - 1964	175	50
☐ 1965 - 1968	65	25
☐ 1969	125	50
☐ 1970 - 1971	25	10
☐ 1972 Tom Seaver	30	10
☐ 1973 Yogi Berra	25	10
☐ 1974 - 1978	20	10
☐ 1979 Willie Mays	20	5
☐ 1980 - 1982	10	3
☐ 1983,1985 Tom Seaver	10	1
☐ 1986 Champions	12	3
☐ 1984,1987-1997	5	1

PROGRAMS & SCORECARDS	Nr-Mt	Ex
☐ 1962	50	15
☐ 1963-1965	25	5
☐ 1966-1969	15	3
☐ 1970-1980	10	1
☐ 1981-1997	5	1
☐ 1962 first game		100

Unscored are the nr-mt price. Scored programs are half the nr-mt price. Early 90's have 9 different covers a year, 80's have 2 different program covers.

SCHEDULES	Nr-Mt	Ex
☐ 1962	100	30
☐ 1963-1965	50	15
☐ 1966-1968	30	15
☐ 1969	50	25
☐ 1970-1979	12	3
☐ 1980-1997	3	1

YEARBOOK (INCLUDES VARIATIONS)	Nr-Mt	Ex
☐ 1962	300	100
☐ 1963 (1st, 2nd, 3rd Rev)	125	65
☐ 1964 (1st, 2nd, final)	65	25
☐ 1964 dedication	75	25
☐ 1965 (1st, 2nd, 3rd)	65	25
☐ 1966 (1st, 2nd , 3rd)	60	20
☐ 1967 (1st, 2ne, 3rd)	45	15
☐ 1968 (1st, 2nd)	45	15
☐ 1969 (Champs)	125	30
☐ 1970,1971	35	10
☐ 1972	15	5
☐ 1973 Mays, Seaver	15	5
☐ 1974	15	5
☐ 1975 Tom Seaver	15	5
☐ 1976	15	5

☐ 1977-1979	15	3
☐ 1980	30	10
☐ 1981-1987	12	2
☐ 1988-1993	10	2
☐ 1994-1997	10	2

Mets Yearbooks have multiple variations during the 60's and 70's. No price difference on variations. "Mets Fan Fare" is the newsletter that the team started issuing in 1966. The most valuable ones are those that feature Nolan Ryan and Tom Seaver.

GENERAL PUBLICATIONS	Nr-Mt	Ex
☐ Yogi Berra (60's)	35	15
☐ Tom Seaver (60's)	40	15
☐ Nolan Ryan (60's)	40	20
☐ Willie Mays (70's)	35	15

For further information on hundreds of Mets publications you can obtain the 'NY Mets Checklist' (249 pages) for 35 from Dave Berman, 377 Golf Dr., Oceanside, NY 11572. If you collect Nolan Ryan you can check out the 'Nolan Ryan Newsletter'.

ORIOLES (BALTIMORE) / ST LOUIS BROWNS

The Baltimore Orioles roots go back to the early American Association days in the 1880's. The team reappeared for a few years (1892-1900) in the National League and then reappeared for a brief period (1901-2) in the American League. Most Baltimore Oriole collectors do not collect the rare and vintage material. However, the most expensive publications are the Pre 1902 Baltimore Oriole programs.

The modern era Orioles start in 1954 and have a solid following throughout the United States. The early 54-60 Oriole material is rather scarce and popular. The prices for their yearbooks, programs and tickets are higher than similar teams of the era. The biggest names that are collected is Brooks Robinson and Cal Ripken Jr. However, Frank Robinson, Boog Powell, and Jim Palmer have solid followings.

The modern era Orioles team was moved from St Louis (Browns). The Browns have a small hard core following who focus around the history of the team. The Browns went to one World Series (1944) and produced two yearbooks (1944 & 1951).

MEDIA GUIDES	Nr-Mt	Ex
☐ 1930-1939 Browns	65	30
☐ 1940-1953 Browns	45	25
☐ 1954 First Oriole MG	75	35
☐ 1955 - 1957	45	25
☐ 1958 - 1965	30	15
☐ 1966 - 1971	20	10
☐ 1972 - 1979	12	5
☐ 1980 - 1997	5	1

PROGRAMS	Nr-Mt	Ex
☐ 1880's	700+	500+
☐ 1890's	600+	400+
☐ 1900-1902	400+	200+
☐ 1940's Browns	40	20
☐ 1950's Browns	35	15
☐ 1954 First Oriole Game	400	200
☐ 1954	75	30
☐ 1955-1956	40	15
☐ 1957-1960	20	10
☐ 1961-1966	15	7
☐ 1967-1971	12	5
☐ 1972-1983	6	2
☐ 1984-1997	5	1
☐ Brooks Robinson Covers	40	15
☐ Frank Robinson Covers	20	10
☐ Cal Ripken Jr	12	5
☐ Jim Palmer	20	10
☐ Cal Ripken Jr Record	30	15
☐ Cal Ripken Jr First Game	100	50
☐ Brooks Robinson First Game	100	50

YEARBOOKS	Nr-Mt	Ex
☐ 1944 St Louis Browns	225	150
☐ 1951 Browns	200	75

☐ 1954	200	75
☐ 1955-1956	120	65
☐ 1957-1959	100	50
☐ 1960-1962	75	35
☐ 1963-1966	50	25
☐ 1967-1970	35	12
☐ 1971-1974	15	5
☐ 1975	15	5
☐ 1976-1979 None Issued		
☐ Photo Album 77,78,79	15	5
☐ 1980-1982	12	4
☐ 1983 Champions	10	5
☐ 1984-1997	9	2

SCHEDULES	Nr-Mt	Ex
☐ 1940-1950	40	15
☐ 1951-1953	35	20
☐ 1954	50	20
☐ 1955-1956	40	20
☐ 1957-1959	30	15
☐ 1960-1969	15	8
☐ 1970-1979	10	5
☐ 1980-1989	3	1
☐ 1990-1997	1	.50

TICKETS	Nr-Mt	Ex
☐ 1882-1890	200	100
☐ 1891-1899	150	75
☐ 1900-1902	100	50
☐ 1940-1945	20	10
☐ 1946-1953	25	15
☐ 1954 First Game	300	150
☐ 1954-1955	30	15
☐ 1956-1966	20	10
☐ 1967-1970	6	3
☐ 1971-1972	4	2
☐ 1973-1980	2	1
☐ 1981-1995	2	1
☐ Ripken Jr Record game	30	15
☐ Ripken Jr First Game	80	40

GENERAL PUBLICATIONS	Nr-Mt	Ex
☐ Jim Palmer Covers	25	10
☐ Cal Ripken Jr Covers	20	10
☐ B. Robinson Covers (50's)	70	35
☐ B. Robinson Covers (60's)	35	10
☐ 'The Oriole-Gram' 55-69	30	15
☐ B. Robinson Covers (70's)	25	10
☐ 'Bird Hits Newsletters	10	4
☐ Pubs (70's-80's)	15	5
☐ Orioles Pubs covers (90's)	10	3
☐ Browns Express NL(53)	25	15

PADRES (SAN DIEGO)

The Padres publication history started in 1969. The team has a few collectors and most of them center on Tony Gwynn.

MEDIA GUIDES	Nr-Mt	Ex
☐ 1969 (First MG)	30	10
☐ 1970 - 1973	12	2
☐ 1974 - 1979	10	2
☐ 1980 Dave Winfield	10	2
☐ 1981 - 1987	6	1
☐ 1988 Tony Gwynn	10	2
☐ 1989 - 1997	5	1

PROGRAMS & SCORECARDS	Nr-Mt	Ex
☐ 1969	35	10
☐ 1970-1980	10	1
☐ 1981-1997	5	1
☐ Tony Gwynn Covers	20	3
☐ Dave Winfield Covers	15	5

SCHEDULES	Nr-Mt	Ex
☐ 1969	22	5
☐ 1970-1979	9	1
☐ 1980-1997	4	1

YEARBOOKS	Nr-Mt	Ex
☐ 1969 (First Yearbook)	75	20
☐ 1970-1978 None Issued		
☐ 1979 Dave Winfield	6	3
☐ 1980 Dave Winfield	6	3
☐ 1981 None Issued		
☐ 1982-1986	10	1
☐ 1987-1991 None Issued		
☐ 1992-1997	6	1

GENERAL PUBLICATIONS	Nr-Mt	Ex
☐ Tony Gwynn (80's)	25	12
☐ Dave Winfield (70's)	20	10
☐ Willie McCovey (70's)	25	10
☐ Steve Garvey (80's)	15	5

PILOTS (SEATTLE)

The Seattle Pilots lasted two years. It is the most collected defunct team in baseball. The Seattle Pilot team collectors look for everything with Seattle Pilot players on them. One of the biggest areas is sports publications. All of the game programs, spring training programs and even the away programs are collected.

MEDIA GUIDES	Nr-Mt	Ex
☐ 1969	75	35
☐ 1970	45	15

PROGRAMS	Nr-Mt	Ex
☐ 1969	75	35
☐ 1969 Spring Training	150	45
☐ 1970	45	15
☐ 1970 Spring Training	150	35

SCHEDULES	Nr-Mt	Ex
☐ 1969	75	35
☐ 1970	50	25

YEARBOOKS	Nr-Mt	Ex
☐ 1969 (Only Yearbook)	200	100

GENERAL PUBLICATIONS	Nr-Mt	Ex
☐ Any Publications	40	20

The Pilot newsletter was produced in 1969 and it was called 'Seattle Pilots Log'. Early copies of the newsletters are rare.

PHILLIES (PHILADELPHIA)

☐ The Phillies is another great sports team from a very old sports town. Phillies fans are very committed to their team. The most popular Phillies team is the 'Whiz Kids' of 1950 along with the 1980 Mike Schmidt era of baseball. Phillies yearbooks seem to be slightly tougher to find than other eastern coast teams. The Phillies Whiz Kids focus around Robin Roberts and Richie Ashburn. The 1980 Champion team is Mike Schmidt, Pete Rose and Steve Carlton.

MEDIA GUIDES	Nr-Mt	Ex
☐ 1930 - 1935 Roster	100	20
☐ 1936 - 1940 Roster	75	15
☐ 1941 - 1948	60	15
☐ 1949 Whiz Kids	75	15
☐ 1950 Whiz Kids	75	15
☐ 1951 - 1953	50	10
☐ 1954 Robin Roberts	50	10
☐ 1955 - 1961	40	7
☐ 1962 - 1970	20	5
☐ 1971 - 1979	10	3
☐ 1980 - 1990	7	1
☐ 1991 - 1997	5	1

PROGRAMS & SCORECARDS	Nr-Mt	Ex

☐ 1901	600	300
☐ 1902	400	200
☐ 1903-1904	300	100
☐ 1905-1909	200	50
☐ 1910-1914	175	50
☐ 1915-1920	125	35
☐ 1921-1925	75	35
☐ 1926-1930	50	25
☐ 1931-1940	35	10
☐ 1941-1950	25	10
☐ 1951-1955	20	10
☐ 1956-1960	20	4
☐ 1961-1969	15	3
☐ 1970-1980	10	1
☐ 1981-1997	5	1

SCHEDULES	Nr-Mt	Ex
☐ 1901-1909	150	50
☐ 1910-1919	100	30
☐ 1920-1929	75	25
☐ 1930-1939	45	15
☐ 1940-1949	30	10
☐ 1950-1959	25	5
☐ 1960-1969	20	5
☐ 1970-1979	9	1
☐ 1980-1997	4	1

YEARBOOKS	Nr-Mt	Ex
☐ 1949	250	100
☐ 1950	150	50
☐ 1951 Six Players (rare)	400	200
☐ 1952	100	35
☐ 1953	35	20
☐ 1954	100	35
☐ 1955	100	50
☐ 1956 Roberts/Ashburn	150	50
☐ 1957	100	35
☐ 1958	80	35
☐ 1959	75	35
☐ 1960	90	30
☐ 1961 First edition	150	75
☐ 1961 2nd edition	150	50
☐ 1962,1963	75	20
☐ 1964 First/2nd	50	20
☐ 1964 3rd	75	20
☐ 1965 Jim Bunning	45	20
☐ 1966	45	15
☐ 1967, 1968	45	10
☐ 1969,1970,1971	45	10
☐ 1972,1973	30	8
☐ 1974	20	4
☐ 1975 Mike Schmidt	30	10
☐ 1976 Schmidt	12	3
☐ 1977	12	3
☐ 1978 Mike Schmidt	12	3
☐ 1979 Mike Schmidt	12	3
☐ 1980 Mike Schmidt	30	5
☐ 1981	30	5
☐ 1982 Mike Schmidt	6	2
☐ 1983-1985 Mike Schmidt	9	1
☐ 1986-1987	6	2
☐ 1988-1997	10	2

GENERAL PUBLICATIONS	Nr-Mt	Ex
☐ Mike Schmidt (70's)	25	10
☐ Jim Bunning (60's)	35	15
☐ Robin Roberts (50's)	45	15
☐ Richie Ashburn (50's)	45	15

Philly had two newsletters/newspapers in its history. The first was called 'News from the Phillies' (1938-1939). The second newsletter/newspaper is called 'The Phillies Scorecard' (6/43 - present). The key values to these are based on the player on the cover and the period.

PIRATES (PITTSBURGH)

The Pirates have a great heritage and a strong following. The early period of collecting (1887-1920) revolves around Honus Wagner and the 1909 championship team. A key book of this era is "Line Drives at the Pittsburgh Pirates", Pittsburgh Press, 1910. The team was ordinary until 1925 & 1927 when they went to the World Series. Then they entered a major drought until 1960 were they beat the Yankees in the World Series. Most publication collectors pursue the greatest Pirate of them all-Roberto Clemente. He did appear on national publications and local ones.

MEDIA GUIDES	Nr-Mt	Ex
☐ 1927 Roster	185	50
☐ 1929-1935 Roster	100	25
☐ 1936-1940 Roster	75	20
☐ 1941-1949 Roster	60	15
☐ 1950-1955	50	10
☐ 1956-1961	40	10
☐ 1962-1964	30	8
☐ 1965-1968	20	5
☐ 1969-1972	15	4
☐ 1973 Roberto Clemente	25	5
☐ 1974-1980	10	3
☐ 1981-1997	6	1

PROGRAMS & SCORECARDS	Nr-Mt	Ex
☐ 1887-1889	1000	450
☐ 1890-1900	750	350
☐ 1901-1902	500	300
☐ 1903-1904	300	100
☐ 1905-1909	200	50
☐ 1910-1914	175	50
☐ 1915-1920	125	35
☐ 1921-1925	75	35
☐ 1926-1930	50	25
☐ 1931-1940	35	10
☐ 1941-1950	25	10
☐ 1951-1955	20	10
☐ 1956-1960	20	4
☐ 1961-1969	15	3
☐ 1970-1980	10	1
☐ 1981-1997	5	1

SCHEDULES	Nr-Mt	Ex
☐ 1901-1909	150	50
☐ 1910-1919	100	30
☐ 1920-1929	75	25
☐ 1930-1939	45	15
☐ 1940-1949	30	10
☐ 1950-1959	25	5
☐ 1960-1969	20	5
☐ 1970-1979	9	1
☐ 1980-1997	4	1

YEARBOOKS	Nr-Mt	Ex
☐ 1951	250	100
☐ 1952	125	75
☐ 1953-1954	100	50
☐ 1955-1957	95	35
☐ 1958	65	20
☐ 1959,1960	65	15
☐ 1961,1962 (First, rev)	60	15
☐ 1963	50	15
☐ 1964	25	10
☐ 1965,1966	30	10
☐ 1967 Bob Clemente	25	10
☐ 1968 Bob Clemente	40	10
☐ 1969	30	8
☐ 1970	70	25
☐ 1971 3 River stad.	30	8
☐ 1971	70	25
☐ 1972 Bob Clemente	15	8
☐ 1973 Bob Clemente	20	10
☐ 1974,75	20	8
☐ 1976-1980	10	2
☐ 1981-1985	6	2
☐ 1986-1997	10	2

GENERAL PUBLICATIONS	Nr-Mt	Ex
☐ Bob Clemente (50's)	100	25
☐ Bob Clemente (60's)	40	15
☐ Willie Stargell (60's)	20	10
☐ Willie Stargell (70's)	20	15

The Pirates newsletter is called 'Pirate Pickin's' which ran from 1946 to date. The most valued newsletters focus on Roberto Clemente.

RANGERS (TEXAS)

The Texas Rangers team originated from Washington and was a below average team. All of the Texas Ranger collectors focus around Nolan Ryan. Most other publications are not very valuable.

MEDIA GUIDES	Nr-Mt	Ex
☐ 1972	20	5
☐ 1973-1975	15	2
☐ 1976-1980	10	1
☐ 1981-1987	6	1
☐ 1988-1997	4	1

PROGRAMS & SCORECARDS	Nr-Mt	Ex
☐ 1972	15	3
☐ 1973-1980	10	1
☐ 1981-1997	5	1
☐ Nolan Ryan Programs	10	3
☐ Key Ryan Programs	40	10
☐ Nolan Ryan Covers	10	3

SCHEDULES	Nr-Mt	Ex
☐ 1972	20	5
☐ 1973-1979	9	1
☐ 1980-1997	4	1

YEARBOOK	Nr-Mt	Ex
☐ 1972-75	None Issued	
☐ 1976	20	4
☐ 1977-1981	12	3
☐ 1982,84,85,88,	8	2
☐ 1983,86,87,89	None Issued	
☐ 1990,91,93	10	3
☐ 1992 Nolan Ryan	8	2

REDS (CINCINNATI)

The Cincinnati Reds are the oldest team in baseball. Most of the sports publication collectors focus on the Big Red Machine Era of 1968-1977 with Pete Rose, Johnny Bench, Tony Perez, and Joe Morgan. Even though the pre-1900 era is collected, the 'Big Red Machine' of the 1970's is where publications are most collected. The Reds were the winners of the 1919 World Series which is easy to forget because the focus is on the scandal. Books were written about the winners 'Official Players Souvenir, The Reds of 1919', Cincinnati Reds (est. 2,500) and 'Souvenir Record Book, World's Championship Series, Chicago vs. Cincinnati' by A. Prusank (est. 2,500). Both of these are among the rarest books in the hobby. Later on a third yearbook was developed called 'Reds" (1930) by Cino Publishing (est. 250).

MEDIA GUIDES	Nr-Mt	Ex
☐ 1927-1929 Roster	125	35
☐ 1930-1935 Roster	100	25
☐ 1936-1940 Roster	80	20
☐ 1941-1949	60	15
☐ 1950-1955	50	10
☐ 1956-1961	40	8
☐ 1962-1964	30	6
☐ 1965-1970	20	4
☐ 1971-1974	10	2
☐ 1975 Johnny Bench	15	3
☐ 1976 Joe Morgan	14	2
☐ 1977 Johnny Bench	15	3
☐ 1978-1985	8	1
☐ 1986 Johnny Bench	8	1
☐ 1987-1997	5	1

PROGRAMS & SCORECARDS	Nr-Mt	Ex
☐ Pre 1890	1000+	450
☐ 1890-1900	750	350
☐ 1901-1902	500	300
☐ 1903-1904	300	100
☐ 1905-1909	200	50
☐ 1910-1914	175	50
☐ 1915-1920	125	35
☐ 1921-1925	75	35
☐ 1926-1930	50	25
☐ 1931-1940	35	10
☐ 1941-1950	25	10
☐ 1951-1955	20	10
☐ 1956-1960	20	4
☐ 1961-1969	15	3
☐ 1970-1980	10	1
☐ 1981-1997	5	1

SCHEDULES	Nr-Mt	Ex
☐ 1900-1909	150	50
☐ 1910-1919	100	30
☐ 1920-1929	75	25
☐ 1930-1939	45	15
☐ 1940-1949	30	10
☐ 1950-1959	25	5
☐ 1960-1969	20	5
☐ 1970-1979	9	1
☐ 1980-1997	4	1

YEARBOOKS	Nr-Mt	Ex
☐ 1948	150	50
☐ 1949	200	50
☐ 1950 None Issued		
☐ 1951 - 1952	100	35
☐ 1953 - 1954	80	30
☐ 1955 (Or/Red)-1956	75	20
☐ 1957 (First, Revised)	65	20
☐ 1958 - 1962	40	15
☐ 1963	65	10
☐ 1964 - 1968	30	5
☐ 1969 Pete Rose & Bench	15	5
☐ 1970 Johnny Bench	20	5
☐ 1971 Rose & Bench	12	5
☐ 1972 Bench	15	5
☐ 1973 Morgan & Bench	15	5
☐ 1974 Pete Rose	20	5
☐ 1975 Joe Morgan	30	10
☐ 1976 Morgan, Bench	12	4
☐ 1977 Morgan, Bench	12	4
☐ 1978 Pete Rose	10	2
☐ 1979 Johnny Bench	10	2
☐ 1980 - 1984	10	1
☐ 1985 Pete Rose	8	1
☐ 1986 None Issued		
☐ 1987 -1997	10	2

GENERAL PUBLICATIONS	Nr-Mt	Ex
☐ Pete Rose (60's)	35	15
☐ Pete Rose (70's)	30	10
☐ Joe Morgan (60's)	25	10
☐ Joe Morgan (70's)	20	10
☐ Tom Seaver(70's)	25	10
☐ Johnny Bench (60's)	25	15
☐ Johnny Bench (70's)	20	10

The Reds newsletter is called 'News of the Reds' which was published from 1946 to present.

RED SOX (BOSTON)

Red Sox collectors tend to focus their sports publication collecting on the key players: Babe Ruth, Ted Williams, Carl Yastremski, Tony Congliaro, and Roger Clemens. The Red Sox was the only team that overproduced its yearbooks making many of them worth very little in the secondary market. They also produced many mid season adjustments, making a normal run of yearbooks to have multiple editions in many years.

MEDIA GUIDES	Nr-Mt	Ex
☐ 1927 Roster sheet	195	100
☐ 1928 - 1933 Roster sheet	150	75
☐ 1934 Fenway-Roster	195	100
☐ 1936 - 1946 Roster sheet	65	45
☐ 1947-1949 Roster sheet	50	25
☐ 1950 First Media guide	65	35
☐ 1951-1954	50	35
☐ 1955 - 1957	40	20
☐ 1958 - 1965	25	12
☐ 1966 - 1971	18	9
☐ 1972 - 1979	10	5
☐ 1980 - 1997	5	1

PROGRAMS	Nr-Mt	Ex
☐ 1901 First Game	1000+	500+
☐ 1901	600+	300+
☐ 1902-1904	400+	200+
☐ 1905-1913	250	100
☐ 1914-1918 Babe Ruth	400+	200
☐ 1914 Babe Ruth First game	1000	500
☐ 1919-1925	65	45
☐ 1926-1930	50	25
☐ 1931-1940	35	15
☐ 1941-1949	25	10
☐ 1950-1960	25	10
☐ 1961-1966	15	7
☐ 1967-1971	12	5
☐ 1972-1983	6	2
☐ 1984-1997	5	1
☐ Ted Williams Covers	50	15
☐ Carl Yastremski Covers	20	10
☐ Tony Congliaro	20	10
☐ Roger Clemens	20	10
☐ Babe Ruth Pitched Program		500

YEARBOOKS	Nr-Mt	Ex
☐ 1951	200	100
☐ 1952	150	50
☐ 1953, 1954	None issued	
☐ 1955	125	50
☐ 1956	95	45
☐ 1957	75	45
☐ 1958	65	30
☐ 1959	65	30
☐ 1960	65	30
☐ 1961,1962	65	30
☐ 1963-1966	50	20
☐ 1967	95	35
☐ 1968	65	20
☐ 1969-1970	40	15
☐ 1971-1972	15	4
☐ 1973	25	15
☐ 1976-1983	9	3
☐ 1984-1988	6	2
☐ 1989-1997	12	4

SCHEDULES	Nr-Mt	Ex
☐ 1901	200	100
☐ 1902-1909	120	60
☐ 1910-1920	100	50
☐ 1921-1930	60	30
☐ 1931-1940	50	25
☐ 1941-1950	30	15
☐ 1951-1960	20	10
☐ 1961-1970	15	8
☐ 1971-1979	8	5
☐ 1980-1989	3	1
☐ 1990-1997	1	.50

TICKETS	Nr-Mt	Ex
☐ 1901	400	200
☐ 1901	200	100
☐ 1902-1909	100	50
☐ 1910-1919	80	40

	Nr-Mt	Ex
☐ 1914-18 Babe Ruth Games	200	50
☐ 1920-1929	50	35
☐ 1930-1939	40	25
☐ 1940-1949	30	15
☐ 1950-1959	21	7
☐ 1960-1970	10	4
☐ 1971-1980	4	2
☐ 1981-1990	3	1
☐ 1991-1997	2	1
☐ Ted Williams First Game	400	200
☐ Ted Williams Last game	200	100
☐ Ted Williams Record gm	200	100
☐ Carl Yastremski First game	200	100
☐ Carl Yastremski Last gm	100	50
☐ Roger Clemens Record	50	25

GENERAL PUBLICATIONS

	Nr-Mt	Ex
☐ Roger Clemens Covers	25	10
☐ Ted Williams Cover (40's)	200	50
☐ Ted Williams Cover (50's)	120	40
☐ Ted Williams Cover (60's)	50	20
☐ R. S. Ramblings NL 46-65	25	15
☐ C. Yastremski Cover(60's)	50	20
☐ R.S. Rambling N.L. 66-on	10	4
☐ Tony Congliaro covers	40	20
☐ Roger Clemens covers	25	10
☐ Babe Ruth covers	400	200

ROYALS (KANSAS CITY)

KC Royals collectibles revolve around George Brett. The KC Royals went to two World Series in its young career. Royal publications are not rare and not in demand.

Media Guide	Nr-Mt	Ex
☐ 1969	30	7
☐ 1970	30	5
☐ 1971-1978	12	3
☐ 1979-1983	7	2
☐ 1984 George Brett	10	2
☐ 1985-1993	6	1
☐ 1994-1997	5	1

PROGRAMS & SCORECARDS

	Nr-Mt	Ex
☐ 1969 First Game	100	25
☐ 1969	30	5
☐ 1970-1972	15	3
☐ 1973-1980	10	1
☐ 1981-1997	5	1

SCHEDULES

	Nr-Mt	Ex
☐ 1969	30	10
☐ 1972	20	5
☐ 1973-1979	9	1
☐ 1980-1997	4	1

YEARBOOKS

	Nr-Mt	Ex
☐ 1969	20	10
☐ 1970 - 1971	15	5
☐ 1972 - 1974	15	5
☐ 1975 Killebrew	20	7
☐ 1976-1982 None Issued		
☐ 1983-1987	9	2
☐ 1988-1997	12	5

GENERAL PUBLICATIONS

	Nr-Mt	Ex
☐ George Brett (70's)	35	15
☐ Harmon Killebrew (70's)	20	10

SENATORS (WASHINGTON)

The Washington Senators is one of the oldest baseball teams in America. It no longer has a major league baseball team. The Senators were a competitive team during the 1920's with a championship team in 1924. These teams were led by the all time great pitcher, Walter Johnson. In fact, Walter Johnson, Frank Howard and Ted Williams are the only three Senator representatives heavily collected.

MEDIA GUIDES

	Nr-Mt	Ex
☐ 1928 Roster	125	50
☐ 1929-1933 Roster	115	25
☐ 1934-1935 Roster	100	20
☐ 1936-1940	75	15
☐ 1941-1949	60	20
☐ 1950-1955	50	10
☐ 1956-1960	40	8
☐ 1961	50	10
☐ 1962-1965	30	8
☐ 1966-1968	25	5
☐ 1969 Frank Howard	25	5
☐ 1970 Ted Williams	35	10
☐ 1971	20	5

PROGRAMS & SCORECARDS

	Nr-Mt	Ex
☐ Pre 1890	1000+	450
☐ 1890-1900	750	350
☐ 1901-1902	500	300
☐ 1903-1904	300	100
☐ 1905-1909	200	50
☐ 1910-1914	175	50
☐ 1915-1920	125	35
☐ 1921-1925	75	35
☐ 1926-1930	50	25
☐ 1931-1940	35	10
☐ 1941-1950	25	10
☐ 1951-1955	20	10
☐ 1956-1960	20	4
☐ 1961-1969	15	3
☐ 1970-1971	10	1

SCHEDULES

	Nr-Mt	Ex
☐ 1900-1909	150	50
☐ 1910-1919	100	30
☐ 1920-1929	75	25
☐ 1930-1939	45	15
☐ 1940-1949	30	10
☐ 1950-1959	25	5
☐ 1960-1969	20	5
☐ 1970-1971 Ted Williams	20	5

YEARBOOKS

	Nr-Mt	Ex
☐ 1947 (First Yearbook)	350	50
☐ 1948 None Issued		
☐ 1949	300	30
☐ 1950	250	25
☐ 1951 None Issued		
☐ 1952	95	25
☐ 1953	25	5
☐ 1954	75	25
☐ 1955	75	25
☐ 1956	100	25
☐ 1957	100	25
☐ 1958 (First or Revised)	100	25
☐ 1959	50	10
☐ 1960 H.Killebrew	65	10
☐ 1961	150	35
☐ 1962	65	15
☐ 1963	30	10
☐ 1963 Revised	45	15
☐ 1964	15	5
☐ 1965	25	10
☐ 1966	20	5
☐ 1967	30	15
☐ 1968	20	5
☐ 1969 Ted Williams	40	10
☐ 1970-71 None Issued		

GENERAL PUBLICATIONS

	Nr-Mt	Ex
☐ Harmon Killebrew (50's)	55	20
☐ Ted Williams (60's)	35	15
☐ Frank Howard (70's)	30	15

The Senators had a short lived newsletter called 'The Senator' (1970-1971).

TIGERS (DETROIT)

The Detroit Tigers is a team with a great heritage. The team started in the National League (1881-1888) and has been in the American League since 1901. Early Tiger collectors revolve around the greatest baseball player of all time, Ty Cobb. Ty Cobb joined the team in 1905 and his career lasted through 1926 when he joined the A's. The Tigers won a few championships with Ty Cobb. The second most popular Tiger is Al Kaline and the 1968 Champion team. Most Tiger collectors will revolve around the 1968 World Series team and players. The only exception is Hank Greenberg, who is a very popular ethnic (Jewish) collected personality.

The rarest books on the Tigers are 'The Detroit Tribune's Epitome of Baseball' ,1887 (est. 1,500) and 'Word's Baseball Album & Sketchbook, Detroit Tigers' by Andrew H. Word, 1912 (est. 700). The first yearbook is 'The 1934 Detroit Tigers in Pictures' by Detroit Free Press (est. 400).

MEDIA & ROSTER GUIDES	Nr-Mt	Ex
☐ 1927 roster sheet	125	50
☐ 1928-1934 roster	100	40
☐ 1935 Champions roster	115	35
☐ 1936-1940	75	20
☐ 1941-1949	60	15
☐ 1950-1955	50	10
☐ 1956 Al Kaline	40	10
☐ 1957-1961	40	10
☐ 1962-1964	30	8
☐ 1965-1968	20	5
☐ 1969-1972	15	4
☐ 1973-1980	10	2
☐ 1981-1987	7	1
☐ 1988-1997	5	1

PROGRAMS & SCORECARDS	Nr-Mt	Ex
☐ Pre 1890	1000+	450
☐ 1890-1900	750	350
☐ 1901-1902	500	300
☐ 1903-1904	300	100
☐ 1905-1909	200	50
☐ 1910-1914	175	50
☐ 1915-1920	125	35
☐ 1921-1925	75	35
☐ 1926-1930	50	25
☐ 1931-1940	35	10
☐ 1941-1950	30	10
☐ 1951-1955	25	10
☐ 1956-1960	20	4
☐ 1961-1969	15	3
☐ 1970-1971	10	1
☐ 1972-1980	6	1
☐ 1981-1997	5	1

SCHEDULES	Nr-Mt	Ex
☐ 1900-1909	150	50
☐ 1910-1919	100	30
☐ 1920-1929	75	25
☐ 1930-1939	45	15
☐ 1940-1949	35	10
☐ 1950-1959	30	5
☐ 1960-1969	25	5
☐ 1970-1971	20	5
☐ 1972-1980	10	3
☐ 1981-1990	5	2
☐ 1991-1997	3	1

YEARBOOKS	Nr-Mt	Ex
☐ 1934(First Yearbook)	400	200
☐ 1939	300	150
☐ 1955	275	75
☐ 1956 None Issued		
☐ 1957 - 1959	150	25
☐ 1960	100	20
☐ 1961 - 1963	80	20
☐ 1964 - 1965	55	10

	Nr-Mt	Ex
☐ 1966 - 1967	40	7
☐ 1968 - 1969 Al Kaline	50	10
☐ 1970	15	5
☐ 1971	20	5
☐ 1972 - 1974	10	2
☐ 1975	12	2
☐ 1976	8	1
☐ 1977- 1978	12	2
☐ 1979 - 1981 Trammell	18	3
☐ 1982 - 1984	10	2
☐ 1985-1988	6	1
☐ 1989 - 1997	7	1

GENERAL PUBLICATIONS	Nr-Mt	Ex
☐ Al Kaline (50's)	35	15
☐ Hank Greenberg	50	25
☐ Ty Cobb	200	100
☐ Alan Trammell	15	5

The Detroit Tigers newsletter is called 'Detroit Tiger Tales' (May 47- Nov 66) and the name was then changed to Tiger News (Dec 1966 - on).

TWINS (MINNESOTA)

The Minnesota Twins have a solid following of sports fans and collectors. Sports publication collectors revolve around the following Twin players: Harmon Killebrew, Tony Oliva, Rod Carew, and Kirby Puckett. Harmon Killebrew did make many sports covers despite the fact Minneapolis is a small media market. Tony Oliva and Rod Carew were not as fortunate because they were not power hitters. Kirby Puckett is perhaps the most adopted man in Minnesota and is heavily collected.

MEDIA GUIDES	Nr-Mt	Ex
☐ 1961	50	20
☐ 1962-1965	30	10
☐ 1966-1969	20	8
☐ 1970 Rod Carew	20	8
☐ 1971-1974	15	4
☐ 1975 Rod Carew	15	4
☐ 1976 Carew/Killebrew	15	4
☐ 1977-1979	12	3
☐ 1980-1986	6	1
☐ 1987 Kirby Puckett	10	2
☐ 1988	6	1
☐ 1989,1990 Puckett	6	1
☐ 1991 Carew/Killebrew	6	1
☐ 1992	6	1
☐ 1993 Kirby Puckett	6	1
☐ 1994-1997	4	1

PROGRAMS & SCORECARDS	Nr-Mt	Ex
☐ 1961	35	4
☐ 1962-1965	20	3
☐ 1966-1970	15	3
☐ 1971-1975	10	2
☐ 1976-1980	8	1
☐ 1981-1997	6	1

SCHEDULES	Nr-Mt	Ex
☐ 1961	35	5
☐ 1962-1969	25	5
☐ 1970-1971	20	5
☐ 1972-1980	10	3
☐ 1981-1990	5	2
☐ 1991-1997	3	1

YEARBOOK	Nr-Mt	Ex
☐ 1961	175	50
☐ 1962	100	30
☐ 1963 Harmon Killebrew	85	25
☐ 1964,65,66	80	20
☐ 1967 Harmon Killebrew	35	15
☐ 1968 Harmon Killebrew	25	10
☐ 1969 Killebrew/Carew	25	10
☐ 1970 Rod Carew	25	10
☐ 1971 Carew/Killebrew	20	7
☐ 1972 Killebrew	15	7
☐ 1973	15	5

	Nr-Mt	Ex
☐ 1974	20	7
☐ 1975	10	5
☐ 1976 Rod Carew	15	5
☐ 1977-1981	12	3
☐ 1982	10	2
☐ 1983-1984 None Issued		
☐ 1985,1986,1987,1988	10	2
☐ 1989 Kirby Puckett	10	2
☐ 1990 Puckett, Carew	6	1
☐ 1991, 1992	6	1

GENERAL PUBLICATIONS	Nr-Mt	Ex
☐ Harmon Killebrew (50's)	50	20
☐ Rod Carew (60's)	25	10
☐ Kirby Puckett	25	10
☐ Tony Oliva (60's)	35	15

WHITE SOX (CHICAGO)

The Chicago White Sox have been in baseball since the creation of the American League (1901). They produced the most infamous team in baseball (the 1919 Black Sox). This team is heavily collected and the key player, Joe Jackson, is just as popular as Ty Cobb. Many publication collectors pursue anything with Joe Jackson in it as well as on it. The second most important era of the Chicago White Sox publication history is the 1959 'Go Go Sox' with its great tandem of Nellie Fox and Luis Aparicio. Today most publication collectors are seeking the great 50's era with Fox or Aparicioon the cover. The modern era personalities collected are Carlton Fisk and Frank Thomas.

ROSTER & MEDIA GUIDES	Nr-Mt	Ex
☐ 1927 Roster Sheet	125	50
☐ 1928-1932 Roster sheet	115	35
☐ 1933-1935 Roster sheet	100	25
☐ 1936-1940 Roster sheet	75	15
☐ 1941-1949 Roster sheet	60	15
☐ 1950-1960	50	12
☐ 1952 Nellie Fox	55	12
☐ 1959 champs	60	25
☐ 1961-1964	30	10
☐ 1965-1966	20	6
☐ 1967-1970	12	4
☐ 1971-1974	10	2
☐ 1975-1979	7	1
☐ 1980-1989	5	1
☐ 1990-1997	4	1

PROGRAMS & SCORECARDS	Nr-Mt	Ex
☐ 1901	600	300
☐ 1902	500	250
☐ 1903-1904	300	100
☐ 1905-1909	200	50
☐ 1910-1914	175	50
☐ 1915-1920	125	35
☐ 1921-1925	75	35
☐ 1926-1930	50	25
☐ 1931-1940	35	10
☐ 1941-1950	30	10
☐ 1951-1955	25	10
☐ 1956-1960	20	4
☐ 1961-1969	15	3
☐ 1970-1971	10	1
☐ 1972-1980	6	1
☐ 1981-1997	5	1

SCHEDULES	Nr-Mt	Ex
☐ 1901	200	100
☐ 1902-1909	150	50
☐ 1910-1919	100	30
☐ 1920-1929	75	25
☐ 1930-1939	45	15
☐ 1940-1949	35	10
☐ 1950-1959	30	5
☐ 1960-1969	25	5
☐ 1970-1971	20	5
☐ 1972-1980	10	3

	Nr-Mt	Ex
☐ 1981-1990	5	2
☐ 1991-1997	3	1

YEARBOOKS	Nr-Mt	Ex
☐ 1947	275	75
☐ 1948	225	50
☐ 1949	175	35
☐ 1950-1951	175	20
☐ 1952-1953 (revised)	95	20
☐ 1954 (First or revised)	100	35
☐ 1955,1956,	65	15
☐ 1957 (First or revised)	75	15
☐ 1958	65	10
☐ 1959 Champs	80	15
☐ 1960 - 1962	45	10
☐ 1963, 1964	40	7
☐ 1965 - 1967	35	6
☐ 1968 - 1969	20	4
☐ 1970	35	15
☐ 1971 - 1981 None Issued		
☐ 1982-1984	9	2
☐ 1985,1987,1989 None Issued		
☐ 1990 - 1997	7	1

GENERAL PUBLICATIONS	Nr-Mt	Ex
☐ Nellie Fox (50's)	50	20
☐ Luis Aparico (50's)	40	20
☐ Luis Aparico (60's)	35	15
☐ Frank Thomas(90's)	15	5
☐ Joe Jackson	300	150

The Chicago White Sox official newsletter is called 'White Sox Yarns' (1948 to present) however they have a minor league newsletter as well called 'Chicago White Sox Farm Club News' (1948 - on). Both of these newsletter values range based upon the material content.

YANKEES (NEW YORK)

The Yankees have the best record in major league baseball. They have won more championships than any other sports team in history. Their publication history really starts with Babe Ruth and his string of championships. Lou Gehrig is also a major name that is heavily collected by Yankee fans. His string of games played record stood for decades. Once the Babe stopped playing Joe DiMaggio took his place. Joe DiMaggio was a national hero and is perhaps the most collected player from the 1940's. Joe was replaced by Mickey Mantle who is the most collected player from the 1950's.

MEDIA GUIDES	Nr-Mt	Ex
☐ 1927-1928 Roster Sheet	175	75
☐ 1929-1931 Roster Sheet	150	50
☐ 1932 champs roster	200	100
☐ 1933-1939 Roster sheet	100	50
☐ 1940-1942	65	20
☐ 1943-1949	60	15
☐ 1950-1955	50	10
☐ 1956-1961	45	8
☐ 1962-1964	35	8
☐ 1965-1968	20	5
☐ 1969-1973	15	4
☐ 1974 Ford/Mantle	20	5
☐ 1975-1978	15	4
☐ 1979 Thurmon Munson	12	3
☐ 1980-1989	6	1
☐ 1990-1997	6	1

PROGRAMS & SCORECARDS	Nr-Mt	Ex
☐ 1903	600	300
☐ 1904	300	100
☐ 1905-1909	200	50
☐ 1910-1914	175	50
☐ 1915-1920	125	35
☐ 1921-1925	75	35
☐ 1926-1930	50	25
☐ 1931-1940	35	10
☐ 1941-1950	30	10
☐ 1951-1955	25	10
☐ 1956-1960	20	4

☐ 1961-1969	15	3
☐ 1970-1971	10	1
☐ 1972-1980	6	1
☐ 1981-1997	5	1

SCHEDULES	Nr-Mt	Ex
☐ 1903-1909	150	50
☐ 1910-1919	100	30
☐ 1920-1929	75	25
☐ 1930-1939	45	15
☐ 1940-1949	35	10
☐ 1950-1959	30	5
☐ 1960-1969	25	5
☐ 1970-1971	20	5
☐ 1972-1980	10	3
☐ 1981-1990	5	2
☐ 1991-1997	3	1

YEARBOOKS	Nr-Mt	Ex
☐ 1950 (First Yearbook)	325	100
☐ 1951	185	75
☐ 1952	150	75
☐ 1953	150	75
☐ 1952 Big League	125	50
☐ 1953 Big League	100	35
☐ 1954	175	50
☐ 1954 Big League	100	35
☐ 1955	220	100
☐ 1955 Big League	100	30
☐ 1956 (red or blue cover)	225	50
☐ 1956 Big League	90	25
☐ 1957 (First or Revised)	200	50
☐ 1957 Big League	90	20
☐ 1958 (First or Revised)	120	35
☐ 1958 Big League	80	20
☐ 1959 (First or Revised)	120	35
☐ 1959 Big League	65	15

☐ 1960 (First or Revised)	75	20
☐ 1960	60	15
☐ 1961 (First or Revised)	100	25
☐ 1961 Big Le Mantle/Mar	100	25
☐ 1962 (First,2nd,3rd ed)	75	15
☐ 1963 (First, 2nd)	65	15
☐ 1964 (First,2nd & Final Rev)	65	15
☐ 1962 - 1965 Big Leag.	50	10
☐ 1964 (2nd & Final Rev)	65	15
☐ 1965 (First, 2nd)	50	10
☐ 1966 (First, 2nd & Final Rev)	50	15
☐ 1967 Mickey Mantle	60	10
☐ 1967 Mickey Mantle (rev)	50	10
☐ 1968	50	10
☐ 1969 Mantle	50	10
☐ 1970	35	7
☐ 1971 - 1972	25	5
☐ 1973 Mickey Mantle	20	4
☐ 1974 Thurmon Munson	35	4
☐ 1975 - 1978	18	4
☐ 1979 - 1983	15	3
☐ 1984 - 1988	10	2
☐ 1980	6	1
☐ 1989 - 1997	6	1
☐ 1983 Spanish Edition	6	1

GENERAL PUBLICATIONS	Nr-Mt	Ex
☐ Babe Ruth (30's)	250	100
☐ Lou Gehrig (30's)	150	75
☐ Joe Dimaggio (40's)	150	50
☐ Joe Dimaggio (50's)	100	35
☐ Mickey Mantle (50's)	75	25
☐ Mickey Mantle (60's)	50	20
☐ Whitey Ford	45	15
☐ Thurmon Munson	40	15
☐ Reggie Jackson	25	10
☐ Newsletter (50's)	30	15

MEDIA GUIDES
1958   **1968**   **1968**   **1970**

1971   **1971**   **1971**   **1974**

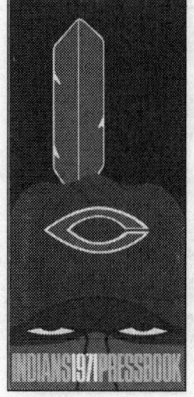   

PROGRAMS
1940   **1947**   **1950**

PROGRAMS

1950

1950

1952

1954

1956

1956

1958

1960

1962

1962

1964

1973

1975

1979

1980

YEARBOOKS
1949

1950

1952

1953

1955

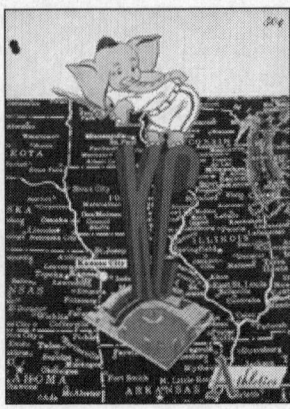

1958

1958

1959

1963

1964

1965

1965

1970

1970

1970

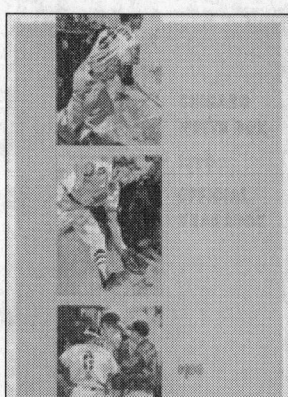

1973

1979

1986

1987

1988

1992

CHAPTER ELEVEN:
World Series / All-Star Publications

WORLD SERIES PROGRAMS

World Series programs are one of the most popular and collected sports programs. Many collectors try to acquire all of them but usually find it cost prohibitive. So most collectors tend to focus on their favorite teams or Series, such as the 1968 Tigers, '69 Mets or '55 Dodgers. Other hobbyists pursue only those programs containing their favorite players. Finally, more than a few people collect the programs just for the great player advertisements.

There are three key factors that determine the value of a World Series program. The first is scarcity. Some games have lower attendance based on lousy weather, smaller stadiums, paper drives and so on. The earliest programs are the rarest and the most valuable, while any from the last 10 years have a nominal value. The second factor is demand. There is great demand for the 1919 Black Sox, the '69 Amazing Mets and the '55 Brooklyn Dodgers. These programs easily can be twice as expensive as other programs from the same era. Finally, the third determinant is condition. Mint and Nr-Mt programs hold their values, while the VG, Ex and Ex-Mt programs have declined in value over the last 10 years.

DATE	HOME TEAM	Nr-Mt	Ex
☐ 1903	Boston (AL)	36,000+	18,000+
☐ 1903	Pittsburgh (NL)	36,000+	18,000+
☐ 1905	New York (NL)	12,000+	6,000+
☐ 1905	Philadelphia (AL)	18,000+	9,000+
☐ 1906	Chicago (AL)	9,000	4,500
☐ 1906	Chicago (NL)	12,000	6,000
☐ 1907	Chicago (NL)	12,000	6,000
☐ 1907	Detroit (AL)	17,000	6,000
☐ 1908	Detroit (AL)	15,000	7,500
☐ 1908	Chicago (NL)	15,000	7,500
☐ 1909	Pittsburgh (NL)	12,000	6,000
☐ 1909	Detroit (AL)	12,000	6,000
☐ 1910	Philadelphia (AL)	12,000	6,000
☐ 1910	Chicago (NL)	9,000	6,000
☐ 1911	Philadelphia (AL)	7,500	4,000
☐ 1911	New York (NL)	6,000	3,000
☐ 1912	New York (NL)	6,000	3,000
☐ 1912	Boston (AL)	4,000	2,000
☐ 1913	Philadelphia (AL)	5,000	2,500
☐ 1913	New York (NL)	5,000	2,000
☐ 1914	Boston (NL)	6,000	3,000
☐ 1914	Philadelphia (AL)	6,000	3,000
☐ 1915	Boston (NL)	4,000	2,000
☐ 1915	Philadelphia (NL)	4,000	2,000
☐ 1916	Boston (AL)	5,000	2,300
☐ 1916	Brooklyn (NL)	6,000	3,000
☐ 1917	Chicago (AL)	6,000	3,000
☐ 1917	New York (NL)	4,000	2,000
☐ 1918	Chicago (NL)	7,000	3,500
☐ 1918	Boston (AL)	12,000	6,000
☐ 1919	Cincinnati (NL)	5,000	2,500
☐ 1919	Chicago (AL)	10,000	5,000
☐ 1920	Cleveland (AL)	7,500	3,500
☐ 1920	Brooklyn (NL)	6,000	3,000
☐ 1921	New York (NL)	3,000	1,500

DATE	HOME TEAM	Nr-Mt	Ex
☐ 1921	New York (AL)	3,000	1,500
☐ 1922	New York (AL)	2,500	1,250
☐ 1923	New York (NL)	3,500	2,000
☐ 1923	New York (AL)	3,000	1,500
☐ 1924	Washington (AL)	2,000	1,000
☐ 1924	New York (NL)	3,000	1,500
☐ 1925	Pittsburgh (NL)	6,000	3,000
☐ 1925	Washington (AL)	1,200	600
☐ 1926	St. Louis (NL)	1,500	750
☐ 1926	New York (AL)	1,600	800
☐ 1927	New York (AL)	3,000	1,500
☐ 1927	Pittsburgh (NL)	6,000	3,000
☐ 1928	New York (AL)	3,000	1,500
☐ 1928	St. Louis (NL)	2,000	800
☐ 1929	Philadelphia (AL)	1,800	750
☐ 1929	Chicago (NL)	1,300	500
☐ 1930	Philadelphia (AL)	1,200	500
☐ 1930	St. Louis (NL)	1,200	300
☐ 1931	St. Louis (NL)	750	300
☐ 1931	Philadelphia (AL)	800	300
☐ 1932	New York (AL)	1,500	700
☐ 1932	Chicago (NL)	1,000	400
☐ 1933	New York (NL)	1,200	500
☐ 1933	Washington (AL)	800	400
☐ 1934	St. Louis (NL)	700	325
☐ 1934	Detroit (AL)	800	400
☐ 1935	Chicago (NL)	600	300
☐ 1936	New York (NL)	400	175
☐ 1936	New York (AL)	400	150
☐ 1937	New York (NL)	400	150
☐ 1937	New York (AL)	400	150
☐ 1938	New York (AL)	400	150
☐ 1938	Chicago (NL)	400	150
☐ 1939	New York (AL)	400	150
☐ 1939	Cincinnati (NL)	400	150
☐ 1940	Cincinnati (NL)	400	150
☐ 1940	Detroit (AL)	375	150
☐ 1941	New York (AL)	300	150
☐ 1941	Brooklyn (NL)	475	300
☐ 1942	St. Louis (NL)	300	125
☐ 1942	New York (AL)	300	125
☐ 1943	New York (AL)	300	125
☐ 1943	St. Louis (NL)	300	125
☐ 1944	St. Louis (NL)	250	100
☐ 1944	St. Louis (AL)	400	200
☐ 1945	Detroit (AL)	425	220
☐ 1945	Chicago (NL)	220	100
☐ 1946	St. Louis (NL)	220	100
☐ 1946	Boston (AL)	265	110
☐ 1947	New York (AL)	280	125
☐ 1947	Brooklyn (NL)	350	170
☐ 1948	Cleveland (AL)	175	75
☐ 1948	Boston (NL)	250	75
☐ 1949	New York (AL)	220	110
☐ 1949	Brooklyn (NL)	325	150
☐ 1950	New York (AL)	250	125
☐ 1950	Philadelphia (NL)	200	110
☐ 1951	New York (AL)	225	110

☐ 1951	New York (NL)	225	110
☐ 1952	New York (AL)	220	100
☐ 1952	Brooklyn (NL)	220	100
☐ 1953	New York (AL)	200	100
☐ 1953	Brooklyn (NL)	330	180
☐ 1954	New York (NL)	250	140
☐ 1954	Cleveland (AL)	200	110
☐ 1955	Brooklyn (NL)	375	200
☐ 1955	New York (AL)	225	100
☐ 1956	New York (AL)	225	100
☐ 1956	Brooklyn (NL)	300	150
☐ 1957	Milwaukee (NL)	200	100
☐ 1957	New York (AL)	150	75
☐ 1958	New York (AL)	150	50
☐ 1958	Milwaukee (NL)	200	100
☐ 1959	Los Angeles (NL)	125	50
☐ 1959	Chicago (AL)	200	100
☐ 1960	Pittsburgh (NL)	120	60
☐ 1960	New York (AL)	120	50
☐ 1961	New York (AL)	150	75
☐ 1961	Cincinnati (NL)	135	50
☐ 1962	New York (AL)	100	50
☐ 1962	Giants (NL)	250	100
☐ 1963	Los Angeles (NL)	75	35
☐ 1963	New York (AL)	75	35
☐ 1964	New York (AL)	75	35
☐ 1964	St. Louis (NL)	135	75
☐ 1965	Los Angeles (NL)	50	20
☐ 1965	Minnesota (AL)	135	35
☐ 1966	Baltimore (AL)	135	20
☐ 1966	Los Angeles (NL)	135	45
☐ 1967	St. Louis (NL)	100	40
☐ 1967	Boston (AL)	220	75
☐ 1968	Detroit (AL)	225	125
☐ 1968	St. Louis (NL)	120	65
☐ 1969	New York (NL)	225	120
☐ 1969	Baltimore (AL)	60	25
☐ 1970	Baltimore (AL)	60	25
☐ 1970	Cincinnati (NL)	60	25
☐ 1971	Pittsburgh (NL)	80	40
☐ 1971	Baltimore (AL)	50	25
☐ 1972	Oakland (AL)	75	40
☐ 1972	Cincinnati (NL)	60	30
☐ 1973	Oakland (AL)	60	30
☐ 1973	New York (NL)	50	25
☐ 1974	Oakland/LA	30	15
☐ 1975	Cin/Bost	30	15
☐ 1976	Cin/NY	30	15
☐ 1977	NY/LA	25	10
☐ 1978	NY/LA	20	10
☐ 1979-1983	....	15	5
☐ 1984-1997	....	10	3

WORLD SERIES TICKETS

World Series tickets rank No. 1 with ticket collectors. The value of these tickets range according to condition, scarcity and completeness. As a rule of thumb, most of them are valued at less than the program price (approximately 50%). But since programs were saved and ticket stubs were thrown out, this percentage can run higher. For example, some experienced collectors estimate that there is one ticket stub to every 10 programs. The prices for World Series complete Mint tickets actually will be higher than the actual game program, and this is especially true after 1970. Tickets that are creased or with other major flaws are about 50% of the Ex value.

There are many ways to store and collect World Series tickets. The best storage method I know of is to either use plastic two-pocket sheets with one section devoted to the ticket and the second part of the plastic sheet devoted to explaining the ticket. You can also use a one-pocket sheet. Also, you can use stamp holder sheet supplies to hold the ticket to a sheet without damaging the ticket. Before you attach the stamp holder corners to a sheet, I suggest putting the history of the game on the sheet (above or below the ticket).

WORLD SERIES SCORECARDS & MEDIA GUIDES

These are not as common as World Series programs but are not in heavy demand. You can purchase these for the same price as World Series programs.

World Series scorecards are usually a one-piece publication that is folded in the middle. These pieces usually are all text with no pictures and have a scorecard in the middle (or on one side). Because of the boring format, the demand for them is low and the price is lower still. You can pick up scorecards for about 35-50% of the similar game program. The only exceptions are well-kept scorecards of significant games.

ALL-STAR GAME PROGRAMS

The MLB All-Star Game is very popular with event collectors. In fact, there are many collectors who enjoy collecting All-Star game programs from all the major sports.

The baseball All-Star Game programs usually have a review of the current All-Stars and a historical review of all the games. The programs range in scarcity based on age and the size of the stadium. All-Star Game programs are about 50% tougher to find than their World Series counterpart, because there is only one All-Star Game a year compared to two to four World Series home games. While programs in lower grades have declined in value during the past few years, those in higher grades (Nr-Mt or better) have held their value.

DATE	HOME TEAM	Nr-Mt	Ex
☐ 1933	Chicago	3,000	1,500
☐ 1934	New York	4,000	2,000
☐ 1935	Cleveland	750	300
☐ 1936	Boston	4,500	2,200
☐ 1937	Washington	1,300	500
☐ 1938	Cincinnati	1,200	600
☐ 1939	New York	1,400	700
☐ 1940	St. Louis	1,000	500
☐ 1941	Detroit	1,000	500
☐ 1942	New York	3,000	1,500
☐ 1943	Philadelphia	800	400
☐ 1944	Pittsburgh	1,300	600
☐ 1945	No game		
☐ 1946	Boston	1,300	600
☐ 1947	Chicago	700	300
☐ 1948	St Louis	700	300
☐ 1949	Brooklyn	1,300	600
☐ 1950	Chicago	600	300
☐ 1951	Detroit	250	100
☐ 1952	Philadelphia	250	100
☐ 1953	Cincinnati	300	150
☐ 1954	Cleveland	300	150
☐ 1955	Milwaukee	225	100
☐ 1956	Washington	225	100
☐ 1957	St. Louis	300	150

DATE		Nr-Mt	Ex
☐ 1958	Baltimore	250	125
☐ 1959	Los Angeles	120	60
☐ 1960	Kansas City	200	100
☐ 1960	New York	140	70
☐ 1961	Boston	360	180
☐ 1961	San Francisco	450	225
☐ 1962	Washington	150	75
☐ 1962	Chicago	150	75
☐ 1963	Cleveland	140	70
☐ 1964	New York	300	150
☐ 1965	Minnesota	75	35
☐ 1966	St. Louis	150	75
☐ 1967	Anaheim	200	100
☐ 1968	Houston	150	75
☐ 1969	Washington	150	75
☐ 1970	Cincinnati	150	80
☐ 1971	Detroit	150	75
☐ 1972	Atlanta	40	20
☐ 1973	Kansas City	120	60
☐ 1974	Pittsburgh	40	20
☐ 1975	Milwaukee	40	20
☐ 1976	Philadelphia	20	10
☐ 1977	New York	20	10
☐ 1978	San Diego	40	20
☐ 1979	Seattle	20	10
☐ 1980	Los Angeles	40	20
☐ 1981	Cleveland	20	10
☐ 1982	Montreal	40	20
☐ 1983-1997		10	4

ALL-STAR GAME TICKETS

All-Star Game tickets are heavily pursued by major event collectors. They are about two to three times tougher to find than programs. Their values range in value, but a good rule of thumb is about 50% of the program value. However, complete tickets and tickets after 1974 will go for more than the game programs. The tougher tickets are usually found at auctions.

AMERICAN/NATIONAL LEAGUE
CHAMPIONSHIP PROGRAMS

Playoff programs are actually tougher to find than World Series programs, because LCS programs are sold only at the games. The rare programs result from a team having only one home game in a Series. The most common tend to be later editions, which are mass produced for collectors.

Most of the programs are also pursued by team collectors, who search high and low for all their favorite teams' postseason programs. Some individual player collectors also pursue playoff programs that feature favorite players on the cover or inside. Finally, special-event collectors enjoy the pursuit of all the playoff programs, regardless of teams or series, such as the ones involving wild-card teams.

DATE	HOME TEAM	Nr-Mt	Ex
☐ 1969	Baltimore	60	30
☐ 1969	Minnesota	100	50
☐ 1969	Atlanta	40	20
☐ 1969	New York Mets	300	150
☐ 1970	Baltimore	40	20
☐ 1970	Minnesota	100	50
☐ 1970	Cincinnati	80	40
☐ 1971	Baltimore	40	20
☐ 1971	Oakland	30	15

DATE		Nr-Mt	Ex
☐ 1971	San Francisco	800	400
☐ 1971	Pittsburgh	200	100
☐ 1972	Detroit	80	40
☐ 1972	Oakland	30	15
☐ 1972	Cincinnati	30	15
☐ 1972	Pittsburgh (Clemente)	40	20
☐ 1973	Baltimore	40	20
☐ 1973	Oakland	24	12
☐ 1973	New York	80	40
☐ 1973	Cincinnati	120	60
☐ 1974	Baltimore	30	15
☐ 1974	Oakland	300	175
☐ 1974	Los Angeles	240	120
☐ 1974	Pittsburgh	180	100
☐ 1975	Boston	50	25
☐ 1975	Oakland	50	25
☐ 1975	Cin/Pitts	12	6
☐ 1976	Phil	12	6
☐ 1976	Cincinnati	60	30
☐ 1976	KC/NY	12	6
☐ 1977	Philadelphia	12	6
☐ 1977	Los Angeles	60	30
☐ 1978	Phil/LA	12	6
☐ 1978	KC/NY	12	6
☐ 1979	Baltimore	60	30
☐ 1979	California	12	6
☐ 1979	Cincinnati	20	10
☐ 1979	Pittsburgh	12	6
☐ 1980	Philadelphia	15	7
☐ 1980	Houston	40	20
☐ 1980	KC/NY	10	5
☐ 1981	NY/Oak	15	5
☐ 1981	KC/Oak	40	20
☐ 1981	NY/Mil	30	15
☐ 1981	Houston/LA	15	7
☐ 1981	Phil/Mont	20	10
☐ 1981	LA/Mont	40	20
☐ 1981	Mont/Phil	40	20
☐ 1981	Mon/LA	10	5
☐ 1981	LA/Houston	200	120
☐ 1982	St. Louis	25	12
☐ 1982	Atlanta	10	5
☐ 1982	California	10	5
☐ 1982	Milwaukee	60	30
☐ 1983	Balt/Chicago	15	7
☐ 1983	Philadelphia	10	5
☐ 1984	San Diego	25	10
☐ 1984	Chicago	15	7
☐ 1984	Detroit	10	5
☐ 1984	Kansas City	20	10
☐ 1985	Toronto	30	15
☐ 1985	Kansas City	30	15
☐ 1985	St Louis	25	10
☐ 1985	Los Angeles	40	20
☐ 1986	Houston	15	7
☐ 1986	New York	25	10
☐ 1986	California	30	15
☐ 1986	Boston	10	5
☐ 1987	Detroit/Minn	15	7
☐ 1987	St. Louis	10	5
☐ 1987	San Francisco	25	15
☐ 1988	LA/NY	10	5
☐ 1988	Boston	10	5
☐ 1988	Oakland	40	20

☐ 1989	Toronto/Oakland	15	7
☐ 1989	SF/Chicago	15	7
☐ 1990	Cin/Pitts	10	5
☐ 1990	Boston/Oakland	10	5
☐ 1991	Toronto/Minn	10	5
☐ 1991	Atlanta	20	10
☐ 1991	Pittsburgh	10	5
☐ 1992	Toronto/Oakland	10	5
☐ 1992	Atlanta	20	10
☐ 1992	Pittsburgh	10	5
☐ 1993-97		10	5

ALL-STAR PROGRAMS

1933

1936

1937

1947

1949

1954

1955

1961

1965

WORLD SERIES PROGRAMS

1988

1903 WORLD CHAMPIONSHIP

1905 WORLD CHAMPIONSHIP

1906 WORLD CHAMPIONSHIP

1910 WORLD CHAMPIONSHIP

1916

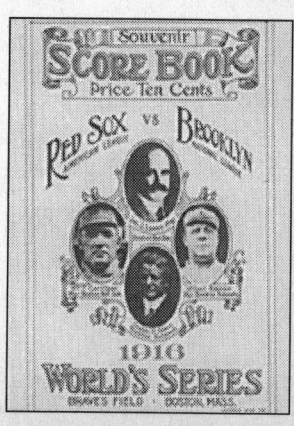

1925

1926

1930

1930

1933

1934

1939

1942

1945

1958

1961

1963

1965

1968

1972

1980

1982

WORLD SERIES TICKETS
1919 WORLD SERIES GAME 1

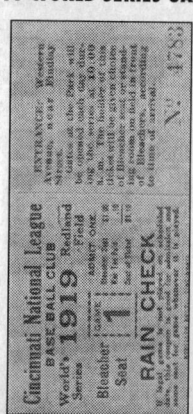

CHAPTER TWELVE:
Collecting Baseball Publications

ACTION SPORTS BASEBALL GUIDE
(Rostam)

DATE	COVER/FEATURE	Nr-Mt	Ex
☐ 1971	Willie Mays/S.McDowell	25	5

ACTION SPORTS BASEBALL
(Rotsam)

DATE	COVER/FEATURE	Nr-Mt	Ex
☐ 1971	Johnny Bench	25	5
☐ 1972	Rose/Blue/Aaron	15	5

ALL SPORTS
(Stanco)

DATE	COVER/FEATURE	Nr-Mt	Ex
☐ 10/62	Warren Spahn	35	10
☐ 7/71	Thurmon Munson	30	5
☐ 9/71	Tom Seaver	25	5

ALL STAR BASEBALL
(Topical Sports Library)

DATE	COVER/FEATURE	Nr-Mt	Ex
☐ 1964	Brooks Robinson/Ken Boyer	25	5
☐ 1965	Sandy Koufax	25	5

ALL STAR SPORTS
(QMG Magazine corp)

DATE	COVER/FEATURE	Nr-Mt	Ex
☐ 8/67	J.Marichal/Durocher vol #1	50	20
☐ 10/67	B. Starr/W. Mays	35	10
☐ 2/68	J Unitas/J. Namath/Bobby Hull	20	10
☐ 4/68	R. Clemente/ E. Stanky	40	20
☐ 6/68	Ernie Banks/Al Kaline/Lou Brock	20	10
☐ 8/68	C. Flood/C. Yaz	30	15
☐ 10/68	B. Robinson/F. Alou	35	15
☐ 12/68	Chamberlain/Gale Sayers/D. McLain	20	10
☐ 2/69	Joe Namath/Bob Gibson/ Bill Russell	20	10
☐ 4/69	Lou Brock/D.McLain/C. Yaz/Wilt Cham	20	10
☐ 6/69	W. McCovey/W.Horton/C.Flood	20	10
☐ 8/69	E. Banks/B.Freeham/J. Namath	20	10
☐ 10/69	W. Mays/F. Robinson	20	10
☐ 12/69	Joe Namath/Kareem Abdul Jabbar	20	10
☐ 2/70	OJ Simpson/Bill Bradley	20	10
☐ 4/70	Jerry Kosman/Boog Powell	20	10
☐ 6/70	H. Aaron/G. Hodges	25	10
☐ 9/70	McLain/Oliva/ Jenkins	25	10
☐ 11/70	D. Lamonica/Aaron/Mays	25	10
☐ 1/71	Wilt Chamberlain/Len Dawson	20	10
☐ 3/71	Kareem Abdul Jabbar	20	10
☐ 5/71	Hank Aaron/Tom Seaver/Bob Gibson	20	10
☐ 7/71	Reggie Jackson/Frank Howard	20	10
☐ 9/71	Rusty Staub/Willie Stargell	20	10
☐ 11/71	Vida Blue/Leroy Kelly	20	10
☐ 1/72	John Brodie/Kareem Abdul Jabbar	20	10
☐ 3/72	Vic Hadfield	20	10
☐ 5/72	Bob Gibson/B. Harrelson	20	10
☐ 8/72	Roger Staubach	20	10
☐ 10/72	College FB Preview	15	10
☐ 5/74	Pete Rose	25	10
☐ 7/75	Reggie Jackson	20	10

AMERICAN LEAGUE RED BOOK

DATE	COVER/FEATURE	Nr-Mt	Ex
☐ 1943-1945		65	25
☐ 1946-1950		40	20
☐ 1951-1959		30	15
☐ 1952	Ted Williams	50	25
☐ 1953	All Stars	40	25

☐ 1954	Best in 53	40	25
☐ 1955	1954 All Star Team	40	25
☐ 1960-1969		20	10
☐ 1960	Cobb/Foxx/DiMaggio	45	25
☐ 1962	Mantle & Maris	55	25
☐ 1964	Killebrew & Yaz	40	15
☐ 1966	Tony Congliaro/Others	30	10
☐ 1967	Frank Robinson	25	10
☐ 1968	Carl Yastrzemski	25	10
☐ 1970-1979		15	5
☐ 1970	Harmon Killebrew	25	10
☐ 1976	Carlton Fisk	15	5
☐ 1980-1989		12	3
☐ 1981	George Brett	15	5
☐ 1983	Robin Yount	15	5
☐ 1984	Carl Ripken Jr	25	10
☐ 1990-1997		10	2

ARGOSY
(Popular Publications)

DATE	COVER/FEATURE	Nr-Mt	Ex
☐ 1976	Pete Rose	20	10
☐ 1977	Mark Fidrych	15	7
☐ 1977	Johnny Bench (WS)	20	10

ATHLON'S BASEBALL

DATE	COVER/FEATURE	Nr-Mt	Ex
☐ 1989	Orel Hershiser	10	5
☐ 1990-1997		10	5

BARNES OFFICIAL BASEBALL GUIDE
Edited by Leslie O'Conor. These were produced in 1945 and 1946. Also produced the 1943 comissioners guide.

BASEBALL
(Whitestone)

DATE	COVER/FEATURE	Nr-Mt	Ex
☐ 1960	Wally Moon #1 - Dodgers	50	20
☐ 1961	Roger Maris - Yankees	40	20
☐ 1962	Joey Jay - Reds	35	10
☐ 1963	Orlando Cepeda -Giants	35	10
☐ 1964	Mickey Mantle - Yankees	50	15
☐ 1965	Mickey Mantle - Yankees	60	15
☐ 1966	Sandy Koufax - Dodgers		

BASEBALL
(NAPBL)

DATE	COVER/FEATURE	Nr-Mt	Ex
☐ 1977	Cobb/Brock	20	10
☐ 1979	Willie Stargell - Pirates	20	10
☐ 1982	Fernando Valenzula - Dodgers	15	7
☐ 1983	Robin Yount - Brewers	15	7

BASEBALL ALBUM

DATE	COVER/FEATURE	Nr-Mt	Ex
☐ 1960	Fox/Mantle/Aaron/Banks	45	15

BASEBALL ALL STARS
(Maco)

DATE	COVER/FEATURE	Nr-Mt	Ex
☐ 1953	Mickey Mantle/Fain/Musial/Robinson	95	20
☐ 1957	Micky Mantle/Musial	65	20
☐ 1958	Mantle/Williams/Burdette/Musial	65	20

BASEBALL ANNUAL
(Whitesone)

DATE	COVER/FEATURE	Nr-Mt	Ex
☐ 1969	Willie Mays/Pete Rose	35	15
☐ 1970	Tom Seaver -Mets	35	10

BASEBALL BEST

(Sport Magazine)

DATE	COVER/FEATURE	Nr-Mt	Ex
☐ 1952	Ashburn/Robinson/Campy/Rizzuto ..	50	20
☐ 1953	Duke Snider/Mantle/Roberts/Musial .	50	20
☐ 1960	Banks/Mays/Fox/Aaron/Mathews ...	45	15

BASEBALL BEST HITTERS

DATE	COVER/FEATURE	Nr-Mt	Ex
☐ 1957	Mantle/Berra/Snider/Kaline/Klu/Mays		
☐	Musial/Williams/Mathews	50	20

BASEBALL DIGEST

DATE	COVER/FEATURE	Nr-Mt	Ex
☐ 8/42	First Issue	300	150
☐ 9/42	Pete Reiser - Dodgers	100	50
☐ 10/42	Double Play	100	50
☐ w/42	Joe DiMaggio - Yankees	125	50
☐ 1-2/43	Baseball Action	50	30
☐ 3/43	Back to School	50	30
☐ 4/43	Action	50	30
☐ 5/43	Action	35	15
☐ 7/43	Yankees #6	45	20
☐ 8/43	Action	35	15
☐ 9/43	Stan Musial - Cardinals	45	25
☐ 10/43	Spud Chandler - Yankees	35	15
☐ 11-12/43	Johnny Lindell - Yankees	35	15
☐ 1-2/44	Bill Johnson - Yankees	30	15
☐ 3/44	Sewell/ Nicholson - Pirates	30	15
☐ 4/44	Dixie Walker - Dodgers	30	15
☐ 5/44	Lou Boudreau - Indians	30	15
☐ 7/44	Vern Stephens - Browns	30	15
☐ 8/44	Bucky Walters - Reds	30	15
☐ 9/44	Charlie Grimm- Cubs	30	15
☐ 10/44	Walker Cooper - Cardinals	30	15
☐ 11/44	Marty Marion - Cardinals	30	15
☐ 1-2/45	Hal Newhouser - Tigers	30	15
☐ 3/45	George McQuinn - Browns	30	15
☐ 4/45	Dixie Walker - Cardinals	30	15
☐ 5/45	Bill Voiselle- Giants	30	15
☐ 6/45	None Issued		
☐ 7/45	Hank Borowy- Yankees	30	15
☐ 8/45	Tommy Holmes - Braves	30	15
☐ 9/45	Stan Hack - Cubs	25	12
☐ 10/45	Hank Greenberg - Tigers	40	20
☐ 11/45	Al Lopez - White Sox	25	10
☐ 1-2/46	Charlie Keller-Yankees	30	12
☐ 3/46	Action	25	10
☐ 4/46	Bobby Doerr -Red Sox	30	15
☐ 5/46	Bob Feller - Indians	35	20
☐ 6/46	None Issued		
☐ 7/46	T. Williams/J. DiMaggio	75	25
☐ 8/46	Joe Cronin - Red Sox	30	15
☐ 9/46	Hank Wyse - Cubs	25	12
☐ 10/46	Dave Ferriss- Red Sox	20	10
☐ 11/46	Red Schoendist - Cardinals	25	12
☐ 1-2/47	Bucky Harris - Braves	20	10
☐ 3/47	J. Rigney - White Sox	20	10
☐ 4/47	Johnny Van Cuyk - Cardinals	20	10
☐ 5/47	Hank Greenberg/B. Herman	25	15
☐ 5/47	PCL Edition (Stengel)	40	20
☐ 7/47	Lou Boudreau/Joe Gordon	20	10
☐ 8/47	Buddy Kerr - Giants	20	10
☐ 9/47	Ewell Blackwell - Reds	20	10
☐ 10/47	Joe DiMaggio - Yankees	75	20
☐ 11/47	Ralph Lapoint - Phillies	20	10
☐ W/48	Joe Page- Yankees	25	10
☐ 2/48	Leo Durocher/Branch Ricky	25	10
☐ 3/48	Phillies player	25	15

☐ 4/48	Joe McCarthy - Giants	25	10
☐ 5/48	Art Houtteman - Tigers	25	10
☐ 6/48	Willard Marshall - Giants	25	10
☐ 7/48	Ralph Kiner - Pirates	25	10
☐ 8/48	Lou Boudreau - Indians	25	10
☐ 9/48	Stan Musial- Cardinals	50	25
☐ 10/48	Hank Sauer - Cubs	25	10
☐ 11/48	Paul Fagan- Indians	25	10
☐ 12/48	None Issued		
☐ W/49	Jim Hegan - Indians	25	10
☐ 2/49	Red Rolfe- Tigers	20	10
☐ 3/49	Ted Williams - Red Sox	60	40
☐ 4/49	Joe DiMaggio - Yankees	70	25
☐ 5/49	Play at Plate	20	10
☐ 6/49	Robin Roberts - Phillies	35	15
☐ 7/49	Johnny Groth - Tigers	20	10
☐ 8/49	Frankie Frisch - Cubs	25	10
☐ 9/49	Vic Raschi -Yankees	20	10
☐ 10/49	Mel Parnell/Birdie Tebbetts	20	10
☐ 11/49	A.Reynolds/T. Henrich	25	10
☐ 12/49	None Issued		
☐ W/50	R.Ashburn/Cubs Player	40	20
☐ 2/50	Dave Koslo - Giants	20	10
☐ 3/50	Baseball Rules	15	10
☐ 4/50	Bob Feller - Indians	20	10
☐ 5/50	Stanky/Kramer/Dark	20	10
☐ 6/50	Joe DiMaggio - Yankees	50	35
☐ 7/50	Phil Rizzuto - Yankees	25	10
☐ 8/50	Dick Sisler - Phillies	20	10
☐ 9/50	L.Jansen/Houtteman	15	10
☐ 10/50	Hoot Evers - Tigers	15	10
☐ 11/50	Jim Konstanty - Phillies	15	10
☐ 12/50	None Issued		
☐ W/51	Berra & Ford - Yankees	20	10
☐ 2/51	Gil Hodges- Dodgers	20	10
☐ 3/51	Eddie Yost - Senators	15	10
☐ 4/51	Joe DiMaggio - Yankees	50	25
☐ 5/51	Earnshaw & Fogg-Phil's	15	10
☐ 6/51	Ted Williams/Mickey Mantle (1st) ...	200	100
☐ 7/51	Irv Norton - Senators	15	10
☐ 8/51	Nellie Fox/P. Richards	30	15
☐ 9/51	Stan Musial - Cardinals	35	15
☐ 10/51	Gil McDougald - Yankees	20	10
☐ 11/51	Charlie Dressen-Dodgers	15	10
☐ 12/51	None Issued		
☐ W/52	Ed Lopat & Phil Rizzuto	20	10
☐ 2/52	Eddie Stanky-Cardinals	15	10
☐ 3/52	Sid Gordan - Braves	15	10
☐ 4/52	Mike Garcia - Indians	15	10
☐ 5/52	George Staley - Cardinals	15	10
☐ 6/52	Pee Wee Reese - Dodgers	35	15
☐ 7/52	Ted Kluszewski - Reds	30	10
☐ 8/52	Bobby Schantz - A's	15	10
☐ 9/52	Sal Maglie - Yankees	20	10
☐ 10/52	Carl Erskine - Dodgers	20	10
☐ 11/52	Duke Snider - Dodgers	40	15
☐ 12/52	None Issued		
☐ W/53	Robin Roberts - Phillies	25	10
☐ 3/53	Billy Martin- Yankees	15	10
☐ 5/53	Carl Furrillo - Dodgers	20	12
☐ 7/53	Logan/Dorish/Kellner	15	10
☐ 8/53	Robin Roberts - Phillies	25	10
☐ 9/53	O'Connell/Trucks/Strickland	15	10
☐ 10/53	Casey Stengel - Yankees	15	10
☐ 11/53	None Issued		
☐ 12/53	None Issued		
☐ W/54	Billy Martin - Yankees	25	10
☐ 2/54	None Issued		
☐ 3/54	Jimmy Piersall - Red Sox	20	10

☐ 4/54	Whitey Ford - Yankees	35	25
☐ 5/54	Harvey Kuenn -Tigers	20	10
☐ 6/54	J.Morgan-Yankees/Mathews	30	20
☐ 7/54	Bob Turley - Orioles	15	10
☐ 8/54	Bob Keegan -White Sox	15	10
☐ 9/54	Willie Mays - Giants	50	25
☐ 10/54	World Series Issue	15	10
☐ 11-12/54	Dusty Rhodes - Giants	15	10
☐ 12/54	None Issued		
☐ W/55	R.Kiner/B.Sarni	15	10
☐ 2/55	None Issued		
☐ 3/55	H Score/Boyer/Howard	30	10
☐ 4/55	Alvin Dark -Giants	15	10
☐ 5/55	D.Mueller & B. Lemon	15	10
☐ 6/55	Bobby Avila-Indians	15	10
☐ 7/55	Bill Skowron - Yankees	15	10
☐ 8/55	Roy McMillian/Al Smith	15	10
☐ 9/55	Don Newcombe - Dodgers	20	10
☐ 10/55	Walt Alston/T. Byrne	20	10
☐ 11/55	Johnny Podres - Dodgers	20	10
☐ 12/55	None Issued		
☐ 1& 2/56	Al Kaline- Tigers	40	20
☐ 3/56	Rookie Report	20	10
☐ 4/56	Luis Apracio - White Sox	30	15
☐ 5/56	Mike Higgens - Red Sox	15	10
☐ 6/56	Clem Labine - Dodgers	15	10
☐ 7/56	Mickey Mantle - Yankees	70	35
☐ 8/56	Dale Long - Pirates	15	10
☐ 9/56	Yogi Berra - Yankees	30	15
☐ 10/56	World Series	15	10
☐ 11/56	Don Larson - Yankees	20	10
☐ 12/56	None Issued		
☐ W/57	Robin Roberts - Phillies	20	10
☐ 2/57	None Issued		
☐ 3/57	Scouting Reports	25	15
☐ 4/57	K. Farrell, Tighe, Scheffing	15	10
☐ 5/57	Don Blasingame-Cardinals	15	10
☐ 6/57	Yankees Breaking up D.P.	15	10
☐ 7/57	Don Hoak/Bob Boyd	15	10
☐ 8/57	Stan Musial - Cardinals	30	15
☐ 9/57	Bobby Shantz -Yankees	15	10
☐ 10/57	Babe Ruth - Yankees	30	15
☐ 11/57	None Issued		
☐ 12/57	None Issued		
☐ W/58	Lew Burdette - Braves	15	10
☐ 2/58	Von McDaniel - Cardinals	15	10
☐ 3/58	Scouting Reports	25	15
☐ 4/58	Willie Mays/Duke Snider	40	25
☐ 5/58	Ted Williams - Red Sox	50	25
☐ 6/58	Stan Musial 3000	45	20
☐ 7/58	Warren Spahn - Braves	35	20
☐ 9/58	Pete Runnels - Red Sox	15	10
☐ 11/58	None Issued		
☐ 12/58	None Issued		
☐ W/59	Turley/Jensen/Roberts	20	10
☐ 2/59	Baseball Daughters	12	8
☐ 3/59	Scouting Reports	20	15
☐ 4/59	Ernie Banks - Cubs	35	15
☐ 5/59	Juan Pizzaro -White Sox	15	10
☐ 6/59	J.Antonelli/J.Landis/C.Pascual ...	12	8
☐ 7/59	Vada Pinson- Reds	15	10
☐ 8/59	Hoyt Wilhlem - Orioles	20	12
☐ 9/59	Roy Face/ Rocky Colavito	20	10
☐ 10/59	World Series	15	10
☐ 11/59	None Issued		
☐ 12/59	None Issued		
☐ W/60	Larry Sherry/J.Roseboro	12	8
☐ 2/60	Harvey Kuenn - Tigers	15	10
☐ 3/60	Scouting Reports	20	12

☐ 4/60	Charlie Neal - Dodgers	20	10
☐ 5/60	Early Wynn - Indians	20	10
☐ 6/60	Jim Bunning - Phillies	15	10
☐ 7/60	Vern Law - Pirates	20	10
☐ 8/60	Dick Stuart - Pirates	15	10
☐ 9/60	Ron Hansen - Orioles	12	8
☐ 10-11/60	Dick Groat - Pirates	15	10
☐ W/61	Bill Virdon /R.Clemente	12	8
☐ 2/61	Ralph Hoak - Yankees	12	8
☐ 3/61	Scouting Reports	15	10
☐ 4/61	Tony Kubek - Yankees	15	10
☐ 5/61	Glen Hobbie- Cubs	12	8
☐ 6/61	Earl Battey- Twins	10	8
☐ 7/61	Wally Moon - Dodgers	12	8
☐ 8/61	Norm Cash - Tigers	10	8
☐ 9/61	Whitey Ford - Yankees	25	10
☐ 10-11/61	Mantle/Maris,Koufax	50	25
☐ W/62	Ralph Terry/Elston Howard	15	10
☐ 2/62	Joey Jay-Reds	12	8
☐ 3/62	Scouting Reports	15	10
☐ 4/62	Orlando Cepeda - Giants	25	15
☐ 5/62	Jim Landis - White Sox	12	8
☐ 6/62	Mickey Mantle - Yankees	45	25
☐ 7/62	Dick Donovan - Indians	12	8
☐ 8/62	Babe Ruth - Yankees	15	10
☐ 9/62	Rick Rollins -Twins	12	8
☐ 10/62	Tom Tresh / Frank Howard	15	10
☐ 11/62	None Issued		
☐ 12/62	None Issued		
☐ W/63	Ralph Terry - Yankees	12	8
☐ 2/63	Ty Cobb & Maury Wills	15	10
☐ 3/63	Scouting Reports	12	8
☐ 4/63	Rosters	20	15
☐ 5/63	Don Drysdale - Dodgers	20	10
☐ 6/63	Al Kaline - Tigers	30	15
☐ 7/63	Jim O'Toole- Reds	12	8
☐ 8/63	Jim Bouton/ODell/Jackson	12	8
☐ 9/63	Denny LeMaster-Braves	12	8
☐ 10/63	Al Downing - Yankees	12	8
☐ 11/63	None Issued		
☐ 12/63	None Issued		
☐ W/64	Koufax/Podres/Drysdale	25	12
☐ 2/64	Roger Maris - Yankees	45	25
☐ 3/64	Scouting Reports	25	15
☐ 4/64	Sandy Koufax - Dodgers	25	12
☐ 5/64	Harmon Killebrew- Twins	25	15
☐ 6/64	Tom Davis & Carl Yastrzemski ...	25	15
☐ 7/64	Jim Maloney - Reds	15	12
☐ 8/64	Dave Nicholson - White Sox	12	8
☐ 9/64	D.Bennett & W Smith	12	8
☐ 10/64	Johnny Evers - Braves	12	8
☐ W/65	Dick Groat - Cardinals	15	8
☐ 2/65	Reds , Larden	12	8
☐ 3/65	Scouting Reports	20	8
☐ 4/65	Cardinals/Cubs(Banks?)	12	8
☐ 5/65	Bill Freeham- Tigers	12	8
☐ 6/65	Tony Congiliaro- Red Sox	25	15
☐ 7/65	Astros/Pirates	12	8
☐ 8/65	Don Drysdale - Dodgers	25	15
☐ 9/65	P.Ward/J.Morgan	15	10
☐ 10-11/65	Sandy Amoros' - Dodgers	15	10
☐ W/66	Sandy Koufax - Dodgers	20	10
☐ 2/66	Willie Mays - Giants	20	10
☐ 3/66	Scouting Reports	15	8
☐ 4/66	Rosters	25	15
☐ 5/66	Sam McDowell - Indians	15	8
☐ 6/66	Rules	12	8
☐ 7/66	Juan Marichal - Giants	15	8
☐ 8/66	Gene Alley/Bill Mazeroski	12	8

□	9/66	George Scott - Red Sox	12	8
□	10-11/66	World Series	12	8
□	W/67	J. Palmer/ D. McNally-O's	15	10
□	2/67	Don Drysdale/Eddie Mathews/others .	20	10
□	3/67	Scouting Reports	12	8
□	4/67	Rosters	20	10
□	5/67	Roger Maris - Cardinals	25	12
□	6/67	G. Perrry/J. Marichal - Giants	20	10
□	7/67	B.Freeham/J.Wynn/others	12	8
□	8/67	Joe Horlen - White Sox	12	8
□	9/67	Tim McCarver - Cardinals	12	8
□	10-11/67	Lew Burdette/Others	12	8
□	W/68	Bob Gibson - Cardinals	20	10
□	2/68	Billy Williams - Cubs/T. Oliva-Twin ..	15	8
□	3/68	J.Bench/Others - Reds	12	8
□	4/68	Rosters	15	10
□	5/68	Rod Carew - Twins/Others	20	10
□	6/68	M.Rojas -Angels/N.Briles-Cardinals .	12	8
□	7/68	Jerry Koosman - Mets	15	8
□	8/68	Andy Kosco - Yankees	12	8
□	9/68	Matty Alou/K.Harrelson	12	8
□	10-11/68	World Series	15	10
□	W/69	Brock/Freeham	15	8
□	2/69	Mickey Mantle - Yankees	55	35
□	3/69	Scouting Reports	12	8
□	4/69	Rosters	15	10
□	5/69	Al Lopez - White Sox	12	8
□	6/69	Ernie Banks- Cubs	20	15
□	7/69	Action - Reds	12	8
□	8/69	Frank Robinson - Orioles	15	10
□	9/69	Cubs/Cardinals	12	8
□	10/69	World Series	20	10
□	11/69	Future Stars	12	8
□	12/69	Tom Seaver - Mets	30	15
□	1/70	Harmon Killebrew-Twins	20	10
□	2/70	Joe Pepitone- Yankees	15	8
□	3/70	Gene Alley - Pirates	12	8
□	4/70	Tony Perez - Reds	15	10
□	5/70	Roberto Clemente-Pirates	40	25
□	6/70	Mel Stottlemyre - Yankees	10	8
□	7/70	Ken Holtzman - Cubs	12	8
□	8/70	Sal Bando - A's	10	8
□	9/70	Tony Perez - Reds	15	8
□	10/70	Jim Palmer - Orioles	15	10
□	11/70	Johnny Bench - Reds	25	12
□	12/70	Billy Williams - Cubs	15	8
□	1/71	Brooks Robinson - Orioles	20	10
□	2/71	Juan Marichal/S. Bando/B.Singer ...	15	10
□	3/71	Carl Yastrzemski - Red Sox	15	10
□	4/71	Bob Gibson - Cardinals	15	10
□	5/71	Willie Mays - Giants	30	15
□	6/71	Tony Oliva - Twins	15	10
□	7/71	Hank Aaron - Braves	20	15
□	8/71	Vida Blue - A's	12	8
□	9/71	Joe Pepitone - Yankees	12	8
□	10/71	Brooks Robinson - Orioles	12	8
□	11/71	Bobby Murcer - Yankees	12	8
□	12/71	Joe Torre- Cardinals	12	8
□	1/72	Steve Blass - Pirates	10	8
□	2/72	Earl Williams - Braves	12	8
□	3/72	Frank Robinson - Orioles	15	10
□	4/72	Bill Melton - White Sox	12	8
□	5/72	Carl Yaz/J. Bench/Others	15	10
□	6/72	Reggie Jackson - A's	15	10
□	7/72	Richie Allen - White Sox	15	10
□	8/72	Bud Harrelson - Mets	12	8
□	9/72	Roberto Clemente -Pirates	35	15
□	10/72	Gary Nolan/J/ Bench	12	8
□	11/72	Carlton Fisk - Red Sox	15	10
□	12/72	Richie Allen - White Sox	10	8
□	1/73	Pete Rose - Reds/A's	20	10
□	2/73	Cesar Cedino -Astros	10	8
□	3/73	Harmon Killebrew-Twins	20	10
□	4/73	Don Kessinger - Cubs	10	8
□	5/73	Nolan Ryan - Angels	40	25
□	6/73	Tom Seaver - Mets	20	10
□	7/73	Pete Rose - Reds	15	10
□	8/73	Richie Allen/B. Melton/D. May-WS	12	8
□	9/73	Ken Holtzman - A's	12	8
□	10/73	Bill Russell - Dodgers	12	8
□	11/73	Jose Cardenal -Cubs	12	8
□	12/73	Willie Stargell - Pirates	15	10
□	1/74	Bert Campaneris/Y Berra	10	7
□	2/74	Bobby Bonds - Giants	10	7
□	3/74	Bobby Grich - Orioles	10	7
□	4/74	Hank Aaron - Braves	20	10
□	5/74	Ted Sizemore - Cardinals	10	7
□	6/74	Felix Millan - Mets	10	7
□	7/74	Brooks Robinson - Orioles	15	7
□	8/74	Gaylord Perry - Indians	12	7
□	9/74	Tommy John - Dodgers	10	7
□	10/74	Richie Allen - White sox	10	7
□	11/74	Jackson/Camy/Bando- A's	20	10
□	12/74	Lou Brock - Cardinals	15	7
□	1/75	Rollie Fingers - A's	10	7
□	2/75	Steve Garvey - Dodgers	15	10
□	3/75	Jeff Burroughs - Rangers	10	5
□	4/75	Jim Hunter - A's	15	10
□	5/75	Mike Schmidt - Phillies	25	15
□	6/75	Rod Carew - Twins	15	10
□	7/75	Nolan Ryan - Angels	35	20
□	8/75	Rick Monday -Cubs	10	7
□	9/75	Johnny Bench - Reds	20	10
□	10/75	Vida Blue - A's	10	7
□	11/75	Fred Lynn - Red Sox	10	7
□	12/75	Joe Morgan - Reds	12	7
□	Special	Lou Brock/Hunter/Carew	40	20
□	1/76	Pete Rose - Reds	20	10
□	2/76	Jim Palmer - Orioles	15	10
□	3/76	George Brett - Royals	20	10
□	4/76	Carlton Fisk - Red Sox	15	10
□	5/76	Frank Tanana - Angels	10	7
□	6/76	Rick Manning - Indians	10	7
□	7/76	Bill Madlock- Pirates	10	7
□	8/76	Randy Jones - Padres	10	7
□	9/76	Larry Bowa- Phillies	10	7
□	10/76	Mickey Rivers - Angels	10	7
□	11/76	Mark Fidrych- Tigers	10	7
□	12/76	Joe Morgan- Reds	15	7
□	1/77	Reds/Yankees	10	7
□	2/77	Thurmon Munson - Yank's	12	7
□	3/77	Amos Otis - Royals	7	7
□	4/77	Mark Fidrych - Tigers	7	7
□	5 /77	John Montefusco -Giants	7	7
□	6/77	Steve Carlton - Phillies	7	7
□	7 /77	Dave Parker- Pirates	7	7
□	8/77	Manny Trillo/Ivan DeJesus	7	7
□	9/77	Carl Yastrzemski - Red Sox	10	10
□	10/77	Steve Garvey- Dodgers	10	7
□	11/77	Bump Wills -Rangers	7	7
□	12/77	George Foster - Reds	7	7
□	1/78	Reggie Jackson -Yankees	20	10
□	2/78	Willie McCovey - Giants	20	10
□	3/78	Rod Carew- Twins	15	10
□	4/78	Tom Seaver -Reds	15	10
□	5/78	Cesar Cedeno - Astros	10	7
□	6/78	Garry Templeton - Cardinals	10	7
□	7/78	Dave Kingman - Cubs	10	7
□	8/78	Jim Rice - Red Sox	10	7

Date	Cover/Feature	Nr-Mt	Ex
☐ 9/78	Ron Guidry - Yankees	10	7
☐ 10/78	C.Hurdle/R.Gale-Royals	10	7
☐ 11/78	Reggie Smith -Dodgers	10	7
☐ 12/78	Dave Parker - Pirates	10	7
☐ 1/79	Dodger/R. Jackson/Yankees	10	7
☐ 2/79	Dave Winfield - Padres	15	7
☐ 3/79	Greg Luzinski - Phillies	10	7
☐ 4/79	Rich Gossage - Yankees	10	7
☐ 5/79	Jack Clark - Giants	10	7
☐ 6/79	Steve Garvey - Dodgers	10	7
☐ 7/79	Al Oliver - Rangers	7	5
☐ 8/79	Bill Buckner - Cubs	10	7
☐ 9/79	Tommy John - Yankees	10	7
☐ 10/79	Mike Schmidt - Phillies	20	10
☐ 11/79	Omar Moreno- Pirates	7	3
☐ 12/79	George Brett - Royals	15	10
☐ 1/80	World Series	7	3
☐ 2/80	Paul Molitor - Brewers	7	5
☐ 3/80	Gary Carter- Expos	7	5
☐ 4/80	Willie Stargell - Pirates	10	3
☐ 5/80	Don Baylor - Angels	7	3
☐ 6/80	Nolan Ryan/JR Richard	20	10
☐ 7/80	Burns/Trout/Bamgarten- WS	7	3
☐ 8/80	Ken Landreaux - Twins	7	3
☐ 9/80	Steve Carlton - Phillies	7	5
☐ 10/80	Reggie Jackson - Yankees	10	5
☐ 11/80	Joe Charboneau - Indians	7	3
☐ 12/80	George Brett - Royals	10	5
☐	Special	15	10
☐ 1/81	Tug McGraw - Phillies	7	3
☐ 2/81	Eddie Murray - Orioles	7	5
☐ 3/81	Ricky Henderson - A's	10	3
☐ 4/81	Mike Schmidt - Phillies	10	5
☐ 5/81	Gary Carter - Expos	7	3
☐ 6/81	Cecil Cooper - Brewers	7	3
☐ 7/81	Carlton Fisk -White Sox	7	3
☐ 8/81	F. Valenzuela- Dodgers	7	3
☐ 9/81	Danny Darwin - Rangers	7	3
☐ 10/81	Ben Davis - Yankees	5	3
☐ 11/81	Pete Rose - Phillies	10	5
☐ 12/81	Tim Raines - Expos	5	3
☐ 1/82	Steve Garvey - Dodgers	5	3
☐ 2/82	Carney Lansford - Red Sox	5	3
☐ 3/82	Rollie Fingers -Brewers	5	3
☐ 4/82	Dave Winfield - Yankees	5	3
☐ 5/82	Nolan Ryan - Astros	20	10
☐ 6/82	Jerry Reuse - Dodgers	5	3
☐ 7/82	Salome Barojas - White Sox	5	3
☐ 8/82	Dale Murphy - Braves	5	3
☐ 9/82	Rickey Henderson - A's	5	3
☐ 10/82	Robin Yount - Brewers	7	3
☐ 11/82	Kent Hrbek - Twins	5	3
☐ 12/82	Ozzie Smith/Lonnie Smith	5	3
☐ 1983-on	Common & Minor Stars	4	2
☐ 1983-on	Major & Popular Stars	2	7

BASEBALL GUIDEBOOK
(Maco Magazine Corp)

DATE	COVER/FEATURE	Nr-Mt	Ex
☐ 1964	Dick Groat - Cards	35	20
☐ 1965	Johnny Callison - Phillies	30	15
☐ 1966	Sam McDowell - Indians	20	10
☐ 1967	Brooks Robinson - Orioles	30	15
☐ 1968	Rusty Staub - Astros	20	10
☐ 1969	Juan Marichal - Giants	20	10
☐ 1969	Denny McLain - Tigers	20	10
☐ 1970	Jim McNally - Orioles	15	10
☐ 1971	Boog Powell - Orioles	15	10
☐ 1972	Vida Blue - A's	15	8
☐ 1974	Tom Seaver - Mets	20	8

Date	Cover/Feature	Nr-Mt	Ex
☐ 1977	Thurman Munson - Yankees	25	10
☐ 1978	Various Stars	15	8
☐ 1979	John Matlock - Pirates	10	8

BASEBALL IN ACTION

DATE	COVER/FEATURE	Nr-Mt	Ex
☐ 7/65	Brooks Robinson - Orioles (vol 1)	50	15

BASEBALL OFFICIAL FORECAST

DATE	COVER/FEATURE	Nr-Mt	Ex
☐ 1964	Sandy Koufax - Dodgers	30	10

BASEBALL ILLUSTRATED
(Complete Sports)

DATE	COVER/FEATURE	Nr-Mt	Ex
☐ 1967	M. Mantle/F. Robinson (first issue)	45	10
☐ 1968	Carl Yastrzemski - Red Sox	35	10
☐ 1969	B. Gibson/D. McLain	30	10
☐ 1970	Tom Seaver - Mets	30	10
☐ 1971	Johnny Bench - Reds	25	10
☐ 1972	Vida Blue - A's	15	10
☐ 1973	Dick Allen - White Sox	15	10
☐ 1975	Reggie Jackson - A's	20	10
☐ 1976	Fred Lynn - Red Sox	15	7
☐ 1978	Reggie Jackson - Yankees	15	7
☐ 1982	Ron Guidry - Yankees	15	7

BASEBALL GUIDEBOOK
(Maco)

DATE	COVER/FEATURE	Nr-Mt	Ex
☐ 1964	Dick Groat - Cards	35	15
☐ 1965	Johnny Callison - Phillies	35	10
☐ 1966	Sam McDowell - Indians	35	20
☐ 1967	Brooks Robinson - Orioles	35	25
☐ 1968	Carl Yastrzemski - Red Sox	35	25
☐ 1969	Frank Howard - Senators	30	15
☐ 1970	Dave McNally - Orioles	25	10
☐ 1974	Tom Seaver - Mets	35	10
☐ 1977	Thurmon Munson - Yanks	25	10

BASEBALL HEROES
(Whitestone)

DATE	COVER/FEATURE	Nr-Mt	Ex
☐ 1958	Hank Aaron/Red Schoendist	25	10
☐ 1959	W. Spahn/J.Jensen/E. Banks/B. Turley	50	15

BASEBALL IN ACTION
(Press Box Series)

DATE	COVER/FEATURE	Nr-Mt	Ex
☐ 7/65	Brooks Robinson - Orioles	30	15

BASEBALL LIFE STORIES

DATE	COVER/FEATURE	Nr-Mt	Ex
☐ 1953	Allie Reynolds-Yankees	50	25

BASEBALL MAGAZINE ISSUES

One of the oldest, longest running Baseball magazines ever made. This magazine is pursued by baseball historians and those who collect older baseball players. The earliest issues (1908-1920) are pursued by collectors. Issues after 1936 are considered common. The issues in the 40's have paper stock that easily decays. The magazine lost its prominance in 1946 when Sport magazine and Baseball Digest came out to cut into Baseball Magazine market share. By the 1950's it ended its monthly magazine program (there are gaps in the run) and ceased production in 1957. The magazine had two revivals in the 1960's and the 1980's. Listed below is the comon issue price and the prices on key cover issues.

DATE	COVER/FEATURE	Nr-Mt	Ex
☐ 5/08	Illustration First Issue	3,000	1,500
☐ 1908	Illustration First Year	500	300
☐ 9/08	Cy Young	500	300
☐ 1909	Common Cover	350	150
☐ 1910	Common Cover	275	100
☐ 11-14	Common Cover	225	75
☐ 15-17	Common Cover	150	65
☐ 18-20	Common Cover	100	40

		Nr-Mt	Ex
☐ 3/16	Joe Jackson Number	600	250
☐ 12/16	Babe Ruth (FC)	500	200
☐ 4/18	George Sisler	300	125
☐ 1/19	Ty Cobb	450	150
☐ 4/20	Babe Ruth	450	200
☐ 6/20	Ty Cobb	450	150
☐ 10/20	Babe Ruth	450	200
☐ 21-24	Common Cover	95	35
☐ 10/21	Babe Ruth	450	200
☐ 12/23	Babe Ruth	450	200
☐ 25-29	Common Cover	70	25
☐ 3/25	Roger Hornsby	200	50
☐ 1/26	Roger Hornsby	200	50
☐ 12/26	Babe Ruth	450	200
☐ 1/27	Ty Cobb	350	150
☐ 9/27	Lou Gehrig (FC)	350	150
☐ 30-36	Common Cover	50	20
☐ 3/30	Lefty Grove	75	30
☐ 7/30	Grover Alexander	75	30
☐ 12/30	Connie Mack	75	30
☐ 2/33	Jimmy Foxx	75	30
☐ 9/33	Walter Johnson	75	30
☐ 12/33	Carl Hubbell	75	30
☐ 1/34	Babe Ruth	350	150
☐ 37-40	Common Cover	45	20
☐ 9/37	Joe DiMaggio (FC)	375	125
☐ 5/38	Joe DiMaggio	300	100
☐ 7/39	Loe Gehrig/others	150	50
☐ 8/39	Lou Gehrig	250	100
☐ 11/39	Joe DiMaggio/Walters	150	75
☐ 12/39	Ted Williams (FC)	150	75
☐ 41-50	Common Cover	35	15
☐ 8/41	Ted Williams Death of Lou Gehrig	75	25
☐ 1/42	Lou Boudreau (Joe DiMaggio) 41 Dodgers	50	25
☐ 2/42	Mell Ott DiMaggio Streak	50	30
☐ 5/42	Hank Greenberg - (Lou Finney)	40	20
☐ 2/43	Phil Rizzuto (Lou Boudreau)	40	20
☐ 2/44	Earl Wynn	35	20
☐ 7/44	Jimmy Foxx/C. Grimm .All Star Game	45	20
☐ 9/44	Mel Ott	45	20
☐ 4/46	Mel Ott (Pee Wee Reese)Yankee Stadium	35	15
☐ 5/46	Bob Feller/Lou Boudreau	40	15
☐ 6/46	Harry Truman	35	15
☐ 10/46	Ted Williams/Bobby Doerr	50	20
☐ 11/46	Bob Feller/Hal Newhouser	45	20
☐ 6/47	Ted Williams	125	35
☐ 3/48	Yogi Berra	35	25
☐ 6/48	Harry Truman	45	25
☐ 7/48	Johnny Mize	45	20
☐ 9/48	Stan Musial	60	35
☐ 10/48	Lou Boudreau	70	35
☐ 11/48	Connie Mack	45	25
☐ 12/48	Lou Boudreau	35	25
☐ 1/49	Williams,Doerr, DiMaggio,	45	25
☐ 5/49	Stan Musial/Ted Williams	75	25
☐ 9/49	Casey Stengel	40	15
☐ 12/49	Casey Stengel	40	15
☐ 5/50	Stan Musial, Schoendiest, Slaughter,Marion	45	15
☐ 10/50	Richie Ashburn	35	15
☐ 51-65	Common Cover	30	12
☐ 4/51	Joe Gargiolla	45	15
☐ 5/51	Warren Spahn	45	15
☐ 8/51	Micky Mantle	250	150
☐ 9/51	Gil Hodges	45	15
☐ 10/51	World Series	35	15
☐ 11/51	Bob Feller	40	15
☐ 12/51	Cy Young	40	15
☐ 2/52	Stan Musial	50	15
☐ 4/52	Roger Hornsby	35	15
☐ 5/52	Richie Ashburn	45	15
☐ 6/52	Willie Mays	45	15
☐ 7/52	Babe Ruth	45	15
☐ S/53	Pee Wee Reese	45	15
☐ 5/53	Johnny Mize	35	15
☐ 6/53	Joe DiMaggio/others	55	15

		Nr-Mt	Ex
☐ 7/53	Billy Bruton/Mickey Mantle	95	25
☐ 8/53	Luke Appling	35	12
☐ 9/53	Mickey Vernon	35	12
☐ 10/53	Gil Hodges	35	12
☐ 11/53	Red Schoendienst/Pee Wee Reese	45	12
☐ 9/54	Casey Stengel	40	12
☐ 6/56	Ted Williams	55	25
☐ 7/56	Mickey Mantle	75	25
☐ 8/56	Bob Friend/Dale Long	25	12
☐ 10/56	World Series/Casey Stengel	25	12
☐ 5/57	Don Larsen - Yanks	25	12
☐ 9/57	Bob Feller	35	12
☐ 11/64	Johnny Callison	25	12
☐ 12/64	Brooks Robinson	35	12
☐ 1/65	Cardinal Team	25	12
☐ 3/65	Frank Howard	30	12
☐ 10/79	Pete Rose	20	12
☐ 4/80	Pete Rose	25	12
☐ 6/80	Bruce Sutter	15	08
☐ 8/80	Carl Yaz	15	08
☐ 10/80	Tommy John	12	08
☐ 4/81	George Brett	15	08
☐ 5/81	DaveWinfield	12	08

BASEBALL MANAGERS' (OFFICIAL) FORECAST

(Official Sports Inc)

DATE	COVER/FEATURE	Nr-Mt	Ex
☐ 1964	Sandy Koufax - Dodgers	25	10

BASEBALL MONTHLY

DATE	COVER/FEATURE	Nr-Mt	Ex
☐ 3/62	Baseball Players	35	10
☐ 4/62	Artist Drawing	25	10
☐ 5/62	Rocky Colavito - Indians	35	10
☐ 6/62	Don Drysdale - Dodgers	30	10

BASEBALL QUARTERLY

DATE	COVER/FEATURE	Nr-Mt	Ex
☐ W/77	Lou Gehrig/Babe Ruth	20	5
☐ F/78	Ron Guidry - Yanks	20	5
☐ 6/79	Reggie Jackson - Yanks	20	5

BASEBALL REGISTER

(The Sporting News)

These are annuals produced by The Sporting News. Not as popular as the Baseball Guide

DATE	COVER/FEATURE	Nr-Mt	Ex
☐ 1940	Ty Cobb	150	100
☐ 1941-1949	Illustrated	50	35
☐ 1947	Walter Johnson	60	35
☐ 1950	Joe DiMaggio	100	45
☐ 1951-1959	Illustrated	40	25
☐ 1960-1965	Illustrated	30	20
☐ 1966	Sandy Koufax	35	20
☐ 1967	Ken Boyer	30	20
☐ 1968	Jim Lonborg	25	15
☐ 1969	Willie Horton	25	15
☐ 1970	Tom Seaver	30	15
☐ 1971	Willie Mays	30	15
☐ 1972	Joe Torre	25	12
☐ 1973	Wilbur Wood	25	12
☐ 1974	Pete Rose	30	10
☐ 1975	Jim Hunter	25	10
☐ 1976	Jim Palmer	25	10
☐ 1977	Joe Morgan	20	10
☐ 1978	Rod Carew	20	8
☐ 1979	Ron Guidry	15	8
☐ 1980	Carl Yastrzemski	25	10
☐ 1981	George Brett	20	10
☐ 1982	Tom Seaver	25	10
☐ 1983	Bruce Sutter	15	8
☐ 1984	John Denny	15	8
☐ 1985	Willie Hernandez	15	8
☐ 86-97	Misc.	15	8

BASEBALL RECORD BOOK
(The Sporting News)

DATE	COVER/FEATURE	Nr-Mt	Ex
☐ 1975	Lou Brock - Cardinals	20	10

BASEBALL RECORDS
(Dell)

DATE	COVER/FEATURE	Nr-Mt	Ex
☐ 1958	....	20	10

BASEBALL REVIEW
(Sport)

DATE	COVER/FEATURE	Nr-Mt	Ex
☐ 1959	Mantle/Banks/Mays/Musial	45	10

BASEBALL SCENE
(Palisides)

DATE	COVER/FEATURE	Nr-Mt	Ex
☐ 1980	Willie Stargell - Pirates	20	10

BASEBALL SPORTS STARS
(Hewfred Publications)

DATE	COVER/FEATURE	Nr-Mt	Ex
☐ 1968	Orlando Cepeda/Carl Yastrzemski ...	30	10
☐ 1969	Denny McLain - Tigers	25	10
☐ 1970	Tug McGraw/Tommy Agee-Mets	20	10
☐ 1971	Johnny Bench - Reds	20	10
☐ 1972	Roberto Clemente - Pirates	35	10
☐ 1973	Johnny Bench - Reds	20	10
☐ 1974	Pete Rose - Reds	20	10
☐ 1975	Reggie Jackson - A's	20	10

BASEBALL STARS
(Dell)

DATE	COVER/FEATURE	Nr-Mt	Ex
☐ 1949	Stan Musial - Cardinals	70	20
☐ 1950	DiMaggio/Williams/Robinson	125	15
☐ 1951	Phil Rizzuto - Yankees	65	25
☐ 1952	Bobby Thompson - Pirates	40	15
☐ 1953	Robin Roberts - Phillies	45	15
☐ 1954	Ted Williams - Red Sox	95	15
☐ 1955	Stan Musial - Cards	55	15
☐ 1956	Mickey Mantle - Yankees	125	25
☐ 1957	Don Larson - Yankees	45	15
☐ 1958	Ted Williams - Red Sox	75	15
☐ 1959	Warren Spahn - Braves	50	15
☐ 1960	Hank Aaron/Earl Wynn/Harvey Kuenn	35	15
☐ 1961	Vern Law - Pirates	30	15
☐ 1962	Colavito/Cepeda/Jay/Gentile	30	15
☐ 1963	Maury Wills - Dodgers	30	15
☐ 1964	Mickey Mantle/Sandy Koufax	50	25
☐ 1965	Dean Chance - Angels	35	15
☐ 1966	Sandy Koufax - Dodgers	35	15
☐ 1967	Sandy Koufax - Dodgers	35	12
☐ 1968	Lou Brock - Cardinals	30	12

BASEBALL SUPERSTARS

DATE	COVER/FEATURE	Nr-Mt	Ex
☐ 1979	Pete Rose/ Ron Guidry	15	5

BASEBALL THRILLS
(Sports Action Magazine)

DATE	COVER/FEATURE	Nr-Mt	Ex
☐ 1961	Mickey Mantle	60	25

BASEBALL TODAY
(Phi Publishing/Ideal Publ/JmJ Ent)

DATE	COVER/FEATURE	Nr-Mt	Ex
☐ 1977	Johnny Bench - Reds	15	7
☐ 1978	Reggie Jackson - Yankees	15	7
☐ 1979	Ron Guidry - Yankees	10	5
☐ 1980	Willie Stargell - Pirates	10	5
☐ 1981	George Brett - Royals	15	5
☐ 1982	Ron Cey - Dodgers	10	5
☐ 1983	Hrbek/Schmidt/Yount/Carter	10	5
☐ 1984	Steve Rogers/Wade Boggs/Moseby .	10	5

BASEBALL YEARBOOK
(True)

DATE	COVER/FEATURE	Nr-Mt	Ex
☐ 1950	Ted Williams -Red Sox	125	25
☐ 1951	Ralph Kiner - Priates	50	20
☐ 1952	Stan Musial - Cards	60	25
☐ 1953	Mantle/Roberts/Sauer/Shantz	50	20
☐ 1954	Campy/Rosen/Mathews/Porterfield ..	50	20
☐ 1956	Mantle/Musial/Berra/Mathews	35	15
☐ 1957	Mickey Mantle - Yankees	55	15
☐ 1958	Mickey Mantle/Stan Musial	55	15
☐ 1959	....	30	15
☐ 1960	Larry Sherry - Dodgers	30	15
☐ 1961	Dick Groat - Pirates	30	15
☐ 1962	Mickey Mantle/Roger Maris	30	15

BASEBALL YEARBOOK
(Popular)

DATE	COVER/FEATURE	Nr-Mt	Ex
☐ 1963	Drysdale/Mantle/Mays	35	15
☐ 1964	Koufax/Yaz,Howard	35	15
☐ 1965	Elston Howard - Yankees	35	15
☐ 1966	Koufax/Mantle/Mays	35	15
☐ 1967	F. Robinson/S. Koufax	35	15
☐ 1968	R. Smith/D. Maxvill	20	10
☐ 1969	Bob Gibson/McLain/Lolich	25	10
☐ 1970	Tom Seaver/ Jerry Koosman	25	10
☐ 1971	Brooks Robinson/Johnny Bench	20	10
☐ 1972	Bob Clemente/Vida Blue	30	10

BIG LEAGUE BASEBALL

DATE	COVER/FEATURE	Nr-Mt	Ex
☐ 1965	Tony Oliva - Twins	35	10

BLACK SPORTS
(Barron Pub)

This magazine covers all sports. It is rather tough to find.

DATE	COVER/FEATURE	Nr-Mt	Ex
☐ 4/71	Lew Alcindor/Oscar Robertson	65	15
☐ 6/71	Bob Gibson	40	15
☐ 7/71	Muhammad Ali	50	15
☐ 8/71	Ernie Banks	45	15
☐ 9/71	Track	25	10
☐ 10/71	Bob Hayes	30	15
☐ 11/71	Bat	20	10
☐ 12/71	OJ Simpson	35	10
☐ 1/72	ABA/NBA merger	20	10
☐ 2/72	Football player	20	10
☐ 3/72	Wilt Chamberlain	30	10
☐ 4/72	Mel Davis	20	10
☐ 5/72	Hank Aaron	30	10
☐ 7/72	Frank Robinson	30	10
☐ 10/72	Wilie Lanier	20	10
☐ 11/72	Bob Clemente	75	30
☐ 1/73	Willis Reed	30	15
☐ 2/73	Franco Harris	25	10
☐ 4/73	Archie Clark	20	10
☐ 5/73	Richie Allen	20	10
☐ 6/73	Willie Mays	35	10
☐ 7/73	Charlie Sifford	20	10
☐ 8/73	Orlando Cepeda	20	10
☐ 10/73	Duane Thomas	20	10
☐ 11/73	Larry Brown	20	10
☐ 12/73	Wilt Chamberlain	25	10
☐ 1/74	OJ Simpson	35	10
☐ 2/74	Nate Archibald	25	10
☐ 3/74	L. Kenon/J. Williams	20	10
☐ 4/74	Pete Maravich	85	40
☐ 5/74	Bobby Bonds	25	10
☐ 6/74	Hank Aaron	40	15
☐ 7/74	Charlie Finley	30	10
☐ 8/74	Dick Allen	20	10
☐ 9/74	Ali/Foreman	35	10
☐ 10/74	J. Brockington	25	10

☐ 11/74	Joe Greene	25	10
☐ 2/77	George Foreman	25	10
☐ 4/78	Marice Lucas	20	10

COMPLETE BASEBALL
(ATLAS)

DATE	COVER/FEATURE	Nr-Mt	Ex
☐ 1949	Ted Williams/Joe DiMaggio/Stan Musial	95	25
☐ 1950	Ted Williams/Stan Musial	95	25
☐ F/50	Musial/Roberts/Doby/Robinson	75	25
☐ W/50	Musial/Rizzuto/,Kell/Others	50	25
☐ S/50	Yogi Berra/Dell Crandall	50	25
☐ s/51	Ralph Kiner - Pirates	50	25
☐ F/51	Robinson/Berra/Kiner/Feller	50	25
☐ S/51	Williams/Musial/Kiner/Others	50	25
☐ S/52	Reese/Musial/Ashburn/Other	50	25
☐ 7/52	Richie Ashburn - Phillies	65	25
☐ 9/52	Gil Hodges - Dodgers	60	25
☐ 11/52	Allie Reynolds - Yankees	60	25
☐ 2/53	Robin Roberts, Sniders,Mantle	75	25
☐ 4/53	Mantle, Musial, others	65	25
☐ S/53	Stan Musial - Cards	50	25
☐ 9/53	Curt Simmons - Phillies	45	25
☐ 12/53	Roy Campanella - Dodgers	55	25
☐ W/53	Ted Williams - Red Sox	95	25
☐ 1961	Dick Groat - Pirates	45	25

COMPLETE SPORTS BASEBALL ILLUSTRATED

DATE	COVER/FEATURE	Nr-Mt	Ex
☐ 1966	S. Koufax/D. Drysdale	25	15
☐ 1967	M. Mantle/F. Robinson	35	15
☐ 1968	Carl Yastrzemski - Red Sox	25	10
☐ 1969	Denny McLain/Bob Gibson	20	10
☐ 1970	Tom Seaver - Mets	25	10
☐ 1971	Johnny Bench - Reds	20	10
☐ 1972	Vida Blue - A's	15	7
☐ 1973	Dick Allen - White Sox	15	7
☐ 1974	Nolan Ryan - Angels	40	15
☐ 1975	Reggie Jackson - A's	25	10
☐ 1976	Fred Lynn - Red Sox	15	7
☐ 1977	Nolan Ryan - Astros	40	15
☐ 1978	Reggie Jackson - Yankees	15	7
☐ 1979	Jim Rice - Red Sox	15	7
☐ 1980	Pete Rose - Reds	15	7

COMPLETE SPORTS DIGEST
(Complete Sports Inc. 5x7 or 5x8 in size)

DATE	COVER/FEATURE	Nr-Mt	Ex
☐ 1964	Jimmy Brown - Browns	20	10
☐ 1965	J. Morris/C.Hennigan	15	10
☐ 1966	Jimmy Brown/Jack Kemp	25	10
☐ 1967	Bart Starr - Packers	30	10
☐ 1968	Joe Namath - Jets	20	10

COMPLETE SPORTS MAGAZINE (BASEBALL)

DATE	COVER/FEATURE	Nr-Mt	Ex
☐ 1962	Mickey Mantle - Yankees	45	25
☐ 5/62	Roger Maris - Yankees	45	25
☐ S/65	Mays/Mantle/Chance	45	25
☐ 9/65	Micky Mantle/Bill Bradley	45	20
☐ 11/65	Fran Tarkenton - Vikings	25	15
☐ 1/66	Cookie Gilchrist - Bronco's	25	15
☐ 3/66	Elgin Baylor - Lakers	25	15
☐ 5/66	Maury Wills - Dodgers	25	15
☐ 7/66	Willie Mays - Giants	35	15
☐ 9/66	Joe Namath - Jets	45	15
☐ 11/66	Johnny Unitas - Colts	25	15
☐ 1/67	Bart Starr/ John Brodie	25	15
☐ 3/67	Oscar Robertson - Royals	25	15
☐ 5/67	Juan Marichal - Giants	35	15
☐ 7/67	Arnold Palmer - Golf	35	15
☐ 9/67	Gale Sayers - Bears	30	15
☐ 11/67	Lenny Dawson - Chiefs	30	15
☐ 1/68	Bart Starr - Packers	20	10
☐ 3/68	Oscar Robertson - Bucks	20	10

☐ 5/68	Mickey Mantle - Yankees	45	20
☐ 7/68	Bradley/Robinson/Beliveau	30	15
☐ 9/68	Roman Gabrial - Rams	20	10
☐ 11/68	Gale Sayers/Leroy Kelly	20	10
☐ 1/69	Johnny Unitas - Colts	20	10
☐ 3/69	Oscar Robertson - Bucks	20	10
☐ 5/69	Al Kaline/Yaz/Hull/Hayes	35	15
☐ 7/69	Bradley/Mays/Unitas	30	15
☐ 9/69	Sonny Jurgensen - Redskins	15	10
☐ 11/69	Fran Tarkenton - Vikings	15	10
☐ 1/70	Dick Butkus - Bears	40	20
☐ 3/70	Walt Frazier - Knicks	30	15
☐ S/70	Reggie Jackson - A's	35	15
☐ S/70	Vikings/Chiefs	20	10
☐ f/70	Johnny Unitas - Colts	20	10
☐ W/70	Roman Gabriel - Rams	15	10
☐ S/71	B.Robinson/Orr/Reed	35	15

CORD SPORTSFACTS BASEBALL NEWS
(Cord Communications Corp 69-74. Went to paperbacks)

DATE	COVER/FEATURE	Nr-Mt	Ex
☐ 1969	Willie McCovey - Giants	35	15
☐ 1969	Lou Brock - Cards	20	10
☐ 1970	Tom Seaver - Mets	35	15
☐ 1971	Wes Parker - Dodgers	20	10
☐ 1971	Brooks Robinson- Orioles	25	10
☐ 1972	Willie Stargell - Pirates	20	10
☐ 1973	Johnny Bench - Reds	20	10
☐ 1974	Reggie Jackson - A's	20	10

CORD SPORTSFACTS BASEBALL REPORT
(Cord Communications Corp. 69-74)

DATE	COVER/FEATURE	Nr-Mt	Ex
☐ 1969	Mickey Lolich - Tigers	20	10
☐ 1970	Frank Robinson - Orioles	20	10
☐ 1970	Johnny Bench - Reds	20	10
☐ 1971		12	7
☐ 1972	Vida Blue - A's	12	7
☐ 1973	Hank Aaron - Braves	20	10
☐ 1974	Pete Rose - Reds	20	10

COUNTRYWIDE SPORTS
This Magazine covers more than just baseball.

DATE	COVER/FEATURE	Nr-Mt	Ex
☐ 6/69	Tony Conigliaro/Mickey Lolich	30	10
☐ 8/70	Tom Seaver/Joe Kapp/Willis Reed	30	10
☐ 10/70	Tom Seaver/Len Dawson	30	10
☐ 2/71	Brooks Robinson	30	10
☐ 4/71	Tom Seaver/Brooks Robinson	30	10
☐ 6/71	Luis Aparico/Bobby Orr	30	10

DELL BASEBALL GUIDE
Originally published by Whitman 37-38. These are 4x5" or 5x7 guide books that cover baseball statistics. Most noted by having a woman baseball player on the back of every book.

DATE	COVER/FEATURE	Nr-Mt	Ex
☐ 1937		35	15
☐ 1938		30	15
☐ 1941	Bob Feller	35	15
☐ 1942	Ted Williams	40	20
☐ 1943	Ted Williams	40	20
☐ 1944	Stan Musial	35	20
☐ 1945	Marty Marion	25	10
☐ 1946	Hal Newhouser	25	10
☐ 1947	Stan Musial	35	10
☐ 1948	Ted Williams	40	20
☐ 1949	Lou Boudreau	35	10
☐ 1950	Joe Page	25	10
☐ 1951	Phil Rizzuto	25	10
☐ 1952	Stan Musial	35	15
☐ 1953	Robin Roberts	35	15

DELL SPORTS
(or Dell Sports Baseball Annual)
This has many titles, see 'Official Baseball Annual', also called Dell sports

magazine Baseball, Dell Sports. No publications were made in 1969.
(Dell Baseball Annual)

DATE	COVER/FEATURE	Nr-Mt	Ex
□ 1953	Mickey Mantle - Yankees	150	50
□ 1954	Billy Martin - Yankees	65	25
□ 1955	Willie Mays- Giants	55	20
□ 1956	Pee Wee Reese - Dodgers	75	25
□ 1957	Mickey Mantle - Yankees	100	35

(Dell Sports Baseball)

DATE	COVER/FEATURE	Nr-Mt	Ex
□ 1958	Lew Burdette - Braves	30	15
□ 1959	Bob Turley - Yankees	35	15

(Dell Sports Magazine Baseball)

DATE	COVER/FEATURE	Nr-Mt	Ex
□ 4/60	Nellie Fox - White Sox	45	15
□ 4/61	Mazeroski/Ford/Richardson	35	15
□ 4/62	Roger Maris - Yankees	30	15
□ 6/62	Jay/Colavito/Cepeda/Gentile	20	10
□ 7/62	Whitey Ford - Yankees	25	10
□ 4/63	Tom Tresh - Yankees	30	10
□ 7/63	Harmon Killebrew - Twins	30	15

(Dell Sports)

DATE	COVER/FEATURE	Nr-Mt	Ex
□ 5/64	Sandy Koufax/Mickey Mantle	45	15
□ 7/64	Dick Stuart - Red Sox	25	10
□ 3/65	Boyer/B. Robinson	25	10
□ 3/66	Sandy Koufax- Dodgers	25	10
□ 7/66	Tony Oliva -Twins	25	10
□ 3/67	Frank Robinson - Orioles	25	10
□ 5/67	Sandy Koufax - Dodgers	25	10
□ 7/67	Boog Powell - Orioles	20	10
□ 1/68	Lew Alcindor- UCLA	20	10
□ 1969	Carl Yastrzemski - Red Sox	25	10
□ 5/68	Lou Brock - Cards	20	10
□ 7/68	Harmon Killebrew - Twins	25	10

(Dell Sports Baseball)

DATE	COVER/FEATURE	Nr-Mt	Ex
□ 1970	Tom Seaver/Jerry Koosman	20	10
□ 1971	Brooks Robinson - Orioles	25	10
□ 1972	Bob Clemente/Vida Blue	35	15
□ 1973	Richie Allen - WhiteSox	25	10
□ 1974	Hank Aaron - Braves	25	10
□ 1975	Lou Brock - Cardinals	25	10
□ 1976	Fred Lynn - Red Sox	20	10
□ 1978	Reggie Jackson - Yankees	20	10

FACTBOOK BASEBALL
(Tommy Kay's)

DATE	COVER/FEATURE	Nr-Mt	Ex
□ 5/75	Garvey/Marshall/Burrough	25	5

FAMOUS SLUGGERS YEARBOOK
These are annuals that are heavily collected.

DATE	COVER/FEATURE	Nr-Mt	Ex
□ 1921	First issue	200	100
□ 22-26	None issued		
□ 27-32	Illustrations	65	35
□ 1933	Jimmy Foxx	75	35
□ 1934	Lou Gehrig/Paul Waner	100	35
□ 1935	Vaughn/Myer	55	25
□ 1936	Lou Gehrig/ Mel Ott	100	35
□ 1937	Charlie Gehringer/Sid Medwick	65	25
□ 1938	Illustration	45	20
□ 1939	Jimmy Foxx/Ernie Lombardi	45	20
□ 1940	Joe DiMaggio	75	35
□ 1941	Joe DiMaggio & others	75	35
□ 1942	Joe DiMaggio & Ted Williams	75	35
□ 1943	Ted Williams	65	35
□ 1944	Stan Musial	50	35
□ 1945	Lou Boudreau	35	25
□ 1946	Illustration	30	20
□ 1947	Stan Musial/Micky Vernon	30	20
□ 1948	Lou Boudreau	30	20
□ 1949	Ted Williams/Stan Musial	40	20
□ 1950	Jackie Robinson/Ted Williams	50	30
□ 1951	Ralph Kiner	30	20
□ 1952	Illustration	25	15
□ 1953	Illustration	25	15
□ 1954	Illustration	20	10

DATE	COVER/FEATURE	Nr-Mt	Ex
□ 1955	Ted Williams	50	30
□ 1956	Al Kaline/Richie Ashburn	45	25
□ 1957	Mickey Mantle/ Hank Aaron	40	20
□ 1958	Ted Williams	40	20
□ 1959	Stan Musial	40	20
□ 1960	Rocky Colavito	40	20
□ 1961	Ernie Banks	40	20
□ 1962	Roger Maris	40	20
□ 1963	T. Davis/P.Runnels	15	10
□ 1964	Carl Yastrzemski/Tommy Davis	15	10
□ 1965	Roberto Clemente	40	20
□ 1966	Roberto Clemente	40	20
□ 1967	Frank Robinson/Matty Alou	15	10
□ 1968	Roberto Clemente/Carl Yaz	40	20
□ 1969	Pete Rose/Carl Yaz	25	10
□ 1970	Pete Rose/Rod Carew	25	10
□ 1971	Johnny Bench	25	10
□ 1972	Willie Stargell	15	5
□ 1973	Dick Allen	15	5
□ 1974	Hank Aaron	15	5
□ 1975	Johnny Bench	15	5
□ 76-78	....	5	2

GREAT MOMENTS IN SPORTS
(Famous Pub, Cape Magazine Mgt, Four Star Mgt) 57-64

DATE	COVER/FEATURE	Nr-Mt	Ex
□ 2/57	Vol 1 #1	25	10
□ 8/57	#2 Don Larsen/Yogi Berra	25	10
□ 2/58	#3 Bob Cousy- Celtics	35	10
□ 5/58	#4 Ted Williams - Red Sox	50	25
□ 7/58	#5 Joe DiMaggio - Yankees	45	25
□ 9/58	#6 Casey Stengel - Yankees	25	10
□ 9/59	#7 Ted Williams - Red Sox	25	10
□ 12/59	#8 Cleveland Browns	25	10
□ 3/60	#9 Ray Robinson	20	10
□ 6/60	#10 Archie Moore	25	10
□ 3/61	#1 Vol 2 Rocky Marcino	25	10
□ 6/61	Kubek/Richardson	25	10
□ 9/61	Willie Mays	25	10
□ 11/61	Bob Schloredt	20	10
□ 1/62	Paul Hornung	25	10
□ 5/62	Whitey Ford	25	10
□ 7/62	Mickey Mantle	25	7
□ 9/62	Mickey Mantle	20	7
□ 11/62	Mantle/Maris	25	10
□ 3/63	Baltimore Colts	15	7
□ 6/63	Stan Musial	20	10
□ 9/63	Frank Thomas	15	7
□ 12/63	Roger Staubach	25	10
□ 3/64	YA Tittle	15	7
□ 6/64	Sandy Koufax	25	10

HANK AARON MEDIA GUIDE

DATE	COVER/FEATURE	Nr-Mt	Ex
....		15	25

HOME RUN HITTERS
(Ideal Publishing)

DATE	COVER/FEATURE	Nr-Mt	Ex
□ 1962	Mantle/Maris/ Ruth	35	15

INSIDE BASEBALL (BIG LEAGUE)
(Weider Publications)

DATE	COVER/FEATURE	Nr-Mt	Ex
□ 7/52	Robinson/Feller/Berra/Musial	85	50
□ 8/52	R. Campy/Gil McDougald	55	25
□ 10/52	Phil Rizzuto/S. Musial	55	25
□ 11/52	Rosen, Sauer/Thomson/DiMaggio ...	55	25
□ 1/53	Stan Musial - Cardinals	55	25
□ 2/53	Jackie Robinson - Dodgers	85	25
□ 3/53	Robin Roberts - Phillies	55	25
□ 6/53	Snider,Rosen, Kiner,Irvin,..	55	25
□ 10/53	Al Rosen - Indians	55	25
□ 2/54	Ed Mathews - Braves	55	25

			Nr-Mt	Ex
☐ 1961	Mickey Mantle/Dick Groat		55	25
☐ 1962	M Mantle/Maris/Robinson,		55	25
☐ 1963	Willie Mays & Maury Wills		45	25
☐ 1964	Sandy Koufax/Al Kaline		45	25
☐ 1965	Ken Boyer/Brooks Robinson		30	25

INSIDE SPORTS

DATE	COVER/FEATURE	Nr-Mt	Ex
☐ 6/53	Casey Stengel - Yankees	50	20
☐ 8/53	Stan Musial - Cardinals	60	20
☐ 11/53	Roy Campanella/Yogi Berra	60	20

MAJOR LEAGUE BASEBALL
(Cavalier)

DATE	COVER/FEATURE	Nr-Mt	Ex
☐ 1961	Bobby Richardson - Yankees	30	20
☐ 1962	Whitey Ford - NY Yankees	35	15
☐ 1963	Willie Mays & Mickey Mantle	40	15
☐ 1966	Sandy Koufax, Maury Wills	30	15

MAZAROSKI BASEBALL
Many regional covers . This highlights the key cover.

DATE	COVER/FEATURE	Nr-Mt	Ex
☐ 1983	Reggie Jackson - Angels	20	10
☐ 1984	Eddie Murray - Orioles	10	5
☐ 1985	Dale Murphy - Braves	10	5
☐ 1985	Ryan Sandberg - Cubs	10	5
☐ 1985	DeCinces or Gooden or Gibson	10	5
☐ 1986	Clark or Valenzuela or Parrish or Barfield	10	5
☐ 1986	George Brett or Rose or Mattingly	15	8
☐ 1987	Sandberg or Schmidt	15	8
☐ 1987	Anderson or Fernandez or Evans or Scott or Carter or Joyner	10	5
☐ 1988	Dawson or Clark or McGwire or Mattingly or Murphy or Trammell or Boggs or Davis or Raines or Bell or Puckett or O.Smith or Hershiser	10	5
☐ 1989	Strawberry or McGriff or Galaragga or Molitor or Maddux or Gibson or Canseco or Greenwell	10	5
☐ 1990	Blyleven or Stewart or Mitchell or Williams or Johnson or Ripken Jr or Sierra or Gruber or Bo Jackson or Guerrero	10	5
☐ 1991	Viola or Fisk or Drabek or Larkin or Griffey Jr or Stieb or Strawberry or Henderson	10	5
☐ 1992-1997	Key players	15	8
☐	Other Players	5	2

MICKEY MANTLE: BASEBALL KING
(SI-News Publishing, Ardsley, N.Y.)

DATE	COVER/FEATURE	Nr-Mt	Ex
☐ 1957	Mickey Mantle	75	30

MICKEY MANTLE BASEBALL MAGAZINE
(H.S. Publications)

DATE	COVER/FEATURE	Nr-Mt	Ex
☐ 6/62	Mickey Mantle - Yankees	45	20
☐ 8/62	Stan Musial - Cardinals	40	15
☐ 10/62	Sandy Koufax - Dodgers	35	15

MAJOR LEAGUE BASEBALL
(DELL) (130 Pg)
These were produced from 37-48 by Whiteman then by Dell. They
stopped production in 1953.

DATE	COVER/FEATURE	Nr-Mt	Ex
☐ 37-39	Illustration	75	35
☐ 1940	None Issued		
☐ 1941	Bob Feller	25	15
☐ 1942	Stan Musial	25	15
☐ 1943	Ted Williams	35	15
☐ 1944	Stan Musial	25	15
☐ 1945	Martin Marion	35	15
☐ 1946	Harold Newhouser	35	10
☐ 1947	Stan Musial	40	15
☐ 1948	Ted Williams	40	20

			Nr-Mt	Ex
☐ 1949	Lou Bourdreau		30	15
☐ 1950	Joe Page		30	15
☐ 1951	Phil Rizzuto		20	12
☐ 1952	Stan Musial		40	12
☐ 1953	Robin Roberts		30	12

NATIONAL LEAGUE GREEN BOOK

DATE	COVER/FEATURE	Nr-Mt	Ex
☐ 1935-1938		75	35
☐ 1939-1947		65	25
☐ 1948-1953		55	20
☐ 1954	NL All Star Team	65	20
☐ 1955	Mays/Musial/Spahn/(others)	65	20
☐ 1956	Dodgers Photo's	65	20
☐ 1957-1958		45	20
☐ 1959	Stan Musial - Warren Spahn	45	20
☐ 1960	Musial/McCovey/Snider/Banks	50	20
☐ 1961	Howard/Spahn/Robinson	40	20
☐ 1962-1963		35	15
☐ 1964	Stan Musial Farewell	40	20
☐ 1965-1969		25	15
☐ 1970	McCovey/Rose/Mets,	40	20
☐ 1971-1972		25	15
☐ 1973	Roberto Clemente	40	20
☐ 1974	Hank Aaron	40	20
☐ 1975	Schmidt/Aaron/Brock/Garvey	25	15
☐ 1976	Bench	25	12
☐ 1977-1980		20	10
☐ 1981	Schmidt/All Stars	15	5
☐ 1982	Nolan Ryan/Schmidt/Rose	20	10
☐ 1983-1985		15	5
☐ 1986	Nolan Ryan/Pete Rose/Gooden	20	10
☐ 1987-1990		12	5
☐ 1991-1997		10	4

NBC COMPLETE BASEBALL

DATE	COVER/FEATURE	Nr-Mt	Ex
☐ 1961	Bill Mazoraski	40	15
☐ 1962	Micky Mantle	45	15

OFFICIAL BIG TIME BASEBALL

DATE	COVER/FEATURE	Nr-Mt	Ex
☐ 1964	Mickey Mantle - Yankees (#1)	45	20

OFFICIAL BASEBALL
(Sport magazine)

DATE	COVER/FEATURE	Nr-Mt	Ex
☐ 1965	Jim O'Toole - Reds (Vol #1)	40	20
☐ 1965	Tony Oliva - Twins	35	20

OFFICIAL BASEBALL ANNUAL
(Dell)

DATE	COVER/FEATURE	Nr-Mt	Ex
☐ 1952	Allie Reynolds - Yankees	40	20

OFFICIAL BASEBALL ANNUAL
(Whitestone Magazine Publicatons)

DATE	COVER/FEATURE	Nr-Mt	Ex
☐ 1962	Rocky Colavito - Tigers	35	15
☐ 1963	Don Drysdale - Dodgers	20	10
☐ 1965	Sandy Koufax - Dodgers	20	10
☐ 1966	Sandy Koufax/Maury Wills	20	10
☐ 1968	Lou Brock/Carl Yastrzemski	20	10
☐ 1969	Willie Mays/Pete Rose	20	10
☐ 1970	Tom Seaver - Mets	25	10
☐ 1971	Johnny Bench - Reds	20	10

OFFICIAL BASEBALL GUIDE
(SPALDING)
Perhaps one of the oldest baseball annuals in the hobby. Spalding produced the series which was eventually acquired by Sporting News. The
covers are artistic work or action scenes. These books are collected by
baseball historians. Many historians are happy with low grade or repro-

ductions. The book eventually mereged with Reach.

DATE	COVER/FEATURE	Nr-Mt	Ex
☐ 1876		1500	900
☐ 1877-1878		1000	500
☐ 1879-1880		500	350
☐ 1881-1885		350	250
☐ 1886-1890		300	150
☐ 1891-1895		275	125
☐ 1896-1900		250	100
☐ 1901-1910		225	75
☐ 1911-1919		200	50
☐ 1920-1922		250	75
☐ 1923-1930		150	50
☐ 1931-1941		125	35

OFFICIAL BASEBALL GUIDE

(The Sporting News) (600 page)
One of the most popular annuals on baseball.

DATE	COVER/FEATURE	Nr-Mt	Ex
☐ 1942	First Issue	250	100
☐ 1943	Illustrated	75	35
☐ 1944	B. Newsom	40	20
☐ 1945	Marty Marion	40	20
☐ 1946	Hal Newhouser	40	20
☐ 1947	Harry Brecheen	35	20
☐ 1948	Ewell Blackwell	35	20
☐ 1949	Lou Boudreau	35	20
☐ 1950	Phil Rizzuto/Pee Wee Reese	50	25
☐ 1951	Red Schoendiest	50	25
☐ 1952	Stan Musial	50	25
☐ 1953	Robin Roberts	40	25
☐ 1954	Casey Stengel	40	25
☐ 1955	Game Play	35	20
☐ 1956	J.Coleman/B. Martin	35	20
☐ 1957	Mickey Mantle	75	25
☐ 1958	Ted Williams	75	25
☐ 1959	Spalding Advertisment	35	20
☐ 1960	Mullin "Bum" Cartoon	35	20
☐ 1961	Relief Pitcher Award	30	15
☐ 1962	Roger Maris	75	25
☐ 1963	Mullin Cartoon	30	15
☐ 1964	Stan Musial	45	20
☐ 1965	Brooks Robinson/Others	40	20
☐ 1966	Willie Mays/Sandy Koufax	40	20
☐ 1967	Roberto Clemente/Others	40	20
☐ 1968	Yaz/Cepeda/Lonborg	30	15
☐ 1969	Pete Rose/Bob Gibson/McLain	30	15
☐ 1970	Willie McCovey/Harmon Killebrew	30	15
☐ 1971	Bench/Gibson/McLain	25	10
☐ 1972	Jenkns/Blue/Torre	15	7
☐ 1973	S.Carlton/Johnny Bench/Gaylord Perry	15	7
☐ 1974	Jim Palmer/R. Jackson/Barry Bonds	15	7
☐ 1975	Lou Brock/ Jim Hunter	15	7
☐ 1976	Tom Seaver/Jim Palmer/Joe Morgan	15	7
☐ 1977	Thurmon Munson/Jim Palmer	15	7
☐ 1978	Nolan Ryan/Steve Carlton/Rod Carew	25	10
☐ 1979	Ron Guidry/ Jim Rice/Dave Parker	12	7
☐ 1980	Keith Hernandez/Don Baylor	10	7
☐ 1981	Steve Carlton	10	7
☐ 1982	Tom Seaver	20	10
☐ 1983	Robin Yount	10	7
☐ 1984	Cal Ripken, Jr.	20	10
☐ 1985	Ryan Sandberg	20	10
☐ 1986	Willie McGee	8	5
☐ 87-97		6	2

OFFICIAL SPORTS MAGAZINE BASEBALL

(Royal Publications)

DATE	COVER/FEATURE	Nr-Mt	Ex
☐ 6/65	Jim O'Toole - Reds	20	7
☐ 10/65	Tony Oliva - Twins	25	10

OFFICIAL WORLD SERIES RECORDS

(The Sporting News)
Very short and unpopular record book series.

DATE	COVER/FEATURE	Nr-Mt	Ex
☐ 53-56		30	15

DATE	COVER/FEATURE	Nr-Mt	Ex
☐ 1957	Don Larsen Perfect Game	30	15
☐ 58-61		20	10
☐ 64-70		20	10
☐ 1962	Yogi Berra	30	15
☐ 1964	Sandy Koufax	30	15
☐ 1965	M. Mantle/B. Richardson	30	15
☐ 1967	Bob Gibson	30	15
☐ 1971	Brooks Robinson	25	12
☐ 72-77		15	5
☐ 1974	Reggie Jackson	20	5
☐ 1976	Pete Rose	20	5
☐ 1977	Johnny Bench	20	5
☐ 1978	Reggie Jackson	15	5
☐ 1979	Thurman Munson/Reggie Jackson	15	5
☐ 1980-1997		10	4

ONE FOR THE BOOK

(The Sporting News)
This is a statistical book that has gone through a few name changes. In 1972 it was changed to 'Baseball Record Book' and then in 1986 it is changed to 'Complete Record Book'.

DATE	COVER/FEATURE	Nr-Mt	Ex
☐ 1949	Stan Musial	40	20
☐ 50-59		25	15
☐ 1954	Roy Campanella	35	15
☐ 1955	Joe Adcock	25	15
☐ 1957	Pee Wee Reese	25	15
☐ 1958	Stan Musial	25	15
☐ 1959	Casey Stengel	20	10
☐ 60-65		20	10
☐ 1960	Roy Face	20	10
☐ 1961	Nellie Fox	35	15
☐ 1962	Warren Spahn	20	10
☐ 1963	Nellie Fox/Aparcio/Hubbs/Wills	20	10
☐ 1967	Willie Mays	20	10
☐ 1968	Mickey Mantle	30	15
☐ 66-72		15	7
☐ 1972	Tom Seaver	20	10
☐ 1974	Nolan Ryan	30	15
☐ 73-80		12	5
☐ 1979	Pete Rose	20	10
☐ 81-97		10	3

PETERSEN'S PRO BASEBALL

(Petersen Publications Inc.)

DATE	COVER/FEATURE	Nr-Mt	Ex
☐ 1977	Brock, Anderson	10	5
☐ 1978	Rod Carew	10	5
☐ 1979	Bench, Garvey	15	5
☐ 1980	Willie Stargell	10	5
☐ 1981-90		10	5
☐ 1991-97		7	3

PRESS BOX BASEBALL

(P.S.L. Publishing)

DATE	COVER/FEATURE	Nr-Mt	Ex
☐ 1964	Mickey Mantle	40	20

PRO SPORTS

(Hammond Assoc)
This magazine covers more than just baseball.

DATE	COVER/FEATURE	Nr-Mt	Ex
☐ 9/65	Mickey Mantle/Willie Mays	60	20
☐ 11/65	Don Drysdale/Mickey Mantle	40	20
☐ 1/66	Paul Hornung	25	10
☐ 3/66	Koufax/J. Brown/Hull/Russell	25	10
☐ 5/66	Willie Mays/Stan Mikita	30	10
☐ 7/66	Juan Marichal/Ken Boyer	20	10
☐ 9/66	Willie Mays/Sandy Koufax	20	10
☐ 11/66	Juan Marichal	25	12
☐ 1/67	Namath/B. Robinson/B. Hull	20	10
☐ 3/67	Namath/Robinson/Koufax	20	10
☐ 5/67	Maury Wills	20	10
☐ 7/67	R. Allen/Mantle/Aparico	20	10
☐ 9/67	Aaron/Maris/Marichal/Cepeda/F Robinson	25	15

☐ 1/68	Donny Anderson - Packers	20	15
☐ 3/68	Joe Namath/Bob Gibson/Carl Yaz ...	20	10
☐ 5/68	Al Kaline/Carl Yaz/Orlando Cepeda ...	20	10
☐ 7/68	Leo Durocher/Jim Kaat	20	10
☐ 9/68	Boog Powell/Lou Brock	20	10
☐ 11/68	Bill Russell/Phil Eagles	20	10
☐ 1/70	Donny Anderson	20	10
☐ 3/70	Micky Lolich	15	7
☐ 5/70	Tommie Agee	15	7
☐ 7/70	Tom Seaver/Koosman/other	20	10
☐ 9/70	A's /Bonds/Allen	15	7
☐ 11/70	Johnny Unitas/ Wilt Chamberlain	15	7
☐ 1/71	Gale Sayers	15	7
☐ 3/71	Jabbar/ Bill Bradley	15	7
☐ 5/71	Hank Aaron/Kareem Abdul Jabbar/Hull	15	10
☐ 7/71	Brooks Robinson/ Johnny Bench ...	20	10
☐ 9/71	Yankee Player	10	7
☐ 11/71	Detroit Lions	10	7
☐ 1/72	49ers	10	7
☐ 3/72	Kareem Abdul Jabbar	15	7
☐ 5/72	Vida Blue	10	7
☐ 7/72	Tom Seaver	20	10
☐ 9/72	Joe Torre	10	5
☐ 11/72	Packers	20	10
☐ 5/73	Bobby Murcer	15	5
☐ 5/74	Tom Seaver	20	10
☐ 7/74	Hank Aaron	20	10
☐ 5/75	Bill Buckner	15	7
☐ 11/76	Pete Rose	15	7
☐ 11/77	Reggie Jackson	15	7
☐ 11/79	Pete Rose	15	7

REACH BASEBALL GUIDE

Reach produced sporting goods and used its Baseball Guide to promote its products. Reach Guides are as popular as Spalding Guides. The catalogs are very popular with historical item collectors. The Baseball guides are packed with baseball statistical information.

DATE	COVER/FEATURE	Nr-Mt	Ex
☐ Pre 1900	....	Auction Prices	
☐ 1903-1907	....	125	75
☐ 1908-1910	....	75	50
☐ 1911-1918	....	60	30
☐ 1919-1929	....	55	25
☐ 1930-1934	....	50	25
☐ 1935-1939	....	50	20

SPORTS ACTION MAG. BASEBALL THRILLS

DATE	COVER/FEATURE	Nr-Mt	Ex
☐ 1961 Mickey Mantle - Yankees		20	50

SPORTS ALBUM

(Dell)
These magazines cover more than just baseball.

DATE	COVER/FEATURE	Nr-Mt	Ex
☐ s/48	Joe DiMaggio	150	35
☐ f/48	T. Minisi	40	20
☐ 1/49	Ed Macauley (St Louis) basketball ...	50	20
☐ 5/49	Joe Gordon/Lou Boudreau	50	20
☐ 8/49	Sid Gordon	50	20
☐ 3/50	Ralph Kiner	55	20
☐ 12/50	Charlie Justice	40	10
☐ 6/50	Stan Musial/Ben Hogan	55	20
☐ 9/50	Curt Simmons	45	20
☐ 12/50	Bill Spivey	35	10
☐ 3/51	Stan Musial/George Kell/Bob Lemon .	50	20
☐ 6/51	Bob Feller/Larry Doby/Robin Roberts	50	20
☐ 3/52	Yogi Berra - Yankees	50	20

SPORTS ALL STARS BASEBALL

(Maco)

DATE	COVER/FEATURE	Nr-Mt	Ex
☐ 1957	Mantle/Musial/H. Score	75	20
☐ 1958	Warren Spahn - Braves (Vol #1)	65	25
☐ 1959	Bob Turley - Yankees	55	25
☐ 1960	Ed Mathews - Braves	45	20

☐ 1961	Vernon Law - Pirates	45	20
☐ 1962	Maris/Mantle - Yankees	55	25
☐ 1963	Willie Mays - Giants	45	15
☐ 1964	Sandy Koufax - Dodgers	35	15
☐ 1965	Sandy Koufax - Dodgers	35	15
☐ 1965	Mickey Mantle - Yankees	50	15
☐ 1966	Willie Mays - Giants	50	25
☐ 1967	Richie Allen - Phillies	35	15
☐ 1967	Rick Reichardt - Angels	25	10
☐ 1967		20	10
☐ 1968	(3 different covers)	15	8
☐ 1969	Reggie Jackson - A's	25	10
☐ 1969	Pete Rose - Reds	20	10
☐ 1970	NY Mets Team	45	15
☐ 1971	Pete Rose - Reds	35	15
☐ 1972	Willie Stargell - Pirates	35	10
☐ 1973	Steve Carlton - Phillies	25	10
☐ 1974	Pete Rose - Phillies	25	10
☐ 1975	Ken Holtzman - A's	20	10
☐ 1976	Rod Carew/Fred Lynn	20	10
☐ 1977	Johnny Bench - Reds	20	10
☐ 1978-1979	....	15	7

SPORT ANNUAL

(Sport Magazine)

DATE	COVER/FEATURE	Nr-Mt	Ex
☐ 1949	Lou Boudreau/Joe Louis	65	25
☐ 1950	Tommy Henrich - Yankees	60	25
☐ 1951	Phil Rizzuto - Yankees	75	25
☐ 1953	Joe Black/Rocky Marciano	70	25
☐ 1954	Roy Campanella/Rocky Marciano ...	75	25
☐ 1962	Roger Maris/Warren Spahn	40	20
☐ 1963	Mickey Mantle - Yankees	45	20
☐ 1964	Mickey Mantle/Sandy Koufax	45	20
☐ 1965	Mickey Mantle - Yankees	40	15
☐ 1966	Mantle/Koufax/Mays/Ali	30	15
☐ 1967	Koufax/F. Robbinson/Hull	20	10
☐ 1968	Mantle/Koufax/Mays/Ali	35	15
☐ 1969	Bob Gibson/Denny McLain	20	10
☐ 1970	Mets Celebrating	20	10

SPORTS ANNUAL

(Hammond Assoc.)
This magazine covers more than just baseball.

DATE	COVER/FEATURE	Nr-Mt	Ex
☐ 9/68	Carl Yaz/Orlando Cepeda vol #1	45	20
☐ 9/69	Frank Robinson/Juan Marichal	25	10
☐ 11/69	Leroy Kelly/Leo Durocher	20	10
☐ 5/70	McCovey/C. Jones/D. McLain	30	15
☐ 8/70	Lou Brock/Pete Rose	20	10
☐ 10/70	Johnny Bench/Hank Aaron	20	10
☐ 4/71	Willie Mays/Pete Rose	25	12
☐ 8/71	Tom Seaver/Hank Aaron	25	10
☐ 10/71	Willie Mays/Vida Blue	22	12
☐ 7/72	Willie Stargell - Pirates	20	10
☐ 9/72	Hank Aaron/Manny Sanguillen	15	10
☐ 7/73	Cesar Cendeno - Reds	15	10
☐ 6/74	Pete Rose/Carlton Fisk/Cleon Jones .	20	10
☐ 6/75	Mike Marshall/Jim Hunter	10	10
☐ 10/77	Pittsburgh Football	10	8
☐ 7/79	Thurmon Munson - Yankees	20	10

SPORTS CAVALCADE

(Complete Sports)

DATE	COVER/FEATURE	Nr-Mt	Ex
☐ 10/62	Bob Feller - Indians	35	20
☐ 1964	Sandy Koufax, Willie Mays	35	20

SPORTS FORECAST BASEBALL

(O'Malley Pub)

DATE	COVER/FEATURE	Nr-Mt	Ex
☐ 5/59	Banks/Jensen/Spahn/Turley	35	15
☐ 5/60	Veeck/Wynn	25	15
☐ 6/60	Team Logo's	20	12

SPORTFOLIO

(Sportsweek)

This small magazine (size of Readers Digest) covers more than just baseball .

DATE	COVER/FEATURE	Nr-Mt	Ex
☐ 08/46	Bob Feller - Indians	40	20
☐ 09/46	Don Budge - Tennis	25	10
☐ 10/46	Glen Davis - Army	25	10
☐ 11/46	Hunting	20	10
☐ 12/46	Bob Waterfield - Rams	25	10
☐ 1/47	St Johns Basketball	25	10
☐ 2/47	Maurice Richard - Hockey	25	10
☐ 3/47	Rocky Grazino - Boxing	20	10
☐ 4/47	Ted Williams - Red Sox	60	25
☐ 5/47	Horseracing (Derby)	20	10
☐ 6/47	Pistol Pete Reiser- Dodgers	20	10
☐ 7/47	Hal Newhouser - Tigers	25	10
☐ 8/47	Zoe Ann Olsen - Diver	20	10
☐ 9/47	Johnny Mize - NY Giants	30	10
☐ 10/47	Johnny Lujack - Notre Dame	35	10
☐ 11/47	Choo Choo Justice/North Carolina	30	10
☐ 12/47	Wilbur Moore - Redskins	20	10
☐ 1/48	Arnie Ferrin - Utah basketball	20	10
☐ 2/48	Wah Wah Jones - Kentucky	25	15
☐ 3/48	Turk Broda - Toronto Hockey	25	12
☐ 4/48	Bob Feller - Indians	35	20
☐ 5/48	Ralph Kiner - Pirates	30	15
☐ 6/48	Joe Louis - Boxing	25	15
☐ 7/48	Ray Maggard (UCLA-Pole Vault)	20	10
☐ 8/48	Bob Elliott -Braves	20	10
☐ 9/48	Charlie Keller - Yankees	25	12
☐ 10/48	Doak Walker -SMU	30	15
☐ 11/48	Chuck Bednarik -Penn	25	10
☐ 1/49	Columbia football	20	10
☐ 2/49	Basketball Players	20	10
☐ 3/49	Bobby Thompson - Giants	20	10
☐ 4/49	Ted Williams - Red Sox	50	25
☐ 5/49	Casey Stengel - Yankees	30	15

SPORTS EXTRA BASEBALL

(Tempest)

DATE	COVER/FEATURE	Nr-Mt	Ex
☐ S/68	Carl Yaz / Bob Clemente	35	15
☐ S/69	Denny Gibson/Bob Gibson	25	10
☐ S/70	Tom Seaver- Mets	30	15
☐ S/71	Johnny Bench - Reds	30	15
☐ S/72	Tom Seaver/Vida Blue	25	10
☐ S/73	Gaylord Perry - Indians	20	10
☐ S/74	Rose/Aaron/Seaver/Ruth	20	10
☐ S/75	Catfish Hunter - Yankees	20	10

SPORTS HEROES

(Complete Sports/Mac)

DATE	COVER/FEATURE	Nr-Mt	Ex
☐ S/66	Oscar Robertson - Royals	35	15
☐ S/66	Sandy Koufax - Dodgers	30	15
☐ F/66	Mickey Mantle/S. Koufax/W. Mays	35	15
☐ W/66	Jim Taylor/Paul Hornung	35	15
☐ W/67	Football Greats	20	10
☐ S/68	Baseball Greats	20	10
☐ W/68	Pro Football greats	20	10
☐ S/69	Pro football Greats	20	10
☐ F/69	Steve Owens - Oklahoma	20	10
☐ W/69	Pro Football Greats	20	10
☐ S/70	Tom Seaver - Mets	30	15
☐ S/70	Hank Aaron/Jim Brown	20	12
☐ F/70	Leroy Kelly/Dick Butkus	40	15
☐ W/70	Johnny Bench - Reds	25	10
☐ S/71	Bobby Orr/Johnny Bench/Jabbar	20	10
☐ S/71	Deacon Jones - Rams	20	10
☐ F/71	Dick Butkus/Floyd Little	40	20
☐ W/71	Calvin Hill/Darryl Lamonica	15	10
☐ F/72	Duane Thomas/Bobby Simth	15	10
☐ W/72	Larry Brown/Larry Csonka	15	10
☐ S/73	Bobby Orr - Bruins	20	10

☐ S/73	Terry Bradshaw - Steelers	25	10
☐ F/73	John Riggins - Redskins	15	7
☐ 1974	Larry Csonka - Dolphins	15	7

SPORT LIFE

(Big Sports Magazine)

Covers more than just baseball.

DATE	COVER/FEATURE	Nr-Mt	Ex
☐ 9/48	Lou Boudreau - Indians #1	65	15
☐ 11/48	Ted Williams - Red Sox	75	25
☐ 12/48	S. Baugh/Tripucka/MaCauley	50	20
☐ 1/49	Otto Graham/W. Pepp	60	20
☐ 2/49	Ralph Beard/Sid Luckman	60	20
☐ 3/49	J. Gordon, L. Boudreau	50	15
☐ 4/49	George Kaftan	50	15
☐ 5/49	Stan Musial - Cards	50	15
☐ 7/49	Joe DiMaggio - Yankees	150	50
☐ 10/49	Ralph Kiner - Pirates	50	25
☐ 2/50	DonNewcombe - Dodgers	50	15
☐ 6/50	Jackie Robinson/Ralph Kiner	70	25
☐ 8/50	Stan Musial - Cards	50	20
☐ 11/50	Phil Rizzuto/George Kell	35	20
☐ 1/51	Otto Graham - Giants	50	20
☐ 3/51	Yogi Berra/R. Kiner/Sam Ranzino	40	20
☐ 5/51	Larry Doby - Indians	50	20
☐ 7/51	J. Konstanty/Roy Campanella	35	20
☐ 9/51	Duke Snider - Dodgers	75	25
☐ 12/51	Sammy Baugh - Bears	45	20
☐ 2/52	S. Maglie/G.Howe/B. Hogan	50	20
☐ 3/52	Rocky Marcino	60	20
☐ 6/52	Roy Campanella	50	20
☐ 8/52	Nellie Fox/C. Carrasquel	50	20
☐ 10/52	Base stealing	35	20
☐ 12/52	Jack Scarbath	30	15
☐ 2/53	Joe Black/Rocky Marciano	30	15
☐ 4/53	Bobby Shantz, Tom Gola	35	20
☐ 6/53	Tommy Collins - Boxing	35	20

SPORTS PARADE

(Print Photograph)

DATE	COVER/FEATURE	Nr-Mt	Ex
☐ 1948	Joe DiMaggio/Johnny Lujack (pin up)	75	25
☐ 4/49	Lou Bourdreau - Indians	50	20
☐ 8/49	Tommy Heinrich - Yankees	50	20

SPORT PIX

(USA com)

DATE	COVER/FEATURE	Nr-Mt	Ex
☐ 2/49	Bob Chappuis	40	20
☐ 4/49	Ed MacAuley/Joe DiMaggio	50	20
☐ 6/49	Bob Feller - Indians	65	30
☐ f/49	Hank Sauer - Giants	65	30

SPORTS QUARTERLY

(Counterpoint inc)

DATE	COVER/FEATURE	Nr-Mt	Ex
☐ 1964	Sandy Koufax/Carl Yaz	50	20
☐ 1965	Ken Boyer - Cards	35	20
☐ 1966	Sandy Koufax - Dodgers	35	20
☐ 1967	Bob Clemente - Pirates	35	20
☐ 1968	Carl Yaz - Red Sox	35	20
☐ 1969	Bob Gibson/M. Lolich	35	20
☐ 1970	Tom Seaver - Mets	35	20
☐ 1971	Brooks Robinson - Orioles	30.	20
☐ 1972	Bob Clemente - Pirates	35	20
☐ 1973	Steve Carlton - Phillies	30	20
☐ 1974	Hank Aaron - Braves	30	10
☐ 1975	Steve Garvey - Dodgers	20	10
☐ 1976	Fred Lynn - Red Sox	12	5
☐ 1980	Willie Stargell - Pirates	12	5

SPORTS QUARTERLY BASEBALL EXTRA

DATE	COVER/FEATURE	Nr-Mt	Ex
☐ 1972	Tom Seaver - Mets	35	15
☐ 1972	Hank Aaron - Braves	35	20

☐ 1973	Johnny Bench - Reds	25	12
☐ 1976	Johnny Bench - Reds	25	12

SPORTS REVIEW

DATE	COVER/FEATURE	Nr-Mt	Ex
☐ 1953	Stan Musial - Cardinals	50	25
☐ 1955	NY Giants player	40	20
☐ 1956	Dodgers (#43, catcher)	50	20
☐ 1957	Mickey Mantle - Yankees	60	15
☐ 1958	Lew Burdette - Braves	40	20
☐ 1959	Hank Aaron- Braves/Musial	50	20
☐ 1960	Luis Aparcio/Nellie Fox	55	25
☐ 1961	Bill Virdon - Pirates	40	20
☐ 1965	Celtics/Angels	25	10
☐ 1966	Sandy Koufax - Dodgers	30	10
☐ 1968	Brock/Yaz/Gibson/Lonborg	25	10
☐ 1969	Bob Gibson/D. McLain	25	15
☐ 1971	Johnny Bench - Reds	25	10

SPORTS SCENE

(Chris Schenkel)

DATE	COVER/FEATURE	Nr-Mt	Ex
☐ 7/71	Johnny Bench - Reds	20	10
☐ 1972	Vida Blue - A's	25	10
☐ 7/72	Harmon Killebrew - Twins	25	10

SPORTS SPECIAL BASEBALL

(Tempest)

DATE	COVER/FEATURE	Nr-Mt	Ex
☐ s/64	R.Maris/M.Mantle/Koufax	50	20
☐ s/65	Mickey Mantle/W Mays	45	20
☐ s/66	Sandy Koufax/J. Marichal	40	20
☐ s/67	B. & F.Robinson/Drysdale/Marichal	30	15
☐ s/68	Carl Yastrzemski/Orlando Cepeda	30	15
☐ s/69	Denny McLain/Pete Rose	30	15
☐ s/70	Hank Aaron/Carl Yastrzemski	30	10
☐ s/71	Tom Seaver/Brooks Robinson	30	15
☐ s/72	Roberto Clemente/Joe Torre	40	20
☐ s/73	Johnny Bench/Dick Allen	25	10
☐ s/74	Reggie Jackson/H. Aaron	40	20
☐ s/75	Catfish Hunter	15	10

SPORTS STARS OFFICIAL 1970 ED

(Photo Album)

DATE	COVER/FEATURE	Nr-Mt	Ex
☐ 1970	Dave McNally (World Series)	50	20
☐ (Stamps Seaver, McCovey, Banks, Bench, Killebrew)			

SUPERSTAR SPORTS

DATE	COVER/FEATURE	Nr-Mt	Ex
☐ 9/72	Tom Seaver - Mets Vol #1	40	20

SPORTS STARS

(USA com)

DATE	COVER/FEATURE	Nr-Mt	Ex
☐ 4/50	Joe Page - NY Yankees	65	20
☐ 8/50	Art Houtteman - Tigers	50	20
☐ 10/50	Ralph Kiner/Pee Wee Reese/Joe DiMaggio	65	20
☐ w/50	Kyle Rote	35	15
☐ 8/51	Phil Rizzuto/Ralph Kiner/Al Rosen	50	25
☐ S/51	Joe DiMaggio - Yankees	95	25
☐ N/51	Jackie Robinson - Dodgers	85	50
☐ F/52	Gil Hodges, Dick Groat	65	25
☐ 5/52	Leo Durocher - Giants	55	25
☐ 7/52	Eddie Stanky - Cardinals	55	20
☐ 8/52	Mike Garcia - Indians	50	20
☐ 9/52	Jackie Robinson/Pee Wee Reese	75	25
☐ 11/52	Mickey Mantle/Roy Campanella/Shantz	150	35
☐ 1/53	F. McPhee/Princeton	65	20
☐ 3/53	Rocky Marciano, Duke Snider	65	25

SPORTS TODAY

(Hewfred Pub)

DATE	COVER/FEATURE	Nr-Mt	Ex
☐ 6/65	Hank Aaron - Braves	35	15

☐ 8/70	Leo Durocher - Cubs	20	10
☐ 10/70	Pete Rose - Reds	25	12
☐ 6/71	Carl Yastrzemski - Red Sox	25	12
☐ 8/71	Harmon Killebrew - Twins	30	12
☐ 8/72	Pete Rose - Reds	20	10
☐ 6/73	Dick Allen - White Sox	20	10
☐ 8/74	Johnny Bench - Reds	25	10

SPORTS WORLD

(Hillman Pub)
Covers more than just baseball.

DATE	COVER/FEATURE	Nr-Mt	Ex
☐ 3/49	Ed Macauley - St Louis Basketball	55	15
☐ 5/49	Joe DiMaggio - Yankees	150	25
☐ 7/49	Stan Musial - Cardinals	75	25
☐ 9/49	Pee Wee Reese - Dodgers	75	20

SPORTS WORLD

(Reese Publishing)
Magazine started in 7/62 and ran through 1985

DATE	COVER/FEATURE	Nr-Mt	Ex
☐ 7/62	Mantle/Mays/Maris/Colavito/Aparico	65	20
☐ 9/62	Clemente/Koufax/Musial/Unitas	45	20
☐ 11/62	Clemente/Kaline/Mays/Koufax	45	20
☐ 12/62	Chamberlain/Cousy/Hull/Geoffrion/Hff	40	20
☐ 4/63	Luis Aparicio/Jim Brown	45	20
☐ 7/63	Mickey Mantle - Yankees	55	20
☐ 8/63	Mays/Aparicio/Kaline/Killebrew	45	20
☐ 10/63	Sandy Koufax - Dodgers	45	20
☐ 12/63	Jim Taylor/Jim Brown/YA Title	45	20
☐ 2/64	Jimmy Brown - Browns	45	20
☐ 4/64	Elston Howard - Yankees	45	20
☐ 6/64	Mays/Mantle/F. Robinson	45	20
☐ 8/64	Whitey Ford, Sandy Koufax	45	20
☐ 10/64	Willie Mays/Casey Stengel	45	20
☐ 12/64	Jimmy Brown - Browns	45	20
☐ 2/65	P. Hornung/J. Brown/Big O	45	20
☐ 4/65	Willie Mays - Giants	45	20
☐ 6/65	Dean Chance/Y Berra	35	20
☐ 8/65	Mantle/Mays/ Bill White	45	20
☐ 10/65	Jimmy Brown - Browns	35	20
☐ 12/65	Johnny Unitas/Sam Huff	30	15
☐ 2/66	Fran Tarkenton/Juan Marichal	30	15
☐ 4/66	Leo Durocher/Willie Mays	30	15
☐ 6/66	Mickey Mantle - Yankees	50	20
☐ 8/66	Willie Mays/Tony Oliva	40	20
☐ 10/66	Sandy Koufax/Willie Mays	35	20
☐ 12/66	John Unitas/Sam Huff	35	20
☐ 2/67	Howe/Wilt/Starr	25	20
☐ 4/67	Frank Robinson, Willie Mays	25	20
☐ 6/67	Mays/Maris/F. Robinson	30	15
☐ 8/67	Clemente/Mays/Killebrew	30	15
☐ 10/67	Mays/Maris/Mantle	50	15
☐ 12/67	B.Bradley/Unitas/Starr	30	15
☐ 2/68	A. Karras/B. Hull	30	15
☐ 4/68	Carl Yaz/O.Cepeda/B Orr/F.Robinson	35	15
☐ 6/68	Bob Gibson/Jim Lonborg	35	15
☐ 8/68	C. Yaz/Hank Aaron/F. Robby	25	15
☐ 10/68	W. Mays/P. Rose/H. Killebrew	25	15
☐ 12/68	Wilt Chamberlain/J. Unitas/B. Starr	30	15
☐ 2/69	B. Hull/B.Starr	20	10
☐ 4/69	Denny McLain/Bob Gibson	20	10
☐ 6/69	J. Marichal/B. Gibson/D. McLain	20	10
☐ 8/69	Carl Yaz/Hank Aaron/W.McCovey	20	10
☐ 10/69	Aaron/T. Conigliaro/J. Namath	25	10
☐ 12/69	Jabbar/Unitas/Namath	20	10
☐ 2/70		12	7
☐ 4/70	Tom Seaver/Frank Robinson	25	10
☐ 6/70	Mays/Seaver/Marichal	25	10
☐ 8/70	Willie McCovey/Frank Robinson	25	10
☐ 10/70	Rose/Aaron/Durocher	20	7
☐ 12/70	Joe Namath/Len Dawson	20	7
☐ 2/71		12	7
☐ 4/71	Tom Seaver/Bob Gibson/Bobby Orr	20	10
☐ 6/71	Tom Seaver/G. Perry/Bob Gibson	20	7

		Nr-Mt	Ex
8/71	Johnny Bench/Carl Yaz	25	10
10/71	Seaver/Mays/Aaron/Namath	20	7
12/71	Namath/Brodie/Jurgensen	15	7
2/72	....	12	7
4/72	Vida Blue - A's/Bill Bradley	20	10
6/72	Tom Seaver, Vida Blue	25	10
8/72	Brooks Robinson/Hank Aaron	25	10
10/72	Frank Robinson/ Tom Seaver	20	10
12/72	Roger Staubach/Bob Griese/J. Brodie	15	7
2/73	Football	20	10
4/73	Hockey -Rangers	20	10
6/73	Micky Lolich - Tigers	15	10
8/73	Johnny Bench/Dick Allen	15	10
10/73	J. Bench/F. Robinson/C. Speier	20	10
2/74	Green Bay Packers	15	10
4/74	Yvan Cournoyers - Canadiens	15	6
6/74	Tom Seaver/Jim Palmer/Jim Hunter .	25	6
10/74	Bobby Bonds/OJ Simpson	15	6
6/75	Nolan Ryan/Luis Tiant/ Jim Hunter ..	30	15
8/75	Jeff Burroughs/Steve Garvey	15	7
10/75	Terry Bradshaw - Steelers	15	7
8/76	Joe Morgan/Fred Lynn	15	7
10/76	Pete Rose/Joe Morgan	15	7
6/77	Mark Fidrych/Tom Seaver	15	7
10/77	Thurmon Munson - Yankees	20	10
2/78	Walter Payton - Bears	20	10
8/78	Reggie Jackson - Yankees	20	10
10/78	Pete Rose - Reds	15	7
8/79	Pete Rose - Reds	20	10
10/80	Reggie Jackson - Yankees	15	7
8/81	Reggie Jackson - Yankees	15	7
8/82	Pete Rose - Reds	15	7

STREET & SMITH'S BASEBALL

This is the standard for preseason annual write-ups.

DATE	COVER/FEATURE	Nr-Mt	Ex
1941	Bob Feller	200	100
1942	Howie Pollet	125	50
1943	NY Giants	125	50
1944	Joe McCarthy	100	50
1945	NY Giants Spring Training	100	50
1946	Dick Fowler	75	35
1947	Leo Durocher	75	35
1948	Joe DiMaggio	75	30
1949	Lou Boudreau	75	30
1950	Joe DiMaggio/Ted Williams	125	30
1951	Joe DiMaggio/Ralph Kiner	120	30
1952	Stan Musial	75	25
1953	Mickey Mantle	125	30
1954	Eddie Mathews	75	25
1955	Yogi Berra	50	20
1956	Mickey Mantle/Duke Snider	100	35
1957	Mickey Mantle/Don Larson/Yogi Berra	100	35
1958	Bob Buhl/Lew Burdette	50	20
1959	Mantle/Spahn/Burdette	70	20
1960	Luis Apracio/Nellie Fox	70	20
1961	Dick Groat	50	15
1962	Roger Maris	50	15
1963	Tom Tresh	40	15
1963	Stan Musial	50	12
1963	Don Drysdale	40	15
1964	Mickey Mantle	60	15
1964	Warren Spahn	40	15
1964	Sandy Koufax	40	15
1965	Brooks Robinson	40	15
1965	Ken Boyer	35	12
1965	Dean Chance	35	12
1966	Ron Swoboda	35	12
1966	Rocky Colavito	40	12
1966	Sandy Koufax	40	12
1967	Andy Etchebarren	30	12
1967	Harmon Killebrew	40	12
1967	Juan Marichal	40	12
1968	Jim Lonborg	30	12
1968	Orlando Cepeda	30	12

		Nr-Mt	Ex
1968	Jim McGlothlin	30	12
1969	Bob Gibson & Denny McLain	25	10
1970	Tom Seaver	40	15
1970	Harmon Killebrew	40	15
1970	Bill Singer	25	10
1971	Boog Powell	25	10
1971	Johnny Bench	30	10
1971	Gaylord Perry	25	10
1972	Roberto Clemente	40	20
1972	Joe Torre	25	10
1972	Vida Blue	25	10
1973	Steve Carlton	25	10
1973	Johnny Bench	25	10
1973	Reggie Jackson	25	10
1974	Hank Aaron	25	10
1974	Pete Rose	25	10
1974	Nolan Ryan	40	15
1975	Lou Brock	20	10
1975	Catfish Hunter	20	10
1975	Mike Marshall	20	10
1976	Fred Lynn	20	10
1976	Joe Morgan	20	10
1976	Davey Lopes	20	10
1977	Thurman Munson	20	10
1977	Mark Fidrych	20	10
1977	Randy Jones	20	10
1978	Reggie Jackson	30	15
1978	Rod Carew	20	10
1978	Steve Garvey	20	10
1979	Ron Guidry	20	10
1979	J.R. Richard	20	10
1979	Burt Hooten	20	10
1980	Mike Flanagan	20	10
1980	Joe Niekro	20	10
1980	Brian Downing	20	10
1981	Mike Schmidt	15	8
1981	Other Covers	12	5
1982	Nolan Ryan	40	20
1983-1986	....	15	8
1986	Nolan Ryan	25	10
1987 - 1997	....	12	8

THE LITTLE RED BOOK

Originally written by Spalding, the Little Red Book became the statistical book for baseball. Collected by baseball historians.

DATE	COVER/FEATURE	Nr-Mt	Ex
1926	....	80	40
1927-1930	....	40	25
1931-1939	....	35	20
1940-1950	....	30	10
1951-1960	....	25	10
1961-1971	....	20	5

THE SPORTING NEWS DOPE BOOK

(The Sporting News)

DATE	COVER/FEATURE	Nr-Mt	Ex
1941	Bob Feller	65	30
1942	Ted Williams	65	30
1948	Joe DiMaggio	40	20
1949	Stan Musial	40	20
1950	Ted Williams	50	25
1955	Willie Mays	40	20
1956	Duke Snider	40	20
1957	Mickey Mantle	55	25
1958	Warren Spahn	35	15
50-60	....	35	15
61-69	....	25	10
1969	Pete Rose	30	15
1970	Willie McCovey	30	15
70-79	....	20	5
80-on	....	15	2

UNITED STATES BASEBALL

DATE	COVER/FEATURE	Nr-Mt	Ex
1964	Koufax/Ford/Mays	30	12

WHO'S BEST IN SPORT

(Sport Magazine)

DATE	COVER/FEATURE	Nr-Mt	Ex
☐ 1959-1962		40	20
☐ 1963-1966		30	15
☐ 1967-1970		25	12

WHO'S WHO IN BASEBALL

(Carmichal)

The annual appears in both hardback and softback editions.
Stars appear on each issue.

DATE	COVER/FEATURE	Nr-Mt	Ex
☐ 1935	Mickey Cochrane/Charlie Grimm	150	50
☐ 36-39		65	35
☐ 1938	Joe DiMaggio/Others	75	40
☐ 1940	Joe DiMaggio/Others	75	40
☐ 41-46		40	25
☐ 1943	Ted Williams & Others	60	30
☐ 1947	Stan Musial & Others	50	25
☐ 1948	Ted Williams/Joe DiMaggio	60	35
☐ 49-51		35	15
☐ 1952	Joe DiMaggio	50	30

WHO'S WHO IN BASEBALL

Produced by Baseball Magazine. This annual is about the size of Readers Digest and it has a red background. Many baseball historians and statistical fans collect every one of them.

DATE	COVER/FEATURE	Nr-Mt	Ex
☐ 1912	Ty Cobb	1000	500
☐ 1916	Ty Cobb or variation	800	400
☐ 1917-1919		400	200
☐ 1920	Babe Ruth	450	200
☐ 1921	Babe Ruth	550	200
☐ 1922	Roger Hornsby	350	150
☐ 1923-1928		150	75
☐ 1929-1936		85	45
☐ 1937	Lou Gehrig	100	50
☐ 1938-1941		85	35
☐ 1942	Joe DiMaggio	100	50
☐ 1943	Ted Williams	100	50
☐ 1944	Stan Musial	75	25
☐ 1945-1951		40	15
☐ 1952	Stan Musial	50	20
☐ 1953-1955		35	10
☐ 1956	Duke Snider	40	15
☐ 1957	Mickey Mantle	65	20
☐ 1958-1960		20	10
☐ 1961	Roger Maris	25	15
☐ 1962	Whitey Ford	30	15
☐ 1963	Don Drysdale	25	10
☐ 1964	Sandy Koufax	25	10
☐ 1965	Ken Boyer	20	10
☐ 1966	Sandy Koufax/Willie Mays	25	10
☐ 1967	Bob Clemente/Sandy Koufax	25	10
☐ 1968	Carl Yastrzemski	25	10
☐ 1969	Denny McLain	20	5
☐ 1970	Tom Seaver	25	5
☐ 1971	Johnny Bench	20	5
☐ 1972	Joe Torre	10	5
☐ 1973	Steve Carlton	10	5
☐ 1974	Pete Rose/Nolan Ryan	25	10
☐ 1975-1980		10	5
☐ 1981-1997		5	3

WHO'S WHO IN THE BIG LEAGUES

(Dell)

Also titled Who's Who in the Major Leagues.

DATE	COVER/FEATURE	Nr-Mt	Ex
☐ 1950	Joe DiMaggio - Yankees	125	20
☐ 1953	Stan Musial - Cardinals	75	40
☐ 1955	Yogi Berra - Yankees	75	40
☐ 1956	Roy Campanella - Dodgers	65	35
☐ 1957	Herb Score - Indians	55	35
☐ 1958	Willie Mays - Giants	55	20
☐ 1959	Mickey Mantle - Yankees	75	35

☐ 1960	Rocky Colavito - Indians	50	25
☐ 1961	Chuck Estrada - Orioles	45	20
☐ 1962	Whitey Ford - Yankees	45	20
☐ 1963	Harmon Killebrew - Twins	45	20
☐ 1964	Dick Stuart - Red Sox	40	20
☐ 1965	Willie Mays - Giants	40	20
☐ 1966	Tony Oliva - Twins	35	20
☐ 1967	Boog Powell - Orioles	25	15

WHO'S WHO IN SPORTS

Features more than baseball.

DATE	COVER/FEATURE	Nr-Mt	Ex
☐ 1950	Ted Williams/George Mikan/Ben Hogan	75	25
☐ 1951	Stan Musial/Bob Lemon/Others	55	20
☐ 1952	Stan Musial/George Mikan	50	20
☐ 1953	Phil Rizzuto - Yankees	50	20

WHO'S WHO IN THE MAJOR LEAGUE

(Dell)

DATE	COVER/FEATURE	Nr-Mt	Ex
☐ 1953	Stan Musial - Cardinals	55	20
☐ 1955	Yogi Berra -Yankees	55	20
☐ 1957	Herb Score -Indians	45	20
☐ 1961	Chuck Estrada -Orioles	35	15

WHO'S WHO IN SPORT

(Sport Magazine)

Covers more than baseball.

DATE	COVER/FEATURE	Nr-Mt	Ex
☐ 1957	Mickey Mantle/Bob Cousy	70	25
☐ 1958	Mickey Mantle/Oscar Robinson	70	25
☐ 1959	Mickey Mantle/Willie Mays	70	25
☐ 1960	Mantle/W. Mays/E. Mathews	60	25
☐ 1961	Mantle/J. Brown/Drysdale	60	25
☐ 1962	Mantle/Mays/S.Koufax/J.Brown	65	20
☐ 1963	Mantle/Mays/ A. Palmer/J.Brown .65	20	

WORLD SERIES

(Complete Sports)

DATE	COVER/FEATURE	Nr-Mt	Ex
☐ 1961	Mickey Mantle -Yankees	55	20
☐ 1962	Yogi Berra -Yankees	45	20
☐ 1963	Hank Aaron -Braves	45	20
☐ 1964	Mickey Mantle/Willie Mays	50	20

BASEBALL DIGEST
1944

1945

1946

1948

1951

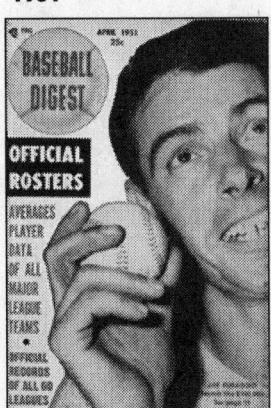

1954

1956

1956

1962

BASEBALL'S BEST 1953

BASEBALL STARS 1950

BASEBALL STARS 1959

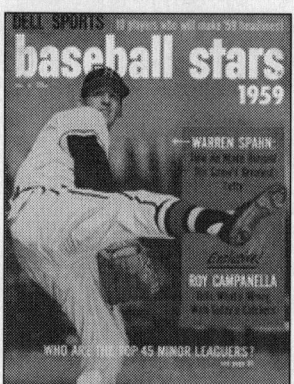

BASEBALL REGISTER 1947

BASEBALL YEARBOOK 1956

BLACK SPORTS 1971

COMPLETE BASEBALL 1950

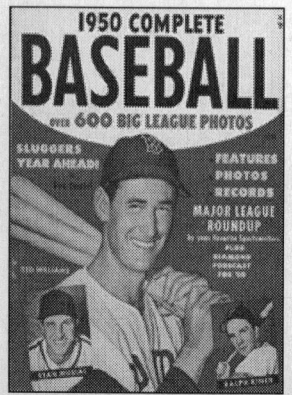

COMPLETE BASEBALL 1952

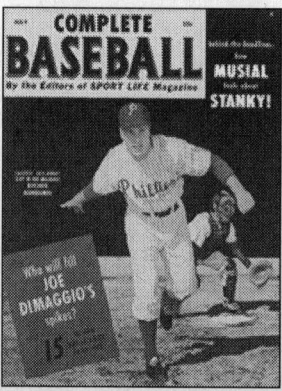

COMPLETE BASEBALL 1952

COMPLETE SPORTS 1966

DELL BASEBALL 1956

DELL BASEBALL 1957

INSIDE BASEBALL 1953

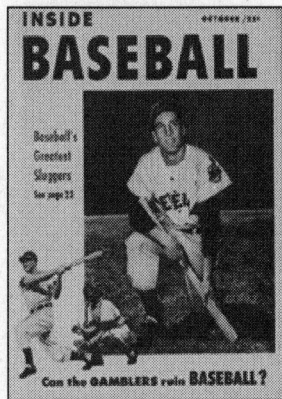

INSIDE SPORTS 1953

MAJOR LEAGUE BB 1962

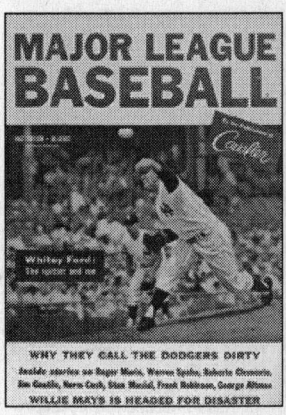

SPORTS ALL-STARS 1959

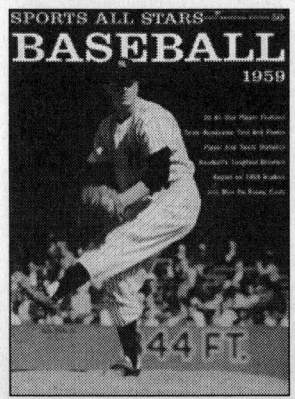

SPORT LIFE 1948

SPORTS PARADE 1949

SPORTS QUARTERLY 1967

SPORTS QUARTERLY 1968

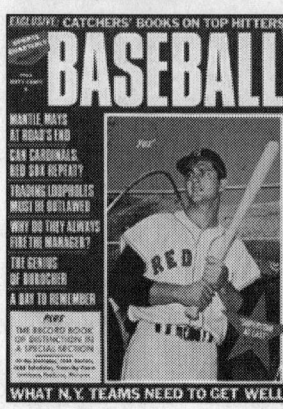

SPORTS STARS 1951

SPORTS WORLD 1949

STREET & SMITH'S 1941

STREET & SMITH'S 1943

TSN DOPE BOOK 1942

WHO'S WHO IN BB 1944

WHO'S WHO IN SPORTS 1951

CHAPTER THIRTEEN:
Collecting Basketball Team Publications

Basketball Publication collecting is fun and difficult. Most basketball publication collectors focus on players such as Michael Jordan, Julius Erving, and Pete Maravich. However, there is a growing demand for teams (Knicks, Suns, Lakers, Bulls, etc.) as well as historical collectibles (pre-1950). This section is a brief overview of the major teams & players publications.

EARLY BASKETBALL PUBLICATIONS

Basketball publications, outside of annual guides, do not date back to the turn of the century. Very few publications are available that are pre-NBA (pre-1949) and prices are very subjective. Basketball publications started to take off during the golden age of publications with both media guides from the pro teams as well as publications that just focus on pro or college basketball. This type of material is not common and surfaces periodically at major shows or ads in trade magazines. Yearbooks, outside of the Boston Celtics, were not made as a rule and very little paper was made on the team until the 1960s. Because of the limited number of released publications on basketball the ability to quantify and qualify this material is difficult. Prices are very subjective and can quickly increase in price once a group of collectors begins to pursue limited material. For example, material on Michael Jordan is the most popular in sports collecting history. Some items have sold in the thousands of dollars in auction. Jordan material is less than 15 years old. How would you value material from the 1930s original Boston Celtics or original Harlem Globetrotters? In the same vein, basketball material circa 1900 is so rare that only a few pieces of material are known to exist.

The most exciting news is that all early basketball material is still undervalued and underrated, giving serious basketball publication collectors ample oppurtunity to make money from any investment. The problem is finding quality early material.

There is so little pre-NBA material that all of it is considered scarce. Most of the pre-NBA material is Industrial League material. Industrial League teams were sponsored by large industrial groups or companies such as Phillips 66. The Industrial League material peaked during the 40s and continued in various forms of play today.

The Harlem Globetrotters team (formed in the 30s) is perhaps one of the more popular non-NBA teams. The Globetrotters squad also is one of the more collected squads outside of the NBA. Globetrotters were not necessarily "showtime" players during the 30s and early 40s but very popular and talented players. The team also offered the premeir showcase for black players to display their talent until the NBA became integrated in the late 50s. Eventually "showtime" basketball was introduced, which evolved into the entertaining shows fans have come to appreciate.

The programs for the Harlem Globetrotters were first produced in the 1940s. Programs range in value from about $50 for 40s-era editions, $35 for the 50s-era editions and $20 for 60s-era editions.

Preceding the NBA was the BAA (the Basketball Association of America, created in 1946 and renamed the National Basketball Association in 1949). The BAA was joined by the Midwest NBA Conference. Both of these early conferences have programs that range in value from $40 to $100 each based on team and scarcity.

The American Basketball League (ABL) was formed in 1961 and lasted two years. Material from the ABL is rare and is expensive. The league had a quality representation of pro players such as Connie Hawkins, but the amount of programs and press release material is very limited. Every piece sells in the $100 to $200-plus range. The ABL teams were the San Francisco Saints, Los Angeles Jets, Honolulu Chiefs, Kansas City Steers, Chicago Majors, Washington Tapers, Cleveland Pipers, and Pittsburgh Rens. This league is sometimes confused with the Industrial League. For example, the Cleveland Pipers were an Industrial League team before they were in the ABL. The Industrial League material is worth only about 50 percent of the ABL league.

The American Basketball League (ABA) was formed in 1967 and lasted until 1977. It is perhaps the most collected defunct league today. A special section is written and devoted to ABA collecting at the end of the NBA team section.

COLLECTING BASKETBALL PUBLICATIONS

If you are a big fan of the greatest name in basketball, Michael Jordan, the sky is the limit. I heard quotes of more than 1,000 different magazine/publication covers featuring Jordan alone. If you were to collect any other player, for example, you would find yourself with less than 500 different covers for a Magic Johnson or Larry Bird and less than 200 different covers for some of the earlier stars such as Pete Maravich and Julius Erving. All the other stars should be featured on less than 100 different publication covers.

Many basketball fans enjoy collecting both items from historical events and content on the game. In those situations you have both the game programs and the yearbooks and guides. Game programs from major events are the most popular (NCAA Final Four, NBA Finals, NBA All Star Game, etc.). The media guide is the best source of information since most NBA teams do not produce a yearbook. Today every NBA team produces its own slick magazine-style guide for its loyal fans.

NBA CHAMPIONSHIP PROGRAMS

The NBA produces many significant, historical programs for teams that reach the NBA Finals. The NBA Finals constitute the second most exciting basketball happening (right after the Final Four). My experience says there are very few pre-1965 NBA Finals programs in the hobby. Because so few change hands, the price listed below is more subjective than, say, Sports Illustrated.

Season	Winner/Loser	Nr-Mt	Ex
☐ 46-47	Warriors/Staggs	2,000	1,000
☐ 47-48	Bullets/Warriors	1,000	500
☐ 48-49	Lakers/Washington	750	350
☐ 49-50	Lakers/Nationals	750	350
☐ 50-51	Royals/Knicks	500	250
☐ 51-52	Lakers/Knicks	500	250
☐ 52-53	Lakers/Knicks	500	250
☐ 53-54	Lakers/Nationals	500	250
☐ 54-55	Nationals/Pistons	500	250
☐ 55-56	Warriors/Pistons	500	250
☐ 56-57	Boston Celtics/Hawks	500	250
☐ 57-58	Hawks/Boston Celtics	400	200
☐ 58-59	Boston Celtics/St. Louis Hawks	400	200
☐ 59-60	Boston Celtics/St. Louis Hawks	400	200
☐ 60-61	Boston Celtics/Los Angeles Lakers	300	150
☐ 61-62	Boston Celtics/Los Angeles Lakers	300	150
☐ 62-63	Boston Celtics/SF Warriors	250	125
☐ 63-64	Boston Celtics/Los Angeles Lakers	250	125
☐ 64-65	Boston Celticsn/Los Angeles Lakers	250	125
☐ 65-66	Boston Celtics/SF Warriors	200	100
☐ 66-67	Sixers/SF Warriors	200	100
☐ 67-68	Boston Celtics/Lakers	200	75
☐ 68-69	Boston Celtics/Lakers	175	75
☐ 69-70	Knicks/Lakers	150	75
☐ 70-71	Bucks/Bullets	85	50

		Nr-Mt	Ex
☐ 71-72	Lakers/ Knicks	85	35
☐ 72-73	Knicks/Lakers	85	35
☐ 73-74	Celtics/Bucks	65	35
☐ 74-75	Warriors/Bullets	65	30
☐ 75-76	Celtics/Suns	50	25
☐ 76-77	Trailblazers/Sixers	50	25
☐ 77-78	Bullets/Supersonics	50	25
☐ 78-79	Supersonics/Bullets	50	25
☐ 79-80	Lakers/Sixers	45	20
☐ 80-81	Celtics/Houston	40	20
☐ 81-82	Lakers/Phil Sixers	40	20
☐ 82-83	Sixers/Lakers	40	20
☐ 83-84	Celtics/Lakers	40	20
☐ 84-85	Lakers/Celtics	40	20
☐ 85-86	Celtics/Rockets	40	20
☐ 86-87	Lakers/Celtics	35	15
☐ 87-88	Lakers/Pistons	35	15
☐ 88-89	Pistons/Lakers	30	10
☐ 89-90	Pistons/Trailblazers	25	10
☐ 90-91	Bulls/Lakers	40	10
☐ 91-92	Bulls/Trailblazers	30	10
☐ 92-93	Bulls/Suns	20	10
☐ 93-94	Rockets/Knicks	14	7
☐ 94-95	Rockets/Magic	14	7
☐ 95-96	Bulls/Sonics	14	7
☐ 96-97	Bulls/Jazz	10	5

Tickets to the NBA Finals are roughly 50% of the program price. Full tickets will be approximately 100%+ of the program price. The only exceptions to this rule of thumb are the later years when the NBA program becomes easy to obtain.

THE NBA ALL STAR GAME

The NBA All Star Game is now a midseason classic. It began in 1951 and has continued ever since. The early games had about 10,000 people in attendance. Attendance increased as stadium size increased.

YEAR	LOCATION	ATTENDANCE	Nr-Mt	Ex
☐ 1951	Boston	10,000	600	300
☐ 1952	Boston	10,000	600	300
☐ 1953	Ft Wayne	10,000	550	300
☐ 1954	N.Y.C.	16,000	500	200
☐ 1955	N.Y.C.	16,000	500	200
☐ 1956	Rochester	8,000	450	300
☐ 1957	Boston	11,000	400	250
☐ 1958	St. Louis	12,000	350	150
☐ 1959	Detroit	10,000	300	150
☐ 1960	Philadelphia	10,000	300	150
☐ 1961	Syracuse	8,000	350	150
☐ 1962	St. Louis	15,000	275	125
☐ 1963	Los Angeles	14,000	275	125
☐ 1964	Boston	13,000	250	125
☐ 1965	St. Louis	16,000	225	100
☐ 1966	Cincinnati	14,000	200	100
☐ 1967	San Franc.	14,000	175	75
☐ 1968	New York	18,000	150	75
☐ 1969	Baltimore	12,000	125	50
☐ 1970	Philadelphia	15,000	125	50
☐ 1971	San Diego	14,000	85	40
☐ 1972	Los Angeles	17,000	75	35
☐ 1973	Chicago	17,000	65	30
☐ 1974	Seattle	14,000	65	30
☐ 1975	Phoenix	13,000	55	20
☐ 1976	Philadelphia	17,000	55	25
☐ 1977	Milwaukee	11,000	45	15
☐ 1978	Atlanta	15,000	45	15
☐ 1979	Detroit	31,000	35	10
☐ 1980	Landover	19,000	35	10
☐ 1981	Cleveland	20,000	35	10
☐ 1982	E. Rutherford	20,000	30	10
☐ 1983	Los Angeles	17,000	30	10
☐ 1984	Denver	17,000	30	10
☐ 1985	Indianapolis	43,000	25	10
☐ 1986	Dallas	16,000	20	10
☐ 1987	Seattle	34,000	20	10
☐ 1988	Chicago	18,000	20	10

☐ 1989	Houston	45,000	20	10
☐ 1990	Miami	15,000	20	5
☐ 1991	Charlotte	23,000	15	5
☐ 1992	Orlando	14,000	15	5
☐ 1993	Salt Lake City	19,000	15	5
☐ 1994	Minneapolis	17,000	15	5
☐ 1995	....		10	5
☐ 1996	....		10	5
☐ 1997	....		10	5

NBA TEAM ISSUED MATERIAL

Each NBA team issues media guides, newspapers, tickets, game programs and the like. In fact, many NBA teams have slick magazines for local newsstands as well as yearbooks. The following listings account for as much team released and related material as possible. You will also be able to find additions at the web site www.asportmall.com.

ATLANTA HAWKS

The key player of the Hawks is Pete Maravich who appeared on the scene in 1970. However, he was eventually traded to the New Orleans Jazz. Early Pete Maravich material on programs and schedules is worth three times more than regular releases. Other key players in Hawks history are Lou Hudson and Dominique Wilkins.

MEDIA GUIDES		Nr-Mt	Ex
☐ 1968-69	Hawks Mascot	40	15
☐ 1969-70	Lou Hudson	25	10
☐ 1970-71	Atlanta	20	10
☐ 1971-72	Richie Guerin	20	10
☐ 1972-73	Hawks Logo	20	10
☐ 1973-74	Overhead	20	10
☐ 1974-75	Lou Hudson	15	7
☐ 1975-76	Tom Van Ardsale	15	7
☐ 1976-77	John Drew	15	7
☐ 1977-78	Hawks logo	15	7
☐ 1978-79	Hawks Logo	15	7
☐ 1979-80	H. Brown, J. Drew	15	7
☐ 1980-81	Dan Roundfield	15	7
☐ 1981-82	Action Art	10	5
☐ 1982-83	Dan Roundfield	10	5
☐ 1983-84	Hawks Art	10	5
☐ 1984-85	Dominique Wilkins	10	5
☐ 1985-86	Dominique Wilkins	10	5
☐ 1986-87	Dominique Wilkins	10	5
☐ 1987-88	Dominique Wilkins	7	3
☐ 1988-89	Dominique Wilkins	7	3
☐ 1989-on	....	5	1

GAME PROGRAMS		Nr-Mt	Ex
☐ 1968	First Game	300	100
☐ 1969	First Pete Maravich Game	300	150
☐ 1968-70	Game Programs	20	10
☐ 1971-75	Game Programs	15	7
☐ 1976-80	Game Programs	12	5
☐ 1981-97	Game Programs	6	1
☐	Key Games	30	10
☐	Key Players on Cover	20	10
☐	Pete Maravich Covers	40	20

SCHEDULES		Nr-Mt	Ex
☐ 1968	First Schedule	20	10
☐ 1969-70	Early Schedules	12	5
☐ 1971-75	Later Schedules	7	2
☐ 1976-80	Regular Schedule	5	1
☐ 1981-90	Regular Schedule	3	1
☐ 1991-on	Regular Schedule	2	1

YEARBOOKS		Nr-Mt	Ex
☐ 1989-90	Wilkins, Rivers, Malone	20	10
☐ 1990-91	Dominique Wilkins	15	7

No other yearbooks made.
Some of the tougher material on Pete Maravich is Hawk magazine & newsletter covers. Newsletters, team magazines have nominal values in the $5-$10 range unless Pete Maravich appears on them.

BOSTON CELTICS

The Boston Celtics are one of the most popular and collected teams in pro basketball. Their string of championships is unmatched. Celtic fans are very loyal and are very dedicated to collecting early Celtic memorabilia.

The pre-NBA Celtic items that date back in the 1920's-1930's are not listed because very little exists from that era. The popular collected eras of Celtic history (1955-1969) and (1977-1990) are usually focused on there heroes: Bob Cousy, Bill Russell and Larry Bird. The most popular of the three is Larry Bird. Larry Bird captured the imagination of basketball fans and his magazine covers are pursued by memorabilia collectors and fans everywhere.

MEDIA GUIDES		Nr-Mt	Ex
☐ 1951-52	Folder report	200	75
☐ 1952-53	....	150	75
☐ 1953-54	....	100	50
☐ 1954-55	Ind. Celtics photos	100	50
☐ 1955-56	Bob Cousy art	100	50
☐ 1956-57	Team photos	75	35
☐ 1957-58	Ind. Celtics photo's	65	30
☐ 1958-59	Frank Ramsell	50	25
☐ 1959-60	Gene Conley	50	20
☐ 1960-61	Boston Garden	50	20
☐ 1961-62	Red Auerbach	50	20
☐ 1962-63	Bob Cousy	45	20
☐ 1963-64	Tom Heinsohn	50	20
☐ 1964-65	Boston Garden	40	15
☐ 1965-66	....	40	15
☐ 1966-67	Bill Russell	40	15
☐ 1967-68	John Havlicek in action	40	15
☐ 1968-69	Bill Russell	40	15
☐ 1969-70	Celtics Mascot	25	10
☐ 1970-71	Cowens, White, Nelson	25	10
☐ 1971-72	Cowens, Havlicek, White	25	10
☐ 1972-73	Cowens, Havlicek	25	10
☐ 1973-74	Cowens, Havlicek, White	25	10
☐ 1974-75	John Havlicek, Paul Silas	25	10
☐ 1975-76	John Havlicek/Dave Cowens	25	10
☐ 1976-77	Championship trophy	15	7
☐ 1977-78	John Havlicek	15	7
☐ 1978-79	Dave Cowens	15	7
☐ 1979-80	Larry Bird	45	20
☐ 1980-81	Larry Bird/Others	25	10
☐ 1981-82	Championship banner	15	7
☐ 1982-83	Celtics w/Bird	20	7
☐ 1983-84	Celtics vs. Hawks	20	7
☐ 1984-85	Championship Trophy	15	7
☐ 1985-86	Larry Bird	20	10
☐ 1986-87	Larry Bird	20	10
☐ 1987-88	Larry Bird/Others	20	10
☐ 1988-89	Celtics	15	7
☐ 1989-90	Red Auerbach	15	7
☐ 1990-on	....	10	5

GAME PROGRAMS

Celtic game programs are actually very popular and collected. The championship years and the early vintage Celtic material is pursued by many collectors. Very few (if any) programs from the original Celtics go up for sale.

		Nr-Mt	Ex
☐ 1920's	Game Programs	400	200
☐ 1946	First NBA Game	600	300
☐ 1947-51	Game Programs	75	35
☐ 1952-55	Game Programs	50	25
☐ 1956-60	Game Programs	40	20
☐ 1961-65	Game Programs	30	15

SCHEDULES

Pre 1970 Schedules are tough to find. Schedules in the early years were not made with the same 'pocket' format as today schedules.

		Nr-Mt	Ex
☐ 1948-50	Schedule	100	50
☐ 1951-55	Schedule	50	25
☐ 1956-60	Schedule	40	20
☐ 1961-65	Pocket Schedule	35	15

☐ 1966-70	Pocket Schedule	30	10
☐ 1971-76	Pocket Schedule	25	10
☐ 1977	Pocket Schedule (Larry Bird)	30	10
☐ 1978-80	Pocket Schedule	25	10
☐ 1981-85	Pocket Schedule	15	8
☐ 1986-90	Pocket Schedule	7	4
☐ 1991-97	Pocket Schedule	2	1

YEARBOOKSx
1955-56 through 1973-74 Yearbooks and Media Guides were the same. The yearbooks were large magazine size and not media guide size.

		Nr-Mt	Ex
☐ 1974-75	Paul Silas	35	15
☐ 1975-76	John Havlicek	35	15
☐ 1976-77	Jo Jo White	25	10
☐ 1977-78	Dave Cowens	25	10
☐ 1978-79		25	10
☐ 1979-80	. . . .	25	10
☐ 1980-81	Larry Bird	40	15
☐ 1981-82	Larry Bird	30	10
☐ 1982-83	Larry Bird, Parrish, Mchale	25	10
☐ 1983-84	Robert Parish	20	10
☐ 1984-85	Larry Bird vs Magic Johnson	30	15
☐ 1985-86	Larry Bird	25	15
☐ 1986-87	Championship banner	20	10
☐ 1987-88	Larry Bird, Parish, McHale	15	7
☐ 1988-89	Larry Bird	12	5
☐ 1989-90	Robert Parish	15	5
☐ 1990-91	Larry Bird	15	5
☐ 1991-97	. . . .	10	5

CHARLOTTE HORNETS
This is a young team that is developing its own fan base. Very few publications have been made for the Charlotte Hornets. They have the traditional publications like media guides, programs (Hoop) and their own newsletter/magazine. The biggest names is Larry Johnson, Alonzo Mourning.

MEDIA GUIDES		Nr-Mt	Ex
☐ 1988-89	Stern	20	7
☐ 1989-90	NBA Banner	10	7
☐ 1990-91	Gene Little	5	3
☐ 1991-97	. . . .	4	1

GAME PROGRAMS		Nr-Mt	Ex
☐ 1988	First Game	40	20
☐ 1988-89	Game Programs	5	2
☐ 1990-97	Game Programs	4	1
	Key Players Featured	20	5

POCKET SCHEDULES		Nr-Mt	Ex
☐ 1988	First Schedule	10	5
☐ 1989-90	Pocket schedule	4	2
☐ 1991-97	Pocket Schedule	2	1

YEARBOOKS
There is none made.

CHICAGO BULLS
The Chicago Bulls have put together one of the greatest teams in basketball history. Led by Michael Jordan, Chicago Bulls publications are the hottest collected sports publications in the last decade. However, most of the Chicago Bulls material that is collect is Michael Jordan related.

Michael Jordan
Michael Jordan has appeared on more sports publications than any other basketball player and perhaps any other professional athlete. He has appeared on at least 1000 publications (sports and business) and will appear on another 100 in the next year. Michael Jordan has recently surpassed Muhammad Ali for the most appearances on Sports Illustrated. The most popular Michael Jordan publication is his first SI cover in 1983 (150 in ex-mt).

The value of Jordan material is based on both scarcity and early history. The most valuable pieces are Michael Jordan high school and college material. Pieces from his high school years would be valued in the $150-$300 range and are very scarce. He did not appear on any publications but was in the McDonald's High School All Star programs. He has high school

game programs and yearbooks. Newspaper articles and the like would also be sought after and very tough.

Michael Jordan first started to appear on sports publications in his college years. His first appearances would be valued in the 100-200 range. His more common sports publication covers would be valued in the 30-50 range (The Sporting News).

Michael Jordan early pro years publications are scarce and they are twice as valuable as his later years (35-50 range). This would also be a realistic range for rare publication appearances on tough to find sports publications. The more common sports publications (Sport, SI, etc.) would have ranges in the 15-35 range.

MEDIA GUIDES		Nr-Mt	Ex
☐ 1966-67	Bulls Logo	40	15
☐ 1967-68	Bulls Logo	35	15
☐ 1968-69	Bulls Logo	35	15
☐ 1969-70	Bulls Logo	25	7
☐ 1970-71	Bulls Logo	25	7
☐ 1971-72	Bulls Logo	15	5
☐ 1972-73	Chet Walker	15	7
☐ 1973-74	Chet Walker	15	5
☐ 1974-75	Bulls Logo	15	5
☐ 1975-76	Bulls Logo	15	5
☐ 1976-77	Bulls art	15	5
☐ 1977-78	Action Photo's	10	5
☐ 1978-79	Artis Gilmore	10	5
☐ 1979-80	Artis Gilmore	10	5
☐ 1980-81	Reggie Theus	10	3
☐ 1981-82	Artis Gilmore	10	3
☐ 1982-83	Rod Thorn	10	3
☐ 1983-84	Kevin Loughery	10	3
☐ 1984-85	Michael Jordan	50	20
☐ 1985-86	Michael Jordan	40	15
☐ 1986-87	Michael Jordan	35	15
☐ 1987-88	Action (Michael Jordan)	35	15
☐ 1988-89	Michael Jordan/others	30	15
☐ 1989-90	Bulls comic	25	10
☐ 1990-on	. . . .	15	5

GAME PROGRAMS		Nr-Mt	Ex
☐ 1966	First Game	250	150
☐ 1966-68	Regular Season Programs	35	15
☐ 1969-72	Regular Season Programs	20	10
☐ 1972-76	Regular Season Programs	15	7
☐ 1977-83	Regular Season Programs	10	4
☐ 1984	Jordan First Game	300	150
☐ 1984-86	Regular Season Programs	20	10
☐ 1987-90	Regular Season Programs	15	5
☐ 1991-93	Champion Season Programs	15	5
☐ 1993-95	Regular Season Programs	5	1
☐ 1995-97	Champion Season Programs	7	2
☐	Issue with Jordan on Cover	20	10
☐	Issue with Pippen on Cover	10	5
☐	Programs when Jordan set records	60	25

POCKET SCHEDULES		Nr-Mt	Ex
Tough to find pre 1970.
☐ 1966-70	Pocket Schedule	30	10
☐ 1971-76	Pocket Schedule	25	10
☐ 1977-80	Pocket Schedule	15	8
☐ 1981-84	Pocket Schedule	10	4
☐ 1984-90	Pocket Schedule (Jordan)	20	10
☐ 1984-90	Pocket Schedule	10	4
☐ 1991-97	Pocket Schedule	2	1
☐ 1991-97	Pocket Schedule (Jordan)	6	3

Chicago Bulls have no yearbooks. Newsletter/magazines were released throughout the history of the Bulls. The issues that have the most value feature Jordan. Early Jordan pieces released by the team (pre-88) have the most value.

CLEVELAND CAVALIERS
The Cleveland Cavaliers appeared on the scene in 1970 and have remained one of the teams that have not generated a major superstar. The demand for their publications is relatively low.

MEDIA GUIDES

		Nr-Mt	Ex
☐ 1970-71	Cleveland Logo	25	7
☐ 1971-72	Cleveland Logo	15	5
☐ 1972-73	Cleveland Logo	15	7
☐ 1973-74	Cav Action	15	5
☐ 1974-75	Cleveland Logo	15	5
☐ 1975-76	Cleveland Stadium	15	5
☐ 1976-77	Cleveland	15	5
☐ 1977-78	Cav's mascot	15	5
☐ 1978-79	Cav's	10	5
☐ 1979-80	A new Era	10	5
☐ 1980-81	Cav's	10	3
☐ 1981-82	Mike Mitchell	10	3
☐ 1982-83	Ron Brewer	10	3
☐ 1983-84	Cav's Logo	10	3
☐ 1984-85	15th Season	10	3
☐ 1985-86	Cav's	10	3
☐ 1986-87	Lenny Wilkins	10	3
☐ 1987-88	Williams, Harper	10	3
☐ 1988-89	Cavs vs Bulls	10	3
☐ 1989-90	20th Season - Lenny Wilkins	10	3
☐ 1990-97		5	3

GAME PROGRAMS

		Nr-Mt	Ex
☐ 1970	First Game	50	25
☐ 1970-71	Game Programs	15	7
☐ 1971-75	Game Programs	12	5
☐ 1976-80	Game Programs	7	3
☐ 1981-85	Game Programs	5	2
☐ 1986-90	Game Programs	3	1
☐ 1991-97	Game Programs	2	1
☐	Key Programs	20	10
☐	Key People on cover	15	5

POCKET SCHEDULES

		NrMt	Ex
☐ 1970-71	Pocket Schedule	15	7
☐ 1971-75	Pocket Schedule	12	5
☐ 1976-80	Pocket Schedule	7	3
☐ 1981-85	Pocket Schedule	5	2
☐ 1986-90	Pocket Schedule	3	1
☐ 1991-97	Pocket Schedule	2	1

YEARBOOKS AND MAGAZINES

Cleveland produced no separate yearbooks but has released team issued magazines and newsletters. They have nominal values in the 5-10 range.

DALLAS MAVERICKS

This is a team that has never done well and does not have a strong fan collector base.

MEDIA GUIDES

		Nr-Mt	EX
☐ 1980-81	Mavericks uniform art	10	3
☐ 1981-82	Dallas Reunion Arena	8	2
☐ 1982-83	Dick Motta art	5	1
☐ 1983-on		4	1

GAME PROGRAMS

		Nr-Mt	Ex
☐ 1980	First Game	30	10
☐ 1980-90	Game Programs	7	1
☐ 1991-97	Game Programs	4	1
	Key Players on cover	15	5

POCKET SCHEDULES

		Nr-Mt	Ex
☐ 1980	First Schedule	10	2
☐ 1981-90	Schedules	7	1
☐ 1991-97	Schedules	4	1

YEARBOOKS & MAGAZINES

		Nr-Mt	Ex
☐ 1987-88	Mark Aguirre	12	2
☐ 1988-89	Roy Tarpley	10	2

No others yearbooks were issued but team release magazines and newsletter may exist.

DENVER NUGGETS (ROCKETS)

The Denver Nuggets were first affiliated with the ABA team the Denver Rockets. The Denver Rockets are heavily collected by devoted Denver fans but the Nuggets lack the hard core following. The Denver Nuggets had a few major superstars: Dan Issel, Dave Thompson, and Alex English.

MEDIA GUIDES

		Nr-mt	Ex
☐ 1967-68	(First ABA Media Guide - rare)	150	50
☐ 1968-69		75	35
☐ 1969-70	Art	60	25
☐ 1970-71		50	25
☐ 1971-72	Ralph Simpson	45	25
☐ 1972-73	Alex Hannum	35	20
☐ 1973-74	Team Photo	35	15
Denver Nuggets (ABA)			
☐ 1974-75	Scheer, L. Brown, M. Calvin	35	15
☐ 1975-76	Thompson, Issel, Scheer, etc.	35	15
☐ 1976-77	Action art	35	15
Denver Nuggets (NBA)			
☐ 1977-78	Logo	25	10
☐ 1978-79	Nuggets mascot	15	7
☐ 1979-80	David Thompson	15	7
☐ 1980-81	Dan Issel	15	7
☐ 1981-82	Thompson, English, Issel	15	7
☐ 1982-83	Nuggets logo	15	7
☐ 1983-84	10th Ann. Action photos	15	7
☐ 1984-85	Action art	15	7
☐ 1985-86	Alex English & Calvin Nat	10	5
☐ 1986-87	Alex English	7	3
☐ 1987-88	Alex English, Fat Lever	6	3
☐ 1988-89	Alex English, Fat Lever	5	3
☐ 1989-90	Alex English, Denver skyline	4	2
☐ 1990-on		4	1

GAME PROGRAMS

		Nr-Mt	Ex
☐ 1967-68	First Game	400	200
☐ 1967-68	First year	60	40
☐ 1968-70	Programs	40	20
☐ 1971-74	Programs	30	10
☐ 1974-77	Denver Nuggets Programs	25	10
☐	Dr J Programs	40+	20
☐ 1977	First NBA Game	100	45
☐ 1978-80	Game Programs	10	5
☐ 1981-97	Game Programs	5	2
	Key Players & games	20	5

POCKET SCHEDULES

		Nr-Mt	Ex
☐ 1967-68	Schedule or Pocket Schedule	50	20
☐ 1968-70	Pocket Schedules	30	15
☐ 1971-76	Pocket Schedules	25	12
☐ 1977-80	Pocket Schedules	7	3
☐ 1981-89	Pocket Schedules	5	2
☐ 1990-97	Pocket Schedules	2	1

YEARBOOKS & MAGAZINES

No Yearbooks were issued. Magazines, newsletters and literature have been made and released periodically by the team. The values range based upon the era (ABA vs NBA) as well as scarcity.

DETROIT PISTONS

The Detroit Pistons is one of the older NBA teams with a quality history of fans and collectibles. The Pistons greatest basketball era would have to be the championship teams led by Isiah Thomas in 88-90. Today, Grant Hill is popular and is becoming heavily collected.

MEDIA GUIDES

		Nr-Mt	Ex
☐ 1954-55	Art	150	50
☐ 1955-56	Art	125	50
☐ 1956-57	Art	100	50
☐ 1957-58	Art	100	50
☐ 1958-59	Art	100	50
☐ 1959-60	Art	100	50
☐ 1960-61	Art	95	45
☐ 1961-62	Art	90	45
☐ 1962-63	Art	80	40
☐ 1963-64	Art	70	35
☐ 1964-65	Art	60	30
☐ 1965-66	Art	55	25

		Nr-Mt	Ex
☐ 1966-67	Art	50	25
☐ 1967-68	Art	40	20
☐ 1968-69		25	10
☐ 1969-70	Art	25	10
☐ 1970-71		25	10
☐ 1971-72		25	10
☐ 1972-73	Coach Earl Lloyd	15	7
☐ 1973-74		15	7
☐ 1974-75	logo	15	7
☐ 1975-76	Action Art	15	7
☐ 1976-77	Art	15	7
☐ 1977-78	Art	15	7
☐ 1978-79	Art	15	7
☐ 1979-80	Logo	15	7
☐ 1980-81		15	7
☐ 1981-82	Isiah Thomas	15	7
☐ 1982-83		15	7
☐ 1983-84	Isiah Thomas	15	7
☐ 1984-85	Isiah Thomas	15	7
☐ 1985-86	Isiah Thomas	10	5
☐ 1986-87	Adrian Dantley	7	3
☐ 1987-88	Adrian Dantley	6	3
☐ 1988-89	(champs)	10	2
☐ 1989-90	(champs)	10	2
☐ 1990-on		4	1

GAME PROGRAMS

		Nr-Mt	Ex
☐	First Game Program	300	150
☐	First Year	75	35
☐ 1950-54	Game Programs	40	15
☐ 1955-59	Game Programs	35	15
☐ 1960-65	Game Programs	20	10
☐ 1966-69	Game Programs	15	7
☐ 1970-75	Game Programs	12	5
☐ 1976-80	Game Programs	10	3
☐ 1981-97	Game Programs	5	1
☐ 1970-97	Key Programs	20+	10
☐ 1970-97	Key Players on cover	20	10

TEAM SCHEDULES

		Nr-Mt	Ex
☐ 1950-54	Schedules	40	15
☐ 1955-59	Schedules	35	15
☐ 1960-65	Schedules	20	10
☐ 1966-69	Schedules	15	7
☐ 1970-75	Schedules	12	5
☐ 1976-80	Schedules	10	3
☐ 1981-97	Schedules	5	1

YEARBOOKS & MAGAZINES
No Yearbooks were issued but team issued newsletter and magazines appeared over the years.

GOLDEN STATE/PHILADELPHIA WARRIORS

The Philadelphia Warriors were one of the original NBA teams. They won the championship in the first official season. The team moved to San Francisco in 1962. Wilt Chamberlain came up with Philadelphia and moved with the team to San Francisco.

The San Francisco Warriors moved to Oakland and became the Golden State Warriors in 1971. However, the fan base for the Warriors extends throughout the Bay Area. The only time they went to the finals and won the championship was with Rick Barry in 1974-75. They have never done well since then.

The Warriors have had a few great stars (Wilt Chamberlain, Rick Barry, Chris Mullin, Nate Thurmond, etc.) but no individual player seems to have drawn a strong Bay Area following.

MEDIA GUIDES

		Nr-Mt	Ex
☐ 1962-63	Art	120	50
☐ 1963-64	Art	70	35
☐ 1964-65	Art	60	30
☐ 1965-66	Art	55	25
☐ 1966-67	Art	50	25
☐ 1967-68	Art	40	20

		Nr-Mt	Ex
☐ 1968-69	Logo	25	10
☐ 1969-70	Nate Thurmond	25	10
☐ 1970-71	Nate Thurmond	25	10
☐ 1971-72	Coach Al Attles	25	10
☐ 1972-73	Nate Thurmond	15	7
☐ 1973-74	Nate Thurmond	15	7
☐ 1974-75	Warriors Art	15	7
☐ 1975-76	NBA Champion	15	7
☐ 1976-77	Al Attles	15	7
☐ 1977-78	Warriors	15	7
☐ 1978-79	Warriors	15	7
☐ 1979-80	Warriors	15	7
☐ 1980-81	Logo	15	7
☐ 1981-82	Al Attles	15	7
☐ 1982-83	Basketball	15	7
☐ 1983-84		15	7
☐ 1984-85	Action	15	7
☐ 1985-86	Chris Mullin	10	5
☐ 1986-87		7	3
☐ 1987-88		6	3
☐ 1988-89	Ralph Sampson	6	2
☐ 1989-90	Chris Mullin	6	2
☐ 1990-97		4	1

GAME PROGRAMS

		Nr-Mt	Ex
☐ 1962	First Game Program SF	300	100
☐ 1962-63	First Year	95	35
☐ 1963-65	Game Programs	40	15
☐ 1966-67	Game Programs	35	15
☐ 1968-69	Game Programs	20	10
☐ 1970-75	Game Programs	12	5
☐ 1976-80	Game Programs	10	3
☐ 1981-97	Game Programs	5	1
☐ 1970-97	Key Programs	20+	10
☐ 1970-97	Key Players on cover	20	10

SCHEDULES

		Nr-Mt	Ex
☐ 1962-63	First Schedule	55	25
☐ 1963-65	Schedule	35	15
☐ 1966-69	Schedule	25	10
☐ 1970-75	Schedule	12	5
☐ 1976-80	Schedule	10	3
☐ 1981-89	Schedule	4	1
☐ 1990-97 Schedule		2	1

YEARBOOKS & MAGAZINES
No Yearbooks were issued. The team has issued magazines, newsletters and press releases. The prices range on this material.

HOUSTON/SAN DIEGO ROCKETS

The Houston Rockets have generated three NBA finalists and two Championships in the last 12 years. The team has had many great names play on their team, including: Cal Murphy, Moses Malone, and Elvin Hayes. However their current team has three of the greatest players of the game: Barkley, Olajuwon and Drexler.

The San Diego Rockets lasted four years and have a small but dedicated following. The Houston Rockets following is mostly confined to the Houston market.

MEDIA GUIDES

		Nr-Mt	Ex
☐ 1967-68	Rockets logo (San Diego)	40	20
☐ 1968-69	Rockets logo	25	10
☐ 1969-70	Elvin Hayes	25	10
☐ 1970-71	Elvin Hayes	25	10
☐ 1971-72	Rockets action (Houston)	25	10
☐ 1972-73	Rockets action	15	7
☐ 1973-74	Newlin/Chamberlain	15	7
☐ 1974-75	Rudy Tomjanovich	15	7
☐ 1975-76	Mike Newlin	15	7
☐ 1976-77	Calvin Murphy	15	7
☐ 1977-78	R. Tomjanovich	15	7
☐ 1978-79	Barry/Malone	15	7
☐ 1979-80	Moses Malone art	15	7
☐ 1980-81	Rockets action art	15	7

		Nr-Mt	Ex
☐ 1981-82	Moses Malone	15	7
☐ 1982-83	Elvin Hayes	15	7
☐ 1983-84	Ralph Sampson	15	7
☐ 1984-85	A. Olajuwon/Sampson	15	7
☐ 1985-86	Olajuwon/Sampson	10	5
☐ 1986-87	Sampson/Olajuwon	7	3
☐ 1987-88	Hakeem Olajuwon	6	3
☐ 1988-89		6	2
☐ 1989-90	Hakeem Olajuwon	6	2
☐ 1990-on		4	1

GAME PROGRAMS

		Nr-Mt	Ex
☐ 1967	First Program	100	50
☐ 1967-68	First Year	35	15
☐ 1968-71	Game Programs	25	5
☐ 1972	First Houston Program	50	35
☐ 1972-75	Game Programs	15	5
☐ 1976-80	Game Programs	10	3
☐ 1981-on	Game Programs	5	1

SCHEDULES

		Nr-Mt	Ex
☐ 1962-63	First Schedule	55	25
☐ 1963-65	Schedule	35	15
☐ 1966-69	Schedule	25	10
☐ 1970-75	Schedule	12	5
☐ 1976-80	Schedule	10	3
☐ 1981-89	Schedule	4	1
☐ 1990-97 Schedule		2	1

YEARBOOKS & MAGAZINES
No separate yearbooks were issued. Magazines and newsletters are issued periodically.

INDIANA PACERS
The Indiana Pacers were one of the original ABA teams that went into the NBA. The ABA Pacers are heavily collected by very devoted NBA fans. The NBA team has a solid fan support in Indianapolis. However all of its championship trophies are from the ABA years. The great players from the early days were Mel Daniels, Roger Brown, and George McGinnis. Once the Pacers entered the NBA they had to wait a few years for a superstar in Reggie Miller.

MEDIA GUIDES

		Nr-Mt	Ex
☐ 1967-68	Rare Media Guide	150	50
☐ 1968-69	Mel Daniels	75	35
☐ 1969-70	Mel Daniels	60	25
☐ 1970-71	Roger Brown	50	25
☐ 1971-72	Bob Leonard cartoon	45	25
☐ 1972-73	Daniels, McGinnis, Leonard	35	20
☐ 1973-74	ABA Trophies	35	15
☐ 1974-75	Market Square Arena	35	15
☐ 1975-76	Pacers logo	35	15
☐ 1976-77		35	15
Indiana Pacers (NBA)			
☐ 1977-78	Coach Bob Leonard	25	10
☐ 1978-79	Market Square	15	7
☐ 1979-80	Pacers logo	15	7
☐ 1980-81		15	7
☐ 1981-82	Coach Jack McKinney	15	7
☐ 1982-83	Herb Williams	15	7
☐ 1983-84	Indianapolis artwork	15	7
☐ 1984-85	Pacer Pride	15	7
☐ 1985-86	Uniform Art	10	5
☐ 1986-87	Herb Williams	7	3
☐ 1987-88	Jack Ramsey, Player art	6	3
☐ 1988-89	S. Stipanovich/Pat Ewing	5	3
☐ 1989-90	Reggie Miller	6	2
☐ 1990-on		4	1

GAME PROGRAMS

		Nr-Mt	Ex
☐ 1967-68	First Program ABA	300	100
☐ 1967-68	Game Programs ABA	95	25
☐ 1968-72	Game Programs ABA	45	20
☐ 1973-76	Game Programs ABA	30	15
☐ 1977	First Program NBA	50	35
☐ 1977-80	Game Programs	10	3

		Nr-Mt	Ex
☐ 1981-97	Game Programs	5	1
	Key Programs & Key Players	20	5

POCKET SCHEDULES

		Nr-Mt	Ex
☐ 1967-68	First Schedule ABA	50	20
☐ 1968-72	Schedules ABA	35	15
☐ 1973-76	Schedules ABA	25	15
☐ 1977-80	Schedules	10	3
☐ 1981-97	Game Programs	2	1

YEARBOOKS & MAGAZINES
No yearbooks were issued but various press releases, magazines and newsletters were issued. Price vary based on scarcity.

LOS ANGELES/SAN DIEGO CLIPPERS (BUFFALO BRAVES)
The Los Angeles Clippers is a team that is not heavily collected. However, the Buffalo Braves have a small committed following from the Buffalo area.

MEDIA GUIDES

		Nr-Mt	Ex
☐ 1970-71	Braves logo	35	10
☐ 1971-72	Braves logo	25	10
☐ 1972-73	Smith/Wilt Chamberlain	25	10
☐ 1973-74	Braves action photo	15	7
☐ 1974-75	Braves action	15	7
☐ 1975-76	Braves action	15	7
☐ 1976-77	Four action photo's	15	7
☐ 1977-78	Buffalo	15	7
San Diego Clippers			
☐ 1978-79	Randy Smith	15	7
☐ 1979-80	Bill Walton	20	10
☐ 1980-81	Paul Silas	15	7
☐ 1981-82	Freeman Williams	15	7
☐ 1982-83	Tom Chambers	15	7
☐ 1983-84	Terry Cummings	15	7
Los Angeles Clippers			
☐ 1984-85	Logo	15	7
☐ 1985-86	Derek Smith	10	5
☐ 1986-87	Benoit Benjamin	7	3
☐ 1987-88	Norm Nixon	6	3
☐ 1988-89	Danny Manning	5	3
☐ 1989-90	Danny Manning	4	2
☐ 1990-on		3	1

GAME PROGRAMS

		Nr-Mt	Ex
☐ 1970	First Game	100	50
☐ 1970-73	Braves Game Programs	45	20
☐ 1973-78	Braves Game Programs	30	15
☐ 1977-84	San Diego Clippers Programs	10	3
☐ 1985-90	LA Game Programs	6	1
☐ 1981-97	Game Programs	2	1
	Key Programs & Key Players	20	5

POCKET SCHEDULES

		Nr-Mt	Ex
☐ 1970-71	First Schedule	35	15
☐ 1972-75	Schedules - Braves	20	10
☐ 1976-78	Schedules - Braves	10	4
☐ 1979-84	Schedules - Clippers	5	2
☐ 1985-90	Schedules - Clippers	2	1
☐ 1991-97	Schedules - Clippers	1	.5

YEARBOOKS & MAGAZINES
No yearbooks were issued but various press releases, magazines and newsletters were issued. Price vary based on scarcity.

LOS ANGELES/MINNEAPOLIS LAKERS
The Minneapolis Lakers date back to the beginning of the NBA. The Lakers generated champion teams, even before they moved to LA. The number one player collected from the Milwaukee period is George Mikan. He led the league in scoring and is one of the greatest players of all time.

The Lakers are one of the most collected teams in the NBA. This is because they are a team of winners with the Jerry West/Wilt Chamberlain era and the Magic Johnson/Kareem Abdul Jabbar era. Today the Lakers have Shaq to lead them to another championship era.

MEDIA GUIDES

		Nr-Mt	Ex
☐ 1954-55	Minneapolis Lakers	150	50
☐ 1955-56	Minneapolis Lakers	150	50
☐ 1956-57	Minneapolis Lakers	150	50
☐ 1957-58	Minneapolis Lakers	150	50
☐ 1958-59	Minneapolis Lakers	150	50
☐ 1959-60	Minneapolis Lakers	150	50
☐ 1960-61	LA Lakers	150	50
☐ 1961-62	. . . .	125	50
☐ 1962-63	. . . .	125	50
☐ 1963-64	. . . .	100	35
☐ 1964-65	. . . .	75	30
☐ 1965-66	. . . .	65	25
☐ 1966-67	LA Laker Logo	50	20
☐ 1967-68	Logo	40	20
☐ 1968-69	Wilt Chamberlain & E. Baylor	35	15
☐ 1969-70	. . . .	30	15
☐ 1970-71		30	15
☐ 1971-72	The Great Team	35	15
☐ 1972-73	Championship Trophy	30	10
☐ 1973-74	Gail Goodrich	25	10
☐ 1974-75	Gail Goodrich	25	10
☐ 1975-76	Kareem Abdul Jabbar	20	10
☐ 1976-77	Jerry West	15	7
☐ 1977-78	Laker Girl	15	7
☐ 1978-79	Kareem Abdul Jabbar	15	7
☐ 1979-80	Magic & Kareem	45	10
☐ 1980-81	Kareem & Magic	25	10
☐ 1981-82	Magic & Kareem	15	7
☐ 1982-83	Magic & Kareem	15	7
☐ 1983-84	The Forum	15	7
☐ 1984-85	Kareem Abdul Jabbar	15	7
☐ 1985-86	Kareem Abdul Jabbar & Trophy . . .	15	7
☐ 1986-97	. . . .	10	3

GAME PROGRAMS

		Nr-Mt	Ex
☐ 1946	First Game	600	250
☐ 1946-48	Programs	100	50
☐ 1949-52	Programs	75	35
☐ 1953-59	Programs	65	25
☐ 1960	First LA Laker Program	350	200
☐ 1960-61	First Game Program	65	40
☐ 1961-64	Programs	40	20
☐ 1965-71	Programs	20	10
☐ 1971-72	Champion Year	25	15
☐ 1973-76	Programs	15	7
☐ 1977-82	Programs	10	3
☐ 1983-90	Programs	7	2
☐ 1991-97	Programs	4	1
☐	First Jerry West Program	100	50
☐	First Kareem Abdul Jabbar	75	35
☐	First Shaq O'Neil	10	5
☐	First Magic Johnson	75	35
☐	Special Issues	30	15
☐	Key Cover Features	20	10

POCKET SCHEDULES

		Nr-Mt	Ex
☐ 1946-48	Schedules	75	35
☐ 1949-52	Schedules	70	25
☐ 1953-59	Schedules	55	20
☐ 1960-61	Schedules	65	40
☐ 1961-64	Schedules	40	20
☐ 1965-71	Schedules	20	10
☐ 1971-72	Schedules	25	15
☐ 1973-76	Schedules	15	7
☐ 1977-82	Schedules	10	3
☐ 1983-90	Schedules	7	2
☐ 1991-97	Schedules	4	1

YEARBOOKS & MAGAZINES

		Nr-Mt	Ex
☐ 1950	George Mikan/Laker Champion . . .	120	50

The magazines, newsletter, and press releases are quality pieces produced by the Laker organization. Early Laker material is hard to find. Value would be based on who is featured and the content of the material.

MIAMI HEAT

Miami Heat is a relatively new team with no major heroes.

MEDIA GUIDES

		Nr-Mt	Ex
☐ 1988-89	Heat Logo	10	5
☐ 1989-90	Rory Sparrow	7	3
☐ 1990-91	Dominique Wilkens	5	2
☐ 1991-97		4	1

GAME PROGRAMS

		Nr-Mt	Ex
☐ 1988	First Game	20	10
☐ 1988-90	Game Programs	5	2
☐ 1991-97	Game Programs	2	1
☐	Feature Covers	15	5
☐	Key Programs	15	5

SCHEDULES

		Nr-Mt	Ex
☐ 1946-48	Schedules	75	35
☐ 1949-52	Schedules	70	25
☐ 1953-59	Schedules	55	20
☐ 1960-61	Schedules	65	40
☐ 1961-64	Schedules	40	20
☐ 1965-71	Schedules	20	10
☐ 1971-72	Schedules	25	15
☐ 1973-76	Schedules	15	7
☐ 1977-82	Schedules	10	3
☐ 1983-90	Schedules	7	2
☐ 1991-97	Schedules	4	1

TEAM SCHEDULES

		Nr-Mt	Ex
☐ 1988	First Game Program	7	3
☐ 1988-90	Game Programs	5	2
☐ 1991-97	Game Programs	2	1

YEARBOOKS & MAGAZINES

No Yearbooks were made. However team issue magazines and press release material does exist.

MILWAUKEE BUCKS

Milwaukee Bucks greatest years were with Lew Alcindor & Oscar Robertson.

MEDIA GUIDES

		Nr-Mt	Ex
☐ 1968-69	Bucks vs Royals	40	15
☐ 1969-70	Bucks Logo	25	7
☐ 1970-71	Kareem in Action	25	7
☐ 1971-72	Kareem in Action	15	5
☐ 1972-73	Kareem in Action vs Suns	15	7
☐ 1973-74	Lucius Allen in action	15	5
☐ 1974-75	Kareem	15	5
☐ 1975-76	Buks vs Bulls	15	5
☐ 1976-77	Gary Brokaw vs Bulls	15	5
☐ 1977-78	Brian Winters vs Suns	10	5
☐ 1978-79	Marques Johnson art	10	5
☐ 1979-80	. . . .	10	5
☐ 1980-81	Art	10	3
☐ 1981-82	Sidney Moncrief	10	3
☐ 1982-83	Bucks - art	10	3
☐ 1983-84	Nelson, Moncrief	10	3
☐ 1984-85	Sidney Moncreif	10	3
☐ 1985-86	Paul Pressey	10	3
☐ 1986-87	Sidney Moncreif	10	3
☐ 1987-88	20th Anniversary	10	3
☐ 1988-89	Bucs vs Rockets	10	3
☐ 1989-90	Del Harris	10	3
☐ 1990-on	. . . .	5	3

GAME PROGRAMS

		Nr-Mt	Ex
☐ 1968	First Game	100	50
☐ 1968-70	Game Programs	20	5
☐ 1971-75	Game Programs	15	3
☐ 1976-80	Game Programs	10	2
☐ 1981-90	Game Programs	5	1
☐ 1991-97	Game Programs	3	1
☐	First Lew Alcindor Program	75	35

		Nr-Mt	Ex
☐	First Kevin Garnett Program	20	10
☐	Other Key Covers	20	10
☐	Other Key Programs		

SCHEDULES

		Nr-Mt	Ex
☐ 1968-70	Schedule	20	5
☐ 1971-75	Schedule	15	3
☐ 1976-80	Schedule	10	2
☐ 1981-90	Schedule	5	1
☐ 1991-97	Schedule	3	1

YEARBOOKS & MAGAZINES

There were no official Yearbooks issued (at least one unofficial yearbook in 1970). However, there have been newsletters, magazines and press releases issued.

MINNESOTA TIMBERWOLVES

This is a young team with some very exciting players on the team today (Kevin Garnett).

MEDIA GUIDES

		Nr-Mt	Ex
☐ 1989-90	....	10	3
☐ 1990-on	....	5	1

GAME PROGRAMS

		Nr-Mt	Ex
☐ 1989	First Game	25	10
☐ 1989-on	Game Programs	5	1
☐	Special Programs	20	5
☐	Cover Subjects	15	3

SCHEDULES

		Nr-Mt	Ex
☐ 1989	First Schedule	5	2
☐ 1989-on	Game Programs	2	1

YEARBOOKS & MAGAZINES

		Nr-Mt	Ex
☐ 1989-90	Timberwolves #1	15	3
☐ 1990-91	Starting Lineup	15	3
☐ 1991-on	....	10	3

Magazines and Newsletters may have been issued.

NEW YORK KNICKS

The New York Knicks are one of the most popular teams in basketball. New York fans are very loyal to their team. The Knicks date back into the 50's. The most collected period of the New York Knicks is the champion years with the great hall of fame players like Bill Bradley, Walt Frazier, Dave Debusshere and Willis Reed. This team lasted until the early 1970's. Unfortunately, the Knicks have not had a champion team until Patrick Ewing brought them into the finals against the Houston Rockets in 1994.

Bill Bradley is heavily collected by both basketball and political fans. His autograph is highly sought after and his two SI's are very popular. The other players are not collected individually but are collected by Knicks fans.

MEDIA GUIDES

		Nr-Mt	Ex
☐ 1958-59	Art Drawing	125	50
☐ 1959-60	Art Drawing	125	50
☐ 1960-61	Art Drawing	125	50
☐ 1961-62	....	125	50
☐ 1962-63	....	100	50
☐ 1963-64	....	80	40
☐ 1964-65	....	50	25
☐ 1965-66	....	50	25
☐ 1966-67	....	45	25
☐ 1967-68	....	40	25
☐ 1968-69	....	35	15
☐ 1969-70	Willis Reed, Dave Debusshere	35	15
☐ 1970-71	....	25	15
☐ 1971-72	....	25	10
☐ 1972-73	Champion Years	25	10
☐ 1973-74	Championship Trophy	20	5
☐ 1974-75	Bill Bradley	20	5
☐ 1975-76	....	20	5
☐ 1976-77	....	15	5
☐ 1977-78	Willie Reed	15	5
☐ 1978-79	Earl Monroe	12	5
☐ 1979-80	Bill Cartwright	10	5

		Nr-Mt	Ex
☐ 1980-81	Bill Cartwright	10	3
☐ 1981-82	NYC skyline	10	3
☐ 1982-83	Hubies Brooks	10	3
☐ 1983-84	Action	10	3
☐ 1984-85	Action	10	3
☐ 1985-86	Patrick Ewing	12	4
☐ 1986-87	Uniform	10	3
☐ 1987-on	....	7	2

GAME PROGRAMS

		Nr-Mt	Ex
☐ 1946	First Game	600	300
☐ 1946-48	Game Programs	100	50
☐ 1949-52	Game Programs	50	25
☐ 1953-56	Game Programs	40	20
☐ 1957-62	Game Programs	20	10
☐ 1963-69	Game Programs	15	5
☐ 1969-70	Championship Season	20	7
☐ 1971-75	Game Programs	12	3
☐ 1976-80	Game Programs	8	2
☐ 1981-89	Game Programs	6	1
☐ 1990-97	Game Programs	5	1
☐	First Bill Bradley Program	75	35
☐	Feature Covers	20	10
☐	Special Issues	20+	10

SCHEDULES

		Nr-Mt	Ex
☐ 1946	First Schedule	200	100
☐ 1947-50	Early Schedules	75	35
☐ 1951-57	Early Schedules	50	25
☐ 1958-62	Early Schedules	40	20
☐ 1963-69	Pocket Schedules	30	15
☐ 1969-70	Championship Schedule	35	20
☐ 1971-75	Pocket Schedules	15	5
☐ 1976-80	Pocket Schedules	10	3
☐ 1981-89	Pocket Schedules	5	2
☐ 1990-97	Pocket Schedules	2	1

YEARBOOKS & MAGAZINES

No Yearbooks were issued. Team magazines, newsletters and press releases have been issued. Prices vary based on vintage and who is featured.

NEW JERSEY NETS

The New Jersey Nets started first in the ABA as the New York Americans. When the ABA and NBA merged in 1977 they changed there name from the New York Nets to the New Jersey Nets.

The second most popular player in basketball history, Julius Erving, played many great years with the Nets before he went to the Philadelphia Sixers. His material is gold on anything that he appeared on.

MEDIA GUIDES

		Nr-Mt	Ex
☐ 1967-68	New Jersey Americans	150	75
☐ 1968-69	New Jersey Nets	75	35
☐ 1969-70	(ABA)	65	35
☐ 1970-71	....	50	25
☐ 1971-72	....	40	20
☐ 1972-73	....	40	20
☐ 1973-74	....	35	15
☐ 1974-75	....	30	12
☐ 1975-76	....	25	10
☐ 1976-77	....	25	10
☐ 1977-78	State of New Jersey art	15	3
☐ 1978-79	B. King & Williamson	15	3
☐ 1979-80	Art	12	3
☐ 1980-81	Action	12	3
☐ 1981-87	....	10	2
☐ 1988-97	....	5	1

GAME PROGRAMS

		Nr-Mt	Ex
☐ 1967	New Jersey Americans first pr	300	150
☐ 1967	New Jersey American Programs ..	100	50
☐ 1968-70	Game Programs (ABA)	40	20
☐ 1970-72	Game Programs (ABA)	30	15
☐ 1972-76	Game Programs (ABA)	25	10
☐ 1977-78	First Game Program (NBA)	50	20

		Nr-Mt	Ex
☐ 1977-80	Game Program	15	3
☐ 1981-on	Game Program	10	2
☐	Julius Erving ABA Covers	50	20
☐	Julius Erving NBA Programs	20	10
☐	Other Special Cover Programs	20	10

SCHEDULES

		Nr-Mt	Ex
☐ 1967	New Jersey Americans	100	50
☐ 1968-70	New Jersey Nets (ABA)	40	25
☐ 1971-76	New Jersey Nets (ABA)	25	15
☐ 1977-80	New York Nets (NBA)	10	5
☐ 1981-89	New York Nets (NBA)	5	2
☐ 1990-97	New York Nets (NBA)	2	1

YEARBOOKS & Magazines

		Nr-Mt	Ex
☐ 1975-76	Dr J (ABA)	45	20

No other Yearbooks were issued. Team issued magazines and press releases values are based on time period (ABA is 25+) and who appears (DR J items 25+).

ORLANDO MAGIC

Orlando Magic appeared on the basketball scene in 1989 and within a few years was a national finalist. The team was lead by Penny Hardiway and Shaq O'Neal. The value of the material is marginal.

MEDIA GUIDES

		Nr-mt	Ex
☐ 1990	....	10	2
☐ 191990-97	....	6	1

GAME PROGRAMS

		Nr-Mt	Ex
☐ 1989	First Game Program	30	10
☐ 1989-on	....	5	1
☐ First Shaq Program	....	35	15
☐ First Penny Hardiway Program	....	30	15
☐ Special cover Features	....	20	5

SCHEDULES

		Nr-Mt	Ex
☐ 1989	First schedule	5	1
☐ 1990-97	....	2	1

YEARBOOKS, MAGAZINES, TICKETS

No Yearbooks but team issued magazines, newsletters and the like have nominal value unless Shaq or Penny Hardiway appears on the cover. Tickets stubs are about 50% of the cover price.

PHILADELPHIA 76ERS

The Sixers had one of the greatest teams of all time with Moses Malone and Julius Erving. This team produced only one Championship trophy but it is forever remembered as one of the best. Julius Erving is the second most collected player of all time. His material is heavily found among Sixer publications.

MEDIA GUIDES

		Nr-Mt	Ex
☐ 1966-67	....	45	25
☐ 1967-68	B.Cunningham/W Chamberlain ...	40	25
☐ 1968-69	Hal Greer	35	15
☐ 1969-70	Hall Greer/B. Cunningham	35	15
☐ 1970-71	Team Pictures	25	15
☐ 1971-72	Sixers mascot	25	10
☐ 1972-73	Team photos	25	10
☐ 1973-74	Gene Shue art	20	5
☐ 1974-75	Shue/Cunningham	20	5
☐ 1975-76	Cunningham	20	5
☐ 1976-77	George McGinnis/Doug Collins	15	5
☐ 1977-78	Julius Erving	20	5
☐ 1978-79	Julius Erving	15	5
☐ 1979-80	Julius Erving	15	5
☐ 1980-81	....	15	3
☐ 1981-82	Julius Erving	15	3
☐ 1982-83	Julius Erving	15	3
☐ 1983-84	Julius Erving/Moses Malone	15	3
☐ 1984-85	Julius Erving	15	3
☐ 1985-86	Moses Malone	12	4
☐ 1986-87	Charles Barkley	10	3
☐ 1987-on	....	7	2

GAME PROGRAMS

		Nr-Mt	Ex
☐ 1966	First Game	300	100
☐ 1966-67	First Year	30	10
☐ 1967-70	Game Programs	20	5
☐ 1971-76	Game Programs	15	3
☐ 1977-87	Game Programs (Dr J played)	15	3
☐ 1988-on	Game Programs	5	1
☐	Special Programs	25+	10
☐	Programs with Dr J on cover	25	5

SCHEDULES

		Nr-Mt	Ex
☐ 1966-69	Schedule	25	15
☐ 1970-76	Schedules	15	5
☐ 1976-79	Schedules (Dr J)	20	10
☐ 1980-85	Schedules (Dr J)	15	7
☐ 1986-90	Schedules	7	4
☐ 1991-97	Schedules	2	1

YEARBOOKS, MAGAZINES, TICKETS

No official yearbooks were made. Magazines, Newsletters with Dr J are highly sought after. Ticket stubs would go for 50% of programs. Full tickets from key games would be worth more.

PHOENIX SUNS

The Phoenix Suns have a very devoted fan based in Arizona. However, a few of their key historic players are collected across the country: Connie Hawkins and Charles Barkley. The Suns have produced a series of media guides, programs, schedules and a newsmagazine for Suns fans.

MEDIA GUIDES

		Nr-Mt	Ex
☐ 1968-69	Suns Logo	35	15
☐ 1969-70	Suns Logo	35	15
☐ 1970-71	Suns Logo	25	15
☐ 1971-72	Connie Hawkins	25	10
☐ 1972-73	Connie Hawkins	25	10
☐ 1973-74	Neil Walk/Charlie Scott	20	5
☐ 1974-75	Suns logo	20	5
☐ 1975-76	Suns logo	20	5
☐ 1976-77	Alvin Adams	15	5
☐ 1977-78	Paul Westphal	20	5
☐ 1978-79	Davis, Westphal, Lee	15	5
☐ 1979-80	John MacLeod - Coach	15	5
☐ 1980-81	Alvin Adams	15	3
☐ 1981-82	Art	15	3
☐ 1982-83	Basketball	15	3
☐ 1983-84	Larry Nance	15	3
☐ 1984-85	Walter Davis	15	3
☐ 1985-86	Logo	12	4
☐ 1986-87	Suns	10	3
☐ 1987-88	Suns	7	2
☐ 1988-89	Tom Chambers, Hornacek	5	2
☐ 1989-90	Tom Chambers, Johnson, ...	5	1
☐ 1990-91	Suns Basketball	4	1
☐ 1991-on	....	4	1

GAME PROGRAMS

		Nr-Mt	Ex
☐ 1968-69	First Game	100	50
☐ 1968-69	First Year Program	30	10
☐ 1969-72	Game Programs	20	7
☐ 1972-77	Game Programs	15	3
☐ 1978-82	Game Programs	10	2
☐ 1983-on	Game Programs	5	1
☐	Key Programs	20	10
☐	Feature Covers	20	10

SCHEDULES

		Nr-Mt	Ex
☐ 1968-69	First Schedule	25	10
☐ 1969-72	Schedules	15	5
☐ 1972-77	Schedules	12	3
☐ 1978-82	Schedules	7	2
☐ 1983-on	Game Programs	4	1
☐	Key Programs	20	10
☐	Feature Covers	20	10

YEARBOOKS/NEWSLETTER/MAGAZINES/TICKETS

No Yearbooks but they started Fastbreak which started out as a newspaper then converted into a slick magazine. The magazine features every Phoenix Suns player. Key players would be worth 10-15 while the lesser cover feature players would be around 5. Ticket stubs go for 50% of the game programs.

PORTLAND TRAILBLAZERS

Portland Trailblazers have one championship season with Bill Walton in 1977 and a run in the finals twice. The key players collected are Bill Walton during his prime and Clyde Drexler. Most Portland fans collect the more recent stars. Publication material includes ticket stubs, pocket schedule, Media guides and game programs.

MEDIA GUIDES

		Nr-Mt	Ex
☐ 1970-71	Rick Adelman	25	5
☐ 1971-72	Geoff Petrie	15	5
☐ 1972-73	Sidney Wicks	15	5
☐ 1973-74	Jack McCloskey	15	5
☐ 1974-75	Bill Walton	15	5
☐ 1975-76	Lenny Steele	15	5
☐ 1976-77	Bill Walton	15	5
☐ 1977-78	Bill Walton (NBA Champs)	20	10
☐ 1978-79	Maurice Lucas	15	5
☐ 1979-80	Walton, Ramsey	10	5
☐ 1980-81	Billy Bates	10	3
☐ 1981-82	Jim Paxson	10	3
☐ 1982-83	Mychal Thompson	10	3
☐ 1983-84	Calvin Natt	10	3
☐ 1984-85	Kiki Vandeweghe, Sam Bowie	10	3
☐ 1985-86	Clyde Drexler	10	3
☐ 1986-87	Kiki Vandeweghe	10	3
☐ 1987-88	Steve Johnson	10	3
☐ 1988-89	Kevin Duckworth	10	3
☐ 1989-90	Rick Adelman	10	3
☐ 1990-91	Western Conference Champs!	5	3
☐ 1991-92 - 97		5	1

GAME PROGRAMS

Most game programs feature major players on the cover. The key programs would be the first game program, key championship programs.

		Nr-Mt	Ex
☐ 1970	First Game	100	50
☐ 1970-71	Game Programs	20	5
☐ 1971-75	Game Programs	10	2
☐ 1976-80	Game Programs	7	1
☐ 1981-97	Game Programs	5	1
☐	Key Players (Jordan, etc)	15	5

SCHEDULES

		Nr-Mt	Ex
☐ 1970-71	Schedules	25	10
☐ 1972-75	Schedules	15	5
☐ 1976-80	Schedules	10	3
☐ 1981-89	Schedules	5	2
☐ 1990-97	Schedules	2	1

YEARBOOKS/MAGAZINES/NEWSLETTERS/TICKETS

None reported.

ROCHESTER/CINCINNATI ROYALS

Rochester Royals was one of the earliest and finest teams of the NBA. Early NBA material is heavily collected, especially teams like the Rochester Royals. It was unfortunate that the team decided to move to Cincinnati. The early Royals had media guides and game programs and schedules. The material is rather rare and expense. The Cincinnati Royals (57-72) were a team that was known for its best player - Oscar Robertson.

MEDIA GUIDES

		Nr-Mt	Ex
☐ 1954-55	Art Drawing	150	75
☐ 1955-56	Art Drawing	150	50
☐ 1956-57	Art Drawing	150	50
☐ 1957-58	World Champions	125	50
☐ 1958-59	Art Drawing	125	50
☐ 1959-60	Art Drawing	125	50
☐ 1960-61	Art Drawing	125	50
☐ 1961-62	Royals	125	50
☐ 1962-63	Royals mascot	100	50
☐ 1963-64		80	40
☐ 1964-65		50	25
☐ 1965-66		50	25
☐ 1966-67		45	25
☐ 1967-68	Art Drawing	40	25
☐ 1968-69	O.Robertson/W.Chamberlain	35	15
☐ 1969-70	Coach Bob Cousy	35	15
☐ 1970-71	Tiny Archibald, Van Arsdale	25	15
☐ 1971-72	Royals Patch	25	10

GAME PROGRAMS

		Nr-Mt	Ex
☐ 1946	First Game	350	150
☐ 1946-47	First Year	95	50
☐ 1947-52	Game Programs	75	35
☐ 1952-55	Game Programs	55	20
☐ 1956-59	Game Programs	45	10
☐ 1960-65	Game Programs	35	10
☐ 1965-70	Game Programs	25	5
☐ 1971-72	Game Programs	20	3
☐	Programs Featuring Key Player	40+	15

SCHEDULES

		Nr-Mt	Ex
☐ 1946-47	First Year	95	50
☐ 1947-52	Schedules	65	30
☐ 1952-55	Schedules	55	20
☐ 1956-59	Schedules	45	10
☐ 1960-65	Schedules	30	10
☐ 1965-72	Schedules	20	5

YEARBOOKS/MAGAZINES/TICKET STUBS

No Yearbooks were issued. Newsletters from Rochester Royals are very scarce. Magazines and other paper release material are tough to find. Ticket stubs are 50% value of the programs.

SACRAMENTO/KANSAS CITY KINGS

The Kings are one of those teams that live at the cellar of pro basketball. However, Sacramento Kings seems to have a fan base but the demand for materials is rather low.

MEDIA GUIDES

		Nr-Mt	Ex
☐ 1972-73	Kings logo art	30	15
☐ 1973-74	Bob Cousy	20	10
☐ 1974-75	Action shot	15	5
☐ 1975-76	Tiny Archibald	15	5
☐ 1976-77	Art	15	5
☐ 1977-78	Art	15	5
☐ 1978-79	Kings Logo	15	5
☐ 1979-80	Kings Logo	10	5
☐ 1980-81	R. King	10	3
☐ 1981-82	Phil Ford	10	3
☐ 1982-83	GM Axelson	10	3
☐ 1983-84	Kings logo	10	3
☐ 1984-85	Kings team photo	10	3
☐ 1985-86	Kings logo	10	3
☐ 1986-87	Kings fans	10	3
☐ 1987-88	Fans	10	3
☐ 1988-89	Karl Malone	10	3
☐ 1989-90	Danny Ainge	10	3
☐ 1990-91	Simmons	5	3
☐ 1991-92 - 97		4	1

GAME PROGRAMS

		Nr-Mt	Ex
☐	First Game	50	35
☐ 1972-73	First Year	15	5
☐ 1973-77	Programs	10	2
☐ 1978-85	Programs	7	1
☐ 1986-97	Programs	5	1
☐ Programs with key players		20	5

SCHEDULES

		Nr-Mt	Ex
☐ 1972-75	Schedules	10	5
☐ 1976-80	Schedules	5	2
☐ 1981-89	Schedules	5	2
☐ 1990-97	Schedules	2	1

YEARBOOKS/MAGAZINES/TICKETS/NEWSLETTERS

No yearbooks were made. However, magazines and newsletters have been issued. Value is nominal. Ticket stubs are worth about 50% of the programs.

SAN ANTONIO SPURS

The San Antonio Spurs were one of the ABA teams that switched over to the NBA. The team has never been the champs but currently has one of the better lineups with Dave Robinson, Sean Elliott and Tim Duncan.

MEDIA GUIDES		Nr-Mt	Ex
☐ 1973-74	Arena	35	10
☐ 1974-75	Logo	35	10
☐ 1975-76	George Gervin, James Silas	35	10
☐ 1976-77	(NBA)	15	5
☐ 1977-78	George Gervin	15	5
☐ 1978-79	Billy Paultz	15	5
☐ 1979-80	Logo	15	5
☐ 1980-81	art	15	5
☐ 1981-82	George Gervin	15	5
☐ 1982-83	Artis Gilmore, George Gervin	15	5
☐ 1983-84	Artis Gilmore	15	5
☐ 1984-85	Cotton Fitzsimmons	15	5
☐ 1985-86	Mike Mitchell	10	5
☐ 1986-87	Alvin Robertson	10	5
☐ 1987-88	Alvin Robertson, Johnny Moore	10	2
☐ 1988-89	Larry Brown	7	2
☐ 1989-90	Dave Robinson, Sean Elliott,	7	2
☐ 1990-91	Dave Robinson	7	2
☐ 1991-on		4	1

GAME PROGRAMS		Nr-Mt	Ex
☐ 1973	First Game	150	50
☐ 1973-76	Game Programs	20	5
☐ 1977-80	Game Programs	15	2
☐ 1981-88	Game Programs	10	1
☐ 1989-97	Game Programs	5	1

SCHEDULES		Nr-Mt	Ex
☐ 1973-74	Schedule (ABA)	25	15
☐ 1974-77	Schedule (ABA)	20	10
☐ 1978-80	Schedules (NBA)	10	5
☐ 1981-89	Schedules (NBA)	5	2
☐ 1990-97	Schedules (NBA)	2	1

YEARBOOKS/MAGAZINES/NEWSLETTERS/TICKETS

No yearbooks were made. Team issued magazines and newsletters are worth more from the ABA years. Ticket stubs are 50% of the program prices.

SEATTLE SUPER SONICS

The Seattle Sonics have been to the finals with some excellent players. Seattle Sonic fans are very loyal to thier team.

MEDIA GUIDES		Nr-Mt	Ex
☐ 1967-68	Sonics	45	15
☐ 1968-69	Bob Rule	35	10
☐ 1969-70	Lenny Wilkens	30	10
☐ 1970-71	Basketball	30	10
☐ 1971-72	Sonics Action	25	10
☐ 1972-73	Spencer Haywood	25	15
☐ 1973-74	Seattle Sky Line	20	10
☐ 1974-75	Bill Russell	15	5
☐ 1975-76	Action	15	5
☐ 1976-77	Sonics Basketball	15	5
☐ 1977-78		15	5
☐ 1978-79		15	5
☐ 1979-80	Dennis Johnson	10	5
☐ 1980-81	Lonnie Shelton	10	3
☐ 1981-82	Jack Skima	10	3
☐ 1982-83	Gus Williams	10	3
☐ 1983-84	Fred Brown	10	3
☐ 1984-85	Sonics Logo	10	3
☐ 1985-86	Sonics art	10	3
☐ 1986-87	Tom Chambers	10	3
☐ 1987-88		10	3
☐ 1988-89		10	3
☐ 1989-90		10	3
☐ 1990-91		5	3
☐ 1991-92 - on		2	1

GAME PROGRAMS		Nr-Mt	Ex
☐ 1967	First Game	300	100
☐ 1967-68	First Year	30	10
☐ 1968-70	Game Programs	20	5
☐ 1971-76	Game Programs	15	3
☐ 1977-87	Game Programs	10	3
☐ 1988-on	Game Programs	5	1
☐	Special Programs	25+	10
☐	Key Cover Programs	20	5

SCHEDULES		Nr-Mt	Ex
☐ 1967-68	First Schedule	25	15
☐ 1968-70	Schedules	20	10
☐ 1971-75	Schedules	15	7
☐ 1976-80	Schedules	10	5
☐ 1981-89	Schedules	5	2
☐ 1990-97	Schedules	2	1

YEARBOOKS/MAGAZINES/TICKETS

No Yearbooks but there were team issued newsletters and info pieces. Prices vary on vintage. Ticket stubs are 50% of programs unless noted.

UTAH/NEW ORLEANS JAZZ

Utah Jazz originated in New Orleans. They never won a championship but were the Western regional champions in 1997. The best player from Jazz history is Pistol Pete Maravich who is the third most popular basketball player of all time. Besides Pistol Pete, Karl Malone and John Stockton are popular players that are collected.

MEDIA GUIDES		Nr-Mt	Ex
☐ 1974-75	New Orleans logo	15	5
☐ 1975-76		15	5
☐ 1976-77	Pete Maravich	30	10
☐ 1977-78		15	5
☐ 1978-79	Pete Maravich	30	10
☐ 1979-80	(move to Salt Lake City)	10	5
☐ 1980-81		10	3
☐ 1981-82		10	3
☐ 1982-83		10	3
☐ 1983-84		10	3
☐ 1984-85		10	3
☐ 1985-86	Karl Malone	12	3
☐ 1986-87		10	3
☐ 1987-88	Karl Malone	12	3
☐ 1988-89	Karl Malone	12	3
☐ 1989-90		10	3
☐ 1990-91		5	3
☐ 1991-92 - on		4	1

GAME PROGRAMS		Nr-Mt	Ex
☐ 1974-76	Game Programs	10	5
☐ 1977-80	Game Programs	9	3
☐ 1981-89	Game Programs	7	3
☐ 1990-97	Game Programs	5	1
☐	Programs with Pete Maravich	20	10
☐	Karl Malone First Game	40	20
☐	John Stockton First Game	40	20
☐	Key Covers	20	10

SCHEDULES		Nr-Mt	Ex
☐ 1974-76	Schedules	20	10
☐ 1976-80	Schedule	10	5
☐ 1981-89	Schedule	5	3
☐ 1990-97	Schedules	2	1

YEARBOOKS/MAGAZINES/TICKET STUBS

The Jazz produced no yearbooks but produced various newsletters and magazines. These items are valued based on who is featured on the cover. Anything with Pistol Pete is worth at least $25. Ticket stubs generally go for 50% of the game programs.

WASHINGTON/BALTIMORE BULLETS

The Washington Bullets were originally the Baltimore Bullets from the 1950's through the 1973. They moved from Baltimore to Washington in 1973. Early Baltimore Bullet material is rare and highly sought after. Washington Bullet material is not as heavily pursued. In 1997 the Washington Bullets changed their name to Washington Wizards. The team won the championship with Wes Unseld.

MEDIA GUIDES		Nr-Mt	Ex
☐ 1954-55	Art Drawing	150	75
☐ 1955-56	Art Drawing	125	50
☐ 1964-65	Gus Johnson	50	25
☐ 1965-66	Media	50	25
☐ 1966-67	Media Equipment	50	25
☐ 1967-68	Baltimore	50	25
☐ 1968-69	Bullets action	25	15
☐ 1969-70	W Unseld, Earl Monroe	35	15
☐ 1970-71	Wes Unseld	20	15
☐ 1971-72	Bullets Action	15	7
☐ 1972-73	Bullets Action	15	5
☐ 1973-74	KC Jones	15	5
☐ 1974-75	Elvin Hayes	15	5
☐ 1975-76	Unseld, Hayes	15	5
☐ 1976-77	Dick Motta	15	5
☐ 1977-78	Hayes, Unseld, Kupchak	15	5
☐ 1978-79	NBA Champs	20	5
☐ 1979-80	Trophy	10	5
☐ 1980-81	Unseld, Hayes	10	3
☐ 1981-82	Action photos	10	3
☐ 1982-83	Lucas	10	3
☐ 1983-84	Jeff Ruland	10	3
☐ 1984-85	Ruland, Ballard	10	3
☐ 1985-86	Action art	10	3
☐ 1986-87	Moses Malone	10	3
☐ 1987-88	Moses Malone	10	3
☐ 1988-89	Wes Unseld	10	3
☐ 1989-90	Wes Unseld	10	3
☐ 1990-91	Wes Unseld	5	3
☐ 1991-92 - 97			

GAME PROGRAMS		Nr-Mt	Ex
☐ 1946	First Game Programs	400	200
☐ 1946-48	Game Programs	75	35
☐ 1949-52	Game Programs	45	20
☐ 1953-57	Game Programs	25	10
☐ 1958-62	Game Programs	20	5
☐ 1963-69	Game Programs	15	4
☐ 1970-75	Game Programs	10	3
☐ 1976-80	Game Programs	7	2
☐ 1981-89	Game Programs	5	2
☐ 1990-97	Game Programs	4	1
☐	Key Players Featured	20+	10
☐	Key Programs	25+	15

SCHEDULE		Nr-Mt	Ex
☐ 1946-48	Early Schedules	100	50
☐ 1949-52	Early Schedules	75	35
☐ 1953-57	Schedules	55	25
☐ 1958-60	Schedules	35	15
☐ 1961-65	Schedules	25	10
☐ 1966-70	Schedules	20	5
☐ 1971-75	Pocket Schedules	15	3
☐ 1976-80	Pocket Schedules	10	3
☐ 1981-89	Pocket Schedules	5	2
☐ 1990-97	Pocket Schedules	2	1

YEARBOOKS/TICKETS		Nr-Mt	Ex
☐ 88-89	Wes Unseld	15	5
☐ 89-90	Wes Unseld	15	5

No other Yearbooks issued. Magazines and newsletter are valued based on time period. Tickets are 50% of Programs.

AMERICAN BASKETBALL ASSOCIATION PUBLICATIONS

The ABA was created in 1967 and ended in 1976. It was the most colorful defunct sports conference known to mankind. The ABA fans were loyal and committed and there is a hardcore group of collectors today who actually collect all the ABA material. The ABA programs, media guides, year-books, and all star programs were more colorful than anything that you will find in the NBA. Each item is worth pursuing.

The ABA had some of the greatest players that ever played professional basketball. The greatest ABA player is Julius Erving who played on the Squires and Nets. His ABA material is the most sought after. After Julius Erving there are a few other key players that are collected like, Connie Hawkins, Artis Gilmore and George Gervin. However, it is one of the few leagues where the teams are sought after more than just the players because of their color and content.

TEAM MEDIA GUIDES

These are tough for the first few years (1967-1970) and get easier by the last season (1975-76). However, the first year will sell for $95 each in nice shape and the second and third year will be around $40-$65 in nr-mt shape. Many will have hole punches for binders. Some teams are tougher than others are and the prices should reflect it. Those teams that went into the NBA in 76 are also noted under the NBA teams.

ROCKETS

1967-68	95	1968-69	65	1969-70	50
1970-71	50	1971-72	50	1972-73	35
1973-74	35				

NUGGETS

1974-75	30	1975-76	30

NETS

1967-68	95	1968-69	65	1969-70	50
1970-71	50	1971-72	35	1972-73	35
1973-74	75*	1974-75	75*	1975-76	50*
Special	Dr. J!!!				

CHAPPARALS

1967-68	95	1968-69	65	1969-70	50
1970-71	50	1971-72	50		

MAVERICKS

1967-68	95	1968-69	65	1969-70	50

PACERS

1967-68	95	1968-69	65	1969-70	50
1970-71	50	1971-72	35	1972-73	35
1973-74	35	1974-75	30	1975-76	25

COLONELS

1967-68	95	1968-69	65	1969-70	50
1970-71	50	1971-72	35	1972-73	35
1973-74	35	1974-75	30	1975-76	25

STARS

1967-68	150	1968-69	65	1969-70	50
1970-71	50	1971-72	40	1972-73	35
1973-74	35	1974-75	35	1975-76	35

FLORIDIANS

1967-68	150*	1968-69	65	1969-70	50
1970-71	50	1971-72	50		
Special	*Minnesota				

PIPERS

1967-68	150	1968-69	75	1969-70	50
1970-71	N/A				

BUCCANEERS

1967-68	150	1968-69	75	1969-70	50

OAKS

1967-68	150	1968-69	75
Special	Rick Barry		

COUGARS

1967-68	N/A	1968-69	N/A	1969-70	N/A
1970-71	50	1971-72	50	1972-73	35

TAMS

1967-68 ....N/A	1968-69 ....N/A	1969-70.......N/A
1970-71 50	1971-72 45	1972-73......40
1973-74.......35	1974-75 35	1975-76.......35

CONDORS

1967-68.......N/A	1968-69 ....N/A	1969-70.......N/A
1970-71 50	1971-72 45	

SQUIRES

1967-68........N/A	1968-69 ....N/A	1969-70........N/A
1970-71 50	1971-72 ....120*	1972-73.........100*
1973-74.......35	1974-75 35	1975-76........35
Special..........DR J		

CAPS

1969-70........50

SPURS

1973-74........45	1974-75 35	1975-76.......35

CONQUISTADORS

1973-74.......50	1974-75 35	1975-76........35
Special..........Wilt Chamberlain		

SPIRIT

1974-75 35	1975-76 35

SAILS

1975-76.........?	Special.............Nope

After Media Guides there are game programs, all star game programs, playoff and championship programs, special programs , yearbooks and ticket stubs.

There are a few yearbooks that were released in the ABA. They are rather scarce and are worth three times the value of the media guides.

CHAMPIONSHIP/PLAYOFF/ALL-STAR GAME PROGRAMS

Usually if you're going to collect only a handful of programs from the ABA it should start with the most significant event. The most significant event is the Championship Program. These programs are rather scarce in the early years and more common in the later years. Playoff programs are about the same. The series has a division playoff, an eastern & western final and then a championship program. The championship program is worth the most but it may not be the toughest to find. Prices are based on general-ized figures because some games are tougher and thus more valuable than other playoff programs. This is the first 'guide' to the subject. Footnote: Dr J items are worth more and sell faster than all the other playoff & champi-onship programs. There were two All Star ABA/NBA programs that do exist. These programs would be in the $250-$350 range.

Year	Div. Playoff	Div. Final	Championship	All Star Game
1967-68	$100	$150	$350 (C. Hawkins)	$300
1968-69	$100	$150	$350 (Rick Barry)	$250
1969-70	$100	$150	$300	$250
1970-71	$100	$150	$250	$225
1971-72	$ 75	$100	$250	$200 (Dr J)
1972-73	$ 50	$ 75	$150	$200 (Dr J)
1973-74	$ 50	$ 75	$175 (Dr J)	$200 (Dr J)
1974-75	$ 50	$ 75	$150	$150 (Dr J)
1975-76	$ 50	$ 75	$150	$125 (Dr J)

REGULAR SEASON PROGRAMS

Regular Season & Preseason Programs are a challenge for even the most advanced collectors. How to go about collecting them is based upon both your priorities and your goals. I have found that most ABA collectors are happy to find any of them. As they get more advanced they head toward variations and styles. There are over 1,500 different programs. The beauty of the ABA is that they had many different types of programs during the course of the year. Therefore one program per year may not be a good sample; you may need 10 to cover all the varieties. The other issue is many great players appeared on the ABA programs (especially Dr. J) which requires even more looking. Finally, the ABA had a lot of games with poor attendance. There are not a lot of certain teams and programs. For exam-ple, Howard 'Smitty' Smith was a pioneer in the sports collecting business.

He stumbled into our wonderful hobby many years ago by buying up fran-chises of the WFL and the ABA. He purchased the entire inventory of the Indiana Pacers. He literary had thousands of programs and thus the market has thousands of programs that surface from time to time.

For collectors this is great, however the value of these is less than some of the teams were they were not saved or sold off to collectors. Many of the early defunct teams materials disappeared and most likely were thrown away. These teams programs are worth two or three times those that are common. Finally, the early year programs are worth the most.

Year	Rare/Defunct Teams	Normal Teams	Special Programs
1967-1968	$75-$125	$35-$75	$100-$200
1968-1969	$50-$100	$35-$75	$100-$200
1969-70	$50-$75	$25-$50	$100+
1970-71	$50-$75	$25-$50	$75+
1971-72	$50-$75	$20-$45	$75+
1972-73	$45-$65	$20-$40	$75+
1973-74	$45-$65	$20-$40	$75+
1974-75	$40-$60	$20-$35	$75+
1975-76	$30-$50	$20-$30	$75+

There are a lot of special issues, pre season releases and the like from the front office. Prices on this type of material is in the $20-$50 range unless is a rare piece or a piece with Julius Erving.

MEDIA GUIDES

1970 CHICAGO BULLS

1970 DETROIT PISTONS

1970 SEATTLE SUPERSONICS

1970 WASHINGTON BULLETS

1971 GOLDEN ST. WARRIORS

1971 PHOENIX SUNS

1972 ATLANTA HAWKS

1972 KANSAS CITY KINGS

1972 MILWAUKEE BUCKS

1975 CLEV. CAVALIERS

1975 ST. LOUIS SPIRITS

1976 NEW ORLEANS JAZZ

1977 INDIANA PACERS

1977 PHILADELPHIA 76'ERS

1977 SAN ANTONIO SPURS

1978 NEW JERSEY NETS

1978 SAN DIEGO CLIPPERS

1979 DENVER NUGGETS

1980 DALLAS MAVERICKS

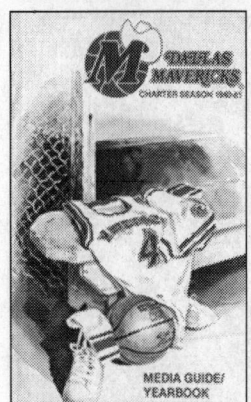

1981 BOSTON CELTICS

1982 WASHINGTON BULLETS

1983 HOUSTON ROCKETS

1985 PORTLAND TRAILBLAZERS

1986 SAN ANTONIO SPURS

1988 CHARLOTTE HORNETS

1989 MINN. TIMBERWOLVES

1990 LA LAKERS

GAME PROGRAMS

1955 PHILLIPS 66 OILERS

1961 NEW YORK KNICKS

1971 NBA PLAYOFF GAME

1973 CELTICS

1973 NBA WESTERN CONF.

1993 NBA ALL-STAR GAME

YEARBOOKS

1971 MILWAUKEE BUCKS

1976 CHICAGO BULLS

1991 NEW YORK KNICKS

CHAPTER FOURTEEN:
Collecting College Basketball Publications

College basketball is as popular as pro basketball. With the invention of cable television and the introduction of ESPN, college basketball is watched across the country. Where traditional fans for any college were localized near the university in the past, today's collegiate basketball fans are scattered across the United States. These fans pursue, to various degree, sports memorabilia from their favorite schools. The most pursued items of these schools is the championship programs and programs from key historical events.

Most colleges have been releasing press guides and programs ever since the game was invented. Some schools have newsletters, official school newspapers (such as LSU's Tiger Tales) or unofficial newspapers and magazines. All of the major basketball schools have some type of magazine or newspaper.

PRESS (MEDIA) GUIDES

The best information about any college team is found in the press (or media) guide. Early press guides, through the 1940s, tend to be very scarce and could be as simple as a carbon-produced information sheet for the media. Most college fans will collect all of their favorite teams' press guides. Media guide values are based on age, scarcity and popularity. For example, a simple rule for media guides is: guides from the 80s and 90s are $2 to $5, guides from the 70s are $5 to $10, guides from the 60s are $10 to $20, guides from the 50s are $20 to $40 and guides from the 40s are $30 to $50. Very few guides date back to the pre-1930s.

The most valued media guides tend to feature star players on their covers: Michael Jordan ($100-$150), Pete Maravich ($150-$200), Julius Erving ($150-$200), Bob Cousy ($100), and Bill Russell ($100). However, there are some rather rare media guides which don't get much media attention, such as guides featuring George Mikan and Jimmy Brown (yes, he played basketball too).

GAME PROGRAMS

Game programs date all the way back to the beginning of basketball. Most people do not collect game programs except for hard core collectors. However, even the non-publication sports collectors would love to have a college program featuring their favorite star. College programs cover a wider range of topics. Some schools use art, while others may featured key players on the cover of their programs.

The most highly sought-after programs feature popular athletes who played in the college games. For example, North Carolina programs with Michael Jordan in them are very popular ($25-$50). And a program from Jordan's very first college game would command at least $250. Julius Erving and Pete Maravich programs are in demand as well.

There are certain schools that command a premium over others. These are considered major basketball powerhouse schools. For example, schools like UCLA and Kentucky are heavily collected. In early basketball history, this would include the Ivy League schools. The demand for programs of major schools from their championship years is especially strong.

YEAR	Major School		Minor School	
	Nr-Mt	Ex	Nr-Mt	Ex
Pre 1900	400	200	200	100
1901-10	250	100	100	50
10-29	100	45	50	25
20-39	75	35	40	20
30-39	55	20	35	10
40-49	35	15	30	5
50-59	25	10	20	4
60-69	20	7	15	3
70-79	10	5	10	2
80-89	10	5	5	1
90-97	10	3	5	1

HISTORICAL EVENT COLLECTING

Finally, historically significant basketball games are pursued by, you guessed it, historical significant basketball event collectors. The only college basketball event that is seriously collected is the NCAA Finals. This tournament determines the NCAA champion ever year. However, the NIT and AAU are both collected.

The NIT tournament usually gets about 50% or less of the NCAA tournament for the same years. AAU Championship is even less. Other historical events, (highest scored game, first games of key basketball figures, etc) are not well known and have not had a chance to mature in value. These events are found by reviewing basketball historical records.

NCAA CHAMPIONSHIP PROGRAMS

YEAR	CHAMPION	KEY PLAYERS	Nr-Mt	Ex
☐ 1939	Oregon	....	5,000	2,000
☐ 1940	Indiana	....	2,000	1,000
☐ 1941	Wisconsin	....	1,500	750
☐ 1942	Stanford	....	1,500	750
☐ 1943	Wyoming	....	1,250	600
☐ 1944	Utah	....	750	500
☐ 1945	Oklahoma St.	....	750	400
☐ 1946	Oklahoma St.	....	700	400
☐ 1947	Holy Cross	George Kaftan	750	400
☐ 1948	Kentucky	Alex Groza	650	250
☐ 1949	Kentucky	Alex Groza	650	250
☐ 1950	CCNY	....	550	250
☐ 1951	Kentucky	....	500	225
☐ 1952	Kansas	....	450	225
☐ 1953	Indiana	....	450	225
☐ 1954	La Salle	Tom Golla	450	200
☐ 1955	San Francisco	Bill Russell	400	200
☐ 1956	San Francisco	Bill Russell	400	200
☐ 1957	North Carolina	Wilt Chamberlain ...	400	200
☐ 1958	Kentucky	Elgin Baylor	400	200
☐ 1959	California	Jerry West	400	200
☐ 1960	Ohio State	Jerry Lucas	300	150
☐ 1961	Cincinnati	Jerry Lucas	300	150
☐ 1962	Cincinnati	....	275	125
☐ 1963	Loyola (Ill)	....	250	125
☐ 1964	UCLA	....	250	125
☐ 1965	UCLA	Bill Bradley	250	125
☐ 1966	UTEP	....	250	125
☐ 1967	UCLA	Lew Alcindor	225	125
☐ 1968	UCLA	Lew Alcindor	225	125
☐ 1969	UCLA	Lew Alcindor	200	125
☐ 1970	UCLA	....	200	100
☐ 1971	UCLA	....	125	50
☐ 1972	UCLA	Bill Walton	125	50
☐ 1973	UCLA	Bill Walton	100	45
☐ 1974	N.C. State	....	75	30
☐ 1975	UCLA	....	100	45
☐ 1976	Indiania	....	75	30
☐ 1977	Marquette	....	75	30
☐ 1978	Kentucky	....	75	30
☐ 1979	Michigan State	Magic/Bird	200	100
☐ 1980	Louisville	....	50	20
☐ 1981	Indiana	Jordan	150	75
☐ 1982	North Carolina	Jordan/Worthy	200	100
☐ 1983	N.C.State	....	50	20
☐ 1984	Georgetown	Pat Ewing	50	20
☐ 1985	Villanova	Ed Pinckley	20	10
☐ 1986	Louisville	Pervis Ellison	20	10
☐ 1987	Indiana	....	15	10
☐ 1988	Kansas	Danny Manning	15	7
☐ 1989	Michigan	Glen Rice	15	7
☐ 1990	UNLV	....	15	7
☐ 1991	Duke	Christian Laettner ...	15	7
☐ 1992	Duke	Grant Hill	15	7
☐ 1993	UNC	Dean Smith	15	7
☐ 1994	Arkansas	....	15	7
☐ 1995	UCLA	....	15	7
☐ 1996	Kentucky	....	10	5
☐ 1997	Arizona	Miles Simon	10	5

MEDIA GUIDES

1960 WV - JERRY WEST

1968 LSU - MARAVICH

1977 MSU - JOHNSON

1973 UCLA

1983 AUBURN

1983 GEORGETOWN

CHAPTER FIFTEEN:
Collecting Basketball Publications

ALL AMERICAN BASKETBALL YEARBOOK

DATE	COVER/FEATURE	Nr-Mt	Ex
☐ F/70	Pistol Pete Maravich	35	15

ALL PRO BASKETBALL

DATE	COVER/FEATURE	Nr-Mt	Ex
☐ 1976	Rick Barry - Warriors	15	10
☐ 1977	John Havlicek - Celtics	15	10
☐ 1978	Julius Erving - Sixers	25	15
☐ 1979	David Thompson - Nuggets	15	10
☐ 1980		15	10
☐ 1981	Larry Bird/Julius Erving	35	15
☐ 1982	Julius Erving - Sixers	25	15

ALL SPORTS

DATE	COVER/FEATURE	Nr-Mt	Ex
☐ 5/71	Jerry West - Lakers	30	10
☐ 3/73	Jerry West - Lakers	25	10

ALL STAR SPORTS

DATE	COVER/FEATURE	Nr-Mt	Ex
☐ 74-75	College Issue	20	10
☐ 75-76		20	10
☐ 77-78	Kareem Abdul Jabbar - Lakers	20	10
☐ 79-80	Julius Erving- Sixers	35	15
☐ 81-82	Larry Bird - Celtics	30	15
☐ 1986	Dave Robinson - Navy	30	15

ANNUAL BASKETBALL
(Complete Sports)

DATE	COVER/FEATURE	Nr-Mt	Ex
☐ 64-65	Oscar Robertson - Royals	40	20
☐ 65-66	Jerry West/Bill Russell	35	15
☐ 66-67	Jerry West - Lakers	35	15
☐ 67-68	Lew Alcindor - UCLA	25	15
☐ 68-69	Chamberlain/Maravich	35	15
☐ 69-70	Jerry West, Pete Maravich	35	15
☐ 70-71	Lew Alcindor - Bucks	25	15
☐ 71-72	Pete Maravich - Jazz	45	20
☐ 72-73	Wilt Chamberlain-Lakers	20	10
☐ 73-74	Bill Walton - UCLA	20	10
☐ 74-75	Isaiah Thomas - NC State	20	10
☐ 75-76	Rick Barry - Warriors	15	10
☐ 76-77	Dave Cowens - Celtics	15	10
☐ 77-78		15	10
☐ 78-79	Artis Gilmore - Bulls	15	10
☐ 79-80	Norte Dame/Duke/North Car.	10	5
☐ 80-81	UCLA/Notre Dame	10	5
☐ 81-82	John Paxson - Notre Dame	10	5
☐ 82-83	Virgina/Georgetown	10	5
☐ 83-84	Alabama/Georgia/Ken.	10	5
☐ 84-85	Kenny Walker-Kentucky	10	5
☐ 85-86	K. Walker-Kentucky/J Will LSU	10	5
☐ 86-87	David Robinson - Navy	10	5
☐ 87-88	Jordan/Barkley/Magic	20	10
☐ 88-89	Magic Johnson/Isiah Thomas	10	5
☐ 89-90		10	5
☐ 90-91		10	5
☐ 91-92	Shaq - LSU	20	10
☐ 92-93	Shaq/Michael Jordan	15	10

BASKETBALL
(Complete Sports)

DATE	COVER/FEATURE	Nr-Mt	Ex
☐ 1964	Oscar Robertson - Royals	30	20

BASKETBALL
(Dell) (Also called Woodward's Basketball)

DATE	COVER/FEATURE	Nr-Mt	Ex
☐ 1950	Don Lofgran - USF	50	20
☐ 1951	Bob Zawoluk - St Johns	50	20
☐ 1952			
☐ 1953			
☐ 1954	Bob Cousy - Celtics	95	25
☐ 1955	Tom Gola - La Salle	55	20
☐ 1956	Tom Heinsohn/Bill Russell	65	25
☐ 1957	Bob Pettit/Chamberlain	65	25
☐ 1958	Wilt Chamberlain - Kansas	65	25
☐ 1959	O.Robertson/J.West	50	25
☐ 1960	Wilt Chamberlain - Warriors	50	15
☐ 1961	Jerry Lucas - Ohio State	40	15
☐ 1962	B. Russell/W.Chamberlain	40	10
☐ 1963	Oscar Robertson - Royals	40	20
☐ 1964	Barry Kramer - NYU	30	15
☐ 1965	Bill Bradley - Princeton	40	20
☐ 1966	Cazzie Russell - Knicks	30	15
☐ 1967	Bill Russell - Celtics	40	20
☐ 1968			

BASKETBALL ACTION

DATE	COVER/FEATURE	Nr-Mt	Ex
☐ 86-87	Larry Bird - Celtics	15	10

BASKETBALL ALL PRO ANNUAL

DATE	COVER/FEATURE	Nr-Mt	Ex
☐ 1971	P.Maravich/R. Mount/Alcindor	25	15
☐ 1972	LewAlcindor/Rick Barry	25	10
☐ 1973	W. Chamberlain/K. Jabbar	25	10

BASKETBALL BEST PICTORIAL REVIEW

DATE	COVER/FEATURE	Nr-Mt	Ex
☐ 1951	Action	75	25
☐ 1952	George Mikan - Lakers	75	25
☐ 1953	Bob Cousy/George Mikan	75	25
☐ 1954	Bob Cousy/George Mikan	60	20
☐ 1955	Red Rocha - Syracuse Nats	40	20
☐ 1956	Action	40	20
☐ 1957	Bob Cousy - Celtics	40	20
☐ 1958	T.Heinsohn/B. Russell - Celtics	50	20
☐ 1959	Frank Ramsey - Celtics	45	20
☐ 1960	Elgin Baylor - Lakers	45	20
☐ 1961	Wilt Chamberlain - Warriors	45	20
☐ 1962	Baylor/West/Chamberlain	45	20
☐ 1963	Jerry West - Lakers	45	20
☐ 1964	Wilt Chamberlain - Warriors	40	15
☐ 1965	Elgin Baylor/Jerry West - Lakers	40	15
☐ 1966	Rick Barry - Warriors	35	15
☐ 1967	Wilt Chamberlain/Bill Russell	35	15
☐ 1968	John Havlicek - Celtics	35	15
☐ 1969	Lew Alcindor - Bucks	35	15
☐ 1970	Wilt Chamberlain - Lakers	35	15
☐ 1971	Lew Alcindor - Bucks	35	15
☐ 1972	Lew Alcindor - Bucks	35	15

BASKETBALL DIGEST

DATE	COVER/FEATURE	Nr-Mt	Ex
☐ 11/73	Dave Cowens - Celtics	35	25
☐ 12/73	Jerry West - Lakers	20	10
☐ 1/74	Norm Van Lier - Bulls	15	10
☐ 2/74	Kareem Abdul Jabbar - Bucks	20	10
☐ 3/74	Walt Frazier - Knicks	20	10
☐ 4/74	Dave DeBusschere - Knicks	20	10
☐ SP/74	Wilt Chamberlain - Lakers	20	10

		Nr-Mt	Ex
☐ 11/74	John Havlicek - Celtics	15	8
☐ 12/74	Bob McAdoo - Bulls	12	8
☐ 1/75	Bob Lanier - Bulls	12	8
☐ 2/75	Bill Walton - Blaziers	12	8
☐ 3/75	Nate Thurmond - Warriors	12	8
☐ 4/75	Rick Barry - Warriors	12	8
☐ 6/75	Bob Lainer - Bulls	12	8
☐ 11/75	Kareem Abdul Jabbar - Bucks	15	10
☐ 12/75	Walt Frazier - Knicks	12	8
☐ 1/76	Pete Maravich - Jazz	30	15
☐ 2/76	Julius Erving - Sixers	25	15
☐ 3/76	Elvin Hayes - Clippers	12	8
☐ 4/76	Dave Cowens - Celtics	15	8
☐ 11/76	Bob McAdoo - Braves	12	8
☐ 12/76	David Thompson/Dr J	25	15
☐ 1/77	Artis Gilmore - Spurs	12	8
☐ 2/77	George McGinnis - Sixers	12	8
☐ 3/77	Earl Monroe - Bullets	12	8
☐ 4/77	Bill Walton - Blazers	12	8
☐ 5/77	Jo Jo White - Celtics	12	8
☐ 6/77	Kareem Abdul Jabbar - Lakers	15	8
☐ 11/77	Maurice Lucas - Blazers	12	8
☐ 12/77	Rick Barry - Warriors	12	8
☐ 1/78	Daryl Dawkins/Moses Malone	12	8
☐ 2/78	Alvan Adams - Suns	12	8
☐ 3/78	Dan Issel - Colonels	12	8
☐ 4/78	Dave Cowens - Celtics	12	8
☐ 5/78	Bob Lanier - Bulls	12	8
☐ 6/78	Bill Walton - Blaziers	12	8
☐ 11/78	Marvin Webster-Sonics	12	8
☐ 12/78	George Gervin - Spurs	12	8
☐ 1/79	David Thompson - Nuggets	12	8
☐ 2/79	Pete Maravich - Jazz	25	12
☐ 3/79	Bob McAdoo - Braves	12	8
☐ 4/79	Elvin Hayes - Clippers	12	8
☐ 5/79	Artis Gilmore - Bulls	12	8
☐ 6/79	Moses Malone - Sixers	12	8
☐ 11/79	Dennis Johnson - Celtics	12	8
☐ 12/79	Kareem Abdul Jabbar - Lakers	12	8
☐ 1/80	Paul Westfall - Suns	12	8
☐ 2/80	Julius Erving - Sixers	25	15
☐ 3/80	Larry Bird - Celtics	25	15
☐ 4/80	Marques Johnson - Trailblazers	12	8
☐ 5/80	Lloyd B. Free - Warriors	12	8
☐ 6/80	Magic Johnson/Dr J	25	15
☐ 11/80	Magic Johnson - Lakers	15	8
☐ 12/80	Phil Ford - Kings	12	8
☐ 1/81	Bill Cartwright - Knicks	12	8
☐ 2/81	Walt Davis - Suns	12	8
☐ 3/81	Darryl Dawkins - Sixers	12	8
☐ 4/81	Andrin Dantley - Bulls	12	8
☐ 5/81	George Gervin - Spurs	12	8
☐ 6/81	Julius Erving - Sixers	25	15
☐ 11/81	Larry Bird - Celtics	20	10
☐ 12/81	Moses Malone - Sixers	12	8
☐ 1/82	Joe Barry Carroll - Warriors	12	8
☐ 2/82	Isaiah Thomas - Pistons	12	8
☐ 3/82	Reggie Theus - Bulls	12	8
☐ 4/82	Sidney Moncrief - Bucks	12	8
☐ 5/82	Alex English - Nuggets	12	8
☐ 6/82	Kareem Abdul Jabbar - Lakers	12	8
☐ 11/82	Magic Johnson - Lakers	20	10
☐ 12/82	Buck Williams - Bucks	12	8
☐ 1/83	Robert Parish - Celtics	12	8
☐ 2/83	Kelly Tripucka - Pistons	10	8
☐ 3/83	Gus Williams - Sonics	10	8
☐ 4/83	Bernard King - Knicks	10	8
☐ 5/83	Artis Gilmore - Bulls	10	8
☐ 6/83	Moses Malone - Rockets	10	8
☐ 11/83	Julius Erving - Sixers	20	10
☐ 12/83	Kiki Vanderweghe - Nuggets	10	8
☐ 1/84	Larry Bird - Celtics	20	10
☐ 2/84	Mark Aquirre - Mavericks	10	8
☐ 3/84	Maurice Lucas - Suns	100	8
☐ 4/84	Jim Paxon - Blazers	10	8
☐ 6/84	Ralph Sampson - Rockets	10	8
☐ 11/84	Larry Bird - Celtics	20	10
☐ 12/84	Jack Sikma - Sonics	12	8
☐ 1/85	Bernard King - Knicks	12	8
☐ 2/85	Isaiah Thomas - Pistons	12	8
☐ 3/85	Jeff Ruland - Bullets	12	8
☐ 4/85	Hakeem Olajuwon - Rockets	20	10
☐ 5/85	Kareem Abdul-Jabbar - Lakers	12	8
☐ 6/85	Michael Jordan - Bulls	40	20
☐ 11/85	Patrick Ewing - Knicks	12	8
☐ 12/85	Rolando Blackman - Mavericks	10	8
☐ 1/86	Kevin McHale - Celtics	12	8
☐ 2/86	Dominique Wilkins - Hawks	12	8
☐ 3/86	Ralph Sampson - Rockets	20	10
☐ 6/86	Larry Bird - Celtics	15	10
☐ 11/86	Hakeem Olajuwon - Rockets	12	8
☐ 12/86	Xavier McDaniel - Sonics	10	8
☐ 1/87	Michael Jordan - Bulls	25	10
☐ 2/87	Moses Malone - Rockets	10	8
☐ 3/87	Terry Cunnings - Bucks	10	8
☐ 4/87	Julius Erving - Sixers	20	10
☐ 5/87	Kevin McHale/Kevin Willis	10	8
☐ 6/87	Magic Johnson - Lakers	10	8
☐ 11/87	Larry Bird - Celtics	20	10
☐ 12/87	Isiah Thomas - Pistons	10	8
☐ 1/88	Karl Malone - Jazz	20	10
☐ 2/88	Charles Barkley - Sixers	10	8
☐ 3/88	Rolando Blackman - Mavericks	8	5
☐ 4/88	Michael Jordan - Bulls	20	10
☐ 5/88	Adrian Dantley - Pistons	8	5
☐ 6/88	Magic Johnson - Lakers	10	6
☐ 11/88	Larry Bird - Celtics	10	6
☐ 12/88	Kevin Duckworth - Bulls	6	4
☐ 1/89	Moses Malone - Hawks	6	4
☐ 2/89	Kareem Abdul Jabbar - Lakers	6	4
☐ 3/89	Patrick Ewing - Knicks	6	4
☐ 4/89		6	4
☐ 5/89	Karl Malone/Hakeem Olajuwon	6	4
☐ 6/89	Michael Jordan - Bulls	20	10
☐ 11/89	Joe Dumars - Pistons	6	4
☐ 12/89	Chris Mullin - Warriors	6	4
☐ 1/90	Michael Jordan/Patrick Ewing	20	10
☐ 2/90	Dennis Rodman - Pistons	6	4
☐ 3/90	Charles Barkley - Sixers	6	4
☐ 4/90	Terry Porter - Blaziers	6	4
☐ 5/90	Michael Jordan - Bulls	20	10
☐ 6/90	David Robinson - Spurs	6	4
☐ 11/90	Kevin Johnson - Suns	6	4
☐ 12/90	Mark Price - Cav's	6	4

BASKETBALL ILLUSTRATED

(Life Size)

DATE	COVER/FEATURE	Nr-Mt	Ex
☐ 1945	Pistons vs All Stars	35	20
☐ 1946	Wisconsin	35	20
☐ 1948	LSU	75	40
☐ 1949	Groza/Beard Kentucky	75	40

BASKETBALL NEWS COLLEGE/PRO YEARBOOKS

DATE	COVER/FEATURE	Nr-Mt	Ex
☐ 1974	D Thompson/Bill Walton	15	10
☐ 1975	Dave Thompson - NC	15	10
☐ 1975	Julius Erving/John Havilek	30	15
☐ 1976	Rick Barry - Warriors	20	10
☐ 1977	Julius Erving - Sixers	25	15
☐ 1978	Bill Walton/Pete Maravich	25	10
☐ 1979	Wes Unseld - Bullets	15	10
☐ 1980	Jack Sikma - Sonics	15	10
☐ 1981	Magic Johnson - Lakers	20	5

BASKETBALL OLDEST YEARBOOK BEST

DATE	COVER/FEATURE	Nr-Mt	Ex
☐ 71-72	Willie Reed - Knicks	25	10

BASKETBALL WEEKLY (NEWSPAPER)

(This is one of a few Newspapers produced on Basketball. It covers Pro and College. The series started in 1967 and has detail coverage. Only key issues listed.)

DATE	COVER/FEATURE	Nr-Mt	Ex
☐ 11/1/68	Jerry West	25	10
☐ 67-70	Common Cover	15	10
☐ 12/19/69	Bill Bradley	20	10
☐ 1/19/70	Jerry West	20	10
☐ 2/02/70	Pete Maravich	50	20
☐ 71-77	Common covers	10	5
☐ 1/18/71	Jerry West	20	10
☐ 3/7/72	Julius Erving	40	20
☐ 5/15/74	Julius Erving	40	20
☐ 5/15/75	Julius Erving	40	20
☐ 11/25/76	Julius Erving	40	20
☐ 1/27/77	Julius Erving	35	20
☐ 2/3/77	Jerry West	20	10
☐ 1/12/78	Larry Bird	30	15
☐ 3/9/78	Larry Bird	25	15
☐ 3/15/79	Larry Bird	20	12
☐ 3/29/79	Larry Bird	20	10
☐ 11/28/79	Larry Bird	20	10
☐ 12/26/79	Julius Erving	20	10
☐ 1980-89	Common Cover	8	3
☐ 2/7/80	Larry Bird	20	10
☐ 3/12/81	Larry Bird	20	10
☐ 1/28/82	Julius Erving	20	10
☐ 5/15/82	Julius Erving/Magic Johnson	20	10
☐ 2/10/83	Julius Erving	20	10
☐ 3/24/83	Michael Jordan	65	25
☐ 3/12/84	Micahel Jordan	50	20
☐ 3/19/84	Michael Jordan	50	20
☐ 12/31/84	Larry Bird	20	10
☐ 5/20/85	Larry Bird	15	7
☐ 2/03/86	Julius Erving	20	10
☐ 5/19/86	Larry Bird	15	7
☐ 1/25/88	Pete Maravich	25	10
☐ 2/8/88	Michael Jordan	30	15
☐ 2/15/88	Michael Jordan	30	15
☐ 5/16/88	Michael Jordan	30	15
☐ 1/3/89	Michael Jordan	30	15
☐ 1990-on	Common Covers	6	3
☐ 11/13/90	Michael Jordan	20	10
☐ 2/25/91	Michael Jordan	20	10
☐ 5/13/91	Michael Jordan	20	10
☐ 5/12/92	Michael Jordan	15	10

BASKETBALL YEARBOOK

(Popular)

DATE	COVER/FEATURE	Nr-Mt	Ex
☐ 1960	Jerry West - West Virginia	40	20
☐ 1961	Jerry Lucas - Ohio State	35	15
☐ 1962	Jerry Lucas - Ohio State	35	15
☐ 1963	Ron Boham - Cincy	30	15
☐ 1964	Gary Bradds - Ohio State	30	15
☐ 1965	B. Bradley/O. Robertson	30	15
☐ 1966	Jerry West/Cazzie Russell	30	15
☐ 1967	Lew Alcindor - UCLA	20	10
☐ 1968	L. Alcindor/B.Bradley/R. Barry	20	10
☐ 1969	L. Alcindor/J. Havlicek/E.Hayes	20	10
☐ 1970	Rick Mount/ Walt Fraizer	20	10
☐ 1971	Lew Alcindor/Willie Reed	20	10
☐ 1972	Lew Alcindor - Bucks	20	10

BECKETT BASKETBALL PRICE GUIDE

Please see the chapter on 'Beckett'.

BLUE RIBBON COLLEGE BASKETBALL ANNUAL

DATE	COVER/FEATURE	Nr-Mt	Ex
☐ 1980-88		15	5
☐ 1989	Shaq O'Neal/Chris Jackson	20	10

CAL-HI SPORTS

DATE	COVER/FEATURE	Nr-Mt	Ex
☐ 11/90	Jason Kidd - Pilots	40	20

CAMERA MAGAZINE

DATE	COVER/FEATURE	Nr-Mt	Ex
☐ 1/51	George Mikan - Lakers	40	20

CELTICS BOOK

DATE	COVER/FEATURE	Nr-Mt	Ex
☐ Through the Hoop		40	20

COLLEGE BASKETBALL HANDBOOK

(All Star Sports - A little larger than Readers Digest.)

DATE	COVER/FEATURE	Nr-Mt	Ex
☐ 1982-1983	(Jordan on Back, Perkins front)	100	50
☐ 83-84	Michael Jordan & Others	100	50

COLLEGE BASKETBALL TODAY

DATE	COVER/FEATURE	Nr-Mt	Ex
☐ 1990	A. Mourning - Georgetown	15	5

COL PRO HIGH SCHOOL BASKETBALL

DATE	COVER/FEATURE	Nr-Mt	Ex
☐ 1967	Lew Alcindor/Rick Barry	25	15
☐ 1968	Bill Bradley/Lew Alcindor	20	10
☐ 1969	Lew Alcindor/JHavlicek	25	15
☐ 1970	Rick Mount/Walt Frazier	20	10
☐ 1971	Lew Alcindor	20	10
☐ 1972	Lew Alcindor	20	10

COMPLETE BASKETBALL

DATE	COVER/FEATURE	Nr-Mt	Ex
☐ 60-61	Wilt Chamberlain - Phila	40	20
☐ 61-62	Bill Russell - Celtics	40	20
☐ 62-63	Oscar Robertson - Royals	35	20
☐ 63-64	Jerry West - Lakers	35	20
☐ 66-67	Elgin Baylor - Lakers	25	15
☐ 67-68	Oscar Robertson - Royals	25	10

COMPLETE SPORTS (BASKETBALL)

DATE	COVER/FEATURE	Nr-Mt	Ex
☐ 1961	Bill Russell - Celtics	30	15
☐ 1963	Jerry West - Lakers	25	10
☐ 1964	Oscar Robertson - Royals	30	15
☐ 1964	(High school - Alcindor)	35	10
☐ 1966	Elgin Baylor - Lakers	25	10
☐ 1967	Oscar Robertson - Royals	25	10
☐ 1968	Oscar Roberston - Royals	20	10
☐ 1969	Oscar Robertson - Royals	20	10
☐ 1971	Clyde Frazier - Knicks	15	10

CONVERSE YEARBOOKS

These are the yearbooks that have the greatest details on high school, college and pro teams in the nation. The early editions are rare and are sought after by basketball historians. They were given out to each Converse shoe store. All the early editions feature art work on the cover.

DATE	COVER/FEATURE	Nr-Mt	Ex
☐ 1922		750	350
☐ 1923		450	250
☐ 1924		250	150
☐ 1925		250	150
☐ 1926-1935		200	100
☐ 1936-1940		150	75
☐ 1941-1950		100	35
☐ 1951-1955		65	30
☐ 1956-1960		50	25
☐ 1961-1965		40	20
☐ 1966-1970		35	15
☐ 1971-1976		30	10
☐ 1977	Julius Erving	45	25
☐ 1978	Larry Bird	40	20
☐ 1979-1983		20	10

COUNTRYWIDE SPORTS BASKETBALL

DATE	COVER/FEATURE	Nr-Mt	Ex
☐ 8/69	L. Alcindor/H. Killbrew	25	15
☐ 12/70	Willis Reed - Knicks	25	15

CORD SPORTSFACT COLLEGE BASKETBALL

DATE	COVER/FEATURE	Nr-Mt	Ex
☐ 1972	Jim Chones - Marquette	15	10
☐ 1973	Bill Walton - UCLA	20	10
☐ 1974	Bill Walton - UCLA	20	10
☐ 1975	David Thompson - NC State	15	10

CORD SPROTSFACT PRO BASKETBALL

DATE	COVER/FEATURE	Nr-Mt	Ex
☐ 1970	Lew Alcindor - Bucks	15	10
☐ 1972	Lew Alcindor - Bucks	15	10
☐ 1973	Kareem A.Jabbar/Jerry West	15	10
☐ 1974	Walt Frazier - Knicks	15	10
☐ 1975	Dave Cowens - Celtics	20	10
☐ 1976	Rick Barry - Warriors	15	10

DELL SPORTS

DATE	COVER/FEATURE	Nr-Mt	Ex
☐ 1965	Bill Bradley - Princeton	40	20

FAST BREAK

DATE	COVER/FEATURE	Nr-Mt	Ex
☐ 1969	Jerry West/Dave Bing	20	10
☐ 1970	Jerry West/J. Havlicek/Alcindor	20	10

GAME PLAN BASKETBALL

(College) (There may be regional college cover issues.)

DATE	COVER/FEATURE	Nr-Mt	Ex
☐ 1977	Phil Ford - NC	15	10
☐ 1978	Larry Bird/Magic (small)	20	10
☐ 1980	Kyle Macy - Kentucky	15	10
☐ 1981	Bernard King - Maryland	15	10
☐ 1982	Sleepy Floyd - Georgetown	15	10
☐ 1983	Sam Perkins - NC	20	10
☐ 1984	Keith Lee - Memphis St	20	10
☐ 1985	Wayman Tisdale - Okla.	10	10
☐ 1986	Mark Price - Georgia Tech	20	10
☐ 1987	Dave Robinson - Navy	15	10
☐ 1988	Charles Smith - Pitt.	12	10
☐ 1989	Jim Harrick - UCLA	12	10
☐ 1990	Derrick Coleman/B.Owens-Syr.	12	10
☐ 1992	Alonzo Mourning - Georgetown	15	10
☐ 1993	Calbert Cheaney - Indiana	10	5
☐ 1994	Eric Montross - NC	10	5
☐ 1995	Lawrece Motten - Syracuse	10	5

GAME PLAN BASKETBALL (PRO)

(There may be regional pro covers.)

DATE	COVER/FEATURE	Nr-Mt	Ex
☐ 1977	Julius Erving - Sixers	25	10
☐ 1978	Doug Collins - Sixers	15	10
☐ 1991	Michael Jordan - Bulls	20	10

GAME PRO

(Electronic Arts) (Video Game Magazine)

DATE	COVER/FEATURE	Nr-Mt	Ex
☐ 4/92	Michael Jordan - Bulls	15	5

GQ MAGAZINE

DATE	COVER/FEATURE	Nr-Mt	Ex
☐ 4/95	Grant Hill - Pistons	20	10

GROW BOOK SPORTS

(TV Guide size)

DATE	COVER/FEATURE	Nr-Mt	Ex
☐ 1970	Oscar Robertson - Royals	15	10

HALL OF FAME

DATE	COVER/FEATURE	Nr-Mt	Ex
☐ 11/61	Commemorative program	50	20

INSIDE BASKETBALL

DATE	COVER/FEATURE	Nr-Mt	Ex
☐ 1964	Bill Russell/ W.Chamberlain	40	15
☐ 1965	Oscar Robertson - Royals	35	15
☐ 1966	Bill Russell - Celtics	35	15
☐ 1967	Lew Alcindor/W. Chamberlain	30	15
☐ 1968	Lew Alcindor - UCLA	25	10
☐ 1969	Lew Alcindor - UCLA	25	10
☐ 1970	Pete Maravich/Rick Mount	35	10
☐ 1971	Jerry West - Lakers	25	10

INSIDE SPORT

(Published by Newsweek.)

DATE	COVER/FEATURE	Nr-Mt	Ex
☐ 4/80	Pete Maravich & others	20	10
☐ 5/80	Magic Johnson	20	10
☐ 11/85	Michael Jordan	40	20
☐ 11/86	Magic & Jordan	30	15
☐ 6/87	Michael Jordan	25	10
☐ 12/87	Michael Jordan & others	25	10
☐ 5/88	Michael Jordan/Bird/Magic	20	10
☐ 11/88	Michael Jordan/Magic/Bird	20	10
☐ 5/90	Michael Jordan	20	10
☐ 10/90	Michael Jordan	20	10
☐ 12/90	Michael Jordan/Magic/Others	20	10
☐ 5/91	Michael Jordan	20	10
☐ 6/92	M.Jordan/Bird/Ewing/Others	20	10
☐ 10/92	Michael Jordan	20	10
☐ 12/92	Michael Jordan	20	10

INSIDE SPORT BOB COUSY MAGAZINE

DATE	COVER/FEATURE	Nr-Mt	Ex
☐ 2/63	Bob Cousy - Celtics	35	15

INSIDE STUFF

(NBA release 1993-on?)

DATE	COVER/FEATURE	Nr-Mt	Ex
☐ 93 #1	Mugsy Bogues - Hornets	30	15
☐ 93 #2	Karl Malone - Jazz	25	10
☐ 93 #3	Michael Jordan - Bulls	30	15

JET

(Produced by Jet magazine. Selected covers listed below.)

DATE	COVER/FEATURE	Nr-Mt	Ex
☐ 7/01/91	Michael Jordan - Bulls	20	10
☐ 11/25/91	Magic Johnson - Lakers	15	5
☐ 7/06/92	Michael Jordan - Bulls	20	10
☐ 8/10/92	M. Jordan/M. Johnson	20	10
☐ 7/12/93	Michael Jordan - Bulls	20	10
☐ 9/06/93	Charles Barkley - Suns	10	5

JOCK

(Published by Sportsworld Communications)
(Magazine started in 1969 and lasted through 1970)

DATE	COVER/FEATURE	Nr-Mt	Ex
☐ 2/70	Cazzie Russell - Knicks	20	10

MAGIC JOHNSON PROMO 92'

DATE	COVER/FEATURE	Nr-Mt	Ex
☐		15	5

MICHAEL JORDAN

DATE	COVER/FEATURE	Nr-Mt	Ex
☐ 1991	MVP/NBA CHAMP	25	10

MORMON SPORTS

DATE	COVER/FEATURE	Nr-Mt	Ex
☐ Vol 1 # 2	Danny Ainge	40	20

NAT HOLMAN BASKETBALL ANNUAL

DATE	COVER/FEATURE	Nr-Mt	Ex
☐ 1951	5 College Players	30	15

NBA BASKETBALL PREVIEW

DATE	COVER/FEATURE	Nr-Mt	Ex
☐ 90-91	M. Jordan/C. Barkley/D. Robinson . . .	30	15

NBA TODAY

(Published by the NBA twice monthly during the basketball season.)

DATE	COVER/FEATURE	Nr-Mt	Ex
☐ 1981-1984	Common Covers	15	5
☐ 1984	Larry Bird Covers	25	10

OFF THE GLASS

DATE	COVER/FEATURE	Nr-Mt	Ex
☐ 11/86	David Robinson - Navy #1	35	15
☐ 12/86	Duke	15	10
☐ 12/86	Jim Valvano - NC State	15	10
☐ 1/87	D. Manning/P. Ellison	15	10
☐ #5	Bobby Knight - Indiana	15	10
☐ #6	Marion Giants H.S.	15	10
☐ 3/87	Jerome Lane - Pitt	10	5
☐ 4/87	JR Reid - NC	10	5
☐ 5/87	Steve Alford - Indiana	10	5
☐ #1	87-88 Chapman - Kentucky	15	5
☐ #11	Derrick Chievous - Missouri	10	5
☐ #2 -4	1988 Harvey Grant - Okla.	15	5
☐ #2 -5	BJ Armstrong/D. Coleman	10	5

OLYMPIAN

DATE	COVER/FEATURE	Nr-Mt	Ex
☐ 2/81	Isiah Thomas	20	10
☐ 11/87	Dave Robinson	25	10

PETERSENS PRO BASKETBALL

(Made Regional Covers from 1987-on. No issues were made between 1981-1987.)

DATE	COVER/FEATURE	Nr-Mt	Ex
☐ 1978	Elvin Hayes	20	10
☐ 1979	Dennis Johnson/Kareem	15	10
☐ 1980	Magic Johnson	15	10
☐ 1987	Michael Jordan	25	15
☐ 1987	All other covers	15	10
☐ 1988	Michael Jordan	25	15
☐ 1988	All other covers	15	10
☐ 1989	Michael Jordan	25	15
☐ 1989	All other covers	15	10
☐ 1990	Michael Jordan	20	15
☐ 1990	All other covers	15	10
☐ 91-on	Michael Jordan	15	10
☐ 91-on	All other Covers	12	5

POPULAR SPORTS BASKETBALL

DATE	COVER/FEATURE	Nr-Mt	Ex
☐ 1973	Bill Walton - UCLA	20	10
☐ 1974	Bill Walton - UCLA	15	10
☐ 1975	John Havlicek - Celtics	20	10
☐ 1976	Rick Barry - Warriors	15	10
☐ 1977	Julius Erving - Sixers	25	15
☐ 1978	Bill Walton - Portland	15	10
☐ 1979	Bill Walton - Portland	15	10
☐ 1980	Larry Bird - Celtics	25	10
☐ 1981	Lew Alcindor/Magic	15	10

PREMIER TELECARD MAGAZINE

DATE	COVER/FEATURE	Nr-Mt	Ex
☐ 12/94	Michael Jordan	20	10

PRESS BOX BASKETBALL

DATE	COVER/FEATURE	Nr-Mt	Ex
☐ 1970	Oscar Robertson	20	10

PRO ACTION SPORTS BASKETBALL

DATE	COVER/FEATURE	Nr-Mt	Ex
☐ 1971	Lew Alcindor/Dan Issel	20	10

PRO BASKETBALL

DATE	COVER/FEATURE	Nr-Mt	Ex
☐ 1964	Wilt Chamberlain	30	15

PRO BASKETBALL (TOPICAL SPORTS)

DATE	COVER/FEATURE	Nr-Mt	Ex
☐ 1964	Bill Russell - Celtics/Howe	40	20
☐ 1965	Phily. Sixers	35	20
☐ 1968	Wilt Chamberlain - Lakers	30	15

PRO BASKETBALL ALL STAR ANNUAL

DATE	COVER/FEATURE	Nr-Mt	Ex
☐ 1958	Bob Cousy - Celtics	45	20

PRO BASKETBALL ALMANAC

DATE	COVER/FEATURE	Nr-Mt	Ex
☐ 1968	Wilt Chamberlain - Lakers	30	15
☐ 1969	Bill Russell/Chamberlain	30	15
☐ 1971	Pete Maravich - Hawks	30	15
☐ 1972	Lew Alcindor/Willis Reed	20	10

PRO BASKETBALL GUIDE

(Cord Sportsfacts)

DATE	COVER/FEATURE	Nr-Mt	Ex
☐ 1970	Lew Alcindor - Bucks	20	10
☐ 1972	Lew Alcindor - Bucks	15	10
☐ 1975	Dave Cowens - Celtics	15	10

PRO BASKETBALL OLDEST YEARBOOK

DATE	COVER/FEATURE	Nr-Mt	Ex
☐ 72-73	Wilt Chamberlain/Alcindor	15	10

PRO BASKETBALL ILLUSTRATED

DATE	COVER/FEATURE	Nr-Mt	Ex
☐ 64-65	Bill Russell - Celtics	35	15
☐ 65-66	Wilt Chamberlain - Sixers	30	15
☐ 66-67	Bill Russell - Celtics	30	15
☐ 67-68	Bill Bradley - Knicks	30	15
☐ 68-69	Jerry West/Chamberlain	25	15
☐ 69-70	Lew Alcindor - Bucks	25	15
☐ 71-72	Lew Alcindor - Bucks	25	15
☐ 72-73	John Havlicek - Celtics	30	15
☐ 73-74	Dave Cowens - Celtics	25	15
☐ 74-75	Julius Erving - Sixers	35	20
☐ 75-76	Bob McAdoo - Braves	25	15
☐ 76-77	Julius Erving - Sixers	25	15
☐ 77-78	Julius Erving - Sixers	25	15
☐ 79-80	Larry Bird/ Magic Johnson	20	10
☐ 83-84	Julius Erving - Sixers	25	15
☐ 85-86	Michael Jordan/Larry Bird	30	15
☐ 86-87	Magic Johnson - Lakers	15	10
☐ 87-88	Michael Jordan - Bulls	25	15
☐ 89-90	Michael Jordan - Bulls	20	10

PRO BASKETBALL SPORTS STARS

DATE	COVER/FEATURE	Nr-Mt	Ex
☐ 1972	Pete Maravich - Jazz	35	15
☐ 1973	Wilt Chamberlain - Lakers	25	15
☐ 1974	Walt Frazier - Knicks	25	10
☐ 1975	Cowens/Havlicek - Celtics	20	10

PRO SPORTS

DATE	COVER/FEATURE	Nr-Mt	Ex
☐ 3/70	Lew Alcindor - Bucks	20	10
☐ 3/71	Lew Alcindor - Bucks	20	10
☐ 1/74	Walt Frazier - Knicks	20	10
☐ 1975	Julius Erving - Sixers	30	10
☐ 3/75	Kareem Abdul Jabbar - Lakers	20	10

PRO VICTORY SPORTS SERIES BASKETBALL

DATE	COVER/FEATURE	Nr-Mt	Ex
☐ 1972	Lew Alcindor/Rick Barry	20	10

SCORE

DATE	COVER/FEATURE	Nr-Mt	Ex
☐ 5/70	Walt Frazier - Knicks	20	10

SPORTS ALBUM

DATE	COVER/FEATURE	Nr-Mt	Ex
☐ W/51	Bill Spivey - Kentucky	50	25

SPORTS ALL STAR BASKETBALL

DATE	COVER/FEATURE	Nr-Mt	Ex
☐ 1970	Lew Alcindor - UCLA	20	10
☐ 1972	O. Robertson/L. Alcindor	20	10

SPORTS CAVALACADE

DATE	COVER/FEATURE	Nr-Mt	Ex
☐ 1/63	Wilt Chamberlain - Phila	35	15

SPORTS FOCUS

DATE	COVER/FEATURE	Nr-Mt	Ex
☐ 1971	Alcindor - Bucks	20	10

SPORT LIFE

DATE	COVER/FEATURE	Nr-Mt	Ex
☐ 4/49	George Kaftan - Holy Cross	45	20

SPORTS QUARTERLY B. SPECIAL

DATE	COVER/FEATURE	Nr-Mt	Ex
☐ 68-69	Bill Bradley/P. Maravich	35	15
☐ 69-70	Lew Alcindor - UCLA/B.Cousy	35	15
☐ 70-71	Austin Carr- Notre Dame	15	10
☐ 70-71	W Reed/Pete Maravich	30	15
☐ 71-72	Alcindor/Pete Maravich	30	15
☐ 71-72	Tom McMillen - MD	15	10
☐ 72-73	Walt Frazier - Knicks	15	10
☐ 73-74	Dave DeBusschere-Knicks	15	10
☐ 74-75	Dr. J/John Havlicek	25	15
☐ 75-76	Rick Barry - Warriors	15	10
☐ 76-77	Alvan Adams/JoJoWhite	15	10
☐ 77-78	Julius Erving - Sixers	25	15
☐ 78-79	Rick Barry/Larry Bird	30	15
☐ 79-80	Bill Walton - Blaziers	15	10
☐ 81-82	Larry Bird - Celtics	30	15

SPORTS REVIEW BASKETBALL

DATE	COVER/FEATURE	Nr-Mt	Ex
☐ 1949	(Life Mag size)	60	25
☐ 1950	(Life Mag size)	60	25
☐ 1951	Bradley/NYC (Life size)	60	25
☐ 1952	(Life Size)	50	25
☐ 1953	Ohio Review/Michigan	50	25
☐ 1954	Indiana/Kansas	45	25
☐ 1955	Rice/St Johns	40	20
☐ 1956	Indiana/Ohio State	35	15
☐ 1957	Hot Rod Hundley	40	20
☐ 1958	Adolph Rupp - Kentucky	40	20
☐ 1959	Adolph Rupp - Kentucky	40	20
☐ 1960	SMU #12 & Coach	35	15
☐ 1961	Adolph Rupp - Kentucky	40	20
☐ 1962	Ohio State/Louisville	35	20
☐ 1963	Cincinnati/Ohio State	35	20
☐ 1967	Jerry West/Oscar Robertson	35	20
☐ 1968	Elgin Baylor/Bill Russell	25	15
☐ 1970	Knicks/Hawks	25	15
☐ 1971	Bucks/Knicks	20	10
☐ 1972	LA Lakers	20	10

SPORTS SCENE

DATE	COVER/FEATURE	Nr-Mt	Ex
☐ 3/71	Jerry West #1 issue	35	20

SPORTS & SOAPS

DATE	COVER/FEATURE	Nr-Mt	Ex
☐ 4/95	Michael Jordan Comes Back	5	2

SPORTS TODAY

DATE	COVER/FEATURE	Nr-Mt	Ex
☐ 3/70	Jerry West - Lakers	25	10
☐ 4/71	Lew Alcindor - Bucks	25	10
☐ 4/72	Jerry West - Lakers	20	10
☐ 2/73	Pete Maravich - Hawks	35	15
☐ 4/73	Wilt Chambelain - Lakers	20	10
☐ 2/75	Dave Cowens - Celtics	20	10

SPORTS WORLD

DATE	COVER/FEATURE	Nr-Mt	Ex
☐ 4/75	Bob McAdoo - Braves	15	10
☐ 4/77	Dave Cowens - Celtics	20	10

STREET & SMITH'S BASKETBALL YEARBOOK

(Began with two Basketball issues in the 50's and then restarted in 1970's. Started off with 3 regions and maintained that into the late 80's. In the late 1980's they split the basketball edition into pro and college. Street and Smith's is still considered one of the best annuals produced on Basketball.)

DATE	COVER/FEATURE	Nr-Mt	Ex
☐ 1957	Charlie Tyra - Louisville	125	50
☐ 1958	Tommy Kearns	125	50
☐ 1970	Jerry West - Lakers	45	25
☐ 1970	Austin Carr - Notre Dame	40	25
☐ 1970	Lew Alcindor - Bucks	40	25
☐ 1971	Lew Alcindor/W. Chamberlain	40	25
☐ 1971	Lew Alcindor/Willis Reed	40	25
☐ 1972	Gail Goodrich - Lakers	40	25
☐ 1972	Dave Cowens/K. Jabbar	40	25
☐ 1972	Bill Walton - UCLA	40	25
☐ 1973	Pete Maravich/John Havlicek	40	25
☐ 1973	Oscar Robertson - Royals	40	25
☐ 1973	Gail Goodrich - Lakers	40	25
☐ 1974	Julius Erving - Sixers	40	25
☐ 1974	Dave Cowens/Kareem	35	20
☐ 1975	Paul Silas/Rick Barry	35	20
☐ 1975	Adrian Dantley/Marques Johnson ...	35	20
☐ 1975	Julius Erving - Sixers	40	20
☐ 1976	Paul Westphal/Dave Cowens	30	15
☐ 1976	Pete Maravich - Jazz	35	15
☐ 1976	John Havlicek - Celtics	30	15
☐ 1977	Bill Walton - Blazers	30	15
☐ 1977	Julius Erving - Sixers	30	15
☐ 1977	Julius Erving - Sixers (Dif. Pose) ...	30	15
☐ 1978	Gene Banks/Kelly Tripucka	25	10
☐ 1978	Kareem Abdul Jabbar - Lakers	25	10
☐ 1978	Kyle Macy - Kentucky	25	10
☐ 1979	Darnell Valentine - Kansas	25	10
☐ 1979	Mike O'Koren/Gene Banks	25	10
☐ 1979	Bill Walton - Blazers	25	10
☐ 1980	Magic Johnson/Kareem	25	10
☐ 1980	Julius Erving/Others	25	10
☐ 1980	Magic Johnson/Larry Bird	25	10
☐ 1981	Moses Malone/Others	20	10
☐ 1981	Larry Bird - Celtics	25	10
☐ 1981	John Paxson/Rod Foster	20	10
☐ 1982	Dr. J./Larry Bird/P. Ewing	20	10
☐ 1982	John Paxson - Notre Dame	20	10
☐ 1982	Sam Perkins - N. Carolina	20	10
☐ 1983	A.C. Green - Oregon State	20	10
☐ 1983	Bobby Knight - Indiana	20	10
☐ 1983	Patrick Ewing - Georgetown	20	10
☐ 1984	Milt Wagner - Louisville	15	10
☐ 1984	Chris Mullin - St Johns	20	10
☐ 1984	Wayman Tisdale - Oklahoma	15	10
☐ 1984	Magic Johnson - Lakers	20	10
☐ 1985	Dwayne Washington - Syracuse	15	7
☐ 1985	Danny Manning - Kansas	15	7
☐ 1985	James Worthy - Lakers	15	7
☐ 1986	David Robinson/Larry Bird	20	15
☐ 1986	Michael Jordan - Bulls	40	25
☐ 1986	Akeem Olajuwon - Rockets	15	7
☐ 1987	Larry Bird - Celtics	35	15
☐ 1987	Bobby Knight/Keith Smart	15	7

DATE	COVER/FEATURE	Nr-Mt	Ex
☐ 1987	Magic Johnson - Lakers	20	10
☐ 1987	Akeem Olajuwon - Rockets	15	7
☐ 1987	Dominique Wilkens - Hawks	15	7
☐ 1987	JR Reid - N. Carolina	15	7
☐ 1988c	Glen Rice - Michigan	15	7
☐ 1988c	Sherman Douglas/Mark Macon	15	7
☐ 1988p	Michael Jordan/Magic/Bird	25	10
☐ 1988c	Danny Ferry - Duke	10	5
☐ 1988c	Stacy King - Oklahoma	10	5
☐ 1989c	Hank Gathers - Pepperdine	10	5
☐ 1989c	Rumeal Robinson - Michigan	10	5
☐ 1989c	Alonzo Mourning - Georgetown	10	7
☐ 1989p	Patrick Ewing - Knicks	10	10
☐ 1989p	Michael Jordan - Bulls	25	12
☐ 1989p	Isiah Thomas - Pistons	10	5
☐ 1990c	Bobby Hurley - Duke	10	5
☐ 1990p	Michael Jordan - Bulls	20	10
☐ 1990c	Larry Johnson - UNLV	7	5
☐ 1990c	Steve Smith - Michigan St.	7	5
☐ 1991c	Shaquille O'Neil - LSU	10	7
☐ 1991-present		7	5
☐ 1991-present Michael Jordan covers		15	10

SUPER SPORTS

DATE	COVER/FEATURE	Nr-Mt	Ex
☐ 12/70	Bill Bradley - Knicks	25	10
☐ 1/73	Illinois St. Akron	15	10
☐ 12/73	North Carolina	15	10
☐ 1974	John Havlicek - Celtics	15	10
☐ 4/74	Nate Thurmond -Warriors	15	10
☐ 4/75	John Havlicek - Celtics	15	10
☐ 1/76	Rick Barry - Warriors	20	10

SUPERSTAR SPORTS

DATE	COVER/FEATURE	Nr-Mt	Ex
☐ 12/72	John Havlicek/Frazier	15	10

THE NATIONAL SPORTS DAILY

(This newspaper came into existence in 1990 and lasted a few years. This is a limited list of Michael Jordan covers.)

DATE	COVER/FEATURE	Nr-Mt	Ex
☐ 4/17/90	Michael Jordan	20	10
☐ 5/21/90	Michael Jordan	20	10
☐ 6/3/90	Kirk Gibson/Michael Jordan	20	10
☐ 12/26/90	Michael Jordan	20	10
☐ 1/15/91	Michael Jordan	20	10
☐ 5/13/91	Michael Jordan/Magic	20	10
☐ 5/29/91	Michael Jordan/Jim Abbott	20	10
☐ 5/28/91	Michael Jordan	20	10
☐ 6/7/91	Magic/Jordan/Pippen	20	10

THE SPORTING NEWS COLLEGE & PRO YEARBOOK

(In 1985 TSN started to produce regional issues. In 1987 they separated the pro from the college edition.)

DATE	COVER/FEATURE	Nr-Mt	Ex
☐ 1982	Patrick Ewing/Jabbar	15	10
☐ 1983	Michael Jordan/Jabbar	40	20
☐ 1984	Varies	15	10
☐ 1985	Michael Jordan	35	20
☐ 1985	All other covers	15	10
☐ 1986	Charles Barkley/Others	20	12
☐ 1986	All other covers	15	10
☐ 1987	College Player Covers	10	5
☐ 1987	Michael Jordan	30	15
☐ 1987	All other pro covers	10	5
☐ 1988	College Player Covers	10	5
☐ 1988	Pro Covers	10	5
☐ 1989	College Player covers	10	5
☐ 1989	Karl Malone	10	5
☐ 1989	Michael Jordan	25	15
☐ 1989	Pro Covers	10	5
☐ 1990-on	Shaquille O'Neal	25	10
☐ 1990-on	All other college covers	10	5

DATE	COVER/FEATURE	Nr-Mt	Ex
☐ 1990-on	Michael Jordan	25	10
☐ 1990-on	All other pro covers	10	5

THE SPORTING NEWS ABA GUIDE

DATE	COVER/FEATURE	Nr-Mt	Ex
☐ 1968	Rick Barry - Oaks	95	35
☐ 1969	Warren Armstrong - Oaks	70	25
☐ 1970	Illustration	55	25
☐ 1971	Mel Daniels - Pacers	50	25
☐ 1972	Artis Gilmore - Cols.	45	20
☐ 1973	Billy Cunningham - Cougars	40	20
☐ 1974	Julius Erving - Nets	40	20
☐ 1975	Artis Gilmore - Spurs	40	20

THE SPORTING NEWS NBA REGISTER

DATE	COVER/FEATURE	Nr-Mt	Ex
☐ 1980	Kareem Abdul Jabbar - Sixers	20	10
☐ 1981	Julius Erving - Sixers	25	10
☐ 1982	Moses Malone - Sixers	20	10
☐ 1983	Moses Malone - Sixers	20	10
☐ 1984	Kareem Abdul Jabbar	20	10
☐ 1985	Kareem Abdul Jabbar	20	10
☐ 1986	Larry Bird - Celtics	25	10
☐ 1987	Michael Jordan - Bulls	35	10
☐ 1988	James Worthy - Lakers	25	10
☐ 1989	Karl Malone - Jazz	15	10
☐ 1990	David Robinson - Spurs	10	5
☐ 1991	Magic Johnson - Lakers	10	5

THE SPORTING NEWS NBA GUIDE

DATE	COVER/FEATURE	Nr-Mt	Ex
☐ 1958	Bob Pettit - Hawks	95	50
☐ 1959	Bill Russell - Celtics	75	50
☐ 1960	Art Picture	50	25
☐ 1961	Bob Pettit - Hawks	40	20
☐ 1962	Tom Hensohn - Celtics	40	20
☐ 1963	Hawks/Royals	60	30
☐ 1964	John Havlicek - Celtics	40	20
☐ 1965	Jerry West - Lakers	40	20
☐ 1966	Gene Wiley - Lakers	40	20
☐ 1967	Wilt Chamberlain - Sixers	35	20
☐ 1968	Oscar Robertson/Jerry West	30	15
☐ 1969	NBA Logos	25	10
☐ 1970	Wilt Chamberlain - Sixers	25	10
☐ 1971	Lew Alcindor - Bucks	25	10
☐ 1972	Wilt Chamberlain - Lakers	20	10
☐ 1973	Dave Cowens - Celtics	20	10
☐ 1974	John Havlick - Celtics	20	10
☐ 1975	Action	20	10
☐ 1976	Garfield Heard - Suns	20	10
☐ 1977	Bill Walton - Blazers	20	10
☐ 1978	Wes Unseld - Bullets	20	10
☐ 1979	Action	15	10
☐ 1980	Larry Bird/Magic Johnson	15	10
☐ 1981	Action	15	10
☐ 1982	Magic Johnson - Lakers	25	10
☐ 1983	Julius Erving - Sixers	25	10
☐ 1984	Larry Bird - Celtics	20	10
☐ 1985	Michael Jordan - Bulls	30	15
☐ 1986	Larry Bird - Celtics	25	15
☐ 1987	Magic Johnson - Lakers	20	15
☐ 1988	Michael Jordan - Bulls	25	10
☐ 1989	Action	12	10
☐ 1990	Isiah Thomas - Pistons	15	10
☐ 1991	Michael Jordan - Bulls	20	10

THE SPORTING NEWS SCHEDULES AND RECORDS

(This is a small pocket book that cost .25 and features basketball players.)

DATE	COVER/FEATURE	Nr-Mt	Ex
☐ 1967	Kansas vs Ohio State	20	10
☐ 1968	Warriors vs Sixers	20	10
☐ 1969	UCLA (Alcindor) vs Providence	20	10
☐ 1970	Denver #24 ABA	20	10

□ 1971	Royals NBA	20	10
□ 1972	Chamberlain/West/Goodrich	20	10
□ 1973	Lew Alcindor/W. Chamberlain	20	10
□ 1974	Braves/Sonics	20	10
□ 1975	Kentucky/Spirit of St. Louis (ABA)	20	10
□ 1976	Sixers vs Suns	20	10

TOMMY KAY BOOK OF PRO BASKETBALL

DATE	COVER/FEATURE	Nr-Mt	Ex
□ 1975	John Havlicek/Others	20	10

TREASURE CHEST

(Comic Book)

DATE	COVER/FEATURE	Nr-Mt	Ex
□ 11/65	Oscar Robertson - Royals	35	10

TV SPORTS

DATE	COVER/FEATURE	Nr-Mt	Ex
□ 2/89	Kareem Abdul Jabbar	20	10

USA OLYMPIC MEN'S
BASKETBALL MEDIA GUIDE

DATE	COVER/FEATURE	Nr-Mt	Ex
□ 1992	M. Jordan/Others	50	30

WHO'S WHO IN BASKETBALL

DATE	COVER/FEATURE	Nr-Mt	Ex
□ 1970	Jerry West/ Lew Alcindor	20	10

WILT CHAMBERLAIN BASKETBALL

DATE	COVER/FEATURE	Nr-Mt	Ex
□ 1963	Wilt Chamberlain - Phila	40	20

SPALDING - BARNES - NCAA ANNUALS

Very little is written on the early years of Basketball and the Spalding Guides are one of the only sources of information on the subject. The guides started in 1894 and ran through 1940. In 1941 Barnes took over and continued the series until 1950. In 1951 the NCAA continued in the tradition and retitled it "Official Collegiate Basketball Guide". This series featured a college player in his day. The "Official Collegiate Basketball Record Book" also started in 1950. I am not sure when this stopped. During the 1980's the NCAA started to use art work and featured both one of the best woman and men's basketball players.

DATE	COVER/FEATURE	Nr-Mt	Ex
□ 1894	Art Work	1000	500
□ 1895	Art work	500	300
□ 1896	Art Work	400	200
□ 1897	Art Work	400	200
□ 1898	Art Work	300	150
□ 1899	Art Work	300	120
□ 1900-1910	Art Work	200	100
□ 11-19	Art Work	150	65
□ 20-29	Art Work	100	50
□ 30-40	Art Work	80	40
□ 1941	Barnes Guides start	80	40
□ 1942		60	30
□ 1943	University of Illinois	60	30
□ 1944		60	30

□ 1945	Barnes Guides	60	30
□ 1946	North Carolina	60	30
□ 1947	Holy Cross in Action	60	30
□ 1948	Kentucky in Action	50	30
□ 1950	NCAA Guides and Record Book Start	40	20
□ 1951	NCAA Guides	45	20
□ 1952	Bill Spivey - Kentucky	40	20
□ 1953	Bob Houbregs - Washington	40	20
□ 1953	Ernie Beck - Pennsylvania (Record Book)	40	20
□ 1954		40	20
□ 1955	Tom Gola - LaSalle	40	20
□ 1956	Dick O'Neal - Texas Christian	40	20
□ 1957		40	20
□ 1958	Bailey Howell - Mississippi State	40	20
□ 1958	Don Hennon - Pitt (Record Book)	40	20
□ 1959		35	20
□ 1960	Wally Frank - Kansas State	35	20
□ 1961	Clyde Rhoden - Arkansas (Record Book)	35	20
□ 1962	Terry Dischinger - Purdue (Record Book)	35	20
□ 1963	Jim Kerwin - Tulane (Record Book)	35	20
□ 1964		35	20
□ 1965		35	20
□ 1966		35	20
□ 1967		30	15
□ 1968		30	15
□ 1969		30	15
□ 1970	Dennis Awtrey - Santa Clara	30	15
□ 1971	Rich Yunkus - Georgia Tech	20	10
□ 1972	Dun Buse - Evansville	20	10
□ 1973	Kermit Washington - American U	20	10
□ 1974	Louis Dunbar - Houston	20	10
□ 1975	Dave Meyers - UCLA	20	10
□ 1976	Chuckie Williams - Kansas State	20	10
□ 1977	Skip Brown - Wake Forest	20	10
□ 1978	Ronnie Perry - Holy Cross	20	10
□ 1979	Craig Finberg - Montana State	20	10
□ 1980	Loyola Marymount	15	5
□ 1981	Action	10	5
□ 1982	Kevin Magee - Cal Irvine	10	5
□ 1983	Anne Donovan/Ralph Sampson	10	5
□ 1984	Akeem Olajuwon/Kim Mulkey	15	5
□ 1985	Cheryl Miller/Patrick Ewing	15	5
□ 1986	Kenny Walker/Kamie Ethridge	10	5
□ 1987	David Robinson - Navy	15	5
□ 1988	Danny Manning/Sue Wicks	10	5
□ 1981-on	NCAA Guides	10	5

REACH BASKETBALL GUIDES

Reach competed against Spalding during the Guide war years. These guides are rare and tough to find.

DATE	COVER/FEATURE	Nr-Mt	Ex
□ 1901	Art Work	500	300
□ 1902	Art Work	300	150
□ 03-04	Art Work	200	100
□ 05-10	Art Work	150	75
□ 11-19	Art Work	100	50
□ 20-26	Art Work	75	35

1971 ALL SPORTS

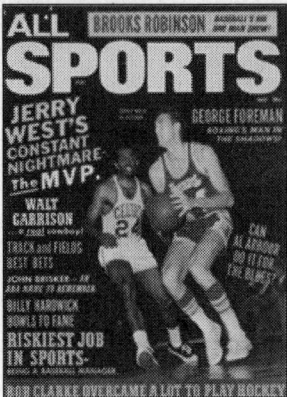

1958 BASKETBALL

1955 BASKETBALL'S BEST

1980 BASKETBALL DIGEST

1948 BASKETBALL ILLUSTRATED

1960 BASKETBALL YEARBOOK

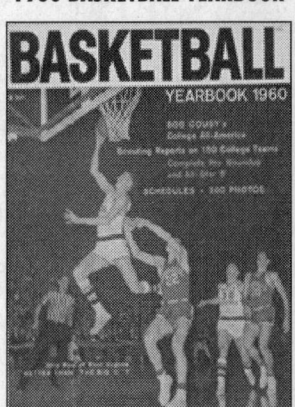

1961 COMPLETE SPORTS

1962 COMPLETE SPORTS

1963 COMPLETE SPORTS

1945 CONVERSE YEARBOOK

1969 COUNTRYWIDE SPORTS

1979 INSIDE SPORTS

1963 INSIDE SPORT BOB COUSY

1991 JET

1957 PROFESSIONAL BK

1964 PRO BASKETBALL

1969 PRO BASKETBALL

1950 SPORTS ALBUM

1963 SPORTS CAVALCADE

1952 SPORTS REVIEW

1967 SPORTS REVIEW

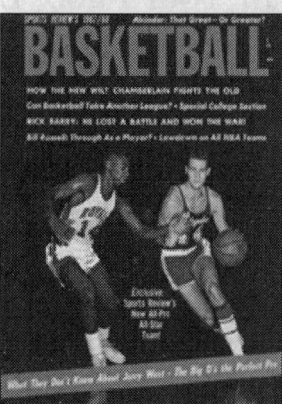

STREET & SMITH'S PRO BASKETBALL
1976-77

1991-92

1994-95

In Your Face, Behind-the-back, No-look, Slam Dunk Hobby Coverage!

EVERY MONTH!

Subscribe to *Beckett Basketball Card Monthly* today!

Looking for a reliable hoops Price Guide with up-to-the-minute info? With a subscription to *Beckett Basketball Card Monthly*, you'll get the hobby's most accurate basketball card Price Guide every month! Plus get great inside info about new product releases, superstar player coverage, off-the-court news and answers to all your collecting questions too!

Beckett Basketball Card Monthly

Name (please print) _____

Address _____

City _____ State _____ ZIP _____

Payment enclosed via: ❏ Check or Money Order   ❏ Bill Me Later

Check One Please: Price   Total

❏ 2 years (24 issues) $44.95 = _____
❏ 1 year (12 issues) $24.95 = _____

All Canadian & foreign addresses add
$12 per year for postage (includes G.S.T.).   = _____

Payable in U.S. funds.
Please do not send cash.   Total Enclosed $ _____

Mail to:
Beckett Basketball Card Monthly
P.O. Box 7646
Red Oak, IA 51591-0646
Photocopies of this coupon are acceptable.

Please allow 4-6 weeks for subscription delivery.

SK0058

CHAPTER SIXTEEN:
Collecting Football Team Publications

There is no easy way to collect every pro football publication made. In the world of Sports Publications most football fans focus on their favorite team or player. The value of pro football programs, media guides, schedules, tickets and the like is based both on the historic importance and the players who appear on the item. Pro football has its key gods of the game (Dan Marino, John Elway, Joe Montana, etc) and when those players appear on a magazine the items go for a premium. However, most football publication related material is modest in pricing.

DEFUNCT PRO FOOTBALL TEAMS

Pro Football had many ups and downs since it was created in 1920. In fact, only one team, the Green Bay Packers, has survived from the beginning. Memorabilia, including programs, are hotly pursued by football historical event collectors. Every team issued a ticket and a program that is pursued by collectors. Some early teams may have had a media information sheet or guide. All of these items are pursued by advanced collectors. It is a challenge for football historic collector to find programs from these early teams. The following are the list of defunct pro teams and the year they first appeared.

1920	Akron Pros, Decatur Staleys, Buffalo All Americans, Rock Island Independents, Dayton Triangles, Canton Bulldogs, Detroit Herald, Chicago Tigers, Rochester Jeffersons, Munice Fliers
1921	Evansville Crimson Giants, Cincinnati Celts, Hammond Pros, Minneapolis Marines, Detroit Panthers, Columbus Panhandlers, Louisville Brecks
1922	Toledo Maroons, Racine Legion, Buffalo All Americans, Akron Pro's, Milwaukee Baders Oorang Indians, Minneaplis Marines, Hammond Pros
1923	Duluth Kelleys, St Louis All Stars
1924	Frankford Yellowjackets, Buffalo Bisons, Kansas City Cowboys, Kenosha Maroons
1925	New York Giants (Jim Thorpe), Detroit Panthers, Columbus Tigers
1926	Los Angeles Bucaneers, Duluth Eskomos, Hartford Blues, Brooklyn Lions, Louisville Colonels.
1927	New York Yankees (Grange)
1928	Orange Toronados
1932	Boston Braves
1934	Cincinnati Reds
1935	Brooklyn Dodgers

Prices for ear.y programs are rather sketchy because only a few programs ever change hands. However, the following are guidelines for defunct team. It should be noted that many of these teams had multiple seasons. Some of these teams also shifted from the NFL to Independent team status. Programs with Jim Thorpe or Ernie Nevers are worth two times the amount of a regular season program.

YEAR	NR-MT	Ex
1920	.450	250
1921	425	225
1922	400	225
1923-27	.300	150
1928-35	200	100

There were three AFL conferences that are considered minor leagues during their appearances (1926- 1946). The All America Football Conference (1946-1949) produced the best looking football programs. However, the league could not survive so it merged into the NFL. The following teams did not merge: Brooklyn Dodgers-New York Yankees, Chicago Rockets, Los Angeles Dons. The average value of a All American Football Conference football program is as follows::

YEAR	NR-MT	Ex
1946	50	35
1947-48	35	20
1949	30	15

The World Football league (1974-1975) is popular with defunct team collectors. None of the 11 teams merged into the NFL:

	NR-MT	Ex
PROGRAMS		
1974	20	10
1975	20	10
MEDIA GUIDES		
1974	25	10
1975	25	10

The USFL (United States Football League) lasted three years. A few of the great stars in the NFL started in the USFL. The conference had 19 teams throughout its time period. The most valuable covers are of key superstars.

	NR-MT	Ex
PROGRAM VALUE		
1983	20	5
1984	20	5
1985	20	5
MEDIA GUIDE VALUE		
1983	20	5
1984	20	5
1985	20	5

SUPER BOWLS & CHAMPIONSHIPS

Most people affiliate the Super Bowl as the beginning and end of the Championship game. However, the best games ever played were in the championship game that dates all the way back to 1933. The first games (1920-1931) were awarded to the team that won the regular season scehdule.

AFL CHAMPIONSHIP

The AFL started its championship season in 1960. They then entered into the Super Bowl in the 1966 season. The Playoff system began in 1968, creating a second round. In 1978, playoff programs go for about 50% of the Championship program.

YEAR	TEAM	Nr-Mt	Ex
☐ 1960	Houston	400	150
☐ 1961	Houston	350	100
☐ 1962	Dallas	350	100
☐ 1963	San Diego	200	100
☐ 1964	Buffalo	200	100
☐ 1965	Buffalo	250	100
☐ 1966	KC Chiefs	200	100
☐ 1967	Oakland	200	100
☐ 1968	NY Jets	200	100
☐ 1969	KC Chiefs	65	45
☐ 1970	Baltimore	55	25
☐ 1971	Miami	55	25
☐ 1972	Miami	55	25
☐ 1973	Miami	55	20
☐ 1974	Pittsburgh	45	20
☐ 1975	Pittsburgh	45	20
☐ 1976	Oakland	40	20
☐ 1977	Denver	40	15
☐ 1978	Pittsburgh	35	15
☐ 1979	Pittsburgh	35	15
☐ 1980	Oakland	35	15
☐ 1981	Cincinati	30	15
☐ 1982	Miami	30	15
☐ 1983	LA Raiders	35	15
☐ 1984	Oakland	30	15
☐ 1985	Patriots	30	15
☐ 1986	Denver	30	10
☐ 1987	Denver	30	10
☐ 1988	Cincinati	30	10
☐ 1989	Denver	30	10
☐ 1990	Buffalo	25	10
☐ 1991	Buffalo	25	10
☐ 1992	Buffalo	25	10
☐ 1993	Buffalo	25	10
☐ 1994	San Diego	25	10
☐ 1995	Pittsburgh	25	10
☐ 1996	Patriots	15	7
☐ 1997	Denver	20	10

		Nr-Mt	Ex
☐ 1955	Browns	400	150
☐ 1956	Giants	400	150
☐ 1957	Lions	400	150
☐ 1958	Colts	400	150
☐ 1959	Colts	400	150
☐ 1960	Eagles	300	150
☐ 1961	Packers	350	100
☐ 1962	Packers	350	100
☐ 1963	Bears	300	100
☐ 1964	Browns	200	200
☐ 1965	Packers	250	100
☐ 1966	Packers	250	100
☐ 1967	Packers	250	100
☐ 1968	Colts	200	100
☐ 1969	Vikings	65	45
☐ 1970	Cowboys	55	25
☐ 1971	Cowboys	55	25
☐ 1972	Redskins	55	25
☐ 1973	Vikings	55	20
☐ 1974	Vikings	45	20
☐ 1975	Cowboys	45	20
☐ 1976	Vikings	40	20
☐ 1977	Cowboys	40	15
☐ 1978	Dallas	35	15
☐ 1979	Rams	35	15
☐ 1980	Eagles	30	15
☐ 1981	49ers	30	15
☐ 1982	Redskins	30	15
☐ 1983	Redskins	30	15
☐ 1984	49ers	30	15
☐ 1985	Bears	30	15
☐ 1986	Giants	30	10
☐ 1987	Redskins	30	10
☐ 1988	49ers	30	10
☐ 1989	49ers	30	10
☐ 1990	Giants	25	10
☐ 1991	Redskins	25	10
☐ 1992	Dallas	25	10
☐ 1993	Dallas	25	10
☐ 1994	49ers	25	10
☐ 1995	Dallas	25	10
☐ 1996	Packers	15	7
☐ 1997	Packers	20	10

NFL CHAMPIONSHIP

So few of the pre 1940 programs are sold that it is hard to gauge these prices. I would make the assumption that all the quality pieces (1933-1950) would only appear in national auctions or sold among the most advanced publication dealers. It should be noted that a playoff system began in 1967 when they created an eastern/western division playoff. This was expanded to two rounds in 1978. The first and second round programs are 50% of the championship program.

SEASON	WINNER	Nr-Mt	Ex
☐ 1933	Chicago	2,000	1,000
☐ 1934	Giants	1,500	500
☐ 1935	Detroit	1,500	500
☐ 1936	Green Bay	1,500	500
☐ 1937	Wash.	1,000	500
☐ 1938	Giants	1,000	500
☐ 1939	Green Bay	1,000	500
☐ 1940	Bears	750	350
☐ 1941	Bears	750	350
☐ 1942	Wash.	600	300
☐ 1944	Green Bay	550	250
☐ 1945	Rams	450	200
☐ 1946	Bears	450	200
☐ 1947	Cardinals	450	200
☐ 1948	Eagles	450	200
☐ 1949	Eagles	450	200
☐ 1950	Browns	400	200
☐ 1951	Rams	400	200
☐ 1952	Lions	400	200
☐ 1953	Lions	400	200
☐ 1954	Browns	400	150

SUPER BOWL PROGRAMS

The most collect championship program is the Super Bowl. Many collectors do not collect anything else but superbowl related material. Super Bowl programs are considered common after Super Bowl XVI. Tthe first ten superbowl programs are the toughest to find in nice shape and are pursued heavily by Super Bowl collectors. The program itself is one of the more attractive programs made in sports. The program has variations (game issue vs. store issue).

SEASON	WINNER	Nr-Mt	Ex
☐ 1966	Green Bay	300	150
☐ 1967	GreenBay	300	150
☐ 1968	Jets	300	150
☐ 1969	Chiefs	200	100
☐ 1970	Baltimore	350	150
☐ 1971	Dallas	150	60
☐ 1972	Miami	150	50
☐ 1973	Miami	75	35
☐ 1974	Pittsburgh	75	25
☐ 1975	Pittsburgh	65	25
☐ 1976	Oakland	65	20
☐ 1977	Dallas	65	20
☐ 1978	Pittsbrugh	45	20
☐ 1979	Pittsburgh	45	20
☐ 1980	Oakland	45	20
☐ 1981	SF	35	15
☐ 1982	Wash.	30	15
☐ 1983	LA Raiders	25	10
☐ 1984	SF 49ers	25	10

☐ 1985	Chicago	20	5
☐ 1986	Giants	20	10
☐ 1987	Wash.	20	5
☐ 1988	SF	15	5
☐ 1989	SF	15	5
☐ 1990	Giants	15	5
☐ 1991	Wash	15	5
☐ 1992	Dallas	15	5
☐ 1993	Dallas	15	5
☐ 1994	SF	10	5
☐ 1995	Dallas	15	5
☐ 1996	Green Bay	10	5
☐ 1997	Denver	12	5

SUPER BOWL TICKETS

Ticket stubs are worth more than the programs. Ticket stubs are harder to find and to find complete. Prices on Super Bowl tickets have climbed over the last four years making them go for near the face value of the used ticket In fact, you can find these stubs offered by many dealers across the country. Many fake and demo Super Bowl tickets exist. Buyers need to know how to tell the demo (usually the ticket location on the front doesn't have a location in the stadium).

SUPER BOWL MEDIA GUIDES

Super Bowl media guides are rare compared to the programs. The demand for the Super Bowl media guides is relatively low and usually are pursued by player or team collectors. I have found that there may be three media guides. One media guide on the superbowl event itself and then one media guide on the AFL team and one on the NFL team. The values is usually two times the Superbowl program the later Super Bowls (25-100).

PRO TEAM PUBLICATIONS

This is where most collectors start when they collect by team or player. Most team related items can be found with regional dealers or national dealers. However, some of the key material only appears in national auctions. Pre-35 sports programs are tough and very few change hands throughout the course of any year.

ATLANTA FALCONS

Average team with small collector team base.

MEDIA GUIDES		Nr-Mt	Ex
☐ 1966	Action	40	20
☐ 1967	Helmet	30	15
☐ 1968	Players	30	15
☐ 1969	Linemen	25	12
☐ 1970	Action	25	10
☐ 1971	Action	25	10
☐ 1972	Action	20	10
☐ 1973	Logo	20	10
☐ 1974	Players	20	7
☐ 1975	Players	15	7
☐ 1976	Players	15	7
☐ 1977	Players	15	7
☐ 1978-80		12	5
☐ 1981-89		10	4
☐ 1990-97		5	2

GAME PROGRAMS		Nr-Mt	Ex
☐ 1966	First Program	100	50
☐ 1966	First Season	35	15
☐ 1967-69	Game Programs	25	12
☐ 1970-75	Game Programs	20	12
☐ 1976-80	Game Programs	15	5
☐ 1981-89	Game Programs	10	3
☐ 1990-97	Game Programs	5	1

TEAM SCHEDULES		Nr-Mt	Ex
☐ 66-69	Schedules	25	15
☐ 70-75	Schedules	15	8
☐ 76-80	Schedules	10	7
☐ 81-89	Schedules	6	3

☐ 90-97	Schedules	2	1

YEARBOOKS, MAGAZINES, NEWSLETTERS		Nr-Mt	Ex

Yearbooks were issued from 1966-1977. Team issue material has been issued but only has marginal value.

☐ 1966	Logo	55	25
☐ 1967	Logo	55	25
☐ 68-70		45	20
☐ 71-77		30	15

BUFFALO BILLS

Awesome team and heavily collected in the Upper New York state area. The A.A.F.C. conference started in 1946 and featured the Buffalo Bisons (Bills) and died in 1950. The early Buffalo Bills material is extremely tough and popular. The name 'Buffalo Bills' reappeared with the creation of the AFL in 1960. Early AFL material is popular. Most collect Buffalo Bills players are Jack Kemp and Jim Kelly. OJ Simpson popularity has now reached an all time low with no special premium on his material.

MEDIA GUIDES		Nr-Mt	Ex
☐ 1960	Bills Logo	50	25
☐ 1961	Bills Mascot	50	25
☐ 1962	Bills Mascot	50	25
☐ 1963	Bills Mascot	50	25
☐ 1964	Bills Logo	40	20
☐ 1965	Bills Logo	40	20
☐ 1966	Team Picture	40	20
☐ 1967	Action	30	15
☐ 1968	Action	30	15
☐ 1969	Action	25	12
☐ 1970	OJ Simpson	30	15
☐ 1971	Action	25	10
☐ 1972	OJ Simpson	25	10
☐ 1973	Stadium	20	10
☐ 1974	OJ Simpson	20	7
☐ 1975	Tony Greene	15	7
☐ 1976	Bills Helmet	15	7
☐ 1977	Bills Logo	15	7
☐ 1978-80		12	5
☐ 1981-89		10	4
☐ 1990-97		5	2

GAME PROGRAMS		Nr-Mt	Ex
☐ 1946	First Bills Program	350	200
☐ 1946	Season	150	75
☐ 47-49	Game Programs	100	50
☐ 1960	First AFL Program	250	100
☐ 1960	First Season	75	35
☐ 61-63	Game Programs	50	25
☐ 64-69	Game Programs	35	20
☐ 70-75	Game Programs	20	12
☐ 76-80	Game Programs	15	5
☐ 81-89	Game Programs	10	3
☐ 90-97	Game Programs	5	1
☐	OJ Simpson first Program	100	50
☐	Jack Kemp First Program	75	35
☐	Jim Kelly First Program	50	25

TEAM SCHEDULES		Nr-Mt	Ex
☐ 1946	First Schedule	150	100
☐ 47-49	Early Schedules	100	75
☐ 1960	AFL First Season	150	100
☐ 61-65	Early Schedules	35	20
☐ 66-69	Schedules	25	15
☐ 70-75	Schedules	15	8
☐ 76-80	Schedules	10	7
☐ 81-89	Schedules	6	3
☐ 90-97	Schedules	2	1

YEARBOOKS, MAGAZINES, NEWSLETTERS		Nr-Mt	Ex

A few yearbooks were issued. Magazines and newsletters, team issue stuff is very valuable in the 46-49 and the 60-65 period.

☐ 1965	Bills in Action	75	35
☐ 1969	OJ Simpson	40	20

☐ 1989	....	10	5
☐ 1990	....	10	5
☐ 1991-on	....	7	3

JACK KEMP
Jack Kemp is popular and is collected by political sports collectors. His oddball material on the Bills is popular (50-75 range).

JIM KELLY
Perhaps one of the greatest quarterbacks of our time. He led the Bills to four Super Bowl losses in a row. His material is still collected by Bills fans.

CHICAGO BEARS
One of the best and oldest teams in pro football. Hard to find pre 1940 material. Quality material can be found among the largest and best dealers in the Chicago area. The fan base for Chicago Bears is high.

MEDIA GUIDES		Nr-Mt	Ex
☐ 1934	Team Name	150	65
☐ 1935	Players	150	65
☐ 1936	Players	150	65
☐ 1937	Players	145	65
☐ 1938	Players	140	55
☐ 1939	Players in Action	140	55
☐ 1940	Players	140	50
☐ 1941	Players in Action	135	50
☐ 1942	Players	140	50
☐ 1943	Players in Action	135	50
☐ 1944	Players in Action	135	50
☐ 1945	Team Picture	135	50
☐ 1946	Picture/Date	135	40
☐ 1947	Players in Action	130	40
☐ 1948	Bears Mascot	135	40
☐ 1949	Bears Mascot	130	40
☐ 1950	Bears Mascot	100	30
☐ 1951	Bears Mascot	100	30
☐ 1952	Players in Action	100	30
☐ 1953	Players in Action	75	30
☐ 1954	Players in Action	75	25
☐ 1955	Players in Action	65	25
☐ 1956	Players in Action	65	25
☐ 1957	Players in Action	55	20
☐ 1958	Bears Mascot	55	20
☐ 1959	Team Picture	55	20
☐ 1960	Bears Mascot	55	20
☐ 1961	Bears Mascot	55	20
☐ 1962	Bears in Action	55	20
☐ 1963	Bears Mascot	55	20
☐ 1964	World Champs	55	20
☐ 1965	Bear in action	55	20
☐ 1966	Bear in Action	55	20
☐ 1967	Bear in action	55	20
☐ 1968	Bears Helmet	35	15
☐ 1969	Bear Helmet	35	15
☐ 1970	Bear Helmet	25	15
☐ 1971	Bear Helmet	25	15
☐ 1972	Bear Helmet	20	15
☐ 1973	Person	20	15
☐ 1974	Bear Helmet	20	5
☐ 1975	Players	20	5
☐ 1976	Bear Helmet	20	5
☐ 1977	Jack Pardee	15	5
☐ 1978	Logo	15	5
☐ 1979	Bears in Action	15	5
☐ 1980	George Halas	15	5
☐ 1981	Logo	15	5
☐ 1982	Mike Ditka	15	5
☐ 1983	Mike Ditka	15	5
☐ 1984	Walter Payton	15	5
☐ 1985	Bears in action	12	3
☐ 1986	Bears in Action	12	3
☐ 1987	Payton, Sayers	12	3
☐ 1988	Bears Helmet	12	3
☐ 1989	Bears.........................	10	2
☐ 1990	Bears Helmet	10	3
☐ 1991-on	....	5	1

PROGRAMS		Nr-Mt	Ex
☐ 1920	First Staleys Program	1000	500
☐ 1920	Game Program	600	300
☐ 1921	First Chicago Game	1000	500
☐ 1921	Game Program	600	300
☐ 1922	First Bear Game	1000	500
☐ 1922	Game Program	500	250
☐ 1923-24	Game Program	500	250
☐ 1925	Red Grange first Gm	600	350
☐ 1925-26	Red Grange Prog	400	200
☐ 1927-30	Game Programs	200	100
☐ 1931-39	Game Programs	150	75
☐ 1940-49	Game Programs	100	50
☐ 190-59	Game Programs	50	25
☐ 1960-69	Game Programs	35	15
☐ 1970-79	Game Programs	15	7
☐ 1980-89	Game Programs	10	5
☐ 1990-97	Game Programs	6	3
☐	Walter Payton First Game	40	20
☐	Brian Piccalo Last Game	30	20
☐	Gale Sayers First Game	40	20

SCHEDULES		Nr-Mt	Ex
☐ 1930's	....	65	40
☐ 1940's	....	45	30
☐ 1950's	....	35	20
☐ 1960's	....	25	10
☐ 1970's	....	12	5
☐ 1980's	....	7	3
☐ 1990's	....	5	1

BEARS YEARBOOKS/MAGAZINES/ NEWSLETTERS
No yearbooks were issued except the superbowl year in 1986 (15). Magazines and newsletters have been released periodically. Values of these are based if they have key players like Walter Payton, Dick Butkus, Gale Sayers, Brian Picallo, Red Grange or Mike Ditka on the cover.

WALTER PAYTON
Definitely the class act from the Bears. His material is pursued by Chicago Bear fans. Most of his material falls in the 20-25 range.

RED GRANGE
His college material and pro material is in the hundreds of dollars. One of the most significant football players of all time.

DICK BUTKUS
The greatest linebacker of all time. Major fans. All of his material goes for 35 and up.

CINCINNATI BENGALS
This team has been to the Super Bowl. Unfortnately no legends make any particular issues special. The team originated in 1968.

MEDIA GUIDES		Nr-Mt	Ex
☐ 1968	Paul Brown	40	20
☐ 1969	Stadium	20	10
☐ 1970	....	20	10
☐ 1971	....	20	10
☐ 1972	....	20	10
☐ 1973	....	20	10
☐ 1974	Cincinnati	15	7
☐ 1975	Bengal in Action	15	7
☐ 1976	Ken Anderson	15	7
☐ 1977	Stadium	15	7
☐ 1978	Stadium	15	7
☐ 1979	Helmet	15	7
☐ 1980	Tiger	10	7
☐ 1981	New Uniform	10	5
☐ 82-90	....	5	3
☐ 91-97	....	4	1

GAME PROGRAMS		Nr-Mt	Ex
☐ 1968	First Program	50	25
☐ 68-70	Game Programs	20	10
☐ 71-75	Game Programs	15	7
☐ 76-80	Game Programs	10	5

		Nr-Mt	Ex
□ 81-89	Game Programs	10	3
□ 90-97	Game Program	5	1

SCHEDULE

		Nr-Mt	Ex
□ 68	First Schedule	30	15
□ 69-70	Schedules	20	10
□ 71-75	Schedules	15	7
□ 76-80	Schedules	10	5
□ 81-89	Schedules	5	2
□ 90-97	Schedules	4	1

YEARBOOKS, MAGAZINE, NEWSLETTERS
None.

CLEVELAND BROWNS

(Also Cleveland Tigers (20), Indians (21-23,31), Bulldogs (24-27). See Rams for Cleveland 36. One of the oldest football franchises. Early material from the Tigers, Indians, and Bulldogs is exceptionally rare and desirable. A Solid fan base is built around the early Cleveland Browns franchise. Quality material can be found among the dealers in the Cleveland area. The historical fan base did not die because the team moved to Baltimore. In fact, the material may go up in value now that htey have a new team with the 'Browns' name and tradition.

MEDIA GUIDES

		Nr-Mt	Ex
□ 1949	Browns Mascot	100	40
□ 1950	Stadium	65	20
□ 1951	Name	65	30
□ 1952	Paul Brown	55	20
□ 1953	Cartoon	65	30
□ 1954	Equipment	55	20
□ 1955	Cartoon	65	25
□ 1956	Cartoon	45	20
□ 1957	Brown Players	55	20
□ 1958	Brown in Action	35	20
□ 1959	Brown in Action	35	20
□ 1960	Helmet	30	20
□ 1961	Helmet	35	20
□ 1962	Jim Brown	35	10
□ 1963	Jim Brown	45	10
□ 1964	Jim Brown	35	10
□ 1965	Helmet	25	10
□ 1966	Action	25	10
□ 1967	Leroy Kelly	25	10
□ 1968	Helmet	20	5
□ 1969	Helmet	20	5
□ 1970	Helmet	20	5
□ 1971	Helmet	20	5
□ 1972	Helmet	15	5
□ 1973	Helmet	15	5
□ 1974	Helmet	15	5
□ 1975	Helmet	15	5
□ 1976	Helmet	15	5
□ 1977	Helmet	15	5
□ 1978	Helmet	15	5
□ 1979	Brown in Action	15	5
□ 80-89	....	10	3
□ 1991-on	....	5	1

PROGRAMS

		Nr-Mt	Ex
□ 1920	First Tigers Game	1000	500
□ 1920	Game Program	600	300
□ 1921	First Indians Game	750	400
□ 1921-31	Game Program	300	100
□ 1949	First Game	300	150
□ 1949	First Season	100	50
□ 1950-59	Game Programs	50	25
□ 1960-69	Game Programs	35	15
□ 1970-79	Game Programs	15	7
□ 1980-89	Game Programs	10	5
□ 1990-97	Game Programs	6	3
□	Jim Brown First Game	120	40

SCHEDULES

		Nr-Mt	Ex
□ 1920's	....	200	100

□ 1930's	....	65	40
□ 1940's	....	45	30
□ 1950's	....	35	20
□ 1960's	....	25	10
□ 1970's	....	12	5
□ 1980's	....	7	3
□ 1990's	....	5	1

(Jim Brown appearances are 50% more.)

YEARBOOKS/ MAGAZINES/NEWSLETTERS
No yearbooks were issued except in 1987 (15). Magazines and newsletters have been released periodically. Values of these are based if they have Jim Brown on the cover.

JIM BROWN
The greatest running back of all time. His Syracuse material and early pro material is hard to find. Most of his publications runs in the 20-50 range. Very rare pieces go for more. Most Brown collectors surround their collection around Jim Brown.

DALLAS COWBOYS

America's Team. This team fan base is only matched by the Green Bay Packers. The Dallas Cowboys are to football what the NY Yankees are to baseball. Early material is especially popular and pursued. Key players like Roger Staubach, Troy Aikman, Tony Dorsett, Emmitt Smith are collected heavily by player collectors.

MEDIA GUIDES

		Nr-Mt	Ex
□ 1960	Cowboys	125	50
□ 1961	In Action	65	35
□ 1962	Uniforms	65	35
□ 1963	Player	65	35
□ 1964	Helmet	50	30
□ 1965	Bob Lilly	55	25
□ 1966	Bob Hayes	45	25
□ 1967	Don Meredith	45	25
□ 1968	Don Perkins	35	20
□ 1969	Tom Landry	35	20
□ 1970	Calvin Hill	25	12
□ 1971	Stadium	25	12
□ 1972	Trophy/Owners	20	10
□ 1973	....	20	10
□ 1974	....	20	7
□ 1975	Roger Staubach	15	7
□ 1976	....	15	7
□ 1977	....	15	7
□ 1978	Superbowl trophies	12	7
□ 79-80	....	10	5
□ 81-89	....	10	4
□ 90-97	....	5	2

GAME PROGRAMS

		Nr-Mt	Ex
□ 1960	First Program	250	100
□ 1960	First Season	75	35
□ 61-63	Game Programs	50	25
□ 64-69	Game Programs	35	20
□ 70-75	Game Programs	20	12
□ 76-80	Game Programs	15	5
□ 81-89	Game Programs	10	3
□ 90-97	Game Programs	5	1
□	R. Staubach First Program	100	35
□	Troy Aikman Cover	15	10
□	E. Smih First Program	40	20
□	E Smith Cover	12	5

SCHEDULES

		Nr-Mt	Ex
□ 1960	First NFL Season	150	100
□ 61-65	Early Schedules	35	20
□ 66-69	Schedules	25	15
□ 70-75	Schedules	15	8
□ 76-80	Schedules	10	7
□ 81-89	Schedules	6	3
□ 90-97	Schedules	2	1

YEARBOOKS, MAGAZINES, NEWSLETTERS
A few yearbooks were issued. Magazines and newsletters, team issue stuff is very valuable in the $60-65 period.

ROGER STAUBACH
Roger Staubach is one of the greatest quarterbacks of all time. He lead the Cowboys his entire career and have taken them to the Super Bowl. His publications are pursued by Dallas Cowboy collectors. His college material ranges in the 35-55 range and his pro material is in the 20-55 range.

EMMITT SMITH
Perhaps one of the two greatest running backs of this decade. When he is healthy the team goes to the superbowl. His college material is in the 20-40 range and his pro material is in the 10-30 range.

TROY AIKMAN
Has led his team to multiple superbowl victories. Collectors love a winner and he wins football games. His college material is in the 20-35 range and his pro material is in the 10-30 range.

DENVER BRONCOS

Awesome team and heavily collected in Colorado. The number one person collected is John Elway. In fact, he is the only major superstar that is collected. Early Denver Bronco AFL material (1960-65) is pursued by advanced collectors.

MEDIA GUIDES		Nr-Mt	Ex
☐ 1960	....	50	25
☐ 1961	....	50	25
☐ 1962	....	50	25
☐ 1963	Bronco Logo	50	25
☐ 1964	L. Taylor	40	20
☐ 1965	Bronco Logo	40	20
☐ 1966	L. Taylor	40	20
☐ 1967	L. Saban	30	15
☐ 1968	Bronco Helmet 15		30
☐ 1969	Mascot	25	12
☐ 1970	Player in Action	30	15
☐ 1971	F. Little	25	10
☐ 1972	F. Little	25	10
☐ 1973	Players	20	10
☐ 1974	Bronco Helmet	20	7
☐ 1975	Otis Armstrong	15	7
☐ 1976	Player	15	7
☐ 1977	Players	15	7
☐ 78-80	....	12	5
☐ 81-89	....	10	4
☐ 90-97	....	5	2
☐	John Elway Covers	10	4

GAME PROGRAMS		Nr-Mt	Ex
☐ 1960	First Program	250	100
☐ 1960	First Season	75	35
☐ 61-63	Game Programs	50	25
☐ 64-69	Game Programs	35	20
☐ 70-75	Game Programs	20	12
☐ 76-80	Game Programs	15	5
☐ 81-89	Game Programs	10	3
☐ 90-97	Game Programs	5	1
☐	J Elway First Program	50	25
☐	John Elway Covers	15	10

SCHEDULES		Nr-Mt	Ex
☐ 1960	First AFL Season	150	100
☐ 61-65	Early Schedules	35	20
☐ 66-69	Schedules	25	15
☐ 70-75	Schedules	15	8
☐ 76-80	Schedules	10	7
☐ 81-89	Schedules	6	3
☐ 90-97	Schedules	2	1
☐	Elway on Schedule	10	3

YEARBOOKS, MAGAZINES, NEWSLETTERS   **Nr-Mt** **Ex**
A few yearbooks were issued. Magazines and newsletters, team issue stuff is very valuable in the 60-65 period.

		Nr-Mt	Ex
☐ 1974	....	40	15
☐ 1986	Player in Action	15	5

JOHN ELWAY
John Elway is one of the greatest quarterbacks of all time. He has lead the Bronco's his entire career and have brought them to four superbowls. John Elway fans pursue his material in all lines of publications. Game programs with him on the cover are worth twice a regular edition, general sports publications of him in college are worth 25-35 range. Early or unusual magazines with him on the cover are in the 30-40 range. More common material is in the 10-15 range.

DETROIT LIONS

One of the oldest teams in pro football. The Detroit Lions originally were the Portsmouth Spartans (1930) before they were bought and moved to Detroit (1934). Hard to find pre 1940 material. The fan base for Detroit Lions revolve around historical collectors and Barry Sanders.

MEDIA GUIDES		Nr-Mt	Ex
☐ 1945	Lions	100	45
☐ 1946	Mascot	100	40
☐ 1947	Team	75	40
☐ 1948	Playert	75	30
☐ 1949	Mascot	75	30
☐ 1950	Lions	65	30
☐ 1951	Doak Walker	65	25
☐ 1952	Name	65	25
☐ 1953	World Champs	65	25
☐ 1954	World Champs	65	25
☐ 1955	Mascot	60	25
☐ 1956	Stadium	55	25
☐ 1957	Players in Action	50	20
☐ 1958	Team Picture	45	15
☐ 1959	Name	45	20
☐ 1960	Lion in Action	45	15
☐ 1961	Jim Gibbons	35	20
☐ 1962	Stadium	35	15
☐ 1963	Mascot	30	10
☐ 1964	Lion in Action	25	10
☐ 1965	Helmet	25	10
☐ 1966	Action	25	10
☐ 1967	Logo	25	10
☐ 1968	Action	20	10
☐ 1969	Action	20	10
☐ 1970	Action	20	10
☐ 1971	Helmet	15	5
☐ 1972	Logo	15	5
☐ 1973	Logo	12	5
☐ 1974	Logo	12	3
☐ 1975	Action	12	5
☐ 1976	Helmet	12	3
☐ 1977	Action	12	5
☐ 1978	Action	12	3
☐ 1979	Monty Clark	10	3
☐ 1980	Action	12	3
☐ 1981	Billy Simms	10	3
☐ 1982	Action	10	3
☐ 1983	50th anniv.	10	3
☐ 1984	Helmet	10	3
☐ 1985	Player	7	3
☐ 1986	Players	5	3
☐ 1987	Lion	5	2
☐ 1988	Lion	5	3
☐ 1989	Player	5	2
☐ 1990	Barry Sanders	10	3
☐ 1991-on	....	5	1

PROGRAMS		Nr-Mt	Ex
☐ 1930	First Spartans Game	600	300
☐ 1930	Game Program	300	150
☐ 31-33	Game Programs	225	125
☐ 1934	First Lion Game	350	200
☐ 34-39	Game Programs	125	50

		Nr-Mt	Ex
☐ 40-49	Game Programs	65	35
☐ 50-59	Game Programs	35	15
☐ 60-69	Game Programs	25	10
☐ 70-79	Game Programs	15	7
☐ 80-89	Game Programs	10	5
☐ 90-97	Game Programs	6	3
☐	Barry Sanders First Game	40	20

SCHEDULES

		Nr-Mt	Ex
☐ 1930's		65	40
☐ 1940's		45	30
☐ 1950's		35	20
☐ 1960's		25	10
☐ 1970's		12	5
☐ 1980's		7	3
☐ 1990's		5	1

YEARBOOKS/ MAGAZINES/ NEWSLETTERS

No official yearbooks were issued. Team issued magazines or newsletters have been released periodically. Values of these are based on age and if Barry Sanders appeared on them.

BARRY SANDERS

Definitely the Lions class act. His material is pursued by fans across the United States. Most of his material falls in the 20-25 range.

GREEN BAY PACKERS

One of the best and oldest teams in pro football. Hard to find pre 1940 material. Quality material can be found among the largest and best dealers. The fan base for Green Bay Packers publications is high.

MEDIA GUIDES

		Nr-Mt	Ex
☐ 1947	Champions	100	40
☐ 1948	C. Lambau	100	40
☐ 1949		100	40
☐ 1950	Name	85	30
☐ 1951	Wisconsin	85	30
☐ 1952	Wisconsin	85	30
☐ 1953	Name	75	30
☐ 1954	Name	75	25
☐ 1955	Wisconsin	65	25
☐ 1956	Wisconsin	65	25
☐ 1957	Players in Action	55	20
☐ 1958	Stadium	55	20
☐ 1959	V. Lombardi	55	20
☐ 1960	Packers in Action	55	20
☐ 1961	Western Champs	55	20
☐ 1962		55	20
☐ 1963	World Champs	55	20
☐ 1964	World Champs	55	20
☐ 1965	Jim Taylor	55	20
☐ 1966	Bart Starr	55	20
☐ 1967	Player in Action	55	20
☐ 1968	Willie Davis	35	15
☐ 1969	Donny Anderson	35	15
☐ 1970	Action	25	15
☐ 1971	Player in Action	25	15
☐ 1972	Player In Action	20	15
☐ 1973	Player in Action	20	15
☐ 1974	Player in Action	20	5
☐ 1975	Bart Starr	20	5
☐ 1976	Bart Starr	20	5
☐ 1977	Player In Action	15	5
☐ 1978	Player in Action	15	5
☐ 1979	Bart Starr/V. Lombardi	15	5
☐ 80-89		12	3
☐ 90-91		6	2

GAME PROGRAMS

		Nr-Mt	Ex
☐ 1921	First Season	1000+	500
☐ 1921	Game Program	600	300
☐ 22-24	Game Program	500	250
☐ 27-30	Game Programs	200	100
☐ 31-39	Game Programs	150	75

		Nr-Mt	Ex
☐ 40-49	Game Programs	100	50
☐ 50-59	Game Programs	50	25
☐ 60-69	Game Programs	35	15
☐ 70-79	Game Programs	15	7
☐ 80-89	Game Programs	10	5
☐ 90-97	Game Programs	6	3
☐	Bart Starr First Game	40	20
☐	Paul Hornung	30	20
☐	Brett Farve First Game	30	15

SCHEDULES

		Nr-Mt	Ex
☐ 1930's		65	40
☐ 1940's		45	30
☐ 1950's		35	20
☐ 1960's		25	10
☐ 1970's		12	5
☐ 1980's		7	3
☐ 1990's		5	1

YEARBOOKS/ MAGAZINES/NEWSLETTERS

Packers Yearbooks, Magazines, Newsletter and anything else released by the team is popular and in demand. Pre 1940 items are highly pursued by the advanced collectors. Modern collectors focus either on Brett Favre, Reggie White from the 90's or the Bart Starr/Vince Lombardi era of the 1957-68 period.

YEARBOOKS

		Nr-Mt	Ex
☐ 1960	Paul Hornung	200	75
☐ 1961	Forrest Gregg	100	50
☐ 1962	Vince Lombardi	100	50
☐ 1963	Jim Taylor	75	35
☐ 1964	Bart Starr	75	35
☐ 1965	Vince Lombardi	75	35
☐ 1966		60	30
☐ 1967	Action Shot	65	30
☐ 1968	Ray Nitschke	50	25
☐ 1969	Donny Anderson	40	20
☐ 1970		35	15
☐ 1971		35	15
☐ 1972		30	15
☐ 1973		25	12
☐ 1974		24	12
☐ 1975	Bart Starr	20	10
☐ 76-80		20	10
☐ 81-89		15	7
☐ 90-97		12	6

BRETT FAVRE

He is currently one of the most popular quarterbacks and has developed a solid following. His covers have values in the 15-30 range.

JIM TAYLOR/PAUL HORNUNG

These two led the team during there championship era. There covers are sold in the 35-60 range.

Green Bay sports covers are the most popular among pro teams in pro football. Fan clubs are scattered across the United States.

INDIANAPOLIS COLTS

(Formerly known as Baltimore Colts)

The Colts originated as the Miami Seahawks in the AAFC in 1946. The team did not survive and moved to Baltimore. The Colts remained in the AAFC until the merger into the NFL in 1950. The Baltimore Colts behind Johnny Unitas was one of the most feared teams in pro football. Even though collectors have been turned off to the Colts for leaving Baltimore, the collectors still pursue the early programs from the AAFC (47-49). The most exciting thing the Indianapolis Colts had was Eric Dickerson.

MEDIA GUIDES

		Nr-Mt	Ex
☐ 1950	Colts Logo	95	50
☐ 1951		75	35
☐ 1952	Colts Logo	75	35
☐ 1953	Colts Logo	55	20
☐ 1954	Colts Logo	45	25
☐ 1955	Colts Logo	45	20

		Nr-Mt	Ex
☐ 1956	Colts Logo	45	25
☐ 1957	Colts Logo	40	20
☐ 1958	Stadium (champs)	40	20
☐ 1959	Colts Logo	40	20
☐ 1960	Banners	40	20
☐ 1961	Helmet	40	20
☐ 1962	Helmet	40	20
☐ 1963	Colts in Action	40	20
☐ 1964	Action	30	15
☐ 1965	Johnny Unitas	40	20
☐ 1966	Cheerleaders	25	15
☐ 1967	Colts in Action	25	15
☐ 1968	John Unitas	25	15
☐ 1969	Colts in Action	25	15
☐ 1970	John Unitas	25	15
☐ 1971	Trophy	20	10
☐ 1972	Colts	20	10
☐ 1973	Player	15	7
☐ 74-80		15	7
☐ 81-89		10	5
☐ 90-97		5	1

GAME PROGRAMS

		Nr-Mt	Ex
☐ 1946	FirstSeahawk Program	200	100
☐ 1946	Game Program	75	50
☐ 1947	First Colt Program	200	100
☐ 47-49	Game Programs	65	35
☐ 50-55	Game Programs	50	35
☐ 56-60	Game Programs	40	20
☐ 61-63	Game Programs	30	15
☐ 64-69	Game Programs	25	10
☐ 70-75	Game Programs	15	7
☐ 76-80	Game Programs	10	5
☐ 81-89	Game Programs	10	3
☐ 90-97	Game Programs	5	1
☐	Johnny Unitas First Program	100	50

SCHEDULES

		Nr-Mt	Ex
☐ 1946	First Schedule	150	100
☐ 47-49	Early Schedules	100	75
☐ 50-55	Early NFL Schedules	50	35
☐ 56-60	NFL Schedules	40	25
☐ 61-65	Early Schedules	35	20
☐ 66-69	Schedules	25	15
☐ 70-75	Schedules	15	8
☐ 76-80	Schedules	10	7
☐ 81-89	Schedules	6	3
☐ 90-97	Schedules	2	1

YEARBOOKS, MAGAZINES, NEWSLETTERS

A few yearbooks were issued. Magazines and newsletters, team issue stuff is very valuable in the 46-49 period.

		Nr-Mt	Ex
☐ 1953	Helmet	100	50
☐ 1958	Stadium	75	35
☐ 1959		75	35
☐ 1960		75	35
☐ 1961		60	30
☐ 1962		60	30
☐ 1963		60	30
☐ 1964		55	30
☐ 1988	Eric Dickerson	15	10

JOHNNY UNITAS

Johnny Unitas is one of the greatest quarterbacks of all time. He is Mr. Colt and fans of the Baltimore Colts collect him. His publication covers run in the 20-50 range.

KANSAS CITY CHIEFS

(Formerly the Dallas Texans)
This is a team that went to the Super Bowl and won it all. The team is popular in the Kansas City area. Most of the demand focuses around the earliest years, the Super Bowl years, and Joe Montana/Marcus Allen years.

MEDIA GUIDES

		Nr-Mt	Ex
☐ 1960	Dallas Texans	95	35
☐ 1961	Texans	50	25
☐ 1962	Texans	55	25
☐ 1963	Len Dawson	50	25
☐ 1964	Action	40	20
☐ 1965	Len Dawson	40	20
☐ 1966	Action	40	20
☐ 1967	AFL Trophy	30	15
☐ 1968	Action	30	15
☐ 1969	Action	25	12
☐ 1970	Superbowl Champions	35	15
☐ 1971	Player	25	10
☐ 1972	Stadium	25	10
☐ 1973	Len Dawson	20	10
☐ 1974	Action	20	7
☐ 1975	Chief Helmet	15	7
☐ 76-77		15	7
☐ 78-80		12	5
☐ 81-89		7	4
☐ 90-97		5	2

GAME PROGRAMS

		Nr-Mt	Ex
☐ 1960	First Program	250	100
☐ 1960	First Season	75	35
☐ 61-62	Game Programs	50	25
☐ 1963	First Chief Programs	200	100
☐ 64-69	Game Programs	35	20
☐ 70-75	Game Programs	20	12
☐ 76-80	Game Programs	15	5
☐ 81-89	Game Programs	10	3
☐ 90-97	Game Programs	5	1
☐	First Len Dawson Programs	100	50
☐	First Joe Montana Programs	20	10

TEAM SCHEDULES

		Nr-Mt	Ex
☐ 1960	First AFL Season	150	100
☐ 61-65	Early Schedules	35	20
☐ 66-69	Schedules	25	15
☐ 70-75	Schedules	15	8
☐ 76-80	Schedules	10	7
☐ 81-89	Schedules	6	3
☐ 90-97	Schedules	2	1

YEARBOOKS, MAGAZINES, NEWSLETTERS

Only one yearbooks was issued in 1972 (35). Magazines, newsletters, and team issue stuff is popular.

LEN DAWSON

Magazines featuringLen Dawson tend to go between $20-$40.

MIAMI DOLPHINS

Awesome team and heavily collected across the USA. The number one person collected is Dan Marino. Miami has had a tradition of winning and has produced quality teams throughout its history. The most famous team is the 1972 undefeated team that went on to win the Super Bowl. That team featured Larry Csonka and Bob Griese.

MEDIA GUIDES

		Nr-Mt	Ex
☐ 1966	G. Wilson	40	20
☐ 1967	Dolphins Helmet	30	15
☐ 1968	Stadium	30	15
☐ 1969	Bob Griese	25	12
☐ 1970	Logo	30	15
☐ 1971	Bob Griese/others	25	10
☐ 1972	(Superbowl!!!)	25	10
☐ 1973	Superbowl Trophy	20	10
☐ 1974	2 superbowl Trophies	20	7
☐ 1975	Griese/Shula	15	7
☐ 1976	Players	15	7
☐ 1977	Bob Griese	15	7
☐ 78-80		12	5
☐ 81-89		10	4
☐ 90-97		5	2
☐	Dan Marino cover	10	4

GAME PROGRAMS

		Nr-Mt	Ex
☐ 1966	First Program	250	100
☐ 1966	First Season	75	35

		Nr-Mt	Ex
☐ 67-69	Game Programs	35	20
☐ 70-75	Game Programs	20	12
☐ 76-80	Game Programs	15	5
☐ 81-89	Game Programs	10	3
☐ 90-97	Game Programs	5	1
☐	Shula Last Program	20	10
☐	Dan Marino First Pro	40	20
☐	Dan Marino on Cover	15	5

SCHEDULES		Nr-Mt	Ex
☐ 66-69	Schedules	25	15
☐ 70-75	Schedules	15	8
☐ 76-80	Schedules	10	7
☐ 81-89	Schedules	6	3
☐ 90-97	Schedules	2	1
☐	Marino on Schedule	10	3

YEARBOOKS, MAGAZINES, NEWSLETTERS
No yearbooks were issued. Magazines , newsletters, and team issue stuff are very valuable in the 66-72 period. Material produced in the perfect season is also popular.

DAN MARINO PUBLICATIONS
Perhaps the most popular quarterback in the 1990's. More people collect Dan Marino than any other quarterback. His college material can be found in the 25-100 range. His pro publications is found in the 20-50 range.

MINNESOTA VIKINGS
Awesome team and heavily collected in Minnesota. People collect Fran Tarkenton and Joe Kapp. Early Viking material (1960-63) is pursued by advanced collectors.

MEDIA GUIDES		Nr-Mt	Ex
☐ 1961	Logo	50	25
☐ 1962	Logo	50	25
☐ 1963	Logo	40	20
☐ 1964	Logo	40	20
☐ 1965	Mascot	40	20
☐ 1966	Logo	40	20
☐ 1967	Fran Tarkenton	30	15
☐ 1968	Joe Kapp	30	15
☐ 1969	Bud Grant	25	12
☐ 1970	Fred Cox	35	15
☐ 1971	J. Marshall	25	10
☐ 1972	Alan Page	25	10
☐ 1973	Fan	20	10
☐ 1974	Players	20	7
☐ 1975	Fans	15	7
☐ 1976	Fran Tarkenton	15	7
☐ 76-77	....	15	7
☐ 78-80	....	12	5
☐ 81-89	....	7	4
☐ 90-97	....	5	2

GAME PROGRAMS		Nr-Mt	Ex
☐ 1961	First Program	225	100
☐ 1961	First Season	55	25
☐ 62-63	Game Programs	35	15
☐ 64-69	Game Programs	25	10
☐ 70-75	Game Programs	20	12
☐ 76-80	Game Programs	15	5
☐ 81-89	Game Programs	10	3
☐ 90-97	Game Programs	5	1
☐	Joe Kapp First Program	50	25
☐	Joe Kapp covers	30	15

SCHEDULES		Nr-Mt	Ex
☐ 1961	NFL Season	100	50
☐ 61-65	Early Schedules	35	20
☐ 66-69	Schedules	25	15
☐ 70-75	Schedules	15	8
☐ 76-80	Schedules	10	7
☐ 81-89	Schedules	6	3
☐ 90-97	Schedules	2	1

YEARBOOKS, MAGAZINES, NEWSLETTERS
Only one yearbooks was issued in 1961 ($150). However, the local newspaper produced a few large magazines/yearbooks that go in the $75-$125 range. Magazines, newsletters, and team issue stuff is very valuable in the $60-$65 period.

JOE KAPP
Joe Kapp has a strong following among hardcore collectors in the latino section. He also has a fan following in the bay area. Most of his material is in the $20-$30 range. His Canadian League material is also hotly pursued.

NEW ENGLAND PATRIOTS
The New England (Boston) Patriots are popular in the New England area. Early Boston Patriots AFL material (1960-64) is pursued by advanced collectors.

MEDIA GUIDES		Nr-Mt	Ex
☐ 1960	....	50	25
☐ 1961	....	50	25
☐ 1962	....	50	25
☐ 1963	Cartoon	50	25
☐ 1964	Helmet	40	20
☐ 1965	G. Cappelletti	40	20
☐ 1966	Nick Buoniconti	40	20
☐ 1967	Jim Nance	30	15
☐ 1968	Logo	30	15
☐ 1969	Player	25	12
☐ 1970	Action	30	15
☐ 1971	Stadium	25	10
☐ 1972	Jim Plunkett	25	10
☐ 1973	Coach	20	10
☐ 1974	Action	20	7
☐ 1975	Fans	15	7
☐ 1976	Patriots	15	7
☐ 1977	Player	15	7
☐ 78-80	....	12	5
☐ 81-89	....	10	4
☐ 90-97	....	5	2

GAME PROGRAMS		Nr-Mt	Ex
☐ 1960	First Program	200	100
☐ 1960	First Season	75	35
☐ 1961-63	Game Programs	35	15
☐ 1964-69	Game Programs	35	15
☐ 1970-75	Game Programs	20	12
☐ 1976-80	Game Programs	15	5
☐ 1981-89	Game Programs	10	3
☐ 90-97	Game Programs	5	1

SCHEDULES		Nr-Mt	Ex
☐ 1960	First AFL Season	100	50
☐ 61-65	Early Schedules	35	20
☐ 66-69	Schedules	25	15
☐ 70-75	Schedules	15	8
☐ 76-80	Schedules	10	7
☐ 81-89	Schedules	6	3
☐ 90-97	Schedules	2	1

YEARBOOKS/MAGAZINES/NEWSLETTERS

		Nr-Mt	Ex
A few yearbooks were issued. Magazines and newsletters, team issue stuff is very valuable in the 60-65 period.

		Nr-Mt	Ex
☐ 1965	Gino Cappelletti	100	30
☐ 1966	Jim Nance	75	25
☐ 1967	Jim Nance	60	20
☐ 1980	Action	20	10
☐ 1985	Action	20	10

NEW ORLEANS SAINTS
This team has never produced a champion team thus never build up the collector fan base. However, Archie Manning has a solid fan base.

MEDIA GUIDES		Nr-Mt	Ex
☐ Year	Feature	NrMt	Ex
☐ 1966	....	35	15

☐ 1967	....	25	12
☐ 1968	....	25	15
☐ 1969	....	25	12
☐ 1970	....	25	15
☐ 1971	....	20	10
☐ 1972	Archie Manning	25	10
☐ 1973	....	20	10
☐ 1974	....	20	7
☐ 1975	....	12	7
☐ 1976	....	15	7
☐ 1977	....	12	7
☐ 78-80	....	12	5
☐ 81-89	....	10	4
☐ 90-97	....	5	2
☐	Archie Manning Covers	15	5

GAME PROGRAMS

		Nr-Mt	Ex
☐ 1967	First Program	250	100
☐ 1967	First Season	75	35
☐ 68-69	Game Programs	35	20
☐ 70-75	Game Programs	20	12
☐ 76-80	Game Programs	15	5
☐ 81-89	Game Programs	10	3
☐ 90-97	Game Programs	5	1
☐	Archie Manning First Program	40	20

SCHEDULES

		Nr-Mt	Ex
☐ 67-69	Schedules	25	15
☐ 70-75	Schedules	15	8
☐ 76-80	Schedules	10	7
☐ 81-89	Schedules	6	3
☐ 90-97	Schedules	2	1

YEARBOOKS, MAGAZINES, NEWSLETTERS

Only one yearbook was made in 1968 ($40). Magazines, newsletters, and team issue material has nominal value.

ARCHIE MANNING PUBLICATIONS

Perhaps one of the most popular quarterback in the 1970's. He is still heavily collected. Magazines go for $20-$40 range.

NEW YORK GIANTS

One of the oldest teams in pro football. Hard to find pre 1940 material. Quality material can be found among the largest and best dealers in the New York area. The fan base for New York Giants publications is found across the United States.

MEDIA GUIDES

		Nr-Mt	Ex
☐ 1945	Player	125	50
☐ 1946	Giants in Action	135	40
☐ 1947		100	40
☐ 1948	Logo	135	40
☐ 1949		100	40
☐ 1950	Polo Grounds	100	30
☐ 1951		100	30
☐ 1952	Microphone	100	30
☐ 1953		65	30
☐ 1954	Logo	75	25
☐ 1955	Logo	50	25
☐ 1956	Logo	65	25
☐ 1957	Logo	45	20
☐ 1958	Logo	55	20
☐ 1959	Logo	40	20
☐ 1960	Logo	55	20
☐ 1961	Logo	35	20
☐ 1962	Logo	55	20
☐ 1963	Logo	30	20
☐ 1964	Logo	55	20
☐ 1965	Logo	25	20
☐ 1966	Mascot	55	20
☐ 1967	Helmet	20	20
☐ 1968	Helmet	35	15
☐ 1969	Helmet	20	15
☐ 1970	Helmet	25	15

☐ 1971	Helmet	15	15
☐ 1972	Helmet	20	15
☐ 1973	Helmet	15	15
☐ 1974	Logo	20	5
☐ 1975	Helmet	15	5
☐ 1976	Stadium	20	5
☐ 1977	Stadium	12	5
☐ 1978	Logo	15	5
☐ 1979	H. Carlson	12	5
☐ 1980	Lawrence Taylor	15	5
☐ 1981	Lawrence Taylor	10	5
☐ 1982	Lawrence Taylor	15	5
☐ 1983	L Taylor/Others	10	5
☐ 1984	Frank Gifford	15	5
☐ 1985	L Taylor/Others	10	3
☐ 1986	Lawrence Taylor	12	3
☐ 1987	Phil Simms	7	3
☐ 1988	Lawrence Taylor	12	3
☐ 1989	Stadium	5	1
☐ 1990	Lawrence Taylor	10	3
☐ 1991-on		5	1

GIANTS PROGRAMS

		Nr-Mt	Ex
☐ 1925	First Program	500	250
☐ 1925	First Season	300	150
☐ 26-29	Game Programs	200	100
☐ 30-39	Game Programs	150	75
☐ 40-49	Game Programs	100	50
☐ 50-59	Game Programs	50	25
☐ 60-69	Game Programs	35	15
☐ 70-79	Game Programs	15	7
☐ 80-89	Game Programs	10	5
☐ 90-97	Game Programs	6	3
☐	Frank Gifford First Game ...,......	100	50
☐	Lawrence Taylor First Game	40	20

GIANTS SCHEDULES

		Nr-Mt	Ex
☐ 1920's	....	200	100
☐ 1930's	....	65	40
☐ 1940's	....	45	30
☐ 1950's	....	35	20
☐ 1960's	....	25	10
☐ 1970's	....	12	5
☐ 1980's	....	7	3
☐ 1990's	....	5	1

GIANTS YEARBOOKS & MAGAZINES & NEWSLETTERS

Giants yearbooks are actually popular with Giants fans. Team magazines and newsletters have been released periodically. Values of these are based if they have key players like YA Title, Lawrence Taylor, and Frank Gifford on them.

YEARBOOKS

		Nr-Mt	Ex
☐ 1964	Ya Tittle	100	50
☐ 1965	Players in Action	75	35
☐ 1966	Player	50	25
☐ 1967	Players in Action	50	20
☐ 1968	Fran Tarkenton	40	20
☐ 1969	Fran Tarkenton	40	20
☐ 1970	Player in Action	40	15
☐ 1976	Player in Action	15	7
☐ 1986	Phil Simms	12	5

LAWRENCE TAYLOR

Perhaps the greatest linebacker of the 1980's. His popularity is still solid in the New York area. His publications tend to have values in the $15-$30 range.

NEW YORK JETS (NEW YORK TITANS 60-63)

New York Jets were best known for Joe Namath and the 1969 Superbowl than anything else. The team originated as the New York Titans in the AFL. The name was converted to the Jets in 1964. The team began its ascent in 1965 when Namath began his career in pro football. The most popular Jet material is the first five years (1960-65), the superbowl season (1968-69) and anything with Joe Namath on the cover.

MEDIA GUIDES

		Nr-Mt	Ex
☐ 1960	Titans	125	50
☐ 1961	Titans	65	35
☐ 1962	Titans	65	35
☐ 1963	Jets Logo	65	30
☐ 1964	Jets Logo	35	15
☐ 1965	Jets Logo	35	15
☐ 1966	Jets Logo	25	15
☐ 1967	Jets Logo	25	12
☐ 1968	Jets Logo	35	15
☐ 1969	Jets Logo	30	15
☐ 1970	Jets Logo	20	12
☐ 1971	Jets Logo	25	12
☐ 1972	Jets Logo	15	7
☐ 1973	Jets Logo	15	7
☐ 1974	Jets Logo	12	7
☐ 1975	Jets Logo	12	7
☐ 1976	Jets Logo	12	7
☐ 1977	Jets Logo	12	7
☐ 78-80		10	2
☐ 81-89		10	2
☐ 90-97		5	1

GAME PROGRAMS

		Nr-Mt	Ex
☐ 1960	First Program	250	100
☐ 1960	First Season	75	35
☐ 61-63	Game Programs	35	15
☐ 64-69	Game Programs	25	15
☐ 70-75	Game Programs	20	10
☐ 76-80	Game Programs	15	5
☐ 81-89	Game Programs	10	3
☐ 90-97	Game Programs	5	1
☐	Joe Namath First Program	100	35

SCHEDULES

		Nr-Mt	Ex
☐ 1960	First AFL Season	150	100
☐ 61-65	Early Schedules	35	20
☐ 66-69	Schedules	25	15
☐ 70-75	Schedules	15	8
☐ 76-80	Schedules	10	7
☐ 81-89	Schedules	6	3
☐ 90-97	Schedules	2	1

YEARBOOKS, MAGAZINES, NEWSLETTERS

A few yearbooks were issued. Magazines and newsletters, team issue stuff is very valuable in the 60-63 period.

		Nr-Mt	Ex
☐ 1960	Titans	150	100
☐ 1961	Titans	100	50
☐ 1962	Titans	75	50
☐ 1963	Jets	65	40
☐ 1964	Jets Players	65	35
☐ 1965	Matt Snell	55	35
☐ 1966	Joe Namath	65	25
☐ 1967	Action	40	20
☐ 1968	Joe Namath	65	35
☐ 1969	Joe Namath	65	35
☐ 1970	Don Maynard	35	15
☐ 1971		35	15
☐ 1972		35	15
☐ 1973		35	15
☐ 1974		30	10
☐ 1975		30	10
☐ 1976		25	10
☐ 1977		25	10

JOE NAMATH

Joe Namath was one of the first football players to obtain national appeal. His promised superbowl victory changed the history of the AFL. Early Joe Namath material is hard to find ($30-$60 range) while his later material is more common ($20-$40 range).

OAKLAND RAIDERS

The Oakland Raiders were the most feared team during the 60's-80's period. The fan base for the old Oakland Raiders is still solid. The team has not obtained many new fans since they left Los Angeles and returned to Oakland. The Oakland Raiders period (60-81) is the most collected. The LA Raiders period (82-94) produced one superbowl team and develop a small but hard core fan base in the LA area. Raider material produced in the 1990's is not collected.

MEDIA GUIDES

		Nr-Mt	Ex
☐ 1960		50	25
☐ 1961	Mascot	50	25
☐ 1962		50	25
☐ 1963		50	25
☐ 1964	Helmet	40	20
☐ 1965	Stadium	40	20
☐ 1966	Helmet	40	20
☐ 1967		30	15
☐ 1968	AFL Ring	30	15
☐ 1969	Player	25	12
☐ 1970	Players	30	15
☐ 1971	Players	25	10
☐ 1972	Logo	25	10
☐ 1973	Players in Action	20	10
☐ 1974	Players	20	7
☐ 1975	Players	15	7
☐ 1976	Players	15	7
☐ 1977	Ring	15	7
☐ 78-80		12	5
☐ 81-89		10	4
☐ 90-97		5	2

GAME PROGRAMS

		Nr-Mt	Ex
☐ 1960	First Program	250	100
☐ 1960	First Season	75	35
☐ 61-63	Game Programs	35	15
☐ 64-69	Game Programs	35	15
☐ 70-75	Game Programs	20	12
☐ 76-80	Game Programs	15	5
☐ 81-89	Game Programs	10	3
☐ 90-97	Game Programs	5	1

SCHEDULES

		Nr-Mt	Ex
☐ 1960	First AFL Season	100	50
☐ 61-65	Early Schedules	35	20
☐ 66-69	Schedules	25	15
☐ 70-75	Schedules	15	8
☐ 76-80	Schedules	10	7
☐ 81-89	Schedules	6	3
☐ 90-97	Schedules	2	1

YEARBOOKS, MAGAZINES, NEWSLETTERS

No yearbooks were issued. Magazines and team issue material is very popular from the 60-65 period.

The most popular players were Ken Stabler, George Blanda, Jack Tatum, Marcus Allen and Jim Plunkett.

PHOENIX CARDINALS

(Formerly located in Chicago, St. Louis)
One of the oldest teams in pro football. Hard to find pre 1930 material. Quality material can be found among the largest and best dealers in the Chicago area. The fan base for Cardinal material is low, with the exception of pre 1940 Cardinal material.

MEDIA GUIDES

		Nr-Mt	Ex
☐ 1947	Logo	120	40
☐ 1948	Logo	105	40
☐ 1949	Logo	100	40
☐ 1950	Logo	100	30
☐ 1951	Logo	100	30
☐ 1952	Logo	100	30
☐ 1953	Logo	55	15
☐ 1954	Logo	55	25
☐ 1955	Logo	45	15
☐ 1956	Logo	45	25
☐ 1957	Logo	35	15
☐ 1958	Logo	55	20
☐ 1959	Logo	35	15

		Nr-Mt	Ex
☐ 1960	Mascot	55	20
☐ 1961	Mascot	25	10
☐ 1962	Mascot	25	10
☐ 1963	Charley Johnson	25	10
☐ 1964	Player in Action	25	10
☐ 1965	Player in action	25	10
☐ 1966	Stadium	25	10
☐ 1967	Larry Wilson	25	10
☐ 1968	Players	25	10
☐ 1969	Player	15	7
☐ 1970	Player in Action	15	7
☐ 1971	Helmet	15	7
☐ 72-79		15	5
☐ 80-89		12	3
☐ 90-on		5	1

PROGRAMS

		Nr-Mt	Ex
☐ 1920	First Program	600	300
☐ 1920	First Season	300	150
☐ 21-24	Game Program	300	150
☐ 25-30	Game Programs	200	100
☐ 31-39	Game Programs	75	45
☐ 40-49	Game Programs	50	25
☐ 50-59	Game Programs	30	15
☐ 60-69	Game Programs	20	10
☐ 70-79	Game Programs	12	6
☐ 80-89	Game Programs	10	5
☐ 90-97	Game Programs	6	3

SCHEDULES

		Nr-Mt	Ex
☐ 1920's		200	100
☐ 1930's		65	40
☐ 1940's		45	30
☐ 1950's		35	20
☐ 1960's		25	10
☐ 1970's		12	5
☐ 1980's		7	3
☐ 1990's		5	1

YEARBOOKS/MAGAZINES/ NEWSLETTERS   **Nr-Mt**   **Ex**

Official yearbooks were issued in the 60's and 80's. Magazines and newsletters have been released periodically but only have nominal value. The exception to this is the early material from the 20's - 40's.

		Nr-Mt	Ex
☐ 1967	Team Picture	45	20
☐ 88-97		7	2

PHILADELPHIA EAGLES

One of the oldest teams in pro football. Hard to find pre 1940 material. Quality material can be found among the largest and best dealers in the Philadelphia area. The fan base for Eagles material is steady, with the exception of pre 1940 Eagles material which is high.

MEDIA GUIDES

		Nr-Mt	Ex
☐ 1947	Logo	75	35
☐ 1948	Logo	75	35
☐ 1949	Logo	60	30
☐ 1950	Logo	60	30
☐ 1951	Logo	60	30
☐ 1952	Logo	55	25
☐ 1953	Logo	55	25
☐ 1954	Logo	50	20
☐ 1955	Logo	45	15
☐ 1956	Player	45	15
☐ 1957	Logo	35	10
☐ 1958	Player	35	10
☐ 1959	Logo	35	10
☐ 1960	Stadium	35	10
☐ 1961	Logo	30	10
☐ 1962	Logo	25	10
☐ 1963	Logo	25	10
☐ 1964	Stadium	25	10
☐ 1965	Norm Snead	25	10
☐ 1966	Player	25	10
☐ 1967	Player	25	10

		Nr-Mt	Ex
☐ 1968	Norm Snead	25	10
☐ 1969	Logo	15	7
☐ 1970	Logo's	15	7
☐ 1971	Logo	15	7
☐ 72-79		15	5
☐ 80-89		12	3
☐ 90-on		5	1
☐	Reggie White cover	12	5

PROGRAMS

		Nr-Mt	Ex
☐ 1933	First Program	400	200
☐ 1933	First Season	250	100
☐ 34-39	Game Programs	125	45
☐ 40-49	Game Programs	55	35
☐ 50-59	Game Programs	30	15
☐ 60-69	Game Programs	20	10
☐ 70-79	Game Programs	12	6
☐ 80-89	Game Programs	10	5
☐ 90-97	Game Programs	6	3

SCHEDULES

		Nr-Mt	Ex
☐ 1930's		65	40
☐ 1940's		45	30
☐ 1950's		35	20
☐ 1960's		25	10
☐ 1970's		12	5
☐ 1980's		7	3
☐ 1990's		5	1

YEARBOOKS & MAGAZINES & NEWSLETTERS   **Nr-Mt**   **Ex**

Official yearbooks were issued since 1972. Magazines and newsletters have been released periodically but only have nominal value. The exception to this is the material from the 30's - 40's.

		Nr-Mt	Ex
☐ 1972	Eagle Pictures	45	20
☐ 73-80		25	10
☐ 81-89		20	8
☐ 90-97		12	5

PITTSBURGH STEELERS (PIRATES 33-40)

The Pittsburgh Steelers are one of the most popular and followed NFL teams. The team originated in 1933 as the Pittsburgh Pirates. They changed their names to the Steelers in 1941. The team is best remembered for its Super Bowl years.

MEDIA GUIDES

		Nr-Mt	Ex
☐ 1947		65	30
☐ 1948	Cartoon	60	30
☐ 1949	Cartoon	50	25
☐ 1950	Cartoon	50	25
☐ 1951	Player	45	20
☐ 1952	Cartoon	55	20
☐ 1953	Steeler kick	50	30
☐ 1954	City	50	30
☐ 1955	Steeler in Action	50	30
☐ 1956	Steelers in Action	50	25
☐ 1957	Players	45	25
☐ 1958	Steelers in Action	45	25
☐ 1959	Logo	40	25
☐ 1960	Steelers in Action	40	25
☐ 1961	Helmet	50	25
☐ 1962	Steelers in Action	50	25
☐ 1963	Helmet	50	25
☐ 1964	Helmet	40	20
☐ 1965	City	40	20
☐ 1966	City	40	20
☐ 1967	Steelers in Action	30	15
☐ 1968	Helmet	30	15
☐ 1969	Stadium	25	12
☐ 70-75		15	7
☐ 76-80		12	7
☐ 81-89		10	4
☐ 90-97		5	2

GAME PROGRAMS

		Nr-Mt	Ex
☐ 1933	First Pirates Program	400	200
☐ 1933	First Season	175	120
☐ 34-36	Pirates Programs	125	55
☐ 37-40	Pirates Programs	100	40
☐ 1941	First Steeler Program	250	125
☐ 1946	First Season	75	25
☐ 47-50	Game Programs	35	20
☐ 51-53	Game Programs	30	15
☐ 54-59	Game Programs	25	12
☐ 60-63	Game Programs	20	12
☐ 64-69	Game Programs	20	10
☐ 70-75	Game Programs	12	6
☐ 76-80	Game Programs	10	4
☐ 81-89	Game Programs	8	2
☐ 90-97	Game Programs	5	1

TEAM SCHEDULES

		Nr-Mt	Ex
☐ 1933	First Schedule	300	150
☐ 34-35	Schedules	200	100
☐ 36-37	Schedules	125	75
☐ 38-40	Early Schedules	100	75
☐ 46-49	Early Schedules	100	75
☐ 50-55	Earl Schedules	35	20
☐ 56-59	Early Schedules	30	15
☐ 60-65	Early Schedules	25	15
☐ 66-69	Schedules	25	15
☐ 70-75	Schedules	15	8
☐ 76-80	Schedules	10	7
☐ 81-89	Schedules	6	3
☐ 90-97	Schedules	2	1

YEARBOOKS, MAGAZINES, NEWSLETTERS

		Nr-Mt	Ex

A few yearbooks were issued. Magazines and newsletters, team issue stuff is very valuable in the pre- 49 period.
Players that are popular with Steelers fans are: Terry Bradshaw, Mean Joe Greene, Jack Lambert, and Franco Harris.

☐ 1979	Terry Bradshaw	25	10
☐ 90-97		10	5

SAN DIEGO CHARGERS

Awesome team and heavily collected in San Diego. The number one person collected is Lance Alworth.
Early San Diego Chargers AFL material (1960-65) is pursued by advanced collectors.

MEDIA GUIDES

		Nr-Mt	Ex
☐ 1960	LA Chargers	95	35
☐ 1961	Logo	50	25
☐ 1962		50	25
☐ 1963	Logo	50	25
☐ 1964	Logo	40	20
☐ 1965	Mascot	40	20
☐ 1966	Charger In Action	40	20
☐ 1967	Stadium	30	15
☐ 1968	Charger in Action	30	15
☐ 1969	John Hadl	25	12
☐ 1970	Lance Alworth	35	15
☐ 1971	Action shot	25	10
☐ 1972	J. Hadl	25	10
☐ 1973	Action	20	10
☐ 1974	Charger Uniform	20	7
☐ 1975	D. Woods	15	7
☐ 76-77		15	7
☐ 78-80		12	5
☐ 81-89		7	4
☐ 90-97		5	2

GAME PROGRAMS

		Nr-Mt	Ex
☐ 1960	First Program	250	100
☐ 1960	First Season	75	35
☐ 61-63	Game Programs	50	25
☐ 64-69	Game Programs	35	20
☐ 70-75	Game Programs	20	12

☐ 76-80	Game Programs	15	5
☐ 81-89	Game Programs	10	3
☐ 90-97	Game Programs	5	1
☐	L Alworth on Cover	50	25
☐	Jack Kemp Cover	75	35

TEAM SCHEDULES

		Nr-Mt	Ex
☐ 1960	First AFL Season	150	100
☐ 61-65	Early Schedules	35	20
☐ 66-69	Schedules	25	15
☐ 70-75	Schedules	15	8
☐ 76-80	Schedules	10	7
☐ 81-89	Schedules	6	3
☐ 90-97	Schedules	2	1
☐	Alworth on Schedule	35	15

YEARBOOKS, MAGAZINES, NEWSLETTERS

No yearbooks were issued. Magazines and newsletters, team issue stuff is very valuable in the 60-65 period.

LANCE ALWORTH

Lance Alworth featured on or in magazines or team issues tend to go between $25-$50.

SAN FRANCISCO 49ERS

The best team since 1980. The fan base continues to grow in the SF bay area. The 49ers started in 1946 and were one of the few teams that merged into the NFL from the AAFC conference. The early AAFC material is popular. The game program covers are beautiful with lots of color.
Most sports fans collect Joe Montana, Jerry Rice and Steve Young material. Mature 49er fans enjoy YA Tittle and John Brodie of the 50's and 60's era.

MEDIA GUIDES

		Nr-Mt	Ex
☐ 1950	49ers Mascot	65	35
☐ 1951	49ers Mascot	55	35
☐ 1952	49ers Mascot	65	35
☐ 1953	49ers Mascot	50	30
☐ 1954	49ers Mascot	50	30
☐ 1955	49ers Mascot	50	30
☐ 1956	49ers Mascot	50	25
☐ 1957	49ers Mascot	45	25
☐ 1958	49ers Mascot	45	25
☐ 1959	49ers Mascot	40	25
☐ 1960	49ers Mascot	40	25
☐ 1961	49ers Mascot	50	25
☐ 1962	49ers Mascot	50	25
☐ 1963	49ers Mascot	50	25
☐ 1964	49ers Mascot	40	20
☐ 1965	49ers Mascot	40	20
☐ 1966	49ers Mascot	40	20
☐ 1967	Action	30	15
☐ 1968	Action	30	15
☐ 1969	John Brodie	25	12
☐ 1970	John Brodie	30	15
☐ 1971	Stadium	25	10
☐ 1972	Stadium	25	10
☐ 1973	Player	20	10
☐ 1974	Helmet	20	7
☐ 1975	Helmet	15	7
☐ 1976	Coach	15	7
☐ 77-80		12	5
☐ 81-89		10	4
☐ 90-97		5	2
☐	Joe Montana cover	15	5

GAME PROGRAMS

		Nr-Mt	Ex
☐ 1946	First Program	300	150
☐ 1946	First Season	100	75
☐ 47-49	Game Programs	45	25
☐ 50-53	Game Programs	35	20
☐ 54-59	Game Programs	25	15
☐ 60-63	Game Programs	20	12
☐ 64-69	Game Programs	20	10
☐ 70-75	Game Programs	12	6

		Nr-Mt	Ex
☐ 76-80	Game Programs	10	4
☐ 81-89	Game Programs	8	2
☐ 90-97	Game Programs	5	1
☐	OJ Simpson Last Program	25	12
☐	Joe Montana First Program	75	25
☐	Jerry Rice First Program	50	25

TEAM SCHEDULES

		Nr-Mt	Ex
☐ 1946	First Schedule	150	100
☐ 47-49	Schedules	100	75
☐ 50-55	Schedules	35	20
☐ 56-59	Schedules	30	15
☐ 60-65	Schedules	25	15
☐ 66-69	Schedules	25	15
☐ 70-75	Schedules	15	8
☐ 76-80	Schedules	10	7
☐ 81-89	Schedules	6	3
☐ 90-97	Schedules	2	1

YEARBOOKS, MAGAZINES, NEWSLETTERS

A few yearbooks were issued. Magazines and newsletters, team issue stuff is very valuable in the 46-49 period.

		Nr-Mt	Ex
☐ 1958	Mascot	75	35
☐ 1963	John Brodie	60	20
☐ 1985	Bill Walsh	15	5
☐ 1986	Joe Montana	15	5
☐ 87-90		12	5
☐ 91-97		10	3

JOE MONTANA

Joe Montana is still popular and collected by die hard 49er fans. His college material (Notre Dame) and his early pro material is the most popular ($25-$50 range).

JERRY RICE

Perhaps the greatest receiver of all time. Each year his material becomes more popular. He appeared only on a handful of items in the early part of his career, thus making the demand for the items rather high ($30-$50).

STEVE YOUNG

Growing steadily in popularity and collectibility. Most covers range in the $15-$30 range.

ST. LOUIS RAMS (FORMERLY LA RAMS)

The Rams have a strong tradition in pro football. They originated in Cleveland in 1937 and played there until 1945 when they moved to LA. The Rams stayed in LA until 1995 when they moved to St. Louis. The Rams have been NFL champs and have been to one Super Bowl.

MEDIA GUIDES

		Nr-Mt	Ex
☐ 1945	Bob Waterfield	70	30
☐ 1946		65	35
☐ 1947	Bob Waterfield	65	30
☐ 1948		60	30
☐ 1949	Rams Head	50	25
☐ 1950	Rams Head	50	25
☐ 1951	Rams Head	45	20
☐ 1952	Rams Head	55	20
☐ 1953	Rams Head	50	30
☐ 1954	Rams Head	50	30
☐ 1955	Rams Head	50	30
☐ 1956	Rams Head	50	25
☐ 1957	Rams Head	45	25
☐ 1958	Rams Head	45	25
☐ 1959	Rams Head	40	25
☐ 1960	Rams Head	40	25
☐ 1961	Rams Head	50	25
☐ 1962	Rams Head	50	25
☐ 1963	Rams Head	50	25
☐ 1964	Rams Head	40	20
☐ 1965	Rams Head	40	20
☐ 1966	Rams Head	40	20
☐ 1967	Rams Head	30	15
☐ 1968	Rams Head	30	15
☐ 1969	Rams Head	25	12
☐ 70-75	Rams Head	15	7
☐ 76-80		12	7
☐ 81-89		10	4
☐ 90-97		5	2

GAME PROGRAMS

		Nr-Mt	Ex
☐ 1937	First Program	300	150
☐ 1937	First Season	125	75
☐ 38-40	Game Programs	75	25
☐ 41-45	Cleveland Rams	75	25
☐ 1946	First Program	150	100
☐ 1946	First Year	75	25
☐ 47-50	Game Programs	35	20
☐ 51-53	Game Programs	30	15
☐ 54-59	Game Programs	25	12
☐ 60-63	Game Programs	20	12
☐ 64-69	Game Programs	20	10
☐ 70-75	Game Programs	12	6
☐ 76-80	Game Programs	10	4
☐ 81-89	Game Programs	8	2
☐ 90-97	Game Programs	5	1

SCHEDULES

		Nr-Mt	Ex
☐ 1937	First Schedule	200	100
☐ 38-40	Schedules	100	75
☐ 46-49	Schedules	100	75
☐ 50-55	Schedules	35	20
☐ 56-59	Schedules	30	15
☐ 60-65	Schedules	25	15
☐ 66-69	Schedules	25	15
☐ 70-75	Schedules	15	8
☐ 76-80	Schedules	10	7
☐ 81-89	Schedules	6	3
☐ 90-97	Schedules	2	1

YEARBOOKS/MAGAZINES/NEWSLETTERS

A few yearbooks were issued. Magazines and newsletters, team issue stuff is very valuable in the pre- 49 period.

		Nr-Mt	Ex
☐ 1958	Cartoon	75	35
☐ 1959	Cartoon	75	35
☐ 1960	Cartoon	75	35
☐ 1961	Cartoon	75	35
☐ 1962	Jon Arnet	60	35
☐ 1963	Dick Bass	60	30

SEATTLE SEAHAWKS

A very young pro football franchise. Most of this material has nominal value but the fan base growns. The most popular player is Steve Largent.

MEDIA GUIDE

		Nr-Mt	Ex
☐ 1976-80		10	5
☐ 1981-90		6	3
☐ 1991-97		4	1

GAME PROGRAMS

		Nr-Mt	Ex
☐ 1976	First Program	55	35
☐ 1976-80	Game Programs	10	5
☐ 1981-89	Game Programs	10	3
☐ 1990-97	Game Program	5	1

SCHEDULES

		Nr-Mt	Ex
☐ 1976	First Schedule	15	6
☐ 1977-80	Schedules	10	5
☐ 1981-89	Schedules	5	2
☐ 1990-97	Schedules	4	1

YEARBOOKS, MAGAZINE, NEWSLETTERS

Two yearbooks were issued by the team (1976 $35, 1989 $15).

STEVE LARGENT

Perhaps the second most popular receiver after Jerry Rice. His material goes between $20-$35.

TAMPA BAY BUCCANEERS

A very young pro football franchise. Most of this material has nominal value.

MEDIA GUIDE		Nr-Mt	Ex
☐ 1976-80	....	10	5
☐ 1981-90	....	6	3
☐ 1991-97	....	4	1

GAME PROGRAMS		Nr-Mt	Ex
☐ 1976	First Program	55	35
☐ 1976-80	Game Programs	10	5
☐ 1981-89	Game Programs	10	3
☐ 1990-97	Game Programs	5	1

SCHEDULES		Nr-Mt	Ex
☐ 1976	First Schedule	15	6
☐ 1977-80	Schedules	10	5
☐ 1981-89	Schedules	5	2
☐ 1990-97	Schedules	4	1

YEARBOOKS, MAGAZINE, NEWSLETTERS
None.

TENNESSEE (HOUSTON) OILERS

One of the original AFL teams. The team moved in 1996 from Houston to Tennessee. The fan base for the Houston material now is among hard core Oiler collectors. The biggest demand is for early AFL material and some items with Earl Campbell.

MEDIA GUIDES		Nr-Mt	Ex
☐ 1960	....	75	35
☐ 1961	Mascot	40	20
☐ 1962	Players	35	12
☐ 1963	Action	30	12
☐ 1964	S. Baugh	30	12
☐ 1965	Helmets	25	12
☐ 1966	Players	25	10
☐ 1967	Logo	25	10
☐ 1968	Stadium	20	10
☐ 1969	Stadium	20	10
☐ 1970	Artwork	15	5
☐ 1971	Sculpture	15	5
☐ 1972	Helmet	15	5
☐ 1973	Helmet	15	5
☐ 1974	Action	10	3
☐ 1975	Action	10	3
☐ 1976-77		7	3
☐ 1978-80		5	2
☐ 1981-89		5	2
☐ 1990-97		5	2

GAME PROGRAMS		Nr-Mt	Ex
☐ 1960	First Game rogram	150	75
☐ 1960	First Season	75	35
☐ 61-63	Game Programs	35	17
☐ 64-69	Game Programs	20	12
☐ 70-75	Game Programs	15	5
☐ 76-80	Game Programs	10	3
☐ 81-89	Game Programs	8	2
☐ 90-97	Game Programs	5	1

SCHEDULES		Nr-Mt	Ex
☐ 1960	First AFL Season	100	50
☐ 61-65	Early Schedules	35	15
☐ 66-69	Schedules	20	10
☐ 70-75	Schedules	12	6
☐ 76-80	Schedules	10	7
☐ 81-89	Schedules	6	2
☐ 90-97	Schedules	2	1

YEARBOOKS, MAGAZINES, NEWSLETTERS
Only one yearbook was ever issued (1965 - $50).

WASHINGTON REDSKINS

The Redskins originated in 1937. Serious collectors pursue programs and material on all of the Redskins publications. However, most sports fans focus on the pre 1960 era with a few fans chasing the superbowl years.

MEDIA GUIDES		Nr-Mt	Ex
☐ 1947	Mascot	100	35
☐ 1948	Mascot	100	35
☐ 1949	Mascot	75	35
☐ 1950	Mascot	65	35
☐ 1951	Mascot	55	35
☐ 1952	Mascot	65	35
☐ 1953	Mascot	50	30
☐ 1954	Mascot	50	30
☐ 1955	In Action	50	30
☐ 1956	In Action	50	25
☐ 1957	In Action	45	25
☐ 1958	Year	45	25
☐ 1959	Helmet	40	25
☐ 1960	Football	40	25
☐ 1961	Silver Ann.	50	25
☐ 1962	Football	50	25
☐ 1963	Capital Building	50	25
☐ 1964	Tomhawk	40	20
☐ 1965	Redskins	40	20
☐ 1966	DC Stadium	40	20
☐ 1967	DC Stadium	30	15
☐ 1968	DC Stadium	30	15
☐ 1969	DC Stadium	25	12
☐ 1970	DC Stadium	30	15
☐ 1971	DC Stadium	25	10
☐ 1972	Helmet	25	10
☐ 1973	Logo	20	10
☐ 1974	Helmet	20	7
☐ 1975	Huddle	15	7
☐ 1976	Logo	15	7
☐ 77-80		12	5
☐ 81-89		10	4
☐ 90-97		5	2

GAME PROGRAMS		Nr-Mt	Ex
☐ 1937	First Program	600	300
☐ 1937	First Season	200	100
☐ 38-39	Game Programs	125	50
☐ 40-46	Game Programs	75	35
☐ 47-49	Game Programs	50	25
☐ 50-53	Game Programs	35	20
☐ 54-59	Game Programs	25	15
☐ 60-63	Game Programs	20	12
☐ 64-69	Game Programs	20	10
☐ 70-75	Game Programs	12	6
☐ 76-80	Game Programs	10	4
☐ 81-89	Game Programs	8	2
☐ 90-97	Game Programs	5	1

SCHEDULES		Nr-Mt	Ex
☐ 1937	First Schedule	250	100
☐ 38-40	Early Schedules	150	75
☐ 41-46	Early Schedules	125	65
☐ 47-49	Early Schedules	100	55
☐ 50-55	Earl Scheds	35	20
☐ 56-59	Early Schedules	30	15
☐ 60-65	Early Schedules	25	15
☐ 66-69	Schedules	25	15
☐ 70-75	Schedules	15	8
☐ 76-80	Schedules	10	7
☐ 81-89	Schedules	6	3
☐ 90-97	Schedules	2	1

YEARBOOKS, MAGAZINES, NEWSLETTERS
A few yearbooks were issued. Magazines and team issue stuff is very valuable in the pre 50 period.

		Nr-Mt	Ex
☐ 1973	George Allen	35	15
☐ 1986	Anniv. Logo	30	10
☐ 87-90		12	5
☐ 91-97		10	3

MEDIA GUIDES

1956 SAN FRANCISCO 49ERS

1962 DALLAS COWBOYS

1966 CHICAGO BEARS

1975 DALLAS COWBOYS

1984 SEATTLE SEAHAWKS

1987 NEW ENGLAND PATRIOTS

GAME PROGRAMS 1943 NEW YORK GIANTS

1947 SAN FRANCISCO 49ERS

1958 SAN FRANCISCO 49ERS

CHAPTER SEVENTEEN:
Collecting College Football Publications

Football publications are the most collected football item outside of football cards. Football publication collectors are fortunate. Compared to baseball and basketball team publication collectors, which may have 40-100 game programs to collect, football program team collectors have at most 20. If you tag on a few media guides and a yearbook you may have at most 25 team related items released in a year.

College football publications date back into the early 1880's. Early programs are very rare and only surface a few times each year in the auction houses. In fact, pre 1900 programs from Michigan, Nebraska, and Ohio State will be over $1,000. Michigan, Notre Dame, Nebraska programs from the1900-1920 era can easily be a few hundred dollars. Early programs are very popular and are pursued by very serious sports historians. Besides game programs, football publications collectors pursue annuals, media guides, pre season and post season guides, and regular publications.

COLLEGE MEDIA GUIDES

Every college today produces a media guide on its football team. Along with media guides are pre season prospectus, post season analysis and team bowl media guides. However, there is no clear specific pattern to anything other than the team media guides and a team bowl media guide.

The values of media guides are mostly driven by popularity of the team or player who appears in them or on them. Popular schools are collected to such a degree that the demand for the older media guides is high. Schools that are considered popular are: Michigan, Ohio State, Alabama, Tennessee, USC, Mississippi, Notre Dame, Texas, Oklahoma and Nebraska. All other schools do not command a premium price for media guides.

Special events are media guides for bowl appearance, pre season prospectus and special releases. These command a special premium because the production is low and even less were saved.

Key Players are those players (Hall of Famers) who appeared or are featured in a team media guide. For example, Dan Marino on a Pitt media guide command a premium. A list of some former players that command premiums: Dan Marino, Ernie Davis (60), Jimmy Brown, Joe Montana, Jerry Rice, Johnny Unitas, Jack Kemp, John Kennedy, Ronald Reagan, Dick Butkus and Gerald Ford.

	Popular Schools		Average Schools		Special Events		Key Players	
YEAR(S)	Nr-Mt	Ex	Nr-Mt	Ex	Nr-Mt	Ex	Nr-Mt	Ex
pre 30	200	100	100	50	300	200	300	200
30-39	200	100	100	50	300	150	300	150
40-49	100	50	50	25	150	75	150	75
50-59	50	25	25	15	80	40	80	40
60-69	25	15	15	5	50	30	50+	30+
70-79	15	7	7	3	30	15	30+	15+
80-89	10	5	5	2	25	15	30+	15+
90-97	5	2	3	1	20	10	20	15+

COLLEGE GAME PROGRAMS

The most popular item to collect is the game program. Serious fans collect all the game programs of their favorite schools. Some only collect their favorite period or home programs. However, very advanced college football collectors collect every game the team went to. The most important college program collected is the bowl program. The toughest programs in demand are the obscure bowl programs that featured popular schools like Nebraska and Michigan.

The college game programs date back into the 1880's. Most teams only have programs dating back to 1890-1910 range. The most valuable college programs are those that date from their earliest years. Demand for college programs is similar to media guides. Checklist for college programs can be developed via team's media guides or with certain football books.

Special events are those programs that are historic in nature. First games played, school or national records made and special series between two key schools like Cal vs Stanford are considered special events.

Key Players perhaps dictate the price of a college program. Joe Montana or Dan Marino college programs command a premium over the same school programs from the year before. If the player is featured on the cover of the program the value doubles. Key Players are limited to the legends in the college or pro game.

COLLEGE FOOTBALL PROGRAM GENERAL PRICE LIST

	Popular Schools		Average Schools		Special Events		Key Players	
YEAR(S)	NM	EX	NM	EX	NM	EX	NM	EX
1880's	1,500+	1,000+	1,000+	750+	3,000+	2,000+	3,000+	2,000+
90-99	1,000+	600+	450+	300+	2,000+	1,000+	2,000+	1,000+
00-09	500	200	250	150	1,000+	500+	1,000+	500+
10-19	200	100	100	50	500+	250+	500+	250+
20-29	100	50	55	25	350+	200+	350+	200+
30-39	60	20	45	20	300+	150+	300+	150+
40-49	45	15	40	15	150+	75+	150+	75+
50-59	40	12	35	12	80+	40+	80+	40+
60-69	30	10	25	5	50+	30+	50+	30+
70-79	20	7	15	3	30+	15+	30+	15+
80-89	15	5	15	2	25+	15+	30+	15+
90-97	10	30	10	1	20+	10+	20+	10+

COLLECTING BOWL PROGRAMS

The passion for football program collecting has to start with the proverbial Big Game. The Big Game for you may be different from everybody else. However, most agree that the bowls (be it your favorite fruit or plant) carry many of the most significant and most important football games ever played.

Bowl programs are sometimes the first programs a football collector will collect. The oldest bowl is the Rose, which played its first game in 1902. The Orange and Sugar bowls started in 1935, the Cotton started in 1937 and the Gator in 1946. The most collected bowl program is for the Super Bowl, which started in 1967.

Bowl programs are valued by demand and scarcity. Some of the most expensive programs are the first 20 Rose Bowl programs (1902, 1916-1926) which can capture prices $400 and up. These programs are rare and don't change hands very often. You should expect to see them pop up about once a year in one of the national auction dealer houses.

On the other hand, Super Bowl programs usually are carried by every publication dealer in the country. The programs after Super Bowl XIII are rather common and inexpensive. In fact, the first 10 are the only ones that command any real value. Shop around for your Super Bowl programs

because they are rather common among the nation's largest publication dealers.

The early years for the Sugar and Cotton bowls are tough but not as popular as the Rose. You will also find that the most popular bowl programs to get are those from heavily collected schools such as Notre Dame, Alabama, USC, Michigan, Ohio State and so forth. The toughest to find are from obscure bowls that appeared once and are long forgotten. Later issues will include articles about other bowls. This issue will focus on the Orange and Rose bowls.

ROSE BOWL

This is the granddaddy of them all and the toughest to complete. I have heard rumors that just a handful of the longest and most devoted collectors have a complete run of these bowl programs. The reasons are obvious. The first bowl program was in 1902 when top-ranked Michigan, which didn't allow a point all year, beat Stanford, 49-0, in front of 8,000 fans. The program is not as attractive as later ones but it is one of the most significant Michigan programs and one of the most important football programs ever released.

Since Michigan defeated Stanford so soundly, the game wasn't sponsored again until 1916, when Washington State beat Brown, 14-0. All of the programs between 1916 and 1926 are scarce and very collectible. They will probably be auction pieces with the most advanced collectors bidding.

Once you enter into the 1920s you have some of the key programs that are collected according to favorite teams. For example, 1921 marks Cal's first Rose Bowl program, 1923 is USC's and 1924 is Washington's.

The biggest program of the 1920s came out in 1925. It is Knute Rockne's only program, when the Four Horsemen of Notre Dame topped Stanford for the mythical national championship in a battle of unbeatens. This is the ultimate program for Notre Dame fans since it is their only bowl appearance until 45 years later. I have not seen one of these on the open market for two years.

With that said, the 1929 game between Cal and Georgia Tech is considered one of the most famous bowl games because of Cal player Roy Riegel's wrong-way run, which actually cost Cal the game when Georgia Tech got a safety to win, 8-7.

In the 1930s the Rose Bowl grew in attendance from 66,000 to 89,000. Most collectors tend to end their Rose Bowl collection in this era. These programs are more plentiful in Southern California. This does not mean that they still don't carry prices in the 100-400 range; it just means you won't have as much trouble finding them. Many of these programs are in nice shape and do trade very well among serious collectors. Shop around for these.

One of the most popular collectible Rose Bowl programs is

from the 1942 game played at Duke University, in which Oregon St. edged Duke, 20-16. The location was changed because at the start of World War II there was fear that L.A. was in danger of being bombed. Within two weeks, Duke Stadium increased its capacity from 35,000 to 56,000 by quickly constructing temporary seating. Valued from $350 to $1,000, the popular collectible sometimes is available at auctions. From 1950 on Rose Bowl programs are relatively easy to obtain and the prices begin to reflect that. Many dealers in Southern California have multiples of the '50s and '60s programs. The '70s and '80s are easy to get in Mint condition. Programs in the 1990s are so common you can pick them up for a few bucks.

If you are going to start collecting Rose Bowl programs, I would recommend that you establish a budget and a goal. I always recommend collecting your favorite team before working into your favorite era. I would also recommend that you purchase a few books on the Rose Bowl from some of the great sports book dealers. This will provide you with some important insights into the game.

Finally, if you are only going to collect your favorite team, I would recommend that you also try to track down Rose Bowl tickets from those games. This will give you additional challenges but finding the tickets will make the hunt worthwhile.

The next list has a detailed breakdown of each Rose Bowl with winners and losers, the score, the attendance and estimated price values. The price values are retail prices from dealers and not necessarily what you may sell them to a dealer for. I would suspect that you can sell your Rose Bowl program to a dealer for 50 percent of the listed price and possibly more for the exceptionally tough Notre Dame program. The earliest programs are rare and only a handful of them change hands each year, making price estimates more difficult.

YEAR	WINNER	LOSER	SCORE	ATT.	Nr-Mt	Ex
1902	Michigan #1*	Stanford*	49-0	8	auction	
1916	Wash St*	Brown*	14 -0	12	auction	
1917	Oregon*	Penn*	14-0	26	auction	
1918	Mare Island	Camp Lewis*	19-7	25	auction	
1919	Great Lakes	Mare Island	17-0	27	auction	
1920	Harvard #1*	Oregon	7-6	30	auction	
1921	Cal #1*	Ohio St*	28-0	42	2,000	1,000
1922	Cal	W & J	0-0	40	2,000	1,000
1923	USC*	Penn St*	14 3	43	2,000	1,000
1924	Washington*	Navy	14-14	40	2,000	1,000
1925	Notre Dame #1*	Stanford	27-10	53	2,000	750
1926	Alabama*	Washington	20-19	50	500	250
1927	Alabama #1	Stanford	7-7	57	600	300
1928	Stanford	Pittsburgh*	7-6	65	500	250
1929	Georgia Tech #1*	California	8 -7	66	800	400
1930	USC	Pittsburgh	47-14	72	350	200
1931	Alabama	Wash. St	2 4-0	60	600	350
1932	USC #1	Tulane	21-12	75	250	150
1933	USC	Pittsburgh	7 -0	78	250	150
1934	Columbia*	Stanford	7- 0	35	350	200
1935	Alabama	Stanford	29-13	84	300	150
1936	Stanford	SMU*	7 - 0	84	200	100
1937	Pittsburgh	Washington	21-0	87	200	100
1938	Cal #1	Alabama	13-0	90	250	150
1939	USC	Duke*	13- 0	89	300	100
1940	USC	Tennessee	14- 0	92	200	80
1941	Stanford	Nebraska*	21-13	91	225	80
1942	Oregon St	Duke*	20-16	52	600	350
1943	Georgia*	UCLA*	9- 0	93	200	80
1944	USC	Washington	29-0	68	200	80
1945	USC	Tennessee	25- 0	91	120	60
1946	Alabama	USC	34-14	93	120	60

1947	Illinois*	UCLA	45-14	93	100	50
1948	Mich #1	USC	49-0	93	95	50
1949	Northwestern*	California	20-14	93	95	50
1950	Ohio State*	California	17-14	100	95	50
1951	Michigan	California	14- 6	100	75	40
1952	Illinois	Stanford	40-7	100	75	40
1953	USC	Wisconsin	7-0	100	60	35
1954	Michigan State	UCLA	28-20	100	60	25
1955	Ohio St #1	USC	20 -7	89	60	25
1956	Michigan State	UCLA	17-14	100	50	25
1957	Iowa	Oregon St	35-19	97	50	25
1958	Ohio St	Oregon	10- 7	100	50	25
1959	Iowa	California	38-12	98	50	25
1960	Washington	Wisconsin	44-8	100	50	25
1961	Washington #1	Minnesota	17 7	97	40	25
1962	Minnisota	UCLA	21- 3	98	40	20
1963	USC #1	Wisconsin	42-37	96	40	20
1964	Illinois	Washington	17- 7	100	40	20
1965	Michigan	Oregon	34 -7	96	40	20
1966	UCLA #1	Mich St	14-12	100	40	20
1967	Purdue	USC	14-13	100	40	20
1968	USC #1	Indiana	14- 3	100	40	20
1969	Ohio St #1	USC	27-16	100	30	15
1970	USC	Michigan	10- 3	100	30	15
1971	Stanford	Ohio St	27-17	100	30	15
1972	Stanford	Mich	13-12	100	25	15
1973	USC #1	Ohio St	42-17	100	30	15
1974	Ohio St	USC	24-21	100	25	15
1975	USC#1	Ohio St	18-1 7	100	25	10
1976	UCLA	Ohio St #1	23-10	100	25	15
1977	USC #1	Michigan	1 4- 6	100	15	10
1978	Washington	Michigan	27-10	100	15	10
1979	USC	Michigan	1 7-10	100	15	10
1980	USC	Ohio State	1 7-16	100	10	5
1981	Michigan	Washington	23- 6	100	10	5
1982	Washington	Iowa	28- 0	100	10	5
1983	UCLA	Michigan	24-14	100	10	5
1984	UCLA	Illinois	45- 9	100	10	5
1985	USC	Ohio State	20-1 7	100	10	5
1986	UCLA	Iowa State	45-28	100	10	5
1987	Arizona State	Michigan	22-1 5	100	10	3
1988	Michigan	UCLA	20-17	100	10	5
1989	Michigan	USC	22-14	100	10	5
1990	USC	Michigan	17-10	100	10	5
1991	Washington	Iowa	46-34	100	10	5
1992	Washington	Michigan	34-14	100	10	5
1993	Michigan	Washington	38-31	100	10	5
1995	Penn St.	Oregon	38-20	100	10	5
1996	USC	Northwestern	41-32	100	10	5
1997	Ohio St.	Arizona St.	20-17	100	10	5

*First appearance. #1 = ranking entering bowl
Attendance in thousands.

ORANGE BOWL

The Orange Bowl is not as sacred or as collected as the Rose Bowl, but it is the bowl of many of the football powerhouses from the 1950s through the '90s. If you collect Nebraska, Oklahoma, Alabama or Georgia Tech, you first start at the Orange Bowl. From 1953 to 1991, the Orange Bowl featured the Big Eight champion versus an at-large team. Since 1992, the teams have been determined by one of the first five picks from the eight-team bowl coalition pool. This format has generated some interesting matchups and a few national championship games. Oklahoma has the most wins of any school with 11. Nebraska, on the other hand, has just five.

The key programs for the Orange Bowl collector are from games between 1935 and 1938. These bowls are generally the toughest to find. However, if your goal is to focus on the key programs in Orange Bowl history, you would need to start with 1953, when Alabama scored 61 points. The most sought after programs are the 1963 and 1965 bowls because of the presence of Alabama quarterback and New York Jets legend-to-be Joe Namath. Another key year for the Crimson Tide was the national championship year of 1966. When you count all those Alabama national championships you can understand the love for legendary head coach Bear Bryant. These programs should be worth double just because of the Alabama and Broadway Joe fans! The next key group of Orange Bowls is the 1971-73 Nebraska championships. These are favorites with the growing Nebraska collecting base.

Other favorite programs are the 1956 game when top-ranked Oklahoma beat Maryland for the title and also the 1954 game when the Sooners knocked off No. 1 Maryland.

YEAR	WINNER	LOSER	SCORE	ATT.	Nr-Mt	Ex
☐ 1935	Bucknell	Miami	26-0	5	auction	
☐ 1936	Catholic	Mississippi.	20-19	6	auction	
☐ 1937	Duquesne	Miss St	13-12	9	auction	
☐ 1938	Auburn	Mich St	6-0	19	auction	
☐ 1939	Tennessee	Oklahoma	17-0	32	auction	
☐ 1940	Georgia Tech	Missouri	21-7	29	275	100
☐ 1941	Miss St	Georgetown	14-10	29	250	100
☐ 1942	Georgia	TCU	40-26	36	250	100
☐ 1943	Alabama	Boston Col	37-21	25	250	100
☐ 1944	LSU	Texas A&M	19-14	25	200	90
☐ 1945	TULSA	Geo.Tech	26-12	23	200	90
☐ 1946	Miami (Fla.)	Holy Cross	13-6	36	175	70
☐ 1947	Rice	Tennessee	8-0	59	150	70
☐ 1948	Georgia Tech	Kansas	20-14	60	150	60
☐ 1949	Texas	Georgia	41-28	60	100	50
☐ 1950	Santa Clara	Kentucky	21-13	65	75	50
☐ 1951	Clemson	Miami	15-14	65	110	40
☐ 1952	Georgia Tech	Baylor	17-14	66	75	30
☐ 1953	Alabama	Syracuse	61-6	66	75	30
☐ 1954	Oklahoma	Maryland	7-0	69	75	30
☐ 1955	Duke	Nebraska	34-7	69	75	30
☐ 1956	Oklahoma#1	Maryland	7-0	76	120	50
☐ 1957	Colorado	Clemson	27-21	73	75	30
☐ 1958	Oklahoma	Duke	48-21	76	75	30
☐ 1959	Oklahoma	Syracuse	21-6	75	75	30
☐ 1960	Georgia	Missouri	14-0	72	75	30
☐ 1961	Missouri	Navy	21-14	72	75	30
☐ 1962	LSU	Colorado	25-7	68	75	30
☐ 1963	Alabama	Oklahoma	17-0	73	75	30
☐ 1964	Nebraska	Auburn	13-7	72	75	30
☐ 1965	Texas	Alabama#1	21-17	72	110	50
☐ 1966	Alabama#1	Nebraska	39-28	72	90	40
☐ 1967	Florida	Geo.Tech	27-12	72	65	30
☐ 1968	Oklahoma	Tenn	26-21	78	50	25
☐ 1969	Penn St	Kansas	15-14	77	40	15
☐ 1970	Penn st	Miss	10-3	77	40	15
☐ 1971	Nebraska#1	LSU	17-12	80	60	35
☐ 1972	Nebraska#1	Alabama	38-6	78	65	35
☐ 1973	Nebraska	Notre Dame	40-6	80	65	35
☐ 1974	Penn St	LSU	16-9	60	30	15
☐ 1975	Notre Dame	Alabama	13-11	71	30	15
☐ 1976	Oklahoma#1	Mich	14-6	80	30	15
☐ 1977	Ohio State	Colorado	27-10	80	25	15
☐ 1978	Arkasas	Oklahoma	31-6	80	20	10
☐ 1979	Oklahoma	Nebraska	31-24	80	20	10
☐ 1980	Oklahoma	Florida State	24-7	80	20	10
☐ 1981	Oklahoma	Florida State	18-17	80	15	7
☐ 1982	Clemson#1	Nebraska	22-15	80	15	7
☐ 1983	Nebraska	LSU	21-20	80	15	7
☐ 1984	Miami Fl#1	Nebraska	31-30	80	15	7
☐ 1985	Washington	Oklahoma	28-17	80	15	7
☐ 1986	Oklahoma#1	Penn State	25-10	80	15	7
☐ 1987	Oklahoma	Arkansas	42-8	80	15	7
☐ 1988	Miami (FL)	Oklahoma	20-14	80	15	7
☐ 1989	Miami (FL)	Nebraska	23-4	80	15	7
☐ 1990	Notre Dame	Colorado	21-6	80	15	7
☐ 1991	Colorado	Notre Dame	10-9	80	15	7
☐ 1992	Miami (FL)	Nebraska	22-0	80	15	7
☐ 1993	Florida St.	Nebraska	27-14	80	15	7
☐ 1994	Florida St.	Nebraska	18-16	80	15	7
☐ 1995	Nebraska	Miami (FL)	24-17	80	15	7
☐ 1996	Florida St.	Notre Dame	31-26	80	15	7
☐ 1997	Nebraska	Virgina Tech	41-21	80	15	7

Attendance in thousands.

ALL AMERICAN BOWL & HALL OF FAME CLASSIC
(This bowl was discontinued after 1990. Played in Birmingham, Alabama at Legion Field. Seats 75,808. Originially called the Hall of Fame Classic from 1977-1984.)

YEAR	WINNER	LOSER	SCORE	Nr-Mt	Ex
☐ 12/77	Maryland	Minnesota	17-7	65	35
☐ 12/78	Texas A&M	Iowa st	28-12	40	25
☐ 12/79	Missouri	S. Carolina	24-14	35	25
☐ 12/80	Arkansas	Tulane	34-14	30	15
☐ 12/81	Mississippi St	Kansas	10-0	25	12
☐ 12/82	Air Force	Vanderbilt	36-28	20	12
☐ 12/83	W. Virginia	Kentucky	20-16	20	12
☐ 12/84	Kentucky	Wisconsin	20-19	20	12
☐ 12/85	Georgia Tech	Michigan St	17-14	20	12
☐ 12/86	Florida St	Indiana	27-13	20	12
☐ 12/87	Virgina	BYU	22-16	20	12
☐ 12/88	Florida	Illinois	14-10	20	12
☐ 12/89	Texas Tech	Duke	49-21	20	12
☐ 12/90	N. Caroli st	Southern Miss	31-27	20	12

ALAMO BOWL
(Played in San Antonio, Texas at the Alamodome. Seats 65,000. Started in 1993.)

YEAR	WINNER	LOSER	SCORE	Nr-Mt	Ex
☐ 1993	California	Iowa	37-3	25	15
☐ 1994	Washington St	Baylor	10-3	15	10
☐ 1995	Texas A&M	Michigan	22-20	15	10
☐ 1996	Iowa	Texas Tech	27-0	15	10

ALOHA BOWL
(Played in Honolulu at Aloha Bowl. Capacity is 50,000.)

YEAR	WINNER	LOSER	SCORE	Nr-Mt	Ex
☐ 12/82	Washington	Maryland	21-20	50	25
☐ 12/83	Penn St	Washington	13-10	40	20
☐ 12/84	SMU	Notre Dame	27-20	35	20
☐ 12/85	Alabama	USC	24-3	30	15
☐ 12/86	Arizona	North Carolina	30-21	25	15
☐ 12/87	UCLA	Florida	20-16	20	12
☐ 12/88	Wash. St	Houston	24-22	20	12
☐ 12/89	Michigan St	Hawaii	33-13	20	12
☐ 12/90	Syracuse	Arizona	28-0	20	12
☐ 12/91	Georgia Tech	Stanford	18-17	20	12
☐ 12/92	Kansas	BYU	23-20	15	10
☐ 12/93	Colorado	Fresno State	41-30	15	10
☐ 12/94	Boston Col	Kansas St.	12-7	15	10
☐ 12/95	Kansas	UCLA	51-30	15	5
☐ 12/96	Navy	California	42-38	15	5

ASTRO-BLUEBONNET BOWL
(Located in Houston Texas. Played at Rice Stadium (1959-67;1985-86) and Astrodome in (1968-84;1987).

YEAR	WINNER	LOSER	SCORE	Nr-Mt	Ex
☐ 1960	Clemson	TCU	23-7	200	100
☐ 1961	Alabama	Texas	3-3	125	50
☐ 1962	Kansas	Rice	33-7	100	50
☐ 1963	Missouri	Georgia Tech	14-10	100	50
☐ 1964	Baylor	LSU	14-7	80	40
☐ 1965	Tulsa	Mississippi	14-7	80	40
☐ 1966	Tennessee	Tulsa	27-6	80	40
☐ 1967	Texas	Mississippi	19-0	80	40
☐ 1968	Colorado	Miami	31-21	60	30
☐ 1969	SMU	Oklahoma	28-27	60	30
☐ 1970	Houston	Auburn	36-7	60	30
☐ 1971	Alabama	Oklahoma	24-24	40	25

YEAR	WINNER	LOSER	SCORE	Nr-Mt	Ex
1972	Colorado	Houston	29-17	40	25
1973	Tennessee	LSU	24-17	40	20
1974	Houston	Tulane	47- 7	35	15
1975	North Carolina	Houston	31-31	35	15
1976	Texas	Colorado	38-21	30	15
1977	Nebraska	Texas Tech	27-14	25	15
1978	USC	Texas A&M	47-28	25	15
12/78	Stanford	Georgia	25-22	25	15
12/79	Purdue	Tennessee	27-22	25	15
12/80	N. Carolina	Texas	16- 7	25	15
12/81	Michigan	UCLA	33-14	30	12
12/82	Arkansas	Florida	28-24	25	12
12/83	Oklahoma St	Baylor	24-14	25	12
12/84	W. Virginia	Texas Christian	31-14	25	12
12/85	Air Force	Texas	24-16	25	12
12/86	Baylor	Colorado	21- 9	25	12
12/87	Texas	Pittsburgh	32-27	25	12

BLOCKBUSTER BOWL (CARQUEST BOWL)

(Played in Miami at Joe Robbie Stadium. Seats 75,000.)

YEAR	WINNER	LOSER	SCORE	Nr-Mt	Ex
12/90	Florida St	Penn St	24-17	35	15
12/91	Alabama	Colorado	30-25	20	10
12/92	Stanford	Penn St	24- 3	15	10
1/94	Boston College	Virginia	31-13	15	10
1/95	South Carolina	West Va.	24-21	15	10
1/96	North Carolina	Arkansas	20-10	15	10
1/97	Miami (Fl)	Virginia	31-21	15	10

CALIFORNIA BOWL

(This is played in Fresno California at BullDog Stadium. Capacity is 30,000.)

YEAR	WINNER	LOSER	SCORE	Nr-Mt	Ex
12/81	Toledo	San Jose St	27-25	50	25
12/82	Fresno St	Bowling Green	29-28	35	20
12/83	N. Illinois	Cal St Fulerton	20-13	35	20
12/84	UNLV	Toledo	30-13	35	20
12/85	Fresno St	Bowling Green	51- 7	35	20
12/86	San Jose St	Miami (OH)	37- 7	30	15
12/87	Eastern Mich	San Jose St	30-27	30	15
12/88	Fresno St	Western Mich	35-30	20	10
12/89	Fresno St	Ball St	27- 6	20	10
12/90	San Jose St	Central Michigan	48-24	20	10
12/91	Bowling Green	Fresno St	28-21	20	10
Others				15	5

COPPER BOWL

(Located in Tucson, Arizona. Capacity is 57,000.)

YEAR	WINNER	LOSER	SCORE	Nr-Mt	Ex
12/89	Arizona	North Carolina St	17-10	40	20
12/90	California	Wyoming	17-15	20	10
12/91	Indiana	Baylor	24- 0	20	10
12/92	Washington St	Utah	31-28	15	10
12/93	Kansas St	Wyoming	52-17	15	10
12/94	BYU	Oklahoma	31- 6	15	10
12/95	Texas Tech	Air Force	55-41	15	10
12/96	Wisconsin	Utah	38-10	15	10

COTTON BOWL

(Originally played in Fair Park Stadium in 1937 and then moved to the Cotton Bowl in Dallas.)

YEAR	WINNER	LOSER	SCORE	Nr-Mt	Ex
1937	TCU	Marquette	16- 6	1,000	450
1938	Rice	Colorado	28-14	750	450
1939	St Marys	Texas Tech	20-13	550	350
1940	Clemson	Boston Col	6- 3	450	250
1941	Texas A&M	Fordham	13-12	450	225
1942	Alabama	Texas A&M	29-21	400	225
1943	Texas	Georgia Tech	14- 7	400	200
1944	Texas	Randolph Fld	7- 7	400	200
1945	Okla. A&M	TCU	34- 0	400	200
1946	Texas	Missouri	40-27	400	200
1947	Arkansas	LSU	0- 0	350	200
1948	SMU	Penn St	13-13	300	200
1949	SMU	Oregon	21-13	275	150

YEAR	WINNER	LOSER	SCORE	Nr-Mt	Ex
1950	Rice	North Carolina	27-13	225	150
1951	Tennessee	Texas	20-14	150	100
1952	Kentucky	TCU	20- 7	150	75
1953	Texas	Tennessee	16- 0	150	100
1954	Rice	Alabama	28- 6	150	100
1955	Georgia Tech	Arkansas	14- 6	125	50
1956	Mississippi	TCU	14-13	125	50
1957	TCU	Syracuse	28-27	120	50
1958	Navy	Rice	20- 7	100	50
1959	Air Force	TCU	0- 0	75	35
1960	Syracuse	Texas	23-14	100	45
1961	Duke	Arkansas	7- 6	75	35
1962	Texas	Mississippi	12- 7	100	35
1963	LSU	Texas	13- 0	75	35
1964	Texas	Navy	28- 6	75	35
1965	Arkansas	Nebraska	10- 7	100	40
1966	LSU	Arkansas	14- 7	75	35
1967	Georgia	SMU	24- 9	75	35
1968	Texas A&M	Alabama	20-16	75	35
1969	Texas	Tennessee	36-13	65	30
1970	Texas	Notre Dame	21-17	125	35
1971	Notre Dame	Texas	24-11	120	35
1972	Penn St	Texas	30- 6	65	30
1973	Texas	Alabama	17-13	55	30
1974	Nebraska	Texas	19- 3	55	25
1975	Penn St	Baylor	41-20	50	25
1976	Arkansas	Georgia	31-10	45	20
1977	Houston	Maryland	30-21	35	15
1978	Notre Dame	Texas	38-10	45	20
1979	Notre Dame	Houston	35-34	45	20
1980	Houston	Nebraska	17-14	45	20
1981	Alabama	Baylor	30- 2	30	15
1982	Texas	Alabama	14-12	35	15
1983	SMU	Pittsburgh	7- 3	30	15
1984	Georgia	Texas	10- 9	30	15
1985	Boston Col	Houston	45-28	25	15
1986	Texas A&M	Auburn	36-16	20	10
1987	Ohio St	Texas A&M	28-12	20	10
1988	Texas A&M	Notre Dame	35-10	20	10
1989	UCLA	Arkansas	17- 3	20	10
1990	Tennessee	Arkansas	31-27	15	10
1991	Miami	Texas	46- 3	15	10
1992	Florida St	Texas A &M	10- 2	15	10
1993	Notre Dame	Texas A & M	28- 3	15	10
1994	Notre Dame	Texas A & M	24-21	15	10
1995	USC	Texas Tech	55-14	15	10
1996	Colorado	Oregon	38- 6	15	10
1997	BYU	Kansas St	19-15	15	10

FIESTA BOWL

(Located in Tempe, Arizona. Stadium capacity of 74,000.)

YEAR	WINNER	LOSER	SCORE	Nr-Mt	Ex
12/71	ASU	Florida St	45-38	75	35
12/72	ASU	Missouri	49-35	50	25
12/73	ASU	Pittsburgh	28- 7	40	20
12/74	Oklahoma	BYU	16- 6	40	20
12/75	ASU	Nebraska	17-14	35	15
12/76	Oklahoma	Wyoming	41- 7	35	15
12/77	Penn St	Arizona St	42-30	35	15
12/78	Arkansas	UCLA	10-10	35	15
12/79	Pittsburgh	Arizona	16-10	35	15
12/80	Penn St	Ohio St	31-19	35	15
1/82	Penn St	USC	26-10	30	15
1/83	Arizona St	Oklahoma	32-21	30	15
1/84	Ohio St	Pittsburgh	28-21	25	15
1/85	UCLA	Miami (FL)	39-37	25	15
1/86	Michigan	Nebraska	27-23	25	15
1/87	Penn St	Miami (FL)	14-10	25	15
1/88	Florida St	Nebraska	31-28	20	15
1/89	Notre Dame	W. Virginia	34-21	20	10
1/90	Florida St	Nebraska	41-17	20	10
1/91	Louisville	Alabama	34- 7	20	10
1/92	Penn St	Tennessee	42-17	20	10
1/93	Syracuse	Colorado	23-10	20	10
1/94	Arizona	Miami (Fl)	29- 0	20	10

☐ 1/95	Colorado	Notre Dame	41-24	15	10
☐ 1/96	Nebraska	Florida	62-24	15	10
☐ 1/97	Penn St	Texas	38-15	15	10

FREEDOM BOWL

(Located in Anaheim, Calif. Stadium seats 70,500.)

YEAR	WINNER	LOSER	SCORE	Nr-Mt	Ex
☐ 12/84	Iowa	Texas	55-17	25	15
☐ 12/85	Washington	Colorado	20-17	25	15
☐ 12/86	UCLA	BYU	31-10	20	10
☐ 12/87	Arizona St	Air Force	33-28	20	10
☐ 12/88	BYU	Colorado	20-17	20	10
☐ 12/89	Washington	Florida	34- 7	20	10
☐ 12/90	Colorado St	Oregon	32-31	20	10
☐ 12/91	Tulsa	San Diego St	28-17	20	10

GATOR BOWL

(Played in Jacksonville, FL at the Gator Bowl. Approx. 82,000 capacity.)

YEAR	WINNER	LOSER	SCORE	Nr-Mt	Ex
☐ 1946	Wake Forest	South Carolina	26-14	300	100
☐ 1947	Oklahoma	North Carolina St	34-13	250	100
☐ 1948	Maryland	Georgia	20-20	200	100
☐ 1949	Clemson	Missoui	24-23	200	100
☐ 1950	Maryland	Missouri	20- 7	100	60
☐ 1951	Wyoming	Washington&Lee	20- 7	100	50
☐ 1952	Miami (FL)	Clemson	14- 0	125	50
☐ 1953	Florida	Tulsa	14-13	125	50
☐ 1954	Texas Tech	Auburn	35-13	90	50
☐ 12/54	Auburn	Baylor	33-13	90	50
☐ 12/55	Vanderbilt	Aubrun	25-13	90	50
☐ 12/56	Georgia Tech	Pittsburgh	21-14	90	50
☐ 12/57	Tennesse	Texas A&M	3- 0	90	50
☐ 12/58	Mississippi	Florida	7- 3	100	50
☐ 1960	Arkansas	Georgia Tech	14- 7	90	40
☐ 12/60	Florida	Baylor	13-12	100	40
☐ 12/61	Penn St	Georgia Tech	30-15	90	40
☐ 12/62	Florida	Penn St	17- 7	90	40
☐ 12/63	North Carolina	Air Force	35- 0	90	40
☐ 1965	Florida St	Oklahoma	26-19	85	40
☐ 12/65	Georgia Tech	Texas Tech	31-21	85	35
☐ 12/66	Tennessee	Syracuse	18-12	80	35
☐ 12/67	Penn St	Florida St	17-17	75	35
☐ 12/68	Missouri	Alabama	35-10	85	45
☐ 12/69	Florida	Tennessee	14-13	65	25
☐ 1971	Auburn	Mississippi	35-28	65	25
☐ 12/71	Georgia	North Carolina	7- 3	55	25
☐ 12/72	Aurburn	Colorado	24- 3	55	25
☐ 12/73	Texas Tech	Tennessee	28-19	55	25
☐ 12/74	Auburn	Texas	27- 3	50	25
☐ 12/75	Maryland	Florida	13- 0	45	25
☐ 12/76	Notre Dame	Penn St	20- 9	40	20
☐ 12/77	Pittsburgh	Clemson	34- 3	40	20
☐ 12/78	Clemson	Ohio St	17-15	40	20
☐ 12/79	N Carolina	Arkansas	17-15	40	20
☐ 12/80	Pittsburgh	S. Carolina	37- 9	35	20
☐ 12/81	N. Carolina	Arkansas	31-27	35	20
☐ 12/82	Florida St	West Virginia	31-12	30	15
☐ 12/83	Florida	Iowa	14- 6	30	15
☐ 12/84	Oklahoma St	S. Carolina	21-14	30	15
☐ 12/85	Florida St	Oklahoma St	34-23	30	15
☐ 12/86	Clemson	Stanford	27-21	20	10
☐ 12/87	LSU	S. Carolina	30-13	20	10
☐ 1989	Georgia	Michigan st	34-27	20	10
☐ 12/89	Clemson	W. Virginia	27- 7	20	10
☐ 1991	Michigan	Mississippi	35- 3	20	10
☐ 12/91	Oklahoma	Virginia	48-14	15	10
☐ 1992	Flordia	NC State	27-10	15	10
☐ 1993	Alabama	North Carolina	24-10	15	10
☐ 1994	Tennessee	Va Tech	45-23	15	10
☐ 1995	Syracuse	Clemson	41- 0	15	10
☐ 1996	N Carolina	West Virginia	20-13	15	10

HALL OF FAME BOWL (OUTBACK BOWL)

(Located in Tampa, Florida. Originally called the Hall of Fame Bowl (86-95) Capacity is 74,315.)

YEAR	WINNER	LOSER	SCORE	Nr-Mt	Ex
☐ 12/86	Boston Col	Georgia	27-24	40	25
☐ 1/88	Michigan	Alabama	28-24	40	20
☐ 1/89	Syracuse	Louisiana	23-10	35	20
☐ 1/90	Auburn	Ohio St	31-14	30	15
☐ 1/91	Clemson	Illinois	30- 0	20	10
☐ 1/92	Syracuse	Ohio St	24-17	20	10
☐ 1/93	Tennessee	Boston College	38-23	15	10
☐ 1/94	Michigan	North Carolina St	42- 7	15	10
☐ 1/95	Wisconsin	Duke	34-20	15	10
☐ 1/96	Penn State	Auburn	43-14	15	10
☐ 1/97	Alabama	Michigan	17-14	15	10

HOLIDAY BOWL

(Played in San Diego at Jack Murphy Stadium. Capacity is 60,750.)

YEAR	WINNER	LOSER	SCORE	Nr-Mt	Ex
☐ 12/78	Navy	Brigham Young	23-16	50	25
☐ 12/79	Indiana	Brigham Young	38-37	40	20
☐ 12/80	BYU	SMU	46-45	40	20
☐ 12/81	BYU	Washington St	38-36	35	15
☐ 12/82	Ohio St	BYU	47-17	30	15
☐ 12/83	BYU	Missouri	21-17	30	15
☐ 12/84	BYU	Michigan	24-17	20	10
☐ 12/85	Arkansas	Arizona St	18-17	20	10
☐ 12/86	Iowa	San Diego St	39-38	20	10
☐ 12/87	Iowa	Wyoming	20-19	20	10
☐ 12/88	Oklahoma	Wyoming	62-14	20	10
☐ 12/89	Penn St	BYU	50-39	20	10
☐ 12/90	Texas A&M	BYU	65-14	20	10
☐ 12/91	Iowa	BYU	13-13	20	10
☐ 12/92	Hawaii	Illinois	27-17	20	10
☐ 12/93	Ohio St	BYU	28-21	15	10
☐ 12/94	Michigan	Colorado St	24-14	15	10
☐ 12/95	Kansas St	Coloroado St	54-21	15	10
☐ 12/96	Colorado	Washington	33-21	15	10

INDEPENDENCE BOWL

(Located in Shreveport, LA. Stadium seats 50,560.)

YEAR	WINNER	LOSER	SCORE	Nr-Mt	Ex
☐ 12/76	McNeese St	Tulsa	20-16	75	35
☐ 12/77	Louisiana Tech	Louisville	24-14	50	35
☐ 12/78	E. Carolina	Louisiana Tech	35-13	40	20
☐ 12/79	Syracuse	McNeese St	31- 7	40	20
☐ 12/80	Southern Miss	McNeese St	16-14	30	15
☐ 12/81	Texas A&M	Oklahoma St	33-16	25	15
☐ 12/82	Wisconsin	Kansas St	14- 3	25	15
☐ 12/83	Air Force	Mississippi	9- 3	25	15
☐ 12/84	Air Force	Virginia	23- 7	25	15
☐ 12/85	Minnesota	Clemson	20-13	25	15
☐ 12/86	Mississippi	Texas Tech	20-17	25	15
☐ 12/87	Washington	Tulane	24-12	25	15
☐ 12/88	Southern Mis	UTEP	38-18	25	15
☐ 12/89	Oregon	Tulsa	27-24	25	15
☐ 12/90	Louisiana Tech	Maryland	34-34	20	15
☐ 12/91	Georgia	Arkansas	24-15	20	15
☐ 12/92	Wake Forest	Oregon	39-35	15	10
☐ 12/93	Va Tech	Indiana	45-20	15	10
☐ 12/94	Virginia	TCU	20-10	15	10
☐ 12/95	LSU	Michigan St	45-26	15	10
☐ 12/96	Auburn	Army	32-29	15	10

LIBERTY BOWL

(Located in Memphis and is played at the Liberty Bowl Stadium with a seating capacity of 63,000. The first game was actually played on 12/59 but is listed as 1960. Games were also played in Philadelphia (59-63) and Atlantic City in 1964. Been located at the Liberty Bowl since 1965.)

YEAR	WINNER	LOSER	SCORE	Nr-Mt	Ex
☐ 1960	Penn St	Alabama	7- 0	150	75
☐ 1961	Penn St	Oregon	41-12	100	50
☐ 1962	Syracuse	Miami (FL)	15-14	100	50
☐ 1963	Oregon St	Villanova	6- 0	75	35
☐ 1964	Mississippi St	Norh Carolina St	16-12	75	35
☐ 1965	Utah	West Virginia	32- 6	60	30
☐ 1966	Mississippi	Auburn	13- 7	60	30
☐ 1967	Miami (FL)	Virginia Tech	14- 7	60	30

	Year	Winner	Loser	Score	Nr-Mt	Ex
☐	1968	NC St	Georgia	14- 7	50	30
☐	1969	Mississippi	Virginia Tech	34-17	50	35
☐	1970	Colorado	Alabama	47-33	50	35
☐	1971	Tulane	Colorado	17- 3	50	30
☐	1972	Tennessee	Arkansas	14-13	50	25
☐	1973	Georgia Tech	Iowa St	31-30	50	25
☐	1974	NC St	Kansas	31-18	40	25
☐	1975	Tennessee	Maryland	7- 3	40	25
☐	1976	USC	Texas A&M	20- 0	40	25
☐	1977	Nebraska	North Carolina	21-17	40	20
☐	1978	Missouri	LSU	20-15	40	20
☐	1979	Penn St	Tulane	9- 6	30	15
☐	1980	Purdue	Missouri	28-25	30	15
☐	1981	Ohio St	Navy	31-28	30	15
☐	1982	Alabama	Illinois	21-15	30	15
☐	1983	Notre Dame	Boston Col.	19-18	40	15
☐	1984	Auburn	Arkansas	21-15	25	10
☐	1985	Baylor	LSU	21- 7	25	10
☐	1986	Tennessee	Minnesota	21-14	25	10
☐	1987	Georgia	Arkansas	20-17	20	10
☐	1988	Indiana	South Carolina	34-10	20	10
☐	1989	Mississippi	Air Force	42-29	15	10
☐	1990	Air Force	Ohio State	23-11	15	10
☐	1991	Air Force	Mississippi St	38-15	15	10
☐	1992	Mississippi	Air Force	7- 0	15	10
☐	1993	Louisville	Michigan St	18- 7	15	10
☐	1994	Illinois	East Carolina	30- 0	15	10
☐	1995	East Carolina	Stanford	19-13	15	10
☐	1996	Syracuse	Houston	30-17	15	10

	Year	Winner	Loser	Score	Nr-Mt	Ex
☐	1943	Tennessee	Tulsa	14-7	250	100
☐	1944	Georgia Tech	Tulsa	20-18	250	125
☐	1945	Duke	Alabama	29-26	200	100
☐	1946	Oklahoma A	St. Mary's	33-13	150	75
☐	1947	Georgia	North Carolina	20-10	175	100
☐	1948	Texas	Alabama	27-7	200	100
☐	1949	Oklahoma	North Carolina	14-6	150	75
☐	1950	Oklahoma	LSU	35-0	150	75
☐	1951	Kentucky	Oklahoma	13-7	150	75
☐	1952	Maryland	Tennessee	28-13	150	75
☐	1953	Georgia Tech	Mississippi	24-7	150	75
☐	1954	Georgia Tech	West Virginia	42-19	150	75
☐	1955	Navy	Mississippi	21-0	150	75
☐	1956	Georgia Tech	Pittsburgh	7-0	120	75
☐	1957	Baylor	Tennessee	13-7	120	60
☐	1958	Mississipi	Texas	39-7	120	60
☐	1959	LSU	Clemson	7-0	120	60
☐	1960	Mississippi	LSU	21-0	100	60
☐	1961	Mississippi	Rice	14-6	100	50
☐	1962	Alabama	Arkansas	10-3	90	45
☐	1963	Mississippi	Arkansas	17-13	90	45
☐	1964	Alabama	Mississippi	12-7	90	45
☐	1965	LSU	Syracuse	13-10	90	35
☐	1966	Missouri	Florida	21-18	75	35
☐	1967	Alabama	Nebraska	34-7	75	35
☐	1968	LSU	Wyoming	20-13	75	35
☐	1969	Arkansas	Georgia	16-2	75	35
☐	1970	Mississippi	Arkansas	27-22	50	25
☐	1971	Tennessee	Air Force	34-13	50	25
☐	1972	Oklahoma	Auburn	40-22	50	25
☐	1973	Oklahoma	Penn St	14-0	50	25
☐	1974	Norte Dame	Alabama	24-23	50	25
☐	1975	Nebraska	Florida	13-10	45	25
☐	1976	Alabama	Penn St	13-6	45	25
☐	1977	Pittsburgh	Georgia	27-3	40	25
☐	1978	Alabama	Ohio St	35-6	40	25
☐	1979	Alabama	Penn St	14-7	35	20
☐	1980	Alabama	Arkansas	24-9	35	20
☐	1981	Georgia	Notre Dame	17-10	40	20
☐	1982	Pittsburgh	Georgia	24-20	40	20
☐	1983	Penn St	Georgia	27-23	35	20
☐	1984	Auburn	Michigan	9-7	35	20
☐	1985	Nebraska	LSU	28-10	35	20
☐	1986	Tennessee	Miami	35-7	35	20
☐	1987	Nebraska	LSU	30-15	35	20
☐	1988	Auburn	Syracuse	16-16	35	20
☐	1989	Florida St	Auburn	13-7	25	15
☐	1990	Miami	Alabama	33-25	25	15
☐	1991	Tennessee	Viriginia	23-22	20	10
☐	1992	Notre Dame	Florida	39-28	20	10
☐	1993	Alabama	Miami (FL)	34-13	15	10
☐	1994	Florida	West Va	41-7	15	10
☐	1995	Va Tech	Texas	28-10	15	10
☐	1997	Florida	Florida St	52-20	15	10

PEACH BOWL

(Played in Atlanta at the Atlanta Fulton County Stadium. Seats 59,800. Also played at Grant Field in 1968-70.)

	YEAR	WINNER	LOSER	SCORE	Nr-Mt	Ex
☐	12/68	Louisiana St	Florida St	31-27	100	50
☐	12/69	W. Virginia	S. Carolina	14- 3	65	35
☐	12/70	Arizona St	N. Carolina	48-26	65	35
☐	12/71	Mississippi	Georgia Tech	41-18	50	35
☐	12/72	N. Carolina	W. Virginia	49-13	50	35
☐	12/73	Georgia	Maryland	17-16	50	30
☐	12/74	Vanderbilt	Texas Tech	6- 6	45	25
☐	12/75	W. Virginia	N. Carolina	13-10	40	25
☐	12/76	Kentucky	N. Carolina	21- 0	35	20
☐	12/77	N. Carolina	Iowa St	24-14	35	20
☐	12/78	Purdue	Georgia Tech	41-21	35	20
☐	12/79	Baylor	Clemson	24-18	25	15
☐	1/81	Miami (FL)	Virginia Tech	20-10	25	15
☐	12/81	W. Virginia	Florida	26- 6	25	15
☐	12/82	Iowa	Tennessee	28-22	25	15
☐	12/83	Florida St	N. Carolina	28- 3	20	10
☐	12/84	Virginia	Purdue	27-24	20	10
☐	12/85	Army	Illinois	31-29	20	10
☐	12/86	Virginia Tech	North Carolina St	25-24	20	10
☐	1/88	Tennessee	Indiana	27-22	20	10
☐	12/88	N. Carolina st	Iowa	28-23	20	10
☐	12/89	Syracuse	Georgia	19-18	20	10
☐	1/92	E. Carolina	N. Carolina St	37-34	20	10
☐	1993	North Carolina	Miss St.	21-17	15	10
☐	12/93	Clemson	Kentucky	14-13	15	10
☐	1995	N. Carolina St	Mississippi St	24-24	15	10
☐	12/95	Virginia	Georgia	34-27	15	10
☐	12/96	LSU	Clemson	10- 7	15	10

SUGAR BOWL

(Played in Tulane Stadium from 1935-1974. Today this is played in New Orleans with a seating capacity of 69,000.)

	YEAR	WINNER	LOSER	SCORE	Nr-Mt	Ex
☐	1935	Tulane	Temple	21-14	400	200
☐	1936	TCU	LSU	3-2	350	150
☐	1937	Santa Clara	LSU	21-14	300	150
☐	1938	Santa Clara	LSU	6-0	300	150
☐	1939	TCU	Carnegie Tech	15-7	300	150
☐	1940	Texas AM	Tulane	14-13	300	150
☐	1941	Boston Col	Tennessee	19-13	225	110
☐	1942	Fordham	Missouri	2-0	200	100

SUN BOWL (JOHN HANCOCK BOWL)

(Name was Sun Bowl from 1936-1986 and then shifted to John Hancock Bowl in 1987. Played in Kidd Field from 1936-1962 and then moved to the Sun Bowl in 1963. Played in El Paso, Texas.)

	YEAR	WINNER	LOSER	SCORE	Nr-Mt	Ex
☐	1936	Hardin-Simm	New Mexico	14-14	450	250
☐	1937	Hardin-Simm	Texas Mines	34- 6	300	150
☐	1938	West Virgina	Texas Tech	7- 6	250	150
☐	1939	Utah	New Mexico	26- 0	250	150
☐	1940	Catholic	ASU	0- 0	250	150
☐	1941	Western Res.	ASU	26-13	250	150
☐	1942	Tulsa	Texas Tech	6- 0	250	150
☐	1943	2nd Army AF	Hardin-Simmin	13- 7	250	150
☐	1944	Southwestern	U of Mexico	7- 0	200	100
☐	1945	Southwestern	U of Mexico	35- 0	200	100
☐	1946	New Mexico	Denver	34-24	200	100
☐	1947	Cincinnati	Virginia Tech	38- 6	250	100
☐	1948	Miami	Texas Mines	13-12	200	100
☐	1949	West Virginia	Texas Mines	21-12	200	100
☐	1950	Texas Western	Georgetown	33-20	150	75

	YEAR	WINNER	LOSER	SCORE	Nr-Mt	Ex
☐	1951	West Texas	Cincinnati	14-13	150	75
☐	1952	Texas Tech	Pacific	25-14	150	65
☐	1953	Pacific	Miss Southern	26- 7	150	65
☐	1954	Texas Western	Miss Southern	37-14	125	55
☐	1955	Texas Western	Florida State	47-20	150	65
☐	1956	Wyoming	Texas Tech	21-14	125	50
☐	1957	George Wash	Texas Western	13- 0	125	50
☐	1958	Louisville	Drake	34-20	100	50
☐	1959	Wyoming	Hardin-Simmon	14- 6	100	50
☐	1960	New Mexico	North Texas St	28- 8	100	50
☐	1961	New Mexico	Utah St	20-13	100	50
☐	1962	Villanova	Wichita	17- 9	100	50
☐	1963	West Texas	Ohio University	15-14	100	50
☐	1964	Oregon	SMU	21-14	100	50
☐	1965	Georgia	Texas Tech	7- 0	100	50
☐	1966	Texas Western	TCU	13-12	75	40
☐	1967	Wyoming	Florida St	28-20	75	40
☐	1968	Texas	Mississippi	14- 7	75	40
☐	1969	Auburn	Arizona	34-10	100	50
☐	1970	Nebraska	Georgia	45- 6	75	35
☐	1971	Georgia Tech	Texas Tech	17- 9	65	25
☐	1972	LSU	Iowa St	23-15	65	25
☐	1973	North Carolina	Texas Tech	32-28	65	25
☐	1974	Missouri	Auburn	34-17	60	20
☐	1975	Miss. St	North Carolina	26-24	60	20
☐	1976	Pittsburgh	Kansas	33-19	50	20
☐	1977	Stanford	LSU	24-14	50	20
☐	1978	Texas	Maryland	42- 0	40	20
☐	1979	Washington	Texas	14- 7	40	20
☐	1980	Nebraska	Mississippi St.	31-17	30	20
☐	1981	Oklahoma	Houston	40-14	30	20
☐	1982	North Carolina	Texas	26-10	30	20
☐	1983	Alabama	LSU	28-7	30	20
☐	1984	Maryland	Tennessee	28-27	25	15
☐	1985	Arizona	Georgia	13-13	25	15
☐	1986	Alabama	Washington	28- 6	20	10
☐	1987	Oklahoma St	W. Virginia	35-33	20	10
☐	1988	Alabama	Army	29-28	20	10
☐	1989	Pittsburgh	Texas A&M	31-28	20	10
☐	1990	Michigan St	USC	17-16	20	10
☐	1991	UCLA	Illinois	6- 3	15	10
☐	1992	Baylor	Arizona	20-15	15	10
☐	1993	Oklahoma	Texas Tech	41-10	15	10
☐	1994	Texas	North Carolina	35-31	15	10
☐	1995	Iowa	Washington	38-18	15	10
☐	1996	Stanford	Michigan St	38- 0	15	10
☐	1969	Richmond	Ohio Univ.	49-42	40	20
☐	1970	Toledo	Davidson	56-33	40	20
☐	1971	Toledo	William and Mary	40-12	40	20
☐	1972	Toledo	Richmond	28- 3	35	20
☐	1973	Tampa	Kent St.	21-18	30	15
☐	1974	Miami (Ohio)	Florida	16- 7	30	15
☐	1975	Miami (Ohio)	Georgia	21-10	30	15
☐	1976	Miami (Ohio)	South Carolina	20- 7	30	15
☐	12/76	Okla. St	BYU	49-21	25	12
☐	12/77	Florida St	Texas Tech	40-17	30	15
☐	12/78	N Carolina	Pittsburgh	30-17	25	12
☐	12/79	LSU	Wake Forest	34-10	25	12
☐	12/80	Florida	Maryland	35-20	25	12
☐	12/81	Missouri	Southern Miss.	19-17	20	12
☐	12/82	Auburn	Boston Col	33-26	20	12
☐	12/83	Tennessee	Maryland	30-23	20	12
☐	12/84	Georgia	Florida St	17-17	20	12
☐	12/85	Ohio St	BYU	10- 7	20	12
☐	1987	Auburn	USC	16- 7	15	10
☐	1988	Clemson	Penn St	35-10	15	10
☐	1989	Clemson	Oklahoma	13- 6	15	10
☐	1990	Illinois	Virginia	31-21	15	10
☐	1991	Georgia Tech	Nebraska	45-21	15	10
☐	1992	California	Clemson	37-13	15	10
☐	1993	Georgia	Ohio St	21-14	15	10
☐	1994	Penn St	Tennessee	31-17	15	10
☐	1995	Alabama	Ohio St	24-17	15	10
☐	1996	Tennessee	Ohio St	20-14	15	10
☐	1997	Tennessee	Northwestern	48-28	15	10

TANGERINE BOWL (FLORIDA CITRUS BOWL)

(Played in Orlando, Florida. Originally played in Tangerine Bowl from 47-97, except for 74 it was held in Florida Field in Gainsville, Fl. The name was Tangerine Bowl from 1947-1982. Then it changed to Florida Citrus Bowl in 1983. Capacity is 52,000.)

	YEAR	WINNER	LOSER	SCORE	Nr-Mt	Ex
☐	1947	Catawba	Maryville	31- 6	300	125
☐	1948	Catawba	Marhshall College	7- 0	175	100
☐	1949	Murray St	Sul Ross	21-21	175	100
☐	1950	St. Vincent	Emory/Henry	7- 6	150	100
☐	1951	Morris Harvey	Emory/Henry	35-14	150	100
☐	1952	Stetson	Arkansas St.	35-20	150	100
☐	1953	East Texas St	Tennessee Tech	33- 0	125	75
☐	1954	E. Texas St	Arkansas St	7- 7	125	75
☐	1955	Omaha	E. Kentucky	7- 6	125	75
☐	1956	Juanita Col	Missouri Val.	6- 6	125	75
☐	1957	W. Texas St	Mississippi St	20-13	125	75
☐	1958	E. Texa St	Miss. Souther	10- 9	125	75
☐	1959	E. Texas St	Missouri VI	26- 9	100	50
☐	1960	M. Tenn St	Presbyterian	21-12	100	50
☐	1961	The Citadel	Tennessee Tech	27- 0	100	50
☐	1962	Lamar Tech	Middle Tenn	21-14	100	50
☐	1963	Houston	Miami (Ohio)	47-28	100	50
☐	1964	W. Kentucky	US Coast Guard	27- 0	100	50
☐	1965	E.Carolina	Mass.	14-13	75	40
☐	1966	E.Carolina	Maine	31- 0	75	40
☐	1967	Morgan St	West Chester St	14- 6	75	40
☐	1968	Tennessee	West Chester St	25- 8	50	25

BOWL PROGRAMS

1934 ROSE BOWL

1953 ROSE BOWL

1955 ROSE BOWL

1969 ROSE BOWL

1979 ROSE BOWL

1949 COTTON BOWL TICKET

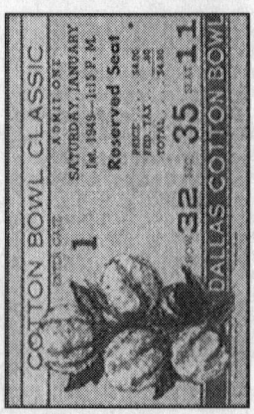

1994 COTTON BOWL TICKET

1983 COTTON BOWL

1984 FIESTA BOWL

1966 SUGAR BOWL

1984 FREEDOM BOWL

1995 SENIOR BOWL

GAME PROGRAMS

1925

1931

1933

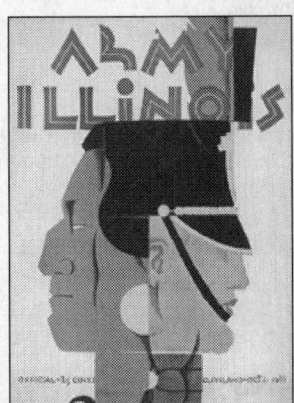

CHAPTER EIGHTEEN:
Collecting Football Publications

This section covers football publications that were either magazines, periodicals or newspapers devoted exclusively to Football. Many fine books have been written on football and a partial list on the subject can be found in the 'Guide to Football Literature' by Anton Grobani published by Gale Research Company in 1972. If you find some magazines that are not listed here (which there are some) you can e-mail me at Regli@aol.com or you can visit the books Web Site at www.asportmall.com.

As a rule of thumb, generic pricing of football publications would go for approximately the following:

1940's - 1950's	$30 - $40
1960's	$20 - $30
1970's	$10 - $20
1980's - 1990's	$ 5 - $10

When you wholesale your magazines expect about 10 - 15% of the common price with the exception of popular players.

ACTION SPORTS PRO FOOTBALL
(Action Sports Group, Rostam Pub)

DATE	COVER/FEATURE	Nr-Mt	Ex
☐ 1971	Yearbook	30	15
☐ 1971	Guidebook	30	15
☐ 1972	Jim Plunkett	25	10

AFL PLAYERS YEARBOOK

DATE	COVER/FEATURE	Nr-Mt	Ex
☐ 1960	Artwork	50	25
☐ 1962	Action	40	20
☐ 1964	Chiefs/Oilers	30	12
☐ 1965	George Blanda - Oilers	35	12
☐ 1966	Action	30	12
☐ 1968	Handbook	25	12
☐ 1969	Matt Snell - Jets	30	12

ALL PRO FOOTBALL
(Maco)

DATE	COVER/FEATURE	Nr-Mt	Ex
☐ 1957	Action Shot - YA Tittle	50	30
☐ 1958	Sports All Stars	45	20
☐ 1959	Johnny Unitas - Colts	45	20
☐ 1960	Johnny Unitas - Colts	45	20
☐ 1961	Kyle Rote - Eagles	35	20
☐ 1962	Y.A. Tittle - Giants	35	20
☐ 1963	Bart Starr - Packers	35	15
☐ 1964	Johnny Unitas - Colts	35	15
☐ 1965	Fran Trakenton- Vikings	35	15
☐ 1966	Frank Ryan - Browns	30	15
☐ 1967	Carrol Dale - Packers	30	15
☐ 1968		20	10
☐ 1969	Joe Namath - Jets	30	15
☐ 1970	Hank Stram- Chiefs	20	10
☐ 1971	John Brodie - 49ers	20	10
☐ 1973	Fran Tarkenton - Vikings	15	10
☐ 1974	Fran Tarkenton -Vikings	15	10

ALL PRO FOOTBALL
(Popular Library)

DATE	COVER/FEATURE	Nr-Mt	Ex
☐ 1963	Y.A. Tittle - Giants	25	10

ALL STAR SPORTS

DATE	COVER/FEATURE	Nr-Mt	Ex
☐ 2/68	Namath/Unitas	25	10
☐ 12/68	G. Sayers/D. Anderson	25	10
☐ 2/69	Joe Namath - Jets	25	10
☐ 8/69	Joe Namath - Jets	25	10
☐ 12/69	Joe Namath - Jets	25	10
☐ 2/70	OJ Simpson - Bills	20	10
☐ 1/71	Len Dawson - Chiefs	20	10
☐ 1/72	John Brodie - 49ers	20	10
☐ 8/72	Roger Staubach-Cowboys	20	10
☐ 10/72	Colorado	20	10

ALL SPORTS

DATE	COVER/FEATURE	Nr-Mt	Ex
☐ 11/70	Len Dawson - Chiefs	35	15
☐ 12/70	Paul Hornung - Packers	25	10
☐ 1/71	John Brodie - 49ers	15	10
☐ 11/71	Jim Plunkett - Patriots	15	10
☐ 1970	Kansas	15	10

ALL TIME FOOTBALL GREATS

DATE	COVER/FEATURE	Nr-Mt	Ex
☐ 1973	J. Brown/J Unitas	15	10
☐ 1974	Jim Brown - Browns	15	10

ARGOSY COLLEGE FOOTBALL
(Popular Publications)

DATE	COVER/FEATURE	Nr-Mt	Ex
☐ 1976	Tony Dorsett - Pitt	20	10
☐ 1977	Browner - Notre Dame	15	10
☐ 1977	J. Davis	10	5
☐ 1978	Joe Montana -Notre Dame	25	5
☐ 1979	Charles Alexander	10	5
☐ 1980-1990		10	5
☐ 1991-1997		5	3

ARKANSAS FOOTBALL ANNUALS
Produced by Dave Campbell in the 60's and 70's.

ATHLONS
College and Pro editions.
Many regional covers are produced of pro and college players.

DATE	COVER/FEATURE	Nr-Mt	Ex
☐ 1982 - 1989		15	5
☐ 1990 - 1997		10	2

AVON SUPERSTAR

DATE	COVER/FEATURE	Nr-Mt	Ex
☐ Dan Marino/Joe Montana		15	5

BECKETT FOOTBALL
See Beckett Magazine

BEN STRONG BOOK OF SPORTS

DATE	COVER/FEATURE	Nr-Mt	Ex
☐ 10/72	Roger Staubach - Cowboys	20	10
☐ 9/73	Bob Griese, Hank Aaron	20	10

BEST SPORTS STORIES

DATE	COVER/FEATURE	Nr-Mt	Ex
☐ 1962	Jim Brown - Browns	25	10

BIG TEN COLLEGE FOOTBALL

DATE	COVER/FEATURE	Nr-Mt	Ex
☐ 1975 & 76	Archie Griffin - Ohio St.	20	10

CALIFORNIA FOOTBALL

DATE	COVER/FEATURE	Nr-Mt	Ex
☐ 1972	John Brodie - 49ers	20	10
☐ 1973	Fred Biletnikoff - Raiders	20	10

CHARLIE CONERLY FOOTBALL

(Popular Library)

DATE	COVER/FEATURE	Nr-Mt	Ex
☐ 1962	Jim Brown - Browns	40	15

CHARGERS WEEKLY

This is the team news weekly

DATE	COVER/FEATURE	Nr-Mt	Ex
☐ 8/21/89	Jim McMahon	10	2
☐	Others	10	2

COLLEGE FOOTBALL

DATE	COVER/FEATURE	Nr-Mt	Ex
☐ 1950	Bob Williams- Notre Dame	40	20
☐ 1976	Tony Dorsett - Pitt	20	10
☐ 1977	Charlie White - USC	20	10

COLLEGE FOOTBALL GUIDE

DATE	COVER/FEATURE	Nr-Mt	Ex
☐ 1971	Tom Gatewood - Notre Dame	20	10

COLLEGE FOOTBALL YEARBOOK

DATE	COVER/FEATURE	Nr-Mt	Ex
☐ 1978	Joe Montana -Notre Dame	30	15

COLLEGE FOOTBALL POP SPORTS

DATE	COVER/FEATURE	Nr-Mt	Ex
☐	Rick Harmon - Purdue	15	10

COLLIERS

Colliers produced an All-American series for years.

DATE	COVER/FEATURE	Nr-Mt	Ex
☐ 1950-60	All America Review	30	15

COMPLETE FOOTBALL

(Sport Life Mag/Interstate Pub Corp)

DATE	COVER/FEATURE	Nr-Mt	Ex
☐ F/49	Dick McKissack - SMU	35	15
☐ 1950	D.Foldberg/Bob Williams	35	10

COMPLETE SPORTS COL FOOTBALL

DATE	COVER/FEATURE	Nr-Mt	Ex
☐ 1961	Roman Gabrial - NC St	30	15

COMPLETE SPORTS PRO FOOTBALL

DATE	COVER/FEATURE	Nr-Mt	Ex
☐ 1961-62	Johnny Unitas - Colts	35	15

COMPLETE SPORTS AFL/NFL YEARBOOK

DATE	COVER/FEATURE	Nr-Mt	Ex
☐ 1964	Jim Brown - Browns	40	20
☐ 1965	Johnny Morris - Bears	35	20
☐ 1966	Jim Brown/Jack Kemp	40	20
☐ 1967	Gale Sayers - Bears	35	20
☐ 1968	Roman Gabrial - Rams	30	15
☐ 1969	Sonny Jurgesen - Redskins	25	15
☐ 1970	Curly Culp - Chiefs	20	10
☐ 1971	Dick Butkus - Bears	30	15
☐ 1972	Larry Csonka/Jim Plunkett	30	15

COMPLETE SPORTS

(Complete Sports Publishing)

DATE	COVER/FEATURE	Nr-Mt	Ex
☐ 1961	Johnny Unitas - Colts	40	15
☐ 1961	Roman Gabrial - NC St	35	15
☐ 10/62	Jim Brown - Browns	45	20

DATE	COVER/FEATURE	Nr-Mt	Ex
☐ 1/63	Tom McDonald - Eagles	30	15
☐ 11/65	Fran Tarkenton Vikings	30	15
☐ 1/66	Cookie Gilchrist - Broncos	25	10
☐ 9/66	Joe Namath - Jets	35	15
☐ 9/67	Gale Sayers - Bears	30	15
☐ 11/67	Len Dawson -Chiefs	30	15
☐ 7/68	Donny Anderson -Packers	30	15
☐ 9/68	Roman Gabriel - Rams	25	10
☐ 11/68	Gale Sayers / Jim Kelly	20	10
☐ 1/69	John Unitas - Colts	25	15
☐ 11/69	Fran Tarkenton - Giants	25	15
☐ 1/70	Dick Butkus - Bears	40	20
☐ 11/70	John Unitas -Colts	25	12
☐ 10/70	Kansas City Chiefs	25	12
☐ F/71	Fran Tarkenton - Vikings	25	12
☐ S/71	Dick Butkus -Bears	25	15
☐ 2/72	Larry Brown - Redskins	15	10
☐ F/72	Duane Thomas-Cowboys	20	10
☐ S/72	Larry Csonka/Jim Plunkett	10	20
☐ F/73	Fran Tarkenton-Vikings	20	10

CORD SPORTSFACTS PRO FOOTBALL GUIDE & REPORT

(Cord Communications Group)

DATE	COVER/FEATURE	Nr-Mt	Ex
☐ 1969	John Mackey - Colts	20	10
☐ 1969	Sonny Jurgensen - Redskins	20	10
☐ 1970	Roman Gabriel - Rams	20	10
☐ 1970	Daryl Lamonica- Raiders	20	10
☐ 1971	Ken Willard - 49ers	20	10
☐ 1971	Ron Johnson - Giants	20	10
☐ 1972	Duane Thomas-Cowboys	20	10
☐ 1972	Dick Butkus - Bears	25	10
☐ 1972	Tom Gatewood-Notre Dame	20	10
☐ 1973	Larry Csonka - Dolphins	20	10
☐ 1973	Larry Brown - Redskins	20	10
☐ 1974	Larry Csonka - Dolphins	15	10
☐ 1974	OJ Simpson - Bills	15	7
☐ 1975	Franco Harris- Steelers	15	7
☐ 1976	Franco Harris- Steelers	15	7
☐ 1977	OJ Simpson - Bills	15	7
☐ 1981	Jack Lambert - Steelers	15	7

COUNTRYWIDE SPORTS

DATE	COVER/FEATURE	Nr-Mt	Ex
☐ 10/71	John Brodie - 49ers	20	10
☐ 1/70	Bryant/Snyder - OU	20	10

DALLAS COWBOYS

Dallas Cowboys weekly.

DATE	COVER/FEATURE	Nr-Mt	Ex
☐ 11/11/89	Tom Rafferty	15	7
☐ 10/13/90	D. Stubbs	15	7

DAVE CAMPBELL TEXAS FOOTBALL

Also published as 'Texas Football'.
Very popular programs. Started in 1960

DATE	COVER/FEATURE	Nr-Mt	Ex
☐ 1960		200	100
☐ 1961-1965		100	50
☐ 1966-1967		40	25
☐ 1968-1970		30	15
☐ 1971-1975		20	10
☐ 1976-1985		20	10
☐ 1986-1990		15	7
☐ 1991-1997		10	5

DELL PRO FOOTBALL

DATE	COVER/FEATURE	Nr-Mt	Ex
☐ 1958	#1 Bobby Layne - Lions	45	15
☐ 1958	#5 Bob Reifsnyder - Navy	35	15
☐ 1959	#10 Johnny Unitas - Colts	40	15
☐ 1959	#11 Bob Anderson - Army	20	10
☐ 1960	#17 Bob Schloredt - Wash	25	10
☐ 1960	D. Meredith/C. Conerly	20	8

☐ 1961	#22 Paul Hornung-Packers	40	15
☐ 1961	#23 Ernie Davis-Syracuse	45	20
☐ 1962	#28 J. Brown/J.Taylor	35	20
☐ 1962	#29 Sonny Gibbs - TCU	20	10
☐ 1963	Bart Starr - Packers	30	15
☐ 1963	Jim Taylor - Packers	30	8
☐ 1964	Y.A. Tittle - Giants	25	8
☐ 1964	#41 Jim Brown - Brown	35	15
☐ 1965	#46 J. Unitas/ J.Namath	30	15
☐ 1965	#47 F.Tarkenton-Vikings	20	10
☐ 1966	#52 P.Hornung/J Taylor	15	10
☐ 1966	#58 Gale Sayers - Bears	30	10
☐ 1967	#59 Bart Starr - Packers	25	10
☐ 1967	#35 Jim Taylor - Packers	25	10
☐ 1967	#40 YA Tittle - Giants	25	10
☐ 1967	#52 P.Hornung/J.Taylor	25	10
☐ 1967	#53 G.Sayers/J. Namath	25	10
☐ 1968	#64 D.Anderson/ Packers	25	10
☐ 1969	Joe Namath - Jets	20	10
☐ 1971	Namath/Lamonica	20	10
☐ 1972	Roger Staubach - Cowboys	15	7
☐ 1973	Bob Griese/Dolphins	15	7
☐ 1974	Larry Csonka - Dolphins	15	7

END ZONE
(Sports Quarterly Pub)

DATE	COVER/FEATURE	Nr-Mt	Ex
☐ 1970	Vince Clements	15	7

ESPN

DATE	COVER/FEATURE	Nr-Mt	Ex
☐ 1995	Troy Aikman - Cowboys	20	10

EAST TEXAS FOOTBALL

DATE	COVER/FEATURE	Nr-Mt	Ex
☐	Don Meredith -Dallas	30	15

FLUOR FOOTBALL FORECASTER
(Fluor Corp)
9/21/46-1/1/49 magazine weekly during Season.

FOOTBALL

DATE	COVER/FEATURE	Nr-Mt	Ex
☐ 1935	Potsy Clark Pro Football	100	150

FOOTBALL ACTION

DATE	COVER/FEATURE	Nr-Mt	Ex
☐ 1976	Joe Namath - Jets	20	10
☐ 1976	OJ Simpson - Bills	20	10
☐ 1981	Jim Plunkett - Raiders	20	10
☐ 1983	Don Shula - Dolphins	15	10
☐ 1986	Dan Marino - Dolphins	25	10

FOOTBALL ALIBIS AND POSTMORTEMS
(Athletic Publications)
1944-46   Weekly during season.

FOOTBALL BETTING GUIDE

DATE	COVER/FEATURE	Nr-Mt	Ex
☐ 1977	OJ Simpson	20	10

FOOTBALL FACTS

DATE	COVER/FEATURE	Nr-Mt	Ex
☐ 1947	....	20	10

FOOTBALL FORM
(Leonard Yormark - Magazine)
10/14/45-12/1/45

FOOTBALL DIGEST
(Simon Publishing)

DATE	COVER/FEATURE	Nr-Mt	Ex
☐ 1947	Johnny Lujack Notre Dame	50	25
☐ 1948	Gene Rosides	40	20

☐ 1949	Emile Sitko - Notre Dame	40	20
☐ 1950	Ohio State	30	15
☐ 1951	Fred Benner SM	30	15
☐ 1952	Hugh McKelley - Wash	30	15
☐ 12/67	....	30	15
☐ 4/68	Bart Starr - Packers	30	15
☐ 8/68	Darryl Lamonica - Raiders	20	10
☐ 11/68	49ers	20	10

FOOTBALL DIGEST
(Century Publishing Co.)

DATE	COVER/FEATURE	Nr-Mt	Ex
☐ 9/71	Gene Washington-49ers	30	15
☐ 10/71	Sonny Jurgenson-Redskins	30	15
☐ 11/71	Bill Munson - Lions	20	10
☐ 12/71	Dick Gordon - Bears	20	10
☐ 1/72	John Brodie-49ers	20	10
☐ 2/72	Osborn - Vikings	15	10
☐ 3/72	John Brockington - Packers	15	10
☐ 4/72	Duane Thomas - Cowboys	15	10
☐ 5/72	Fran Tarkenton - Vikings	15	10
☐ 6/72	Darryl Lamonica-Raiders	15	10
☐ 7/72	Darryl Lamonica - Raiders	15	10
☐ 9/72	Dick Butkus - Bears	25	15
☐ 10/72	Len Dawson - Chiefs	15	10
☐ 11/72	Joe Namath - Jets	20	10
☐ 12/72	Mercury Morris - Dolphins	20	10
☐ 1/73	Dick Butkus - Bears	30	15
☐ 2/73	Terry Bradshaw - Steelers	20	10
☐ 3/73	John Brockington - Packers	20	10
☐ 4/73	Bob Griese - Dolphins	20	10
☐ 6/73	Norm Snead - Eagles	15	10
☐ 8/73	OJ Simpson - Bills	15	10
☐ 9/73	Larry Csonka - Dolphins	15	10
☐ 10/73	Joe Greene -Steelers	15	10
☐ 11/73	Bobby Douglas - Bears	15	10
☐ 12/73	Daryle Lamonica -Raiders	15	10
☐ 1/74	Chuck Foreman - Vikings	15	10
☐ 2/74	John Hadl - Chargers	15	10
☐ 3/74	OJ Simpson - Bills	15	10
☐ 4/74	Larry Csonka- Dolphins	15	10
☐ 6/74	Calvin Hill - Cowboys	15	10
☐ 8/74	Archie Manning - Saints	35	20
☐ 9/74	Bob Griese /John Hadl	15	10
☐ 12/74	John Brockington - Packers	15	10
☐ 1/75	Ken Stabler - Raiders	15	10
☐ 2/75	Jim Hart-Cards	15	10
☐ 3/75	Ken Stabler - Raiders	15	10
☐ 4/75	Pittsburgh Steelers	15	10
☐ 6/75	Ken Anderson - Bengals	15	10
☐ 8/75	Otis Armstrong -Chiefs	15	10
☐ 9/75	Terry Bradshaw -Steelers	15	10
☐ 10/75	Jim Plunkett - Patriots	15	10
☐ 11/75	Wally Chambers - Bears	15	10
☐ 12/75	Joe Namath - Jets	15	10
☐ 1/76	Mercury Morris - Dolphins	15	10
☐ 2/76	Jeff Siemon - Vikings	10	5
☐ 3/76	OJ Simpson - Bills	10	5
☐ 4/76	Super Bowl	10	5
☐ 6/76	Dan Pastorini - Oilers	10	5
☐ 8/76	Bert Jones - Colts	10	5
☐ 9/76	Jack Lambert - Steelers	12	5
☐ 10/76	Roger Staubach- Cowboys	10	5
☐ 1/77	Fran Tarkenton - Vikings	10	5
☐ 2/77	Jim Langer - Vikings	10	5
☐ 3/77	Ken Stabler - Raiders	12	5
☐ 4/77	Superbowl	10	5
☐ 6/77	Steve Grogan - Patriots	10	5
☐ 8/77	Greg Pruitt - Browns	10	5
☐ 9/77	Joe Namath - Jets	12	5
☐ 10/77	T. Bardshaw/K. Stabler	12	5
☐ 11/77	Walter Payton - Bears	15	5
☐ 12/77	Ken Anderson - Bengals	10	5
☐ 1/78	Jack Youngblood - Rams	10	5

☐ 2/78	Bert Jones - Colts	10	5
☐ 3/78	Tony Dorsett - Cowboys	12	5
☐ 4/78	Craig Morton - Cowboys	12	5
☐ 6/78	Jim Zorn - Seahawks	12	5
☐ 8/78	Chuck Foreman - Vikings	10	5
☐ 9/78	Roger Staubach - Cowboys	15	5
☐ 10/78	Ron Jaworski - Eagles	10	5
☐ 11/78	OJ Simpson - Bills	10	5
☐ 12/78	Franco Harris - Steelers	12	5
☐ 1/79	Pat Haden - Rams	10	5
☐ 2/79	Don Shula - Dolphins	10	5
☐ 3/79	Earl Campbell - Oilers	12	5
☐ 4/79	Terry Bradshaw - Steelers	12	5
☐ 6/79	Archie Manning - Saints	15	5
☐ 8/79	Craig Morton -Cowboys	15	5
☐ 9/79	Steve Grogan - Patriots	10	5
☐ 10/79	Bill Bergey-Eagles	10	5
☐ 11/79	Dan Fouts - Chargers	10	5
☐ 12/79	David Whitehurst - Packers	10	5
☐ 1/80	Larry Csonka - Dolphins	12	5
☐ 2/80	Terry Bradshaw - Steelers	12	4
☐ 3/80	Dan Fouts - Chargers	10	4
☐ 4/80	Lynn Swann - Steelers	10	4
☐ 6/80	Lee Roy Selmon - Cowboys	10	4
☐ 10/80	Harry Carson - Giants	8	4
☐ 11/80	Walter Payton - Bears	20	10
☐ 12/80	Russ Francis - 49ers	8	4
☐ 1/81	Wilbert Montgomery - Eagles	8	4
☐ 2/81	Bert Jones- Colts	8	4
☐ 4/81	Phil Simms - Giants	8	4
☐ 6/81	Steve Bartkowski - Eagles	8	4
☐ 8/81	Joe Ferguson - Bills	8	4
☐ 9/81	Jim Plunkett - Raiders	10	5
☐ 10/81	Tommy Kramer - Vikings	8	4
☐ 11/81	OJ Anderson - Bengels	8	4
☐ 12/81	Danny White - Cowboys	10	4
☐ 1/82	David Woodley - Dolphins	8	4
☐ 2/82	Ron Jaworski - Eagles	8	4
☐ 3/82	George Rogers - Saints	8	4
☐ 4/82	Ken Anderson - Bengels	8	4
☐ 6/82	Joe Montana - 49ers	20	10
☐ 8/82	Joe Theismann - Redskins	8	4
☐ 9/82	Bert Jones - Colts	8	4
☐ 10/82	Joe Klecko - Jets	8	4
☐ 11/82	Terry Bradshaw - Steelers	10	5
☐ 12/82	Joe Montana- 49ers	15	10
☐ 1/83	Dan Fouts - Chargers	10	5
☐ 2/83	William Andrews	8	4
☐ 3/83	Randy White - Cowboys	10	5
☐ 4/83	Marcus Allen - Raiders	10	5
☐ 6/83	John Riggins - Redskins	8	4
☐ 8/83	Herschel Walker- Cowboys	10	5
☐ 9/83	Lawrence Taylor - Giants	8	4
☐ 10/83	Doug Williams - Redskins	8	4
☐ 11/83	Kellen Winslow - Chargers	8	4
☐ 12/83	Lynn Dickey -Steelers	8	4
☐ 1/84	Brian Sipe - Browns	8	4
☐ 2/84	Danny White-Cowboys	10	5
☐ 3/84	Eric Dickerson - Rams	8	4
☐ 4/84	Joe Theismann - Redskins	8	4
☐ 6/84	Dan Marino - Dolphins	20	10
☐ 8/84	Curt Warner - Seahawks	8	4
☐ 9/84	Marcus Allen - Raiders	12	4
☐ 10/84	Franco Harris - Steelers	8	4
☐ 11/84	John Elway - Broncos	20	10
☐ 12/84	Billy Sims - Lions	8	4
☐ 1/85	Tony Dorsett - Cowboys	8	4
☐ 2/85	Joe Montana - 49ers	20	10
☐ 3/85	Walter Payton - Bears	12	4
☐ 4/85	Dan Marino - Dolphins	20	10
☐ 6/85	Eric Dickerson - Rams	8	4
☐ 8/85	Doug Flutie - Generals	8	4
☐ 9/85	Dave Kreig - Seahawks	8	4
☐ 10/85	Danny White - Cowboys	8	4
☐ 11/85	Mark Gastineau - Jets	8	4

☐ 12/85	Neil Lomax - Cards	8	4
☐ 1/86	Howie Long - Raiders	8	4
☐ 2/86	Jim McMahon - Bears	8	4
☐ 3/86	Dieter Brock - Rams	8	4
☐ 4/86	Marcus Allen - Raiders	8	4
☐ 6/86	Super Bowl XX	8	4
☐ 8/86	Joe Morris - Giants	8	4
☐ 9/86	Jim McMahon - Bears	8	4
☐ 10/86	Louis Lipps - Steelers	8	4
☐ 11/86	James Lofton - Packers	8	4
☐ 12/86	Dan Fouts - Chargers	8	4
☐ 1/87	Herschel Walker - Cowboys	8	4
☐ 2/87	Walter Payton - Bears	10	5
☐ 3/87	Jay Schroeder - Giants	8	4
☐ 4/87	Lawrence Taylor - Giants	8	4
☐ 6/87	SuperBowl XX1	8	4
☐ 8/87	Dan Marino - Dolphins	15	10
☐ 9/87	Bernie Kosar - Browns	8	4
☐ 10/87	Tommy Kramer - Vikings	8	4
☐ 11/87	Tony Eason - Patriots	8	4
☐ 12/87	Curt Warner - Seahawks	5	3
☐ 1/88	Joe Montana - 49ers	10	5
☐ 2/88	Walter Payton - Bears	10	5
☐ 3/88	Eric Dickerson - Rams	5	3
☐ 4/88	Jerry Rice - 49ers	15	10
☐ 6/88	Super Bowl XXII	5	3
☐ 8/88	John Elway - Broncos	15	10
☐ 9/88	Phil Simms - Giants	5	3
☐ 10/88	Morten Anderson - Saints	5	3
☐ 11/88	Bennett/ Conlan	5	3
☐ 12/88	Chris Doleman - Vikings	5	3
☐ 1/89	Brian Bosworth - Seahawks	5	3
☐ 2/89	Mike Singletary - Bears	5	3
☐ 3/89	Keith Jackson - Eagles	5	3
☐ 4/89	Boomer Esiason - Bengels	5	3
☐ 6/89	Troy Aikman - Cowboys	5	3
☐ 8/89	Warren Moon - Oilers	5	3
☐ 9/89	Jim Everett - Rams	5	3
☐ 10/89	Vinny Testaverde - Bucs	5	3
☐ 11/89	Jim Kelly - Bills	12	5
☐ 12/89	Lawrence Taylor - Giants	5	3
☐ 1/90	Roger Craig - 49ers	5	3
☐ 2/90	John Elway - Broncos	15	5
☐ 3/90	Barry Sanders- Lions	15	5
☐ 4/90	Joe Montana - 49ers	10	4
☐ 6/90	Keith McCants - Bucs	5	3
☐ 8/90	Christian Okoye - Chiefs	5	3
☐ 9/90	James Brooks - Bengals	5	3
☐ 10/90	Bill Fralik - Falcons	5	3
☐ 11/90	Randall Cunningham - Eagles	5	3
☐ 12/90	Bo Jackson - Raiders	5	3
☐ 91-97	Common cover	4	2
☐ 91-97	Joe Montana - 49ers	10	4
☐ 85-97	Walter Payton - Bears	10	5
☐ 85-97	Dan Marino - Dolphins	15	4
☐ 85-97	John Elway-Broncos	15	5
☐ 85-97	Barry Sanders - Lions	15	5
☐ 85-97	Emmit Smith - Cowboys	15	5

FOOTBALL DIGEST YEARBOOK

DATE	COVER/FEATURE	Nr-Mt	Ex
☐ 1986	Marino/Montana	15	5
☐ 1987	Marino/Montana	15	5

FOOTBALL FIGURES WEEKLY

(Zimmerman)
9/29/41-12/41 Newspaper

FOOTBALL FORECAST

(Fawcett Publications)

DATE	COVER/FEATURE	Nr-Mt	Ex
☐ 1962	YA Tittle - Giants	30	15
☐ 1963	Bart Starr - Packers	35	15

FOOTBALL FORECASTER
(Lexington Library)

DATE	COVER/FEATURE	Nr-Mt	Ex
☐ 1970	Jim Plunkett	12	5
☐ 1976	OJ Simpson	10	5
☐ 1977	Bert Jones	10	5
☐ 1978	Tony Dorsett	10	5
☐ 1979	Earl Campbell	10	5
☐ 1980	Dan Fouts	10	5
☐ 1981	Walter Payton	15	5
☐ 1982	Richard Todd	10	5
☐ 1983	Mark Gastineau	10	5
☐ 1984	Riggins/Allen	10	5
☐ 1985	Walter Payton	10	5
☐ 1986	Marcus Allen	10	5
☐ 1987	Eric Dickerson	10	5

FOOTBALL FORM AND DIGEST
(7Up Bottling Company - Newspaper)
1938-1945 Weekly during season. Covers pro and college.

FOOTBALL NEWSLETTER
(National Sports Bureau)

DATE	COVER/FEATURE	Nr-Mt	Ex
☐ 1954-1956 12 issues per year		30	15

FOOTBALL PREVIEW

DATE	COVER/FEATURE	Nr-Mt	Ex
☐ 1978	Ken Stabler - Raiders	10	5
☐ 1980	Ken Stabler - Raiders	10	5

FOOTBALL PREVUES

DATE	COVER/FEATURE	Nr-Mt	Ex
☐ 1947	Johnny Lujack	45	10

FOOTBALL ROUNDUP
(Sports Quarterly Publications)

DATE	COVER/FEATURE	Nr-Mt	Ex
☐ 1960	Mike Ditka - Pitt.	40	20
☐ 1961	Joe Romig - Colorado	30	20
☐ 1962	Sonny Gibbs -Texas Christian	30	15
☐ 1963	George Mira -Miami	30	15
☐ 1964	Jim Grisham - Oklahoma	30	15
☐ 1965	Donny Anderson - Texas Tech	30	15
☐ 1966	Bob Griese - Purdue	35	20
☐ 1967	Lenny Snow	20	10
☐ 1968	Jim Seymour	20	10
☐ 1969	Ron Carpenter - NC St	20	10
☐ 1970	Bob Jacobs - Wyo.	20	10
☐ 1971	Ed Marinaro- Cornell	20	10
☐ 1972	Jerry Sisemore - Texas	20	10
☐ 1973	Randy Gradishar - Ohio St	20	10
☐ 1974	P. Donovan/R.Stillwell	20	10
☐ 1975	Bill Marek	15	7
☐ 1976	Jim Smith	15	7
☐ 1977	Wes Chandler	15	7
☐ 1978	Chuck Fusina - Penn. St	15	7
☐ 1979	Johnny Johnson - Texas	15	7
☐ 1980	Leonard Mitchell	15	7
☐ 1981	Hershel Walker - Georgia	15	7
☐ 1982	Joe Montana - Notre Dame	20	7

FOOTBALL SPORTSCENE

DATE	COVER/FEATURE	Nr-Mt	Ex
☐ 1972	Joe Namath - Jets	25	10

FOOTBALL STARS - DELL

DATE	COVER/FEATURE	Nr-Mt	Ex
☐ 1952	Harry Agganis - Boston	40	20
☐ 1953	Gial - Minnesota	35	15

FOOTBALL STORY

DATE	COVER/FEATURE	Nr-Mt	Ex
☐ 1959		30	15

FRANK GIFFORD FOOTBALL
(Popular Library)

DATE	COVER/FEATURE	Nr-Mt	Ex
☐ 1961	Paul Hornung - Packers	40	20

GAME PLAN COLLEGE FOOTBALL

DATE	COVER/FEATURE	Nr-Mt	Ex
☐ 1970	Archie Manning	20	10
☐ 1971	Marinaro/Bertelsen	15	10
☐ 1972	Rich Glover - Nebraska	20	10
☐ 1973	R. Gradisher - Ohio St.	20	10
☐ 1974	Pat Haden - USC	15	10
☐ 1975	Tony Dorsett - Pitt	20	10
☐ 1976	Tony Dorsett - Pitt	20	10
☐ 1977		15	8
☐ 1978	Joe Montana - Notre Dame	25	12
☐ 1979	Bobby Bowden - Fla. St.	15	8
☐ 1981-1990		15	8

GAME PLAN PRO FOOTBALL

DATE	COVER/FEATURE	Nr-Mt	Ex
☐ 1971	George Blanda- Raiders	20	10
☐ 1972	Roger Staubach/ Bob Griese	25	10
☐ 1973	Larry Csonka - Dolphins	20	10
☐ 1974	Fran Tarkenton -Vikings	20	10
☐ 1975	Franco Harris-Steelers	20	10
☐ 1976	Roger Staubach - Cowboys	20	10
☐ 1977	Walter Payton-Bears	20	10
☐ 1978	Bert Jones - Colts	15	10
☐ 1979	Archie Manning - Old Miss	40	20
☐ 1980	Joe Ferguson - Bills	15	10
☐ 1981	Ricky Bell - Bucs	15	7
☐ 1983	J.Theisman/ K.Anderson	15	10
☐ 1985	John Elway - Bronco's	20	10
☐ 1986	Phil Simms - Giants	15	7
☐ 1987	John Elway - Bronco's	20	10
☐ 1989	Neil Lomax - Cardinals	10	5
☐ 1990	Dan Marino/Dolphins	15	5

GOAL POST COLLEGE FOOTBALL
(JMJ enterprises)

DATE	COVER/FEATURE	Nr-Mt	Ex
☐ 1975	Sedrick McIntyre	10	5
☐ 1976	Ricky Bell	10	5
☐ 1977	George Woodard	10	5
☐ 1978	IM Hipp	10	5
☐ 1979	Billy Sims	10	5
☐ 1980	Amos Lawrence	10	5
☐ 1981	John Fourade	10	5
☐ 1982	Jim Kelly	30	20
☐ 1983	Wayne Peace	10	5

GOAL POST PRO FOOTBALL
(JMJ Enterprises)

DATE	COVER/FEATURE	Nr-Mt	Ex
☐ 1975	OJ Simpson - Bills	15	10
☐ 1976	Fran Tarkenton/C. Foreman	10	7
☐ 1977	Lawrence McCutheon - Rams	10	7
☐ 1978	Craig Morton - Broncos	15	10
☐ 1979	Brian Sipe - Browns	10	5
☐ 1980	Terry Bradshaw - Steelers	15	5
☐ 1981	Joe Ferguson - Bills	10	5
☐ 1981	Ken Anderson - Bengels	10	5

GREAT MOMENT IN SPORTS
(Famous Pub)

DATE	COVER/FEATURE	Nr-Mt	Ex
☐ 12/59	Jim Brown - Browns	25	10
☐ 1961	Bob Schloredt - Redskins	25	10
☐ 1962	Paul Hornung- Packers	25	10
☐ 3/63	Baltimore Colts	25	10
☐ 12/63	Roger Staubach - Cowboys	25	10
☐ 3/64	YA Tittle - Giants	25	10

GRIDIRON'S COLLEGE YEARBOOK
(Champion Sports Publishing)

DATE	COVER/FEATURE	Nr-Mt	Ex
☐ 1972	Pruitt/Sixkiller	15	8
☐ 1973	Mark Harmon	15	8
☐ 1974	Ara Parseghian	15	8

GRIDIRON PRO YEARBOOK
(Champion Sports Publishing)

DATE	COVER/FEATURE	Nr-Mt	Ex
☐ 1972	Gale Sayers/Namath/OJ	20	10
☐ 1973	OJ Simpson/Bob Griese	20	10
☐ 1974	OJ Simpson - Bills	20	10
☐ 1975	Harris/Bradshaw	15	10
☐ 1976	Simpson/Namath/Stabler	15	10
☐ 1977	Csonka/Stabler	15	10
☐ 1978	Staubach/T.Bradshaw	15	10
☐ 1979	Terry Bradshaw - Steelers	15	8
☐ 1980	Franco Harris - Steelers	15	8
☐ 1993	Steve Young - 49ers	15	5

GRIDIRON WEEKLY
(Athletic Publications - Newspaper)
1944-1946

HALL OF FAME FOOTBALL
(Modern Day Periodicals)

DATE	COVER/FEATURE	Nr-Mt	Ex
☐ 1974	Brown/Grange/Graham	15	8

INSIDE FOOTBALL
(Sport Mag)

DATE	COVER/FEATURE	Nr-Mt	Ex
☐ 1961	Johnny Unitas/ Ernie Davis	30	15
☐ 1962	Jim Taylor -Packers	35	10
☐ 1963	J.Brown/G.Mira	30	10
☐ 1963	Roger Staubach - Navy	30	10
☐ 1964	Roger Staubach - Navy	30	10
☐ 1965	Joe Namath - Jets	30	10
☐ 1967	Terry Hanratty-Notre Dame	25	10
☐ 1968	OJ Simpson - USC	25	10
☐ 1969	Sunny Jurgenson/Lombardi	20	10
☐ 1971	Sonny Sixkiller - Wash	15	8
☐ 1978	Ken Stabler-Raiders	15	10

INSIDE FOOTBALL
(Sports Quarterly Pub)

DATE	COVER/FEATURE	Nr-Mt	Ex
☐ 1977	Joe Namath Jets	15	8
☐ 1978	Ken Stabler - Raiders	15	8
☐ 1979	Terry Bradshaw - Steelers	15	8
☐ 1980	Franco Harris - Steelers	15	8
☐ 1981	Mark Van Eeghan -Raiders	15	8

INSIDE SPORTS PAUL HURNUNG
FOOTBALL MAGAZINE
(H.S. Publications)

DATE	COVER/FEATURE	Nr-Mt	Ex
☐ 1962	Paul Hornung - Packers	35	15

ILLUSTRATED FOOTBALL

DATE	COVER/FEATURE	Nr-Mt	Ex
☐ 1932	Art Drawing	100	50
☐ 1933	none issued		
☐ 1934	Art Drawing	55	35
☐ 1935	Art Drawing	50	35
☐ 1936	Art Drawing	50	35
☐ 1937	Art Drawing	50	35
☐ 1938	Art Drawing	50	35
☐ 1939	Art Drawing	50	35
☐ 1940	Art Drawing	50	35
☐ 1941	Art Drawings	40	25
☐ 1942	Frank Sinkwich	40	25
☐ 1943	Douglas Kenna	40	25
☐ 1944	Joe Sullivan	40	25
☐ 1945	Bill Hacket	40	25
☐ 1946	H.Wedemeyer	40	25
☐ 1947	Bobby Layne	40	25
☐ 1948	Chuck Bednarik	30	15
☐ 1949	J. Owens	30	15
☐ 1950	Bobby Cox	30	15
☐ 1951	L.Richter	30	15
☐ 1952	Bob Kenned	30	15
☐ 1953	Art Drawing	30	15

LINDY'S PRO FOOTBALL
These magazines started in 1987. May have regional covers

DATE	COVER/FEATURE	Nr-Mt	Ex
☐ 1990	Bo Jackson - Raiders	10	5
☐ 1991	Raiders	10	5
☐ 1995	Troy Aikman - Cowboys	10	5

LOMBARDI
(Macfadden-Bartell)

DATE	COVER/FEATURE	Nr-Mt	Ex
☐ 1970	Vince Lombardi	25	10

KICK OFF FOOTBALL YEARBOOK

DATE	COVER/FEATURE	Nr-Mt	Ex
☐ 1956	Jim Swink - TCU	30	15
☐ 1957	Walt Kowalczyk - MS	30	15
☐ 1958	Bob Anderson - Army	30	15
☐ 1959	Billy Cannon - LSU	30	15
☐ 1960	Alan Ameche - Colts	30	15
☐ 1961	Ernie Davis - Syracuse	45	25
☐ 1962	George Mira - Miami	30	15
☐ 1963	George Mira - Miami	30	15
☐ 1964	Roger Staubach - Navy	40	25
☐ 1966	Floyd Little-Syracuse	20	10
☐ 1967	Terry Hanratty - Notre Dame	20	10
☐ 1968	OJ Simpson -USC	20	10
☐ 1969	Rex Kern- Ohio St.	20	10
☐ 1970	Archie Manning - Old Miss	40	20
☐ 1971	Sixkiller/Gatewood	20	10
☐ 1972	John Hurnagel -Penn St	15	10
☐ 1973	Archie Davis - USC	20	10
☐ 1974	Archie Griffin - Ohio St	15	7

MICHIGAN SPORTS SCENES

DATE	COVER/FEATURE	Nr-Mt	Ex
☐ 11/67	Duffy Daugherty	15	10

MOBIL PIGSKIN PROPHET
(LB Chapman, Mobil Oil Corp)
1940-1941 Newspaper format

MOBIL TOUCHDOWN TIPS
(Mobil Oil Corp)
1946-1948 Newspaper

NATION-WIDE FOOTBALL
1961-present 12 weekly issues during the season

NEWSWEEK
See 'Newsweek in General Magazines

NFL PLAYERS AUTOGRAPH YEARBOOK

DATE	COVER/FEATURE	Nr-Mt	Ex
☐ 1969	Roman Gabriel	20	10

NFL PREVIEW
(Lexington Libary)

DATE	COVER/FEATURE	Nr-Mt	Ex
☐ 1981	Steve Bartkowski - Falcons	12	8
☐ 1982	Billy Simms - Oilers	12	8
☐ 1983	John Riggins - Redskins	15	8
☐ 1984	Marcus Allen - Raiders	15	8
☐ 1985	Dan Marino - Dolphins	20	8
☐ 1986	Dan Marino/Montana	20	8

NATIONAL LEAGUE YEARBOOK

DATE	COVER/FEATURE	Nr-Mt	Ex
☐ 1959	....	35	15
☐ 1960	....	25	15
☐ 1961	....	25	15

NOTRE DAME FOOTBALL PREVIEW

DATE	COVER/FEATURE	Nr-Mt	Ex
☐ 1991	Rick Mirer	15	10
☐ 1992	Jerome Bettis	15	10
☐ 1993-1997	....	10	5

OFFICIAL AUTOGRAPH YEARBOOK

DATE	COVER/FEATURE	Nr-Mt	Ex
☐ 1968	....	30	15
☐ 1969	Roman Gabriel -Rams	30	15

OFFICIAL FOOTBALL
(Official sports Inc)

DATE	COVER/FEATURE	Nr-Mt	Ex
☐ 1964	Jim Brown - Browns	30	15

OFFICIAL PRO FOOTBALL
(Official Sports Inc.) ....

DATE	COVER/FEATURE	Nr-Mt	Ex
☐ 1964	YA Tittle - Giants	25	12

OFFICIAL PRO FOOTBALL YEARBOOK
(Reliance Publications) ....

DATE	COVER/FEATURE	Nr-Mt	Ex
☐ 1979	Payton/Dorsett/Campbell	20	12
☐ 1980	Bradshaw/Payton/Fouts	20	10
☐ 1981	Four Quarterbacks	20	10
☐ 1982	Tony Dorsett	15	7
☐ 1983	John Elway/L. Taylor	20	10
☐ 1984	Dickerson/Allen	15	10

OFFICIAL SPORTS MAGAZINE

DATE	COVER/FEATURE	Nr-Mt	Ex
☐ 12/65	Frank Ryan/Jim Brown	25	15

PAC-8

DATE	COVER/FEATURE	Nr-Mt	Ex
☐ 1967	Gary Beban	20	10

PETERSON COLLEGE FOOTBALL

DATE	COVER/FEATURE	Nr-Mt	Ex
☐ 1980	A.Schlicter/R.Campbell	20	10

PETERSON PRO FOOTBALL

DATE	COVER/FEATURE	Nr-Mt	Ex
☐ 1956	First issue Ron Waler	50	15
☐ 1957	Frank Gifford - Giants	35	15
☐ 1958	Jon Arnett - Rams	35	15
☐ 1959	Action	35	15
☐ 1960	Action	35	15
☐ 1961	Action	30	15
☐ 1962	Jim Brown - Browns	40	20
☐ 1963	YA Tittle - Giants	30	15
☐ 1964	Jim Brown - Browns	30	15
☐ 1965 - 1969		None Issued	
☐ 1970	Roman Gabrial - Rams	20	10
☐ 1971	Bart Starr - Packers	20	10
☐ 1972	Washington Redskins	15	10
☐ 1973	Bob Griese - Dolphins	20	10
☐ 1974	OJ Simpson - Bills	20	10
☐ 1975	Pittsburgh Steelers	20	10
☐ 1976	Bert Jones - Colts	20	10
☐ 1977	Ken Stabler - Raiders	25	10
☐ 1978	Roger Staubach - Cowboys	25	10
☐ 1979	Terry Bradshaw-Steelers	15	7
☐ 1980	V.Ferragamo/P. Haden	15	7
☐ 1981	Jim Plunkett - Patriots	15	7
☐ 1982	Joe Montana - 49ers	30	15

DATE	COVER/FEATURE	Nr-Mt	Ex
☐ 1983	Joe Theisman - Redskins	15	7
☐ 1984	Wendell Tyler-49ers	15	7
☐ 1985	Calvin Muhammad	15	7
☐ 1986	Walter Payton - Bears	20	10
☐ 1987	H.Walker/Moon	12	7
☐ 1988	Jerry Rice- 49ers	15	7
☐ 1989	Joe Montana - 49ers	15	7
☐ 1990	Joe Montana - 49ers	15	7
☐ 1995	Troy Aikman - Dallas	15	7
☐ 1991-1997	....	10	3

PIC QUARTERLY

DATE	COVER/FEATURE	Nr-Mt	Ex
☐ Fall/49	(Justice/NC)	40	10

PIGSKIN PREVIEW
(Sportstime Publ)

DATE	COVER/FEATURE	Nr-Mt	Ex
☐ 1979	Charles White	15	8
☐ 1979	Roger Staubach	20	10
☐ 1980	Jack Youngblood	15	10
☐ 1981	Jim Kelly	25	10
☐ 1981	Billy Simms	15	8
☐ 1982	Rod Elkins	15	8
☐ 1982	Pete Johnson	15	8
☐ 1983	Col/Pro	15	8

PIGSKIN SALUTE

DATE	COVER/FEATURE	Nr-Mt	Ex
☐ 1951	Art	20	10

PIGSKIN PREVIEW

DATE	COVER/FEATURE	Nr-Mt	Ex
☐ 1980	J.Youngblood-Rams	20	10
☐ 1981	Jim Kelly - Miami	40	15

SPORTS COLLEGE FOOTBALL PREVIEW

DATE	COVER/FEATURE	Nr-Mt	Ex
☐ 10/80	(B.Bryant/J.Elway)	20	10

POPULAR SPORTS KICK OFF

DATE	COVER/FEATURE	Nr-Mt	Ex
☐ 1972	John Huffnagel - Penn St.	20	10
☐ 1973	Davis - USC	20	10
☐ 1974	OJ Simpson - Bills	20	10
☐ 1975	Archie Griffin-Ohio St.	20	10
☐ 1976	Rickey Bell - USC	15	7
☐ 1977	Terry Miller - Okla.	10	7
☐ 1978	T.Dorsett/J.Montana	25	15
☐ 10/79	M.Herrmann/ Purdue	10	7
☐ 10/80	John Elway/Bear Bryant	15	7

POPULAR SPORTS

DATE	COVER/FEATURE	Nr-Mt	Ex
☐ 1978	Joe Montana/Tony Dorsett	20	10

POPULAR SPORTS KICK OFF

DATE	COVER/FEATURE	Nr-Mt	Ex
☐ 1975	Archie Griffen- Ohio St.	20	10
☐ 1976	Rickey Bell- USC	15	7
☐ 1977	Miller-Okla.	15	7

POPULAR SPORTS COLLEGE FOOTBALL PREVIEW
(CBS-Popular Magazine Group) ....

DATE	COVER/FEATURE	Nr-Mt	Ex
☐ 1979	Mark Herrmann	15	7
☐ 1980	John Elway - Stanford	30	15

POPULAR SPORTS FOOTBALL PREVIEW/
PRO FOOTBALL PREVIEW
(CBS Publications/Popular Magazine Group)

DATE	COVER/FEATURE	Nr-Mt	Ex
☐ 1978	Bert Jones - Colts	15	7
☐ 1979	Roger Staubach - Cowboys	15	7
☐ 1980	Tony Dorsett - Cowboys	15	7
☐ 1981	Jim Plunkett - Raiders	15	7

POP SPORTS PRO FOOTBALL

DATE	COVER/FEATURE	Nr-Mt	Ex
☐ 10/78	Tony Dorsett	15	7

POP SPORTS TOUCHDOWN

DATE	COVER/FEATURE	Nr-Mt	Ex
☐ 1974	OJ Simpson	20	7

PRO/COLLEGE FOOTBALL
(Whitestone)

DATE	COVER/FEATURE	Nr-Mt	Ex
☐ 1965	#1 Browns-Giants	40	20
☐ 1966	Lenny Moore-Colts	25	10
☐ 1977	Bert Jones-Colts	15	7
☐ 1979	Terry Bradshaw-Steelers	15	7

PRO & COLLEGE FOOTBALL TODAY
(Phil Publ/Ideal Pub)

DATE	COVER/FEATURE	Nr-Mt	Ex
☐ 1976	Fran Tarkenton	15	8
☐ 1977	Bert Jones	12	8
☐ 1978	Roger Staubach	15	8
☐ 1979	Terry Bradshaw	12	8
☐ 1980	Jack Tatum	10	8

PRO & COLLEGE FOOTBALL SPORTS STARS
(Hewfred Pub)

DATE	COVER/FEATURE	Nr-Mt	Ex
☐ 1968	OJ Simpson	20	8
☐ 1969	J. Namath/F. Tarkenton	20	8
☐ 1970	Len Dawson	20	8
☐ 1971	Roman Gabrial	15	8
☐ 1972	Jim Plunkett	15	8
☐ 1973	Bob Griese	15	8
☐ 1974	Larry Csonka	15	8
☐ 1975	Ken Stabler	15	8

PRO FOOTBALL 1964
(Dell)

DATE	COVER/FEATURE	Nr-Mt	Ex
☐ 1964	Gordie Howe/Bill Russell	20	10

PRO FOOTBALL
(Fawcett)

DATE	COVER/FEATURE	Nr-Mt	Ex
☐ 1961	Paul Hornung - Packers	40	15
☐ 1962	Jim Taylor - Packers	40	15
☐ 1963	Jim Taylor - Packers	35	12

PRO FOOTBALL CHEERLEADERS
Team issued calendars

DATE	COVER/FEATURE	Nr-Mt	Ex
☐ 1981	Raiderettes	20	10

PRO FOOTBALL ALL STARS

DATE	COVER/FEATURE	Nr-Mt	Ex
☐ 1957	Frank Gifford	50	25

PRO FOOTBALL ACTION

DATE	COVER/FEATURE	Nr-Mt	Ex
☐ 1971	Bills /Rams	15	10
☐ 1972	Jim Plunkett - Patriots	15	10

PRO FOOTBALL ALMANAC
(Sport)

DATE	COVER/FEATURE	Nr-Mt	Ex
☐ 1965	Johnny Unitas - Colts	25	15
☐ 1966	John Brodie - 49ers	20	10
☐ 1970	J.Namath/R.Gabriel	20	10
☐ 1971	J. Brodie/K.Willard	15	10

PRO FOOTBALL
(Dell)

DATE	COVER/FEATURE	Nr-Mt	Ex
☐ 1956	Football Action	40	20

☐ 1957	Football Action	40	20
☐ 1958	Bobby Layne - Bears	45	15
☐ 1959	Johnny Unitas - Colts	40	15
☐ 1960	C.Conerly/D Meredith	35	15
☐ 1961	Paul Hornung - Packers	40	15
☐ 1962	Jim Brown/Jim Taylor	40	15
☐ 1963	Y.A. Tittle/NY Giants	35	15
☐ 1964	Jim Brown - Browns	35	15
☐ 1965	J.Namath/J.Unitas	20	10
☐ 1966	Gale Sayers- Bears	25	10
☐ 1967	Bart Starr-Packers	25	10
☐ 1968	Donny Anderson-Packer	20	10
☐ 1969	Joe Namath -Jets	25	10
☐ 1970	Len Dawson -Chiefs	20	10
☐ 1971	Joe Namath-Jets	25	10
☐ 1972	Roger Staubach-Cowboys	25	10
☐ 1973	Bob Griese-Dolphins	20	10
☐ 1974	Larry Csonka-Dolphins	20	10

PRO FOOTBALL
(Hewfred Publicatins)

DATE	COVER/FEATURE	Nr-Mt	Ex
☐ 1971	Joe Namath	20	10
☐ 1972	Roger Staubach	20	10
☐ 1973	Joe Namath	20	10
☐ 1974	OJ Simpson	20	10

PRO FOOTBALL ILLUSTRATED
(Ted Elbert, ed.)

DATE	COVER/FEATURE	Nr-Mt	Ex
☐ 1961	Johnny Unitas - Colts	35	15
☐ 1962	Rams/49ers	35	15
☐ 1962	Green Bay Packers	45	20
☐ 1963	Jim Brown - Browns	30	15
☐ 1964	Jim Brown - Browns	30	15
☐ 1966	Gale Sayers - Bears	45	20
☐ 1967	Joe Namath/J.Unitas	35	15
☐ 1968	Joe Namath - Jets	30	15
☐ 1969	Joe Namath/R.Gabriel	25	10
☐ 1970	Gale Sayers/Leroy Kelly	30	10
☐ 1971	John Brodie/Joe Namath	20	10
☐ 1972	Len Dawson/R.Staubach	25	10
☐ 1972	Joe Namath/F.Tarkenton	20	10
☐ 1973	Larry Csonka - Dolphins	15	5
☐ 1974	OJ Simpson - Bills	15	5
☐ 1975	OJ Simpson/C.Foreman	15	5
☐ 1976	Ken Anderson - Bengels	15	5
☐ 1977	OJ Simpson - Bills	15	5
☐ 1978	Walter Payton - Bears	20	10
☐ 1979	Terry Bradshaw-Steelers	15	10
☐ 1980	OJ Anderson Cardinals	10	5
☐ 1981	Bill Simms	10	5
☐ 1983	Tony Dorsett - Cowboys	10	5
☐ 1985	J. Elway/D.Marino/Mon	15	5
☐ 1986	Jim McMahon - Bears	10	5
☐ 1987	Elway/Marino/Simms	15	5
☐ 1988	Herschel Walker	10	5
☐ 1989	Boomer Esiason - Bengels	7	5
☐ 1990	Joe Montana - 49ers	20	10
☐ 1991 - 1997	....	8	5

PRO FOOTBALL MONTHLY

DATE	COVER/FEATURE	Nr-Mt	Ex
☐ 11/79	R. Staubach/Cowboys	25	10

PRO FOOTBALL NEWSLETTER
1965   (26 issues)

PRO FOOTBALL SPORTS STARS OF
(Hewfred Publications)

DATE	COVER/FEATURE	Nr-Mt	Ex
☐ 1968	Bart Starr - Packers	20	10
☐ 1969	Joe Namath - Jets	20	10

☐ 1970	Len Dawson - Chiefs	15	10
☐ 1971	John Brodie - 49ers	15	7
☐ 1972	Jim Plunkett - Patriots	15	10
☐ 1973	Larry Brown - Redskins	10	5
☐ 1973	Bob Griese - Dolphins	15	5
☐ 1974	Larry Csonka - Dolphins	15	10
☐ 1974	Bob Griese - Dolphins	15	5
☐ 1975	Terry Bradshaw-Steelers	10	5

PRO FOOTBALL WEEKLY

This newsprint started in 1967 an ran through 1978. Many stars were featured on the cover.

PRO FOOTBALL YEARBOOK- RENSE

DATE	COVER/FEATURE	Nr-Mt	Ex
☐ 1957	Pro Football All Star	35	15

PROLOG

DATE	COVER/FEATURE	Nr-Mt	Ex
☐ 1971	(First Cover)	20	10
☐ 1972	Calvin Hill - Cowboys	20	10
☐ 1973	Larry Brown - Redskins	15	5
☐ 1974	Mercury Morris-Dolphins	15	5
☐ 1975	Franco Harris - Steelers	15	5
☐ 1976	Fran Tarkenton - Vikings	15	5
☐ 1977	Bert Jones - Colts	12	5
☐ 1978	Walter Payton - Bears	15	5
☐ 1979	Terry Bradshaw - Steeler	10	5
☐ 1980	Jim Youngblood - Rams	10	5
☐ 1981	Jim Plunkett - Raiders	10	5
☐ 1982	Joe Montana - 49ers	20	10
☐ 1983	Freeman McNeil - Jets	10	5
☐ 1984	Eric Dickerson - Rams	10	5
☐ 1985	Walter Payton - Bears	20	10
☐ 1986	Marcus Allen - Raiders	10	5
☐ 1987	Walter Payton - Bears	10	5
☐ 1988	Jerry Rice - 49ers	20	10
☐ 1989-1997		10	5

PRO SPORTS

DATE	COVER/FEATURE	Nr-Mt	Ex
☐ 1/67	Joe Namath - Jets	20	10
☐ 1/67	Football Action	20	10
☐ 1/68	D. Anderson - Packers	20	10
☐ 11/68	Eagles	20	10
☐ 11/69	J.Unitas - Colts	20	10
☐ 11/70	Jets	20	10
☐ 11/71	Lions	20	10

PRO SPORTS STARS OF

DATE	COVER/FEATURE	Nr-Mt	Ex
☐ 1972	Jim Plunkett - Patriots	20	10
☐ 1974	Larry Csonka - Dolphins	25	10

PRO FOOTBALL

(Sports Today)

DATE	COVER/FEATURE	Nr-Mt	Ex
☐ 1971	Joe Namath - Jets	20	10

PRO FOOTBALL

(Fawcett)

DATE	COVER/FEATURE	Nr-Mt	Ex
☐ 1963	Jim Taylor - Packers	20	10

PRO FOOTBALL

(Charlaston Comics)

DATE	COVER/FEATURE	Nr-Mt	Ex
☐ 1/69	Landry,Sayers,Tarkenton		15

PRO FOOTBALL ALMANAC

DATE	COVER/FEATURE	Nr-Mt	Ex
☐ 1964	Action	25	10
☐ 1965	Johnny Unitas - Colts	25	10
☐ 1966	John Brodie - 49ers	25	10
☐ 1967	Bart Starr - Packers	25	10

☐ 1968	Johnny Unitas - Colts	25	10
☐ 1969	Gale Sayers/ Joe Namath	20	10
☐ 1971	Joe Namath - Jets	20	10

PRO FOOTBALL ALL STARS

DATE	COVER/FEATURE	Nr-Mt	Ex
☐ 1957	....	35	15

PRO FOOTBALL ILLUSTRATED

DATE	COVER/FEATURE	Nr-Mt	Ex
☐ 1964	J. Brown - Browns	35	10
☐ 1967	J. Unitas/Namath	25	10
☐ 1968	Joe Namath - Jets	20	10
☐ 1969	J.Namath/Gabriel	20	10
☐ 1971	Joe Namath - Jets	20	10
☐ 1972	Joe Namath - Jets	15	10
☐ 1973	Larry Csonka - Dolphins	15	10
☐ 1975	OJ Simpson /C. Foreman	15	10
☐ 1976	....	15	10
☐ 1977	OJ Simpson - Bills	15	10
☐ 1978	Walter Payton - Bears	20	10

PRO FOOTBALL EXCLUSIVE

(Fritz Van Enterprises - Newspaper)

DATE	COVER/FEATURE	Nr-Mt	Ex
☐ 1969	Monthly	20	10

PRO FOOTBALL FORECAST #1

DATE	COVER/FEATURE	Nr-Mt	Ex
☐ 1959	....	20	10

PRO FOOTBALL LINDY'S

This may have cover variations across the U.S.

DATE	COVER/FEATURE	Nr-Mt	Ex
☐ 1990	....	10	
☐ 1991	Troy Aikman - Cowboys	10	5
☐ 1992-1997		7	5

PRO FOOTBALL YEARBOOK

DATE	COVER/FEATURE	Nr-Mt	Ex
☐ 1953	....	60	30
☐ 1954	....	45	20
☐ 1955	....	30	15

PRO FOOTBALL SPORTS QUARTERLY

DATE	COVER/FEATURE	Nr-Mt	Ex
☐ 1963	....	25	10

PRO FOOTBALL GUIDE

(Goldwin Publications Inc. - Newspaper)
1969 to date. Weekly during season Monthly during off season.

PRO FOOTBALL GUIDE

DATE	COVER/FEATURE	Nr-Mt	Ex
☐ 8/70	Joe Namath - Jets	20	10
☐ 10/70	John Unitas - Colts	25	10
☐ 12/70	Oakland Raiders	20	10
☐ 2/71	Jim O'Brian-Colts	20	10
☐ 1977	OJ Simpson - Bills	20	10

PRO FOOTBALL - MONTHLY

DATE	COVER/FEATURE	Nr-Mt	Ex
☐ 11/79	Roger Staubach-Cowboys	20	10

PRO FOOTBALL REPORT

DATE	COVER/FEATURE	Nr-Mt	Ex
☐ 1969	Sonny Jurgenson - Redskins	30	15
☐ 1973	Larry Csonka - Dolphins	35	10

PRO FOOTBALL (SPORTS) REVIEW

(Dell)

DATE	COVER/FEATURE	Nr-Mt	Ex
☐ 1958	Bobby Layne - Bears	75	25
☐ 1959	Johnny Unitas - Colts	50	20

	DATE	COVER/FEATURE	Nr-Mt	Ex
☐	1960	D Meredith/C. Conerly	30	15
☐	1961	Paul Hornung - Packers	30	15
☐	1962	Taylor/Horung/Brown	35	15
☐	1963	Y.A. Tittle - Giants	35	15
☐	1964	Jim Brown - Browns	40	15
☐	1965	Namath/Unitas	30	15
☐	1966	Gale Sayers - Bears	30	15
☐	1967	Bart Starr - Packers	25	10
☐	1968	Johnny Unitas/Bart Starr	20	10
☐	1969	Leroy Kelly - Browns	20	10
☐	1970	Vikings/Rams	20	10
☐	1971	Colts/Cowboys	20	10
☐	1972	Roger Staubach - Cowboys	20	10
☐	1973	Bob Griese - Dolphins	20	10
☐	1974	Larry Csonka - Dolphins	20	10

PRO FOOTBALL SPORTS SPECIAL

	DATE	COVER/FEATURE	Nr-Mt	Ex
☐	F/64	YA Tittle/Wade	25	10
☐	F/66	Gale Sayers- Bears	30	15
☐	F/67	Bart Starr/Joe Namath	20	10
☐	F/69	Joe Namath - Jets	20	10
☐	f/70	Len Dawson/OJ Simpson	20	10
☐	F/71	John Brodie - 49ers	20	10

PRO FOOTBALL SPORTS STAR

	DATE	COVER/FEATURE	Nr-Mt	Ex
☐	1975	Terry Bradshaw - Steelers	20	10

PRO FOOTBALL STARS OF

	DATE	COVER/FEATURE	Nr-Mt	Ex
☐	1972	Jim Plunkett - Patriots	15	10
☐	1974	Larry Csonka -Dolphins	20	10
☐	1975	Terry Bradshaw - Steelers	15	10

PRO FOOTBALL STARS
(Whitestone)

	DATE	COVER/FEATURE	Nr-Mt	Ex
☐	1959	Frank Gifford- Giants	35	15
☐	1960	Johnny Unitas - Colts	30	15
☐	1961	Jim Brown - Browns	25	10
☐	1962	Bart Starr - Packers	20	10
☐	1963	Jim Taylor - Packers	25	10
☐	1964	Paul Hornung/Rams	20	10
☐	1968	Joe Namath - Jets	20	10
☐	1969	Joe Namath - Jets	20	10
☐	1970	Vikings Front Four	15	8
☐	1971	Duane Thomas/Cowboys	15	8

PRO FOOTBALL TODAY

	DATE	COVER/FEATURE	Nr-Mt	Ex
☐	1977	Bert Jones-Colts	15	10
☐	1979	Terry Bradshaw-Steelers	20	10

PROLOG & PRO

	DATE	COVER/FEATURE	Nr-Mt	Ex
☐	1973	Washington-Miami	20	10
☐	1974	M. Morris - Dolphins	20	10
☐	1977	Bert Jones - Colts	20	10
☐	1981	Jim Plunkett - Raiders	15	10
☐	1985	John Elway- Broncos	25	10
☐	1987	John Elway- Broncos	20	10

PRO NEWS
(Pro News Publishing Co)

	DATE	COVER/FEATURE	Nr-Mt	Ex
☐	1957	Weekly during season	25	10

PRO PIGSKIN

	DATE	COVER/FEATURE	Nr-Mt	Ex
☐	1961	Weekly during season	30	15

PRO PREVIEW

	DATE	COVER/FEATURE	Nr-Mt	Ex

☐	1988	Bo Jackson	20	10

PRO PHOTOSTAMP ALBUM #1

	DATE	COVER/FEATURE	Nr-Mt	Ex
☐	1970		25	10

PRO SPORTS

	DATE	COVER/FEATURE	Nr-Mt	Ex
☐	1/66	Paul Hornung - Packers	25	10
☐	1/67	Joe Namath - Jets	20	10
☐	11/67	Giants/Cards	20	10
☐	11/68	Phillies	20	10
☐	1/68	D. Anderson-Packers	20	10
☐	1/69	D. Anderson-Packers	20	10
☐	11/69	Johnny Unitas-Colts	20	10
☐	1/70	Leroy Kelly - Browns	20	10
☐	11/70	Jets/Giants	20	10
☐	1/71	Gale Sayers - Bears	20	10
☐	11/71	Detroit Lions	20	10
☐	1/72	San Francisco 49ers	20	10
☐	9/74	Larry Csonka-Dolphins	20	10

QUARTERBACK/PRO QUARTERBACK

This magazine changes names from Quarterback to Pro Quarterback during its tenure. Very popular with football fans.

	DATE	COVER/FEATURE	Nr-Mt	Ex
☐	10/69	Joe Namath - Jets	50	15
☐	11/69	Gale Sayers - Bears	35	20
☐	12/69	Johnny Unitas - Colts	35	15
☐	1/70	Superbowl	30	15
☐	2/70	Mike McCoy - Colts	15	10
☐	3/70	Len Dawson- Chiefs	20	10
☐	4/70	OJ Simpson - Bills	20	10
☐	5/70	Hank Stram - Chiefs	15	5
☐	6/70	Don Shula - Dolphins	15	5
☐	7/70	Pete Rozelle	15	5
☐	8/70	Terry Bradshaw - Steelers	20	10
☐	11/70	Len Dawson -Chiefs	20	10
☐	12/70	Roman Gabriel -Rams	20	10
☐	1/71	Joe Namath -Jets	20	10
☐	2/71	Unitas/Dawson/Gabrial	20	10
☐	3/71	Manning/Theismann	25	10
☐	5/71	Dallas Cowboys	20	10
☐	7/71	J.Unitas/G.Sayers	20	10
☐	9/71	Bart Starr - Packers	20	10
☐	10/71	John Brodie - 49ers	15	10
☐	11/71	OJ Simpson - Bills	15	10
☐	12/71	Norm Snead -Eagles	15	5
☐	Spec. 1971	Joe Namath - Jets	20	10
☐	1/72	Calvin Hill - Cowboys	20	10
☐	2/72	Superbowl Issue	15	5
☐	3/72	Walt Patulski - Bills	15	10
☐	5/72	Dallas Cowboys	20	10
☐	7/72	Len Dawson - Chiefs	20	10
☐	9/72	Charlie Sanders-Lions	15	10
☐	10/72	Fran Tarkenton-Vikings	15	10
☐	11/72	Joe Namath - Jets	20	10
☐	12/72	Larry Csonka- Dolphins	20	10
☐	An/72	Roger Staubach - Cowboys	20	10
☐	1/73	Superbowl Issue	20	10
☐	2/73	Larry Brown - Redskins	20	10
☐	3/73	Franco Harris - Steelers	15	10
☐	5/73	Don Shula - Dolphins	15	10
☐	7/73	J.Brockington - Packers	15	10
☐	8/73	Bob Griese - Dolphins	15	10
☐	9/73	T. Bradshaw- Steeler	20	10
☐	10/73	Dick Butkus - Bears	20	10
☐	11/73	Joe Namath - Jets	20	10
☐	12/73	N.Buoniconi/Dolphins	15	10
☐	1973	B.Griese/J.Namath	20	10
☐	1/74	B.Griese/T.Bradshaw	15	10
☐	2/74	OJ Simpson-Bills	20	10
☐	4/74	Franco Harris-Steelers	15	10
☐	10/74	Shula/OJ Simpson	15	10
☐	12/74	C.Hill/L. Csonka	15	10

		Nr-Mt	Ex
☐ 2/75	Bob Griese/K Stabler	15	10
☐ 4/75	Franco Harris - Steelers	15	10
☐ 11/75	Franco Harris - Steelers	15	10
☐ 12/75	Joe Namath - Jets	15	10
☐ 1/76	OJ Simpson - Bills	15	10
☐ 2/76	Super Bowl	15	10
☐ 9/76	O.J. Simpson - Bills	15	10
☐ 11/76	Fran Tarkenton - Vikings	15	10
☐ 12/76	K. Anderson/Bradshaw	15	10
☐ 1/77	F.Harris/Bob Griese	15	10
☐ 2/77	R Staubach/K. Stabler	15	10
☐ 9/77	Bert Jones - Colts	15	10
☐ 10/77	Otis Sistrunk - Raiders	12	10
☐ 11/77	C. Foreman-Vikings	15	10
☐ 12/77	R.Staubach/C.Morton	15	10
☐ 1/78	Ken Stabler - Raiders	12	8
☐ 10/78	Tony Dorsett - Cowboys	12	8
☐ 11/78	Tarkenton/Staubach	15	10
☐ 11/79	Fouts/Bradshaw	12	8
☐ 11/80	Terry Bradshaw - Steelers	12	8
☐ An 80	Violence in the Game	10	8
☐ An 81	Jim Plunkett - Raiders	10	8
☐ 2/81	Terry Bradshaw - Steelers	10	8
☐ An 82	Joe Montana - 49ers	20	10
☐ 2/82	Joe Ferguson - Bills	10	8

REAL MAGAZINE YEARBOOK

DATE	COVER/FEATURE	Nr-Mt	Ex
☐ 1957		30	15

SAGA'S FOOTBALL SPECIAL

DATE	COVER/FEATURE	Nr-Mt	Ex
☐ 1979	Jack Lambert	15	8
☐ 1980	Tony Dorsett	15	8
☐ 1981	Earl Campbell	15	8

SID FOOTBALL REPORT

DATE	COVER/FEATURE	Nr-Mt	Ex
☐ 1987	Walter Payton	15	10

SPALDING FOOTBALL GUIDES

The early issues are rare and are highly sought after.

DATE	COVER/FEATURE	Nr-Mt	Ex
☐ 1891-1892		800	700
☐ 1893-1895		400	300
☐ 1896-1905		250	150
☐ 1906-1916		150	100
☐ 1917-1930		75	50
☐ 1931-1940		40	25

In 1941 IT became the NCAA Guides

DATE	COVER/FEATURE	Nr-Mt	Ex
☐ 1941-1950		40	25
☐ 1951	Reynolds	25	15
☐ 1952	Lattner/Notre Dame	25	15
☐ 1953	Garrett	25	15
☐ 1954	Burris-Okla.	25	10
☐ 1955	J.Childress	25	10
☐ 1956	J.Arnett	25	10
☐ 1957	Fondren/Texas	25	10
☐ 1958	Groseup-Utah	20	10
☐ 1959	Billy Cannon - LSU	20	10
☐ 1960	Mautiro-Syracuse	20	10
☐ 1961	Romig-Colo.	20	10
☐ 1962	S. Gibbs	20	10
☐ 1963	Simmon-Tulsa	20	10
☐ 1964	Dick Butkus	40	15
☐ 1965	Obillovich	20	10
☐ 1966	Talbolt-N.C.	20	10
☐ 1967	Meylan-Neb.	20	10
☐ 1968	Gonso-In.	20	10
☐ 1969	Picture	20	10
☐ 1970	Dicus-Arkansas	20	10
☐ 1971	Ah You-ASU	20	10
☐ 1972	Glover-Nebraska	15	7
☐ 1973	Randy Grandisher	15	7
☐ 1974	Todd Rutledge	15	7

		Nr-Mt	Ex
☐ 1975	Thomas-Texas	15	7
☐ 1976	Roth-Cal	15	7
☐ 1977	Joey Browner-Notre Dame	15	7
☐ 1978	Hugh Green-Iowa ST	15	7
☐ 1979	Notre Dame	15	7
☐ 1980		15	7
☐ 1981	Jim McMahon-BYU	15	7
☐ 1982	Dave Rimington/Neb.	15	7
☐ 1983	Jerry Hoage-Georgia	15	7
☐ 1984	Tony Zendajas-ASU	15	7
☐ 1985	Keith Byers-Ohio St.	15	7
☐ 1986 - 1997		10	5

SPORTS ALL STARS PRO FOOTBALL

(Maco)

DATE	COVER/FEATURE	Nr-Mt	Ex
☐ 1958	LA Rams	45	20
☐ 1959	Johnny Unitas - Colts	35	20
☐ 1960	Johnny Unitas - Colts	35	15
☐ 1961	New York Giants	30	15
☐ 1962	Paul Hornung - Packers	40	20
☐ 1963	Jim Taylor - Packers	25	10
☐ 1964	Jim Brown - Browns	35	15
☐ 1965	Charley Johnson- Cards	30	15
☐ 1966	Dick Butkus - Bears	40	20
☐ 1967	Don Meredith - Cowboys	30	15
☐ 1968	Johnny Unitas - Colts	25	12
☐ 1969	Roman Gabrial - Rams	20	10
☐ 1970	Don Maynard - Jets	15	10
☐ 1971	Larry Brown - Redskins	15	10
☐ 1972	Jim Plunkett - Patriots	15	7
☐ 1973	Mercury Morris - Dolphins	12	7
☐ 1974	Roger Staubach - Cowboys	20	10
☐ 1975	Terry Bradshaw - Steelers	15	7
☐ 1976	Terry Bradshaw - Steelers	15	7

SPORTS EXTRA PRO FOOTBALL

(Tempest Pub's)

DATE	COVER/FEATURE	Nr-Mt	Ex
☐ 1967		20	10
☐ 1968	Starr/Namath/Hayes)	20	10
☐ 1969	Joe Namath	20	10
☐ 1970	Sayers/Dawson	20	10
☐ 1971	Tarkenton/Brodie	20	10
☐ 1972	Griese/Staubach/Tark	15	8

SPORTS FORECAST FOOTBALL ISSUES

(EJ O'Malley)

DATE	COVER/FEATURE	Nr-Mt	Ex
☐ 1958	Don Meredith - SMU	20	10
☐ 1959	College/Pro	20	10

SPORTSCASTER BULLETIN

(Sportscasters, Inc)

DATE	COVER/FEATURE	Nr-Mt	Ex
☐ 1967 11	weekly issues	20	10

THE FOOTBALL WORLD

(Football World Publishing Co)

DATE	COVER/FEATURE	Nr-Mt	Ex
☐ 9/21 - 11/21		200	100

Succeeded by The Athletic World

☐ 1/22-12/23		100	50

THE SPORTING NEWS AFL GUIDE

DATE	COVER/FEATURE	Nr-Mt	Ex
☐ 1962	Action Shot	75	35
☐ 1963	Action Shot	65	25
☐ 1964	Action Shot	40	20
☐ 1965	Tobin Rote - Chargers	40	15
☐ 1966	Sherrill Headrick -Chiefs	40	15
☐ 1967	Bobby Burnett - Bills	40	15
☐ 1968	Blanda/Lamonica	40	15
☐ 1969	Jets (Super Bowl)	35	15
☐ 1970	Lance Alworth - Chargers	35	15

This merged into a NFL Football Guide . . . .

☐ 1970	Hank Stram - Chiefs	30	10
☐ 1971	Jim Bakken - Cards	30	10
☐ 1972	Roger Staubach - Cowboys	30	10
☐ 1973	Mercury Morris - Dolphins	30	10
☐ 1974	Larry Csonka - Dolphins	30	10
☐ 1975	Franco Harris - Steelers	30	10
☐ 1976	Lynn Swann - Steelers	30	10
☐ 1977	Ken Stabler - Raiders	30	10
☐ 1978	Roger Staubach - Cowboys	30	15
☐ 1979	Terry Bradshaw - Steelers	30	15
☐ 1980	John Stallworth/Swann	25	10
☐ 1981	Billy Sims - Lions	25	10
☐ 1982	Ken Anderson - Bengels	20	10
☐ 1983	Mark Moseley - Redskins	20	10
☐ 1984	Eric Dickerson - Rams	30	15
☐ 1985	Dan Marino - Dolphins	30	15
☐ 1986	Marcus Allen - Raiders	20	10
☐ 1987	Phil Simms - Giants	20	10
☐ 1988	John Elway - Broncos	25	10
☐ 1989	Steve Largent - Seahawks	20	10
☐ 1990	Joe Montana - 49ers	20	10
☐ 1991 -1997		15	5

THE SPORTING NEWS FOOTBALL GUIDES & RULES
These are early guides

DATE	COVER/FEATURE	Nr-Mt	Ex
☐ 1945	Record Book	40	20
☐ 1946	A.A. Stagg Rules	30	15
☐ 1947	Pop Warner	30	15
☐ 1948	Frank Leahy	30	15
☐ 1949	Sammy Baugh	50	25
☐ 1950	Greasy Neale	50	25

THE SPORTING NEWS COLLEGE FOOTBALL
There may be regional covers.

DATE	COVER/FEATURE	Nr-Mt	Ex
☐ 1982	Dan Marino/John Elway	30	15
☐ 1983	Blair Kiel-Notre Dame	15	10
☐ 1984	Bill Frulia-Pitt	15	10
☐ 1984	Tomczak/Trudeau	15	10
☐ 1985	Allen Pinkett - Notre Dame	12	7
☐ 1985	Keith Byars - Ohio St.	12	7
☐ 1985	Robie Bosco-BYU	12	7
☐ 1985	Bo Jackson - Raiders	12	7
☐ 1986	Lorenzo White - Michigan St	12	7
☐ 1986	Shane Conlan -Penn St	12	7
☐ 1986	Gaston Green-UCLA	10	7
☐ 1988	Troy Aikman - UCLA	20	10
☐ 1989	Brian Cox - Fresno State	10	7
☐ 1990	Todd Marnovich- USC	10	7
☐ 1991	Washington	10	7
☐ 1992-1997		7	3

THE SPORTING NEWS FOOTBALL REGISTERS

DATE	COVER/FEATURE	Nr-Mt	Ex
☐ 1966	St. Louis Cardinals	45	20
☐ 1967	Mike Garrett - Chiefs	35	15
☐ 1968	Quarterback	35	15
☐ 1969	Dick Butkus - Bears	40	20
☐ 1970	Roman Gabriel - Rams	25	10
☐ 1971	Sonny Jurgensen-Redskins	20	10
☐ 1972	Larry Wilson - 49ers	20	10
☐ 1973	Terry Bradshaw - Steelers	30	10
☐ 1974	O.J. Simpson - Bills	25	10
☐ 1975	Ken Stabler - Raiders	25	10
☐ 1976	Fran Tarkenton - Vikings	25	10
☐ 1977	Bert Jones - Colts	20	10
☐ 1978	Walter Payton - Bears	20	10
☐ 1979	Earl Campbell - Oilers	20	10
☐ 1980	Dan Fouts- Chargers	20	10
☐ 1981	Brian Sipe - Browns	20	10
☐.1982	George Rogers - Saints	20	10
☐ 1983	Marcus Allen - Raiders	20	10
☐ 1984-1990		15	7

☐ 1991-1997		10	5

THE SPORTING NEWS PRO FOOTBALL
This title may have multiple covers

DATE	COVER/FEATURE	Nr-Mt	Ex
☐ 1981	Brian Sipe - Browns	20	7
☐ 1982	Kellen Winslow-Chargers	15	7
☐ 1983	John Jefferson-Packers	20	10
☐ 1984	Payton/Dorsett	15	7
☐ 1984	M.Gastineau/L Taylor	15	7
☐ 1984	Marcus Allen-Raiders	15	7
☐ 1985	Joe Montana/D. Marino	15	7
☐ 1986	Jim McMahon -Chargers	20	10
☐ 1987	Jim Kelly - Bills	20	10
☐ 1987	Eric Dickenson - Colts	15	7
☐ 1987	B. Kosar/B.Esiason	15	7
☐ 1988	Eric Dickerson - Rams	15	7
☐ 1988	Jerry Rice - 49ers	20	8
☐ 1989	Roger Craig-49ers	15	7
☐ 1990	Joe Montana- 49ers	15	7
☐ 1991-1997		10	5

THE SPORTING NEWS SUPER BOWL BOOK

DATE	COVER/FEATURE	Nr-Mt	Ex
☐ 1981	Jim Plunkett - Raiders	10	5
☐ 1982	Joe Montana - 49ers	15	7
☐ 1983	John Riggens- Redskins	10	5
☐ 1984	Raiders	10	5
☐ 1985	Joe Montana - 49ers	20	10
☐ 1986	Dan Hampton - Giants	12	7
☐ 1987	Mark Bavaro - Giants	10	5
☐ 1988	Doug Williams - Redskins	10	5
☐ 1989	Jerry Rice - 49ers	10	5
☐ 1990	Joe Montana- 49ers	15	5
☐ 1991 -1997		9	3

THE SPORTING NEWS USFL GUIDE

DATE	COVER/FEATURE	Nr-Mt	Ex
☐ 1984	Hershel Walker - Generals	40	20
☐ 1985	Jim Kelly - Gunslingers	30	15

SPORTS ACTION MAGAZINE

DATE	COVER/FEATURE	Nr-Mt	Ex
☐ F/61	Jim Brown - Browns	35	15
☐ 2/63	Packers/Rams	25	15

SPORTS ALBUM

DATE	COVER/FEATURE	Nr-Mt	Ex
☐ 1948	Tony Minisi	40	15
☐ 1949	Charlie Justice (Winter)	30	15
☐ 1951	Bobby Reynolds (Fall)	30	12

SPORTS ALL STARS PRO FOOTBALL
(Maco Magazine)

DATE	COVER/FEATURE	Nr-Mt	Ex
☐ 1958	Rams	30	12
☐ 1959	Johnny Unitas - Colts	35	15
☐ 1960	Johnny Unitas - Colts	35	15
☐ 1961	New York Giants	20	10
☐ 1962	Paul Hornung - Packers	35	15
☐ 1963	Jim Taylor - Packers	35	15
☐ 1964	Jim Brown - Browns	35	15
☐ 1965	Charley Johnson - Cards	20	10
☐ 1966	Dick Butkus - Bears	40	20
☐ 1967	Don Meredith - Cowboys	30	15
☐ 1967	Gale Sayers - Bears	30	15
☐ 1968	John Unitas - Colts	25	10
☐ 1968	Roman Gabrial - Rams	20	10
☐ 1969	Fran Tarkenton - Vikings	20	10
☐ 1969	Leroy Kelly - Browns	20	10
☐ 1970	Don Maynard - Jets	20	10
☐ 1971	Larry Brown - Redskins	20	10
☐ 1972	Jim Plunkett - Patriots	15	10
☐ 1973	M. Morris - Dolphins	15	10
☐ 1974	Roger Staubach - Cowboys	15	7

	1975	Terry Bradshaw - Steelers	15	7
☐	1975	Terry Bradshaw - Steelers	15	7
☐	1976	Terry Bradshaw - Steelers	15	7
☐	1977	Bert Jones - Colts	10	5
☐	1979	Ken Anderson - Bengals	10	5

SPORTS CAVALCADE
(Com. Sports)

DATE	COVER/FEATURE	Nr-Mt	Ex
☐ 1965	YA Tittle - Giants	20	10

SPORTS EXTRA PRO FOOTBALL

DATE	COVER/FEATURE	Nr-Mt	Ex
☐ 1968	Bart Starr - Packers (Fall)	20	10
☐ 1969	Joe Namath - Jets (Fall)	20	10
☐ 1970	Len Dawson - Chiefs (Fall)	15	7
☐ 1972	Bob Griese - Dolphins (Fall)	15	7

SPORTSFOLIO
(Sports Week inc) See Baseball Sectio

SPORTS HERO'S

DATE	COVER/FEATURE	Nr-Mt	Ex
☐ 1967	Starr/Unitas/Sayers (Winter)	20	10
☐ 1972	Joe Namath - Jets (Summer)	20	10
☐ 1973	Terry Bradshaw/Steelers (Summer)	15	10

SPORT LIFE
This magazine features other than football stars.
Football stars listed.

DATE	COVER/FEATURE	Nr-Mt	Ex
☐ 12/48	Frank Tripucka	50	25
☐ 2/49	Sid Luckman-Bears	50	25
☐ 2/50	D.Royal/Newcombe	50	20
☐ 1/51	B. Cox/Otto Graham	45	20
☐ 12/51	Fred Benners - SMU	45	20
☐ 12/52	J.Scarbath - Maryland	40	20
☐ 2/53	Marlow/Marciano/Black	40	20

SPORTS PIX

DATE	COVER/FEATURE	Nr-Mt	Ex
☐ 2/49	Bob Chappuis	50	20

SPORTS QUARTERLY FOOTBALL ROUNDUP

DATE	COVER/FEATURE	Nr-Mt	Ex
☐ 1965	Donny Anderson	25	15
☐ 1966	Bob Greiese - Purdue	20	10
☐ 1967	Lenny Snow - Ga Tech	20	10
☐ 1968	Jim Seymour- Notre Dame	20	10
☐ 1969	Ron Carpenter - NC St	20	10
☐ 1970	Bob Jacobs - Wyoming	15	10
☐ 1971	Ed Marinaro - Cornell	15	10
☐ 1973	Randy Gradishar - Ohio St.	15	10
☐ 1972	Jerry Sisemore - Texas	15	10
☐ 1974	OJ Simpson	15	10
☐ 1975		15	10
☐ 1978	Chuck Fusina	15	10
☐ 1977	Wes Chandler	15	10

SPORTS REVIEW FOOTBALL
(Elbak Pub) Also referred to as Pro Football Illustrated.

DATE	COVER/FEATURE	Nr-Mt	Ex
☐ 1941	NY Giants	125	50
☐ 1942	Action shot	125	50
☐ 1943	Sammy Baugh	100	45
☐ 1944	Action Shot	65	25
☐ 1945	Action Shot	65	25
☐ 1946	Action (Pro) Life size	65	25
☐ 1946	Action (College)	65	25
☐ 1947	Action (Pro)	65	25
☐ 1947	College	65	25
☐ 1948	College	65	25
☐ 1948	Pro	65	25
☐ 1949	Action (Pro)	50	25
☐ 1949	Action (College)	45	25

DATE	COVER/FEATURE	Nr-Mt	Ex
☐ 1950	Action (College)	45	20
☐ 1951	Action	45	20
☐ 1952	Action	45	20
☐ 1953	Action (regular size)	35	20
☐ 1954	Action	35	20
☐ 1955	Action	35	20
☐ 1956	Action	35	20
☐ 1957	Action	35	20
☐ 1958	Duffy Daughterty	35	20
☐ 1959	Univ of Iowa	35	20
☐ 1960	Johnny Unitas	35	20
☐ 1961	Colts/Giants	30	15
☐ 1962	Colts vs Bears	30	15
☐ 1963	Hall of Famers	30	15
☐ 1965	Johnny Unitas	25	15
☐ 1966	Bears/49ers	25	15
☐ 1967	Bart Starr	30	15
☐ 1968	J.Unitas/B. Starr	25	10
☐ 1969	Joe Namath	35	15
☐ 1970	Joe Kapp	20	10
☐ 1971	Cowboys/Colts	15	7

SPORTS QUARTERLY PRO FOOTBALL

DATE	COVER/FEATURE	Nr-Mt	Ex
☐ 63	Jim Taylor/SamHuff	25	15
☐ 64	NY Giants	25	15
☐ 65	Bart Starr - Packers	25	10
☐ 66	Jim Taylor - Packers	25	10
☐ 67	Sayers/Namath/Meredith	25	10
☐ 68	Don Anderson/Packers	20	10
☐ 69	Joe Namath-Jets	20	10
☐ 70	Sonny Jurgensen - Redskins	20	10
☐ 71	Roman Gabrial-Rams	20	10
☐ 72	Oakland Raiders	15	10
☐ 73	Bob Griese/Larry Csonka	20	10
☐ 74	OJ Simpson - Bills	15	10
☐ 75	Carl Eller-Vikings	10	5
☐ 76	Lynn Swann - Steelers	10	5
☐ 78	Lyle Alzado - Raiders	10	5
☐ 79	Terry Bradshaw-Steelers	10	5

SPORTS SCENE
(American Graphics Inc.)

DATE	COVER/FEATURE	Nr-Mt	Ex
☐ 11/71	S. Jurgensen/Redskins	15	7
☐ 10/72	Fred Dryer - Rams	15	7
☐ 11/72	Fran Tarkenton - Vikings	15	7
☐ 12/72	Pete Rozelle	15	7
☐ 1/73	Bob Lilly - Cowboys	12	5
☐ 2/73		10	5

SPORTS SPEC. PRO FOOTBALL
(Tempest Pub)

DATE	COVER/FEATURE	Nr-Mt	Ex
☐ 1964	Hornung/Brown/Tittle	25	5
☐ 1965	Brown/P. Hornung	25	5
☐ 1966	J. Namath/G. Sayers	25	5
☐ 1967	Namath/Sayers/Starr	20	5
☐ 1968	G. Sayers/R. Gabriel	15	5
☐ 1969	Joe Namath - Jets	10	5
☐ 1970		10	5
☐ 1971	G. Sayers/J. Brodie	10	5
☐ 1972	R. Staubach/J. Namath	10	5
☐ 1973	OJ / Griese/ Brown	10	5
☐ F/72	Roger Staubach - Cowboys	20	10

SPORTS WORLD
This magazine has multiple sports. Only Football covers are listed.

DATE	COVER/FEATURE	Nr-Mt	Ex
☐ 12/63	Jim Taylor - Packers	45	20
☐ 12/64	Jim Brown - Browns	35	15
☐ 2/65	Paul Hornung- Packers	30	15

		Nr-Mt	Ex
☐ 10/65	Jim Brown - Browns	30	15
☐ 12/65	John Unitas - Colts	30	15
☐ 12/66	Gale Sayers - Bears	25	10
☐ 2/68	Steelers/Packers	20	10
☐ 2/69	Bart Starr - Packers	25	10
☐ 2/66	Fran Tarkenton -Vikings	20	10
☐ 2/67	Taylor/Hornung, Starr	20	10
☐ 12/67	Meredith/Unitas, Starr	25	10
☐ 2/69	Bart Starr - Packers	20	10
☐ 12/69	Namath/ Unitas	20	10
☐ 2/70	Atlanta Falcons	20	10
☐ 12/70	Namath/Dawson	20	10
☐ 2/71	Rams/Packers	15	10
☐ 12/71	Gabriel/ Namath	15	10
☐ 2/72	R. Staubach-Cowboys	15	10
☐ 12/72	R. Staubach -Cowboys	15	10
☐ 2/73	Cowboys/Vikings	15	10
☐ 12/73	Namath/Griese	15	10
☐ 10/74	OJ Simpson - Bills	15	10
☐ 2/75	Dallas Cowboys	15	10
☐ 12/79	Terry Bradshaw - Steelers	15	10

SPORTS STARS

DATE	COVER/FEATURE	Nr-Mt	Ex
☐ 11/52	D.Walker, M.Mantle	60	30
☐ 1/53	Frank McPhee	40	20
☐ 2/53	Bob Williams/Notre Dame	40	20

SPORTS TODAY FOOTBALL

DATE	COVER/FEATURE	Nr-Mt	Ex
☐ 1971	Joe Namath - Jets	15	10
☐ 2/72	John Brodie - 49ers	15	10
☐ 10/72	Roger Staubach - Cowboys	15	10
☐ 12/72	Joe Namath - Jets	20	10
☐ 1973	Joe Namath - Jets	15	10
☐ 12/74	Larry Csonka - Dolphins	15	10
☐ 1974	OJ Simpson - Bills	15	10

STANLEY WOODWARD FOOTBALL

DATE	COVER/FEATURE	Nr-Mt	Ex
☐ 1949	Dan Foldberg	55	20
☐ 1950	Bobby Williams	40	15
☐ 1951	Smith Texas AM	45	15
☐ 1952	Scarbath - Maryland	45	15
☐ 1953	Burkhart/WSU	40	15
☐ 1954	Guglielmi/Notre Dame	40	15
☐ 1955	George Welsh - Navy	40	15
☐ 1956	McDonald - Oklahoma	35	15
☐ 1957	Bobby Cox - Minn.	35	15
☐ 1958	Reifsnyder - Navy	35	15
☐ 1959	Bob Anderson	30	15
☐ 1960	Bob Schloredt	25	12
☐ 1961	Joe Romig - Colorado	25	12

STREET & SMITH'S PRO FOOTBALL YEARBOOK

Perhaps the most popular football annual ever issued. Many regional covers were issued in the 80's. Most collectors want all variations.

DATE	COVER/FEATURE	Nr-Mt	Ex
☐ 1963	Milt Plum-Lions	60	30
☐ 1963	Roman Gabriel - Rams	60	30
☐ 1963	YA Tittle - Giants	80	40
☐ 1964	Terry Baker - Rams	60	30
☐ 1964	Jim Katcavage - Giants	60	30
☐ 1964	Bart Starr - Packers	60	30
☐ 1965	Frank Ryan - Browns	50	25
☐ 1965	Johnny Unitas - Colts	50	25
☐ 1965	Dick Bass-Rams	50	25
☐ 1966	Charley Johnson - Cards	50	25
☐ 1966	Ken Willard- 49ers	50	25
☐ 1966	LaLonde/Hillebrand	50	25
☐ 1967	Dick Bass - Rams	45	20
☐ 1967	Sayers/Rabold	45	20
☐ 1967	Lorick & Vogel- Colts	35	20
☐ 1968	Norm Snead - Eagles	25	15
☐ 1968	Hewritt Dixon - Raiders	30	15

		Nr-Mt	Ex
☐ 1968	Don Meredith - Cowboys	40	20
☐ 1969	Joe Namath - Jets	50	20
☐ 1969	Concannon & Seals	35	15
☐ 1969	John Brodie - 49ers	25	10
☐ 1970	Roman Gabrial - Rams	30	15
☐ 1970	Joe Namath - Jets	25	12
☐ 1970	Joe Kapp-Vikings	25	12
☐ 1971	Earl Morrall - Colts	25	12
☐ 1971	Duane Thomas - Cowboys	25	12
☐ 1971	John Brodie - 49ers	25	12
☐ 1972	Roger Staubach-Cowboys	25	12
☐ 1972	John Hadl-Chargers	25	12
☐ 1972	Bob Griese - Dolphins	25	12
☐ 1973	Steve Spurrier-49ers	25	12
☐ 1973	Chester Marcol - Packers	25	12
☐ 1973	Larry Csonka-Dolphins	25	12
☐ 1974	Jim Bertelsen	20	12
☐ 1974	OJ Simpson - Bills	30	15
☐ 1974	Roger Staubach - Cowboys	30	15
☐ 1975	Jim Hart-Cardinals	25	12
☐ 1975	Franco Harris- Steelers	20	12
☐ 1975	Lawrence McCutcheon - Rams	15	10
☐ 1976	Ken Stabler-Raiders	15	10
☐ 1976	Terry Bradshaw - Steelers	20	10
☐ 1976	Roger Staubach - Cowboys	20	10
☐ 1977	Walter Payton - Bears	25	10
☐ 1977	John Capalletti - Patriots	15	5
☐ 1977	Bert Jones - Colts	15	5
☐ 1978	Bob Griese - Dolphins	20	5
☐ 1978	Mark Van Eagan - Raiders	15	5
☐ 1978	Tony Dorsett - Cowboys	20	5
☐ 1979	Jim Zorn - Seahawks	15	5
☐ 1979	Terry Bradshaw-Steelers	12	6
☐ 1979	Roger Staubach - Cowboys	20	10
☐ 1980	Dan Fouts - Chargers	15	6
☐ 1980	Walter Payton - Bears	20	10
☐ 1980	Terry Bradshaw-Steelers	10	6
☐ 1981	Jim Zorn/Jim Plunkett	15	6
☐ 1981	Earl Campbell - Oilers	15	6
☐ 1981	Joe Ferguson - Bills	15	6
☐ 1981	Tommy Kraer/Brian Sipe	12	5
☐ 1982	Joe Montana - 49ers	30	15
☐ 1982	Tony Dorsett - Cowboys	15	6
☐ 1982	Ken Anderson - Bengals	15	6
☐ 1982	Lawrence Taylor - Giants	15	6
☐ 1983	Joe Theisman - Redskins	15	6
☐ 1983	Marcus Allen - Raiders	15	6
☐ 1983	AJ Duhe - Dolphins	10	6
☐ 1983	Ken Anderson - Bengals	15	6
☐ 1984	Dan Marino - Dolphins	20	10
☐ 1984	John Riggins - Redskins	10	6
☐ 1984	Marcus Allen - Raiders	15	6
☐ 1984	Walter Payton- Bears	20	10
☐ 1985	Walter Payton - Bears	20	10
☐ 1985	Dan Marino - Dolphins	20	10
☐ 1985	Phil Simms - Giants	10	6
☐ 1985	Joe Montana- 49ers	20	10
☐ 1986	Eric Dickerson - Rams	10	5
☐ 1986	Mike Singletary - Bears	10	5
☐ 1986	Joe Morris - Steelers	10	5
☐ 1986	Dan Marino - Dolphins	15	6
☐ 1987	Dan Marino - Dolphins	20	10
☐ 1987	Bernie Kosar - Browns	10	6
☐ 1987	John Elway - Bronco's	20	10
☐ 1987	Phil Simms - Giants	10	5
☐ 1987	Tony Dorsett - Cowboys	10	5
☐ 1988	John Offerdahl - Dolphins	10	5
☐ 1988	Doug Williams - Redskins	10	5
☐ 1988	Anthony Carter - Vikings	10	5
☐ 1988	Ozzie Newsome - Browns	10	5
☐ 1988	Jerry Rice - 49ers	10	5
☐ 1988	Warren Moon - Oilers	10	5
☐ 1989	Mike Singletary-Bears	10	5
☐ 1989	Boomer Esiason - Bengals	10	5
☐ 1989	Jim Kelly - Bills	10	5

		Nr-Mt	Ex
☐ 1989	Herschel Walker-Cowboys	10	5
☐ 1989	Jim Evertt- Rams	10	5
☐ 1989	Roger Craig - 49ers	10	5
☐ 1989	Morten Anderson - Saints	10	5
☐ 1989	Randall Cunningham - Eagles	10	5
☐ 1990-on except for:		7	3
☐	Joe Montana	10	5
☐	Dan Marino	15	5
☐	John Elway	15	5
☐	Barry Sanders	15	5
☐	Emmitt Smith	10	5

STREET & SMITH'S
COLLEGE FOOTBALL YEARBOOK

DATE	COVER/FEATURE	Nr-Mt	Ex
☐ 1940	Illustration	180	75
☐ 1941	Frankie Alberts-Stanford	75	40
☐ 1942	Allen Cameron- Navy	75	40
☐ 1943	Steve Juzwik - Navy	70	35
☐ 1944	Bob Kelly- Notre Dame	70	35
☐ 1945	Bob Jenkins - Navy	60	35
☐ 1946	Ferraro - USC	60	35
☐ 1947	Connor- Notre Dame	60	35
☐ 1948	Jack Cloud -WM	65	25
☐ 1949	Charley Justice - NC	65	25
☐ 1950	Leon Heath - OKLA.	55	25
☐ 1951	Bob Smith - Texas A&M	55	20
☐ 1952	John Olszewski - Cal	55	20
☐ 1953	Ike Eisenhower- Navy	65	30
☐ 1954	Ralph Gugliemi - Notre Dame	45	20
☐ 1955	Hopalong Cassady - Ohio St.	75	25
☐ 1956	Jim Swink-TCU	45	20
☐ 1957	Clendenon Thomas-Okla.	35	15
☐ 1958	Bob White -Ohio St.	35	15
☐ 1959	Izo, Brennan Notre Dame	35	15
☐ 1960	Rich Mayo - Air Force	35	15
☐ 1961	Ronnie Bull- Baylor	35	15
☐ 1962	Jay Wilkinson- Duke	35	10
☐ 1963	Pete Beathard - USC	35	10
☐ 1963	Tom Myers - NW	35	10
☐ 1963	Paul Martha - Pitt	35	15
☐ 1964	Craig Morton - USC	35	10
☐ 1964	Roger Staubach - Navy	45	20
☐ 1964	Dick Butkus - Ill	45	25
☐ 1965	Roger Bird-Nebraska	35	10
☐ 1965	Phil Sheridan - Notre Dame	35	10
☐ 1965	Ray Handley - Stanford	35	10
☐ 1966	Steve Spurrier - Florida	35	10
☐ 1966	Gary Beban - UCLA	30	10
☐ 1966	Bob Griese - Purdue	40	10
☐ 1967	Terry Hanratty - Notre Dame	25	10
☐ 1967	Ted Hendricks - Miami	25	10
☐ 1967	Ron Drake - USC	25	10
☐ 1968	OJ Simpson - USC	25	10
☐ 1968	Chris Gilbert - Texas	25	10
☐ 1968	Larry Smith - Florida	25	10
☐ 1969	Billy Main - USC	25	10
☐ 1969	Steve Kiner - Tennessee	25	10
☐ 1969	Rex Kern -Ohio St.	25	10
☐ 1970	Jim Plunkett - Stanford	35	10
☐ 1970	Archie Manning - Miss	45	20
☐ 1970	Steve Worcester - Texas	25	10
☐ 1971	Sunny Sixkiller - Washington	25	10
☐ 1971	Pat Sullivan - Auburn	25	10
☐ 1971	Joe Ferguson - Arkansas	25	10
☐ 1972	John Hufnagel - Penn St.	20	10
☐ 1972	Pete Adams- USC	20	10
☐ 1972	Brad Van Pelt- Mich St	20	10
☐ 1973	Kermit Johnson - UCLA	20	10
☐ 1973	Champ Henson - Ohio St.	20	10
☐ 1973	Wayne Wheeler - Alabama	20	10
☐ 1974	Brad Davis - LSU	20	10
☐ 1974	Pat Haden - USC	15	10
☐ 1974	Tom Clements - Notre Dame	15	10

		Nr-Mt	Ex
☐ 1975	Richard Todd- Alabama	15	10
☐ 1975	John Sciarra - UCLA	15	10
☐ 1975	Archie Griffin - Ohio St.	15	10
☐ 1976	Tony Dorsett - Pitt	15	10
☐ 1976	RobLyttle - Michigan	15	10
☐ 1976	Ricky Bell - USC	15	10
☐ 1977	Guy Bejamnn - Stanford	15	10
☐ 1977	Ben Zambiasi - Georgia	15	10
☐ 1977	Ken McAfee-Notre Dame	15	10
☐ 1978	Jack Thompson-Wash St	15	10
☐ 1978	Jeff Rutledge - Alabama.	15	10
☐ 1978	Rick Leach - Michigan	15	10
☐ 1979	Charles White -USC	15	10
☐ 1979	Jeff Pyburn -Georgia	15	10
☐ 1979	Mark Herrmann- Purdue	15	10
☐ 1980	Scott Woerner - Georgia	15	10
☐ 1980	Art Schlichter - Ohio St.	15	10
☐ 1980	Rick Campbell - Cal	15	10
☐ 1981	John Elway - Stanford	30	15
☐ 1981	Dan Marino - Pitt	30	20
☐ 1981	Anthoy Carter/B. Crable	15	10
☐ 1981	Bryant/Walker	15	10
☐ 1982	Tony Eason - Illinios	15	10
☐ 1982	Herschel Walker - Georgia	15	10
☐ 1982	Dan Marino - Pitt.	25	10
☐ 1982	John Elway - Stanford	20	10
☐ 1983	Mike Rozier - Neb.	15	10
☐ 1983	Kenny Jackson - Penn St	15	10
☐ 1983	Marcus Dupree - Ok	15	10
☐ 1983	Jacque Robinson - Wash.	15	10
☐ 1984	Jack Trudeau - Illinois	15	10
☐ 1984	Doug Flutie - Boston Col.	15	5
☐ 1984	Bo Jackson - Auburn	20	10
☐ 1984	Del Rio-USC	15	5
☐ 1985	DJ Dozier- Penn St	15	5
☐ 1985	Keith Byers - Ohio St.	15	5
☐ 1985	Jeff Wickersham - LSU	12	5
☐ 1985	Robbie Bosco - BYU	12	5
☐ 1986	Lorenzo White - Michigan St.	15	5
☐ 1986	Joe Paterno/DJ Dozier	15	5
☐ 1986	Vinny Testaverde - Michigan	15	5
☐ 1986	UCLA Bruins	15	5
☐ 1987	Kerwin Bell - Florida	15	5
☐ 1987	GordonLockbaum - Holy Cross	15	5
☐ 1987	Tim Brown - Notre Dame	15	5
☐ 1987	Gaston Green - UCLA	12	5
☐ 1988	Mike Power - Boston	15	5
☐ 1988	Steve Taylor - Nebraska	15	5
☐ 1988	Todd Ellis - SC	12	5
☐ 1988	Bobby Humphry-Alabama	12	5
☐ 1989	Tony Rice - Notre Dame	15	5
☐ 1989	Demetrius Brown - Michigan	15	5
☐ 1989	Emmitt Smith - Miami	20	10
☐ 1989	Mark Carter - USC	12	5
☐ 1989	Troy Taylor - Cal.	10	5
☐ 1989	Major Harris - West Virgina	10	5
☐ 1989	Demetrius Brown -Michigan	10	5
☐ 1989	Bill Musgrave - Oregon	10	5
☐ 1989	Mike Gundy - Okla.	10	5
☐ 1990	50th Anniv Issue	10	5
☐ 1991-1997		7	3

SUPER SPORT

This magazine had multisporte covers. Only the football issues are listed.

DATE	COVER/FEATURE	Nr-Mt	Ex
☐ 1/69	Don Meredith - Cowboys	20	10
☐ 3/69	Roman Gabriel - Eagles	15	10
☐ 11/69	Leroy Kelly - Browns	15	10
☐ 1/70	Bart Starr - Packers	15	10
☐ 3/70	R.Gabriel - Rams	15	10
☐ 2/71	Leroy Kelly- Browns	15	10
☐ 12/71	Roman Gabriel - Rams	15	10
☐ 10/73	Los Angeles Rams	15	10
☐ 8/74	OJ Simpson - Bills	15	10

THE FOOTBALL GRAPHIC

(NFL - Newspaper)

DATE	COVER/FEATURE	Nr-Mt	Ex
☐ 1954	(9 weekly issues)	35	15

THE FOOTBALL REVIEW

Northern Collegiate Sports - Newspaper
1950   (weekly Sept - Dec)

THE 5TH DOWN

(Newsletter) (Football Writers Association of America)
1964-date (6 monthly issues)

THE QUARTERBACK

(The Sporting News)
☐ 10/5/46-1/12/47
Football Newpaper insert in The Sporting News. 12 weekly issues.

TOUCHDOWN ANNUAL

(Popular Library/sports)

DATE	COVER/FEATURE	Nr-Mt	Ex
☐ 1963	First Issue	45	20
☐ 1964	Ron Bull - Eagles	20	10
☐ 1965	C.Gilchrist/J.Unitas	20	10
☐ 1966	Jim Taylor - Packers	25	15
☐ 1967	Fran Tarkenton - Vikings	20	10
☐ 1968	Donny Anderson	25	10
☐ 1969	K. Lincoln /Rob Bull	25	15
☐ 1969	Joe Namath - Jets	25	15
☐ 1970	R.Gabrial/C. Hill	20	10
☐ 1971	Mike Curtis/F. Tarkenton	20	10
☐ 1972	Calvin Hill - Cowboys	15	10
☐ 1973	Larry Brown - Redskins	15	10
☐ 1974	OJ Simpson - Bills	15	10
☐ 1975	Joe Namath - Jets	15	10
☐ 1976	Franco Harris - Steelers	15	10
☐ 1977	Ken Stabler - Raiders	15	7
☐ 1978	Joe Montana/T. Dorsett	25	7

TRUE FOOTBALL YEARBOOK

DATE	COVER/FEATURE	Nr-Mt	Ex
☐ 1948	Anderson - Army	40	20
☐ 1949	....	30	15
☐ 1950	Action	50	25
☐ 1951	Kyle Rote	45	20
☐ 1952	O. Graham/ B.Mathias	45	20
☐ 1953	Johnny Lattner - Notre Dame	50	25
☐ 1954	....	40	20
☐ 1955	....	40	20
☐ 1956	Action	40	20
☐ 1957	Action	40	20
☐ 1958	Jim Brown - Browns	45	20
☐ 1959	John Unitas - Colts	40	20
☐ 1960	Ernie Davis - Syracuse	45	20
☐ 1961	Roman Gabriel- NC St	35	15
☐ 1962	Paul Hornung - Packers	40	20
☐ 1963	Ed Meador - Rams	30	15
☐ 1964	Jim Brown - Brown	30	15
☐ 1965	Johnny Unitas - Colts	25	12
☐ 1966	Bart Starr - Packers	25	12
☐ 1967	Bart Starr - Packers	25	12
☐ 1968	Johnny Unitas - Colts	20	10
☐ 1969	Earl Morall - Colts	20	10
☐ 1970	Len Dawson - Chiefs	20	10
☐ 1971	Dallas/Cowboys	20	10
☐ 1972	Roger Staubach - Cowboys	20	10
☐ 1978	Roger Staubach - Cowboys	20	10
☐ 1979	Earl Campbell - Oilers	10	5
☐ 1980	Joe Greene - Steelers	10	5
☐ 1981	Jim Plunkett - Raiders	10	5

TEXAS FOOTBALL

DATE	COVER/FEATURE	Nr-Mt	Ex
☐ 1972	....	15	5

THE FOOTBALL NEWS

(Weekly newspaper during season)
9/14/39 - 1997 Values range depending on cover photos.

VARSITY MAGAZINE

DATE	COVER/FEATURE	Nr-Mt	Ex
☐ 10/48	Doak Walker - SMU	35	20

WEEKLY FOOTBALL GUIDE

1967   12 weekly issues

WEEKLY GRIDRON RECORD

(Athletic Publications 1947-1962)

DATE	COVER/FEATURE	Nr-Mt	Ex
☐ 10/22/51	Doak Walker	25	10
☐ 11/26/51	Dick Kazimier	25	10

WHAT'S WHAT IN FOOTBALL

(10 weekly issues during football season)

DATE	COVER/FEATURE	Nr-Mt	Ex
☐ 1937-1941	....	40	20

WHO'S WHO IN PRO FOOTBALL

(Topical Magazine Inc.)

DATE	COVER/FEATURE	Nr-Mt	Ex
☐ 1935	(First Issue)	185	50
☐ 1936	....	150	50
☐ 1961	YA Tittle	60	35
☐ 1964	Mike Ditka	60	35

WHO'S WHO IN PRO FOOTBALL

(Agard Publ. Corp)

DATE	COVER/FEATURE	Nr-Mt	Ex
☐ 1961	Frank Gifford	20	10

1975 ALL-STAR SPORTS

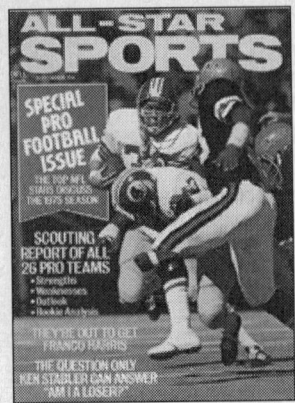

1977 ALL-STAR SPORTS

1962 BEST SPORTS STORIES

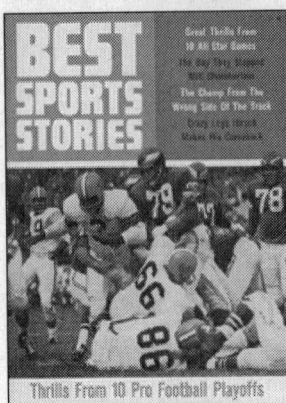

1962 CHARLIE CONERLLY'S FB

1947 COLLEGE FOOTBALL

1964 DELL SPORTS

1967 DELL SPORTS

1961 INSIDE FOOTBALL

1962 PETERSON PRO FOOTBALL

1960 PRO FOOTBALL STARS

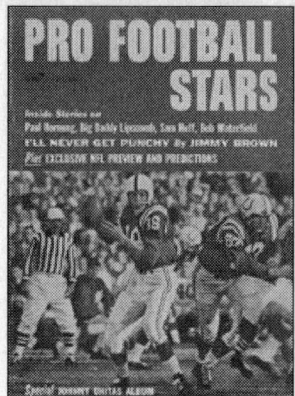

1943 PRO FOOTBALL ILLUST.

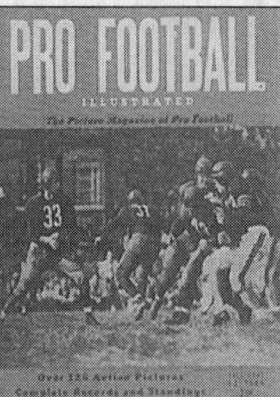

1962 TSN AFL GUIDE

1968 TSN REGISTER

1962 SPORT WORLD

1955 NFL YEARBOOK

1960 AFL YEARBOOK

1957 STREET & SMITH'S COL YB

1960 TEXAS FOOTBALL

CHAPTER NINETEEN:
Collecting Hockey Publications

The growing popularity of hockey throughout the United States and Canada has caused the demand in quality older publications to increase in value, especially early (pre-1960) quality material. However, most serious hockey collectors still focus their collections around the greatest players in the game, such as Wayne Gretzky, Bobby Hull, Bobby Orr and Gordie Howe.

For the hockey historians there are annual registers and guides that date back into the 1930s. Also NHL team-issued materials such as media guides and yearbooks give quality detail about a particular hockey team.

The second best resource is The Hockey News. This news publication dates back to the 1940s. Aside from team-issued publications and The Hockey News is the group of monthly hockey publications: Hockey Digest, Hockey Blueline Magazine, Hockey Pictorial and Hockey World.

Finally, a lot of quality hockey material comes in the form of artifacts from the games. The Stanley Cup and All-Star programs are coveted by many collectors. The tickets to these games are also pursued by many hobbyists. Regular season NHL game programs and ticket stubs also are collected. Also popular are key historical games — examples being Gretzky's 802nd NHL goal and Mario Lemieux's 600th goal — along with game programs with star players on the covers.

NHL GUIDES

The NHL Guides were started with Mr. Hendy who produced the guides from 1932-1951. These issues had players featured on the cover. These were replaced by the NHL Logo from 1951-1968. Then in 1969 they went back to featuring players.

YEAR	COVER/FEATURE	Nr-Mt	Ex
☐ 1932	(1st issue)	400	150
☐ 1932-33		300	100
☐ 1934-1940		200	75
☐ 1941-1948		150	50
☐ 1949-1959	NHL Logo	100	35
☐ 1960-1968	NHL Logo	75	25
☐ 1969	Phil Esposito	50	15
☐ 1970	Gordie Howe	35	10
☐ 1971-1979	Many Stars	22	5
☐ 1980	Wayne Gretzky	40	20
☐ 1981-1989	Many Stars	15	5
☐ 1982,84,85,87	Wayne Gretzky	20	5
☐ 1990-1997	Many Stars	10	3

The Official NHL Record Book (1948-present) goes for 50% of the NHL Guide.

THE SPORTING NEWS NHL GUIDE

This is a very popular series among hockey collectors

YEAR	COVER/FEATURE	Nr-Mt	Ex
☐ 1967-68	Detroit Goalie	150	40
☐ 1968-69	Bobby Hull	75	25
☐ 1969-70	Bobby Orr	60	20
☐ 1970-71	Gordie Howe	55	15
☐ 1971-72	Phil Esposito	55	15
☐ 1972-73	Bobby Orr	55	15
☐ 1973-79	Various	35	10
☐ 1980-82	Various	25	7
☐ 1982-85	Wayne Gretzky	35	10
☐ 1986-88	Various	20	5
☐ 1989-97	Various	15	3

THE SPORTING NEWS NHL REGISTERS

These tend to be less in value (about 70%) with the exception of the 1980 edition with Wayne Gretzky (40).

THE HOCKEY NEWS

The Hockey News has tons of history and great information. The newspaper is rather thin in the early years and easy to damage. Very few nice editions are bound to exist of the early years. Later years the mailing label is commonly found on the paper.

The key to hockey news is the first appearances of the great players like Wayne Gretkzy, Bobby Orr, etc.

YEAR	COVER/FEATURE	Nr-Mt	Ex
☐ 10/1/47	First Issue	500	250
☐ 1947 (year)	Various	100	50
☐ 1948 (year)	Various	50	25
☐ 1949 (year)	Various	35	17
☐ 12/3/49	Gordie Howe (FC)	130	45
☐ 1950 - 1955	Various	30	15
☐ 1950's	Championship/All Star	50	15
☐ 4/4/53	Gordie Howe	130	35
☐ 1956 - 1959	Various	25	10
☐ 4/27/56	Gordie Howe	75	10
☐ 10/26/57	Rocket Richard (500th)	150	50
☐ 12/20/58	Gordie Howe (400th)	75	20
☐ 1950's	Championship/All Star	40	15
☐ 1950's	Gordie Howe covers	40	15
☐ 1960 - 1964	Various	20	5
☐ 1960 - 1964	Bobby Hull Covers	40	15
☐ 1960 - 1964	Gordie Howe Covers	40	15
☐ 11/16/63	Gordie (545 goal)	100	30
☐ 1960 - 1964	Championship issue	40	15
☐ 1965 - 1970	Various	15	5
☐ 1965 - 1970	Champ/All star/stars	30	10
☐ 1971 - 1975	Various	15	5
☐ 1971 - 1975	Champ/All Star	30	10
☐ 1976 - 1980	Various	12	4
☐ 10/27/78	Wayne Gretzky (FC)	100	25
☐ 1981 - 1989	Various	8	2
☐ 1980's	Champs/Key Stars	15-20	5
☐ 1980's	Wayne Gretzky Covers	20-40	10
☐ 1990 - 1997	various	5	1

THE NHL ALL-STAR PROGRAMS

All-Star teams were selected since the 1930-31 season, but the first official All-Star tilt occurred in 1947 when the Stanley Cup champ Leafs played a group of All-Stars at the beginning of the season. This format continued until the 1966-67 season, when the league moved the All-Star Game to midseason. Another change came in 1969, when the NHL changed the format to have the East and West clash annually. The only exceptions to this format came in 1979 and 1987 when the All-Stars met the Soviet Union and in 1995 when the work stoppage iced the midseason classic.

YEAR	SITE	Nr-Mt	Ex
☐ 1947-48	Toronto	500	200
☐ 1948-49	Chicago	350	150

☐ 1949-50	Toronto		350	150
☐ 1950-51	Detroit		350	150
☐ 1951-52	Toronto		300	100
☐ 1952-53	Detroit		250	100
☐ 1953-54	Montreal		250	100
☐ 1954-55	Detroit		200	100
☐ 1955-56	Detroit		175	75
☐ 1956-57	Montreal		175	75
☐ 1957-58	Montreal		175	75
☐ 1958-59	Montreal		175	75
☐ 1959-60	Montreal		175	75
☐ 1960-61	Montreal		150	75
☐ 1961-62	Chicago		150	50
☐ 1962-63	Toronto		150	50
☐ 1963-64	Toronto		100	50
☐ 1964-65	Toronto		100	50
☐ 1965-66	Montreal		100	50
☐ 1966-67	Montreal		100	35
☐ 1967-68	Toronto		100	35
☐ 1968-69	Montreal		75	35
☐ 1969-70	St. Louis		75	35
☐ 1970-71	Boston		70	30
☐ 1971-72	Minnesota		70	30
☐ 1972-73	New York		65	30
☐ 1973-74	Chicago		65	30
☐ 1974-75	Montreal		65	30
☐ 1975-76	Philadelphia		65	25
☐ 1976-77	Vancouver		50	25
☐ 1977-78	Buffalo		35	20
☐ 1978-79	New York		35	20
☐ 1979-80	Detroit (Russia)		35	20
☐ 1980-81	Los Angeles		35	20
☐ 1981-82	Washington		25	10
☐ 1982-83	New York		25	10
☐ 1983-84	New Jersey		25	10
☐ 1984-85	Calgary		25	10
☐ 1985-86	Hartford		20	10
☐ 1986-87	Quebec		20	10
☐ 1987-88	St. Louis (Russia)		20	10
☐ 1988-97	Various		10	5

THE NHL STANLEY CUP PLAYOFF AND FINALS PROGRAMS

Hockey championship and playoff programs are very underrated in both scarcity and demand. Very few people could attend the early games and only a percentage of them saved their programs and ticket stubs. Thus, these programs are more scarce than baseball championship programs from the same era. Key championship programs go for more and some are tougher than others to find. Also some teams are more popular than others.

YEAR	COVER/FEATURE		Nr-Mt	Ex
☐ 1929-1932	Various		1500	500
☐ 1933-1935	Various		1000	400
☐ 1936-1944	Various		750	350
☐ 1945-1949	Various		500	300
☐ 1950-1953	Various		400	200
☐ 1954-1960	Various		300	100
☐ 1961-1966	Various		220	75
☐ 1967-1968			180	60
☐ 1969-1972			120	60
☐ 1973-1975			90	50
☐ 1976-1979			80	40
☐ 1980-1987			45	25
☐ 1988	Edmonton/Boston		75	35
☐ 1989-1991	Various		40	20
☐ 1992-1997	Various		15	5

Playoff programs go for 30-50% of the championship program. They are not as popular as championship programs but just as tough. Key playoff programs will go for more than average playoff programs.

REGULAR GAME PROGRAMS

Regular game programs are not as popular as championship programs or all star programs but still have a following. Most game program collectors pursue special games or teams. It is very common to find an Edmonton Oiler program collector who just wants a sample from each year. On the other hand, there are program collectors who pursue special events (example: Gordie Howe sets record) and historical events (example: First game played by Wayne Gretzky). Many collectors also pursue game programs because of who is on the cover (Wayne Gretzky). All these exceptions make certain regular game programs worth two to ten times the listed price.

YEAR	COVER/FEATURE		Nr-Mt	Ex
☐ 1929-1932	Various		100-200	50-100
☐ 1933-1935	Various		100-125	40- 75
☐ 1936-1944	Various		75-100	35- 45
☐ 1945-1949	Various		50- 75	30- 40
☐ 1950-1953	Various		40- 50	20- 30
☐ 1954-1960	Various		30- 40	10- 20
☐ 1961-1966	Various		22- 30	7 - 12
☐ 1967-1968	Various		18- 25	6 - 10
☐ 1969-1972	Various		12 - 20	6 - 10
☐ 1973-1974	Various		9 - 18	5 - 7
☐ 1976-1979	Various		8 - 15	4 - 10
☐ 1980-1997	Various		5 - 10	2 - 4

HOCKEY MAGAZINES

There are two types of hockey sports publication collectors, those who collect everything and those who collect their favorite stars. Hockey Magazines are very low in production and are mostly found in the major hockey cities and Canada.

HOCKEY BLUELINE

This is a quality early pro hockey monthly magazine (54-59). This publication has many, if not all, the major stars of that period.

YEAR	COVER/FEATURE	Nr-Mt	Ex
☐ 10/54	Gordie Howe (1st issue)	100	250
☐ 11/54	Marice Richard	50	100
☐ 12/54-3/55	Various	25	65
☐ 3/55	Jean Beliveau	50	100
☐ 4/55-8/56	Various	25	65
☐ 9/56 & 11/56	Maurice Richard	50	100
☐ 10/56 & 5/57	Gorden Howe	50	100
☐ 12/56-5/59	Various	25	45

HOCKEY DIGEST

The most common hockey magazine to be found and the least valued. This is a monthly program that started in 11/72. Hockey Digest valued is based on cover & condition. Hard to find without the mailing label.

YEAR	COVER/FEATURE	Nr-Mt	Ex
☐ 11/72	Bobby Orr	60	20
☐ 12/72-12/75	Various	15	5
☐ 1/76-1/80	Various	8	3
☐ 3/80-12/89	Various	6	2
☐ 1/90-present	Various	4	1
☐	Bobby Hull covers	20	5
☐	Bobby Orr covers	20	5
☐ 5/80	Wayne Gretzky (first)	40	20
☐	Wayne Gretzky covers	29	10
☐ 3/86	Mario Lemieux	25	5

HOCKEY ILLUSTRATED

This magazine started in the 60's and ran into the 80's. Hockey Illustrated is one of many general hockey magazines.

YEAR	COVER/FEATURE	Nr-Mt	Ex
☐ 11/62	Jacques Plante (1st issue)	100	25
☐ 12/62	Andy Bathgate	45	20
☐ 1/63	Jean Beliveau	45	20
☐ 2/63	Bobby Hull	50	20
☐ 1963-1970	Various	30	10
☐ 3/63	Gordie Howe	60	20
☐	Bobby Hull Covers	45	10
☐	Gordie Howe	40	10
☐	Bobby Orr	35	10

☐	1971-1981		
☐	Various	12	3

HOCKEY PICTORIAL

Hockey Pictorial is nice monthly publication that started in the 1950's.

YEAR	COVER/FEATURE	Nr-Mt	Ex
☐ 10/55	Jean Beliveau	125	35
☐ 11/55-12/56	Various	85	20
☐ 1/57-12/57	Various	65	20
☐ 1/58-12/59	Various	45	15
☐ 12/57	Gordie Howe	100	30
☐ 11/59	Bobby Hull	75	25
☐ 1/60-12/67	Various	30	15
☐	Bobby Hull Covers	45	20
☐	Gordie Howe Cover	45	20
☐ 1/68-12/71	Various	18	10
☐ 1/72-12/80	Various	10	5
☐	Bobby Orr Covers	20	10

GUIDES

1931 SPALDING GUIDE

1982 SPORTING NEWS

PROGRAMS

1950 NY RANGERS

1970

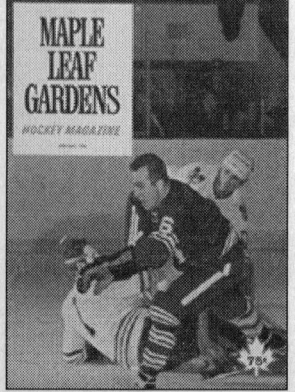

1979

1994

Stick With Beckett's All-Pro Hockey Coverage!

Subscribe to *Beckett Hockey Card Monthly* today!

Wondering where "in-the-know" hockey collectors get their monthly Price Guide? A subscription to *Beckett Hockey Card Monthly* gives you the hobby's most accurate hockey card Price Guide <u>every month</u>! Plus great info about new product releases, superstar player coverage, off-ice news and answers to all your collecting questions too!

Beckett Hockey Card Monthly

Name (please print) _____

Address _____

City _____ State _____ ZIP _____

Payment enclosed via:　❑ Check or Money Order　❑ Bill Me Later

Check One Please:	Price	Total
❑ 2 years (24 issues)	$44.95 =	_____
❑ 1 year (12 issues)	$24.95 =	_____

All Canadian & foreign addresses add
$12 per year for postage (includes G.S.T.).　=
_____

Payable in U.S. funds.
Please do not send cash.　Total Enclosed $ _____

Mail to:
Beckett Hockey Card Monthly
P.O. Box 7647
Red Oak, IA 51591-0647
Photocopies of this coupon are acceptable.

Please allow 4-6 weeks for
subscription delivery.

SH0058

CHAPTER TWENTY:
Collecting Golf Publications

GOLF PUBLICATIONS

Perhaps the hottest growth area in publications collecting is golf. Golf collectors tend to focus on physical items like clubs and balls, but there is a lot of growth in golf publications collecting, especially in the area of books, magazines and programs.

Golf collectors love their sport and tend to decorate their homes with memorabilia of golf legends along with scenes of great golf courses. There are four great legends of golf and one up and coming star. There are hundreds of great golf course views (but this book is about publications, not prints).

The two key legends are Ben Hogan and Bobby Jones. In the world of golf, these are the names that bring out the true golf historic sports fans. Any item that features these two players commands a premium. The next two legends are Arnold Palmer and Jack Nicklaus. Palmer is known by his Arnold's Army of fans. His charisma was said to be greater than that of John F. Kennedy. Nicklaus is the man with the most records and trophies. His material is plentiful everywhere.

The up and coming legend is Tiger Woods, who has the fan appeal no golfer has possessed since Nicklaus came on the pro scene. However, he still has 10 years to catch up with Nicklaus.

The facet of collecting with the strongest niche is perhaps the area of golf books. The best books are the earliest, and those autographed by legends such as Jones, Hogan, etc., are the most sought after. Prices are best reflected in the auction catalogs of the major golf auction houses.

GOLF MAGAZINES

There are many golf publications, and only the most popular ones are heavily collected. There are many titles that have been produced over the last 100 years. The most expensive are not necessarily the oldest but are instead those that feature Jones or Hogan. Then it is followed by age and vintage.

Outside of those two legends the remaining golf magazines have more of a general price that you can obtain from magazine dealers. The American Golfer (1922-1925) is perhaps one of the finest golf magazines made during the early period of golf history. This magazine was followed by Sports Illustrated (1925-1939). All of these magazines command $100 as a base in ex condition. After WWII, various golf magazines appeared on the national scene (Golf Digest, Golf, Golfing, Golf Illustrated). These magazines cover specific pro golfers and how to play the game.

Golf is now growing so rapidly that a multitude of regional and local golf magazines are being produced. General price guidelines would be $20-$30 for those in the 1940s, $15-$30 for those in the '50s and $10-$20 for those in the '60s. Golf magazines in the 1970s-1990s tend to have nominal prices in the $5-$10 range. However, there are exceptions.

Jones' pieces are rather pricey. The least inexpensive piece on Jones is the '59 SI magazine, which lists at $40. The most expensive magazine is the 1930 Time in nr-mt for $900.

Most of the remaining magazines from the 1920s and 1930s, such as vintage items like 1931's Spalding Golf Annual and Bobby Jones on Golf, will fall between $150 - $350. Items from later years (1940s-1960s) will fall in the $45-$150 range.

Jones passed away in 1972. His autographed books will fetch $900-plus. You never have to worry about selling Jones material.

Hogan is the Babe Ruth of golf. His material sells and continues to rise in value. During his prime he was unbeatable. The hottest Hogan item tends to be an autographed Time magazine. Hogan was a very generous autograph signer and was willing to sign through the mail until just before he passed away in 1997.

Ben does appear on items like Golf, Golf Digest, Golf Illustrated, etc. He was also featured on SI (twice) and on other magazine covers. His magazines tend to go between $50 and $100. His better or earlier pieces range from $100 to $200.

Nicklaus is perhaps the greatest golfer ever. He has more major wins than any other player. His consistency over two decades is simply tough to beat. Nicklaus is also approachable at golf tournaments and has been willing to sign for his fans. This makes his SI very desirable.

He has a lot of magazine cover appearances that do not command any premium. However, he does have a growing following and many golf fans are recognizing his investment potential. Currently you can find his magazines in the $10-$50 range.

Palmer has more charisma and charm than all the other pro golfers put together. He established the way golfers should treat their fans. His material is pursued heavily because he will sign them all. A great accomplishment is to get all 14 SIs signed. His magazine material is rather inexpensive and very undervalued ($10-$50 range).

Woods is perhaps the man to watch for the next decade. Already the youngest Masters champion and money winner, he has golf collectors going gaga over all of his items. His material may be perhaps the best to pick up now because his potential is so great. Mint material that features Woods is in the $15-$20 range. His autograph can easily command $75 on a quality item.

GOLF PROGRAMS

Perhaps the most underrated collectible is the golf program and ticket. The most collectible golf items rarely change hands and perhaps never get cataloged. Golf programs are desired by both historical event collectors as well as player collectors. The most popular golf programs will be the majors, with the Masters being the most sought after.

Minor tournaments do not command much of a premium unless it is won by one the of the more popular players. Ticket stubs, press passes and the like are collected by golfers, but values are not well determined. This is great news for the collector, because many items can be picked up relatively inexpensively. However, expect those pieces that relate to the major tournaments to be rather expensive.

1964 GOLF DIGEST

1964 GOLF

1994 GOLF

1995 GOLF

1995 GOLF DIGEST

1996 GOLF WORLD

1996 GOLF WORLD

1996 GOLF WORLD

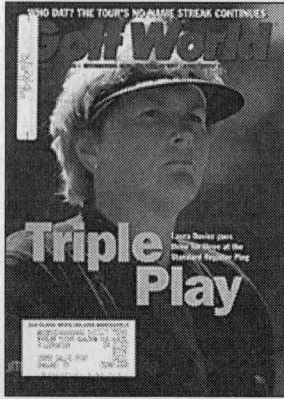

BYRON/NELSON PROGRAM

CHAPTER TWENTY-ONE:
Collecting Boxing Publications

Boxing certainly stirs a passion in fans worldwide. It's a passion that has fueled one of the fastest growing groups of publication collecting.

Collectors have long been fascinated with ring heroes, from the first heavyweight champion, John L. Sullivan, to Evander Holyfield, the latest idol of boxing champs. However, there is one fighter who is collected by everyone: Muhammad Ali, the three-time heavyweight champion and 1960 Gold medalist. Ali is also one of the most recognizable figures in any field.

Ali collectibles are among the most sought after items in all of sports. However, any boxer who has held a title or appeared in a title bout will find collectors who will seek out their items. These include Jack Johnson, Jack Dempsey, Joe Louis, Sonny Liston, Rocky Marciano, Sugar Ray Robinson, Jake Lamotta, Roberto Duran, Sugar Ray Leonard, Joe Frazier, George Foreman, Larry Holmes, Mike Tyson, Julio Cesar Chavez and Oscar De La Hoya.

The most sought after boxing publications fall into two distinct groups: programs and periodicals. Programs are produced for two venues: the actual venue where the fight is held, and the various closed circuit outlets that show the bouts on a large screen. The programs from the actual venue are known as on-site programs and are the most collectible and demand a large dollar premium. Scarcity is a major factor in determining the value of an on-site program.

How many people attended the bout and where the bout occurred are key ingredients in the value of a program. Examples of these factors would be two Muhammad Ali fights from the same year. Ali met Joe Frazier on July 25, 1975, at Madison Square Garden. Nearly 20,000 people viewed the fight. This program in ex-mt condition is routinely sold for $150-$175. Ali then challenged George Foreman for the heavyweight crown on Oct. 30. Estimated attendance for that bout exceed 25,000. But because of the bout location

(Kinshasa, Zairee) very few programs have entered the marketplace. In ex-mt condition, the programs command a minimum of $1,500.

Although many programs command a premium due to scarcity or historical significance, others can be found at very reasonable prices and could prove over time to have a fine collectible future. Programs of recent champions can be purchased rather inexpensively, with a price ranging from $10 to $50.

PROGRAMS - ON SITES (UNLESS NOTED)

DATE	COVER SUBJECT	Nr-Mt	Ex
☐ 7/14/19	Willard - Dempsey	1800	1000
☐ 7/23/26	Dempsey - Tunney	800	650
☐ 9/22/27	Tunney - Dempsey	850	700
☐ 6/19/36	Louis - Schmelling	550	400
☐ 6/22/37	Braddock - Louis	450	325
☐ 6/22/38	Louis - Schmeling	500	375
☐ 10/24/51	Louis - Margiano	600	450
☐ 2/14/51	Lamotta - Robinson	400	300
☐ 4/16/52	Robinson - Graziano	325	200
☐ 9/23/52	Walcott - Marciano	400	275
☐ 9/21/55	Marciano - Moore	350	225
☐ 9/25/62	Patterson - Liston	275	175
☐ 2/25/64	Liston - Clay	600	400
☐ 6/21/66	Ali - Cooper	250	150
☐ 3/22/67	Ali - Folley	375	250
☐ 3/ 8/71	Frazier - Ali	325	200
☐ 10/23/73	Ali -Lubbers	850	550
☐ 10/1/75	Ali - Frazier	1250	850
☐ 10/1/75	Ali - Frazier Closed Circuit	100	75
☐ 10/2/80	Holmes - Ali	100	75
☐ 6/20/80	Leonard - Duran	125	85
☐ 1/22/88	Tyson - Holmes	100	75
☐ 2/11/90	Tyson - Dollars	100	75

Boxing publicaitons have been on our newsstands for nearly 100 years. Many have had long and successful runs while others have failed miserably. The most sought after by collectors has been "the Ring". Known as the 'Bible' of boxing. Ring was founded by Nat Flesher in 1922. Nearly every popular pugilist has appeared on the cover at least once. Collectors have followed three distinct patterns when collecting htis publication. 1) collecting magazines from a certain era, 2) collecting magazines that feature a favorite boxer or boxers on the cover, 3) collecting a complete "run" of the periodicals. Other boxing publications that are popular with collectors are Arena, Police Gazzette, Boxing Illustrated, "KO" and International Boxing Digest.

Although in some cases the periodicals do not command the dollars of similar 'Ring Magazine' they are often sought after because they feature their favorite boxers and the art work is beautiful.

RING MAGAZINE

DATE	COVER SUBJECT	Nr-Mt	Ex
□ 2/11/22	First Issue	750	450
□ 8/22	Benny Leonard	175	100
□ 9/27	Jack Dempsey	75	50
□ 2/32	Max Schmelling	50	35
□ 8/37	Joe Louis	50	35
□ 7/42	Joe Louis	35	20
□ 10/49	Jake Lamotta	30	20
□ 10/53	Rocky Marciano	30	20
□ 1/55	Archie Moore	25	15
□ 8/60	Cassius Clay (first cover)	75	45
□ 7/67	Demsey, Louis, Clay	20	10
□ 1/73	George Foreman	15	10
□ 2/77	Roberto Duran	10	5
□ 2/82	Holmes - Cooney	7.5	4
□ 11/91	Mike Tylson	5	3

CHAMPIONSHIP TICKETS

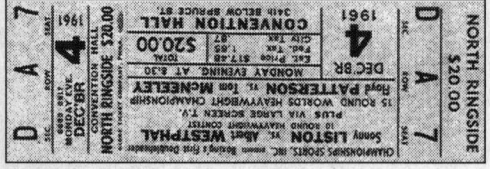

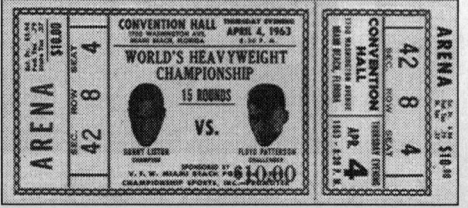

1929 ARENA

1932 ARENA

CHAMPIONSHIP PROGRAM

CHAMPIONSHIP PROGRAM

CHAMPIONSHIP PROGRAM

CHAMPIONSHIP PROGRAM

CHAMPIONSHIP PROGRAM

CHAMPIONSHIP PROGRAM

RING MAGAZINE

CHAPTER TWENTY-TWO:
Collecting Auto Racing Publications

This is a special unique aspect of the sports publication hobby because Auto Racing magazines are not normally found at the traditional 'sports shows' or 'hobby stores'. This distinct group of publications is growing fast with the growth in the NASCAR hobby collecting business. The reflection of this trend is how major magazines, like Beckett and Sports Illustrated, created special issues on the subject of NASCAR racing.

Most of the hobby focuses on race programs with less emphasis on monthly or annual publications. The bulk of the value is in the actual race programs, especially from the early part of the racing days. The number one collected auto program is the Indy 500 program.. This is followed by Daytona 500. There is a small following of beach race events and regional events. The best book written on Auto Racing programs is 'The Baseball & Sports Publications Price Guide - 1st edition' by Century of Sports Publications (Cretshol & Alexander 1995).

INDY 500 PROGRAMS

DATE	COVER	Nr-Mt	Ex
☐ 1911	....	3500+	1,000
☐ 1913-1914	....	1700	300
☐ 1915	....	1200	250
☐ 1916	500 Mile Race	1900	500
☐ 1917	Very Rare	3000+	1500
☐ 1919-1920	....	1000	300
☐ 1921-1924	....	600	200
☐ 1925-1931	(oversize versions)	450	100
☐ 1932-1937	Art Deco	300	70
☐ 1938-1941	....	225	50
☐ 1942-1945	WWII - no programs		
☐ 1946-1949	....	100	30
☐ 1950-1955	....	60	20
☐ 1956-1961	....	30	10
☐ 1962-1979	....	20	5
☐ 1980-on	....	10	3

DAYTONA 500

The Ultimate NASCAR event. This program is a must for all NASCAR collectors.

DATE	COVER	Nr-Mt	Ex
☐ 1959	1st event	600	200
☐ 1960	....	280	100
☐ 1961	....	175	65
☐ 1962-1963	....	130	40
☐ 1964	Richard Petty	200	70
☐ 1965-1967	....	100	30
☐ 1968	Andretti/Petty	75	25
☐ 1969	Richard Petty	75	25
☐ 1970	LeRoy Yarborough	60	20

☐ 1971-1972	....	50	15
☐ 1973-1977	....	40	10
☐ 1978-1986	....	25	5
☐ 1987-1997	....	15	3

It should be noted that The Daytona Firecracker event is held at Daytona on July 4th and it is not as valuable as the Daytona program.

Early programs from Daytona Beach in the 30's-40's will be in the hundreds of dollars. In fact Daytona Beach classics are very tough and popular among auto buffs. Other minor car racing programs would be similar to the Daytona 500 except 35% less in value.

CAR RACING MAGAZINES

This is pursued by die hard car racing fanatics. Most of these titles carry general values. However, there are short print runs that create premiums along with specific superstar features that create a value about two times the common price.

The following is a simple guide to prices for the following car magazines:

Auto Age (1950's), Auto Racing (1966-1970's), Auto Racing Digest (1973-present), Auto Racing Memories (1981-1989), Auto Speed and Sport (1953), Auto Sport Review (1952-1953), Auto Sports(1962-1963), Best Hot Rods (1952-1960), Challenge 1975-1976, Circle Track (1982-1997), Circle Track and Highway (1971-72), GT Motosports (1986), Indy Car Racing (1983-1997), Motor Racing Stars (1969), Motor Speed (1953-1959), Motorsport (1950-1956), Official Racing Guide (1955), On the Grid (1960-1962), Open Wheel (1981-present), Racing Cars (1977-1981), Racing Pictorial (1959-1980) Speed Age (1947-1969 & 1987-1988), Stock Car Racing (1966-present), USAC Magazine (1970-1975), and US Auto Sports (1964-1965). Grand National Illustrated (1982-present) are more popular than the general magazines and go for twice the listed price.

The general magazine prices are

DATE	COVER	Nr-Mt	Ex
☐ 1940's	General	45-60	10-20
☐ 1950's	General	45-60	10-20
☐ 1950's	Special/1st issues	100+	30+
☐ 1960's	General	15-25	5- 7
☐ 1960's	Special/1st issues	40	5- 7
☐ 1970's	General	10-20	5
☐ 1970's	Superstars	15-25	5
☐ 1980's	General	7-10	2
☐ 1980's	Superstars	15-20	4
☐ 1990's	General	4-10	2
☐ 1990's	Superstars	10-15	2

CAR MAGAZINES

The second area that is heavily collected by a different type of auto collector is auto magazines. Such magazines as 'Car & Driver' & 'Road/Track' are pursued by automobile collectors. The most popular of all car magazines that are collected revolve around Corvette and Mustangs. However, there is a strong following in many types of automobiles. Early auto related material is pursued by both ad collectors and by type car collectors.

Again auto buffs love early car racing material, especially from the beach events in the 1930's. Auto magazines from the 1950's are typically pursued by car lovers who are willing to spend 20-25 for nice copies. Magazines from the 1960's bounce around 15-20 with the exception of special features with stars like Reggie Jackson (50) or cool corvette magazines (25). Magazines from the 70's bounce around 10 and 5 from the 1980's-1990's. Car magazines are usually not well preserved and are hard to find in nice condition.

1994 DRAG RACING

1994 WINSTON CUP ILLUST.

1995 RACING FOR KIDS

1996 RACER

1996 RACER

1996 WINSTON CUP ILLUST.

1995 BECKETT RACING HEROES

1996 BECKETT RACING PREVIEW

1996 BECKETT TRIBUTE

CHAPTER TWENTY-THREE:
Collecting Sports Newspapers

When Cal Ripken Jr. of the Baltimore Orioles broke Lou Gehrig's consecutive games played record in 1995, baseball collectors began searching frantically for Gehrig's 1939 newspaper chronicling the end of his legendary streak.

"Immortal Cal!" and "Cal-Lossal!" screamed the headlines of the Baltimore Sun for their hometown hero, perhaps a bit louder than " 'Iron Man' Lou Benches self after 2,130 games!" some 56 years earlier.

Whether you follow a particular player or team, vintage newspapers offer the collector a relatively inexpensive display piece. And, like a program or ticket, whether you collect the World Series or the Super Bowl, a heavyweight boxing match or the NCAA Tournament, newspapers are a wonderful way to complete a collection.

Since newspapers were meant to be read and discarded, only a limited number over the years have survived. Though most major city editions published several million each day, most of those didn't survive more than a week or so, creating the present market for low supply and high demand. Older editions, especially those published before 1960, may be difficult to find, but not necessarily impossible.

Collecting newspapers probably began to catch on in the 1970s, when libraries around the country started converting their bound volumes onto microfilm because of storage limitations. These bound volumes were either discarded or sold to dealers, who pulled out the important dates and began selling them as authentic artifacts of sports and world history.

HISTORY OF SPORTS NEWSPAPERS

The modern newspaper as we know it, with its front page banner headlines, began circulating around 1898 with the outbreak of the Spanish American War. Sports periodicals of that era, such as The Sporting News and Sporting Life, have their share of collectors, too. Other 19th century editions of note are Harper's Weekly and Frank Leslie's Illustrated, which followed the evolution of baseball from the 1850s. Each published early artist illustrations — known as wood blocks (engravings on wood or metal plates) — of the players and the game, featuring teams such as the 1869 Cincinnati Red Stockings, the first professional baseball club.

SOURCES OF SPORTS NEWSPAPERS

Finding particular sports newspapers can be difficult if you don't know where to look. Antique stores and garage sales sometimes offer them, but don't expect these sources to provide much of a selection. Large newspaper dealers who offer birth date papers may be a good source, but many of the important dates already have been cherry-picked. And don't bother calling The Miami Herald or The Los Angeles Times and expect them to find you a mint edition of Sandy Koufax's perfect game in 1965. Most daily newspapers only carry up to three months of back inventory before discarding them.

In fact, I've found that just a handful of dealers carry sports newspapers. The world's leading vintage sports newspaper firm, Box Seat Collectibles in Halesite, N.Y., is one of the few companies dealing in vintage sports newspapers and the only one that issues a catalog for specific newspaper prices. (You can order the catalog at 516-423-1025.)

DISPLAYING SPORTS NEWSPAPERS

Capturing a memorable sports moment on the front page can turn a 50-cent piece of newsprint into a valuable work of art. Consider some of the most legendary home runs in baseball history, for example, and picture what the page would look like framed in your office. "Bobby Thomson Hits Short Heard Around the World," "Mazeroski Homer Wins Series," and "Maris Slams 61st" are just three that come to mind. But every team has had its share of heroic moments, from Babe Ruth's called shot in the '32 World Series to Kirk Gibson's thrilling home run in the 1988 Series.

"I have many items from significant games," explains prominent collector Barry Halper, whose favorite newspapers revolve around Shoeless Joe Jackson and the 1919 Black Sox scandal. "Displaying an item with a newspaper adds greatly to the presentation of the piece. It also helps place the item into its proper historical context."

Football is another sport with an endless history of stars and headlines, from Red Grange and the Four Horsemen to Barry Sanders and Brett Farve. For Colts fans, there's the 1958 NFL title game when Alan Ameche scored the winning touchdown in sudden-death overtime. How about the legendary Ice Bowl game nine years later when Green Bay's Bart Starr left the Cowboys literally frozen in their shoes with a quarterback sneak with 13 seconds remaining? The possibilities are endless.

Joe Namath's victory guarantee and ensuing Super Bowl III upset, Franco Harris' Immaculate Reception, and Joe Montana's TD pass with no time left in the 1982 title game make wonderful eye catching mementos of the game.

RARITY AND PRICING

Some newspapers are easier to find than others. In basketball, for example, Wilt Chamberlain's 100-point game in 1962 is especially valuable and hard to find, while papers chronicling Michael Jordan's five NBA championships are easier to track down and remain relatively inexpensive pieces of Chicago Bulls' legacy memorabilia.

In boxing, bouts of Tunney-Dempsey, Schmeling-Louis, Clay-Liston, Ali-Frazier, and anything with Rocky Marciano are highly coveted.

Golf's major tournaments, featuring players from Bobby Jones to Tiger Woods, make great gifts for the golf enthusiast. And the United States' stunning 4-3 victory over the Soviets in the 1980 Olympics made headlines and believers all over the world.

So how does one go about placing a price tag on sports history? There are five essential factors involved: the significance of the event (Hank Aaron's 715th home run was much more important than his 716th); the size and placement of the headline; whether a picture of the subject accompanies the story; a complete edition versus a single page; and overall condition.

While some believe owning a hometown edition (where the game was played) is a necessity — especially in a championship paper — most collectors don't care where the paper was printed as long as it is displayable. That may explain why in many cases a prestigious newspaper such as The New York Times, with its smaller headline style, may not be nearly as valuable as The Chicago Tribune which boasts larger and bolder headlines.

Story clippings cut from the page have little or no market value.

STORAGE

Once you've found what you are looking for, newspapers are great items to have autographed. Most athletes enjoy reminiscing upon a defining moment in their careers and are glad to sign them. Whether they are autographed or not, framing a newspaper is a good way to preserve it. When framing, acid-free material should be used, and, once framed, avoid direct sunlight, which tends to fade newsprint. Otherwise, keeping them opened flat with a backboard in a polyethylene bag (large archival bags which insulate against moisture) is a good idea. Newspapers should be stored in dehumidified rooms and handled sparingly.

Article contribution by Michael Solomowitz.

SPORTING NEWS

The Sporting News is the longest running periodical on sports today. It originally competed against newspapers in its day (Sporting Life) but all of the newspapers folded by the early 1910's. The Sporting News then became the Baseball bible for decades. After WWII The Sporting News began to cover topics like Football, Basketball and Hockey. This subject matter was relegated to the back of the periodical. However, the best photos of major superstars are covered in these articles. The magazine format was developed in the 1940's and then color was introduced in the 1960's. In the 1990's the format has gone to a magazine style size and shape with its focus on the major four sports.

Most Sporting News collectors are historical collectors who enjoy doing baseball research. There are groups that focus on their key players like Joe DiMaggio, Mickey Mantle and other superstars. Most of the player collectors now focus in the 1960's and up. Heavy emphasis is now on Michael Jordan covers. Autographing of Sporting News does occur but is not as frequent as Sports Illustrated. Therefore, I did not list autograph values on them.

The best book written on The Sporting News is "The Baseball and Sports Publications Price Guide" (1996) by Robert Crestohl and David T. Alexander. The book lists every issue and the keys to each issue.

YEARS	COVER	FEATURE	Nr-Mt	Ex
☐ 1886-89	Common cover	....	400	200
☐ 1890-99	Common cover	....	350	150
☐ 1900-10	Common cover	....	200	125
☐ 1911-15	Common cover	....	150	100
☐ 1916-20	Common cover	....	100	75
☐ 1921-25	Common cover	....	75	50
☐ 1926-30	Common cover	....	55	45
☐ 1931-35	Common cover	....	45	30
☐ 1936-40	Common cover	....	35	20
☐ 1941-45	Common cover	....	25	15
☐ 1946-50	Common cover	....	22	15
☐ 1951-60	Common cover	....	20	12
☐ 1961-70	Common cover	....	17	10
☐ 1971-80	Common cover	....	12	5
☐ 1981-97	Common cover	....	7	3

Key issues worth noting: Major Stars, World Series and All Stars issues are worth 2x the common cover price. However, the following are key issues that are noted for demand:

YEARS	COVER	FEATURE	Nr-Mt	Ex
☐ 1/21/1899	Roy Thomas Phillies Rare good condition			150
☐ 10/17/12	Joe Wood World Series issue ....vg			150
☐ 10/09/19	Black Sox World Series	....	400	200
☐ 10/16/19	Black Sox World Series	....	400	200
☐ 9/30/20	Black Sox Case	....	400	200
☐ 10/7/20	Black Sox Case	....	500	200
☐ 7/28/21	Black Sox Trial	....	400	200
☐ 8/4/21	Black Sox Trial	....	400	200
☐ 8/11/21	Black Sox Trial (Banned for life)	.....	500	250
☐ 3/16/22	Ty Cobb	....	200	100
☐ 9/27/22	Babe Ruth (1st cover)	....	400	200
☐ 3/20/24	Lou Gehrig (1st cover)	....	400	200
☐ 5/1/24	Ty Cobb	....	300	150
☐ 5/22/24	Ty Cobb	....	300	150
☐ 5/14/24	Ty Cobb	....	250	125
☐ 9/3/25	Babe Ruth	....	400	200
☐ 3/4/26	Babe Ruth	....	300	150
☐ 9/29/27	Babe Ruth/Lou Gehrig	....	300	150
☐ 10/6/27	Babe Ruth sets record	....	300	150
☐ 7/10/30	Babe Ruth	....	300	150
☐ 11/19/30	Babe Ruth	....	300	150
☐ 11/19/31	Babe Ruth	....	300	150

YEARS	COVER	FEATURE	Nr-Mt	Ex
☐ 10/6/32	Babe Ruth/Lou Gehrig	....	400	200
☐ 7/6/33	First All Star Game Featured	....	600	300
☐ 7/5/34	Second All Star Game Featured	.....	400	200
☐ 6/6/35	Babe Ruth Retires	....	250	125
☐ 7/9/36	Lou Gehrig		150	75
☐ 10/8/36	Lou Gehrig	....	225	100
☐ 10/29/36	Joe DiMaggio (first appearance)	....	150	100
☐ 12/31/36	Carl Hubbell #1 men of year	....	150	75
☐ 4/29/37	Lou Gehrig/Joe DiMaggio	....	150	75
☐ 9/23/37	Lou Gehrig	....	150	75
☐ 6/23/38	Babe Ruth as Braves Coach	....	150	75
☐ 7/14/38	Babe Ruth/All Star Game	....	150	75
☐ 4/13/39	Ted Williams with Rookies	....	200	125
☐ 6/22/39	100 yr of Baseball Commemorative Issue (4 teams pictured)	....		100
☐ 12/28/39	Joe DiMaggio #1	....	200	125
☐ 8/22/40	Ted Williams	....	200	100
☐ 1/2/41	Bob Feller #1	....	175	100
☐ 6/5/41	Lou Gehrig Dies (article)	....	250	125
☐ 6/19/41	Ted Williams	....	200	125
☐ 11/20/41	Joe Jackson/Williams/others	....	250	125
☐ 1/1/42	Ted Williams	....	200	100
☐ 1/29/42	Ted Williams	....	200	100
☐ 7/2/42	Ruth/Gehrig/Williams/others	....	200	100
☐ 9/24/42	Shoeless Joe Jackson	....	200	100
☐ 12/31/42	Ted Williams	....	200	100
☐ 11/4/43	Stan Musial (MVP)	....	75	35
☐ 11/18/43		....		25
☐ 1/20/44	Branch Rickey	....		25
☐ 1/ 27/44		....		25
☐ 4/6/44	Carl Hubbell	....		30
☐ 5/4/44	Herb Pennock	....		25
☐ 5/11/44	Babe Ruth	....		40
☐ 5/18/44	Connie Mack	....		35
☐ 5/25/44	Clark Griffith	....		30
☐ 6/1/44	Babe Adams	....		30
☐ 6/29/44	Walter Johnson	....		40
☐ 7/6/44	All Star Game issue	....		70
☐ 7/13/44	Stan Musial	....		75
☐ 9/21/44	George Sisler	....		30
☐ 11/2/44	Bill Veeck	....		25
☐ 11/9/44	Frank Chance	....		30
☐ 11/16/44	Luke Sewell	....		35
☐ 11/23/44	Marty Marion MVP	....		35
☐ 11/30/44	Judge Landis dies	....		35
☐ 11/1/45	Jackie Robinson signs (article)	.....	100	40
☐ 1/11/45	44 All-Star team	....		60
☐ 1/25/45		....		20
☐ 2/22/45	Jimmie Foxx	....		30
☐ 3/01/45	Ruth/Gehrig	....		40
☐ 4/5/45	Leo Durocher	....		20
☐ 4/26/45	St Louis Browns	....		25
☐ 5/03/45	Happy Chandler	....		25
☐ 5/10/45	Tommy Holmes	....		25
☐ 5/17/45	Jimmie Dykes	....		25
☐ 5/24/45	Happy Chandler	....		25
☐ 5/31/45	Mort Cooper	....		25
☐ 6/7/45	Dave Ferris	....		25
☐ 6/14/45	Howard Schultz	....		25
☐ 6/21/45	Cy Young	....		40
☐ 6/28/45	Dodger Bum	....		25
☐ 7/05/45	Hank Greenberg	....		45
☐ 7/19/45	Happy Chandler	....		25
☐ 7/26/45	Charley Grimm	....		25
☐ 8/02/45	Larry MacPhail	....		25
☐ 8/09/45	Mel Ott	....		35
☐ 8/23/45	Joe McCarthy	....		40
☐ 8/30/45	Bob Feller	....		50
☐ 9/06/45	Leo Durocher	....		25
☐ 9/20/45	Dick Fowler	....		25
☐ 10/25/45	Andy Pafko	....		20
☐ 11/08/45	Sam Breadon	....		20
☐ 11/15/45	Eddie Dyer	....		20
☐ 1/31/46	Joe DiMaggio/Ted Williams	....	250	150

YEARS	COVER	FEATURE	Nr-Mt	Ex	YEARS	COVER	FEATURE	Nr-Mt	Ex
☐ 1/03/46	Hall of Fame			25	☐ 3/17/48	Yogi Berra			20
☐ 1/10/46	Sam Breadon			20	☐ 3/31/48	Joe McCarthy			20
☐ 1/17/46	Larry MacPhail			20	☐ 4/07/48	Hank Greenberg			25
☐ 1/24/46	Happy Chandler			30	☐ 4/14/48	Joe McCarthy			20
☐ 1/31/46	DiMaggio/Williams			200	☐ 4/21/48	Opening Day issue			50
☐ 3/07/46	Bob Feller			35	☐ 4/28/48	Joe DiMaggio			40
☐ 3/14/46	Ted Williams			40	☐ 5/05/48	Ty Cobb			40
☐ 3/28/46	Cardinal Outfielders			20	☐ 5/12/48	Leo Durocher			35
☐ 4/04/46	Johnny Mize			25	☐ 6/16/48	Yankee Stadium			35
☐ 4/11/46	Mickey Owen			20	☐ 6/23/48	Babe Ruth says goodbye		400	200
☐ 4/18/46	Opening Day Issue			50	☐ 6/30/48	Bob Lemon			35
☐ 5/16/46	46 Bos. Sluggers			35	☐ 7/21/48	All Star Game			40
☐ 5/23/46	Ted Williams			35	☐ 7/28/48	Leo Durocher			35
☐ 7/03/46	Veeck Buys Indians			30	☐ 8/04/48	Joe Tinker dies			35
☐ 9/04/46	Larry MacPhail			25	☐ 8/11/48	Tinkers/Evers/Chnce			25
☐ 9/18/46	Ted Williams			60	☐ 8/25/48	Babe Ruth Dies Issue Memorial Section			
☐ 9/25/46	Ted Williams/Stan Musial		125	100		(Key Sport News Issue)		800	500
☐ 10/02/46	Eddie Collins			35	☐ 9/1/48	Joe DiMaggio		150	75
☐ 10/09/46	World Series Issue			75	☐ 9/01/48	Babe Ruth Stories			150
☐ 11/20/46	Ted Williams MVP			44	☐ 9/08/48	Phil Rizzuto, B Ruth			40
☐ 11/27/46	Stan Musial MVP			45	☐ 9/15/48	Richie Ashburn			30
☐ 12/11/46	Bill Goodman			20	☐ 9/22/48	Satchel Paige			35
☐ 1/1/47	Stan Musial		150	75	☐ 9/29/48	Bill Southworth			20
☐ 12/31/47	Ted Williams #1		200	100	☐ 10/13/48	World Series			80
☐ 1/ 22/47	46 TSN All Star			35	☐ 10/20/48	World Series			80
☐ 2/26/47	Speaker/Hornsby			35	☐ 11/03/48	Casey Stengel			20
☐ 3/05/47	Williams/Musial			45	☐ 11/24/48	Red Rolfe			20
☐ 3/12/47	Durocher			40	☐ 12/01/48	Lou Boudreau			20
☐ 3/19/47	Leo Durocher			25	☐ 12/08/48	Stan Musial			40
☐ 3/26/47	Durocher			25	☐ 12/15/48	Jackie Robinson			25
☐ 4/02/47	Jackie Robinson			45	☐ 1/05/49	Pete Reiser			50
☐ 4/09/47	Berra			45	☐ 1/12/49	Red Schoendienst			20
☐ 4/16/47	Opening Day			70	☐ 2/2/49	Bill Veeck			20
☐ 4/23/47	Babe Ruth Special 8 page section -				☐ 2/23/49	Joe DiMaggio			70
	Jackie Robinson 1st game		400	200	☐ 3/02/49				25
☐ 4/30/47	Pete Reiser			30	☐ 3/09/49	Honus Wagner			25
☐ 5/07/47	Babe Ruth Day			70	☐ 3/16/49	Red Sanford			20
☐ 5/14/47	Hank Greenberg			30	☐ 3/23/49	George Earnshaw			20
☐ 5/21/47	Johnny Mize			50	☐ 3/30/49	Bill Dickey			30
☐ 5/28/47	Hal Chase dies			25	☐ 4/06/49	Gene Woodling			20
☐ 6/04/47	Dugout Jockeys			20	☐ 4/13/49	Joe DiMaggio/Ted Williams (photo)		350	200
☐ 6/11/47	George McQuinn			20	☐ 4/20/49	Opening Day			90
☐ 6/18/47	Bobby Thomson			35	☐ 4/27/49	Lou Boudreau			30
☐ 6/25/47	Warren Spahn			35	☐ 5/04/49	Frank Crosetti			25
☐ 7/02/47	Ewell Blackwell			25	☐ 5/11/49	Charley Gehringer			25
☐ 7/16/47	Larry Doby			75	☐ 5/18/49	Gene Breadon			35
☐ 7/23/47	Yanks Win			35	☐ 5/25/49	Yogi Berra			25
☐ 7/30/47	15 HoF			45	☐ 6/01/49	Larry Doby			25
☐ 8/06/47	Burt Shotton			25	☐ 6/08/49	Red Schoendienst			25
☐ 8/13/47	Hugh Casey			35	☐ 6/14/49	Hank Greenberg			35
☐ 8/20/47	Ted Williams			40	☐ 6/22/49	Frank Frisch			35
☐ 8/27/47	Connie mack			35	☐ 6/29/49	Ray Boone			25
☐ 9/03/47	1st Negro Pitcher			40	☐ 7/06/49	Joe DiMaggio			75
☐ 9/10/47	Honus Wagner			35	☐ 7/20/49	All-Star Game			35
☐ 9/17/47	Jackie Robinson ROY (article)		150	75	☐ 7/27/49	Casey Stengel			35
☐ 9/24/47	Dikie Walker			35	☐ 8/03/49	Stan Musial			45
☐ 10/29/47	Larry MacPhail			20	☐ 8/10/49	Joe McCarthy			35
☐ 11/05/47	Red Ruffing			25	☐ 8/17/49	Luke Appling			25
☐ 11/12/47	Muddy Ruel			20	☐ 8/24/49	Yogi Berra			40
☐ 11/19/47	47 retirees			20	☐ 8/31/49	Connie Mack Day			25
☐ 11/2/47	Bob Elliott MVP			20	☐ 9/7/49	Berra/J.Robinson			60
☐ 12/17/47	Leo Durocher			25	☐ 9/14/49	Yogi Berra			25
☐ 12/24/47	Hugh Casey			20	☐ 9/21/49	Enos Slaughter			25
☐ 12/31/47	Ted Williams #1			150	☐ 9/28/49	Ty Cobb			35
☐ 1/07/48	47 Sports Thrills			40	☐ 10/05/49	World Series			75
☐ 1/14/48	Joe DiMaggio			40	☐ 10/12/49	Casey Stengel			70
☐ 1/21/48	Sam Breadon Ret.			20	☐ 10/19/49	J. Robinson			75
☐ 1/28/48	Bill Veeck			40	☐ 11/09/49				20
☐ 2/04/48	Joe McCarthy			20	☐ 11/16/49	Berra/Garagiola			20
☐ 2/11/48	Herb Pennock dies			25	☐ 11/23/49	Jackie Robinson			40
☐ 2/18/48	Babe Ruth			20	☐ 11/30/49	Ted Williams MVP			40
☐ 2/25/48	M. Brown Dies			25	☐ 12/07/49	Ted Williams			30
☐ 3/30/48	Pennock HOF			25	☐ 12/14/49	Bobby Thomson			30
☐ 3/10/48	Joe McCarthy			20	☐ 12/21/49	Jackie Robsinson			40

YEARS	COVER	FEATURE	Nr-Mt	Ex		YEARS	COVER	FEATURE	Nr-Mt	Ex
☐ 12/28/49	Ted Williams #1	....	150	75		☐ 3/3/54		....		12
☐ 1/18/50		....		20		☐ 3/17/54	Walt Alston			15
☐ 1/25/50		....		20		☐ 3/24/54		....		12
☐ 2/01/50	Jackie Robinson	....		40		☐ 3/31/54		....		12
☐ 2/22/50				20		☐ 5/12/54	Stan Musial			65
☐ 1/3/51	Phil Rizzuto #1	....	100	50		☐ 5/19/54		....		12
☐ 1/31/51	First Mantle Story	....	200	125		☐ 6/2/54		....		12
☐ 4/25/51	Mickey Mantle Cover	....	400	200		☐ 6/30/54		....		12
☐ 6/27/51	W. O'Malley	....		15		☐ 8/11/54		....		12
☐ 7/04/51				15		☐ 9/22/54	Casey Stengel			15
☐ 8/29/51	Bob Feller	....		20		☐ 6/17/53	Mickey Mantle	....	100	50
☐ 10/17/51				15		☐ 7/1/53	Mickey Mantle		100	50
☐ 10/10/51	Stan Musial/Others	....	150	75		☐ 1/5/55	Willie Mays #1	....	100	50
☐ 1/02/52	Stan Musial	....	150	75		☐ 6/1/55	Al Kaline (first appearance)	....	75	50
☐ 2/06/52	Club Uses Negroes	....		40		☐ 1/4/56	Duke Snider	....	75	50
☐ 4/9/52		....		20		☐ 7/4/56	Ted Williams/Joe DiMaggio	....	125	50
☐ 4/16/52		....		60		☐ 7/11/56	Stan Musial		125	50
☐ 4/23/52				40		☐ 10/10/56	Mantle /others	....	150	100
☐ 4/30/52	Walter O'Malley	....		20		☐ 10/17/56	Don Larsen perfect game (article)	...	150	100
☐ 5/07/52	Ted Williams	....		40		☐ 1/2/57	Mantle #1	....	200	100
☐ 5/14/52	R. Hornsby	....		20		☐ 1/1/58	Ted Williams #1		80	40
☐ 5/21/52	Jackie Jensen	....		20		☐ 5/14/58	Stan Musial		80	40
☐ 5/28/52	Dale Mitchell	....		20		☐ 8/17/60	Ted Williams player of decade	......	200	100
☐ 6/04/52	Jimmy Piersall	....		20		☐ 6/28/61	Mantle/Maris		100	50
☐ 6/11/52	Cobb/Hornsby	....		25		☐ 1/3/62	Roger Maris #1	....	100	50
☐ 6/25/52	Jimmy Piersall	....		25		☐ 10/20/62	Roger Maris/Mickey Mantle	....	50	20
☐ 7/02/52	Paige/Veeck	....		25		☐ 12/14/63	Sandy Koufax #1	....	50	20
☐ 7/16/52	All-Star Game	....		25		☐ 2/22/64	Pete Rose	....	40	20
☐ 7/23/52	Ty Cobb	....		25		☐ 5/2/64	McCovey/Mays/Cepeda	....	40	20
☐ 7/30/52		....		25		☐ 9/5/64	Roberto Clemente	....	75	35
☐ 8/06/52	Roger Hornsby	....		25		☐ 8/21/65	Pete Rose	....	40	20
☐ 8/13/52	Jackie Jensen	....		20		☐ 4/6/68	Mickey Mantle (color)	....	50	30
☐ 8/20/52	Mickey Mantle	....		20		☐ 11/01/69	NY Mets	....	40	20
☐ 8/27/52	Leo Durocher	....		20		☐ 2/28/70	Roberto Clemente	....	40	20
☐ 9/03/52	Robin Roberts/Mantle	....		40		☐ 10/30/71	Roberto Clemente	....	40	20
☐ 9/10/52	Early Wynn	....		20		☐ 4/8/72	Roberto Clemente	....	40	20
☐ 9/17/52	Jackie Robinson	....		20		☐ 5/5/73	Nolan Ryan	....	50	25
☐ 9/24/52	Joe Black	....		20		☐ 4/20/74	Hank Aaron/Babe Ruth	....	40	20
☐ 10/01/52	World Series	....		75		☐ 5/17/75	Nolan Ryan	....	40	20
☐ 10/15/52	Rizzuto/Berra	....		50		☐ 4/19/80	Nolan Ryan	....	30	15
☐ 10/29/52	Ted Williams	....		20		☐ 1/9/82	Wayne Gretzky	....	30	15
☐ 11/12/52	Mickey Mantle Story	....		100		☐ 3/28/83	Michael Jordan	....	50	30
☐ 11/19/52	Duke Snider	....		25		☐ 5/9/83	Nolan Ryan	....	30	15
☐ 11/26/52	All Star Team	....		25		☐ 2/13/84	Michael Jordan/Sam Perkins	....	30	15
☐ 11/11/53	Nap Lajoe	....		20		☐ 3/26/84	Michael Jordan	....	30	15
☐ 1/06/54	Baseball Thrills	....		15		☐ 10/29/84	Michael Jordan	....	30	15
☐ 2/17/54		....		12		☐ 3/23/87	Michael Jordan/Dr J	....	30	15
☐ 2/24/54	Willie Mays	....		25		☐ 87 on	Michael Jordan covers	....	25	15

THE SPORTING NEWS
1967

1968

1988 BASEBALL YEARBOOK

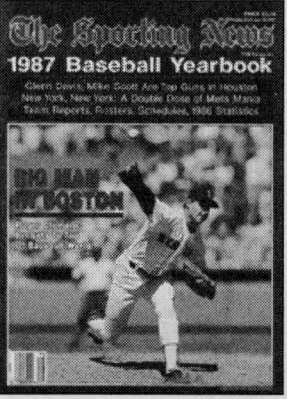

CHAPTER TWENTY-FOUR:
Alphabetical Index

Many players have appeared on the cover of Sports Illustrated, Time, Life, Beckett, Sport and Sports Illustrated for Kids that it took more than 35 pages to complete this alpha index. The index is not totally complete. It does not include some issues that a player is in the background for SI and Sport. It also does not list every Beckett issue released. This tool is a quick reference guide to the cover issues of your favorite player. The index lists each player covers by the magazine it is (si = Sport Illustrated), then the date of the magazine. Sports Illustrated will also have a few with initials' YIS for Year in Sports, and COM for commemorative.

The magazine references are coded below:
si = Sports Illustrated   sk = Sports Illustrated for Kids
sp = Sport Magazine   ti = Time
li = Life   bk = Beckett (all sports)
sip = Sports Illus. Presents   yis = Year In Sports (SI)
siod = Olympic Daily

NAME/TEAM	TITLE/PUBLICATIONS LISTING
Aaron, Hank	si) 8/18/69, 5/25/70, 4/15/74, 9/19/94 sp) 6/62, 7/68, 8/70, 5/74 bk) #4
Abbott, Jim	sk) 9/94 bk) #54
Abdul-Jabbar, Kareem (Lew Alcindor)	si) 12/5/66, 4/3/67, 1/29/68, 4/1/68, 3/31/69,10/26/69, 3/9/70, 4/27/70, 2/8/71, 4/19/71, 4/24/72, 2/19/73,10/14/74, 2/14/77, 5/23/77,5/5/80, 12/15/80, 5/9/83, 6/10/85, 6/17/85, 12/23/85, 5/26/86, 6/22/87,4/18/88,, 1/23/89, 11/11/96, 83 YIS, sp) 2/74, 2/78 bk) #12 li) 3/24/72
Abele, John	si) 6/18/62
Abercrombie, Walter	si) 1/7/85
Adams, Alvin	si) 6/7/76
Adcock, Joe	si) 7/30/56 sp) 8/57
Adleman, Rick	si) 10/15/73
Affirmed/Aldar	si) 6/19/78
Agassi, Andre	si) 7/13/92, 3/13/95
Agganis, Harry	sp) 11/50, 11/52
Aquirre, Mark	si) 12/1/80
Aikman, Troy	si) 8/21/89, 8/27/90, 2/8/93, 8/1/94, 1/16/95 95,96,97 SIP Pro Ft, sk) 3/93, 10/94, 9/88, 7/92, 7/93, 8/93, 10/93, 2/94, 7/94, 8/94,
Ainge, Danny	si) 5/2/83, 3/30/90
Akers-Stahl, Michelle	sk) 9/92
Alabama/Penn St	si) 7/8/79
Alarie, Mark	si) 12/1/80
Albright, Tenley	si) 1/30/56
Alcindor, Lew	sp) 4/67, 3/68, 2/70, 5/71
Alexeyev, Vasili	si) 4/14/75
Ali, Muhammad	si) 6/10/63, 2/24/64/, 3/9/64,11/16/64, 5/24/65, 6/7/65, 11/2/65,
(Cassus Clay)	4/11/66, 2/6/67, 7/10/67, 12/22/67 (flap), 5/5/69, 3/1/71 3/15/71, 7/26/71, 4/23/73,2/4/74, 10/28/74, 11/11/74,12/23/74, 9/15/75, 10/13/75, 10/13/80, 77YIS, 4/25/88, 11/15/89, 1/13/92, 9/19/94, 9/3096

NAME/TEAM	TITLE/PUBLICATIONS LISTING
	li) 3/6/64, 1023/70, 3/5/71, 3/19/71, 1/91 sp) 3/64, 9/74, 2/75 ti) 3/22/63, 3/8/71, 2/27/78
Allen, Dick (Richie)	si) 3/23/70, 6/12/72, sp) 7/67
Allen, George	si) 7/9/73
Allen, Marcus	si) 10/5/81, 12/13/82, 12/16/85, 9/2/96, 9/2/96(r) sp) 8/83, 11/85, 2/87, 8/88,9/91, 10/94
Allen, Ray - CT	si) 95 sip Col Basket
Alomar, Roberto	si) 10/26/92, 10/14/96 sk) 4/92 bk) #86,#91
Alomar, Sandy Jr.	sk) 4/92
Alson, Jo	si) 3/7/55
Allstar Peview	si) 7/9/56
Alston, Walt	si) 9/26/55, 5/15/67, 5/19/69,
Alt, Carol (swimsuit)	si) 2/8/82
Alworth, Lance	si) 12/13/65
Alzado, Lyle	si) 7/8/91 sp) 12/83
American Birds	si) 5/16/55
American Cup	si) 5/12/58, 7/9/62, 8/24/64
Anderson, Bob (Army)	si) 11/24/58, sp) 11/58
Anderson, Brad	si) 97 sip Pro Baseball
Anderson, Don	si) 12/16/68
Anderson, Kenny	si) 97sip Pro Basketball
Anderson, Mary	si) 11/5/62
Anderson, N.	Bk) f#71
Anderson, Otis	si) 1/28/91
Anderson, Rotnei	si) 11/16/87
Andrie, George	si) 9/9/63
Antonelli, Johnny	sp) 6/55, 1/58
Aparicio, Luis	si) 8/10/59, 9/22/59, 4/30/62 sp) 7/60
Arcaro, Eddie	si) 6/17/57 ti) 5/17/48
Archer, George	si) 4/21/69
Archibald, Tiny	si) 10/15/73
Armour, Tommy	si) 3/30/59
Armstrong, Debbie	si) 2/20/84
Arnett, John	si) 10/23/61
Artist's View /Sp. Training	si) 3/7/60
Ashburn, Richie	si) 5/19/53
Ashe, Arthur	si) 8/29/66, 7/14/75, 12/21/92, 2/15/93, li) 9/20/68
Athlete, U.S.S.R.	si) 12/2/57
Atkins, Ace	si) 1993 Alabama Com.
Augmon, Stacey	si) 4/2/90, 11/19/90 bk) #22
Austin, Tracy	si) 3/22/76, 9/17/79, 1981 YIS
Australia:World's Sports C.	si) 5/16/60
Auto Racing at Lime Rock	si) 10/19/59
Autograph Madness	si) 8/13/90
Autumn Leaves in Nova Scotia	si) 10/28/57
Avery, Dan	bk) #82, 86
Babashoff, Shirley	si) 7/19/76
Bagwell, Jeff	si) 97 sip pro baseball
Bailey, Damon	si) 12/13/93
Bailey, Donovan	96siod
Bailey, Thurl	si) 4/11/83
Baird, Amy	si) 12/16/57
Baiul, Oksana	sk) 2/94
Bagwell, Jeff	bk) #83
Baker, Terry	si) 10/16/61, 1/7/63
Baker, Vin	si) 97 sip pro Basketball
Ballesteros, Steve	si) 4/21/80
Bamberger, George	si) 4/30/79
Bando, Sal	si) 10/21/74
Banks, Ernie	si) 7/7/58, 9/8/69 sp) 9/69
Banks, Gene	si) 3/13/78, 4/3/78
Banks, Tyra	si) 1/29/96, w97
Bannister, Roger	si) 1/3/55 (sportsman of the Year)
Banzai Pipeline (Surfing)	si) 3/8/82

APPENDIX I
Sports Illustrated Promotions and Other Material

In addition to rare publications, some collectors also accumulate items sponsored and sold by Sports Illustrated. In this category are posters, lithographs, films, games, books, and puzzles. The estimated value for these items will range depending upon player and demand. However, many of these items are tough to find. It should be noted that this is not a comprehensive list of material and that more is added daily through the Sports Illustrated Store.

BOOKS
Books are a natural fit for Sports Illustrated. Many times books were released, sponsored, and promoted, in Sports Illustrated pages and outside of the magazine. I compiled a very short list of books and the first year they were promoted within the pages of Sports Illustrated.

1957
"Spectacle of Sports"
"The Pros"
"Book of the Outdoors"
"Golf is My Game" Bob Jones
"Modern Fundamentals of Golf " Ben Hogan
"Tips from the Top"
"Bonnie Prudden's Fitness Book"
"Wind on My Wings"
"The Best 18 Golf Holes in America"
"Jack Nicklaus - Take a Tip From Me"
"The Wonderful World of Sport"

1966 - 1976
The Sports Illustrated Library of Book series was created to help instruct people on how to play different sports. The books were promoted over a period of time. Listed below is a partial list of the many book subjects:

* Badmitton
* Basketball
* Diving
* Fencing
* Football
* Football Offense
* Gaited Riding
* Handball
* Ice Hockey
* Junior Sailing
* Safe Driving
* Skin Diving
* Soccer
* Swimming/Diving
* Tennis
* Training - Weights
* Wet Fly Fishing
* Baseball
* Boating
* Dog Training
* Fly Fishing
* Football Defense
* Football Quarterback
* Golf
* Horseback Riding
* Judo
* Powerboating,
* Skiing
* Small Boat Sail
* Squash
* Table Tennis
* Track & Field
* Volleyball

1971
"Golf Lessons"
" Inside Major League Baseball"

1977
SI Book club - Many different Time-Warner books were promoted and advertised through the SI Book Club.

CALENDARS
Today's Sports Illustrated Swimsuit Calendar is one of the top ten most recognized calendars made in America. Outside of the traditional large swimsuit calendar is the daily box calendar and the monthly regular size calendar. The most collectable calendar is the Swimsuit calendars which can range from $10 - $100 depending upon year and demand. There are Sports Illustrated calendars that date back to 1970.

GAMES/PUZZLES
From 1978-1987 Sports Illustrated offered board games. The games are collected by game collectors and tend to range in value from $15 - $50 depending upon the game and the condition. Some of the games were released each year with the ability to buy updated cards of each sport. Games originally sold between $15 - $20 each. Games are listed below.

BOARD GAMES

All Time All Star Baseball	College Football
Football Strategy	Golf for the Green
Challenge Golf	Paydirt
Baseball Strategy	Statis-Pro Football
Bowl Bound	Statis- Pro Baseball
Superstar Baseball	Title Bout
Speed Circuit	Auto Racing
Horse Racing	Regatta
Pro Tennis	Decathlon

PUZZLES
1969 - Ski, Best 18 Holes
1977 - Oscar Robertson, and others

LEARNING PROGRAMS
1975 - This package contained SI posters, boxes, and SI education books. It may not have lasted long because it was only advertised a few years.

POSTERS
Posters is one area that Sports Illustrated pushed throughout its history. Many of these earlier posters are now sought after by advanced collectors.

1957
Sports Illustrated offered your choice of any color photograph or painting, which ever appeared in Sports Illustrated. The cost was $1.00 half page, $1.50 full page and $2.50 for a two page

spread. Therefore many photos of the original Sports Illustrated covers may exist.

1961

Russell Hoban paintings prints were offered in 1961 for $1 each. These 3-feet by 12-inch color prints are seldom seen in the market and therefore are classified as scarce. The prints were offered only through Sports Illustrated in 1961. I would estimate the value around $100 to $300 each:

1. Carol Heiss skating at Squaw Valley
2. Ted Williams hitting home run no. 500
3. Johnny Unitas winning the championship
4. Rafer Johnson wins the Olympic Decathlon
5. Arnold Palmer winning second Masters title
6. Floyd Paterson beating Ingemar Johansson

1963

Posters are from the pages of Sports Illustrated. These are beautiful sports scenes that range in sizes from 20 x 27 to 34 x 36. The value of the scenes is unknown, but I would estimate them to be about $25 - $50 each.

"Skiing in the Sangre De Cristo Mountains, Taos, N.M."
"Tennis at Wimbledon"
"Harness Racing - High stepping trotters at Goshen" 36x14
"Sports Car Racing - the start of the 24 hour race at LeMans"
"Ocean Racing" cover of SI 7/4/60
"Crew - on the Seventh River"
"Golf - The 12th hole at Augusta"

1968 - 1972

The most popular sports posters. These were done over a four year period and were marketed through various means. Originally, there were Baseball, Football, Basketball and Hockey individual player posters.

SI Posters had an insert poster that had pictures of 54 different players that were going to be on a Sports Illustrated Poster. These pictures were all baseball players. The major players were: Mantle, Aaron, Mays, Kaline, Clemente, Seaver, Banks, Rose, Gibson, Robinson, and Killebrew. The value of this insert poster ranges from $5 to $10.

1968-1972 SI BASEBALL POSTERS

PLAYER- TEAM	YR	PRICE
☐ Hank Aaron - Braves	68	50
☐ Tommy Agee - Mets	68	20
☐ Richie Allen - Phillies	68	20
☐ Gene Alley - Pirates	68	15
☐ Felipe Alou - Braves	68	12
☐ Max Alvis - Indians	68	20
☐ Mike Andrews - Red Sox	69	12
☐ Bob Aspromonte -Astros	68	15
☐ Ernie Banks - Cubs	68	25
☐ Glen Beckett - Cubs	70	20
☐ Gary Bell - Indians	68	25
☐ Gary Bell - Pilots	68	15
☐ Bobby Bonds - Giants	70	25
☐ Clete Boyer - Braves	68	15
☐ Lou Brock - Cards	68	20
☐ Johnny Callison - Phillies	68	20
☐ Bert Campaneris - A's	68	20
☐ Leo Cardenas - Reds	68	12
☐ Rod Carew - Twins	70	25
☐ Paul Casanova - Orioles	68	15
☐ Orlando Cepeda -Card	68	15
☐ Roberto Clemente - Pirates	68	350
☐ Tony Conigliaro - Red Sox	68	20
☐ Mike Cuellar - Orioles	70	15
☐ Tommy Davis - Pilots	68	15
☐ Willie Davis - Dodgers	68	20
☐ Don Drysdale - Dodgers	68	30
☐ Mike Epstein - Senators	70	15
☐ Al Ferrara - Dodgers	68	15
☐ Curt Flood - Cards	68	15
☐ Bill Freeham - Tigers	68	20
☐ Jim Fregosi - Angels	68	12
☐ Bob Gibson - Cards	68	20
☐ Bud Harrelson - Mets	68	15
☐ Ken Harrelson - Red Sox	68	15
☐ Ken Holtzman - Cubs	70	12
☐ Joe Horlen - White Sox	68	15
☐ Tony Horton - Indians	68	15
☐ Frank Howard - Senators	68	20
☐ Reggie Jackson - A's	68	150
☐ Ferguson Jenkins - Cubs	69	50
☐ Tommy John - White Sox	68	30
☐ Cleon Jones - Mets	68	25
☐ Al Kaline - Tigers	68	25
☐ Harmon Killebrew - Twins	68	25
☐ Jerry Koosman - Mets	68	15
☐ Lets Go Mets - Mets	69	35
☐ Mickey Lolich - Tigers	68	25
☐ Jim Lonborg - Red Sox	68	20
☐ Jim Maloney - Reds	68	25
☐ Mickey Mantle - Yankees	68	300
☐ Juan Maricha l- Giants	68	25
☐ Willie Mays - Giants	68	200
☐ Willie Mays - Mets	72	100
☐ Bill Mazeroski -Pirates	68	12
☐ Tim McCarver - Cards	68	12
☐ Mick McCormick - Giants	68	25
☐ Willie McCovey - Giants	68	100
☐ Sam McDowell - Indians	68	25
☐ Denny McLain -Tigers	68	15
☐ Don Mincher - Angels	68	30
☐ Don Mincher - Pilots	69	20
☐ Rick Monday - A's	68	12
☐ Bobby Murcer - Yankees	68	20
☐ Phil Niekro - Braves	68	20
☐ John Odom - A's	70	20
☐ Tony Oliva - Twins	68	17
☐ Wes Parker - Dodgers	68	25
☐ Tony Perez - Reds	70	25
☐ Rico Petrocelli - Red Sox	68	20
☐ Boog Powell - Orioles	68	25
☐ Rich Riechart - Angels	68	12
☐ Brooks Robinson - Orioles	68	100
☐ Frank Robinson - Orioles	68	50
☐ Pete Rose - Reds	68	50
☐ Ron Santo - Cubs	68	20
☐ Tom Seaver - Mets	68	150
☐ Chris Short - Phillies	68	15
☐ Bill Singer -Dodgers	68	20
☐ Reggie Smith - Red Sox	68	20
☐ Rusty Staub - Astros	68	15

☐ Mel Stottlemyre - Yankees	....	68	20
☐ Ron Swoboda - Mets	....	68	15
☐ Cesar Tovar - Twins	....	68	20
☐ Roy White -Yanks	....	68	20
☐ Walt Williams - White Sox	....	68	15
☐ Earl Wilson - Tigers	....	68	20
☐ Jim Wynn -Astros	....	68	15
☐ Carl Yastrzemski - Red Sox	....	68	15

1968-1972 SI BASKETBALL POSTERS

Basketball was not the most popular sport during the 68-72 era. However a few superstars still had a poster made. These posters are considered rare, except for the Billy Cunningham.

PLAYER/TEAM		YR	PRICE
☐ Bill Bradley - Knicks	....	68	100
☐ Billy Cunningham - 76ers	....	68	15
☐ John Havlicek - Celtics	....	68	40
☐ Elvin Hayes - Bullets	....	70	40
☐ Spencer Hayward - Bullets	....	71	12
☐ Willis Reed - Knicks	....	71	20
☐ Oscar Robertson - Bucks	....	71	45
☐ Pete Maravich - Hawks	....	71	150
☐ Lew Alcindor - Bucks	....	71	100

1968-1972 SI FOOTBALL POSTER

There were many Football SI Posters made during this era and it would take a page to list all of the common posters. The common posters value around $15-$40 based on demand and scarcity. Many of the posters are considered scarce. Star posters tend to go between $50-$150.

Some of the posters are listed below:

Lance Alworth (150)	Jim Bakken
Pete Nanaszak	Lem Barney
Mike Battle	Fred Biletnikoff (75)
George Blanda (75)	John Brockington
John Brodie (50)	Bill Brown
Larry Brown	Norm Bulaich
Dick Butkus (150)	Vince Carter
Junior Coffey	Greg Cook
Larry Csonka (75)	Mike Curtis
Ben Davidson (50)	Len Dawson (75)
Carl Eller (50)	Mel Farr
Roman Gabriel (50)	Mike Garrett
Jim Grabowski	Joe Greene (75)
Bob Griese (100)	John Hadl
Ben Hawkins	Bob Hayes (50)
Rich Jackson	Charley Johnson
Ron Johnson	Decon Jones (50)
Homer Jones	Sonny Jorgensen
Joe Kapp (150)	Alex Karras
Leroy Kelly	Jack Kemp (50)
Billy Kilmer	Daryle Lamonica
Greg Landry	Bob Lilly
Floyd Little	Spider Lockhart
John Mackey	Archie Manning
Tom Matte	Don Maynard
Craig Morton	Jim Nance
Bill Nelson	Kent Nix
Ray Nitschke	Tommy Nobis
Joe Namath	Merlin Olsen
Alan Page	Jim Plunkett
Dan Reeves	Tim Rossovich

Andy Russell	Frank Ryan
George Sauer	Gale Sayers
Ron Sellers	Dennis Shaw
OJ Simpson (75)	Jackie Smith
Norm Snead	Matt Snell
Bart Starr (100)	Roger Staubach (100)
Charley Taylor	Otis Taylor
Paul Warfield	Gene Washington
George Webster	Larry Wilson
Marv Woodson	

1968-1972 SI HOCKEY POSTERS

These are tougher than the baseball and football posters. Common posters tend to be between $15-$40 each. The tougher ones are the superstars which go between $40-$150 each. Here is a sampling:

Red Berenson (50)	Phil Esposito (40)
Ed Giscomin (40)	Vic Hadfield (30)
Gordie Howe (75)	Bobby Hull (75)
Dave Keon (25)	Bobby Orr (150)
Derek Sanderson (25)	Gump Worsley (25)

1973-1983 SI POSTERS

Sports Illustrated changed marketing companies and Marketcom became the producer of Sports Illustrated posters. Marketcom produced varities with and without the SI promotional name.

The difference between the 1973-1983 series is it was produced on a slick surface compared to the grainy 68-72 series. These posters were not part of any large poster find and tend to be scarce. This series included such variety as baseball, football, basketball, horseracing, hockey, etc.

Sports Illustrated also developed non-direct individual posters. In 1971 it created an Ali vs Frazier fight poster along with Olympic posters. In 1979 the company started in with the SI Signature series.

1971: Ali vs. Frazier fight poster

1972: Nature posters

1972: Secretariat SI poster

1975: More Sports posters - Basketball, Horseracing, etc.

1976: Montreal Olympic poster

1976: 28 small Olympic posters

1979: SI Signature Sports posters

1983 SPORTS ILLUSTRATED POSTERS

These posters were handled by Marketcom and were advertised in 1983 in Sports Illustrated. The posters had the name of the athlete at the top with a border around the player. These posters do appear from time to time. Commons tend to go around $10 - $15 and superstars go for $25 - $50. They also created a series of mini posters (5 1/2" x 8 1/2") in full color.

Most of the posters featured big name sports (football, baseball, basketball), however, this generation of Sports Illustrated posters had many different types of sports offered. Listed below are the key posters and a total listing of posters by sport:

FOOTBALL 53+ POSTERS (PARTIAL LIST):

Jim Zorn	Ron Jaworski
Wesley Walker	Craig Morton
Ottis Anderson	Dan Dierdorf
Jim Hart	Earl Campbell
Harvey Martin	Ray Guy
Pat Haden	Tony Dorsett
Roger Staubach	Joe Montana
Walter Payton	Roland Harper
Franco Harris	Ken Anderson
Chris Collinsworth	Brian Sipe
Jack Youngblood	Steve Grogan
Terry Bradshaw	Randy Gradishar
Wallace Francis	robert Brazille
Ken Burrough	Phil Simms
Gary Danielson	Joe Theisman
Jack Ham	Joe Greene
Vince Ferragamo	Charlie Waters
Randy White	Jack Lambert
Lee Roy Selmon	Regggie McKenzie
Joe Ferguson	Kellen Winslow
George Rogers	Tommy Kramer
Mike Pruitt	Steve Bartkowski
Dan Fouts	Rob Carpenter
Mark Gastinaeu	Richard Todd
Jimmy Cefalo	Marcus Allen
Dwight Clark	Lawrence Taylor
Eric Hipple	

BASEBALL 44+ POSTERS (PARTIAL LIST):

Rod Carew	Wilie Randolph
Pete Rose	Jim Palmer
Keith Hernandez	Eddie Murray
Rick Cerone	George Brett
Wilie Stargell	Johnny Bench
Gary Maddox	Graig Nettles
Jim Rice	Bill Buckner
Jack Clark	Gary Matthews
Ron Guidry	Buddy Bell
Joe Charboneau	Dale Murphy
Bob Horner	Paul Molitor
Steve Carlton	Reggie Jackson
Mike Schmidt	Dave Parker
Gorman Thomas	Kirk Gibson
Gary Carter	Jerry Remy
Darrell Porter	Bruce Sutter
Willie Wilson	Mookie Wilson
Steve Sax	Roy Smalley
Steve Garvey	Tom Seaver
Jim Sundberg	Robin Yount

BASKETBALL 26+ POSTERS:

Julius Erving	Bill Walton
Alvan Adams	Dennis Johnson
Austin Carr	Larry Bird
Isiah Thomas	Jamaal Wilkes
Magic Johnson	Darrell Griffith
Marvin Webster	Marques Johnson
Jack Sikma	Mychal Thomson
Gus Williams	Mark Aguirre
Moses Malone	Artis Gilmore
Dominque Wilkins	Darryl Dawkins
Kareem Abdul Jabar	Buck Williams
Frank Johnson	George Gervin
Rick Robey	

TENNIS 11 POSTERS:

Jimmy Connors	Bjorn Borg
Ilie Nastase	Evonne Goolagong
Rosie Casals	Vitas Gerulaitis
Billie Jea King	Guillermo Vilas
Virginia Wade	John McEnroe
Martina Navratilova	

MISCELLANEOUS POSTERS

US Ski Team - (5)

Boxing - (1) - Sugar Ray Leonard

Hockey (3)- Phil Esposito, Dave Maloney, Wayne Gretzky

Golf - (4) - Hale Irwin, Laura Baugh, Jan Stephenson, Nancy Lopez

Bowling - (5)

Body Building - (1)

1986 SPORTS ILLUSTRATED POSTER TEST STICKERS

These stickers were released to stores to promote the 86 Sports Ilustrated Poster. There were 20 in the set and they were issued only to stores. When the business went under a few of the sticker sets emerged. The average price is $15 each.

☐ Lawrence Taylor - Giants	15
☐ Herschel Walker - Cowboys	15
☐ John Elway - Bronco's	35
☐ Andre Dawson - Cubs	15
☐ Eric Davis - Reds	15
☐ Dwight Gooden - Mets	15
☐ Darryl Strawberry - Mets	15
☐ Ricky Henderson - Yankees	20
☐ Gary Carter - Mets	15
☐ Dale Murphy - Braves	20
☐ Wade Boggs - Red Sox	20
☐ Ryne Sandberg - Cubs	25
☐ Ozzie Smith - Cards	25
☐ Kirby Puckett - Twins	25
☐ Roger Clemens - Red Sox	25
☐ Don Mattingly - Yankees	20
☐ Michael Jordan - Bulls	150
☐ Dominique Wilkins - Hawks	25
☐ Magic Johnson - Lakers	25
☐ Larry Bird - Celtics	25

1987 SPORTS ILLUSTRATED QUACKER CHEWY GRANOLA BARS (3 x 5) MINI POSTERS

These posters are similar to the 1983 posters except in size. Values range from $5 to $30 based on player and condition.

FOOTBALL 57 POSTERS (PARTIAL LIST):

Payton, Killy, Elway, Dorsett, Staubach,Walker, Marino, Montana, Taylor, Largent, Bradshaw

BASEBALL 40 POSTERS (PARTIAL LIST):

Jackson, Yount, Sandberg, Ripken, Gwynn,Schmidt, Bench, Rose, Brett

BASKETBALL 28 POSTERS (PARTIAL LIST):

Jordan, Bird, Johnson, Jabbar, Thomas, Barkley, Erving

MISCELLANEOUS:

Ice Skating & Running - (5)

Surfing - (2)

Water Skiing - (2)

Snowmobile - (2)

Golf - (4)

Racquetball - (2)

Hockey - (1) - Dave Maloney

Boxing - (1) - Sugar Ray Leonard

US Ski Team - (5)

Soccer - (2)

PRINTS

Sports Illustrated twice offered limited edition autographed lithographs of great atheletes during great events. These were all signed in pencil by the athletes. The original price when they were released was $100 each. The litho's were limited to 1,000 or 1,500 each. The most valuable ones will be of the great deceased players.

1974

PRINTS	PRICE RANGES
☐ Jack Dempsey/Gene Tunney	250 - 400
☐ Joe Louis vs Max Schmiling	400 - 600
☐ Arnold Palmer	150 - 250
☐ Eddie Aracado	75 - 100
☐ Joe DiMaggio	250 - 500
☐ Johnny Unitas	100 - 150

1976

PRINTS	PRICE RANGES
☐ Jack Nicklaus	150 - 250
☐ Chamberlain/Havlicek	100 - 200
☐ Stan Musial	75 - 150
☐ Billie Jean King	50 - 100
☐ Rod Laver	75 - 150
☐ Red Grange	250 - 350

PROMOTIONAL ITEMS

These are salesman representative giveaways, samples and the like that have various Sports Illustrated logos on them. I have found belt buckles, buttons, pins, magazines and books as some of the items that were developed for this purpose. The demand for these items is low because they usually don't directly relate to a particular person or sport. Some of the neatest items are special posters of players that were used in displays.

VIDEOS

The Sports Illustrated Store continues to offer new and exciting videos on a range of subjects. The ones that are offered exclusively by Sports Illustrated are the ones most coveted by Sports Illustrated collectors. Two very popular series produced by Sports Illustrated are "The Year in Sports" and "The Swimsuit Issue." There were also Beta Sports Illustrated (no longer made) videos (the smaller cartridge that didn't make it) that do exist in the market. In earlier years action films (1971) and SI highlight films were released.

APPENDIX II

SI Cover Appearance Leaders

1. Michael Jordan	42	
2. Muhammad Ali	34	
3. Kareem Abdul-Jabbar	28	
4. Jack Nicklaus	23	
5. Earvin "Magic" Johnson	23	
6. Larry Bird	20	
7. Pete Rose	17	
8. Arnold Palmer	14	
9. Bill Walton	14	
10. Wayne Gretzky	14	
11. Mike Tyson	14	
12. Joe Montana	13	
13. Sugar Ray Leonard	13	
14. Mickey Mantle	12	
15. Patrick Ewing	12	
16. Reggie Jackson	10	
17. John McEnroe	10	
18. Emmitt Smith	10	

19. Jimmy Connors	9
20. Roberto Duran	9
21. Chris Evert	9
22. "Marvelous" Marvin Hagler	9
23. Larry Holmes	9
24. Sonny Liston	9
25. Joe Namath	9
26. OJ Simpson	9
27. Herschel Walker	9
28. Julius Erving	8
29. Willie Mays	8
30. Floyd Patterson	8
31. Bill Russell	8
32. Dan Marino	8

*SOURCE: Sports Illustrated's "35 Years of Covers" issue and updated through 1997.

APPENDIX III
Dealers and Supplies

MAGAZINE SUPPLIES
Larry E. Krein Co.
3725 Portland Ave So.
PO Box 7126
MN Minn 55407
612-824-9422

SPECIALTY DEALERS
The Sports Illustrated Store
P.O. Box 60042
Tampa, FL 33660-0042

SPORTS PUBLICATION DEALERS
Concord Collectibles (Lou Madden)
15875 Greenway-Hayden Loop,
Suite 112
Scottsdale, AZ 85260

Tom Gitto - Auto Time/SI Collector
7 Wilson St.
Staten Island, NY 10304

SCI - Boxing / Autographs
8925 Riverbend Ct.
Indianapolis, IN 46250

Horance "Ace" Martchant
232 Rockrimmon Rd.
Belchertown, MA 01007

Big Al
37 Seville Way
San Mateo, CA 94402
415 341 5735

Baseball Dreams - (Ed Taylor)
982 Monterey St.
San Luis Obispo, CA 93401
805-541-6432

B & E Collectibles, Inc -
(Joe & Jay Esposito)
950 Broadway
Thornwood, NY 10594
914-769-1304

Box Seat Collectibles - Newspapers
PO Box 2013
Halesite, NY 11743-0852

Sportslore - (Joe Campius)
P.O. Box 43256
Upper Montclair, NJ 07043

P&R Publications (Phil Regli)
P.O. Box 65778
Tucson AZ 85728-5778
(520) 531-8880 fax 8881
e-mail Regli@aol.com
www.asportmall.com

Adelson Sports
13610 N Scottsdale Rd.
Scottsdale, AZ 85254

Scott Smith - Signed Issues Only
53 Sherwood Ave.
Englewood Cliffs, NJ 07632
(201) 567-2723

Todd Mueller- Signed Issues Only
PO Box 701182,
Dallas, TX 75370-1182

Wayne Greene
945 W. End Ave, 5d
New York, NY 10025

Headline Sports
Kurt Backhaus
3404 Nottingham
Pearland, TX 77581
713-485-7622

Scott Daloisio Sports
12475 Central Ave #286
Chino, CA 91710

The Golf Hounds
16612 Green Dolphin Lane
Corrnelius, NC 28031

YesterYear Sports
Bill Harris
4 Cedar Way
Charleroi, PA 15022
(412) 483- 8508

Jeff Baseball Books
5536-A Port Royal Rd
Springfield, VA 22151

Bailey's Collectible
2910-B Girad NE
Albuquerque, NM 87107

George Kaufer
4104 E. 14th st.,
Vancouver, WA 98661

Paul Cards & Collectible
3879 E. 120th Ave #308
Thornton, CO 80233

Robert Dick
3 Ambrose Lane
South Barrington, IL 60010

R. Plapinger- Baseball Books
po box 1062
Ashland, OR 97520

Van Daniel c/o Happier Day Collectible
5104 Jimmy Carter Blvd.
Norcross, GA 30093

Label Removal Service
Greg York c/o
Speciality Sports
15213 S. W. Freeway #115
Sugarland, TX 77478
713-491-0997

NOTES

NOTES

NOTES